THE GOTHIC QUEST
A HISTORY OF THE GOTHIC NOVEL

PLATE I

M.G. LEWIS Esqr M.P.

AUTHOR OF THE MONK.

Pubd for the Proprietors of the Monthly Mirror Novr 1796 by T. Bellamy, King Str Covent Garden

MATTHEW GREGORY LEWIS
Aetat. 21

[Frontispiece

THE GOTHIC QUEST

A HISTORY OF THE GOTHIC NOVEL

by

MONTAGUE SUMMERS

NEW YORK

RUSSELL & RUSSELL · INC

1964

FIRST PUBLISHED IN 1938
REISSUED, 1964, BY RUSSELL & RUSSELL, INC.
L. C. CATALOG CARD NO: 64—8919

PRINTED IN THE UNITED STATES OF AMERICA

CONTENTS

CHAPTER   PAGE

      INTRODUCTION 7

I.   THE ROMANTIC FEELING 17

II. THE PUBLISHERS AND THE CIRCULATING LIBRARIES . 60

III. INFLUENCES FROM ABROAD 106

IV. HISTORICAL GOTHIC 153

V. MATTHEW GREGORY LEWIS 202

VI. FRANCIS LATHOM; T. J. HORSLEY CURTIES; WILLIAM
     HENRY IRELAND; AND OTHERS 309

     SURREALISM AND THE GOTHIC NOVEL . . . 382

     GENERAL INDEX 413

     INDEX OF NOVELS 432

LIST OF ILLUSTRATIONS

PLATE

FACING PAGE

I. M. G. Lewis Esqr : M.P. (1775-1818). Engraved by Ridley, from a picture by Drummond. *The Monthly Mirror*, October, 1796.
Samuel Drummond, A.R.A. Portrait painter. 1765-1844.
William Ridley, Engraver. 1764-1838.
From the Author's Collection . . . . . . *Frontispiece*

II. The Gothic Shrine. The seer Duncannon at his devotions. An incident from William Child Green's *The Prophecy of Duncannon; or, The Dwarf and the Seer.* A Caledonian Legend. 1824. Chapter XIX
From the Author's Collection 22

III. Frontispiece to *The Spectre.* By Charles Andrews. 2 vols. Stockdale. 1789. *W. Bromley sculp. Published Feb.* 12, 1789, *by J. Stockdale.*
Henry Wilmot, walking at night on the lonely shore, beholds (as he imagines) the spectre of his adored Maria Hamilton, falsely supposed dead. Vol. I, pp. 21-5.
From the Author's Collection 50

IV. An original watercolour drawing, one of six inserted in a copy of Mrs. Radcliffe's *The Italian; or, The Confessional of the Black Penitents.* The Second Edition. T. Cadell, Jun. and W. Davies, (Successors to Mr. Cadell) in the Strand. 1797
Frontispiece to *Ancient Records; or, The Abbey of Saint Oswythe.* A Romance. In Four Volumes. By T. J. Horsley Curties. Minerva Press, 1801.
Constantine has been surprised by his demoniac brother, Gondemar, whose grim-visaged attendant aims a deadly shaft at the hero's heart. Just as the horrid deed is a-doing, Lady Rosaline St. Oswythe, distracted and dishevelled, appears in the portal.
From the Author's Collection 82

V. Frontispiece to *Le Panache Rouge; ou le Spectre de Fer,* " imité de l'anglais de Mrs. Radcliffe," by Mme la Comtesse de Nardouet. (Pseudonym of Madame la Comtesse de Ruault de la Haye.) 2 tom. Paris, 1822; and 1824.
Ines abstracts the mysterious keys from the skeleton's hand.
By courtesy of the British Museum 108

VI. Frontispiece to *The Castle of Saint Donats; or, The History of Jack Smith.* By the Rev. Charles Lucas. 3 vols., Minerva Press. 1798 *J. Storer Sc.*
At Turin, Jack Smith is rescued by the English girl from the dagger of the courtezan Flametta. Vol. II, p. 176.
From the Author's Collection 134

VII. *Longsword, Earl of Salisbury.* An Historical Romance. By Thomas Leland. [The First Edition]. W. Johnston, in Ludgate-Street. 1762.
Frontispiece to Vol. I. *S. Wale del. C. Grignion sculp.*
A Cistercian monk succours the distressed Earl.
Samuel Wale, R.A., *ob.* 1786.
Charles Grignion, 1716-1810.
From the Author's Collection 160

VIII. Sophia Lee (1750-1824). Engraved by Ridley, from an Original Drawing by Lawrence. *The Monthly Mirror*, July, 1797.
Sir Thomas Lawrence, 1769-1830
From the Author's Collection 186

IX. An interesting Scene from the Novel of *Margiana* by Lady Sykes, 5 vols., Minerva Press, 1808.
Margiana ; or, Widdrington Tower, A Tale of the Fifteenth Century (Richard II– Henry IV) is a typical Historical Gothic romance. The illustration depicts the abduction of the heroine, Margiana, by hired ruffians. Vol. III, ch. 7.
From the Author's Collection 204

X. Frontispiece to *The Mysterious Warning : including the Memoirs of the Solitary Man of the Desolated Mansion*. By Mrs. Parsons. London. S. Fisher. 151. St. John Street. West Smithfield. 1824. *W. Hopwood del. S. Russell sculp.*
Ferdinand, whilst watching by his dead father, seems to hear the lifeless lips utter the words : " *Pardon and peace* ! " Chapter II.
The Mysterious Warning, A German Tale. In Four Volumes. [With a Frontispiece] *By Mrs. Parsons*. Author of Voluntary Exile, &c. Minerva Press. 1796.
The Mysterious Warning is one of the " Northanger Novels."
William Hopwood, son and pupil of James Hopwood the elder.
Lady Matilda weeping over the coffin of Lord Leicester. An illustration from *The Recess ; or, A Tale of other Times*, by Sophia Lee. London. S. Fisher, 151, St. John Street, West Smithfield. 1824. *W. Hopwood del. W. Ponormo sculp.*
The Recess ; or, A Tale of Other Times by Sophia Lee, Vol. I, 1783 ; Vols. II and III, 1785. T. Cadell, in the Strand.
From the Author's Collection 232

XI. *Agnes ! Agnes ! thou art mine !* The Bleeding Nun of Lindenberg. Illustration, Vol. II, p. 87, to *Le Moine*, " traduit de l'anglais," 4 tom., Paris, chez Maradan, an X [1801–2]. Translation of *The Monk*.
By courtesy of the British Museum 252

XII. *Thus I secure my prey !* The Fate of Ambrosio. Illustration, Vol. IV, p. 186, to *Le Moine*, 4 tom., Paris, chez Maradan, an X [1801–2].
Ambrosio, " abbot of the Capuchins " in the English original, becomes " prieur des Dominicains " in the French translation.
By courtesy of the British Museum 280

XIII. Frontispiece, Vol. I, to *La Cloche de Minuit*, " traduit de l'anglais," 3 tom., Paris, an VII, 1799. Translation of *The Midnight Bell*, 1798, by Francis Lathom.
Count Alphonsus, acting as sacristan at the Convent of St. Helena, secretly conveys a *billet doux* to the fair novice Lauretta.
By courtesy of the British Museum 312

XIV. William Henry Ireland (1777–1835) at the age of five and twenty. " *Engraved by Mackenzie from an Original Picture in the possession of Mr. Ireland.*" *Published by Longman & Rees Paternoster Row May* 1803.
Samuel Mackenzie, Scotch portrait-painter, 1785–1847.
From the Author's Collection 342

XV. William Child Green, Esqr. *Painted by Le Comte De Carné. P. Roberts Sculpt.*
This portrait was used as a frontispiece to several of Green's novels : *The Prophecy of Duncannon*, Joseph Emans, Ivy Lane, Paternoster-row, 1824 ; *Abbot of Montserrat, or, The Pool of Blood*, 2 vols., A. K. Newman and Co., Leadenhall-Street, 1826.
From the Author's Collection 372

XVI. Frontispiece, Vol. I, to *Manfredi, Baron St. Osmund. An Old English Romance* by Sarah Lansdell of Tenterden. 2 vols., Minerva Press, 1796.
Elinor and Catherine discover the beautiful recluse in her Gothic retreat. " The appearance of the ruins was extremely grand . . . and the sculptored arches closely entwined by mantling ivy seemed to say that magnificence had once there held its lofty reign." Vol. II, pp. 6–8.
From the Author's Collection 404

INTRODUCTION

My love for the romances of Mrs. Radcliffe dates from my very first years. Among my earliest recollections is an edition of her Works in one rather formidable fat volume, double-columned—which offered no difficulties then—and embellished with woodcuts that were a perpetual delight, not least because of their close affinity to the plays of Webb and Pollock of which one was giving nightly performances. Bound in dull black morocco, gilt-tooled, Mrs. Radcliffe lived on the summit of the highest shelves in a sombre and shadowy but by no means large old library, where the books stood ranged in very neat rows in tall mahogany cases behind heavy glass doors. Most sections were locked and keyless, but the particular bookcase whence Mrs. Radcliffe could be reached by mounting upon a chair and stretching rather far was always left unfastened, as I suppose containing standard literature and works approved for general and uncensored perusal, Scott, Dickens, Thackeray, Trollope, Marryat, Fenimore Cooper, Lingard, Miss Strickland, Prescott, and the more sober historians. *Tom Jones*, I remember, was banished to the remotest altitudes, and jailed beyond all hope of release. What a day it was—diem numera meliore lapillo, as old Persius bids—that day when I discovered how an alien key would fit the bookcase locks !

I now recognize that I began my acquaintance with Mrs. Radcliffe— an acquaintance that was soon to warm into affection and then to love— from Limbird's edition of 1824. A schoolboy friend—we were not in our 'teens—lent me a copy of *The Bravo of Venice* he had picked up on some twopenny stall. *The Monk* was not to follow until some years later. Next I was attracted by a title, *Manfroné ; or, The One-Handed Monk*, the four volumes of which I espied in a dingy little shop, and soon proudly possessed for one shilling. Thus I may be said to have been fairly started on my Gothic career. Very early too do I remember *Horrid Mysteries*, to which I did not make my way viâ Jane Austen, for when I came to read *Northanger Abbey*, how delighted I was to find the recommendation of sweet Miss Andrews.

7

In the mid-nineties there lived not far from my home an ancient lady,—she must then have been nearer her eightieth than her seventieth year—who yet retained all her faculties in a most surprising manner. Her house, small and thoroughly old-fashioned, and exceedingly comfortable, contained a numerous collection of books, and the bulk of these consisted of long-forgotten romances with which she was most intimately familiar, which she read occasionally even then, of which she was always ready to talk, and which she was ever willing— kind soul!—to lend. When quite young, hardly more than twenty years old, I suppose, she had been married to a gentleman very greatly her senior. As a youth he lived in London, he had written some verse, a closet drama or two (printed but never acted), and at least one fiction which appeared anonymously from the house of Newman. He had mixed in literary circles and personally known not a few of the writers whose duodecimos crowded those tight-packed shelves. His widow, whose memory remained excellent and clear, often spoke of Harriet Lee, Jane Porter, Charles Lucas, William Child Green, Robert Huish, Hannah Jones, Eleanor Sleath, some of whom she had herself met, some of whom she knew from her husband's anecdotes and reminiscences. How often have I since wished that I had taken notes of her tea-table talk, or that her husband's diaries and papers had been preserved.

I may add that she died rather suddenly, and being myself in Italy at the time, I only heard of her decease through correspondence. The estate went to distant relatives, who had little or no interest in her branch of the family. The books, accounted mere lumber, were dispersed ; the letters and personal papers were all destroyed.

Thirty-five years ago, indeed, the fiction of the late eighteenth and early nineteenth centuries was with few exceptions regarded as the veriest draff of the shelves, universally and most deservedly and for ever forgotten. It is true that W. Nicholson & Sons of Wakefield (late of Halifax) reprinted in their " Cottager's Library " at one shilling a volume *The Children of the Abbey*, Mrs. Helme's *The Farmer of Inglewood Forest* and *St. Clair of the Isles*, Charlotte Smith's *Ethelinde, or, The Recluse of the Lake*, and even *Fatherless Fanny*, and Mrs. Ward's *The Cottage on the Cliff* with its sequel *The Fisher's Daughter*. But such books were literally for the peasant and the poor. Milner reprinted *Manfroné*, of which romance (perhaps because of the fudge attribution to Mrs. Radcliffe) there was an edition at least as late as 1870. *The Children of the Abbey* and *The Farmer of Inglewood Forest* were included by Milner both in his " Two Shilling Red Library " and " One Shilling Red and Blue Library." *St. Clair of the Isles* was in the " One Shilling

Red and Blue Library." Other Gothic flotsam might be traced. I
can call to mind a sixpenny edition of *The Children of the Abbey* in 1890.
Mrs. Roche's novel, indeed, was immensely popular, and had been
issued time after time. Mrs. Helme's two favourite romances, also,
maintained their place in a sixpenny series. Now and again, moreover,
there had been published a poor edition of some novel by Mrs. Radcliffe. *The Monk*, generally under the title *Rosario*, and more fully
Rosario, or, The Female Monk, was circulated as a work of semiporno-
graphy· in surreptitious sniggering fashion, and presented on vile
paper with execrable type in the cheapest flimsiest wrappers.

It may be that I shall be reminded how in 1891 was issued (Percival
& Co.) " The Pocket Library of English Literature," a collection, in
separate 16mo volumes, of extracts and short pieces. Volume I,
bearing the title " Tales of Mystery," consisted of fragments from
Mrs. Radcliffe, Lewis and Maturin. The experiment was not well
conceived, and but poorly executed. Mrs. Radcliffe, Lewis and
Maturin do not lend themselves to selection and cannot be read in
parcels and samples.

In Chapter III of *Melmoth the Wanderer*, when Stanton is confined in
the madhouse and Melmoth so mysteriously appears, to tempt him
with a fearful bargain, the wretched victim " heard his heart beat
audibly, and could have exclaimed with Lee's unfortunate heroine,—
" It pants as cowards do before a battle ; Oh the great march has
sounded ! " Upon this the editor of " Tales of Mystery " (p. 315)
observes : " All Lee's heroines are as unfortunate as they can possibly
be. This might be Statira, or Narcissa, or any of them, and I have
not yet identified her : though I spent some time in endeavouring to
do so." It may be worth while, then, to point out that the lines thus
quoted by Maturin are spoken by the dying Semandra in *Mithridates,
King of Pontus*, Act V ; 4to, 1678, p. 64 :

> *Ziphares.* Speak, speak, *Semandra*.
> I feel a trembling warmth about thy heart :
> It pants.
> *Semandra.* As Cowards do before a Battel.
> Oh, the Great March is sounded.

On April 11th, 1891, *The Saturday Review*, speaking of " A Forgotten
Writer," remarked : " It may safely be said that not one reader in a
hundred, unless he be a close student of Balzac, or the literature of the
English stage, has ever heard of the author of *Melmoth the Wanderer*.
References to him in Byron's letters are passed over without comment,
and few histories of literature do more than chronicle his existence."

Balzac's *Melmoth Reconcilié* appeared in 1835. Edmund Kean won
a great success as Bertram in Maturin's *Bertram, or the Castle of St.
Aldobrand*, which was produced at Drury Lane on May 9th, 1816, and
achieved a run of twenty-two nights, being, moreover, very frequently
revived with applause. On Whit Monday, 1847, during his third
season at Sadler's Wells, Phelps played Bertram, " and in some parts
of it was very fine." The tragedy was revived at the Marylebone
Theatre as late as 1853. First published by Murray in 1816, *Bertram*
went through seven editions that year.

In 1892, at the suggestion of Walter Pollock, *Melmoth the Wanderer*
was reprinted, Three Volumes, Richard Bentley & Son, *cura* Robert
Ross and More Adey. Unfortunately this excellent edition attracted
no notice.

It should, perhaps, be mentioned in passing that a German scholar
or two, delving into the dustiest corners of English literature for a
thesis, were not unnaturally attracted to the English *Schauerromantik*,
but their academic dissertations have little, if any, value. They are
often inaccurate, they give us nothing new, and here they aroused
scant interest. Such were *The Gothic Romance* of Hans Möbius, Leipzig,
1902 ; Max Rentsch's *Matthew Gregory Lewis. Mit besonderer Berück-
sichtigung seines Romans " Ambrosio or The Monk,"* Leipzig, 1902 ;
Willy Müller's *Charles Robert Maturin's Romane " The fatal Revenge " und
" Melmoth the Wanderer." Ein Beitrag zur Gothic Romance*, Weida, 1908 ;
and Oscar F. W. Fernsemer's *Die Dramatischen Werke Charles Robert
Maturins, mit einer kurzen Lebensbeschreibung des Dichters*, München,
1913.

Well might Andrew Lang in *The Cornhill Magazine*, July, 1900, so
plaintively inquire : " Does anyone now read Mrs. Radcliffe, or am I
the only wanderer in her windy corridors, listening timidly to groans
and hollow voices, and shielding the flame of a lamp, which, I fear,
will presently flicker out, and leave me in darkness ? "

When in January, 1917, I lectured before the Royal Society of
Literature upon *A Great Mistress of Romance* : *Ann Radcliffe*, 1764–1823
(printed in *The Transactions of the Royal Society of Literature* : *Second
Series*, Volume XXXV), the subject was considered something quite
new. In a subsequent lecture (printed *ibid.*, Volume XXXVI),
delivered before the same Body on October 24th, 1917, the Jane
Austen Centenary Lecture, I particularly emphasized the Northanger
Novels, the seven romances of which mention is made in Chapter VI
of the First Volume of *Northanger Abbey*.

In his *Mainly Victorian*, 1925, my friend the late Mr. S. M. Ellis
reprinted an article from *The Contemporary Review*, February, 1923,

which he had written for the centenary of Ann Radcliffe, and whilst attention had already begun to concentrate upon things Victorian it also became evident that the Gothic Romance was fast coming into vogue among the inner circles of the advanced and elect.

How far indeed there is any true appreciation and understanding of the Gothic Novel among its latest admirers, how far there exists any actual knowledge is a question. It is significant that the Introduction to the most recent cheap reprint of *The Mysteries of Udolpho* was furnished by a popular writer of detective fiction.

I may perhaps remark that this present work was originally planned, and in great part actually written as long as five and twenty years ago.

It was in 1924 that I edited *The Castle of Otranto* and *The Mysterious Mother*. In 1927 I projected a series of the seven Northanger Novels, of which, however, only *Horrid Mysteries* and *The Necromancer of the Black Forest* were published. *The Mysterious Warning* was privately printed. In 1928 I edited *Zofloya*, by Charlotte Dacre, whom I had previously made the subject of a particular study in my *Essays in Petto*.

It was inevitable that the Gothic Romance should attract the attention of the academic and the amateur, and that itching pens should rush in to attack this theme. The majority of such studies are obviously "crammed" stuff; hastily conceived, ill directed, badly written theses, a deplorably jejune output of the Universities. Moreover, as was pointed out in a notice of what is probably quite the worst and most feckless of these dissertations (reviewed in *The Times Literary Supplement*, May 17th, 1934), our undergraduates and sophomores are hampered, and something more than hampered, by the fact that they have not access to sufficient material, and in consequence such tiros are apt to analyse *in extenso* some quite negligible novel whilst they ignore, because they have no knowledge of, romances which are really significant and historically important. Thus they have no critical perspective, and their information is soon seen to be undependable and insincere, at the very best to have been acquired second-hand, if indeed they reach so far, from *The Critical Review*, *The Monthly Review*, and Watt's *Bibliotheca Britannica*.

In refreshing contrast to these banalities we welcome such a work as Mr. Niilo Idman's *Charles Robert Maturin*, in which the writer is not only in sympathy with, and indeed discreetly enthusiastic for, his subject, but in which moreover he affords ample evidence of real research, of original reading and judgement.

Baroque and Gothic Sentimentalism, which first appeared in an Oxford magazine, *Farrago*, No. 3, October, 1930, and in a revised form was published separately in February, 1931, is a thoughtful and suggestive

Essay by my late friend Peter Burra, who was keenly interested in the
Gothic period.

Although the heyday of the Gothic Novel in England may be said
to have flourished during the 1790's, I shall hope to show in a further
study that it remained immensely popular and how its influence
extended far later than is generally supposed, until indeed it was
absorbed, essentially unchanged, in the pages of Bulwer Lytton,
Harrison Ainsworth, George Herbert Rodwell, and G. W. M. Reynolds ; nay, even later yet in the romances of Malcolm J. Errym,
Margaret Blount, and Eliza Winstanley, as in the far finer work of
Le Fanu, Miss Braddon, Florence and Gertrude Warden.

The Gothic Novel with its romantic unrealities, its strange beauties,
its very extravagances—if you will—was to a great extent the Novel of
Escape from the troubles and carking cases of everyday life. Men
wearied of fiction which, clever and pointed as the strokes might be,
presented too nearly the world almost as they saw it around them.
Sidney Bidulph and Lady Barton were found to be distressing ; the
heroines of Mrs. Lennox, Henrietta and Euphemia ; Mrs. Gibbes'
Sukey Thornby ; George Walker's Cinthelia ; were all voted ordinary.
The novel of real life to achieve complete success must have mingled
with it something of surprise, something of romance. There was
nobody more adroit in supplying this blend than Mrs. Charlotte Smith.
In her *The Old Manor House* (1793), although the *Critical Review* might
complain that the housekeeper's niece, Monimia, remained in the end
precisely what she was at the beginning, whereas the reader had a right
to expect she would prove to be " a very different personage," Mrs.
Smith has presented her rambling old Hampshire mansion, its
mysterious sights and sounds, its antique and deserted rooms, its secret
passages haunted by smugglers, an estate so imperiously ruled by a
high and haughty chatelaine, Mrs. Rayland, the last daughter of a long
and lordly line, with as fully Gothic a flavour as though it were a
frowning castle in the awful heart of the Apennines or an eyrie convent
in the remotest Abruzzi where some harsh and despot abbess held
sovran sway, unquestioned and uncontrolled.

Celestina (1791), *Montalbert* (1795), Mrs. Parsons' *Lucy* (1794), the
anonymous *Eloise de Montblanc* (1796), Charles Lucas' *The Castle of Saint
Donats* (1798), Mrs. Roche's *The Children of the Abbey* (1798), and to
come to a later date the same lady's *The Tradition of the Castle* (1824),
are notable examples of this kind, romances whose titles I have picked
just at random.

The novel of domestic life with its Richardsonian sensibilities and
the didactic novel of course persisted, nor would it be difficult to quote

not a few important names, as, for instance, Mrs. Inchbald's *A Simple Story* (1791, but written some fourteen years earlier), Cumberland's *Henry* (1795), Mrs. Helme's *The Farmer of Inglewood Forest* (1796), and Mrs. Bennett's admired *The Beggar Girl and her Benefactors* (1798). Mrs. Parsons, Mrs. Roche, Lathom, even Maturin, who it has been said so amply " earned his title to the Headship of the School of Terror," and many more (but not, be it noted, Mrs. Radcliffe), wrote domestic as well as romantic tales. Yet if served with Gothic sauce the domestic novel was generally considered far more appetizing fare.

The explanation is that both at home and abroad dark shadows were lowering ; the times were difficult, full of anxiety and unrest ; there was a sense of dissatisfaction to-day and of apprehension for the morrow ; there were wars and rumours of wars. Readers sought some counter-excitement, and to many the novel became a precious anodyne. There is something in this which may be closely paralleled at the present time, and never before than now were readers so greedy for " fictional anæsthetics." The modern public has been frankly debauched by a surfeit of crime fiction and " Thrillers," which belie their very name and fail most lamentably in their function, since for the most part they are of the lineage of *The Lady Flabella*, and there is not a line in them, " from beginning to end, which could, by the most remote contingency, awaken the smallest excitement in any person breathing." I do not speak of the spate of nameless scribblers, but I have in mind " detective novels " and " thrillers " by authors who are brazenly boosted and boomed, and I believe that there is no uglier symptom to-day than the shameless blazoning of such unhealthy and unwholesome rubbish. These novels are unhealthy and unwholesome not because of their subjects, however coarse and crude, but because they are bad to rottenness in their conception, in their execution, in their presentation. The spineless detective novel, the " thriller " which cannot thrill, are the most useless, the most worthless and most boring books of any sort or kind.

I may perhaps claim to have read a very fair number of Gothic romances, but so far as my knowledge extends not even the poorest and most erratic novel of that school sinks to a bathos within measurable distance of the dull draff which amongst us is so puffed and advertised amain.

Setting aside such masterpieces as *The Woman in White* and *The Moonstone*, no small pleasure may be derived from mystery and detective novels of the second or even the third rate. They are often absurd, but 'tis an enviable relaxation to seek the answer to the riddle, and many a happy hour have I spent by the fireside all agog to know Who

did the murder ? or, Who stole the jewels ?   This candid acknowledgement of weakness, for it is a weakness, will make it plain that so far
from having any sort of prejudice against detective novels, I can enjoy
them with gusto.   The good " thriller " is most excellent fare.   To-day
the good detective novels which I light upon are few and far between.
The bad detective novels, the bad " thrillers " which flood the land, I
nauseate and abhor as the ultimate degradation of letters.

I regret that in the following pages I have barely been able to touch
upon the vogue of the Gothic Romance in France, where " tout le
décor du *gothique* anglais paraît se retrouver."   Fortunately the Gothic
influence is being dealt with by Mons. Maurice Heine, whose two
valuable articles *Le Marquis de Sade et le Roman Noir* and *Promenade
à travers le Roman noir* lead us eagerly to await a fuller study from his pen.

Even in England alone so vast is the field that an explorer may well
hesitate before he ventures.   The present work in fine is the outcome
of more than forty years of reading Gothic romances, and more than
thirty years of definite concentration and research, a labour, not light,
but of love, often and seriously interrupted by duty and inquiry in
other fields.   The quantity of Gothic material alone at once presents a
Gordian dilemma.   Either in the endeavour to cover all the ground a
writer will show himself superficial and thin ; or else he must select,
and that somewhat arbitrarily, whence his plan will be open to criticism,
facile enough yet not always easy to answer.   This latter method, since
a choice had to be made, I have preferred, although fully conscious
that such an approach is not without difficulties and drawbacks, which
must be as far as possible obviated and counterchecked.

In a second volume, then, I propose to treat in detail the work of
Mrs. Radcliffe, Mrs. Charlotte Smith, Mrs. Parsons, Mrs. Roche, Mrs.
Meeke, Mrs. Helme, Mrs. Bennett, Godwin, Charlotte Dacre, Jane and
Anna Maria Porter, Mrs. Shelley, Maturin, Robert Huish, Charles
Lucas, Mrs. Yorke, Catherine Ward, and very many more, the central
place being, of course, held by " the mighty magician of *The Mysteries
of Udolpho*."

It is my intention further to publish a Bibliography of the Gothic
Novel.

In the present volume I have elected to deal mainly with those
aspects of Gothic Romance which in some sense find their fullest
expression in the work of that most notable and significant figure,
Matthew Gregory Lewis.

One reason, perhaps, which inclined me to this course is that whilst
both Mrs. Radcliffe and Maturin have formed the subject of particular
studies, there is no work (if we except the hundred-year-old and not

very satisfactory *Life and Correspondence of M. G. Lewis*) which concentrates upon Lewis alone, and Lewis not merely in his literary output but in his life is a character of extraordinary interest, and, I will add of an influence that is not exhausted even to-day. It may not be unfitting to remind ourselves that his fantasticisms, his absurdities if you will, were those of his time from which no man can wholly scape, that his power and his genius were his own, and of a quality to which both Scott and Byron bore testimony with no uncertain meed of praise.

Not long ago I was asked a curious question : Did Matthew Gregory Lewis really believe in ghosts ? Shelley said that Lewis at times " did not seem to believe in them," but this scepticism was very superficial, for bold as he might be in the broad daylight, when darkness and loneliness fell the " Monk " obviously thought " more respectfully of the world of shadows." Lewis certainly confided to Byron that before any important crisis in his life, especially before any untoward happening, he was visited (as in warning) by the shade of his brother Barrington. In Chapter V I have quoted, as Medwin reports, two ghost stories which Lewis was wont to relate, and, there can be no reason to doubt, which he firmly believed, the haunted house at Mannheim and the Florentine lovers. In Shelley's *Journal* will be found " four other stories—all grim " that Lewis loved to tell. Of these, three (as is known from other sources) are absolutely authentic. For the tales themselves see Mrs. Shelley's *Essays Letters from Abroad*, 1840, and Shelley's complete *Works*, edited Ingpen and Peck, 1929, Vol VI, pp. 147-50.

It gives me great pleasure to thank Mr. Michael Sadleir, a high authority upon the Gothic Novel as in many other fields of literature, for so courteously permitting me to quote in Chapter II from his published work. Especially am I indebted to him for his kindness in bringing to my notice and supplying me in regard to these points with many new and important details, which he has established in the course of his more recent investigations.

Mr. W. Gaunt's *Bandits in a Landscape*, a study of Romantic Painting, from Caravaggio to Delacroix, is not only a delightful book in itself, but a most valuable companion to any who desire to understand how the Gothic spirit found expression in art ; and to a real appreciation of romanticism such knowledge is essential. The anonymous author of *An Epistle in Rhyme to M. G Lewis*, 1798, writes :

> Thou not'est, like Radcliffe, with a painter's eye
> The pine-clad mountains, and the stormy sky,
> And at thy bidding, to my wondering view
> Rise the bold scenes Salvator's pencil drew . . .

Mrs. Radcliffe, who was indeed a painter in words, used to name Salvator Rosa and Claude Lorraine as her favourite artists. Chapters on both these masters will be found in Mr. Gaunt's study, from which he has generously allowed me to make quotation.

The claims put forward by the Surrealists that their new movement is influenced by and draws vital inspiration from the Gothic romance are sufficiently surprising to necessitate an inquiry into the significance and quality of this connexion—if indeed any such there be. I have accordingly added a brief survey of the arguments they urge in support of their contention, and attempted to arrive at some understanding of their aims and principles.

To Mons. Maurice Heine, a great authority upon " le roman noir," I desire to express my heartiest thanks for the time and trouble he has so generously given to discussing with me the influence of the Gothic Novel in France. I am especially obliged to him for clearing up by his researches many obscure points concerning that multitude of authors whose romances, " démodés, furent dédaignés par les plus humbles bouquinistes, vendus au poids comme vieux papiers, détruits en grand nombre," and of which in consequence (as in England) exemplars have become of the very last rarity.

I have to thank the Editor of *The Connoisseur*, Mr. Granville Fell, for the kind loan of blocks for those of the Illustrations which accompanied my article " The Illustrations of the ' Gothick ' Novels," *The Connoisseur*, November, 1936, as also for permission to quote from my previous work.

During the course of my work, Mr. Hector Stuart-Forbes has ungrudgingly helped me by his fruitful and valuable suggestions, by as valuable and fruitful criticism, and in many more ways beside than I am able adequately to acknowledge.

MONTAGUE SUMMERS.

THE GOTHIC QUEST

CHAPTER I

THE ROMANTIC FEELING.

As for novels, there are some I would strongly recommend, but romances infinitely more. The one is a representation of the effects of the passions as they should be, the other as they are. The latter is falsely called nature ; it is a figure of corrupt or depraved society. The other is the glow of nature.

SHERIDAN.

Le romanticisme, c'est l'étoile qui pleure, c'est le vent qui vagit, c'est la nuit qui frissonne.

DE MUSSET.

LITERATURE in every age presents itself under one of two forms, neither of which can ever be arbitrary or accidental, since both, however separate in their tendencies and aims have their roots deep down in man's philosophical or religious speculation. In the one case literature expresses and discusses under various shapes, as elegantly and masterly as its exponents are able, the prevailing ideas concerning the problems, material and metaphysical, of the current hour. It is a clear reflection, and brightly burnished is the mirror, of everyday life. The common man, to take a phrase from Dr. Johnson, " feels what he remembers to have felt before, but he feels it with a great increase of sensibility." He is pleased because he finds the fleet yet haunting thoughts he was seeking to disentangle and digest in his own mind are set out before him in order, far better than he himself could have arranged his ideas. The answers to the problems and the conclusions may not be such as he approves or would accept, but no matter, the inquiry has been made, and even by his mere regard, his reading the pages quite cursorily, he feels that he has in some sort taken his individual part and had a main share in the argument.

On the other hand literature may lead a man away from life, as it were, that is to say it may direct him from the long and often fruitless contemplation of the circumstances which surround him, his journey-work, to many distasteful, monotonous to most, and invite his attention to other realities and aspirations, flinging wide

> Magic casements, opening on the foam
> Of perilous seas, in faery lands forlorn.

This is the essence of the romantic spirit. Romanticism weans our thought and care from the sordid practicalities of the repeated round ; it offers us a wider and fuller vision ; and it is therefore subjective ; it is reactionary in its revolt against the present since it yearns for the loveliness of the past as so picturesquely revealed to us in art and poem ; and informed by a passionate desire for the beautiful, which can never be entirely satisfied but is always craving for more, it must by its very nature remain always unappeased, that is to say in some sense dimly seeking adventure in the realms of the mind, intellectually restless and aspiring.

Walter Pater wrote : " It is the addition of strangeness to beauty that constitutes the Romantic character in art. . . . It is the addition of curiosity to the desire of beauty that constitutes the Romantic temper. . . . The essential elements, then of the Romantic spirit are curiosity and the love of beauty ; and it is as the accidental effects of these qualities only that it seeks the middle age."[1] " The ages are all equal," says William Blake, " but genius is always above its age," and Romanticism is beyond it.

Romanticism is, in effect, a supernaturalism, and the highest form of Romanticism, in its purest and best endeavour, raised upwards to the sublime, is Mysticism.[2] Indeed some definitions of Mysticism would well nigh serve for Romanticism, although of course we have passed from literature to an even higher sphere.[3] Von Hartmann, however, extends the name of mystic to " eminent art-geniuses who owe their productions to inspirations of genius, and not to the work of their consciousness, e.g. Phidias, Æschylus, Raphael, Beethoven," since " Mysticism is the filling of the consciousness with a content (feeling, thought, desire), by an involuntary emergence of the same out of the unconscious." Bouchitté pregnantly observes : " Mysticism consists in giving to the spontaneity of the intelligence a larger part than to the other faculties." Dean Inge has a very striking and pertinent passage : " The phase of thought or feeling which we call Mysticism has its origin in that which is the raw material of all religion, and perhaps of all philosophy and art as well, namely, that dim consciousness of the *beyond*, which is part of our nature as human beings." [4]

Romanticism is literary Mysticism.

J.-K. Huysmans has said : " Le tout est de savoir s'y prendre, de savoir concentrer son esprit sur un seul point, de savoir s'abstraire suffisamment pour amener l'hallucination et pouvoir substituer le rêve de la réalité à la réalité même." It is interesting to recall how he had concluded the Avant-Propos to the second edition[5] of *Marthe* with the following profession : " Je fais ce que je vois, ce que je sens et ce que j'ai vécu, en l'écrivant du mieux que je puis, et voilà tout. Cette explication n'est pas une excuse, c'est simplement la constatation du but que je poursuis en art."

Romanticism is generally contrasted with Classicism, but this can only hold good when the latter term is narrowed to apply merely to treatment and form, and not to subject-matter. It is true that in English literature the classical writers, by whom pre-eminently are to be understood the Augustans of the reign of Queen Anne, resolutely limited their themes, and as in their own religious beliefs, worship, and respectable devotional practice they had deliberately and with care reduced the supernatural to a cipher so they resolutely excluded all feelings of Mystery and Awe, all gentle enthusiasm,[6] chiaroscuro, and supernatural imagination from their literature. They thought that they were following Horace ; their master, as a matter of fact, was Boileau. They aimed at an elegant and correct serenity ; they achieved a systematized and monotonous frigidness.

The motto, indeed, of the Augustan Classicists was " Follow Nature," which sounds not a little surprising until we ask what they meant by " Nature," and then we discover that to them Nature implied nothing more than the cold business of plain Common-Sense, as they conceived it. They wished to reproduce upon entirely stereotyped and didactic lines the manners and landscape they observed around them, and they were bitterly opposed to any irregularity, anything emotional and disturbing, or evoked by a vivid imagination. Hence the formal adjective, the thrice-chimed rhyme, the trite metaphor, the threadbare trope—they all saw, or essayed to see with the same eyes.

Genius, although it could not break through, at least might inform these limitations in its own way, and, even if trammelled by the convention of admired models and academic rule, it did not suffer its own brilliance to be extinguished or eclipsed. Unhappily genius is rare, and talents albeit of a high order were chilled to mediocrity and simulation by the rigid principles and dogma of a tyrant authority.

Alexander Pope was the one great poetic genius of his day, and there is more romanticism in Pope than either he or his disciples would have cared to admit. In 1716 when writing to Lady Mary Wortley Montagu with unusual frankness he says : " The more I examine my own mind, the more romantic I find myself. . . . Let them say I am romantic ; so is every one said to be that either admires a fine thing or praises one ; it is no wonder such people are thought mad, for they are as much out of the way of common understanding as if they were mad, because they are in the right." [7]   Romanticism here has not indeed as yet quite the full richness of meaning it later developed, but Pope means that he prefers the content of an exquisite sensibility, the reverie of imagination which suggests pictures of beauty and inspired loveliness not to be discerned in daily life, to the clear cold vision that sees things precisely as they are, or rather as they appear to the prosaic and unvaried mind.   It is not impertinent to recall an anecdote I have often heard George Moore tell.   One day when Corot was painting *en plein air* a pupil looking at the canvas said : " Maître, it is superb. But where do you see all this beauty ? "   " There," replied Corot with a wave of the hand to the woods and sky before him.   Once at a dinner at Bourgival Degas, looking at some large trees massed in shadow, exclaimed : " How beautiful they would be if Corot had painted them ! "

No whole-hearted or single-mind Classicist—using the word strictly in the Augustan sense—could have conceived and builded that delicious ' Ægerian grot ' at Twickenham, the *Museum* in which Pope took so much pleasure and so much pride.   It was at the end of 1717, just after his father's death that Pope bought his Twickenham estate, and Martha Blount declared that from first to last in gems, shells and lucent spars he spent no less than a thousand pounds upon the Grotto, which was originally devised to avoid the necessity of crossing the high road from Twickenham to Teddington, when the poet was desirous of rambling through the whole extent of his gardens.   Minerals, stones, and ores came from Mount Vesuvius, the Hartz Mountains, Mexico, the West Indies, Italian quarries of marble, Cornish mines, and even from the stalactite caves of Wookey Hole to adorn the Grotto, and Bishop Warburton remarks that " the beauty of Pope's poetic genius appeared to as much advantage in the disposition of these romantic materials as in any of his best contrived poems." [8]   It was, as Pope desired, " a study for virtuosi and a scene for contemplation."   Even now the Grotto remains, although alas ! long since despoiled of its ornament.[9] The poet thus describes it in a letter to Edward Blount, June 2nd, 1725 : " From the river Thames you see thro' my arch up a walk of the wilderness, to a kind of open temple, wholly composed of shells in the rustic manner, and from that distance under the temple you look down through a sloping arcade of trees, and see the sails on the river passing suddenly and vanishing as through a perspective glass.   When you shut the doors of this grotto it becomes on the instant, from a luminous room, a camera-obscura ; on the walls of which all objects of the river, hills, woods, and boats are forming a moving picture in their visible radiations. . . . It is furnished with shells interspersed with pieces of looking-glass in regular forms ; and in the ceiling is a star of the same material, at which, when a lamp (of an orbicular figure of thin alabaster) is hung in the middle, a thousand pointed rays glitter, and are reflected over the place. . . . You'll think I have been very poetical in this description, but it is pretty near the truth." Here we have a baroque romanticism no genuine Augustan would have tolerated for a moment.

Pope may not untruly be said to be more than ' romantic ' in one poem at least, for there are lines and whole passages of *Eloisa to Abelard* [10] which show such Gothic influences as might almost be paralleled in Mrs. Radcliffe herself. Even the opening strikes this note :

> In these deep solitudes and awful cells,
> Where heav'nly-pensive contemplation dwells,
> And ever-musing melancholy reigns ; . . .
> Shrines ! where their vigils pale-ey'd virgins keep,
> And pitying Saints, whose statues learn to weep !

The following lines have not a little of the pale spirit of Monk Lewis :

> See in her cell sad Eloïsa spread,
> Propt on some tomb, a neighbour of the dead.
> In each low wind methinks a Spirit calls,
> And more than Echoes talk along the walls.
> Here, as I watch'd the dying lamps around,
> From yonder shrine I heard a hollow sound.
> " Come, sister, come ! " (it said, or seem'd to say)
> " Thy place is here, sad sister, come away ! "

True, the form is the classic couplet, so-called, but the expression and the feeling are Gothic to a degree. One line, indeed, Pope has taken entire from Crashaw, the metaphysical, the mystic :

> Obedient slumbers that can wake and weep.

These exquisite and pregnant words occur in the *Description of a Religious House and Condition of Life*.

We have then a Poem which is classical in form, but—to a very large extent at any rate—in its theme and matter intensely romantic, for the Gothic influence is the very osmazome of quintessential romanticism. We are now near concluding that classicism is a question of form, a circumstance extremely important in itself, for if definite forms be prescribed by the critical canon and it is found that certain subject-matter can hardly, or at best, very awkwardly, be cast in those straitly ordained patterns and moulds, at no very distant date all such difficult and intractable material will be discarded and deemed uncouth, extravagant, and unfit for use.

The contrast and the contest are not then so much between classicism and romanticism, for this resolves itself into a discussion concerning form and the consequences, as between realism and romanticism, a passage which seeks to decide the legitimate sphere of artistic treatment, and this cuts something deeper. The real root of the whole business, stripped of logomachy and all its trappings, lies in the eternal jar between materialism and the Supernatural.

In *The Confessions of a Young Man*[11] George Moore said : " One thing cannot be denied to the realists : a constant and intense desire to write well, to write artistically. . . . What Hugo did for French verse, Flaubert, Goncourt, Zola, and Huysmans have done for French prose. No more literary school than the realists has ever existed, and I do not except even the Elizabethans." Upon which we comment that the very desire to write well, to write artistically, betrayed the realist in spite of himself, and he became a romanticist. By the side of *Madame Bovary* we set *La Tentation de Saint Antoine* and *Salammbô*. Of Goncourt, Huysmans shrewdly remarked, "Goncourt l'a bien comprise, l'erreur du naturalisme, et il l'a évitéa"; in *Madame Gervaisais*, as Arthur Symons so penetratingly observes, Edmond and Jules de Goncourt have given us the soul of Rome, which Zola with all the documentation of *Rome* was unable to do. As regards Huysmans himself no man turned his face more steadfastly towards, and steeped his very being more saturatingly in, the faith and ideals of Mediævalism ; even in 1884 when he published *A Rebours*, " Zola sentit tout de suite que le disciple sur lequel il comptait le lâchait. . . . Zola lui reproche d'avoir porté un coup terrible au naturalisme, et conseilla au déserteur de revenir à l'étude de mœurs " [12] ; and Huysmans himself declared, " le naturalisme est fini. . . . La masturbation a été traitée, la Belgique vient de nous donner le roman de la syphilis, oui ! Je crois que, dans la domaine de l'observation pure, on peut s'arrêter la ! " [13] Of Huysmans Zola generously allowed : " Tenez, il y en a un, d'écrivain, qui ne l'aime pas, le siècle, et qui le vomit d'une façon superbe, c'est Huysmans, dans *Là-Bas*, son feuilleton de *l'Echo de Paris*. Et il est clair, au moins, celui-là, et c'est avec cela un peintre d'une couleur et d'une intensité extraordinaires." [14] Zola too, the master of realism, wrote his *La Faute de l'Abbé Mouret* and *Le Rêve* ; he cast a wistful eye towards romanticism and complained half-playfully, half in earnest, that when

PLATE II

Lorrimond advanced cautiously down the avenue, as if fearful of disturbing his devotion

THE GOTHIC SHRINE

Green's " Prophecy of Duncannon," 1824

[Face p. 22

he was engaged upon *Pot-Bouille* he could allow himself " No *bravura*, not the least lyrical treat." "My novel," he wrote in a letter from Grandcamp, August 24th, 1881, " does not give me any warm satisfactions, but it amuses me like a piece of mechanism with a thousand wheels, of which it is my duty to regulate the movement with the most minute care." [15] In 1890 Rémy de Gourmont prophesied : " Je pourrais m'aventurer à dire que la littérature prochaine sera *mystique*. . . . Un peu d'encens, un peu de prière, un peu de latin liturgique, de la prose de Saint Bernard, des vers de Saint Bonaventure,—et des secrets pour exorciser M. Zola ! " [16]

It is inevitable that throughout the centuries of literature the pendulum should swing, Romanticism-realism, and Realism-romanticism again ; whilst the spirit of Romanticism in its immortality will assume a thousand varied shapes, sometimes a shape of exquisite beauty, sometimes a shape of wild extravagance with affectations that are almost vulgar and crude, whilst the body of Realism can but clothe itself in the prevailing modes and fashions of the hour and hold up a mirror to reflect what' is passing around and about, often indeed exhibiting pictures of extraordinary interest and value, if seldom however visions of what is loveliest and best. Wherein seems to lie the reason why poets upon whom was imposed an artificial pseudo-classical form often became didactic in their art,[17] or satirists. Pope himself, having necessarily accepted definite limitations, excelled in both these kinds, and not irrelevantly has Mr. Austin Dobson shrewdly observed that so supreme is the genius of Hogarth, the dramatist of the brush, who " without a school, and without a precedent . . . has found a way of expressing what he sees with the clearest simplicity, richness, and directness," [18] that we are apt to forget his " specific mission as a pictorial moralist and satirist."

Dr. F. H. Hedge has given it as his opinion that the Romantic feeling has its origin in wonder and mystery, the essence of Romanticism being Aspiration. " It is the sense of something hidden, of imperfect revelation. . . . The peculiarity of the classic style is reserve, self-suppression of the writer. . . . The Romantic is self-reflecting. . . . To the Greeks the world was a fact, to us it is a problem. . . . Byron is simply and wholly Romantic, with no tincture of classicism in his nature or works." [19] Similarly Professor Boyesen had said : " Romanticism is really on one side retrogressive, as it seeks to bring back the past, and on the other hand, progressive as it seeks to break up the traditional order of things. . . . The conventional machinery of Romantic fiction ; night, moonlight, dreams. . . . Romantic poetry invariably deals with longing, . . . not a definite desire, but a dim, mysterious aspiration." [20]   These critics present us with a good deal of the truth, not the whole truth, perhaps, for volumes might be penned and no completely satisfactory definition of Romanticism in all its facets and phases arrived at, but at any rate their insistence upon Aspiration, yearning desire, mystery, wonder, certainly approaches near the heart of the matter, and we shall find that from those essential elements spring the characteristics of the Gothic Novel.

As Horace Walpole wrote so excellently well : " Visions, you know, have always been my pasture ; and so far from growing old enough to quarrel with their emptiness, I almost think there is no wisdom comparable to that of exchanging what is called the realities of life for dreams. Old castles, old pictures, old histories, and the babble of old people, make one live back into centuries that cannot disappoint one. One holds fast and surely what is past." [21]

Having thus reviewed some general and preliminary conceptions of Romanticism we may inquire what Romance meant during the latter half of the eighteenth century amongst us in England in the mind of the average observer, or more precisely in the mind of the observer, who although no analytic virtuoso or psychologist, was rather above the average.

Horace Walpole, when he published *The Castle of Otranto* in 1764, termed his work " A Story. Translated by William Marshal, Gent. From the Original Italian of Onuphrio Muralto," and in the second edition (of the next year) he calls it " A Gothic Story." [22]   In a letter to the Earl of Hertford, whom he presents with a copy, he writes on January 27th, 1765, " the enclosed novel is much in vogue." On March 17th, 1765, he speaks of it in a letter to Joseph Warton as " partially an imitation of ancient romances ; being rather intended for an attempt to blend the marvellous of old story with the natural of modern novels," and on the following day he reminds Élie de Beaumont, " I believe I told you that I had written a novel. . . . I have since that time published my little story . . . how will you be surprised to find a narrative of the most improbable and absurd adventures ? How will you be amazed to hear that a country of whose good sense you have an opinion should have applauded so wild a tale ! . . . To tell you the truth, it was not so much my intention to recall the exploded marvels of ancient romance, as to blend the wonderful of old stories with the natural of modern novels." [23]   *The Castle of Otranto* was then to Walpole, primarily a Story, a Novel, a Narrative. It is true that in a letter to the Rev. William Cole, March 9th, 1765,[24] he says : " Shall I even confess to you, what was the origin of this romance ? " But he is writing very familiarly here.

The fact is that the term Romance [25] as applied to a story or a work of fiction did not convey in the middle of the eighteenth century quite what we should understand by the term. The distinction, such as it is, may be vague; but a Romance in 1750 often carried with it uncertain suggestions of the Sagas of Chivalry, Amadis, the Palmerins, Tirante the White, as well as very distinct memories of *Artamenes*; *Or, The Grand Cyrus*," that Excellent Romance. In Ten Parts. Written By that Famous Wit of *France*, *Monsieur* de Scudery, Governour of *Nostre-Dame*," [26] *Parthenissa*, "That most Fam'd Romance. *The Six Volumes Compleat*. Composed By the Right Honourable The Earl of Orrery," [27] and *Cassandra* "the fam'd Romance." [28] It must be remembered that the long-lived popularity in England of the Romances by La Calprènede and Mademoiselle de Scudéry was simply amazing. There are continual references. In *The Spectator*, No. 37, Addison among the books in Leonora's library notes *Cassandra, Cleopatra, Astræa*, "The Grand Cyrus, with a pin stuck in one of the middle pages," and "Clelia, which opened of itself in the place that describes two lovers in a bower." One of his lady correspondents (*Spectator*, No. 92), advised him to put "*Pharamond* at the head of my catalogue, and, if I think proper, to give the second place to *Cassandra*." In Farquhar's *The Constant Couple*, 1699, Lady Lurewell read *Cassandra*, dreamed of her lover all night, and in the morning made Verses. In *The Beaux Stratagem*, 1707, Archer candidly informs Mrs. Sullen, "Look'ye, Madam, I'm none of your *Romantick* Fools, that fight Gyants and Monsters for nothing"; whilst Aimwell exclaims "call me *Oroondates, Cesario, Amadis*, all that Romance can in a Lover paint"; Cesario being the son of Julius Cæsar and Cleopatra in "*that so much admir'd Romance intituled Cleopatra*," and not an allusion to *Twelfth Night* as editors of Farquhar will still persist in supposing. Pope's "advent'rous Baron"

> to Love an Altar built,
> Of twelve vast *French* Romances, neatly gilt,

and the poet himself gave a copy of the *Grand Cyrus* to Martha Blount. In 1705 Steele in his comedy *The Tender Husband* : *Or, The Accomplished Fools*, produced at Drury Lane in April of that year, satirized the passion for French Romances in his fair heroine Biddy Tipkin (created by Nance Oldfield) who on coming to Years of Discretion assumed the name Parthenissa and, since her case was "exactly the same with the Princess of the *Leontines* in *Clelia*," sighed to give "Occasion for a whole Romance in Folio" before one-and-twenty, whose reading, her Aunt Bersheba protested, was all "idle Romances of Fights and Battles of Dwarfs and Giants."

Until the middle of the eighteenth century (and even later) the translations of La Calprenède and Mademoiselle de Scudéry were still widely read in England as is proved by the famous novel of Mrs. Charlotte Lennox,[29] *The Female Quixote ; or the Adventures of Arabella,* 1752, the humour of which must almost entirely be lost upon the reader who has not at least a very fair acquaintance with *Cassandra, Cleopatra, The Grand Cyrus, Clelia,* and the rest. Further we may remark that the Fourth Edition of Cotterell's *Cassandra* was published 5 Vols. 12mo, Price 15s. in 1739 by Richard Ware " at the *Bible* and *Sun* in *Amen-Corner* " and appears in his catalogue alongside novels by Mrs. Haywood, Mrs. Aubin, and *Robinson Crusoe. The Female Quixote* has been characterized as " an agreeable and ingenious satire upon the old romances ; not the more ancient ones of chivalry, but the languishing love romances of the Calprenèdes and Scuderis." Arabella, the daughter of a nobleman living in a far retirement, is brought up in the country, and as she discovers a great fondness for reading she has the use of the Castle library, " in which unfortunately for her, were great store of romances, and, what was still more unfortunate, not in the original French, but very bad translations. . . . Her ideas, from the manner of her life, and the objects around her, had taken a romantic turn ; and supposing romances were real pictures of life, from them she drew all her notions and expectations. By them she was taught to believe that love was the ruling principle of the world ; that every other passion was subordinate to this ; and that it caused all the happiness and miseries of life " (Chapter I). She lives then in the realm of romance, and her ideas, conversation, and manners are all based on the models of " the divine Mandane," " the inexorable Statira," Parisatis, Candace, "the admirable Clelia," "the fair Artemisa," " the beautiful Thalestris," Elismonda, Alcionida, Cleorante, Amalazontha, Cerinthe, Olympia, " the beauteous Agione," Albysinda, Placida, Arsinoe, and a thousand other whimsies. Thus she imagines Edward, a young under-gardener on her father's estate, to be " a person of sublime quality " who submits to that disguise in order to have the happiness of gazing on her charms. She dismisses a lover who does not know that Artaxerxes was the brother of Statira, and who makes the horrid mistake of supposing Orontes and Oroondates to be two several persons, not guessing that Oroondates, Prince of the Scythians, assumed the name Orontes and gave himself out as Prince of the Massagètes, to conceal his identity (in *Cassandra*). She engages an Abigail to relate the adventures of her mistress, which happen to be of a nature not fit to be talked of, and quite nonplusses a classical scholar by her acquaintance with the intimate details of Greek and

Roman history which by some chance neither Thucydides, nor Livy, nor Tacitus, nor Plutarch have chronicled. In a fit of heroics, whilst walking on the river bank at Twickenham, she imagines she is about to be abducted, and to imitate the renowned Clelia she plunges into the Thames intending to swim over it, as that heroine traversed the Tiber. Happily she is rescued, senseless and half-drowned. A dangerous fever is the result, and during her illness she is visited by a pious and learned divine whose solid discourse throughout her convalescence clears her imagination of its myriad extravagances and puts an end to her follies so that a serenity of mind is restored with health of body.

The catastrophe of Arabella's leap into the river was perhaps suggested to Mrs. Lennox by Adrien Thomas Perdou de Subligny's [30] satire *La fausse Clélie. Histoire française galante et comique*, 1670.[31] This was translated into English as *The Mock-Clelia. Being a comical History of French Gallantrie and Novels. In Imitation of Dom* [sic] *Quixote. Translated out of French*, 8vo., 1678. Juliette d'Arviane imagines she is Clélie, and imitates the exploits of this peerless heroine, even to the extent of throwing herself into a canal which she supposes must be the Tiber.

As we have emphasized, by its continual allusions to, and lengthy quotations from French romances, *The Female Quixote* shows how deeprooted was the love for these heroic volumes in England in 1750. As late as 1796 Robert Bage was able to write in the last of his six novels, *Hermsprong : or, Man as he is not*, that Miss Brown's mind " was adorned with all the literature which this learned age has produced for the service of the ladies. To the novels of the present day were added the Cassandras and Cleopatras—the classics of a century or two preceding " (Chapter I). There is a mild touch of satire, for even if Miss Brown were the daughter of a mercer in Exeter, she showed excessively genteel. Moreover young Gregory Glen " was allowed to read the sublime Cassandra to her, while she worked in the summer evenings in a little alcove at the bottom of the garden." " What draughts of love I drank ! " he exclaims, " whilst I read the sublime meltings of the soul of Oroondates." Mrs. Barbauld, however, writing in 1810, criticizes the performance of Mrs. Lennox as being at a disadvantage, " namely, that the satire has now no object." She adds, however, with a bob at the Scudéry romances : " No doubt there were many things in them to admire ; nor is it very improbable that, in the rage for reviving every thing that is old, they may make their appearance again in a modern quarto of hot-pressed paper, with a life and an engraving from the original portrait of Mad[lle] Scudéry by Nanteuil, with her elegant verses under it."

In 1760 the Prologue, spoken by King, who acted Scribble, to George Colman's *Polly Honeycombe*, produced at Drury Lane on December 5th, has the following lines :

> ROMANCE *might strike our grave Forefather's pomp,*
> But NOVEL *for our Buck and lively Romp !*
> *Cassandra's Folios now no longer read,*
> *See, Two Neat Pocket Volumes in their stead !*

The novel, which was at first romantic or at least picaresque, soon partook of a certain realism. Then gradually fiction grew more realistic and less romantic, until romance again asserted its sway in the efflorescence of the Gothic Novel, where it was the supreme quality, and in the Sentimental Novel where it was blended with such an undercurrent of contemporary life as should make the fair reader delightedly exclaim, " Why, all this might easily happen to me ! " She could not, mayhap, be very well able to imagine herself being carried off by a Montoni to a remote castle in the robber-haunted Apennines ; or abducted by a treacherous Montaldo to a rock, furthest of the Isles of Tremiti, like Ariadne in *The Bandit Chief*; or even confined in a sullen cloister beneath the rigid rule of some ancient devotee, Mother S. Agatha or the cruel cadaverous Superior of S. Ursula. None the less it was clearly within the bounds of possibility that our heroine might so fascinate the heart of some bad bold baronet, that as she was returning from the Hotwells assembly or the Lower Rooms at Bath, he would whirl her away in his four-horsed chaise to the heavy Gothic magnificence of Arundel Hall amid the loneliest Cornish moors, where a grim-visaged steward would fit the rôle of gaoler well enough and a mysterious silent housekeeper prove as veritable a dragon-duenna as any Abbess of the Abruzzi. Did not the elder O'Farrel abduct his innocent victim Mrs. Parsons' Lucy from Lady Campley, Mrs. Murray and Henrietta, even in Whitehall itself, and hurry her off viâ Harwich and Ostend as far as Verona before she was rescued ? Did he not even contrive to kidnap her from Verona to Vicenza, so strange and extravagant were his schemes ? Life—on the printed page—was full of thrills !

It was by a happy stroke that Mrs. Charlotte Smith gave her collection of tales from the *Causes Célèbres*, such a title as *The Romance of Real Life*, 1787, selecting from Gayot de Pitavel and Richter narratives that " might lead us to form awful ideas of the force and danger of the human passions." *The Romance of Real Life* was a first-rate " selling " title.

It is possible indeed to some extent to differentiate between the

" terror-Gothic " and the " sentimental-Gothic," but it would scarcely be possible to say which of the two kinds proved most popular. Among the " terror-Gothic " are certainly to be classed the huge majority of novels that owe their inspiration to a German source, even if they are not—as so often proves the case—direct translations from the German. To give long lists were tedious, but we may say that the work of Matthew Gregory Lewis (generally speaking), is to be accounted " terror-Gothic," as also are such novels as—to give some fifteen titles— *The Necromancer; or, The Tale of the Black Forest,* 1794: *Horrid Mysteries,* 1796: *The History of Rinaldo Rinaldini, Captain of Banditti,* 1800 (all three translations from the German): George Walker's *The Three Spaniards,* 1800: *The Eve of San Pietro,* anonymous, 1804: G. T. Morley's *Deeds of Darkness; or, The Unnatural Uncle,* 1805: W. H. Ireland's *Gondez the Monk,* 1805: Charlotte Dacre's *Zofloya; or, The Moor,* 1806: T. P. Lathy's *The Invisible Enemy; or, The Mines of Wielitska,* 1806: Charles Robert Maturin's *The Fatal Revenge; or, The Family of Montorio,* 1807: Edward Montague's *The Demon of Sicily,* 1807: T. J. Horsley Curties' *The Monk of Udolpho,* 1807; Mary Anne Radcliffe's *Manfroné; or, The One-Handed Monk,* 1809: Maturin's *Melmoth the Wanderer,* 1820; William Child Green's *Abbot of Monserrat; or, The Pool of Blood,* 1826. (We may note that Ainsworth's *Rookwood* was published in 1834.)

The ingenious Richard Sickelmore has a romance *Osrick; or, Modern Horrors,* 1809, of which there is more to be said in a later chapter.

Among the " sentimental-Gothic " novels we can list some very famous titles, for example Mrs. Charlotte Smith's *Emmeline, or, the Orphan of the Castle,* 1788; *Ethelinde, or, the Recluse of the Lake,* 1789; *Celestina,* 1791; Mrs. Roche's *The Children of the Abbey,* 1796; *Clermont,* 1798; *The Tradition of the Castle, or, Scenes in the Emerald Isle,* 1824; Miss Cuthbertson's *Romance of the Pyrenees,* 1803; *Santo Sebastiano, or, The Young Protector,* 1806; *Forest of Montalbano,* 1810. Indeed, all the novels of these three ladies (as of very many more) might well be described as " sentimental-Gothic." In the *Forest of Montalbano,* however, there is a distinct leaning to " terror-Gothic." " Sentimental-Gothic," again, are Mrs. Parsons' *Lucy,* 1794, and *The Girl of the Mountains,* 1795; the anonymous *Eloise de Montblanc,* 1796; Mrs. Eleanor Sleath's *The Orphan of the Rhine,* 1798; *Ariel, or, the Invisible Monitor,* 1801; *Vesuvia, or Anglesea Manor,* 1807; *Rosalie, or, The Castle of Montalabretti* (very inclining to " terror "), 1811; Agnes Lancaster's *The Abbess of Valtiera, or, The Sorrows of a Falsehood,* 1816; Catherine G. Ward's *The Cottage on the Cliff, A Sea Side Story* (an elegant and enchanting specimen), 1823 ; Hannah Maria Jones' *Emily Moreland, or, The Maid of the Valley*, 1829.

So easily, however, do the two kinds, the terror-Gothic and the sentimental-Gothic, blend in one novel that it is often impossible to consign any particular fiction to the one category. The work of Mrs. Meeke, for example, and much of the work of Mrs. Helme, might be called sentimental with a strong admixture (in many instances) of terror. Mrs. Meeke whilst writing of a contemporary Duke of Orkney with sons at Eton and Oxford none the less creates a Gothic atmosphere, which she contrives to supply with an almost individual colouring.

Mrs. Radcliffe's genius is so great that it may be considered to stand above and apart, yet if we must analyse her romances we shall find both terror and a sentimental interest.

A third kind of Gothic novel should be particularized, the historical. As this is to be dealt with in detail later it will suffice to say that historical Gothic does not so much derive its inspiration from Leland's *Longsword, Earl of Salisbury*, 1762, all-important pioneer as this romance is, but rather from Sophia Lee's *The Recess*, 1783–85, a romance of the days of Queen Elizabeth, who herself appears in these pages together with a number of other well-known persons of the reign. Indeed, the skill with which Miss Lee introduces us to famous characters almost rivals that of Harrison Ainsworth and his vast gallery. *The Recess*, as will be emphasized in another chapter, is a work of considerable note, and exercised upon the novel of the day an influence which yet waits to receive its due meed of recognition and esteem. Miss Lee was followed by a lengthy train. In 1790 Mrs. A. M. Mackenzie published her *Monmouth* ; in 1794 appeared the anonymous *Edward de Courcy*, a tale of the Wars of the Roses ; in 1795 Anne Yearsley issued *The Royal Captives*, a solution of the Man in the Iron Mask ; and in the same year appeared *The Duke of Clarence*, an Historical Novel, by E. M. F. ; in 1802 was published Anna Millikin's tale of the twelfth century, *Plantagenet, or Secrets of the House of Anjou* ; Leslie Armstrong in 1806 went even further down the years with *The Anglo-Saxons, or, the Court of Ethelwald*, and a few months earlier Francis Lathom had issued one of the best of his novels, *The Mysterious Freebooter ; or, The Days of Queen Bess*, who appears *in propriâ personâ* on the scene. A quarter of a century later, in 1830, Lathom wrote " A Romantic Legend of the Days of Anne Boleyn," *Mystic Events ; or, The Vision of the Tapestry*, chapters in which as we shall see, not only Anne Boleyn and her father Sir Thomas Boleyn play their part, but Henry VIII is an actor in the tale, whilst we catch a glimpse of Wolsey and Queen

Catherine of Arragon.   Only a dozen years more and all these historical personages were drawn by Ainsworth with much detail in *Windsor Castle*. ²

The historical-Gothic novel for the most part can easily be distinguished from the historical novel which, often rather clumsily, follows in the footsteps of Scott, and even before *Ivanhoe*, *The Monastery*, *The Abbot* and *Kenilworth*, there appeared such Historical Novels as Miss Prickett's *Warwick Castle*, "containing, amongst other desultory information, the Descent and Achievements of the ancient Earls of Warwick, from the earliest period of their creation to the present time. With some Account of Warwick, Birmingham, Lemington, etc., etc., interspersed with Pieces of local Poetry, incidental Biography, and Anecdotes of English History"; Baldwin, Cradock, and Joy: 3 vols., 1817.

Curiously enough Mrs. Radcliffe's *Gaston de Blondeville, or The Court of Henry III Keeping Festival in Ardenne*, written in the winter of 1802, but not issued (posthumously) until 1826, can hardly be called a historical-Gothic novel, even although not intending to publish these chapters she gratified herself by the introduction of a true spectre.   It does not appear that she was inspired by Scott, but she writes in a vein which looks forward to the earlier work of Ainsworth, particularly *Crichton* (1837) and *The Tower of London* (1840), and I think it probable that he was much influenced by *Gaston de Blondeville*, since he was a professed admirer of Mrs. Radcliffe and steeped himself in her romantic pages.   *Sir John Chiverton*, 1826, is obviously modelled upon *Gaston de Blondeville*, but this must be regarded as mainly (if not almost entirely) the work of John Partington Aston, and Ainsworth had a very small share in the book.

In William Heseltine's *The Last of the Plantagenets*: " An Historical Romance, Illustrating Some of the Public Events, and Domestic and Ecclesiastical Manners of the Fifteenth and Sixteenth Centuries," published in 1829, that is to say, a year before *Mystic Events*, although there is distinctly a Gothic atmosphere in several passages, archæology is beginning to assert itself, and we meet with such terms as " *genouillières*, or knee-pieces " ; " *sollerets*, or polished iron shoes " ; "white wassellbread " ; " an Esquire or *Coustillier* " ; " *hucque*, or mantle " ; " the courteous *Antè* and *Retrò* reverence " ; " Paske-tide " ; and many more.   The story, which is well-written, shows the influence of Scott. It tells the adventures of Richard Plantagenet from 1485 to 1549. Richard, the son of King Richard III, has been brought up in obscurity at Ely Monastery, and is only recognized by his father on the eve of Bosworth.   The flight of Lord Lovel after the battle of Stoke enters into the narrative, together with the concealment of that nobleman in a secret cell at Minster Lovel, and his death there.

Perhaps Anne Fuller most candidly represents the attitude of the Gothic novelist to history when in the preface to *Alan Fitz-Osborne, an Historical Tale*, 1787, she declares : " I mean not to offend the majesty of sacred truth by giving her but a secondary place in the following pages. Necessity, stronger than prudence, obliges me to give fiction the pre-eminence ; but . . . I have preserved her genuine purity as unblemished as circumstances would admit," and necessity in this case had the upper hand all along the line. T. J. Horsley Curties placed his first novel, *Ethelwina, or, The House of Fitz-Auburne*, 1799, " In the reign of the illustrious Edward the Third," and early in the story the monarch visits Auburne Castle, but the author's sole purpose is " to fascinate the senses with a delusive picture of ' times for ever past.' " Lathom has a shrewd observation in the Preface to *The Mysterious Freebooter*, answering the reviewers who gird at Romance for assuming " the right of placing deceased characters in situations through which they never passed, and of giving to historical facts false dates, and erroneous terminations." He answers such cavillers " ' A Romance,' says Dr. Johnson, ' means a fiction, a tale of wild adventures of love and war ' ; which explanation must, I think, be sufficient to prevent anyone from reading them under the idea of gaining from them correct historical information ; and prepare them to encounter those anachronisms and misstatements which the author has been guilty of, for the purpose of augmenting or enriching his tale."

Ethelwina, which Horsley Curties had sent " into the world as an orphan, whose father feared to acknowledge it, under his *Christian* appellation of HORSLEY," proved very popular with the votaries of the Circulating Library, but was rather scurvily handled by the reviewers, whereupon in the Preface [33] to his second Romance, *Ancient Records, or The Abbey of Saint Oswythe* (1801), Horsley Curties remarks : " As this species of writing has of late been feebly attacked, I will venture a few observations on the subject.—Authors of Novels are nearly allied to those of Romance—are twin-sisters, and should be equally allied in affection ; but as sisters will sometimes envy and disagree when the one has been more admired than the other, so the Writers of Novels, jealous of us humble architects, will not suffer us to build our airy castles, or mine our subterranean caverns, unmolested." The sentence is something of a hermaphrodite, but the meaning is quite plain. He continues : " Let me enlarge a little further on this theme.—Ought the female Novelist, in order to display a *complete* knowledge of human nature, to degrade that delicate timidity, that shrinking innocence which is the loveliest boast of womanhood, in drawing characters which would ruin her reputation to be acquainted with ?—Ought she to describe scenes which bashful modesty would blush to conceive an idea, much less avow a knowledge of ?—Oh no ! let the chaste pen of female delicacy disdain such unworthy subjects ;—leave to the other sex a description of grovelling incidents, debased characters, and low pursuits :—there is still a range wide and vast enough for fanciful imagination." The significant point here is that Horsley Curties emphatically differentiates between the writer of romances and the writer of novels. A little earlier, indeed, he acclaims Mrs. Radcliffe, " *Udolpho's* unrivalled Foundress " as the finest and supreme writer of romances.

In an important note upon the First Dialogue of *The Pursuits of Literature*, first published in 1794, Thomas James Mathias is very severe upon " Mrs. Charlotte Smith, Mrs. Inchbald, Mrs. Mary Robinson, Mrs. etc., etc.," who, though all of them " very ingenious ladies," are " too frequently *whining* or *frisking* in novels, till our girls' heads turn wild with impossible adventures, and are now and then tainted with democracy, and sometimes with infidelity and loose principles. Not so the mighty magician of THE MYSTERIES OF UDOLPHO, bred and nourished by the Florentine Muses in their sacred solitary caverns, amid the paler shrines of Gothic superstition, and in all the dreariness of enchantment ; a poetess whom Ariosto would with rapture have acknowledged as the

La nudrita
Damigella Trivulzia AL SACRO SPECO.

I would say a word on Romances and Novels. . . . No works can be read with more delight and advantage, when they are selected with discrimination ; they animate and improve the mind." Mathias quite justly lays down that it is *necessary* to read Cervantes, *Gil Blas* and " that great comic Epic poem " *Tom Jones*. He allows that " Mrs. Charlotte Smith has great poetical powers, and a pathos which commands attention." He praises Miss Burney, and concludes : " I cannot descend among all the modern farrago of novels, which are too often ' receipts to make w——s.' " The first portion of this note, so far as the quotation from Ariosto, was written in 1794 ; the latter part was added in 1798. We have here, then, the same distinction drawn between romances and novels.

The author of that amusing satire *The Age* (1810), " A Poem : Moral, Political, and Metaphysical," in the rubric to his Book VII has : " Soliloquy of a Votaress of Romance. The Fashion of Romances

Described. Novelists. Description of their Productions." He gives a description of the Temple of romance : [34]

> Here vot'ries crowd of all conditions
> To view the fleeting exhibitions ;
> And, well as crazy brain permits
> Sketch down each vision as it flits :
> While deeper mysteries are brewing
> They see at first a gothic ruin.
> (This seems to be a rule of late
> From which none dare to deviate),
> 'Tis castle large with turrets high
> Intruding always on the sky . . . .
> On ev'ry tow'r, to please the sight,
> The moon bestows a speck of light . . .
> The stairs and passages so wind,
> The way's impossible to find ;
> And who to venture in them durst
> Must always lose himself at first.
> The windows close, thro' which, about
> Each hour, some curious Ghost peeps out ;
> As if he had a slight suspicion
> Folks might walk in without permission : . .
> Woods all around are thickly set
> Which 'stead of green, are black as jet.
> Beyond these rise a ridge of rocks
> At which imagination shocks. . . .

The hero follows, and later the heroine,

> Next comes a monk with disposition
> Endeav'ring solely for perdition ;
> Without design or end in view
> For which the devil's work he'll do.

Novelists are rather cruelly and unfairly ridiculed :

> These novelists who boast one school
> Can ne'er depart a general rule :
> To make (before one page they move)
> Two creature fall in fits of love :
> One always masculine in gender
> The other female, and more tender.

The course of true love never did run smooth :

> Starts up a father, guardian, aunt,
> Morose and ever slyly creeping,
> Suspiciously thro' keyholes peeping ;
> As hateful as the pen can draw
> In hideousness without a flaw :
> For these in novels hold that place
> Which wizards in romances grace.

In a note upon this passage the author of *The Age* gives us very precise instructions how we may nicely distinguish between the romance and the novel, together with a useful receipt for turning one into the other.   He writes as follows : " The conduct of the poet in considering romances and novels separately, may be thought singular by those who have penetration to see that a novel may be made out of a romance, or a romance out of a novel with the greatest ease, by scratching out a few terms, and inserting others.   Take the following, which may, like machinery in factories, greatly accelerate the progress of the divine art.

From any romance to make a novel.

Where you find :—

A castle	put	An house.
A cavern		A bower.
A groan		A sigh.
A giant		A father.
A blood-stained dagger .		A fan.
Howling blasts . . .		Zephyrs.
A knight		A gentleman without whiskers.
A lady who is the heroine .		Need not be changed, being versatile.
Assassins		Killing glances.
A monk		An old steward.
Skeletons, skulls, &c. .		Compliments, sentiments, &c.
A lamp		A candle.
A magic book sprinkled with blood . . .		A letter bedewed with tears.
Mysterious voices . .		Abstruse words (easily found in a Dictionary.)
A secret oath . . .		A tender hint accompanied with naiveté.
A gliding ghost . . .		A usurer, or an attorney.
A witch		An old housekeeper.
A wound		A kiss.
A midnight murder . .		A marriage.

The same table of course answers for transmuting a novel into a romance.

It however must be acknowledged that something is required from the author's judgement.   Though the loom is prepared, none but the weaver can make the web.   So the mind, educated in the school of nature, and afterwards sent to the college of fancy ; refined, rectified, and sublimed, is necessary for the formation of this intellectual tapestry. There is that ardour necessary which laughs at impossibilities ; that ingenuity and persuasion which bring together and reconcile those circumstances that were justly considered time immemorial the most irreconcileable ; and that force which bursts the whole asunder when it can be continued no longer, or that the author is losing his way in his own labyrinth.

As to the plots of mystery which are inseparable from these pro-ductions, there is one rule in forming them, which is this : For the author to suppose secretly, under any thing ostensible, whatever it is almost impossible could be there : which the reader never can suspect, unless by the extraordinary shuffling and fuss commonly used about that part, as in legerdemain."

The poem gives lengthy and very clever descriptions of a hero and a heroine in a novel together with amplest directions how to manage the whole conventional business.   Of the lady we are told :

> If out she trips, we always find
> Some Zephyr fans, not vulgar wind ;
> Contriv'd by Æolus's throat,
> On which her " silver locks " may float ;
> Or " roseate garments " and her hair
> Together take a dance in air.
> She never walks, she always *trips*
> And 'stead of running, *wildly skips*.
> To pass away her leisure hour,
> From nature's breast she plucks a flow'r;
> On which should drop of rain appear,
> The lover takes it for a tear,
> With rapture sips it tho' thin-pated
> Is by the draught intoxicated.
> The maid immediate to her spark
> Makes some original remark ;
> Such sentiment thro'out it glows!
> About the fragrance of the rose ;
> And of its prickles, and its thorn;
> Then flies away in virgin scorn :
> But reasons why she capers so
> The most inquisitive can't know.
> For pranks like these, now frown, now smile,
> Show soul refin'd and versatile,
> So whimsical, so wildly gay
> Like monkey or an April day.

A good deal of ungenerous exaggeration seems inseparable from early nineteenth century satire, but we can easily enough discount all that, and it does not in the slightest affect our enjoyment of Mrs. Charlotte Smith, Mrs. Roche, Mrs. Bennett, Mrs. Meeke, Miss Cuthbert-son, Mrs. Ward, to find certain contemporary conventions of the novelist, modes and phrases in themselves quite pleasing and often

felicitous, laughed at by Pasquin and Marfurio, even though a disagreeable tang of malice not unseldom sour the jest.   The lampoons are
interesting, and often accidentally throw light upon the literary
theories and fashions of the moment.

Of romances, the author of *The Age* remarks :

> In these days, the Gothic sect
> Can scribble with a good effect,
> Whene'er these tales like lighted match
> Can fire imagination's thatch.

And concerning the novels he adds less than twenty lines later :

> In physiognomy we trace
> The vestige of a Gothic race.

The word " Gothic," which was to play so important a part
in later days, and which now has so very definite and particular
a meaning (especially in relation to literature) originally conveyed
the idea of barbarous, tramontane and antique, and was merely
a term of reproach and contempt.   From its application to
architecture—and Gothic building, as we shall see, was long enough
held in very low esteem—it came to connote almost anything
mediæval, and could be referred to almost any period until the
middle, or even the end, of the seventeenth century.   In such
extension, of course, it comes loosely to signify little more than
old-fashioned, grannam and out-of-date.[35]
    In reference to architecture, the sovran disdain with which Gothic
was regarded is repeatedly emphasized.   John Evelyn, a virtuoso of
the most cultured talent, writing *An Account of Architects & Architecture*, in *A Parallel of Architecture Both Ancient & Modern* by Roland
Freart Sr De Chambray, folio, 1664, in his Epistle Dedicatory instructs
Sir John Denham : " You will know, that all the mischiefs and
absurdities in our modern *Structures* proceed chiefly from our busie
and *Gotic* triflings in the *Composition* of the *Five Orders*."   Gothic is
unworthy to be called an Order, those who envisaged it were " low
and reptile *Souls* " severely to be reprobated on account of the " idle
and impertinent *Grotesks*, with which they have ever infected all our
Modern Architecture " (p. 3), and no words are bad enough for those
who dare " to *Engotish* (as one may say) after their own capricious
Humour " (p. 5).   Evelyn speaks of " *Arched Doors* or *Windows* "
(p. 131), and observes, " This *Barbarity* therefore we may look upon as
purely *Gotique*."

The great Sir Christopher Wren in his ample description of and notes upon S. Paul's Cathedral, printed in *Parentalia*, folio, 1750,[36] speaks of abandoning " the *Gothick* Rudeness of the old Design " for " a good *Roman* Manner." His aim was " a Cathedral-form . . . so rectified, as to reconcile, as near as possible, the *Gothick* to a better Manner of Architecture ; with a *Cupola*, and above that, instead of a Lantern, a lofty Spire, and large Porticoes." He remarks : " This we now call the *Gothick* Manner of Architecture (so the *Italians* called what was not after the *Roman* Style) tho' the *Goths* were rather Destroyers than Builders ; I think it should with more reason be called the *Saracen* style. . . . The *Crusado* gave us an Idea of this Form." In England, Salisbury is " one of the best patterns of *Gothick-building*." He again insists " what we now vulgarly call the *Gothick*, ought properly and truly to be named the *Saracenick Architecture refined by the Christians*," and developed from " Mosques, Caravansaras, and Sepulchres " built by Mohammedans.

Sir Christopher Wren quotes with warm approval Evelyn,[37] and speaks of buildings demolished by " the Goths, Vandals, and other barbarous Nations . . . introducing in their stead, a certain fantastical and licentious Manner of Building, which we have since called *Modern* or *Gothick*. Congestions of heavy, dark, melancholy and monkish Piles, without any just Proportion, Use, or Beauty, compared with the truly ancient . . . a judicious Spectator is rather distracted or quite confounded, than touched with that Admiration, which results from the true and just Symmetry, regular Proportion, Union, and Disposition." In final condemnation Wren sums up Gothic Cathedrals as " vast and gigantick Buildings indeed, but not worthy the Name of Architecture."

We are the less surprised then to find that the Augustan Addison, who incidentally in his *Remarks on Several Parts of Italy, etc. In the Years*, 1701, 1702, 1703, never misses an opportunity of lewdly aspersing the manners and impiously reviling the religion of the country in which he was a stranger, shook his head sadly enough when he saw the Certosa [38] of Pavia. He perforce allowed " the convent of *Carthusians* " to be " very spacious and beautiful," yet added, " Their church is extremely fine, and curiously adorned, but of a *Gothic* structure."[39] When he approaches Siena he is rabid with resentment : " There is nothing in this city so extraordinary as the Cathedral, which . . . can only be looked upon as one of the master-pieces of *Gothic* Architecture. When a man sees the prodigious pains and expence, that our forefathers have been at in these barbarous buildings, one cannot but fancy to himself what miracles of Architecture they would have left us, had they been only instructed in the right way ; for when the devotion of those ages was much warmer than that of the present, and the riches of the people much more at the disposal of the Priests, there was so much mony consumed on these *Gothic* Cathedrals, as would have finished a greater variety of noble buildings, than have been raised either before or since that time.

One would wonder to see the vast labour that has been laid out on this single Cathedral . . . nothing in the world can make a prettier show to those who prefer false beauties, and affected ornaments, to a noble and majestick simplicity." And this of the Duomo with its black and white chequered marbles, memorials of the Sorrowful and Joyful Mysteries of Our Lady, whereby, as she told S. Bridget, " her life was ever divided between grief and happiness," the Duomo with the Capella del Voto, the bronze work of Beccafumi, Donatello's statue of S. John Baptist, Neroccio's S. Catharine, and the wonderful mosaics of that pavement !

The fact is that the antipathy of Wren and Addison to Gothic does not consist in any mere matter of taste or liking, but sets much deeper than that ; it is psychological. Wren, unconsciously perhaps, betrays the secret when he speaks of " monkish Piles " without any use. The Gothic Cathedral was an aspiration towards God, a place where the Most Holy Sacrifice of the Altar might be ever offered to the Father. The Gothic Cathedral was built for the Mass and on account of the Mass. Minds of the type of Wren and Addison had no conception of the Christian Sacrifice ; what they supposed the Catholic Faith to be they loathed. Their churches were empty lecture-rooms, " luminous and disencumbered " to echo Addison's approving phrase. Here was no priest, but a preacher who should discourse lukewarm logic and moral common-sense to his auditors. It was all very didactic and very respectable, and it would be difficult to imagine anything more utterly lacking in any sense of religion.

The classicists were wont to hold up Horace as the supreme master and model, not Horace of the Odes and Satires, not even a genuine Horace of the *De Arte Poetica*, but a Horace who had been tailored in the velvet court-coat and made to wear the mighty periwig of the " regent of Parnassus," Nicolas Boileau Despréaux.

As we might expect, Boileau uses the word *gothique* in sternest reprobation, as for example when in his famous ninth Satire he lashes the clerk who in the parterre for " quinze sous " can

Traiter de visigoths tous les vers de Corneille.

In England, too, the use of the word was soon conveniently extended from its direct application to architecture, and Dryden in his critical preface containing *A Parallel betwixt Painting and Poetry*, to *The Art of Painting*, 4to, 1695, his English prose translation of Charles Alphonse du Fresnoy's Latin poem *De Arte Graphica*,[40] precisely says : " The Gothique manner, and the barbarous ornaments, which are to be avoided in a picture, are just the same with those in an ill-ordered play. For example, our English Tragi-comedy must be confessed to be wholly Gothique, notwithstanding the success which it has found upon our theatre." (How unjust Dryden is to his own genius here is an inquiry we must waive as impertinent to our matter.) [41] Again, he defines : " All that has nothing of the Ancient gust is call'd a barbarous or Gothique manner." Echoing these very words the vaguely philosophical third Earl of Shaftesbury in his *Characteristicks of Men, Manners, Opinions and Times* (1711) writes : " We are not so Barbarous or Gothick as they pretend." Bishop Burnet in his *History of his Own Time* (published posthumously 1723-34) described the temper of Charles XII as growing " daily more fierce and Gothick."

" Ah Rustick, ruder than *Gothick*," cries Mrs. Millamant to the loutish Sir Wilfull in *The Way of the World*, 1700 ; and well nigh half a century later Mrs. Western rebuked her irate brother with " O ! more than Gothick ignorance ! " *Tom Jones*, vii, chapter 3. In 1773 Mrs. Hardcastle complains of her good spouse's " Gothic vivacity," whilst a modish young lady in *The Example ; or, the History of Lucy Cleveland* (1778) deemed " husband " a " gothic word." In Miss Cuthbertson's *Rosabella ; or, A Mother's Marriage*, 5 volumes, 1817, Mrs. O'Dowd with horror speaks of Rotherhithe whither she has accompanied her husband, Captain O'Dowd, on business as " Gothland " (Vol. III, p. 254), and in the same novel we hear that the Marchioness of Quizland cried shame on Lady Townhurst's rusticity, declaring " it was Gothic barbarity to patronize children." Even as late as 1841, in his novel *The Parish Clerk*, J. T. Hewlett spoke of eating dinner " at the gothic hour of one o'clock." Very rarely was there any adverse comment upon the extended use of the word ' Gothic,' although it is true that a reviewer in the *Gentleman's Magazine*, July, 1778, takes exception to the description of *The Champion of Virtue* (*The Old English Baron*) as a Gothic story, since Englishmen of the days of King Henry V and King Henry VI were certainly not Goths.[42] Wisely enough Clara Reeve ignored such futile pedantry, and in good set terms made it plain that her literary offspring was intended " to unite the most attractive and interesting circumstances of the ancient Romance and modern Novel," and that it was " distinguished by the appellation of a Gothic story, being a picture of Gothic times and manners." In *The Novice of Saint Dominick*, 4 volumes, 1806, by Miss Sydney Owenson (afterwards

Lady Morgan), chapter V, the pious and learned lady Magdelaine de Montmorell exclaims : " female sanctity is, I am afraid, a treasure still rarer than female genius, to be found in this Gothic age."

The term ' Gothic.' so long slandered and traduced, found at length a learned and powerful defender in Bishop Richard Hurd of Worcester (1720–1808),[43] whose *Letters on Chivalry and Romance,* published anonymously in 1762, must be accounted not only a work of paramount importance in the history of English romanticism, but also regarded as among the finest critical essays of our literature. Bishop Hurd was greatly influenced by Joseph and Thomas Warton, yet he is something far more than the mere disciple of the two brothers, for his pages in every period show a forceful originality, conviction, and matured reflection, whilst he goes much further than they had ventured openly to advance.

The very first of the twelve *Letters* boldly throws down the gauntlet with its opening words : " The ages, we call barbarous, present us with many a subject of curious speculation. What, for instance, is more remarkable than the Gothic CHIVALRY ? or than the spirit of ROMANCE, which took its rise from that singular institution ? " A little later in the same letter he observes : " The greatest geniuses of our own and foreign countries, such as Ariosto and Tasso in Italy, and Spenser and Milton in England, were seduced by these barbarities of their forefathers ; were even charmed by the Gothic Romances. Was this caprice and absurdity in them ? Or, may there not be something in the Gothic Romance peculiarly suited to the views of a genius, and to the ends of poetry ? And may not the philosophic moderns have gone too far, in their perpetual ridicule and contempt of it ? " To answer which questions he proposes as the Subject and Plan to explain the rise, progress and genius of Gothic Chivalry. " Reasons, for the decline and rejection of the Gothic taste in later times must be given." In the third *Letter* Hurd notes the several Characteristics of Chivalry ; the passion for arms ; the spirit of enterprize ; the honour of knighthood ; the rewards of valour ; the splendour of equipages ; their romantic ideas of justice ; their passion for adventures ; their eagerness to run to the succour of the distressed ; the pride they took in redressing wrongs, and removing grievances ; their courtesy, affability, and that refined gallantry, which carried the notions of chastity, the fairest and strongest claim of the female sex, to so platonic an elevation ; and above all, the " character of Religion." Every one of these characteristics, under a varied form, but yet plain to distinguish, is to be found in the Gothic Novel, the " character of Religion " becoming an intense pre-occupation with the cloister, abbots, monks, nuns, friars, convents, priories and the anchoret's retreat.   The fourth *Letter* draws some very striking parallels between the *old Romances* and the poems of Homer, " circumstances of agreement between the *heroic* and *gothic* manners," [44] and the author commences the fifth *Letter* by emphasizing " that the resemblance between the heroic and Gothic ages is very great."   In the sixth *Letter* he justly remarks that " so far as the heroic and Gothic manners are the same, the pictures of each, if well taken, must be equally entertaining.   But I go further, and maintain that the circumstances, in which they differ, are clearly to the advantage of the Gothic designers."   Not a few of his contemporaries must have been horrified when they read these sentences, nor would their amaze decrease, when, speaking of the manners of the feudal age, he adds that as Homer was a citizen of the world, could the poet have seen the manners of the feudal age he would certainly have preferred them to Grecian manners, " And the grounds of this preference would, I suppose, have been ' *The improved gallantry of the feudal times* ; and the *superior solemnity of their superstitions.*' "   This last phrase is very significant, and strikes the key-note of much that was to follow in novel and romance.   As to *religious machinery,* " for the more solemn fancies of witchcraft and incantation, the horrors of the Gothic were above measure striking and terrible.   The mummeries of the pagan priests were childish, but the Gothic Enchanters shook and alarmed all nature.   We feel this difference very sensibly in reading the antient and modern poets.   You would not compare the Canidia of Horace with the Witches in Macbeth.   And what are Virgil's myrtles dropping blood to Tasso's enchanted forest ? "   With a tribute of enthusiastic praise to the " terrible sublime " of Shakespeare, he continues :   " I can't but think that, when Milton wanted to paint the horrors of that night (one of the noblest parts in his *Paradise Regained*) which the Devil himself is feigned to conjure up in the wilderness, the Gothic language and ideas helped him to work up his tempest with such terror. . . . And without more words you will readily apprehend that the fancies of our modern bards are not only more gallant, but, on a change of the scene, more sublime, more terrible, more alarming, than those of the classic fablers.   In a word, you will find that the *manners* they paint, and the *superstitions* they adopt, are the more poetical for being Gothic."

The seventh *Letter* considers in some detail the effect of the Gothic upon Spenser [45] and Milton.   No doubt each of these bards kindled his poetic fire from classic lore, but when most inflamed they are the more particularly rapt with the Gothic fables of chivalry.   With regard to Shakespeare too, whose " genius kept no certain rout, but rambled at hazard into all the regions of human life and manners . . . one thing is clear, that even he is greater when he uses Gothic manners and machinery, than when he employs classical." The eighth *Letter* entirely cuts the ground from under the feet of Wren and Evelyn. " When an architect examines a Gothic structure by Grecian rules he finds nothing but deformity. But the Gothic architecture had its own rules, by which when it comes to be examined, it is seen to have its merit, as well as the Grecian. The question is not, which of the two is conducted in the simplest or truest taste : but, whether there be not sense and design in both, when scrutinized by the laws on which each is projected.

The same observation holds of the two sorts of poetry. Judge of the *Faery Queen* by the classic models, and you are shocked with its disorder : consider it with an eye to its Gothic original, and you find it regular. The unity and simplicity of the former are more complete : but the latter has that sort of unity and simplicity, which results from its nature.

The *Faery Queen* then, as a Gothic poem, derives its METHOD, as well as the other characters of its composition, from the established modes and ideas of chivalry.

. . . So that if you will say anything against the poet's method, you must say that he should not have chosen this subject. But this objection arises from your classic ideas of Unity, which have no place here ; and are in every view foreign to the purpose." There is, in fact, not the classic Unity, " which consists in the representation of one entire action," but " an Unity of another sort, an unity resulting from the respect which a number of related actions have to one common purpose. In other words, It is an unity of *design*, and not of action." The Gothic Novel,—*The Romance of the Forest*, *The Mysteries of Udolpho*, *The Italian*, for example—has this unity of design.

In the ninth *Letter* the author considers the beauties of Tasso, which afford a fresh confirmation of the point upon which he principally insists, *The pre-eminence of the Gothic manners and fictions, as adapted to the ends of poetry* [and certainly *romance*] *above the classic.*

Bishop Hurd with urbanest satire just laughs out of court my Lord Shaftesbury and his critical cant upon the tritest theme—" it is not to be told with what alacrity and self-complacency he flourishes upon it " in his *Soliloquy or Advice to an Author*, 1710. " The *Gothic manner*, as he calls it," is the favourite object of my Lord's raillery. This ingenious nobleman is so perfectly enamoured " of his *noble antients*," whose spirit and precepts he misunderstands, that he will fight any man who contends there may be other elegances and beauties in literature besides those in the behalf of which he jousts so slashingly.

The cold Boileau " happened to say something of the *clinquant* of Tasso ; and the magic of this word, like the report of Astolfo's horn in Ariosto, overturned at once the solid and well-built reputation of the Italian poetry."

This potent word occurs in the ninth of Boileau's satires, *A Son Esprit*, where he attacks a whole catalogue of poets, almost as long as Homer's list of ships, and unmercifully belabours the courtier-wits :

> Tous les jours, à la cour, un sot de qualité
> Peut juger de travers avec impunité ;
> À Malherbe, à Racan, préférer Théophile,
> Et le clinquant du Tasse, à tout l'or de Virgile.

You are, no doubt, a vastly superior critic, Monsieur Nicolas Boileau Despréaux, but did it never occur to you that a man may yield to none in his devotion to Vergil, and yet may love and admire Tasso also ?

Yet " the *clinquant* of Tasso " became a sort of watchword among the critickins. On a sudden nothing was heard but this abracadabra, and the respectable Mr. Addison, " who gave the law in taste here, took it up and sent it about the kingdom in his polite and popular essays."

These considerations lead to some very pointed remarks in regard to those who profess so exactly to follow what they are pleased to call nature : " But the source of bad criticism, as universally of bad philosophy, is the abuse of terms. A poet, they say, must follow *Nature* ; and by Nature we are to suppose can only be meant the known and experienced course of affairs in this world. Whereas the poet has a world of his own, where experience has less to do, than consistent imagination.

He has, besides, a supernatural world to range in. He has Gods, and Faeries, and Witches at his command : And,

> — — — — O ! who can tell
> The hidden *pow'r* of herbes, and might of magic spell ?
> SPENSER, B. i, C. 2.

Thus in the poet's world, all is marvellous and extraordinary ; yet not *unnatural* in one sense, as it agrees to the conceptions that are readily entertained of these magical and wonder-working Natures.

This trite maxim of *following Nature* is further mistaken in applying it indiscriminately to all sorts of poetry."

Sublime and creative poetry and romance may be regarded as a species addressing itself solely or principally to the Imagination.

Therefore the poet or romantic writer may say : " I leave to the realist, to the classicist (so-called) the merit of being always broad awake, always in their dull sober senses ; The *divine dream* (Homer's " theios oneiros "),[46] and mystic fancy are among the noblest of my prerogatives."

The cry of the Augustans was : Magic and enchantment are senseless things. This crass materialism is met by the simple truth that witchcraft is a very real and terrible thing, for we are wiser in this than they ; that the supernatural is all about and around us ever ; that the veil trembles and is very thin.

The concluding *Letters* sum up and emphasize with a few general reflexions and particular applications Hurd's views upon Gothic Romance.

One of the writer's strongest arguments—although never explicitly advanced as such—lies in the fact that he on no occasion expresses himself narrowly, as one who wishes entirely to banish and disallow any school of poetry save the chivalrous and romantic ; he freely acknowledges the legitimate claim and position of classical poetry, he merely refuses to grant it a monopoly and an exclusive tyranny of place and power. He urges and insists that Gothic poetry shall be judged by its own standards, by its own particular claims, method, and end.

In the direct opposite to this catholic spirit consists one of the many, perhaps the greatest of the many, weaknesses of Addison and his followers. We may take Addison, as being the most influential, to typify a school. Addison has the hall-mark of the completest prig. He steadfastly refuses to allow worth or beauty in poem or prose which he conceives as not conforming to the stereotyped rules and prejudices that had become in the world of letters a kind of canon law. Any author who does not speak the polite and popular cant is disbarred. This is the very essence of egotistical Philistinism, and if it so ill befits a writer such as Addison, who had parts, what are we to think when we meet it in men of a much lesser grade and narrower intellects such as Thomas Babington Macaulay ? It were superfluous to dwell upon the point since this latter writer, both as critic and historian, is now so badly blown upon and generally discredited.

Gibbon has justly declared that he could mention " few writers more deserving of the great though prostituted name of the critic " than Richard Hurd, and to over-estimate the importance of the *Letters on Chivalry and Romance* in the history of English letters is almost impossible. The anonymous publication of the book did not burst with a sudden resonance in literary circles and compel clamant attention in every quarter, but its influence very swiftly coursed and permeated the channels of taste and thought. The change thereafter was immediate. There had, of course, already been symptoms of a certain vacillation of fashion, but this transition was incalculably accelerated by the authoritative pronouncements and acknowledged learning of so eminent a man as Hurd, for the authorship of the *Letters* was no great secret. Not merely did a few scholars, a few poets, a handful of critics echo his dicta and range themselves beneath his banner, but a Gothic flavour rapidly became fashionable with all classes of society.

Following closely in the footsteps of their father, who died in 1745, and who is by no means an unimportant name in the history of the revival of romanticism, the Rev. Thomas Warton of *Philander, an Imitation of Spencer*, and the two Runic Odes, the Warton brothers, Joseph and Thomas, were already known as ardent romanticists, and as early as 1746 Joseph in the Advertisement prefixed to his *Odes* fairly challenged didactic poetry, and declared his conviction that "the fashion of moralizing in verse has been carried too far," asserting that "he looks upon Invention and Imagination to be the chief faculties of a Poet."

It might be an exaggeration to say that Thomas Percy's *Reliques of Ancient English Poetry* which appeared in three volumes, February, 1765, was a performance inspired by the *Letters on Chivalry and Romance*, since early in 1761 he was in treaty with Dodsley concerning the publication of a collection of old ballads, but Hurd's championship of the Gothic immensely helped and encheered him, although the original Preface is apologetic to the last degree, and as is well known he polished, printed and pruned the ballads in a perfectly preposterous fashion. The *Reliques* were not much approved of by Hurd himself, and Percy found little encouragement from many of the most eminent literary men, but for all that the success of his collections was overwhelming, and the reading public vehemently applauded, whilst Walpole, on February 5th, 1765, acknowledged "the flattering and agreeable present of the *Reliques of Ancient Poetry*" in a letter[47] of most cordial compliment, requesting the honour of the editor's acquaintance, and protesting, "If it should ever lie within my slender power to assist your studies or inquiries, I hope, Sir, you will command me. I love the cause, I have a passion for antiquity . . ." A second edition of the *Reliques* was called for in 1767; a third in 1775; but the fourth did not appear until 1794. The influence of the *Reliques* upon the younger generation was openly acknowledged by such men as Scott and Wordsworth. It should, however, be remarked that Matthew Gregory Lewis for his ballads, *The Tales of Wonder*, *The Tales of Terror*, and others drew his inspiration from contemporary Germany, from Bürger, Schiller, Goethe, and from J. G. von Herder's *Stimmen der Völker in Liedern*.

Whatever we may think of *Ossian* to-day, and myself I sometimes imagine that even the few of us who yet linger to read with real enjoyment and admiration Macpherson's perfervid rhetoric and lyrical flights are hardly able to judge his very remarkable work with completest candour, there can be no question that the Ossianic poems created an ineffaceable impression upon the age. Nor can a book be without deep significance which was hailed with enthusiasm by Gray, David Hume, John Home, and many another eminent name ; which gave Herder such extraordinary pleasure ; which strongly influenced Goethe and Schiller ; which was imitated by Coleridge and Byron ; which was praised and carefully studied by Chateaubriand, " épicurien à l'imagination catholique," as Sainte-Beuve [48] once named him.

Dr. Hugh Blair, in his essay *A Critical Dissertation on the Poems of Ossian, the Son of Fingal* (1763), defined Ossian's two principal characteristics as tenderness and sublimity. " The events recorded are all serious and grave ; the scenery throughout, wild and romantic. The extended heath by the seashore ; the mountains shaded with mist ; the torrent rushing through a solitary valley ; the scattered oaks, and the tombs of warriors overgrown with moss, all produce a solemn attention in the mind, and prepare it for great and extraordinary events." The same might be said of numberless Gothic novels. Ossian's address to the Sun, his lament over the Desolation of Balclutha, the Songs of Selma, and many passages more, are repeated and but little varied again and again in romantic fiction.

The spectres of *Ossian* which, Dr. Drake said, seem to " rush upon the eye with all the stupendous vigour of wild and momentary creation," have their ghostly progeny in the thousand phantoms of a thousand Castles.

In that poignant scene in Mrs. Charlotte Smith's *Emmeline ; or, The Orphan of the Castle*, when Lady Adelina walking in the woods encounters Fitz-Edward, quite naturally comes the phrase : " The wind blew chill and hollow among the half-stripped trees, as they passed through the wood ; and the dead leaves rustled in the blast. 'Twas such a night as Ossian might describe."

There are even, one might truly say, many Caledonian Gothic novels which show the influence of Ossian, another and entirely separate thing from the imitation of Sir Walter Scott, although some daring spirits essayed a commixture of the two. Mrs. Radcliffe's first book, *The Castles of Athlin and Dunbayne*, " A Highland Story," 1789 ; Horsley

Curties' *The Scottish Legend, or The Isle of St. Clothair*, 1802 ; Mrs. Helme's *St. Clair of the Isles* : *or, The Outlaws of Barra*, " A Scottish Tradition," 1803 ; and William Child Green's *The Prophecy of Duncannon, or, The Dwarf and the Seer*, " A Caledonian Legend," 1824 ; all show a certain indirect Ossianic influence, whilst *Otho and Rutha*, 1781, is servilely imitative.

The impetus given to the Romantic Movement by the two Wartons by Percy, and by Ossian, was very great, and had far-reaching consequences, but it was Hurd's *Letters* [49] which not only vindicated Gothicism but made the Gothic fashionable.   In 1749, as we have already seen, Squire Western's sister used the epithet " Gothick " [50] as a term of unqualified opprobrium and contempt ; seventeen years later, in 1766, the wealthy Mrs. Heidelberg, "the very flower of delicacy and cream of politeness," invites Lord Ogleby to take a dish of tea or " a sullabub warm from the cow " in her " little Gothic dairy, fitted up entirely in my own taste," whilst the old city merchant, Sterling, who apes luxury and courts the mode, builds a spire in a field against a tree to terminate the prospect—" One must always have a church, or an obelisk, or something to terminate the prospect, you know "—and spends one hundred and fifty pounds to put his ruins in proper repair, so that " you would think them ready to tumble on your head."

The famous, but unfinished *Sir Bertrand*, which so powerfully impressed Leigh Hunt, is too obviously inspired by *The Castle of Otranto*, and the introductory essay *On the Pleasure Derived from Objects of Terror* was certainly suggested by the work of Bishop Hurd, as indeed were other discourses in this kind such as *On Romances, an Imitation*, and *An Enquiry into those Kinds of Distress which Excite Agreeable Sensations*, appearing in the same collection *Miscellaneous Pieces in Prose, by J. and A. L. Aikin*, 1773.   *Sir Bertrand* has often been ascribed to Anna Laetitia Aikin (who married in 1774 the Rev. Rochemont Barbauld), but Miss Lucy Aikin in her *Memoir* prefixed to Mrs. Barbauld's *Works*, 1825, specifically gives the fragment to Dr. Aikin, and the essay on pleasurable terror to Miss Aikin.   Walpole, it is true, in a letter to Robert Jephson, January 27th, 1780, wrote of *The Castle of Otranto* : [51] " Miss Aikin flattered me even by stooping to tread in my eccentric steps.   Her *Fragment*, though but a specimen, showed her talent for imprinting terror " ; but Miss Lucy's testimony is conclusive, and it is borne out by Leigh Hunt who comments that John Aikin was " a writer from whom this effusion was hardly to have been looked for," *Book in a Corner*, 1849 ; and who was assuredly at no pains to advance his authorship of *Sir Bertrand*.

Miss Aikin in her essay shrewdly observed the positive pleasure which arises from curiosity. Imagination thus stimulated " rejoices in the expansion of its poweis." A supernatural terror is on a higher psychological plane than terror aroused by natural objects of repulsion. When there is excess of pain scenes of terror drive " too near our common nature " ; it is far more agreeable when the circumstances are " wild, fanciful and extraordinary." This is a true difference, and nicely discerned. We do not, however, stay now to consider this very vital point, since there will be much more to say on the subject and more pertinently when considering the work of Mrs. Radcliffe.

John Aikin set out to combine both kinds of terror in *Sir Bertrand*, which Walpole thought " excellent," but although it must remain a question of opinion, I cannot persuade myself that the Fragment achieves success. The commencement is striking. A knight, as he wanders in darkness over a desolate and dreary moor, hears the sullen tolling of a bell, whose funeste curfew guides him by the aid of a flickering light to " an antique mansion " with turrets at the coins. All is wrapped in darkness. He enters to grasp a death-cold hand, which he severs with one stroke of his sabre. Mysterious armed figures menace him, and he sees a hideous chevalier " thrusting forwards the bloody stump of an arm." Eventually he gains a far chamber where a lady in a shroud and black veil arises from a coffin. As he kisses her the horrid enchantment dissolves, and he finds himself set at a banquet in a splendid room, when the lady thanks him as her deliverer. Here the fragment ends. The opening is, as I have said, a powerful piece of work and grue, but the story rapidly loses, and the wakening kiss with its reminiscences of *La Belle au Bois Dormant* is utterly incongruous, bringing the whole structure to the ground. We are not with Amadis and Esplandian now.

At the very eagre of the Gothic movement there appeared a work of particular value and importance which not only takes up, but elaborates and enlarges upon the arguments and exposition of " the most learned and elegant " Hurd, perhaps even expanding the theme and carrying the inquiry further than the good Bishop would have altogether approved. Dr. Nathan Drake, whose *Literary Hours* originally first appeared in 1798, was an essayist and critic of authority. Born in 1766, he practised as a physician at Sudbury, Suffolk, 1790–92, and at Hadleigh from 1792 to 1836, in which latter year he died.

The first edition of *Literary Hours*, consists of thirty numbers. No. 2 is : On the Government of the Imagination. No. 3 : On the Tender Melancholy which usually follows the acuter feelings of sorrow. No. 6 : On Gothic superstition. Nos. 7 to 9 comprise,

Henry Fitzowen, a Gothic Tale. No. 15 : On objects of Terror. *Montmorenci*, a Fragment. No. 20 : *The Abbey of Clunedale*, a Tale. Nos. 28 and 29 : On the Superstitions of the Highlands of Scotland.

The Second Edition, 2 vols., 1800, " Corrected and Greatly Enlarged," adds nine new Numbers, and with some re-arrangement we have Forty Numbers.

The Third Edition, 3 vols., 1804, has no less than Sixty Numbers. *Sir Egbert*, a Gothic Tale, takes up Numbers 45–47 [52] ; and No. 59 is *The Spectre*, A Legendary Tale, a long ballad in quatrains clearly modelled upon the poems of Monk Lewis, " a specimen of that species which endeavours to interest, through the medium of gothic superstition." [53]

Since we have just spoken of Percy's *Reliques* the views of Drake on the subject are pertinent. Discussing Ballads, Historical Songs, and Metrical Romances,[54] he remarks that all these kinds are " well known to the poetic antiquary," and continues : " The style and poetry of these ancient ballads, must necessarily as they were the product of a rude age be, in general, extremely unequal ; and though the simplicity, the strokes of character, and description, which are frequently discoverable in these pieces, be truly interesting, they are, for the most part, so strangely intermixed with indecencies and vulgarities of every kind, as greatly to injure their effect. To remedy this inconvenience, to preserve the touching simplicity, the dramatic cast and manner of these antique compositions, at the same time avoiding their occasional grossness of diction and sentiment, has been the aim of many modern writers," amongst whom must be ranked Drake himself, since he gives a Legendary Tale, *Arthur and Edith*, [55] an attempt to copy the manner though not the obsolete diction of the ancient ballad," and *The Spectre*, to which latter reference has already been made.

Drake's analytical essays are, as we have said, of the very first importance and interest, and among these perhaps even the most thoughtful and penetrating is Number VI, where he writes on Gothic superstition. " Of the various kinds of superstition which have in any age influenced the human mind, none appear to have operated with so much effect as what has been termed the Gothic. Even in the present polished period of society, there are thousands who are yet alive to all the horrors of witchcraft, to all the solemn and terrible graces of the appalling spectre. The most enlightened mind, the mind free from all taint of superstition, involuntarily acknowledges the power of gothic agency ; and the late favourable reception which two or three publications in this style have met with, is a convincing proof of the assertion. The enchanted forest of Tasso, the spectre of Camoëns,

PLATE III

THE SPECTRE
Frontispiece, 1789

[*Face p.* 50

and the apparitions of Shakespeare, are to this day highly pleasing, striking, and sublime features in these delightful compositions." Gothic superstition may be divided into horror and the gloomy on the one part, and the romantic delighting in sportive and elegant imagery on the other.

" Next to the Gothic in point of sublimity and imagination comes the Celtic, which if the superstition of the Lowlands be esteemed a part of it may into equal propriety, be divided into the terrible and the sportive." The former is displayed in Ossian, who has given supernatural agents " employments new to gothic fiction." The latter appears in songs and ballads.

" It has been, however, too much the fashion among critical writers to condemn the introduction of any kind of supernatural agency though perfectly consonant with the common feelings of mankind." [56] Genius none the less ever had a predilection for such imagery, and if we resolve to banish powerful superstitions from our writings " the sublime, the terrible, the fanciful in poetry, will no longer exist." Mere morality, criticism, satire, alone remain.

In the Second Edition Drake appends an *Ode to Superstition*. He differentiates two kinds of Superstition, the one " Of ghastly Fear, and darkest Midnight born," a " fiend whose breath Poisons the passing hours," the other " Of Hesper born and Cynthia pale " " in Fancy's garb array'd " a " magic maid " found

> 'Mid moon-light scenes, and woody vales,
> When Elves, and Fays, and Sprites disport,
> And nightly keep their festive court.

Henry Fitzowen, A Gothic Tale, follows. In the reign of Edward IV there dwelt " at his paternal castle in Yorkshire, a piece of fine old gothic architecture, and seated in a romantic glen," Henry Fitzowen. He loves Adeline de Montfort, who resides with her mother in " a small but elegant house on the skirts of the forest adjoining to the Fitzowen estate." However, Henry has a demoniac rival, Walleran, Earl of Meullant, " of great hauteur and family pride." Among this wizard's haunts is a forest where trees coeval with druid days are the lurking-place of preternatural beings. Not long before the wedding Fitzowen, whilst hunting, is led far out of his path by a strangely fleet stag and an elusive phantom monk. He returns home amid thunder and storm to find his castle wrapped in pitchy darkness, whilst the old steward expires in his arms. He learns from his mother and sister, prisoned in a distant chamber, that Adeline has been carried off by masked ruffians. Being convinced that this is due to Walleran, immediately Fitzowen sets out in search of the evil wretch. After many wanderings he is beguiled into a decayed Gothic castle,[57] whose gates are hung with black, by the craft of a horrible witch, " a wrinckled Hagg, with Age grown double," [58] and here he is welcomed by peal after peal of horrible and infernal laughter. Spectres throng round him, and presently he meets Walleran, who wields a battle-axe, but Fitzowen, " sheathed his falchion in the breast of his opponent." The enchantment is dissolved. Espying Adeline slumbering on a couch he awakes her with a kiss. Amid the roar of thunder a whirlwind sweeps the castle of horror into air, and the lovers " found themselves seated on some mossy turf, and around them the sweet and tranquil scenery of a summer's moon-light night." Strains of harmony are heard ; warlike knights and elegant nymphs thread a bransel on the mead ; a female form of exquisite beauty announces, " from Hecate's dread agents we have freed you, from wildering fear and gloomy superstition," whilst as the spirits vanish and the music dies away Henry and Adeline are on a pleasant road, with " a village at a little distance, on whose spire the rising sun had shed his earliest beams."

Montmorenci, a Fragment is introduced by an Essay *On Objects of Terror* due to "the agency of supernatural beings" and that terror " excited by the interference of simple material causation," which " requires no small degree of skill and arrangement to prevent its operating more pain than pleasure." For example, the old ballad *Edward* could not be rendered tolerable to any person of sensibility. Walpole's *The Mysterious Mother* is condemned on the ground that the catastrophe only produces horror and repulsion. Shakespeare has seldom if ever been exceeded in his management of terror, for *Titus Andronicus* is dismissed from the count as " now generally allowed not to be his." Dante and Shakespeare both confine themselves within the " bounds of salutary and grateful pleasure." The scenes in *The Italian* when Schedoni, shocked yet self-accusing, is about to assassinate Ellena but recoils on discovering that she is (as he thinks) his daughter " appall yet delight " the reader. In the work of Mrs. Radcliffe " the Shakespeare of Romance Writers, and who to the wild landscape of Salvator Rosa has added the softer graces of a Claude, may be found many scenes truly terrific in their conception, yet so softened down, and the mind so much relieved, by the intermixture of beautiful description, or pathetic incident, that the impression of the whole never becomes too strong, never degenerates into horror, but pleasurable emotion is ever the predominating result." This is well said, and no mean tribute to the genius of Mrs. Radcliffe. Drake instances as admirable examples of the fear excited by natural causes, the sixty-third chapter of *Ferdinand, Count Fathom*, where at midnight, whilst mourning over her very tomb Renaldo beholds his lost Monimia at his side ; the description of Danger in Collins' *Ode to Fear* ; and the Scottish ballad, *Hardyknute*.

Personally I am unable to go with Drake in his observations upon *Edward* and *The Mysterious Mother*.[59] The famous old ballad *Edward* was printed in Percy's *Reliques*, 1765, Vol. I, p. 53, from a manuscript communicated by Sir David Dalrymple (Lord Hailes). It was by some thought not to be genuine, but such suspicion is altogether unfounded. There are exact parallels in Swedish, Danish, and Finnish of this extremely fine piece.[60] (The Finnish ballad, even if from the Swedish, has original turns of its own.) *Hardyknute*, on the other hand, is not antique, but " a most spirited and beautiful imitation of the ancient ballad." [61] Some writers indeed believed it to be a genuine old ballad, and Pinkerton, unfortunately for his own critical perception, went so far as to attribute it to Sir John Bruce of Kinross. It is included in Allan Ramsay's anthology *The Evergreen*, 2 vols., 1724–27. It were impertinent here to enter into any discussion of Shakespeare's authorship of *Titus Andronicus*, which seems to me beyond question. There is, in fact, no reason at all to suppose the contrary save the qualms and dislike of certain critickins, who with all their scraping can find nothing to bolster their hypothesis beyond a sentence of Ravenscroft,[62] a mere hearsay upon which it were eminently unsafe to rely. I am very certain that anyone who saw the revival of *Titus Andronicus* at the Royal Victoria Theatre, the " Old Vic," on October 8th, 1923, when George Hayes so masterly acted Aaron and Florence Saunders Tamora, can have no doubt but that 'tis all Shakespeare's hand.

Montmorenci, a Fragment, sets out to combine " picturesque description with some of those objects of terror which are independent of supernatural agency." " The sullen tolling of the curfew was heard over the heath," when Henry De Montmorency and his two attendants hurry from the ancient castle into the darkness of a storm-tossed night. They speed through a wild glen, where a swollen torrent pours over a sheer precipice. A clang of falling armour breaks through the murk, and they come upon an expiring knight on whose ghastly features is depicted horror unutterable ! Shrieks rend the air, and Montmorency finds a maiden who is being carried off by savage banditti. Montmorency cuts down the leader—" lifeless he dropped prone upon the ground and the crash of his armour bellowed through the hollow rock "—but the robbers seize him and bind him to a tree overhanging the abyss into which he is to be hurled. When he leaned over the illimitable void " his eyes were starting from their sockets, and, as he looked into the dark abyss, his senses, blasted by the view, seemed ready to forsake him." By a superhuman effort he escapes from his bonds, when suddenly—— * * * *, and there the narrative abruptly breaks off, *hiatus valde deflendus*.

The Abbey of Clunedale is a tale in which what appear to be super-natural happenings are explained, much in the style of Mrs. Radcliffe, a rationalism one cannot but think to be a blemish. The mouldering abbey, which is excellently described and at great length, is nightly visited by Clifford, as an act of penance. Owing to unfounded jealousy he has killed his wife's brother. Accompanied by his sister, Caroline, and bearing a light, he threads the Abbey ruins, and kneels in deepest humiliation and sorrow before his wife's tomb. This midnight visitant is espied and taken for a phantom. The period of the story is August, 1587.

Sir Egbert, a Gothic tale, is far more ambitious. Founded upon an ancient legend associated with Gundulph's Tower, the great Tower of Rochester Castle, it introduces us to Sir Egbert of the Order of the Oak of Navarre, who is in quest of his friend Conrad, a Chevalier who has mysteriously disappeared. From the Knights Templar of the Teutonic Order at Strood, Sir Egbert learns that the Constable of the Castle, Robert de Weldon, is rumoured to hold two amiable young people, a Lady and her Lover, in a profound and deathlike slumber. He resolves to attempt the adventure and to essay to draw from its sheath the gigantic sword which separates them, thus restoring them to conscious-ness and liberty. Many have failed, and Egbert vows " should success attend his arduous enterprise, to erect a choral shrine with daily dirges, over the sepulchre of those who have fallen in the same attempt." He enters the Castle, and is entertained at a lordly revel, " whose pomp and splendour seemed the effect of enchantments." Suddenly a con-vulsive shriek is heard. The company fly in horror, and Sir Egbert all alone is confronted by a spectral corse, which amid dreadful omens beckons him to a vault, where in characters that flamed with fire are writ the words : *Death to him who violates the mysteries of Gundulph's Tower*. A blue yet faint sulphureous light flashes forth, and as Sir Egbert presses on amid the execrations of demons phantom horrors encompass his path. He is then tempted by voluptuous delusions. At last he unsheaths the mighty sword ; Conrad and Bertha awake from their trance ; " the wild imprecations of disappointed fiends rebellowed through the air " ; and the whole glamour of ensorcellment vanishes. Conrad relates how, six years before, he and Bertha who had been lured by a vain fire to a luxurious cavern drank a magic potion offered by fair nymphs. The wretched Constable, Robert de

Weldon, confesses himself a warlock, and expires in agony and terror. The tale concludes with the nuptials of Conrad and Bertha, and of Egbert and Matilda, a sister of one of the victims of the foul enchanter's spell.

Dr. Drake is undeniably happier in his criticism and analysis than in the tales which he wrote to exhibit his Gothic principles. This is not to say that his legends are ill-told or without interest. They have romantic beauty, and *The Abbey of Clunedale* in particular shows very considerable power of narrative. We feel that *Henry Fitzowen* and *Sir Egbert* just miss the thrill and atmosphere of the true Gothic inasmuch as they trench a little too nearly upon faery lore. The enchantments, agreeable and curiously devised as they are, look towards Huon and " the sage and serious Spenser " rather than towards Mrs. Radcliffe or Lewis. Drake, no doubt, was unconsciously hampered by the limitations he imposed upon himself; he offers us an abstract, an epitome. The Gothic novel does not permit of any abbreviation; a certain leisure, a certain length allowing of long-drawn suspense ; a certain hesitation even, seem essentials in the true Gothic romance. We must be held in expectation. Events cannot hurry on their course. The Gothic novel which aims at brevity or concision is never entirely successful or to be approved. As we shall have occasion to note, this is just the point where the chap-books wilt and show so thin.

Dr. Drake well knew all that was necessary for the equipment of the Gothic novel and why, but throughout his experiments he has not allowed himself the space in which to make use of his material. He has written the prescription with rare skill ; but he has not mixed the draught. His searching analysis of pleasurable fear, although we may not agree with him in some details—I mean his repudiation of *Edward*, *The Mysterious Mother*, and *Titus Andronicus*—is a critical and psychological piece of permanent value. How admirably does he write : " When well conducted, a grateful astonishment, a welcome sensation of fear, will creep through the bosom of the Sage and of the Savage, and it is, perhaps, to the introduction of such well-imagined agency, or when not introduced upon the scene, to a very frequent allusion to it, that Shakespeare, beyond any other poet, owes the capability of raising the most awful, yet the most delightful species of terror." Dr. Drake further points out that Terror " requires no small degree of skill and arrangement " when introduced into fiction, and it must be very artfully contrived to " induce that thrilling sensation of mingled astonishment, apprehension and delight so irresistibly captivating to the generality of mankind." Curiosity must be stimulated by the "texture of the fable, or by the uncertain and suspended fate of an interesting personage," and the mind must be so agreeably relieved "that the impression of the whole never becomes too strong, never degenerates into horror, but pleasurable emotion is ever the predominating result." He gives us an example, *The Italian*, in which the genius of Mrs. Radcliffe is so masterly as to "appal yet delight the reader, and it is difficult to ascertain whether ardent curiosity, intense commiseration, or apprehension that suspends almost the faculty of breathing, be, in the progress of this well-written story, most powerfully excited."

It was, as we shall have occasion to emphasize, not an accidental circumstance that the terror-novel was in the fullest flush of popularity during the seventeen-nineties, and it was also in this decade that Mrs. Radcliffe wrote and published her most characteristic works, *A Sicilian Romance*, 1790 ; *The Romance of the Forest*, 1791 ; *The Mysteries of Udolpho*, 1794 ; and *The Italian, or, The Confessional of the Black Penitents*, 1797, a mournival of Gothic masterpieces.

NOTES TO CHAPTER I

1. *Macmillan's Magazine*, Vol. XXXV.
2. Even Max Nordau, in his clumsy, utterly perverse way, recognized and gave utterance to this. He speaks of Mysticism as "Musing and dreaming, the free ranging of imagination, disporting itself at its own sweet will along the meandering pathways of association," which is, of course, entirely erroneous, but significant. In another place he remarks : "In one part or another of his mental field of vision each of us therefore is a mystic." He includes a vast number of painters and writers in his curious topsy-turvy chapters on Mysticism : the Pre-Raphaelites, Rollinat, Haraucourt, Mallarmé, Verlaine, Jean Moréas, Tolstoi, Wagner, Stanislas de Guaita, Péladan, Walt Whitman, Maeterlinck. *Degeneration*, by Max Nordau, first English translation, 1895 ; popular edition, 1898. The difference between the German *Mystik* and dyslogistic *Mysticismus* should not be overlooked.
3. I should perhaps safeguard myself by saying that I deliberately refrain so far as possible here from touching upon Religious Mysticism.
4. *Christian Mysticism*, 1899, pp. 4–5.
5. *Marthe, histoire d'une fille*, Paris, Derveaux (Bibliothèque naturaliste), 1879.
6. The word "Enthusiasm" was anathema to the polite in the eighteenth century. Hogarth expressed much of the current idea in his *Enthusiasm Delineated*, when, as he said, he designed to give "a lineal representation of the strange effects of literal and low conceptions of Sacred Beings, as also of the Idolatrous tendency of Pictures in Churches and Prints in Religious Books, etc." The picture is so extremely irreverent and profane that he was persuaded to modify the details and to introduce many alterations. The result was the plate *Credulity, Superstition, and Fanaticism : A Medley*, published in March, 1762. It is quite incomprehensible that Walpole should have professed to regard this as the "most sublime" of Hogarth's works "for useful and deep satire." It is noteworthy that even as late as 1848 we find a Tractarian novel, *Enthusiasm not Religion*. "A Tale, By the late M. A. G.," pub. Masters.

7. *Pope's Works*, ed. Elwin and Courthope, Vol. IX, p. 360. Lady Mary hated and was in some way afraid of Romanticism. The idea might be contagious, and must be avoided altogether. Thus when perforce she was bound to admire Theocritus she hastened to declare : " I no longer look upon Theocritus as a romantic writer." *Ibid.*, Vol. IX p. 374.

8. *Pope's Works*, ed. Warburton, Vol. VI, p. 63.

9. On the death of Sir John Briscoe in 1807 Lady Howe bought Pope's villa and, desiring a commodious family residence, with insensate barbarity razed the house to the ground and destroyed the garden.

10. Printed 1717. The poem was composed for the most part during a visit of the poet to Oxford in 1716. Is it too fanciful to suppose Pope was influenced by the ancient colleges ?

11. 1886.

12. *Oeuvres Complètes de J.-K. Huysmans* ; VII, *A Rebours*, G. Crès, 1929, Note de Lucien Descaves, p. 357.

13. Jules Huret, *L'Evolution Littéraire*, 1901, pp. 177–8.

14. *Ibid.*, pp. 174–5.

15. *Emile Zola*, by R. H. Sherard, London, 1893, Chapter XIV, p. 192. The whole letter is singularly illuminating.

16. Huret, *ut cit.*, p. 142.

17. What Mr. H. W. Garrod intends by the profound observation that the whole trouble about didactic art is that it has nothing to teach, neither I nor (as I suppose) anybody else can hope to understand.

18. Sidney Colvin, *Portfolio*, III, p. 153.

19. *Atlantic Monthly*, Vol. LVII.

20. " Novalis and the Blue Flower " ; *Atlantic Monthly*, December, 1875.

21. Letter to George Montagu from Paris, January 5th, 1766. *Letters of Horace Walpole*, ed. Toynbee, Vol. VI, pp. 387–8.

22. *The Castle of Otranto, and The Mysterious Mother*, edited by Montague Summers, Constable, 1924. *Otranto* issued Christmas Eve, 1764, has title-page 1765.

23. *Letters of Horace Walpole*, ed. Toynbee, Vol. VI, pp. 180, 198, 200–1.

24. *Ibid.*, p. 195.

25. It is interesting to note that as early as 1667 Dryden is using ' Romance ' as ' an idle story,' ' a fib,' since Mrs. Millisent in Act II of *Sʳ Martin Mar-all* (produced Duke's House, August 15th, 1667), says to Sir John's expostulations and surmises, " This is Romance—I'll not believe a word on't——" The O.E.D. defines Romance as " A tale in verse, embodying the adventures of some hero of chivalry, esp. of those of the great cycles of mediæval legend, and belonging both in matter and form to the ages of knighthood." Thus a Romance is often in the vernacular as distinct from a Latin chronicle. Later, a Romance is " A fictitious narrative in prose of which the scene and incidents are very remote from those of ordinary life ; *esp.* one of the class prevalent in the 16th and 17th centuries, in which the story is often overlaid with long disquisitions and digressions." In this sense Romance is derived from the French *roman*.

26. 12mo, 1691. The first English translation of the *Grand Cyrus* is 2 vols., folio, 1653–4.

27. Folio, 1676.

28. Translated by Sir Charles Cotterell, London, folio, 1652 ; folio, 1676 ; and " by Several Hands," 3 vols., 8vo, 1703. Third edition, corrected, translated by Sir Charles Cotterell, five vols., 12mo, 1725.

29. Charlotte Ramsay, born in 1720 at New York, where her father was lieutenant-governor. She came to England when a child. Died at London, January 4th, 1804.

30. For whom see A. Jal, *Dictionnaire critique de biographie et d'histoire*, Paris, 1872, p. 1154.

31. There is a later and more general satire on these romances, *Voyage merveilleux du Prince Fan-Férédin dans la Romancie*, 1735, by Guillaume Hyacinthe Bougeant, S.J., 1690–1743. This *Voyage* is a dream by a gentleman of Languedoc, M. de la Brosse, who as Prince Fan-Férédin takes a tour " dans ce pays merveilleux des romans " peopled by heroes

and heroines. In the land of Romancie the only manufacture is the fabrication of Romances. The adventures and the satire are often amusing but rather too prolix. They conclude tamely enough when M. de la Brosse awakes.

32. First issued in *Ainsworth's Magazine*, commencing in 1842. First edition, 3 vols., 1843.

33. Not reprinted in the second edition of *Ancient Records*, 4 vols., A. K. Newman & Co., 1832.

34. *The Age.* In Ten Books. London. For Vernor, Hood, and Sharpe. 1810, pp. 200–21, ll. 242–604, and the footnotes.

35. In the reign of Charles II the current phrase was " the old Elizabeth way." Thus Lady Dupe, in Dryden's *Sʳ Martin Mar-all* (acted 1667) describes old Moody as one who "stands up for the old *Elizabeth* way in all things." In *The Gentleman Dancing-Master* (acted in 1672) Mrs. Flirt, arranging her *ménage*, is quick to tell Monsieur : " Don't you think we'll take up with your old Queen Elizabeth furniture as your Wives do."

36. *Parentalia*, folio, 1750, pp. 282, 297, 304, 306, 308.

37. *An Account of Architects and Architecture*, folio, 1664, p. 9.

38. Founded by Gian Galeazzo Visconti. The façade (1491) is one of the world's loveliest things. The interior paintings are mostly by Borgognone, although there are examples of the work of Perugino, Mantegna, Pordenone, and other artists.

39. My quotations are from the edition in The *Works of the Honourable Joseph Addison, Esq.*, four volumes, London, Tonson, 1721, Vol. II, p. 10 ; and *Sienna*, pp. 135–6.

40. Du Fresnoy, 1611–65. *De Arte Graphica* was published posthumously at Paris three years after his death with a French prose translation by De Piles.

41. Dryden even speaks of his own The *Spanish Fryar* as " unnatural mingle," although he acknowledges his partiality to the play. Yet there can be a regular as well as an irregular and unfitting alternation of gravity and mirth, as Dryden shows us in his masterpiece of drama, *Don Sebastian*. Here our pleasure during the lighter episodes in no way encroaches upon our concernment for the tragic scenes.

42. *The Castle of Otranto* might, of course, be criticized along the same lines.

43. His editions of Horace, *Ars Poetica*, 1749, and *Epistola ad Augustum*, 1751, were warmly praised by Warburton. In 1776 Hurd, then Bishop of Lichfield and Coventry (translated to Worcester, 1781), was appointed preceptor to the Prince of Wales, and in 1783 he was offered the Primacy, which he declined.

44. *Letters on Chivalry*, 1762, p. 32. " Nay, could the very castle of a Gothic giant be better described than in the words of Homer :

> High walls and battlements the courts inclose,
> And the strong gates defy a host of foes.
> Od. B. xvii, ver. 318."
> Udolpho in the *Odyssey* !

It does not appear to me that Hurd owes anything to Sainte-Palaye's *Mémoires sur l'ancienne Chevalerie*, 2 vols., 1759, (Vol. III, 1781), although he may, of course, have known the book.

45. The Spenserian revival in the eighteenth century, important as it is in its influence upon Romanticism, must barely be indicated in a brief word. It is interesting to note that Oldham (1653–83) wrote a *Satyr*, " The *Person of* Spencer *is brought in, Dissuading the Author from the Study of* Poetry." The Augustans hardly understood " Old Spenser," who, as Addison was pleased to write, failed to " charm an understanding age," *Account of the Greatest English Poets*, 1694. Prior thought that he had imitated the Spenserian stanza, but he could not even make the colouring look like Spenser's. In 1713 Samuel Croxall published a political satire as *An Original Canto of Spenser*, and in 1715 appeared an edition of Spenser edited by John Hughes, who ventured to say that to compare *The Fairie Queene* " with the novels of antiquity, would be like drawing a parallel between the *Roman* and the *Gothick* architecture." Towards the middle of the eighteenth century, however, many imitations of Spenser appeared, such, for example, as the three poems of William Thompson, who was a complete romanticist in spirit and form. Richard Owen Cambridge (1717–1702) imitated Spenser in his *Archimage*, as did Gilbert West in his *On the Abuse of Travelling*, 1839, with which Gray was " enraptured and enmarvailed." William Shenstone (1714–63)

is deservedly famous for his " ludicrous imitation " *The School-Mistress* (the final revision is 1742) ; and there were many other mock-Spenserian poems, such as Christopher Pitt's *The Jordan*, the subject of which finds a parallel in Francesco Berni's capitolo *In Lode dell'Orinale*. In 1748 appeared James Thomson's *The Castle of Indolence*, in one passage of which, Canto II, stanza 52, the poet speaks of " my master Spenser." Moses Mendez, a professed admirer of Thomson, published *The Seasons* in 1751, and a few years later *The Squire of Dames*, which latter in particular shows a close study and no tepid appreciation of Spenser. In 1754 appeared that very important critical study, Thomas Warton's *Observations on the Faery Queene*.

46. *Iliad*, II, 22. Leaf and some scholars read ' oulos,' ' baneful,' Autenrieth-Keep. Pope translates, " the flatt'ring *Dream*."

47. *Letters of Horace Walpole*, Toynbee, 1904, Vol. VI, pp. 181–3

48. *Chateaubriand et son groupe*, t. I, p. 89.

49. Samuel Jackson Pratt (who wrote chiefly under the name Courtney Melmoth) in his *Family Secrets, Literary and Domestic*, 5 vols., 1797, has a disquisition, *The use and abuse of the ancient romance*, Chapter XLVI, Vol. I, pp. 359–70 (see also the two following chapters), which is of considerable interest, and in which the very proper praise is significant.

50. It is worth noting that in Mrs. Behn's *The Emperor of the Moon* (acted in 1687), 4to, 1687, II, 3, some splendid Masking Habits are described as " *à la Gothic* and *Uncommune*." A little later we have : " *Enter* Charmante *and* Cinthio, *dress'd in their Gothic Habits*."

51. *Letters of Horace Walpole*, ed. Toynbee, 1904, Vol. XI, p. 113. Miss Aikin had visited Strawberry Hill on June 14th, 1774. " She desired to see the Castle of Otranto," and, says Walpole, " I let her see all the antiquities of it." On April 8th, 1778, Walpole, in a letter to Mason, remarked, " Mrs. Barbut's *Fragment* was excellent," but, as he was not even at the pains to learn the lady's correct name, he is hardly to be relied upon as regards the authorship. *Letters of Horace Walpole*, ed. Toynbee, 1904, Vol. IX, p. 217, where the footnote is slightly inaccurate, *Sir Bertrand* not *Don Bertrand*.

52. Vol. III (1804), pp. 89–171.

53. *Ibid.*, p. 497.

54. *Ibid.*, No. LII, pp. 257–72.

55. *Ibid.*, p. 264.

56. A curious example of this materialism and anti-romanticism was seen in a production of *Macbeth*, April, 1934, at the Royal Victoria Theatre, the " Old Vic." The witch scenes were heavily cut on the score that they were not written by Shakespeare ! In consequence of this deplorable error on the part of a producer capable of much better things, the play broke to pieces.

57. It is significant that Drake has a long note on Gothic architecture ; p. 108.

58. *The Orphan ; or, The Unhappy-Marriage*, II, 1.

59. See *The Mysterious Mother* in my edition of 1924. Constable's edition, with *The Castle of Otranto*.

60. *Edward* is in very many collections, *e.g. Ballads of Scotland*, ed. W. E. Aytoun, 4th ed., 1870, Vol. II, p. 19 ; *English and Scottish Ballads*, ed. F. J. Child, 5 vols., 1882–98.

61. *Minstrelsy of the Scottish Border*, ed. by Sir Walter Scott ; new and revised edition (four volumes), by T. F. Henderson, 1932 ; Vol. I, pp. 25 and 44.

62. *Titus Andronicus ; or, The Rape of Lavinia*, " Alter'd from Mr. Shakespears Works, By Mr. Edw. Ravenscroft," 4to, 1687. " To the Reader " : " I have been told by some anciently conversant with the Stage, that it was not Originally his, but brought by a private Author to be Acted, and he only gave some Master-touches to one or two of the Principal Parts or Characters."

CHAPTER II

THE PUBLISHERS AND THE CIRCULATING LIBRARIES

Sir Anthony. In my way hither, Mrs. Malaprop, I observed your niece's maid coming forth from a circulating library !—She had a book in each hand—they were half-bound volumes, with marble covers !—From that moment I guess'd how full of duty I should see her mistress !
Mrs. Malaprop. Those are vile places, indeed !
Sir Anthony. Madam, a circulating library in a town is, as an ever-green tree of diabolical knowledge !—It blossoms throughout the year !—And depend on it, Mrs. Malaprop, that they who are so fond of handling the leaves, will long for the fruit at last.
R. B. SHERIDAN, The Rivals (1777), Act I, scene 2.

Last enter, what I call my *consumers*—lasses, young and old, who run over a novel of three, four or five volumes faster than book-men can put them into boards : three sets a day ; morning vols, noon vols, and night vols ; pretty caterpillars, as I call them, because they devour my leaves. Devilish troublesome though ; but write as much as they read, corresponding misses, and so make it up to me in stationery.
Family Secrets (1797), By Mr. Pratt (Courtney Melmoth) :
Vol. I, chap. xlviii, The secrets of a circulating library.

I have written much against the circulating library, and I have read a feeble defence or two ; but I have not seen the argument that might be legitimately put forward in its favour. It seems to me this : the circulating library is conservatism, art is always conservative ; the circulating library lifts the writer out of the precariousness and noise of the wild street of popular fancy into a quiet place where passion is more restrained and where there is more reflection.
GEORGE MOORE, Confessions of a Young Man (1886).

NOT the least significant and a very remarkable feature of to-day is the extraordinary expansion of the Circulating Library, which within but a few years has extended beyond all imagination. The modern system of Chain Libraries, where no deposit is asked and a humble twopence per volume is the fee, is spreading, and is warmly welcomed amongst us far and wide, in the smallest and remotest towns, even in sleepy villages.

To our fathers and mothers, uncles and aunts, half a century and more ago, with their boxes from Mudie, or their local libraries discreetly supplied from Mudie, so vast a dispersion and increase would have been extremely surprising, if not indeed a little disquieting, and even those of us who belong to the Victorian generation and hold the Victorian tradition, who seem a little too conservative, a little old-fashioned and slow perhaps, are apt to find the novelty of the thing unusual, and to question within ourselves the possible influences of such prodigality. For myself I confess I am of that age which saw with regret the passing of the three-volume novel ; inevitable no doubt, but none the less for many who loved and were accustomed to that spacious and solid form not without a certain melancholy and very real repining.

George Moore in his whimsical yet wholly delightful *Confessions of a Young Man* (1886) cried out upon " the circulating library, at once the symbol and glory of villaism," but actually he was denouncing, and not without amplest warrant, " the voracious censorship exercised by the librarian," when literature was " rocked to sleep in the motherly arms of the librarian " whose aim was " to reconcile those two irreconcilable things—literature and young girls." [1] When we remember the horrid scandals of the day, the outcry against the published translations of Zola and the shameful imprisonment of Henry Vizetelly in 1889, the prurient activities of the National Vigilance Association, the nauseous clamour of Emily Crawford in the *Fortnightly Review* (January, 1889),[2] that " the underlings of the naturalist school are like dogs battening upon carrion offal " ; and the grimace of a scribbler in *Society* (April, 1888), who declared that " Realism according to latterday French lights means nothing short of sheer beastliness," we realize that no indictment of the existing pharisaism and organized cant could be too strongly worded and expressed. In 1892, Sir Edmund Gosse wrote : " If we could suddenly arrive from another planet and read a cluster of novels from Mudie's without any previous knowledge of the class, we should be astonished at the conventionality, the narrowness, the monotony. . . . What is the use of this tyranny which they [the novelists] wield if it does not enable them to treat life broadly and to treat it as a whole ? . . . The one living novelist who has striven to give a large, competent, and profound view of the movement of life is M. Zola." [4] Hypocrisy was being beaten out of the field by the very impulse of the time. As Sir Edmund Gosse again said : " A public which has eaten of the apple of knowledge will no longer be satisfied with marionettes." [5]

These dangers have passed away ; one dare not write " never to return," for who knows what new Samuel Smith, what modern Comstock, may arise to muzzle and mask us all ? As George Moore once remarked to me, these outbreaks are continual and sporadic. It is well to remind ourselves of the past. At the present, literature in the circulating library enjoys, I believe, for the most part a reasonable liberty ; at any rate I cannot conceive that the works of Zola, Maupassant, Flaubert, Bourget, would be banned.

In spite of Sir Anthony Absolute's reprehension of a circulating library " as an ever-green tree of diabolical knowledge," [6] history informs us that he was entirely out in his censure, and actually the first circulating-library (in no very exaggerated or strained sense of the word) owed its inception to a canonized Saint.

S. Pamphilus of Cæsarea,[7] who was ordained priest and governed a college there, being of great wealth and immense learning, had founded a library of 30,000 volumes, many of which were copies of the Scriptures (some transcribed with his own hand), and these he lent out to religiously disposed persons. It has been well said that Pamphilus combined the literary man and the Saint, the philosopher and the martyr, for in 309, after several years imprisonment and many tortures, he expired a victim of the persecution under Maximin. S. Jerome [8] mentions his splendid library and the fact that books were lent out to scholars, upon which Dr. Adam Clarke elegantly observes : " This is, if I mistake not, the first notice we have of a circulating library."

Plomer in his *Dictionary of Booksellers and Printers*, 1726–75, gives an *Index of Circulating Libraries in England and Scotland*,[9] the first of which is Benjamin Matthews of Bath, 1725–55. He also notes three later Bath libraries ; Samuel Hazard, 1772–1806 ; Lewis Bull, *c*. 1773–90 ; Mrs. M. Bally, 1774. In London he lists : Francis and John Noble, 1739–92 ; Wright, 1740 ; Willoughby Minors (Mynors), 1744 ; John Fuller, 1755–76 ; Thomas Lowndes, 1756–84 ; A. Cooke, 1765 ; Samuel James, *c*. 1770 ; Thomas Jordan Hookham, *c*. 1775 ; Samuel Noble, *c*. 1775 ; and C. Rice, *c*. 1775.

The Bath circulating libraries will be dealt with in detail a little later. Of the London libraries the most important mentioned by Plomer are Francis and John Noble ; Lowndes ; and Hookham.

Francis Noble kept his extensive and widely-patronized circulating library at No. 324, Middle Row, Holborn, retiring from business when his daughter obtained a share of the first £30,000 prize that ever was sold. He died at Kentish Town, at a very advanced age, on June 7th, 1792. His brother, John Noble, kept a much frequented circulating library in S. Martin's Court, near Leicester Square.[10]

The two Nobles were originally together in business and their library, which commenced in 1739, was one of the first four established in London. In 1746 the Nobles issued a catalogue of children's books and second-hand works. Sir Ambrose Heal has in his Collection a trade-card of Francis Noble, engraved by Ravenet, showing the interior of the library. *The Gazeteer and Daily Advertiser*, October 7th, 1765, advertises *The History of Miss Clarinda Cathcart*, " Printed for and sold by Francis Noble at his Circulating Library opposite Gray's Inn Gate,

Holborn, and John Noble near Leicester Square." In 1788 was issued *The Niece*; or *the History of Sukey Thornby*, a novel in 3 vols., by Mrs. P. Gibbes, "Printed for F. Noble at his Circulating Library, No. 324, Holborn."

The Nobles were attacked by the *London Magazine* the editor of the Impartial Review declaring that they maintained underpaid hack-writers to supply their shelves. They answered this accusation in an *Advertisement to the Public*, January 14th, 1769, and a *Rejoinder*, February 2nd of the same year, both prefixed to *The Rational Lovers*, a novel of 1769. Three years later two novels published by the Nobles, *The Way to Lose him* and *The Way to Please him* were described by the *London Magazine* of November, 1772 (p. 543), as "very proper to debauch all young women who are still undebauched," to which charge of immorality the Nobles replied by *An Appeal to the Public* in the following January. This they afterwards enlarged and published as an appendix to *The Self-Deceived*; or, *The History of Lord Byron*, 1773. Here they gave their correspondence with the editor of the *London Magazine*, Baldwin, and commented upon his censure. They also warned country booksellers in an advertisement that since Baldwin was not to be supplied with any more books printed for them, either at Holborn or S. Martin's Court, there was reason to believe that provincial orders would not be complied with by him, and therefore all such orders should be sent direct to the Nobles themselves.

There was at that time no "sending-out" or formal distribution of review copies. A critic noticed the works which were issued by his own publishing-house, and at leisure collected from other booksellers such volumes as he might deem worthy his survey. Hence it often happened that a very popular romance might not receive attention until the second edition, since if the first edition were quickly sold out the reviewer was too late in his application.

Thomas Lowndes had his very extensive circulating library in Fleet Street from 1756 to 1784. Born in 1719, he died November 7th, 1784, and is buried in S. Bride's.[11] His character has been drawn with masterly strokes by Miss Burney in *Cecilia* where he appears as the ubiquitous sycophant, Mr. Briggs.

Thomas Hookham, who was well known for his circulating library, appears from his trade-cards at several fashionable addresses : New Street, Hanover Square, opposite Maddox Street ; 15 Old Bond Street, opposite Stafford Street ; and from 1772 to 1775, New Bond Street, at the corner of Bruton Street. The exact dates when he occupied these various premises cannot be well determined, but in Sir Ambrose Heal's Collection is a bill-head dated from New Street,

Hanover Square, of 1772. About 1775 to 1776 he was succeeded by his son Thomas Jordan Hookham at 100 New Bond Street. In the Heal Collection is a trade-card showing his circulating library.

A fashionable library of later date was that of J. Andrews " Bookseller, Stationer, and Librarian. 167 New Bond Street. Boxes and Tickets *for the* Opera *by the* Night *or* Season *and Private Boxes for* Covent Garden *&* Drury Lane Theatres. Visiting & other Cards neatly Engraved & Printed. Please Return the Books as Soon as Read." [12]

Timperley [13] under 1770 says : " At this time there were only four circulating libraries in London and its neighbourhood."

A very popular and important circulating library at this period was of George Riley in Queen Street, Berkeley Square (1771) where he succeeded William Cooke ; George Riley is said to have originally come from York.[14] According to his advertisement at the end of *Heathen Mythology made Easy*, 1779, he kept an extensive stock of stationery of all kinds. Riley died at Greenwich on January 12th, 1829, aged eighty-six years, " and was nearly the oldest proprietor of a newspaper in the kingdom."

In *The Gentleman's Magazine*, October, 1783,[15] a correspondent asks " Your correspondent and the publick would be glad of information on the rise of circulating libraries, and who were the first that were so obliging as to lend out their books to the world by subscription. I am certain the custom began very late in the present century. From the contents of some letters now before me, this practice was not in vogue so early as the year 1724."

A reply was printed in the following number.[16] The writer in his letter stated, " an honoured relation of mine says, ' that he well remembers having frequently heard that the first circulating library was opened by the Rev. Mr. Fancourt, a dissenting minister 50 or 60 years ago : the place where it was first opened he does not recollect, but it was afterwards removed to Crane-court, Fleet-street.' "

In Franklin's *Autobiography* [17] he mentions, when speaking of his first visit to England, that whilst lodging in Little Britain, he made the acquaintance of his next door neighbour, Wilcox, a bookseller, who had a large collection of second-hand books. " Circulating libraries were not then in use ; but we agreed that on reasonable terms which I have now forgotten, I might take, read, and return any of his books." This was in 1725.

In 1740 Bathoe had established a circulating library at his shop in the Strand, and the same year there came into existence, Cawthorn and Hutt's " British Library."

It was between 1740 and 1745 that Samuel Fancourt,[18] who is spoken of above, established a Library in Crane Court. A first scheme by which subscribers paid a guinea a year was much modified at Michaelmas, 1745. His Catalogue,[19] published in parts between 1746–48 ; 2 vols., 8vo, 1748, states that each member is required to disburse an initial fee of one guinea for the purchase of books, and a quarterly payment of twelve pence out of which the rent of the rooms, the librarian's salary, and other expenses were to be met. The library was vested in twelve or thirteen trustees, and Fancourt was to continue librarian so long as he discharged his duties diligently and well. The library contained between 2,000–3,000 bound volumes, and an equal number of pamphlets. The works were of a serious cast, theology, history, biography and travels. Each member could take out one volume and one pamphlet, to be read in a reasonable time according to their size. If the books were not required by other readers they could be kept so long as the member had a mind. For some reason the library excited a good deal of ill feeling, and eventually, after several changes of address, the last of which was " the corner of one of the streets in the Strand," about 1759–60 the scheme collapsed.

The circulating library established in 1776 by William Dangerfield on the north side of Berkeley Square was purchased in 1810 by Mr. Rice, who greatly extended it, and later it moved to Mount Street, and passed into the hands of John and Charles Day successively. In 1913, Cawthorn and Hutt's " British Library " was incorporated with Day's Library.

Towards 1790 R. Dillon established a circulating Library in " Lombard Street, near the Church, Chelsea." About 1800 he was succeeded by Thomas Mudie at " 39 Cheyne Walk, near Chelsea Church." This library was enriched with a variety of travels, histories, biographies, novels, plays, " as cannot fail to gratify every class of readers—The Daily Papers are taken in," and the Terms were : For Four Books, Yearly, one guinea ; half-yearly, 12s. 6d. ; Quarterly, 7s. 6d. ; Monthly, 3s. 6d. For Two Books, Yearly, 16s. ; half-yearly, 9s. ; Quarterly, 5s. ; Monthly, 2s. 6d. Books read by Non-Subscribers charged according to size. A week was allowed for new books ; a month for older volumes. This regulation was enforced under penalty of paying for such book or books, and the Proprietor apologized for strictly obliging the same, yet would not relax, since it was in the general interest of the Subscribers.

The modern Mudie's Library was founded in 1842 at 28 Upper King Street (now Southampton Row), Bloomsbury, by Charles Edward Mudie (1818–90), the son of Thomas Mudie.

In time there crept into a shabby existence the humbler circulating libraries which have left no name and no trace in the shape of labels on their well-worn second-hand books. Such Thackeray has described in the circulating library which, in conjunction with her school and a small brandy-ball and millinery business Miss Minifer kept in New-castle Street, Strand, where pretty Fanny Bolton, who had been a pupil, devoured those darling greasy volumes from whose very pages Arthur Pendennis seemed to her to have stepped as a hero in real life. Miss Flinders, too, who lived near Walpole Street, Mayfair, had a small establishment of lollipops, theatrical characters and ginger-beer and a stock of novels for the ladies of the upper servants' table. Behind her counter John James Ridley, the son of Mr. Samuel Ridley, butler and confidential valet to the Right Honourable John James Baron Tod-morden, spent many happy hours teaching himself to read out of her novels. The whole library passed through his hands, *Manfroné*; *or, The One-Handed Monk*; *Abellino, the Terrific Bravo of Venice*; *The History of Rinaldo Rinaldini, Captain of Banditti*; *William Wallace, the Hero of Scotland*; and the heroic *Thaddeus of Warsaw*, whose pages were blistered with his tears. By such vivid sketches the homeliest and poorer circulating libraries have been brought before us by the genius of Thackeray. Miss Minifer and Miss Flinders supplied their shelves from the novels which had been discarded by the better booksellers as beyond service, copies for the most part overworked and torn and tattered, but so long as the pages somehow held together these were again passed from hand to hand, and read and read until they were literally read to pieces. It is this which to some extent accounts for the extreme rarity to-day of so many of the novels in vogue a century and a quarter ago, books which ran into their second, third and fourth editions.

Mr. Mortimer Knag, who in 1837 was an ornamental stationer and small circulating library keeper in a by-street off Tottenham Court Road and who let out the newest old novels, boasted a shop about the size of three hackney coaches. He specialized not so much in the Gothic romance as in the sentimental and social novels written by ladies of the school of Mrs. Gore, such works as *Osmond* and *The Favourite of Nature*, the doings of drawing-rooms and the ton.

Of circulating libraries nearer London, Rowley's Circulating Library at Edmonton supplied a large district as also did Wall's Circulating Library at Kew. Wall died, a very old man, in 1811.[20]

The provincial circulating libraries were also very important. *The New Bath Guide for the Year* 1778, p. 56, notes : " Books. There are three or four Booksellers who keep Circulating Libraries, where the

Inhabitants subscribe by the Year, and Strangers by the Month or Season; viz. Shrimpton's, near *York House*; Taylor's, in *Church Street*; Bull's, opposite Gyde's *Rooms* (the Lower Assembly Rooms on the Walks leading from the Grove to the Parades); Tennent's in *Milsom Street*; and Bally's in *Milsom Street*." A dozen years later there is a decided increase as no less than seven circulating libraries are given in the *New Bath Directory of* 1792 : Lewis Bull, Lower Walks; James Barrett, Milsom Street; Campbell & Gainsborough, Burton Street; William Meyler, Orange Grove; James Marshall, Milsom Street; Edward Russell, Miles's Court; and William Taylor, Church Street.

It was from Lewis Bull's in the Lower Walks that Miss Sukey Saunter one fine morning in 1775 had fetched away Pierre Henri Treyssac de Vergy's *The Mistakes of the Heart; or, the Memoirs of Lady Caroline Pelham, and Lady Victoria Nevil* (1769)—the second volume, *The Mistakes of the Heart*, appearing in 1771—and thus disappointed Miss Lydia Languish who was all agog for these seductive chapters.[21] Some nine novels may be certainly assigned to de Vergy,[22] and he probably wrote many more. They gave scandal and were regarded as inflammables. The reviewers denounced him and all his works— " too indelicate for the eye or ear of a modest woman "[23] in no uncertain chorus. Yet he had parts, and reflects something of the grace and profligacy of a Voisenon or a Crébillon. *The Nun, or, the Adventures of the Marchioness de Beauville* (1771) was long discreetly popular, and who could resist *The Memoirs of an Hermaphrodite* ?

It will be remembered that among the books Miss Languish receives piping hot from the circulating libraries of Bath and strews about her dressing-room are Sterne's *A Sentimental Journey* (1768); Smollett's *Roderick Random* (1748); *Peregrine Pickle* (1751); and *Humphry Clinker* (1771). Since Lucy seems to distinguish *The Memoirs of a Lady of Quality, written by herself,* which she produces from her pockets from *Peregrine Pickle,* it is possible that this book is *The Memoirs of an Unfortunate Lady of Quality,* 1774, which according to the *Monthly Review* tells the story of Lady Jane Douglas, rather than *The Memoirs of a Lady of Quality,* a true tale written by Lady Vane, inserted in *Peregrine Pickle,* Smollett having been bribed to admit the extraneous narrative.[24] The *Memoirs* might be considered (by those who wished to think so) to belong to the province of gallant literature, and I imagine some would fondly place *Lord Aimworth,*[25] which is *The History of Lord Aimworth and Charles Hartford,* 3 vols., in the same category. *The Memoirs of Lady Woodford,* 1771, which is anonymous, might also be deemed gently erotic. *The Innocent Adultery* is, I incline to think,

Scarron's novel, so often translated and immensely popular throughout the eighteenth century, rather than the contemporary *Harriet, or the Innocent Adultress*, 2 vols. The remaining novels read by Miss Languish are all of the most exquisite sensibility. *The Reward of Constancy, The Fatal Connection*, and *The Tears of Sensibility*,[26] by John Murdoch, 1773, are, as indeed their titles alone would show, three novels of ultra-Richardsonian sentiment. *The Man of Feeling*, published anonymously (1771) is by Henry Mackenzie. In 1757 Elizabeth Griffith (which was also her maiden surname), who had some six years before married Richard Griffith, published *A Series of Genuine Letters between Henry and Frances*, that is to say, the actual correspondence (perhaps polished a trifle) which passed between her husband (Henry) and herself (Frances) before they were united. In 1769 ' Frances ' obliged the world with *The Delicate Distress*, a novel in letters, and the following year ' Henry ' issued a companion novel in epistolary form, *The Gordian Knot*, 4 volumes.

To these we must add Frederick's, of rather earlier date, a library to which Miss Lydia Languish was a subscriber, not here listed, since towards the end of 1774 the proprietor was selling off the majority of his lending stock and desirous of closing his library department to concentrate upon bookselling alone. William Frederick died on August 1st, 1776. He was educated at the Grammar School, was articled and learned his business with Leake. He commenced on his own account at No. 18 The Grove about 1740, his first book being published in 1742. *The Bath Chronicle*, October 2nd, 1766, has : " Last week, Mr. Frederick, Bookseller of this City was elected a member of this Corporation in the room of Mr. Thomas King, deceased." The same paper, August 2nd, 1776, announces : " Thursday sennight died Mr. William Frederick, many years an eminent bookseller in The Grove, and one of the Common Council of this City." *The Bath Abbey Registers*, (Vol. II, p. 462) record : " Burials August 4th, 1776. Mr. William Frederick was carried away." *The Bath Chronicle*, August 22nd, 1776, prints an advertisement : " Orange Grove, Bath, Aug. 19, 1776. A. Tucker, Executrix and successor to the late Mr. Frederick, very respectfully solicits a continuance of her late Master's Customers and at the same time takes the liberty to inform them, that the Circulating Library will be opened on Monday next ; a regular supply of New Publications will be procured and every endeavour and attention exerted to merit a continuance of their favours, &c."

Brighton, naturally, was not furnished with circulating libraries at so early a date as Bath, but directly it began to become the resort of wealth and fashion the votaries of romance must be provided with their modish fare. *The Brighthelmston Directory*, a new edition (no date, but about 1795), was sold at " Thomas's Circulating Library on the Steyne, Brighthelmston." In the account of the Steyne we read: " Here likewise are some shops, and Thomas's circulating library which is stocked with a good collection of books, of which the company has the use for the season, on subscribing at pleasure." [27]

A subsequent edition of the *Directory* [1800 ?] was sold " at Mr. Baker's Circulating Library on the Steyne, Brighthelmston." [28]

The Directory : or, The Ancient and Present State of Tunbridge Wells,[29] 1816, draws particular attention to " the public rooms, lodging-houses, libraries, post-office," for the convenience of visitors to the salubrious spot, where " the prevailing spirit suggests ease as the criterion of enjoyment."

To come to a far later date, and one indeed beyond our purview, it may be noted that in *A Picture of the New Town of Herne Bay*, 1835,[30] the frontispiece particularly marks " a long range of buildings on the Parade." " These are an assemblage of extremely handsome shops. . . . These shops are spacious, and are finished in a superior style and elegance. Among them is a circulating library."

It is impossible and even superfluous to attempt to give any list of the circulating libraries throughout England, and therefore some four or five names chosen at random [31] will serve as the types of hundreds more.

C. Evans's Circulating Library was in the " Market-Place, Abingdon : Where may be had Books of Every Description, also Every Article of General and Ornamental Stationary. Letter-Press and Copper-Plate Printing *executed with neatness and dispatch*. Books, Plainly or Superbly Bound. Albums, Scrap, and Sketch Books, of Plain or Tinted Papers ; arranged and Bound to Order. Music cases, Guard Books, and Port Folios made to any Size."

At Cheltenham Saunder's Public Library opened in 1822 as The Literary Saloon, of which their trade-card gives a fine exterior view. Another Circulating Library in great repute at Cheltenham was that of J. & G. Parker, 82 High Street, established in 1820, where books were " lent by the volume, and charged for according to the time they are kept, size or newness of the work."

Chapman's Circulating Library was at Newport-Pagnell. S. White's Circulating Library, Moretonhampstead, was " Open every day except Sundays, from *Eleven* till *One*, and from *Two* till *Five* in the After-noon ; on Saturdays from *Ten* in the *Morning* till *Eight* in the Evening."

At James Briddon's Circulating Library, 7 Cross Street, Ryde, the subscription was, Single : Annual, 15*s*. ; Half-year, 8*s*. ; Quarter, 4*s*. 6*d*. ; Month, 2*s*. 6*d*. ; Week, 1*s*. 6*d*. There was also a Double Subscription which allowed " *Three* Sets at the same time." Non-Subscribers, 3*d*. per volume for New, and 2*d*. per volume for Old Works. A fine of 2*d*. per day for each book kept over the specified time. A London Parcel of Books, Periodicals, Etc., was received every Saturday. " J. B. returns thanks to the Gentry and Inhabitants of Ryde and the Isle of Wight generally for the liberal patronage bestowed upon him since his commencement in business."

" At J. B. Fulcher's Circulating Library Near the Church, Wisbeach, Books Are Let to Read on the following Terms : viz. Subscribers, By the Year to pay 16*s*. 0*d*. ; Half Year, 9*s*. 0*d*. ; Quarter, 5*s*, 0*d*. ; Month, 2*s*. 0*d*. And are allowed two Books at a time." " Non-Subscribers To pay one Penny per volume per Night, or three-pence per volume per Week for every new Novel or Play. . . . No Book exchanged before eight o'clock in the morning, nor after eight in the Evening."

Yearly Subscribers at Hodges's Library, Cheap-Street, Sherborne, paid 18*s*., and Quarterly Subscribers, 5*s*. for the Use of one Book at a Time. Guinea Subscribers were entitled to full Sets and reading the new Books first. Non-Subscribers paid on a scale of fees graduated according to the value of the Books. Not exceeding 3*s*. 6*d*. Mr. Hodges charged 2*d*. a volume ; from 10*s*. 6*d*. to 20*s*. One Shilling was asked. " Both Subscribers and Non-Subscribers are to engage not to lend any Books to any other Person on any Account, without making the same known to W. HODGES ; such lending of books being unfair and unjust." [32]

By far the greater number of these circulating libraries were established throughout the country by William Lane and stocked from the Minerva Press. Thus the hero of *Frederic and Caroline*, published by Lane in 1800, entering a circulating library at Margate, found it "furnished from the Minerva," a somewhat ingenious advertisement.

Forty years ago the descendants of these circulating libraries still lingered in some out-of-the-way little towns. I myself remember in a village by the sea a library where children's toys, delightful theatres, buckets and spades, china, paper-weights with views, fascinating pebble-brooches, woolwork, albums and stationery, held one spellbound by their quaint array, and in a little back-room, the library proper, rows of three-volumed novels invited the reader, shelves upon which were still to be found Mrs. Parsons and Mrs. Meeke, Mrs. Bonhote, Mrs. Roche and the Porters, mingling with G. P. R. James,

Ainsworth, Lytton, Miss Braddon, Mrs. Trollope, Miss Warboise and Mrs. Crowe.

Samuel Jackson Pratt in his *Family Secrets, Literary and Domestic* [33] (1797) has an amusing picture of a London circulating library and contemporary readers. Dilettanti scholars are chattering and proclaiming books they have not read " dull, Sir, very dull " ; a lady bustles in for " the last plays and novel," whilst another declares the books of last week "old as Poles," and a virtuosa demands only metaphysics, yet informs the librarian he may " throw in some nonsense for the servants." As the learned lady goes out another cries : " Pray is not that Lady Sarah Dingey who makes all the novels smell so of spirits, and is so generous of her snuff among the pages ? " Another damsel is asking for *The Cruel Disappointment* ; *Reuben, or Suicide* ; *Seduction* ; *The Mutual Attachment* ; *The Assignation* ; and *Frederick, or, The Libertine* ; which will serve her (she thinks) until the day after to-morrow at least. Then there are the toilette-students who glance at a chapter whilst their hair is being dressed, and send back the books all covered with powder, pomatum and perfume. Finally there are the devourers of books, who run through three sets a day, and a sprinkling of old dons who read Master Gibbon, Dominie Robertson, Old Verulam, and bold Sir Isaac. Many of these touches are exceedingly modern, and as one reads one might almost be listening to an account of a morning hour spent at Smith's or Boot's to-day.

There were, of course, very many satires on the circulating libraries, and there are some pretty smart bobs in the pages of the novels themselves. Sometimes, even, an author is aggressively hostile and denunciatory. Thus in the Prefatory Epistle to *Santa-Maria ; or, The Mysterious Pregnancy*, 3 vols., G. Kearsley, 1797, a romance which will be considered in detail later, Joseph Fox declares that the provincial libraries receive the hacked productions of literature by waggon-loads, and urges that no surprise can be felt if novels are condemned for their heaviness, sameness, and insipidity. He himself in order to break new ground has imitated in *Santa-Maria* " the romanzos of the Italians." He girds at the libraries for new facing old romances and giving them as new when all that is original consists in the type and paper. There is another sore point :—" Besides, the librarians (at least most of them) cannot afford to pay reputed authors liberally—they therefore employ hacknied copies." [34] Perhaps one of the liveliest pasquinados on the circulating library is a play, of which something may not improperly be said here, since the piece in itself has considerable merit and fun.

" A Novel is the only thing to teach a girl life, and the way of the world, and elegant fancies, and love to the end of the chapter," cries

Polly, the heroine of *Polly Honeycombe*, " A Dramatick Novel of One Act," by George Colman, which was produced at Drury Lane, as the afterpiece to Hill's tragedy, *Merope*, on December 5th, 1760. *Polly Honeycombe* is a brisk, bright farce satirizing the Circulating Library with a good deal of humour and zest. Honeycombe and Mrs. Honeycombe, the foolish fond old couple, were played by Yates and Mrs. Kennedy, whilst Miss Pope achieved a tremendous success in Polly, whose head is well-nigh turned by her glut of novel-reading, and who ranks herself as one of the

Girls of Reading, and superior notions,
Who from the fountain-head drink love's sweet potions.

" These damn'd Story Books ! " ejaculated old Honeycombe. " And a man might as well turn his daughter loose in Covent Garden, as trust the cultivation of her mind to

A CIRCULATING LIBRARY."

When published, 8vo, 1760, Colman prefixed a list of some 182 novels, with an amusing Preface, to his play. Here we meet *Joseph Andrews* ; *Peregrine Pickle* ; *Amelia* ; *Tom Jones* ; *Daphnis and Cloe* ; *David Simple* ; Mrs. Haywood's *History of Miss Betsy Thoughtless*, and *Jemmy and Jenny Jesammy* ; *Chrysal* ; *Pompey the Little* ; Cleland's *Memoirs of Fanny Hill*, and *Memoirs of a Coxcomb* ; *The Adventures of a Rake* ; *The Amorous Friars, or the Intrigues of a Convent* ; *The Fair Adulteress* ; *History of a Woman of Quality, or the Adventures of Lady Frail* ; *History of some of the Penitents in the Magdalen-House* ; *Memoirs of a Man of Pleasure* ; *Prostitutes of Quality, or Adultery a la Mode, being authentic and genuine Memoirs of several Persons of the highest Quality* ; *The Sopha* ; *The Theatre of Love, cum multis aliis*. Sentimental, social, erotic, and pseudo-improper, all appear pell-mell in Colman's catalogue.

From the circulating libraries we may retrace our steps, as it were, to the fountain head of fiction, and indeed of all printed books, the publishers. It will, of course, only be possible to make particular mention of the more famous houses, of which first and foremost must be ranked the Minerva Press.

Born in 1738, William Lane first set up business at the Minerva printing office, which in 1763 was in Leadenhall Street. Thus his name occurs as a bookseller in Henry Kent's London Directory, 1776, at 33 Leadenhall Street.[35] In *The Gentleman's Magazine*, April, 1774,[36] under the Catalogue of New Publications, we have : " *Christiani Cultus : or the Ornaments of a Christian* ; being a collection of Christian virtues and graces : also their opposite vices, &c. By Hugh Stopley.

12mo. 1s. Lane." Timperley [37] notes : " 1814, *January*. *Died* William Lane, formerly of the *Minerva* printing-office, London ; from which concern he had retired about ten years, in favour of his late partner, Mr. Newman. He was long distinguished for his copious publication of novels, and for the energy with which he established circulating libraries in every town, and almost every village, of the empire. For many years he was senior captain of one of the regiments of the London militia. No man knew the world better, and none better knew how to manage and enjoy it. He was twice married, but left no children. He died at Brighton, aged seventy-six." As early indeed as 1786 Lane was advertising (see *Anthony Varnish*) that he would advise and stock any person genuinely desirous of establishing a circulating library.

" Lane made a large fortune by the immense quantity of trashy novels which he sent forth from his Minerva-press. I perfectly well remember the splendid carriage in which he used to ride, and his footmen with their cockades and gold-headed canes.

" Nowadays, as soon as a novel has had its run, and is beginning to be forgotten, out comes an edition of it as a ' standard novel.' " [38]

On the title-page of Mrs. Bennett's *Anna ; or, Memoirs of a Welch Heiress*, 4 vols., 1785, we have " Printed for William Lane, Leadenhall Street." The title-page of *Anna Melvil*, 2 vols., 1792, carries : " *London :* Printed for William Lane, at The Minerva Press, Leadenhall Street," as also does Mrs. Gunning's *Anecdotes of the Delborough Family*, 5 vols., 1792. William Lane's name appears alone on the title-page of T. J. Horsley Curties' *Ancient Records*, 4 vols., 1801, whilst on the title-page of *Independence*, by Gabrielli, 4 vols., 1802, we have ' Lane and Newman,' the printer being Lane, Minerva Press, Leadenhall Street. The title-page of *The Three Old Maids*, 3 vols., 1806, has Lane, Newman and Co., the printers being Lane, Darling, and Co., Leadenhall Street. The title-page of *Laurette*, 3 vols., 1807, also carries Lane, Newman and Co., the printers being the same. The title-page of Edward Moore's *Sir Ralph de Bigod*, 4 vols., 1811, has : " *London :* Printed at the Minerva-Press, For A. K. Newman and Co. (*Successors to Lane, Newman, and Co.*), Leadenhall-street." *Who Is The Bridegroom?* by Mrs. Green, 3 vols., 1822, was printed for A. K. Newman and Co., Leadenhall Street, by J. Darling, Leadenhall Street, London. *Eustace Fitz-Richard*, 4 vols., 1826, is printed for the same by the same. The third edition, 4 vols., 1828, of *Manfroné ; or, The One-Handed Monk*, was printed for A. K. Newman and Co. by Sloman, Printer, King Street, Yarmouth. A. K. Newman remained in business until the mid-thirties.

The Minerva Press had, of course, no monopoly in Gothic romance. Lane did not publish Mrs. Radcliffe or Monk Lewis or Charlotte Dacre, and his house was one of half a dozen other publishing houses, as was the Minerva Library one of half a dozen other libraries. None the less he achieved an eminence in the Gothic field of fiction that has left behind a tradition and a name even to-day. One can, so to speak, always be sure of a Minerva Press novel.

The following is the circular of the Minerva Library in 1822 :

MINERVA PUBLIC LIBRARY, LEADENHALL-STREET.

THE Proprietors of the above Establishment beg leave to return their sincere thanks to Subscribers who honour them with their patronage, and beg to assure them, no endeavour shall be wanting on their part to merit a continuance, and trust the increased supply and new regulations will entirely obviate any delay that may have arisen in procuring an early perusal of new Publications. Ladies and Gentlemen subscribing to this Library will have access to near Eleven Thousand Standard Works, in History, Voyages, Travels, Divinity, Poetry, Plays, Miscellaneous Literature, Novels, Romances, &c. on the following low terms :

First Class.—Subscribers paying £5. 5s. per Year, £2. 16s. per Half-Year, £1. 11s. 6d. per Quarter, are entitled to Twenty-four Volumes in Town, or Thirty-six in the Country.

Second Class.—Subscribers paying £4. 4s. per Year, £2. 8s. per Half-Year, or £1. 6s. per Quarter, are entitled to Eighteen Volumes in Town, or Twenty-four in the Country.

Third Class.—Subscribers paying £3. 3s. per Year, £1. 16s. per Half-Year, or £1. 1s. per Quarter, are entitled to Twelve Volumes in Town, or Eighteen in the Country ; but not more than three new Works at one time.

Fourth Class.—Subscribers paying £2. 2s. per Year, £1. 6s. per Half-Year, or 15s. per Quarter, are entitled to Six Volumes in Town, or Twelve in the Country, and excluded from new Quarto Works, but entitled to Periodical Publications. (This Class are not allowed more than two new Works at one time.)

Fifth Class.—Subscribers paying £1. 11s. 6d. per Year, 18s. per Half-Year, or 10s. 6d. per Quarter, are entitled to Four Volumes in Town, or Eight in the Country ; but are totally excluded from new Publications and Quartos.

Publications are termed New, if published within Twelve Months from the date of subscribing.

Folios and Quartos are counted as Four, and Octavos as Two Volumes.

CONDITIONS AND REGULATIONS

OF THE

MINERVA LIBRARY.

I. The Subscription to be paid at the time of subscribing, and at the commencement of every subsequent term. Should the Books not be returned at the expiration of a Subscription, it will be deemed a renewal of the period already subscribed for, and they will be charged accordingly, whether read or not.

II. A Box, Catalogue, Postage, Carriage to and from the Library, and every Expence, to be defrayed by the Subscriber.

III. If a Subscriber lends a Book to a Non-Subscriber, he forfeits his Subscription ; neither is it allowable to transfer Books to other Subscribers.

IV. No Subscriber to keep any new Book in Duodecimo or Octavo longer than three Days, or Quarto beyond one Week ; for old Works double this time is allowed ; but no Work to be kept more than one Month. Plays, Magazines, and Reviews, must be returned in two Days. Books kept after the above time will be charged as if on deposit. To Subscribers residing more than ten miles from Town, double the time above specified is allowed.—N.B. Those Subscribers who strictly attend this Rule, will have the first reading of the new Publications.

V. If a Book be written in, torn, or damaged, whilst in the possession of a Subscriber, the Book, or the Set, if part of one, to be paid for.

*₊*Subscribers are requested to observe, that they will not, under any consideration, be allowed more Books than their Subscription entitles them to ; and to prevent disappointments, a list of twenty or thirty numbers should be sent.

Non-Subscribers to deposit the Value of the Books required.

The publisher of *The Monk* was Bell ; of *The Mysteries of Udolpho*, Robinson ; of *The Italian*, Cadell junior and Davies ; of Ireland's *Gondez the Monk*, Hemet and Earle ; to whom, together with the famous names of Longman, Crosby, and Colburn, some brief notice must necessarily be given here.

John Bell, " than whom few men have contributed more, by their industry and good taste, to the improvement of the graphic and typographic art, " was born in 1745. He succeeded in the winter of

1768, near Exeter Change, in the Strand, William Bathoe, a well-known publisher and bookseller, who died on October 2nd of that year. On October 20th, 1769, Bell married a Miss Dover, of Ongar, in Essex. He was one of the original proprietors of the *Fashionable World*, the *Oracle*, and the *Morning Post*, and proprietor of the long popular Sunday newspaper *Bell's Weekly Messenger*. In 1774 began to appear his duodecimo edition of *Shakespeare's Works*, and two years later his *British Theatre*. It was in the course of issuing this latter book that about 1795 Bell first set the fashion, which soon became general, of discarding the long " s." He died at Fulham on February 26th, 1831, in the eighty-sixth year of his age. Timperley, *History of Printing* [39] (p. 916) sums up his character thus : " He was one of the most marked men of his day ; he possessed a masculine understanding, which a long course of observation, and a particular quickness and facility in observing had very highly cultivated—so as to have given him a judgement as just and exact as his powers of conception were vigorous and acute. He had an instinctive perception of what was beautiful in every possible combination of the arts."

George Robinson, the founder of the firm of Robinson, and described by Nichols as " one of the most eminent booksellers of his time," was born at Dalston, in Cumberland, and came to London in 1755. He was apprenticed to John Rivington, bookseller and publisher, in S. Paul's Churchyard, 1740–92.[40] From Rivington's, George Robinson went to William Johnston, bookseller at the Golden Ball, S. Paul's Churchyard, 1748–73,[41] one of the foremost publishers in London. In 1764 Robinson commenced business as an independent bookseller at Addison's Head, 25 Paternoster Row, in partnership with Mr. John Roberts, who died about 1766. At first Robinson was much helped by Thomas Longman, who assisted him with considerable loans. " The uniform habits of industry and punctuality, which Mr. Robinson had displayed, while managing the affairs of others," together with his " active spirit, knowledge of business, and reputable connexion," soon enabled him to achieve the higher branches of the business, and become the rival of the most formidable of the old houses ; so that before the year 1780 he had the largest wholesale trade that ever was carried on by an individual. " To the rise and progress of so great a concern, Mr. Robinson was an eminent proof how much may be done by attention, industry, and above all, inflexible integrity and perseverance." In 1784 he took into partnership his son George and his brother John, who succeeded him in business.

George Robinson (the father) died at five o'clock on Saturday morning, June 6th, 1801. Nichols,[42] who has a very ample account of this remarkable man, speaks in terms of warmest admiration of his many excellent qualities, not the least of which was the fact that he paid his authors very fairly, justly believing that in this he was carrying out the true spirit of bookselling.

George Robinson, junior, and his uncle John now carried on the business conjointly. They " were men of the highest integrity and skill in their profession." A disastrous fire which destroyed much of their property involved them in serious difficulties, from whence, it is said, they emerged with the highest honour to themselves and a credit which had gathered strength from the shock.

George Robinson died May 22nd, 1811.

John Robinson, the last surviving member of the firm of G. and J. Robinson, after the failure of the firm, went into partnership with Mr. George Wilkie, a well-known bookseller and publisher, in S. Paul's Churchyard. He died at Putney on December 2nd, 1813, in his sixty-first year, leaving a widow and two sons, John and Richard, the former for some time carrying on a successful business as a bookseller in Paternoster Row, and being assisted by his brother.

Thomas Cadell the elder was the son of Thomas Cadell, a bookseller in Wine Street, Bristol, where he was born in 1742. In 1758 he was sent to London and apprenticed to Andrew Millar, one of the most eminent booksellers of the eighteenth century. He rose rapidly, was admitted as a partner in the firm in 1765, and succeeded to the business on the retirement of Millar two years later. On April 1st, 1769, Cadell married the daughter of Mr. Thomas Jones, in the Strand. He was a most liberal patron of authors, and, says Timperley, [43] " munificent remunerations were held out to writers of the most eminent talents." He retired from business in 1793, leaving as his successors Thomas, his only son, who jointly with Mr. William Davies preserved the high reputation acquired from the liberality, honour and integrity of their predecessors. Thomas Cadell senior died at his house in Bloomsbury Place in the sixtieth year of his age on December 27th, 1801. [44]

William Davies died in 1820, after which date Thomas Cadell's name stood alone. Thomas Cadell died at his residence in Fitzroy Square, London, on November 26th, 1836, aged sixty-three. In 1802 he married a daughter of Robert Smith, Esq., of Basinghall Street. Of his numerous family, however, none continued in his profession. " For nearly half a century, Mr. Cadell followed his father's example, and preserved the reputation the house had acquired for liberality, honour, and integrity." [45]

Of the firm of Hemet and Earle, John Hemet, a native of France, was eventually obliged to dissolve partnership with Earle, and, under the Aliens Act of January, 1793, to leave the country. He was himself an elegant author of some reputation. In 1798 he published *Reflections for Every Day in the Year on the Works of God and His Providence throughout all Nations*, "from the German of C. C. Sturm. Translated and abridged chiefly for the use of Schools."[46] In 1799 he issued *Contradictions, or Who Could Have Thought It?* "a Novel from the French," and a little later in the same year *Misanthropy and Repentance*, "a Novel. From the German," being the romance whence Kotzebue took the plot of his famous drama, *Menschenhass und Reue*, which, when adapted by Benjamin Thompson as *The Stranger*,[47] had so remarkable and enduring a success upon the English stage. With Lane and Newman, 1802, Hemet published *Odd enough, to be sure! or Emilius in the world*, 2 vols., a version of August Lafontaine's *Der Sonderling*.[48]

William Earle, junior, the son of William Earle, was a minor dramatist. In 1799 was published by his father's house : " *Natural Faults*, a Comedy, as written by W. Earle, Junior ; so like *First Faults*, as performed at the Theatre Royal Drury Lane, for the Benefit of Miss de Camp, that the reader will immediately conclude it is the same. Price 2s."

First Faults was produced at Drury Lane, May 3rd, 1799. Earle in his Preface says he sent his MS. to Miss De Camp and that she coolly conveyed his play. In a letter to the *Morning Post*, June 10th, 1799, the lady absolutely denied ever having seen *Natural Faults*, and declared she had no acquaintance with Earle.[49]

An interlude, *The Villagers*, of which Earle speaks as his work, was probably not printed. On December 13th, 1817, was given, at Drury Lane, a light opera in three acts, *Outwitted at Last*, libretto by Earle, music by Lanza. It was performed four times.

Further details concerning Earle and Hemet will be found when we speak of Henry Colburn.

One of the most famous of all Gothic robber-romances, *The History of Rinaldo Rinaldini*, 3 vols., 1800, was published by Longman and Rees, Paternoster Row, and C. Geisweiler, Parliament Street. A very important figure was Thomas Longman, the founder of the firm Longman & Co., a bookseller at the Ship and Black Swan, Paternoster Row, 1726–55. The firm was carried on after the death of the founder under the same title, for, although in 1746, on the death of his father-in-law, J. Osborn, Longman took Thomas Shremrell into partnership, this only lasted two years. In 1754 a nephew, Thomas Longman, became a partner, and the title-pages of their firm carry : " Printed for T. & T. Longman at the Ship in Paternoster Row." On June 18th, 1755, Thomas Longman (the uncle) died. The nephew, Thomas

Longman, who was born in 1731, had entered the firm when 15 years old as an apprentice, and was at the time of the founder's death only 24. He showed himself extraordinarily shrewd and capable. He married a Miss Harris, and by her had three sons, of whom Thomas Norton Longman, born in 1771, began to take his father's place in business about 1792. In 1794 Owen Rees was admitted a member, and the title of the firm was altered to Longman & Co. Thomas Longman, the nephew of the original founder, died February 5th, 1797, at Hampstead, in his sixty-sixth year. " He was a man of the most exemplary character, both in his profession and in private life, and as universally esteemed for his benevolence as for his integrity." Thomas Norton Longman, who succeeded him in the business " with a considerable portion of the well-earned wealth, inherited the good qualities of his father." 50

Owen Rees retired at midsummer, 1837, from the firm of Messrs. Longman & Co., booksellers, Paternoster Row, London, and withdrew to his estate, Gelligran, near Neath, Glamorganshire, where he died after an indisposition of a few weeks on September 5th of the same year, aged sixty-seven. Mr. Rees was highly spoken of as a great lover and patron of literature, an excellent dramatic critic, and one who was much lamented by all literary men.

Another well-known house purveying Gothic romances was that of Crosby, who with Richardson published in 1809 *The Castles of Marsange & Nuger*, 3 vols. Benjamin Crosby, of Stationer's Hall Court, London, was the youngest son and the last of a large family of a considerable grazier who lived at a village near Leeds. Born in 1768, young Crosby came up to Town from Yorkshire at an early age, and commenced apprentice with Mr. James Nunn, a well-known bookseller of Great Queen Street. His industry and attention to business won him the respect and confidence of that worthy man. From Mr. Nunn he went to the house of Robinson, in Paternoster Row. His next step was successor to Mr. Stalker, of Stationer's Hall Court, where he raised himself to eminence in the trade. He was one of the first London booksellers who regularly travelled through the country effecting sales and extending his connexion, in which he was extremely successful, as his mode of business combined with the urbanity of his manners procured him widespread friendship and esteem. He long maintained a high rank in the trade, and was one of the largest buyers at trade sales when the stocks of publishers were being sold off and dispersed.

In the winter of 1814 an attack of paralysis decided him to dispose of his business. A certain portion of it was sold to Mr. Robert Baldwin,

The Rose, 47 Paternoster Row, and Messrs. Cradock and Joy, whilst the remainder with the premises was acquired by Crosby's assistants, Messrs. Simpkin and Marshall.

A few days after this business was completed Benjamin Crosby suffered a second stroke, which so weakened his mind that for a while he was placed under restraint. He so far recovered, however, as to be able to accept an invitation to stay with an old friend, Mr. Jackson, bookseller, of Louth. He seemed to rally, but one morning his servant, upon entering the bedchamber, found he was no more, having died apparently without a struggle. He was buried in the parish church at Louth, under its magnificent steeple. He left a widow, who survived him some years, and two children, a son and a daughter.

Actually Henry Colburn, "Three Volume Novels and Light Literature," [51] might be judged to fall a little outside the period of the Gothic novel, but none the less a brief account of this famous publisher is certainly not impertinent, as it was he who issued Mrs. Radcliffe's posthumous *Gaston*. As a lad Henry Colburn was placed in the establishment of William Earle, the bookseller, of Albemarle Street.[52] Earle and Hemet have already been dealt with as a well-known firm, and published, amongst others, for Mrs. Helme, whose *St. Margaret's Cave* they issued in December, 1801. Earle and Hemet also published Mrs. R. P. M. Yorke's *The romance of Smyrna*, 4 vols., price 14s., February, 1801, and the same lady's *The Haunted Palace : or, The Horrors of Ventoliene*, 3 vols., in the following June. In December, 1801, Earle published *The Mysterious Friendship*, 2 vols., anonymous, and in December, 1804, W. H. Ireland's *Gondez the Monk*, 4 vols., 12mo, at 16s. From Earle and Hemet, Henry Colburn went to Morgan's, a large circulating library in Conduit Street, to the proprietorship of which he succeeded in 1816, conducting this business with the greatest success and resigning it upon his removal to New Burlington Street to Saunders and Otley.

However interesting the tale, it is clearly beyond our scope here to follow Colburn in his relations with Harrison Ainsworth, G. P. R. James, Theodore Hook, Banim, Marryat, Benjamin Disraeli, Bulwer Lytton, Alaric Watts, Lady Morgan, Agnes Strickland, and many another famous writer of the day, or to relate the history of the publication of Evelyn's Diary in 1818, and Pepys in 1825, the foundation of *The Court Journal* in 1828, and the series of Colburn's *Modern Standard Novelists*, better known as Bentley's " Standard Novels," [53] which commenced on February 25th, 1831, with Fenimore Cooper's *The Pilot*.

In 1830 Colburn took Richard Bentley (1794–1871), his principal printer, into partnership, but this was dissolved in August, 1832.

After a brief retirement Colburn opened a house in Great Marlborough Street, paying a forfeiture for breaking his agreement with Bentley. He finally retired in favour of Messrs. Hurst and Blackett, but still kept his name attached to certain copyrights. He was twice married, the second time to Eliza Anne, the only daughter of Captain Crosbie, R.N. Henry Colburn died August 16th, at his house in Bryanston Square.

George Walker (1772–1847), who had been apprenticed to a bookseller named Cuthell, started in business for himself with a capital of only a few shillings, and yet by his industry and application he did so well that in 1800 he was established at No. 106 Great Portland Street, whence later he removed to Golden Square. He issued his own works, which proved extremely popular, for he was not only a writer of Gothic romances but of anti-Godwin novels to boot. Thus *The House of Tynian*, 4 vols. (1795), and *Theodore Cyphon ; or, The Benevolent Jew*, 3 vols. (1796), were much admired. The theme of the latter is a relentless persecution, and the imprisonment of the hero in a private madhouse allows the author urgently to criticize the shameful abuses permitted by these institutions, for Walker was a zealous but by no means a fanatical reformer. The madhouse episode occurs in many other novels, of which it will suffice to mention Mrs. Parsons' *Lucy*, 1794 ; Henry Cockton's *Valentine Vox*, 1840 ; Wilkie Collins' *The Woman in White*, 1860 ; G. W. M. Reynolds' *Joseph Wilmot*, 1865 ; and Sheridan Le Fanu's *The Rose and the Key*, 1871. I do not find the villainy of the two Cyphons, Theodore's father and uncle, at all exaggerated, since I have known the hideous baseness of two similar ruffians in real life. *Theodore Cyphon* was one of the novels reprinted, 1822–23, by S. Fisher, 151 St. John Street, West Smithfield, " with 7 *excellent* Engravings, the 3 volumes in 6 Sixpenny Numbers, or in boards 3s. 6d." In *Cinthelia ; or The Woman of Ten Thousand*, 4 vols. 1797, Walker does not hesitate to make his heroine a tradesman's daughter, and, what is more surprising, to keep her so without any amazing history of babes changed in the cradle or the like.

The Vagabond, 2 vols., 1799, was dedicated to the Bishop of Llandaff, and by the following year had run into a fourth edition. Here Walker is writing with a very definite and direct purpose. He has a lesson to teach ; an example to point ; a warning to give. He clearly sees how great a menace to all society and to human welfare is the false philosopher, the infidel fanatic, who has keen intelligence but no scruples, who has those gifts which can sway the mob. Dr. Alogos, Fenton the young Oxonian, and Stupeo, the tutor, logically carry out the principles, or rather the lack of principles, of Godwin to their fullest extent, and, although the author treats his theme rather too fantastically, arguing from the accepted premises, there is no evading the truth of the picture he draws.

The Three Spaniards, 3 vols., 1800, has a brief preface : " In compliance with the Present Taste in Literary Amusement, this work is presented to the Public." It is an exceedingly well written and interestingly told romance. Whilst avoiding extravagance, Walker successfully introduces all the typical features of Gothic adventures, mystery, and love. The opening scene, at the splendid entertainment given by the Duke D'Alcantara at his palace in Madrid, where the Marquis Antonio De los Velos and Albert de Denia spy the lovely Almira so guarded by the dark and stern Don Tevarro Padilla, is admirably done, and the reader's attention is held to the very end. The ruins of a Moorish castle, seen through the gloom of night ; a lovely miniature ; Almonsor the Caballist ; the tales of mountain banditti ; the Convent of Dominican Nuns and its Lady Mother with the " grand Anthem and Requiem" ; would all have been most palatable fare. Walker has inserted in his chapters a ballad and lyrics which give a pleasing idea of his talent. He had indeed already published a volume of *Poems* which was received not without favour.

Of Walker's second Gothic romance, 3 vols., 1803, *Don Raphael*, who was " led into enormous crimes by the extravagance of his passions, not the badness of his heart," and who very wisely retires " to the quiet recess of a serene monastic establishment," I am able to give an equally good report. George Walker must certainly be accounted as an author of uncommon merit, and one who exhibits no little power in unfolding and sustaining a narrative.

" Publisher, Re-publisher, Printer, Book-buyer," [54] Thomas Tegg (1776–1848), lord of " the remainder trade," must not be passed over without brief notice. We have seen how the humbler circulating libraries catered for their myriad patrons, but there was—to quote the cookery books—" another way " in which the tastes of juveniles, schoolboys for the most part, and other simple folk could be conveniently gratified and indulged. The Gothic novel, a lengthy affair, in its four volumes or three volumes, as the case might be, was abridged, compressed and imitated upon a small scale, and the cheaper presses began to pour out in undiminished spate legions upon legions of " bluebooks " which were the lineal descendants of the earlier chapbooks, and which were bought in infinity by exactly the same class of purchaser. The bluebooks, " so designated from their covers . . . are or were to be bought for sixpence, and embodied stories of haunted castles, bandits, murderers, and other grim personages—a most

PLATE IV

THE ITALIAN
Contemporary water-colour drawing

ANCIENT RECORDS
Frontispiece, 1801

[*Face p.* 82

exciting and interesting food for boys' minds." [55] Their closely printed pages were roughly stitched into a cover of flimsy blue paper ; they were generally adorned with an appropriate frontispiece of most startling nature, sometimes plain, but more often decked in gaudiest colouring ; they were ' Price Sixpence.' Some publishers, indeed, purveyed two lengths, definitely measured—thirty-six pages for sixpence, and seventy-two for a shilling.

There was no busier house in this particular trade than that of Thomas Tegg, No. 3 Cheapside, and it may be remarked that his bluebooks are far better printed than the majority of these miniature romances, whilst his frontispieces are often of a quality, the illustrations (for example) to *The Castle of the Apennines* and *The Irish Assassin* being by Rowlandson.

Amongst other well-known publishers of bluebooks were Langley & Belch, 173 High Street, Borough ; T. & R. Hughes, 35 Ludgate Street ; J. Ker, 4 Greek Street, Soho Square ; R. Harrild, 20 Great Eastcheap ; J. Roe, 90 Houndsditch, and afterwards 38 Chiswell Street, Finsbury Square ; Ann Lemoine, White Rose Court, Coleman Street ; and a multitude of even obscurer names, both in town and country.

It was the aim of the writer of the bluebook first to give his narrative as exciting a title as possible ; secondly, to cram into his limited space as many shocking mysterious and horrid incidents as possible. Accordingly he must at once rush *in medias res* and waste no time in explanation or descriptions, save it be a brief descant on his hero's valour, or his heroine's beauty, or the unknown secrets of the ruined castle. His readers must be like Henry Tilney, and gulp down his pages with their " hair standing on end all the time."

With regard to titles, a few specimens will suffice : *Romano Castle, or, the Horrors of the Forest* ; *The Mysterious Omen, or, Awful Retribution* ; *The Black Forest, or, the Cavern of Horrors* ; *The Secret Oath, or, Bloodstained Dagger* ; *Midnight Horrors, or, The Bandit's Daughter* ; *The Hag of the Mountains, or, Mysterious Memoirs of the Marquis De La Terra and His Supposed Friend The Count Di Suza, Including Those of Lucetta and Vittoria, The Lovely Daughters of a Vintager, at Montmelian, in Savoy* ; *The Sicilian Pirate, or The Pillar of Mystery,* " A Terrific Romance " ; *The Convent Spectre* ; *The Abbess of St. Hilda. A dismal, dreadful, horrid Story !*

Occasionally the bluebook was to some extent original, but far more frequently a popular romance of the day was abbreviated and epitomized into the required number of pages, not unseldom with a considerable sacrifice of clarity and connexion. These piracies seem to have been entirely shameless and unabashed. Names were altered, and that was all. The more famous romances were abridged in this way times out of number, and were printed as separate bluebooks under a variety of sufficiently lurid and entrancing titles. I am only able to devote but a little space to the bluebooks, to which a chapter of considerable length might well be given. Moreover, I confine my examples to those which have a place in my own collection, but the following list, which I could double and redouble and amplify again from my shelves, will serve to show how ruthlessly famous and popular novels were plundered and hashed up at sixpence apiece.

Lovel Castle, or the Rightful Heir Restored, a Gothic Tale, is Clara Reeve's *The Old English Baron*. Mrs. Radcliffe's *The Italian* becomes *The Midnight Assassin, or, Confession of the Monk Rinaldi ; containing a Complete History of his Diabolical Machinations and Unparalleled Ferocity*. Rinaldi is Schedoni ; Amanda, Ellena ; and the Marchioness di Sardo, the Marchesa di Vivaldi.

The Monk was plundered a thousand times. *The Castle of Lindenburg, or The History of Raymond & Agnes* (1799) frankly acknowledges itself as an extract, unaltered save by omissions. *Almagro and Claude, or Monastic Murder ; Exemplified in the Dreadful Doom of an Unfortunate Nun* (1803) disguises its origin as well as may be, but with scant success. *Father Innocent, Abbot of the Capuchins, or The Crimes of the Cloister* (Tegg, 1803), which also appeared in the *Marvelous Magazine*, again can hardly be said to conceal Ambrosio.

Sometimes the titles were boldly preserved. In 1810 Tegg published *Vancenza ; or, The Dangers of Credulity*, by Mrs. Robinson, in two parts of 28 pages each ; whilst *Fatherless Fanny* is reduced to 32 pages. *The Midnight Bell ; or, The Abbey of St. Francis*, 34 pages, is Lathom's *Midnight Bell* ; *The Priory of St. Clair, or, Spectre of the Murdered Nun*, 36 pages, is Sarah Wilkinson's *Priory of St. Clair*. *Rayland Hall*, 1810, 40 pages, is Charlotte Smith's *The Old Manor House*, and Orlando Somerville keeps his name, but for some reason Monimia becomes Juliana. In *The Dæmon of Venice*, Tegg, 1810, 28 pages, which is Charlotte Dacre's *Zofloya*, Victoria di Loredini becomes Arabella di Lenardi ; her brother Leonardo, Orlando ; Berenza, Count Amiens ; Lilla, Agnes ; Zofloya, Abdallah ; and the names are, in fact, changed throughout the whole narrative.

It must be remembered that these little bluebooks were sold in their hundreds upon hundreds for a tester apiece, and the reason why now exemplars are of the very last rarity, and good clean copies will sometimes fetch as many pounds as they were sold for pence, lies in the fact that they were read and read on every side by schoolboys, by prentices, by servant-girls, by the whole of that vast population which longed to be in the fashion, to steep themselves in the Gothic romance—but the circulating library was too expensive or inaccessible for them, and so the Gothic chapbook passed from hand to hand and was literally read to pieces. Even if a virgin copy or two by some chance survived, they would not have been for a moment deemed worthy of the bookshelf, or even of a cardboard cover. They were thrown out contemptuously ; the babies crawling over the nursery floor were allowed to play with them for the sake of the pretty painted pictures, and little hands soon had them in scraps and tatters. So what were thought rubbish by our grandmothers have become unique treasures to-day, a thing which is no new phenomenon in the annals of bibliography.

In order to appreciate the swarm of Gothic romances and novels that came from the press it may be useful rapidly to cast our eyes over the more prominent output of a few years, without any idea at all of giving a complete or exhaustive list, but merely to familiarize ourselves with a few titles and publishers at the beginning of the nineteenth century, and thus to some extent at any rate visualize the conditions of the day.

Between July and October, 1804, appeared Henrietta Rouvière's [56] *Lussington Abbey*, 2 vols., Lane ; *The Captive of Vallance*, 2 vols. ; Mrs. Meeke's *The Nine Days Wonder*, 3 vols., Lane ; W. Frederic Williams' *The Witcheries of Craig Isaf*, 2 vols., Lane ; *Valambrosa, or The Venetian Nun*, 3 vols., Lane ; *Durston Castle, or the Ghost of Eleonora, a Gothic story.* Between October, 1804, and January, 1805, may be noted Ireland's *Gondez the Monk*, 4 vols., Earle ; Sarah Ann Hook's *Secret Machinations*, 4 vols. ; Sophia Woodfall's *Rosa ; or, The Child of the Abbey*, 4 vols. ; *Edmund Ironside*, 3 vols. ; Lewis' *The Bravo of Venice*, J. F. Hughes ; *The Fisherman's Hut*, 3 vols. ; *Dolgorucki and Menzikoff*, a translation from Lafontaine, 2 vols. ; *The Abbey of Weyhill*, Lane, 2 vols., and Mrs. Yorke's *My Master's Secret*, 2 vols. Between January and April, 1805, we may note : Godwin's *Fleetwood*, 3 vols ; *The Mysterious Father, or, Trials of the Heart*, 4 vols., Cundee ; Mrs. Opie's *Adeline Mowbray*, 3 vols. ; Charlotte Dacre's *Confessions of the Nun of St. Omers*, 3 vols. ; and *Donalda, or The Witches of Glenshiel*, 2 vols. From April to July, 1805, were published : *The Nun and her Daughter, or Memoirs of the Courville Family*, 4 vols., Lane ; H. M. Cecil's *The Mysterious Visitor, or, Mary the Rose of Cumberland*, 2 vols. ; *The Banks of the Douro, or, The Maid of Portugal*, by Emily Clark, 3 vols. ; Mrs. Burke's *The Secret of the Cavern*, 2 vols., Lane ; *The Nuns of the Desert, or the Woodland Witches*, by Eugenia de Acton,[57] 2 vols., Lane ;

L. A. Conolly's *The Friar's Tale*, 2 vols., Cadell; G. T. Morley's *Deeds of Darkness, or, The Unnatural Uncle*; a Tale of the 16th Century, including interesting *Memoirs founded on Facts*, 2 vols., Tipper & Richards. July to October, 1805, furnishes us with *The Idiot Heiress*, 2 vols., Lane; *Glenmore Abbey, or the Lady of the Rock*, 3 vols.; *The Castle of Roviègo; or, Retribution*, an Italian romance, 4 vols., Lane; G. D. Hernon's *Louisa, or, The Black Tower*, 2 vols.; *Eugene and Eugenia; or, One Night's Horrors*, 3 vols., Lane; Lathy's *The Paraclete*, 5 vols.; Miss Owenson's *The Novice of St. Dominick*, 5 vols.; Richard Phillips' *The Mysterious Protector*, 2 vols., Robinson. The fall of the year brought Mrs. Rice's *Monteith, founded on Scottish History*, 2 vols.; *The Mysterious Sisters*, 2 vols.; *Eversfield Abbey*, 3 vols., Crosby; *Ferdinand and Amelia*, 3 vols., Crosby; *The Eventful Marriage*, 4 vols., Crosby; Horsley Curties' *St. Botolph's Priory, or The Sable Mask*, 5 vols.; Richard Sickelmore's *Rashleigh Abbey or The Ruin on the Rock*, 3 vols., Lane; Lathom's *The Impenetrable Secret*, 2 vols.; *Hyppolitus, or The Wild Boy*, from the French, 4 vols., Lane; Henrietta Rouvière's *The Heirs of Villeroy*, 3 vols., Lane; and Mrs. Helme's *The Pilgrim of the Cross*, 4 vols., published by Norbury, Brentford.

In the first quarter of 1806 there came J. Powell's translation from the favourite Lafontaine, *The Village of Friedewalde*, one of the " familien-geschichten," 3 vols.; *Vivonio, or the Hour of Retribution*, 4 vols.; Lathom's *The Mysterious Freebooter*, 4 vols., Lane; *Siegwart, a Monastic Tale*, from the German of J. M. Müller, by Laetitia M. Hawkins; Miss Hamilton's *The Forest of St. Bernardo*, 4 vols.; another translation by Powell, *Wolf, or The Tribunal of Blood*, 2 vols., " From the German of Weber," and Jane Harvey's *The Castle of Tynemouth*, 2 vols., Vernor.

Jane Harvey specialized in castles, as witness, among her other novels, *Minerva Castle*, 3 vols., Lane, 1802; *Wakefield Castle*, 3 vols., Lane, 1802; *Brougham Castle*, 2 vols., Newman, 1816. The latter was suggested by a striking passage in Mrs. Radcliffe's *Journey Through Holland . . . and . . . A Tour to The Lakes*, 1795, pp. 426–31, where she describes at length " Brougham Castle, venerable for its well-certified antiquity, and for the hoary masses it now exhibits." She romantically remarks of the hawthorn and ash springing from the ruins that " at the transforming hour of twilight, the superstitious eye might mistake them for spectres of some early possessor of the castle, restless from guilt, or of some sufferer persevering from vengeance."

Castles and abbeys still continued to be built by the novelists at a great rate, for during the next three years, to select but a few from many, we have : *Dellingborough Castle; or, The Mysterious Recluse*,

2 vols., Lane, 1806 ; *Mountbrasil Abbey, or Maternal Trials*,[58] 2 vols., 1806 ; Edward Montague's *The Castle of Berry Pomeroy*, 2 vols., Lane, 1806, of which the reviewer in the *Literary Journal*, October, 1806, remarked that " Although *castles* generally produce incidents of a similar nature, Mr. Montague has diversified his materials so happily as to give an original air to the principal story, which keeps up the attention and interests the feelings in a manner that is not very common."

In the winter of 1806 was published *The Convent of Notre Dame ; or, Jeanette*, 2 vols., by the author of *A Tale of Mystery ; or, Celina*.

In 1807 we have : *Mandeville Castle, or the Two Ellinors*, 2 vols., Booth ; Theodore Melville's *The Benevolent Monk, or The Castle of Olalla*, 3 vols., Crosby ; Edward Montague's *The Legends of a Nunnery*, 4 vols., Hughes ; *Griffith Abbey, or, Memoirs of Eugenia*, 2 vols., by Mrs. Charlotte Matthews ; and Mrs. Mary Pilkington's *Ellen, Heiress of the Castle*, 3 vols., Crosby. In the winter appeared *Mountville Castle, or, The Village Story*, by James N. Brewer, 3 vols. ; Lathom's *The Fatal Vow, or St. Michael's Monastery*, 2 vols. ; and *Ludovico's Tale, or The Black Banner of Castle Douglas*, by A. A. Stewart, 4 vols.

In 1808 some particularly lurid romances saw the light. " A Citizen of the World " published *The Atrocities of a Convent, or the Necessity of Thinking for ourselves, exemplified in the History of a Nun*, 3 vols. *The Monks and the Robbers*, 2 vols., is " A Tale of the Fifteenth Century." *The Convent of St. Marc*, 4 vols., is well in the Gothic tradition. Mrs. Mary A. Hanway's *Falconbridge Abbey*, 3 vols., was published by Lane in December.

Ruins also gave a real thrill. *The Ruins of Rigonda ; or The Homicidal Father*, by Helen St. Victor, 4 vols., Chapple, 1808, is a title not to be resisted. Almost equally good are F. Clifford's *The Ruins of Tivoli*, a romance, 1810 ; *The Ruins of Selinunti ; or, The Val de Mazzara*, 3 vols., Newman, 1813 ; and Mrs. C. D. Golland's [59] *The Ruins of Ruthvale Abbey*, 4 vols., Newman, 1826.

The Gothic Novel was a power in the land, and its votaries were drawn from all classes, high and low. With Mrs. Radcliffe, with Monk Lewis and Maturin, to mention no other names, it touched genius. It was able to sink to bathos and the most formal absurdity, although I am bound to acknowledge that in the whole course of my reading of fiction of the eighteenth and nineteenth centuries, which has involved not a little delving in dusty and forgotten corners, I have never come across any novel, however feeble, however immature, which can be deemed such dreary and dead rubbish as are only too many of our modern trite and yawny novels.

The reviewers, for the most part, were traditionally opposed to fiction. I say " traditionally," since in January, 1788, the *Monthly Review* is complaining bitterly of a long-standing grievance : " The Reviewer of the modern novel is in the situation of Hercules encountering the Hydra, one head lopped off, two or three immediately spring up in its place," [60] and in August, 1790, the same *Review* grumbles that " The manufacture of novels has been so long established," adding, " We are indeed so sickened with this worn-out species of composition, that we have lost all relish for it." [61]   It is true that Mrs. Radcliffe won respect and admiration,[62] but it is notorious how vehemently and maliciously attacks were launched upon Matthew Gregory Lewis and even his personal character lewdly assailed, whilst lesser writers again and again protest that their lives are made miserable owing to the unprovoked antagonism of ignorant reviewers. Perhaps this sort of thing is sporadic, for it cannot escape remark that precisely the same conditions prevail to-day, and now our critics have passed, the fry of reviewers seem normally to be actuated by a brutal malevolence and urged by a spleen that often does not seek to disguise a personal enmity and hate.

It is surprising, for example, to remark the bitterness of the censure in *The Ghost*, a bi-weekly Journal, published at Edinburgh in 1796, by Felix Phantom, who was a Portuguese student, named Constantia, at Edinburgh University.   No. 24 of *The Ghost*, August 24th, sweepingly condemns all fiction " so much in fashion among the Misses," and the writer adds " I deem highly probable, that even the best Novels are pernicious to youth."   Knox and Calvin could hardly have said much more.

It will not be uninstructive to consider a few specimens—and those by no means the harshest or most unfair—of criticism one hundred and forty years ago.

The Monthly Mirror, June, 1796,[63] observes of *Adela Northington*, a Novel, 3 vols., Cawthorn, 1796, that " This novel is neither well-written nor well-conducted.   A heroine without principle . . . had the author studied effect, he must have known could never interest ; but he seems to have had no object."

Angelo : a Novel, founded on melancholy facts, written by Edward Henry Iliff (late of the Theatre Royal, Haymarket), Allen and West, 1796, is curtly given its congé as " Wild, incongruous, pedantic, and uninteresting."

The Mansion-House, a Novel Written by a Young Gentleman, 2 vols., Lane, 1796, is dismissed as " neither above nor below mediocrity ; it will do neither good nor harm : it can demand no praise, and deserves no censure.[64]

The Neapolitan, or The Test of Integrity, a Novel by Ellen of Exeter, 3 vols., Lane, 1797, has a crumb of comfort thrown, " An incongruous performance ; sometimes interesting, but often dull ; negligently written, and immethodically conducted : it is, nevertheless, not wholly destitute of merit." [65]

The same *Mirror*, November, 1796, trounces *Louis de Boncœur, A domestic Tale*, by Catherine Lara, 2 vols., Ridgway, as " A translation from the French, abounding with bastard sentiment and unnatural incident, fit only for those to read who can dispense with nature and common sense." [66]

In July, 1797, *The Monthly Mirror*,[67] noticing *Eloise de Montblanc, a Novel*, 4 vols., Lane, 1796, said : " We have contrived to get through this novel ourselves ; but we do not mean to be revenged on the author by recommending the same duty to any one of our readers." Against so harsh a sentence I vehemently protest, and will not allow it. The writer, who was only seventeen, disarms attack by her preface. " And when too she recollects the perfect Pen of a Burney, a Radcliffe, a Bennet, or a Smith, she shrinks at meeting the scrutinizing Eye of Criticism." The story has youthfulness, but it also shows very considerable talent, and it is not without charm. I have more than once read it with a great deal of pleasure, and although I cannot name any other novel as the work of this fair anonyma, I should be sorry to think that she did not again contribute to the world of fiction.

In August, 1797,[68] the *Mirror* is uncommonly severe upon *The Wanderer of the Alps, or Alphonso, A Romance*, 2 vols., Lane, 1796, and says : " If we merely apprize our readers that there exists a novel bearing the title above mentioned, we think we shall do sufficient honour to the *Wanderer of the Alps*, and the author ought to thank us for not proceeding any further."

The Monthly Mirror, March, 1799, thought Gabrielli's *The Sicilian*, 4 vols., Lane, was " one of those works which possess just interest enough to prevent the reader's throwing the book aside in disgust."

The Critical Review, January, 1801, damned *Jaqueline of Olzeburg ; or Final Retribution*, 1 vol., Chapple, 1800, as : " Another ghostly story, with a bombastic beginning, and an horrible termination, but with no incident between of the least consequence or interest. The author seems to have adopted the adage of the kitchen, ' Light the fire well at both sides, and the middle will take care of itself.' "

The Monthly Review, July, 1801,[69] thus proceeds to pulverize G. A. Graglia's *The Castle of Eridan*, " or, the entertaining and surprising History of the valiant Don Alvares, and the beautiful Eugenia, Duchess of Savoy," one vol., Hurst, 1800 ; " Improbable in its events, unnatural in its characters, mean in its sentiments, and trifling in its description, this tragical tale is *sad* in nothing but its composition, and excites no sorrow but for its author."

Of the anonymous *The Cavern of Strozzi*, one vol., Lane, 1800, *The Critical Review*, March, 1801, thought that " the supposed statement of the crimes, and consequent horrors and death of an abandoned woman of quality " in this age of rhodomontade and fiction might " strut its hour among the other wonders and incongruities of the circulating library."

The Critical Review, November, 1805,[70] p. 326, remarks of *Mental Recreations, Four Danish and German Tales*, one vol., Baldwin, 1805 : " This publication at this season may safely be recommended as a fire-screen : it will shield the face from the fire, and employ the eyes, without arresting the attention so much as to prevent the holder from participating in the pleasure of the conversation of the company."

The Last Man, or Omegarus and Syderia, a Romance in Futurity, 2 vols., Dutton, 1806, is thus noticed in *The Critical Review*, August, 1806 [71] : " A most potent narcotic, which we strongly recommend to all apothecaries and druggists, as a substitute for opium, producing all the good, without any of the bad qualities of that soporific medicine."

When Mrs. Norris published *The Strangers*, 3 vols., Vernor, 1806, the uxoriousness of Mr. Norris [72] rashly induced him to send *The Critical Review* [73] a notice of this production of his spouse " replete with the most overstrained panegyric. In revenge for the insult of supposing that we should prostitute our journal by inserting a critciism which contained no word of truth, we are almost tempted to expose in an unceremonious manner the present senseless volumes to the ridicule they deserve, but

Nullum memorabile nomen
Foemineâ in paenâ est, neque habet victoria laudem.[74]

We therefore silently consign them to oblivion."

In November, 1806, *The Critical Review*, Series the Third, Vol. IX, No. 3 (p. 328), thus noticed Thomas Pike Lathy's *The Invisible Enemy* ; *or, the Mines of Wielitska. A Polish Legendary Romance*, 4 vols., Lane, " We were sorry to find the Mines so unproductive. The romance of Mr. L. has but little to recommend it to the discriminating reader. The plot is threadbare and irregular, composed of a few incidents thrown together in an unmeaning confusion, tedious where they concern and where they do not, as indifferent and uninteresting as they are unnecessary, and seldom endowed with any pretensions to originality." Of the same romance *The Monthly Mirror*, January, 1807, said that there might be " some *salt* expected but these are *lead* mines.

. . . We dug and dug with that exemplary patience, which by exercise Mr. Lane has so much improved in us, but found no vein of precious ore. All is trite and trumpery." [75]

Lathy, born at Exeter in 1771, was the author of four other novels,[76] *The Paraclete*, 5 vols., 1805; *Usurpation; or, The Inflexible Uncle*, 3 vols., 1805; *Gabriel Forrester, or, The Deserted Son*, 4 vols., 1807; *Love, Hatred and Revenge, a Swiss Romance*, 3 vols., 1809; *The Misled General*, a serio-comic romance, 1 vol., 1870, is by Barrett, and not his.

In 1800, whilst in America, he wrote *Reparation, or the School for Libertines*, a dramatic piece published at Boston, "for the benefit of the author," as having been performed at the Boston Theatre with great applause. In 1819, he dedicated to the Prince Regent his *Memoirs of the Court of Louis XIV*, 3 vols., 8vo, a work of some historical research. In the same year Lathy imposed upon Godson, the well-known publisher, an original poem on angling which was issued as *The Angler, a Poem in ten cantos with notes*, etc., by Piscator [T. P. Lathy, Esq.] embellished with a symbolical full-length portrait of himself. After a number of copies de luxe had been printed it was discovered that *The Angler* was transcribed from a work of Dr. Thomas Scott of Ipswich,[77] *The Anglers*, London, 12mo, 1758.

I must enter another protest against the reviewers. *The Invisible Enemy; or, the Mines of Wielitska*, is a first-rate specimen of the more lurid Gothic romance. Lathy has not, of course, a tithe of the genius of Mrs. Radcliffe, indeed he is of the school of Lewis, and he handles his secret chapels where are sculptured death's heads, his mouldering black palls, his skulls, pistols, and daggers, his scaffolds covered with hearse cloths, blocks and scimitars, with lavish profusion. Rhodiska and Theresia read with a terrific surprise threats of fearful vengeance traced in characters of fire : Gramani's whole life " has been one continued scene of blood, pillage, and infamy" ; and it is all very thick and slab, and Leopold Rosomaski loves Rhodiska, and Rhodiska loves Leopold ; but *The Invisible Enemy* is full of first-class thrills.

Gabriel Forrester is probably the best of Lathy's work. Modelled both in subject and style upon Tom Jones, it is by no means a lifeless and wooden imitation of Fielding, although of course Lathy is not to be compared with his great predecessor. His characters, if strictly unoriginal, have yet a vigour and briskness of their own. The part of Squire Western is taken by Sir Hector Gabion, " who had fought all the battles he would ever fight in this world, both in the fields of Mars and Venus " ; Sophia appears as his daughter Jemima to whom (with his permission) Lord Tandem, a regency black-leg, is paying matrimonial addresses. Jemima and Gabriel Forrester are deeply in love, but some diplomatic attentions offered by the latter to Miss Diana Gabion, an antique sibyl, Sir Hector's sister, are misconstrued by this lady as "tenders of affection." The acute Lord Tandem employs Parrott, an accommodating levite, who also has cast a sheep's eye on Miss Diana, to spy out the land on his behalf, and Parrott's zealous service to his patron leads to many complications, perplexities and delays in the course of true love. Not the least amusing episodes are those scenes "drawn with so much warmth, that we wonder the paper did not take fire," as a contemporary has it.

Theodore Melville [78] is the author of *The White Knight*; or, *The Monastery of Marne*, 3 vols., 1802; *The Benevolent Monk*; or, *The Castle of Ollala*, 3 vols., Crosby, 1807; *The Irish Chieftain and his Family*, 4 vols., Newman, 1809.

In spite of the fact that *The Benevolent Monk* was sufficiently well received to run into a second edition, 2 vols., 1810, *The Critical Review*, September, 1807,[79] is unmercifully crushing in its notice of this romance: " We strenuously recommend to Theodore Melville the advice which Dr. Johnson gave to the Irishman, to reperuse everything he writes, and whenever he meets with *shall* to alter it to *will*, and *vice versâ*. By so doing he will write intelligible English. As to the plot, it is stale ; a wicked brother conspires against the life of a brother, to succeed to his estates, and to gain possession of his wife's person ; trap-doors and subterranean passages, tapestry, and all the armoury of novels, are brushed up for the occasion."

The Critical Review, September, 1801,[80] so disapproved of *Martyn of Fenrose*; or, *The Wizard and the Sword*, A Romance by Henry Summersett,[81] 3 vols., Dutton, 1801, that " disgust compelled us to throw the book on the floor, and we confess we have never since proceeded to the perusal. Is it not enough that the English are already condemned by all Europe for the multiplicity of their oaths and blasphemies, that our circulating libraries must furnish their readers with a new set of anathemas ? ' May the spirit of my father strangle me in savageness ! ' and ' By the ruler of the world of angels, I will level all my rage and resentment at these smiling devils ' are the only two instances of our author's invention with which we will pollute our journal." The dragoon or boatswain's mate who finds " himself disposed to improve in the delectable science of swearing is invited to study the curses and imprecations in these three volumes." " The German dramatists are here absolutely *out-heroded*."

The Monthly Mirror, June, 1805, not unjustly derides " the witches of Glenshiel, in their car of broom, suspended in the air "[82] as they appear to Donalda in *Donalda, or The Witches of Glenshiel*, A Caledonian

Legend, by Mary Julia Young, 2 vols., Hughes, 1805. Miss Young, however, is possessed of as much merit as the generality of those ladies " who are so constantly teeming, and so easily and so speedily delivered of their offspring, by the circulating man-midwife of Leadenhall-street." Miss Young, who was a relative of the poet of *Night Thoughts*, had described a former novel, *Moss Cliff Abbey* ; or, *The Sepulchral Harmonist*, 4 vols., Crosby, 1803, as " A Mysterious Tale," and indeed mysteries abound. George and Harriet Newton in this romance are not too poor an imitation of Booth and Amelia.

Miss Eliza Museat of Bromley was rebuked for the moral of her *Cave of Corenza*, " a Romance of the 18th Century, Altered from the Italian," 2 vols., Robinson, 1803. A girl of seventeen passionately loves a married man of fifty whose amiable wife dies in pudding-time to make possible their union. The romance abounds in caves and bandits.

In Eugenia de Acton's *The Nuns of the Desert* ; or, *the Woodland Witches*,[83] 2 vols., Lane, 1805, we have Hindo, an ape, and Brimo, a talking dog, who answer questions put by the witches. At the end all this is bunglingly attempted to be ascribed to ventriloquism. *The Monthly Mirror*[84] tartly remarked, " We, however, can ascribe it to nothing but ' a native weakness of intellect ' in the writer," and condemns wholesale such miserable artifice.

Even favourite authors were sometimes taken to task.[85] Thus Mrs. Parsons learns that her *Voluntary Exile*, 5 vols., 1795, has merit, but " horror is crowded upon horror till our sympathy becomes exhausted and we read of faintings, death and madness with perfect apathy." The lady is reminded that " The heart can suffer long and severely without breaking," and she is bidden clear her pages of this plethora of swoonings and dyings.

In regard to his *Astonishment* ! ! ! 2 vols., 1802, Lathom is told that he has " almost thrown away his time in attempting this work," [86] whilst his *Human Beings*, 3 vols., Crosby, 1807, was thus criticized : " This novel bears very few marks of the genius which dictated *Men and Manners*. . . . The characters are insignificant and the story improbable." [87]

Edric the Forester ; or *The Mysteries of the Haunted Chamber*, by Mrs. Anne Ker, 3 vols., Newman, was popular enough to run into more than one edition, and to be reprinted 1841 for " The Romancist and Novelist's Library," yet it was severely handled in the *Monthly Review* of June, 1818. " A total want of grammatical accuracy is among the least faults of this paltry performance," says the reviewer. " *The ladies Ellen and Elgiva for that were their names* ' [88] are confined in a dungeon,

' as it was not Lord Fitzosric's *intentions to marry,*' and they are released by Lady Jane, who had imprisoned herself during thirteen years in a haunted room and performed the part of a ghost from pure good will although she constantly possessed the means of escaping and of claiming a noble fortune." [89]

The period of *Edric* is in the days of William the Conqueror, but naturally we do not look for any attempt at historical accuracy, and it is only fair to say that the reviewer practically burlesques the romance, which is in its own way well told and interesting. Anne Ker also wrote *The Heiress Di Montalde*, 1793 ; *Adeline St. Julian* ; *or, The Midnight Hour*, 2 vols., 1804 ; *Emmeline* ; *or The Happy Discovery* (to be distinguished from Charlotte Smith's *Emmeline*) ; *The Mysterious Count*, 1802, and *Modern Faults.*

Deeds of Darkness, or the Unnatural Uncle, a Tale of the Sixteenth Century, by G. T. Morley, 2 vols., 12mo, Tipper and Richards, March, 1805 (12*s.*) is a typical Gothic novel, whence an exciting incident may be quoted : " Watching with straining eyes the painted canvass her fears were at last confirmed, and, dreadful to behold, it was slid back, and a man, masked and armed, stepped softly through the aperture, followed by three others !

" The terrified and trembling Josephina could scarcely believe her eyes, and with difficulty drew her breath. The men, all of whom were masked, beckoned silence to each other, and advanced towards the bed, where our heroine, giving a faint scream, fainted. Lifting her up, they seized upon their prey, and bore her through the pannel, closing it after them, and extinguishing the lamp." Upon this *The Critical Review*,[90] January, 1806, remarks : " As our fair readers must burn with impatience to learn the fate of the unhappy Josephina, we may beg leave to inform them that they may safely gratify their curiosity, for (as is our bounden duty) we have taken care to ascertain that the sentiments in this tale are proper, and the moral is good."

Frankenstein, 3 vols., Lackington, 1818, was regarded by the *Monthly Review* [91] as " An uncouth story . . . setting probability at defiance and leading to no conclusion either moral or philosophical. A serious examination is scarcely necessary for so excentric a vagary of the imagination as this tale presents."

There was, however, from time to time some protest, and not on the part of authors alone, against this bitter prejudice of the reviewers which served to bring the art of the novelist into contempt.

Rimelli, a correspondent of the *Monthly Mirror*,[92] August, 1802, writing against the " anti-novelists " who urge that young persons, especially females, become so totally absorbed in lamenting and condoling with the melancholy situation of a Julia, an Emily, or a Matilda so hot with admiration of some *all-perfect* novel hero, that they forget the common duties and obligations of ordinary life often to the risk of domestic happiness, allows that this may sometimes be the case, and that some modern novels are " mere catchpenny trash, and *some* immoral and even impious ; though the press teems with ' Midnight Bells,' ' Black Castles,' ' Haunted Towers,' ' Mysterious Monks,' etc., etc., with a long train of ghosts, phantoms, etc.," yet by far the greater number of novels do inculcate excellent precepts and morals, and as for the rest they should be censured as *absurd, improbable, and ill-written*, rather than as tending to corrupt the mind.   " I except some few, such as ' The Monk,' by Mr. Lewis, which is not only immoral, but blasphemous, *cum paucis aliis*." Yet the romances of " the ingenious and amiable Mrs. Ann Radcliffe " and of Dr. Moore both please and instruct ; a rare coalition !

To conclude this chapter a few words may fittingly be given to the distribution by publishers and the prices of novels.

The problems of the exact " original condition " of the novel as issued towards the end of the eighteenth century and at the beginning of the nineteenth century are technicalities which lie almost entirely beyond my scope, and accordingly I will refer those who wish to investigate such matters in ampler detail to the work of Mr. Michael Sadleir, the recognized authority upon these difficult and intricate questions.   From the period 1730 to 1770, and indeed until about 1800, says Mr. Sadleir, the publisher and the wholesale bookseller were one. The latter department distributed the book (still in sheets) to the retail trade.   The retail bookseller, who may or may not have been the proprietor of a circulating library bound the sheets in leather or half leather binding as best suited his purpose.   For his own library, if any, he would bind in a strong cheap style to stand the wear and tear of circulation ; for his stock he would bind in those styles he considered were best calculated to attract his customers ; for important private buyers he would undertake the binding in the style each particularly affected.

It is highly probable that copies of the books from this period which have survived in plain wrappers are merely the residue of an edition. Whilst it cannot be proved that no wrappered books were ever sent out by the publisher's wholesale department, it is extremely significant that, in no single engraving known of the interior of a bookseller's shop of this period is there any sign of stock in other than leather bound shape.   It seems, therefore, likely that, after the selling life of a book had ceased and it became necessary to dispose of the balance of edition, the publisher-wholesaler might wrapper up this balance for jobbing to persons outside the regular trade, who had not the resources or facilities for immediate leather binding possessed by the retail bookseller proper. Mr. Sadleir has a note enumerating certain "typical examples of *unstiffened*, unlettered wrappering from the last and transitional decade of the eighteenth century : *Fatal Follies* (4 vols., 1788) ; *The Knight of the Rose*, by Lucy Peacock (1 vol., 1793) ; *Clermont*, by Regina Maria Roche (4 vols., 1798) ; *The Haunted Palace or The Horrors of Ventoliene*, by Mrs. Yorke (4 vols., 1801).[93]

The earlier unstiffened wrapper was generally blue, and hence in *The Rivals*, I, 2, when Lydia Languish says to her maid : "Give me the *sal volatile*," Lucy asks : "Is it in a blue cover, Ma'am ? "

I have in my own collection many examples of the novel in its primitive unstiffened, unlettered wrapperings, and incidentally these also show that not in every case was the smaller circulating library at the cost and trouble to have their novels bound. I may instance *The Castle of Tariffa ; or The Self-Banished Man*, 4 vols., Crosby, 1812, in limp blue paper wrappers, no lettering on spine save the volume marked (I . . . IV), and *Castle of Tariffa* written in ink, from S. White's Circulating Library, Moretonhampstead. T. J. Horsley Curties' *Ethelwina ; or The House of Fitz-Auburne*, 3 vols., Minerva Press, 1799, from the same Circulating Library, is in an exactly similar condition. On the other hand, *The Abbess of Valtiera ; or the Sorrows of a Falsehood*, by Agnes Lancaster, 4 vols., A. K. Newman (Minerva Press), 1816, has been put in stiffened covers with a rough leather spine, on which are marked the several numbers of the volumes.

For the shelves of the large country manors and noblemen's seats the bindings, no doubt often personally designed by My Lord or His Grace, were generally elaborate and rich. The presentation copies, again, offered to the patron or patroness of the writer would be particularly splendid in their dress.

Presentation copies form an exceedingly interesting chapter in bibliography, but we must not be tempted to stray aside here. Our greater libraries afford many examples, not the least remarkable of which is Nathaniel Lee's *The Tragedy of Nero, Emperour of Rome*, 4to, 1675, in the Bodleian. Malone, unfortunately, stripped this of its binding in order to include it in one volume with the rest of his Lee quartos.[94] *The Tragedy of Nero* is dedicated to Rochester. On a blank leaf facing "The Persons" Malone has a MS. note : *When this play fell into my hands it was bound in a splendid cover. The gilding of the leaves is not yet worn off. I imagine it was the presentation copy given probably to Lord Rochester, and that the corrections*

throughout in MS. were made by Nat Lee himself [95] *. . . E. M.*
1780.

The Congratulatory and Occasional Poems written by Elkanah
Settle frequently appear in very special and magnificently ornamented
presentation bindings.

" They form an interesting and unique group of English bindings,
as, although ' armorial ' bindings are in themselves common enough,
this is the only instance in which a particular binder has consistently
ornamented a large series of bindings with heraldic designs." [96] Thus
a copy of Settle's *Augusta Lacrimans. A Funeral Poem, to the Memory
of the Honoured Charles Baynton, Esq.*, 1712,[97] is bound with the coat-
of arms " of Baynton impaling Keenlyside " ; and a copy [98] of Settle's
*Thalia Lacrimans. A Funeral Poem to the Memory of the Right Honourable
Baptist Earl of Gainsborough*, 1714, is bound in black morocco with the
arms of the Earl of Gainsborough on the cover, and contains the
book-plate of the Rt. Hon. Dorothy, Countess of Gainsborough.
*Honori Sacellum. A Funeral Poem to the Memory of the Honoured Clement
Pettit, Esq.*, . . . By E. Settle, 1717, is bound in black morocco, and
the cover, panelled in gold, bears the Pettit arms.[99] Even when
Settle's poems were not printed he caused the MS. to be bound for
presentation, as in the case of *Augusta Triumphans*, written in 1705,
and addressed to the Right Hon. Sir Thomas Rawlinson, Kt., Lord
Mayor, which the author caused to be bound in black morocco with
the Rawlinson arms tooled in gold on the covers.[100]

When Jean Marishall, dedicating her *Clarinda Cathcart* to Queen
Charlotte, was enabled to present a copy to that royal lady, she soon
found that no ordinary format " stitched in blue paper " was per-
missible on such an occasion, but that an elaborate tooled binding was
the essential court dress.

With the appearance of the printed spine label, comes the first sign
that the publisher-wholesaler is regarding the wrappering or boarding
of his books as conceivably part of his job. " We know of cases,"
Mr. Sadleir says, " where a page of undivided labels still survives in
books of the 18th century ; and inasmuch as these labels were printed
at the time the book itself was printed, they argue a possible wrappering
or boarding at some stage of the book's career, probably at the hands
of the wholesale department of the publisher." To attempt to date
anything so gradual and confused as the chronology of binding
practice is impossible. " Particularly," Mr. Sadleir warns us, " must
one beware of arguing from boards or wrappers of possible later date
than the title pages they embrace." Only when labels can prove to
have been printed with the book, and so be part of the sheet is it

possible safely to suggest that the book's publisher envisaged some kind of casing, of however temporary a nature.

I possess novels from circulating libraries which still retain on their spines nothing more than the mere number of the volume in the set—1, 2, 3, and so on—and when ranged in the shelves it is often extremely difficult to find among the uniform rows the precise novel of which one may be in search. In a large circulating library such a mere numeration of untitled sets must have presented a serious problem and have involved a considerable loss of time and patience. Examples of untitled sets, only numbered with a figure designating the order of volumes, are : Mrs. Meeke's *What Shall Be, Shall Be* 4 vols., A. K. Newman, 1823, from Evans's Library, Abingdon ; *The Bandit Chief*, 4 vols., A. K. Newman 1818, from the Moretonhampstead Library ; *Romantic Facts*, 4 vols., A. K. Newman, 1816. The Sedbergh Book Club tried to obviate this difficulty by assigning a number to each set. Thus *The Bravo of Bohemia*, 4 vols., Lane, 1806, is No. 28. I also have many examples of novels, not circulating library copies, which have only the figure of the order of volumes on the spine. I may instance *Women as They Are*, by Mrs. Parsons, 4 vols., Lane, 1796.

It soon appeared, however, that certain buyers—both private persons and libraries—desired to keep their books more or less permanently in the condition they had purchased the volumes. Probably this was often due to a wish to spare the expense of binding. Hence evolved the paper label.

Actually there are examples—though rare—of paper labels in the seventeenth century. I have a copy of Gerard Langbaine's *An Account of the English Dramatick Poets*, Oxford, 1691, in the original calf binding with a paper label. Moreover, a duplicate paper label printed " Laingbaine's Account of the *Dramatick Poets* " is supplied to replace an outworn original.

I know copies of several novels—for example, *Who Is The Bridegroom* ? by Mrs. Green 3 vols., Newman, 1822 ; *Manfroné*, by Mary Anne Radcliffe, 4 vols., A K. Newman, 1828, The Third Edition— which provide the actual labels intended for the eventual boards. These are not the modern duplicate labels generously furnished to replace a tired original.

Novels were expensive for the private purchaser. In 1673 *Hymen's Præludia*—that is, Loveday's translation of *Cléopâtre*, cost, bound, 20s. ; in 1675 *Cassandra* (Cotterell's translation), folio, bound, was 18s. ; but smaller volumes were, of course, less, as in 1678 *The Mock Clelia*, 8vo, translated from Perdou de Subligny's burlesque of the heroic romances *La Fausse Clelie*, cost, bound, 4s. " The Secret

History of the most renowned Queen *Elizabeth* and the E. of *Essex*,"
12mo, published by Bentley, cost 1*s*. in 1680. One shilling was the
usual price for the duodecimo novella. This was the price of the
scandalous *Venus in the Cloyster, or The Nun in her Smock*, by Du Prat,
1683 ; of *Auristella* and *Paul of Ségovia*, in one volume, 1683 ; *Love
Victorious*, 1684 ; *The Amorous Abbess, or Love in a Nunnery*, " A Novel
Translated from the French by a Woman of Quality," 1684 ; *The
Gallant Hermaphrodite*, " An Amorous Novel," 1687 ; Mrs. Behn's
Oroonoko; *The Fair Jilt*; and *Agnes de Castro*; all three, 1688 ; Congreve's
Incognita, 1693 ; and of the majority of novels. *The Adventures of
Lindamira* (Tom Brown) in 1703 cost 2*s*. ; and in 1705 *All the Histories
and Novels of the late Mrs. Behn, entire, in One Volume*, the Fifth Edition
was published at 5*s*.

In 1739 Richard Ware, " at the *Bible* and *Sun* in *Amen-Corner*,"
published the Fourth Edition of *Cassandra*, in 5 vols., 12mo, at 15*s*.
Mrs. Haywood's *Secret Histories, Novels, Love-Letters and Poems*, 3rd ed.,
4 vols., 12mo, cost 10*s*. ; Mrs. Aubin's *The Life of Charlotte Dupont, an
English Lady* ; *taken from her own Memoirs*, 1 vol. cost 2*s*. Towards the
end of the eighteenth century, from approximately 1770 to 1790, they
cost per volume, bound, 3*s*. ; sewed, with a thick paper cover, 2*s*. 6*d*. ;
and in sheets for the country libraries (or for those who wished to bind
their own books), 2*s*. Mrs. Radcliffe's *The Castles of Athlin and
Dunbayne*, one vol., 1789, Hookham, cost 3*s*. *The Romance of the
Forest*, 3 vols., sewed, Hookham, 1792, is 9*s*. By this time, indeed,
there had been an advance in prices. *The Mysteries of Udolpho*, 4 vols.,
Robinson, 1794, cost £1 5*s*. In 1796, Lewis' *The Monk* was published
by Bell in 3 vols. at half-a-guinea. In 1801 Bell was advertising the
Fifth Edition, 3 vols., " Price 12*s*. in boards." Certain passages had
been modified, but Bell informed the public that a few copies of the
First edition might still be had at the Publisher's, price One Guinea.
In 1826, J. Limbird, 143, Strand, London, published " The whole of
the Works " of Mrs. Radcliffe, " embellished with numerous Engravings," Vols. I and II " for the trifling sum of Ten Shillings in
boards." Vols. III and IV, 5*s*. each. In 1808 *The Romance of the
Forest*, 3 vols., 7th ed., Longmans, cost 15*s*. in boards ; and from the
same house *The Mysteries of Udolpho*, 4 vols., 6th ed., £1 4*s*., boards,
whilst the Fifth Edition of *Thaddeus of Warsaw*, 4 vols., was 14*s*. boards.

In 1805 Lathom's *The Impenetrable Secret*, 2 vols., Lane, cost 9*s*.
sewed. In 1806 Pigault Lebrun's *The Barons of Felsheim*, 3 vols., Lane,
was 12*s*. sewed ; Lafontaine's *Hermann and Emilia*, 4 vols., Lane,
13*s*., sewed. In 1807 J. F. Hughes' prices are : *A Summer at Brighton*,
3 vols., 13*s*. 6*d*. ; Lewis' *Feudal Tyrants*, 4 vols., £1 8*s*. ; Horsley

Curties' *The Monk of Udolpho*, 4 vols., £1 2*s*.; the same author's *St. Botolph's Priory*, 5 vols., £1 5*s*.; Mrs. Edgeworth's *Adelaide*, 4 vols., 18*s*.; Miss Hamilton's *Forest of St. Bernardo*, 4 vols., 18*s*.; and Mrs. Fortnum's *Victor Allen*, second ed., 2 vols., 8*s*.

The *Novice of Saint-Dominick* by Miss Sydney Owenson, 4 vols., Phillips, 1806, was " Price Eighteen Shillings, in boards." In 1811 A. K. Newman at the Minerva Press generally charges 5*s*. a volume, but there are some variations. Mrs. Pilkington's *Sinclair*, 4 vols., Gabrielli's *Laughton Priory*, 4 vols., Theodore Melville's *Irish Chieftain*, 4 vols., all cost £1 a set; Sickelmore's *Osrick*, 3 vols., is 15*s*.; but *Man as he is Not*, 3rd ed., 3 vols., is 12*s*.; Horace Vere's *Guiscard*, 2 vols., is 10*s*.; whilst Orlando's *The Chamber of Death*, 2 vols., is 9*s*. In 1828 Newman charges 5*s*. or 6*s*. a volume with few exceptions; *Ambition*, 3 vols., is £1 4*s*.; Ann of Swansea's *Deeds of the Olden Time*, 5 vols., £1 10*s*.; Mrs. Roche's *Discarded Son*, 5 vols., £1 10*s*.; Lathom's *Midnight Bell*, 3 vols., second ed., 15*s*.; but C. A. Bolen's *The Mysterious Monk*, 3 vols., 16*s*. 6*d*.; and *Tales of Fault and Feeling*, 3 vols., £1 1*s*.

Novels were very seldom illustrated, although the Minerva Press sometimes embellished a romance with an elegant frontispiece such as we find in Sarah Lansdell's *Manfredi*, 1796; Miss Mackenzie's *Mysteries Elucidated*, 1795; Charles Lucas' *The Castle of Saint Donats*, 1798; *The Castle of Santa Fé*, 1805; Mrs. Parsons' *Voluntary Exile*, 1795; *Women As They Are*, 1796; and *The Mysterious Warning*, 1796; Mrs. Meeke's *Which Is the Man?* 1801; Curties' *Ancient Records*, 1801, a frontispiece not reproduced in the Second Edition, 1832.

A feature, however, was made of the illustrations in later editions, and in later novels. Thus Mrs. Charlotte Smith's *Ethelinde* (1789), in the one volume Robins reprint, is embellished with six elegant engravings; Mrs. Roche's *Children of the Abbey* (1796), one volume, Gleave, 1823, erroneously called " Third Edition," has an engraved title and eight plates; Mrs. Helme's *Farmer of Inglewood Forest* (1796, with a Frontispiece), Virtue, n.d., " Seventh Edition "; and Lathom's *Mysterious Freebooter* (1806), Jaques reprint, 1826, are also fully illustrated. William Child Green's *The Woodland Family* (1824) and *Prophecy of Duncannon* (1824); Robert Huish's *Castle of Niolo*, 2 vols., 1820; and many of the novels of the prolific Mrs. Catherine G. Ward, have the most fascinating plates.

An edition of *The Monk*, published in Paris, 3 vols., 1807, has three frontispieces, *Lafitte*, *Del.*, *L'Epine*, *Sculp.*, and the translation, *Le Moine*, Paris, Maradan, an X, 4 vol., is " avec gravures." In fact, most of the French translations of English novels were illustrated. The 1808 edition, 6 vols., 12mo, Paris, of Victorine de Chastenay's translation from Mrs. Radcliffe *Les Mystères d'Udolpho*, has half-a-dozen charming frontispieces in which all the characters wear the costumes of the directoire and the ladies are robed and coiffed *à la grecque*.

Il Castello di Otranto, Storia Gotica, the famous Italian translation of *The Castle of Otranto*, was published, London, 1795, with seven illustrations by Miss Clarke, which were used by Jeffery in his edition of 1796, when the plates were beautifully coloured. These seven coloured engravings were reproduced when I edited (1924) *The Castle of Otranto* and *The Mysterious Mother*, Constable's Edition.

Engravings were a feature of Fisher's Editions, those admirable little books " Printed and Sold by S. Fisher, 151 St. John Street, West Smithfield," which might " be had in *single* Six-penny Numbers or in one Volume " in boards. Fisher proclaims with just pride at the end of his catalogue : " *None of the above Works are* One-Third of the Price *of the most common unembellished editions.*" *The Castles of Athlin and Dunbayne* " with 3 *beautiful* engravings " comprised 2 Sixpenny Numbers ; in boards 1*s.* 6*d.* : *The Mysteries of Udolpho*, 13 Nos., 15 Engravings, boards 2 vols., 7*s.* 6*d.* : *The Recess*, 7 Nos., 8 Engravings, boards, 4*s.* : *The Castle of Wolfenbach*, 4 Nos., 5 Engravings, boards, 2*s.* : *The Mysterious Warning*, 9 Nos., 10 Engravings, boards, 5*s.* : Mrs. Kelly's *Ruins of Avondale Priory*, 5 Nos., 6 Engravings, boards, 3*s.* This collection began to be issued about 1815, and continued until the late twenties. For some reason these dumpy little books now appear to be excessively scarce. The engravings are excellently done in the true spirit of the tales, and the whole series affords ample evidence that the Gothic novels did not lose their popularity so early as has often been supposed. Not only Mrs. Radcliffe, who in one sense stands apart, but Mrs. Parsons, Charlotte Smith, and Mrs. Kelly were being widely read and enjoyed until the middle years of the Victorian era, whilst some especial favourites, Mrs. Roche's *The Children of the Abbey*, Mrs. Helme's *The Farmer of Inglewood Forest* and *St. Clair of the Isles*, were more than once reprinted even in the twentieth century.

NOTES TO CHAPTER II

1. George Moore, *Literature at Nurse ; or, Circulating Morals*, 1885.
2. " Emile Zola," *Fortnightly Review*, January, 1889.
3. *Society*, 21st April, 1888.
4. " The Tyranny of the Novel," *National Review*, 1892.
5. " The Limits of Realism in Fiction," *Questions at Issue*, 1893.

6. In *The Progress of Romance*, 1785, Clara Reeve in all seriousness is almost equally severe and stigmatizes circulating libraries as " one source of the vices and follies of our present times."

7. Roman Martyrology, June 1st; full office in the Greek Church, February 15th; in the Coptic calendar, May 16th ; at Jerusalem (Latin rite), June 1st, duplex.

8. *De Viris Illustribus*, cap. iii.

9. Appendix V. The other towns besides London and Bath are : Edinburgh, Bristol, Cambridge, Birmingham, Dover, Glasgow, Barnstaple, Southampton, Chelmsford, Margate, Aberdeen, and Canterbury.

10. Nichols, *Literary Anecdotes*, Vol. III. (1812), p. 648, note.

11. Nichols, *Literary Anecdotes*, Vol. III (1812), p. 646.

12. Trade card in my collection.

13. Page 721.

14. Timperley, *Encyclopædia of Literary and Typographical Anecdote*, 2nd. ed., Bohn, 1842, p. 908.

15. Page 832.

16. Page 941.

17. Edited by Jared Sparks, London, 1850, p. 40. See also p. 243, n. 1.

18. 1678-1768. There is a life in the *Dictionary of National Biography*, by Edwin Cannn.

19. *An Alphabetical Catalogue of Books and Pamphlets in English, French and Latin belonging to the Circulating Library in Crane Court*. London, 1748.

20. Timperley, *Encyclopædia, ut cit. sup.*, p. 843.

21. Dr. E. A. Baker in his *History of the English Novel*, Vol. V, *The Novel of Sentiment and the Gothic Romance*, has the following in reference to the Novels mentioned in *The Rivals* : " No serious person wants to identify them now." This eagerness that his subject matter should be " consigned to oblivion "—a favourite phrase—is scarcely indicative of serious scholarship.

22. Treyssac de Vergy came to England in 1764, when aged about thirty. He was attached to the French embassy, but took sides with the Chevalier d'Eon de Beaumont, who quarrelled with the Ambassador, de Guerchy. The literary career of de Vergy commenced in 1769, and continued until 1772. In the autumn of 1774 he is spoken of as dying in his lodgings at Blackheath. *The Monthly Review*, February, 1776, p. 162, speaks of him as deceased.

23. *The Gentleman's Magazine* thus reprehends the Second Part of *The Lovers*. *The Memoirs of an Hermaphrodite* was published in 1772.

24. See Howard Swazey Buck, *A Study of Smollett, chiefly Peregrine Pickle*, 1925.

25. In some editions *Lord Ainsworth*. I have used the Fifth Edition, 1791.

26. Which borrows four stories from Baculard d'Arnaud's *Les Epreuves du sentiment*, tomes I and II, 1772.

27. Page 10.

28. The same passage as just quoted occurs on p. 12, but " Thomas's circulating library " is " the circulating library."

29. *Tunbridge Wells : Published & Sold by J. Sprange, Bookseller*, 1816, p. 24.

30. By a Lady, p. 11.

31. I take the names and details from trade-cards and labels in my collection. The libraries were by no means poorly stocked. As early as 1771 Humphry's Circulating Library, Chichester, had over 900 volumes according to the label in the British Museum copy of the *Genuine Memoirs of Miss Faulkner* (1771).

32. The " Conditions of the Shakespeare Circulating Library, *No. 25, School Street*," Boston, U.S.A., " C. Callender's," were " Subscribers are entitled to *four volumes* at a time, paying *in advance*—Per Year, Seven Dollars ; Half Year, Four Dollars ; Quarter, Two Dollars, 50 Cents ; Month, One Dollar." Non-subscribers paid 6¼ cents a week for a 12mo ; 12½ cents a week for an 8vo.

33. Vol. I, chapter xlviii.

34. There is a good deal of truth in these strictures of Fox. To give only one example of old dishes rehashed under new names, in January and February, 1772, *The Monthly*

Review commented upon " the shameless plunder of superannuated and worthless novels," one a publication of the notorious Edmund Curll, forty years before. *Love in a Nunnery*, from the French, had already been translated as *The Fortunate Country Maid*, but a spicier title was needed ; *The Oxonian* was none other than *The Adventures of Charles Careless* ; whilst the old *Spanish Amusements* adopted the more blatant catch-title *The Reclaimed Prostitute*. With regard to hack-work the attack by *The London Magazine* upon the Nobles has already been noticed.

35. See also *Kent's Directory*, 1780 ; " Lane William, Bookseller, 33, *Leadenhall-street* " (p. 106) ; and succeeding years.

36. Page 181.

37. *Encyclopædia of Literary and Typographical Anecdote*, 2nd ed., Bohn, 1842, p. 853. I have corrected Timperley's *March*. " Died on Saturday last, at his house, No. 3 Glouces-ter Place, W. Lane, esq., formerly of the Minerva Printing-Office, London. His strong mental power and great fortitude he supported to the last hour. As a publisher few excelled him in the novel line. He was a friend to the distressed, and a zealous supporter of his country." *Sussex Weekly Advertiser* ; *Or, Lewes and Brighthelmston Journal*. Monday, January 31st, 1814.

38. *Recollections of the Table-Talk of Samuel Rogers*, London, 1856, p. 138. Edited and published by the Rev. Alexander Dyce. Samuel Rogers was born in July, 1763, and died December, 1855.

39. Ed. Bohn, 1842.

40. See S. Rivington, *The Publishing Family of Rivington*, 1919.

41. Retiring from business in 1773, Johnston died at a very advanced age in 1804.

42. *Literary Anecdotes*, 1812, Vol. III, pp. 445-9.

43. Page. 804.

44. 1802 according to H. R. Plomer, *Dictionary of Printers and Booksellers*, 1726 to 1775 : 1932 (for 1930), p. 42.

45. Timperley, p. 946.

46. Price 5s. bound. Christoph Christian Sturm (died 1786) was an evangelical minister and a very prolific writer. His *Betrachtungen über die Werke Gottes im Reiche der Natur und der Vorsehung auf alle Tage des Jahres* was first published at Halle in 1772, and ran into many editions ; 4th ed., 1797.

47. Produced at Drury Lane, March 24th, 1798, with Kemble as the Stranger ; and Mrs. Siddons, Mrs. Haller.

48. The ascription of *Augusta*, a novel from the French, 3 vols., 1799, to Hemet seems to be incorrect, as it is stated to have been Englished " By a Lady."

49. See Genest, *English Stage*, VII, pp. 417-19.

50. See Henry Curwen, *A History of Booksellers* (1873), pp. 79-109, " The Longman Family."

51. Curwen, *History of Booksellers*, 1873, pp. 279-95.

52. C. Stower, King Street, Covent Garden, was one of Earle and Hemet's chief printers.

53. A paper, privately printed, 1932, which also appeared in an American magazine, *The Colophon, Bentley's Standard Novel Series. Its History and Achievement*, by Michael Sadleir, deals in detail with this series.

54. Curwen, *A History of Booksellers*, 1873, pp. 379-98.

55. Thomas Medwin, *The Life of Percy Bysshe Shelley*, ed. Oxford, 1913, p. 25.

56. Afterwards Mrs. Mosse.

57. She also wrote *A Tale without a Title*, 3 vols., Lane, 1804 ; *The discarded Daughter*, 4 vols., Lane, 1810 ; *The Microcosm*, 5 vols., Mawman, 1801 ; and *Essays on the Art of Being Happy*, 2 vols., Lane, 1803. These essays are upon such subjects as " Economy of Time," " Simplicity of Manners," " Drama," " Genteel Situation," " Sunday Duties," " General Utility," and are by no means ill written. They might, indeed, be read by many with much profit to-day. The novels, highly praised by the critics as presenting " exquisite views of nature, accurately delineated, and forcibly coloured," in some jealous quarters received but negative plaudits.

58. *The Bandit's Bride ; or, The Maid of Saxony*, 4 vols., 1807, a full-flushed romance, is by the same author.

59. Better known as Miss Haynes. She also wrote *The Foundling of Devonshire*, 5 vols., 1817 ; *Augustus and Adelina*, 4 vols., 1819 ; *Eleanor ; or, The Spectre of St. Michael's*, 5 vols., 1820 ; and *The Maid of Padua, or Past Times, a Venetian Tale*, 4 vols., 1834—all published by Newman.

60. January, 1788, p. 82.

61. August, 1790, p. 463.

62. *The Monthly Review*, December, 1789, found the incidents in *The Castles of Athlin and Dunbayne* " insipid, if not disgustful," p. 563.

63. *Monthly Mirror*, Vol. II, p. 99.

64. *Ibid.*, Vol. III, p. 27 ; January, 1797.

65. *Ibid.*, Vol. III, p. 297 ; May, 1797.

66. *Ibid.*, Vol. II, p. 416.

67. *Ibid.*, Vol. IV, p. 37.

68. *Ibid.*, Vol. IV, p. 92.

69. Vol. XXXV, p. 333.

70. Series the Third, Vol. VI, No. 3.

71. *Ibid.*, Vol. VIII, No. 4.

72. In addition to *The Strangers*, Mrs. Norris wrote *Second Love, or The Way to be Happy*, 2 vols., 1805 ; *Olivia and Marcella*, 3 vols., 1807 ; *Julia of England*, 4 vols., 1808 ; and *Euphrasia, or the Captive*, 3 vols., 1810.

73. Vol. VIII, p. 443.

74. *Æneid*, II, 583-4.

75. *Critical Review*, Series the Third, Vol. IX, No. 3, p. 328 ; *Monthly Mirror*, Vol. XXIII, p. 47.

76. Watt gives Lathy, *The Rising Sun*, 3 vols., 1807 ; and *The Setting Sun*, 3 vols., 1809, two novels by Eaton Stannard Barrett.

77. 1705-75. Scott's great-nephew, who possessed the original manuscript, exposed the fraud. *Gentlemen's Magazine*, 1819, II, p. 407.

78. *A Biographical Dictionary of the Living Authors of Great Britain and Ireland*, 1816 p. 232, has : " Melville, Theodore, Esq. Under this name, real or fictitious we know not, have appeared *The White Knight, The Benevolent Monk, The Irish Chieftain*."

79. Series the Third, Vol. XII, No. 1, p. 104.

80. New Series, Vol. XXXIII, p. 112.

81. Henry Summersett also wrote *The Worst of Stains*, a novel, two vols., Dutton, 1804 ; and *All Sorts of Lovers*, 3 vols., 1805. He is the author of a comedy, *Happy at heart*, 8vo, 1805, and *Maurice the rustic and other poems*, 8vo, 1805.

82. Vol. I, p. 270.

83. The lady was said, Preface, p. x, to have imitated Fielding !

84. August, 1805, Vol. XX, pp. 110-11.

85. *Critical Review*, July, 1795, Vol. XIV, p. 352.

86. *Ibid.*, January, 1803.

87. *Ibid.*, Series III, Vol. X, No. 1, January, 1807.

88. In 1843 : " for such were their names."

89. *Monthly Review*, Vol. 86, pp. 218-19.

90. Series the Third, Vol. VII, No. 1, pp. 107-8.

91. April, 1818.

92. Vol. XIV, pp. 81-82.

93. *The Evolution of Publishers' Binding Styles*, 1770-1900, (*Bibliographia*, No. 1 ; 1930).

94. Malone 137. Twelve dramas by Lee (not all first editions) bound together, calf, and labelled " Lee's Plays." Owing to the carelessness of the binder the contents were misplaced. The inserted general title-page, " The Works of Mr. Nathaniel Lee, . . . *London*, Printed for R. Bently, . . . 1694," has nothing to do with this made-up volume.

95. There are several important emendations and additions (including two whole lines) in the text. The gilding of the leaves is easily discernible.

96. See " Elkanah Settle, City Poet," by Cyril Davenport, *The Connoisseur* (London), VI, pp. 160-3, 210-11.

97. British Museum copy, C. 66, f. 19. Presented, Dec., 1838, by G. C. Gorham, to whom this copy descended from the Bayntons.

98. British Museum, G. 19057.

99. Bodley. Malone F. 11, 20. This seems to be the only exemplar extant. It contains an interesting but ill-natured MS. note in a contemporary hand.

100. Bodley. Rawlinson, B. 361. Enclosed is a letter from Settle to Sir Thomas Rawlinson, offering his poem in lieu of a public triumph, since the Vintner's Company declined to be at the expense of a pageant.

CHAPTER III

INFLUENCES FROM ABROAD

Peut-être devrions-nous analyser ici ces romans nouveaux, dont le sortilège et la fantasmagorie composent à peu près tout le mérite en plaçant à leur tête *le Moine*, supérieur sous tous les rapports, aux élans de la brillante imagination de *Radgliffe* ; mais cette dissertation serait trop longue ; convenons seulement que ce genre, quoi qu'on en puisse dire, n'est assurément pas sans mérite ; il devenait le fruit indispensable des secousses révolutionnaires dont l'Europe entière se ressentait. Pour qui connaissait tous les malheures dont les méchants peuvent accabler les hommes, le roman devenait aussi difficile à faire que monotone à lire ; il n'y avait point d'individu qui n'eut plus éprouvé d'infortunes en quatre ou cinq ans, que n'en pouvait peindre en un siècle le plus fameux romancier de la littérature ; il fallait donc appeler l'enfer à son secours, pour se composer des titres à l'intérêt, et trouver dans le pays des chimères, ce qu'on savait couramment en ne fouillant, que l'histoire de l'homme dans cet âge de fer. Mais que d'inconvénients présentait cette manière d'écrire ! l'auteur du *Moine* ne les a pas plus évités que Radgliffe ; ici nécessairement de choses l'une, ou il faut développer le sortilège, et dès lors vous n'intéressez plus, ou il ne faut jamais lever le rideau, et vous voilà dans la plus affreuse invraisemblance. Qu'il paraisse dans ce genre un ouvrage assez bon pour atteindre le but sans ce briser contre l'un ou l'autre de ces écueils, loin de lui reprocher ses moyens, nous l'offrirons alors comme un modèle.

DE SADE, Idée sur les Romans.

Hail ! Germany most favored, who
Seems a romantic rendezvous ;
Thro'out whose large and tumid veins
The unmixt Gothic current reigns !
Much thou hast giv'n of precious hosts
Of monsters, wizards, giants, ghosts :
Yet, give our babes of fancy more
Impart to novelists thy store !
Till classic science dull monastic
Dissolves in flood enthusiastic.

THE AGE. A Poem. 1810. Book VII, 407-16.

" THE French," said Lisideius, " have many excellencies not common to us," and although it is possible (as has indeed been done by some critics) to exaggerate the influence of France upon English literature at the Restoration, it cannot be denied that French taste and French manners largely moulded our modes of thought, although—and this is an essential circumstance—there was always maintained a strong traditional and native growth. In the theatre the plays of Molière, Pierre and Thomas Corneille, Racine, Quinault, Scarron, Rotrou, Rosimond, and lesser authors, were adapted and re-handled again and again. Fiction in England was mainly represented by the heroic romances of La Calprenède, De Gomberville, Mlle de Scudéry, Desmaretz, and that "vain amatorious poem," as Milton[1] dubbed it, the golden *Astrée* of Honoré d'Urfé.

All the great romances, which of course were also widely read in the original here in England, were soon translated. The *Astrée* (1607–19), appeared in 3 vols. folio, London, 1657–58, *Astrea . . . translated by a Person of Quality, i.e.* John Davies of Kidwelly ; De Gomberville's *Polexandre* (1632) was *Done into English* by W. Browne, London, folio, 1647 ; the *Ariane* (1632) of Desmaretz, was published London, folio, 1636 (a second edition, 4to, 1642), *Ariana, in two parts. As it was translated out of the French.* La Calprenède's romances in particular enjoyed an astonishing vogue. *Cassandre* (1642–50) was first made English by Sir Charles Cotterell, folio, 1652, a version which ran into no less than four editions and was reprinted as late as 1738, whilst there was also another translation "by Several Hands" ; *Cléopâtre* (1647–58), was first translated in 1652 by Robert Loveday, later parts being the work of John Coles, James Webb, and John Davies, complete editions being issued, folio 1659, 1663, 1665, and by Loveday, 2 vols. folio, 1674 ; *Faramond* (1661–70), with the conclusion by Vaumorière, was translated by Milton's nephew, John Phillips, *Pharamond*, 2 vols. folio, 1677.[2] Of Mlle. de Scudéry's works, *Ibrahim, ou l'Illustre Bassa* (1641), was Englished by Henry Cogan, folio 1652 ; *Artamène, ou le Grand Cyrus* (1649–53), English translation, folio, 1653, several times reprinted ; *Clélie* (1654–60), translated by John Davies, folio, London, 1656–61, and 1678 ; and *Almahide* (1660) as *Almahide, or, The Captive Queen. An excellent New Romance. Never before in English. The whole Work . . . Done into English* by J. Phillips, Gent, London, 1677, Folio.[3]

The only English imitators of the heroic romance of "that ceremonious nation" the French—the phrase is Crowne's—were the Earl of Orrery in his *Parthenissa* (the first five parts, 1654 ; Part Sixth, 1669 ; and the romance "compleat"—actually it never was finished, folio, 1676), and Crowne himself with *Pandion and Amphigenia ; or, the History of the Coy Lady of Thessaly*, 8vo, 1665.

There were, of course, other translations from the French : Charles Sorel's *Francion* (1622), who as Professor Paul Morillot remarks, dwells in "un vilain monde . . . mais comme il est réel et vivant ! "—was given an English dress (probably by Robert Loveday) in 1655, folio ; and the same author's *Berger extravagant* (1628) was turned by John Davies as *The Extravagant Shepherd, the anti-romance*, folio, 1653, and second edition, 1660 ; Scarron's *Roman comique* (1651) and his *Nouvelles* proved immensely popular in English versions, and were reprinted again and again. In *The Comical Romance* ; *or, A facetious History of a company of strowling Stage-players*, folio, 1676 (Price, bound, 6s.), the original has been acclimatized, thus for Paris we find London, and when the poet brags of his acquaintance with Corneille and Rotrou, we also have Shakespeare, Fletcher, and Jonson. *The Whole Comical Works of Mons. Scarron*, containing his *Comical Romance*, " in Three Parts compleat," together with *All his Novels and Histories* were translated by Mr. Thomas Brown, Mr. Savage, and others, " and Illustrated with several Copper-cutts. Octavo. Price 6s.," 1700. There had been earlier versions of the novels, separately translated by Davies, and collected, 1682, in one volume, which in 1700 reached a fourth edition.

Antoine Furetière's *Roman Bourgeois* (Molière tout entier) published in 1666, crossed the Channel in 1673 as the *City Romance*, " A Book of Wit and Humour," 8vo, Price, bound, 2s.

Madame de la Fayette's *Zayde* (1670) was published in English, 8vo, Price 2s., in 1677 as *Zayde, An excellent new Romance*, whilst *La Princesse de Clèves*, 1677, " The most fam'd Romance. Written in French by the greatest Wits in *France*.[4] Englished by a Person of Quality, at the request of some Friends." was published early in 1679, and attained a great celebrity.[5]

Smaller and less important works, also, such as the novels of Gabriel de Bremond, Madame Villedieu, Mlle. de Brillac,[6] and other " admired Wits," were being translated in a steady stream of success throughout the last forty years of the seventeenth century.

Charles De Saint-Denis-Le-Guast, Seigneur De Saint-Evremond (1613–1703), was a very considerable figure amongst the Wits of the Court of Charles II, and he has left his appreciation of the culture of the Restoration in many a page of his works, which were widely read and of weight both in France and at home. He even attempted—not very successfully, it is true,—a French comedy on English lines, *Sir Politick Would-Be*, " Comedie A la manière des Anglois." [7]

Another important link between French and English literature is the easy and elegant pen of Anthony Hamilton the famous author of the *Mémoires du Comte de Grammont*, who died at St. Germain in April, 1720, aged about 74. His Oriental Tales achieved an immense vogue, and as for the *Mémoires* (of which an edition was printed with a dedication to Madame du Deffand at Strawberry Hill in 1772), in January, 1775, Walpole wrote to the Countess of Upper Ossory,[8] " I can scarce read Grammont and Madame de Sévigné, because I know them by heart." *Les Quatre Facardins*, the most celebrated and perhaps the most entertaining of Hamilton's fictions, written about 1710–15, was

PLATE V

LE PANACHE ROUGE
Frontispiece, 1824

[*Face p.* 108

admirably translated and wittily completed by Matthew Gregory Lewis in 1808.

In November, 1728, there arrived in England a notable fugitive from justice, a monk of thirty-one, Dom Antoine-François Prévost, O.S.B., of the Congregation of St. Maur. Educated by the Jesuits he had twice entered the novitiate of the Society only to abandon the clerical state, first to join the army, and secondly in consequence of a tragic love-affair, which is believed in outline and emotion at least to have inspired *Manon Lescaut*. In the autumn of 1720 he commenced his third essay of religion, this time in a Benedictine house near Rouen. He was professed and proceeded to Holy Orders, but he was unhappy ; and in 1728, after having obtained a brief of translation, he so indiscreetly left his house, Saint-Germain des Prés, on October 18th or 19th, without waiting for the due formalities to be observed that the Abbot to avoid open scandal applied for his arrest, and a warrant was issued on November 6th, which impelled him to fly to England.

Prévost had already published earlier in 1728 Volumes I and II of the *Memoires d'un Homme de Qualité*, and Volumes III and IV followed the same year. Volumes V. and VI appeared at Amsterdam in 1731 ; together with Vol. VII, an appendix, quite independent of the rest, containing the *Histoire du Chevalier des Grieux et de Manon Lescaut*. There are two English translations, which differ very slightly, of the *Homme de Qualité*, 1738, for J. Wilford, and 1770 for F. Newberry. *Manon Lescaut* was translated by Charlotte Smith, *Manon L'Escaut : or, The Fatal Attachment. A French Story*. London, Cadell, 2 vols., 6s.

In Vol. V of the *Homme de Qualité* the Marquis de Renoncour and his young pupil the Marquis de Rosemont come to England, when their residence in London and a tour through the provinces—they visit Tunbridge, Rye, Winchelsea, Chichester, Portsmouth, Winchester, Salisbury, Blandford, Dorchester, Weymouth, Exeter, Bristol, Oxford, and many other towns, even penetrating into Cornwall—are described in great detail.[9] It may be remarked that Prévost has something to say of the theatre, of the acting of Mrs. Oldfield, and he highly applauds *Hamlet, Don Sebastian, The Orphan, Venice Preserv'd, The Way of the World, The Constant Couple, The Provok'd Husband*, and other plays.

Dom Prévost was in England from 1728 to 1730 as companion and tutor to Francis, the only son of Sir John Eyles, a prominent figure in the political and civic life of the day. From London Prévost went to Holland, and here concentrated upon literary work, completing as has been noted above the *Homme de Qualité*, and commencing his more famous romance *Le Philosophe anglais ; ou, histoire de M. Cléveland, fils naturel de Cromwell*, 8 vols., 1732–39. Early in 1733 Prévost was back in London, accompanied by a mistress owing to whose bad influence (as it is thought) in December of that year he most unhappily falsely made a promissory note of £50 under the signature of his old pupil, Francis Eyles. He was arrested, but with rare generosity young Eyles, who had lodged the complaint on oath, refused to prosecute and the case was quashed, Prévost being discharged. The details are obscure, and it is not plain how a criminal charge could have been withdrawn. It may be young Eyles acknowledged the note and declared himself mistaken, or it may be that the great influence of Sir John Eyles effectually composed matters. It is not necessary to discuss details, but it is difficult to see how Prévost can be held innocent, so that we must perforce account him weak, foolish, and even in this instance ungrateful to his benefactors and friends.[10]   Prévost now obtained a formal and complete dispensation from his monastic vows from Pope Clement XII, whereupon he was able to return to France in the autumn, of 1734, and thereafter reconciled with the Church, he lived honoured and admired by all, devoting himself to immense literary labours.   He died suddenly at Courteuil, on November 25th, 1765.[11]   Perhaps even more famous than *Cléveland* is *Le Doyen de Killérine* : *historie morale, composée sur les mémoires d'une illustre famille d'Irlande*, which occupied his pen from 1735–40, and of which an English version *The Dean of Coleraine* appeared in 1742.

Dunlop observes that the chief defect of the novels of Prévost consists in a perplexed arrangement of the incidents : " he has an appearance of advancing at hazard, without having fixed whither he is tending ; he heaps one event on another, and frequently loses sight of his most interesting characters." However, if there is no regularity there is an extreme sensibility in his pages, and we might truly remark that he has taken as his text the title of that play of Dryden's which in 1735 he turned into his native tongue,[12] *All For Love : Or, The World well Lost.* " Fierté, raison, et richesse, il faudra que tout se rende. Quand l'amour parle, il est le maître." [13]   Love excuses everything ; there are no moral lapses in the light of the divine law of the tender passion ; the true lover must be prepared to risk all, to endure even dishonour and shame, for love's sake.   The *Homme de Qualité* is full of passion, but Prévost makes it clear at every turn that love does not bring happiness, an inevitable concomitant is that " chère et délicieuse tristesse," the very soul of sensibility.   Moreover his heroes and lovers are marked by no ordinary sorrow ; their hearts are the very throne of melancholy.   A succession of tragic events pursues the Marquis de Renoncour ; his sister Julie is shot by ravishers and expires in his arms ; his mother dies of shock on hearing the tragic news ; his father withdraws to a Carthusian monastery. When he loses his beloved Sélima in a few hours of a malignant fever he immerses himself in a room shrouded with funereal black, alone with a golden casket containing her heart. Cléveland is persecuted by his terrible father, and later wanders far and wide to find his beloved Fanny Axminster, whom he weds among the forests of America. Jealousy, brooded over in silence, corrodes their happiness, and this leads to new adventures, sombre and dreadful catastrophes. Cléveland becomes deeply enamoured of a young girl, Cécile, only to discover that she is his daughter. The incidents, says Dunlop with considerable acumen, " are wild and incredible, but the characters are marked, impassioned, and singular." Patrice in *Le Doyen de Killérine* is just such another *âme sensible* as Cléveland. In fact, we have quite clearly in Prévost the first movements of the novel of sensibility. We have something more ; we have the antepast of many features of the " horrid " Gothic romance. Prévost creates an atmosphere of shuddering dread, suspense, and a mysterious melancholy which broods over his castles such as Corogne, his impenetrable forests and primæval prairies of the New World ; the dark recesses of Rumney Hole ; his anchorholds, Carthusian abbeys and Trappist cloisters in which his heroes take refuge from the world. Mons. Servais Étienne has well spoken of " le roman noir dont l'essential était dans Prévost." [14]

The Gothic novel of sensibility, however, draws its emotionalism and psychology from a far greater than Prévost, from the work of Samuel Richardson. It were superfluous to emphasize the universal success and immense influence of *Pamela*, 1740 ; *Clarissa*, 1747 ; and *Sir Charles Grandison*, 1753, books which set not only England but all Europe a-sobbing. In Germany, Klopstock, Gellert, and Wieland were to hail these three novels in glowing terms such as perhaps only genius may fitly apply to genius. Diderot, in his *Eloge de Richardson*, declared that history merely showed us individuals ; Richardson painted man. Jean Jacques Rousseau gave it as his opinion that nothing equal to nor even approaching *Clarissa* had ever been written in any language. In later days Alfred de Musset has spoken of *Clarissa* as " le premier roman du monde." Prévost hastened to translate the novels as they appeared : *Paméla*, 1742 ; *Clarisse Harlowe*, 1751 ; and *Sir Charles Grandisson*, 1754–58,

It is difficult, perhaps impossible, to draw a satisfactory dividing-line between sentiment and sensibility. Any definition must be artificial, almost personal, and therefore it were nugatory—except we allow that we are merely using convenient labels, and labels are mighty convenient things—to allocate and codify sentimental novels and the novels of sensibility. Except in certain specific instances the latter term will be employed here, and the distinction, such as it is, may be made plainer, if we say that sensibility is, in fact, little other than an elegantly exaggerated sentimentalism. This is not to say that from a psychological point of view both sentimentalism and sensibility are not very real and very poignant emotions.

The sentimental, of course, appears in English literature long before Richardson. There are even passages in Chaucer, infrequent but none the less marked, which are sentimental, and it would be easy to write at length upon the sentimentalism of the Elizabethan dramatists. There is a strong vein of sentimentalism in the Beaumont and Fletcher plays, the figure of Bellario in *Philaster*, Urania in *Cupid's Revenge*, Viola and Ricardo in *The Coxcomb*,[15] in *The Faithful Shepherdess*, *The Night-Walker*, *The Elder Brother*, and many more ; both Dekker and Heywood are steeped in sentiment—one need but refer to *The Honest Whore* and *A Woman Kill'd with Kindness*. A generation later there are sentimental scenes in the comedies of Mrs. Behn, *The Town Fop*, and the whole story of Bellmour and Leticia in *The Luckey Chance*. Wycherley has sentimental scenes in *Love in a Wood*, and he has also drawn Fidelia Grey, whose language and love are pure Richardson, in *The Plain-Dealer*. In fact, there is only one eminent dramatist of the Restoration —I do not speak of the men who wrote one play—who is almost without sentiment and that is the brilliant but hard and unattractive Etherege. *The Man of Mode* is, I think, the most immoral and brutal piece in the English language. Yet there are scenes, very false and second-rate, in *The Comical Revenge*, where he has made an essay at sentiment, but it rings hollow, tawdry, and untrue. It is a fundamental error, then, to suppose, as Mr. Bernbaum imagines,[16] that sentimentality in the theatre had its beginnings as late as Colley Cibber's *Love's Last Shift* ; or, *The Fool in Fashion*, produced at Drury Lane in January, 1696. Cibber had not an atom of sentiment under his fashionable periwig, but he wrote sentimental plays as they were tending to become the mode, and he with Steele immensely aided to direct public taste. Throughout the eighteenth century sentimentalism in the theatre became more and more pronounced, but to talk with Mr. Bernbaum of the " Inhibition of Sentimentalism, 1660–95," [17] is unsound and untrue. Charles Shadwell, Charles Johnson, Edward Moore, and lesser men contributed important plays to the sentimental drama, as also did Cibber's successor in the bays, William Whitehead, with his *School for Lovers*, produced February 10th, 1762. There came the efflorescence of Sentimental Comedy—the *comédie larmoyante*—with Arthur Murphy, Hugh Kelly, Mrs. Griffith, Cumberland, Burgoyne, the younger Colman, Mrs. Inchbald, and many more. I have, it will be remarked, but barely glanced at sentiment in the theatre, and to treat of sentimental tragedy, the influence of Otway's *The Orphan*, Southerne, Lillo, would I fear take us too far from the path.

The English sentimental drama had a marked influence at Paris, whilst the plays of Destouches, La Chaussée, Gresset, Christophe Fagan, and above all Marivaux, were much read and admired in England. *Le Philosophe Marié* (1727) of Destouches was actually written during his six years residence in London, and his scenes evince such a fine sensibility that when John Kelly adapted the piece as *The Married Philosopher*, given at Lincoln's Inn Fields, March 25th, 1732 ; 8vo. 1732 ; he saw fit to emphasize the more humorous episodes, and in some respects to modify the sentiment, with the result that his scenes lost interest and the production found little favour.

In England *Pamela* was dramatized by James Dance and presented at Goodman's Fields, November 9th, 1741. This version was very successful, partly because Garrick, new to fame, acted Jack Smatter, and partly—for the same reason that so many novels are attractive in the form of plays—because the piece offered a series of living illustrations of the most popular book of the day. A poor adaptation, *Pamela, or Virtue Triumphant*, 8vo., 1742, was never acted and indeed not required in the theatre. On the French stage *Pamela* was dramatized from Prévost's translation three times, by La Chaussée, 1743 ; by Louis de Boissy in the same year, as *Paméla en France, ou la vertu mieux éprouvée* ; and by Voltaire *Nanine*, 1749.

"The novel of *Pamela* had been for some time delighting Italy,"[18] says Goldoni in his *Memorie*, ". . . and surrounded as I was, both at Mantua and Venice, by people who urged me to dramatize it, I consented willingly enough." *Pamela Nubile* was given at Milan in the summer of 1750, and afterwards at Venice at the Teatro Sant' Angelo during the autumn season, which lasted from the first week of October to December 15th.[19] *Pamela Nubile* was received with rapturous applause : " Provai una Commedia senza le Maschere, e questa fu la *Pamela* : vidi che non dispiacque, ed io ne feci alcun' altre, felici tutte egualmente."[20] Nine years later, in 1759, *Pamela Maritata*, written before July of that year, was given at the Capranica Theatre, Rome.[21]

The novels of Marivaux " l'histoire du cœur humain "[22] were even better known in England than his plays. *La Vie de Marianne* (1731–41) was translated as *The Virtuous Orphan*; *or, The Life of Marianne*, London, 8vo., 1784, and *Le Paysan Parvenu* (1735–36) almost immediately upon its appearance. It has been said not without a good deal of truth that *Marianne* is picaresque and in the tradition of *Gil Blas*. " Mais les héros de Marivaux se distinguent de ceux du Lesage parce qu'ils ont des âmes sensibles." Marivaux himself very neatly summed up the matter : " Les personnes qui ont du sentiment sont bien plus abattues que d'autres dans de certaines occasions, parce que tout ce qui leur arrive les pénètre." [23]

A *Suite* to *Marianne* was supplied with the benison of Marivaux by Madame Riccoboni (Marie Jeanne Laboras de Mazières, 1714–92), whilst the Kingdom of Prévost was divided by this lady and Baculard d'Arnaud. The former took over his sensibility, with large drafts from Richardson ; the latter the mystery and melancholy, the terror, which he has all the more highly coloured from his study of the *Inferno*, and above all his devotion to *Paradise Lost* and the *Night Thoughts* of the admired Young. Even before the days of this poet of the tomb French critics had marked *le goût du sombre* as an English characteristic, *un feu sombre* is the striking phrase of Resnel in 1730. The Anglomania which began in France early in the Regency, and the after-effects of which pervaded the Romantic movement of 1830 were immensely stimulated by the *Night Thoughts*, published (we may remind ourselves) 1742–46 in seven successive instalments. *La tristesse des Nuits* was a veritable passion. Richardson, Young, and Ossian are the three great masters and models, and of Le Tourneur's translation of the *Night Thoughts* in 1760 edition succeeded edition. Restif de la Bretonne quite ordinarily uses the words *Digne d'Young et de Shakespeare*.[24]

Moreover, both in English and in French, the *Night Thoughts* were embellished with engravings which represented a moonlit churchyard and shadowed tomb, a bleaching skull, a lanthorn, a mattock, yews or cypresses, and a man of melancholy deeply musing upon the fragments of mortality.[25]

It should be observed in passing that such pieces as Robert Blair's *The Grave*, 1743, with its magnificent passage upon a great church at night—See yonder hallow'd fane !—; *The Deity*, 1739, by the lugubrious Samuel Boyse ; *Death*, 1759, by Bishop Beilby Porteus, were held in great esteem by elegant piety of the Georgian school. Above all, James Hervey's *Meditations among the Tombs*, published in 1745, with its romantic descriptions and gentle pathos, in spite of the sharp sterile criticism of John Wesley, had reached a twenty-fifth edition in 1791, and is a work yet regarded with affection by certain old-fashioned people. Be its faults what they may in the eyes of an infidel and modern world, it is not the least of their praise that the *Meditations among the Tombs* have soothed many a sick-bed and comforted many a mourner.

Following closely in Richardson's steps Madame Riccoboni favoured the epistolary form of the novel. Her works are always

‿ ‿efully, and sometimes beautifully composed, but there is generally suffering or at least unhappiness in her pages. The *Histoire de M. le marquis de Cressy* (1758) tells of a man who sacrifices the young girl whom he loves and whom he has taught to love him all too tenderly for the sake of an alliance with a beautiful widow who is able to aid his ambitions. The forsaken Adelaide de Bugei enters a cloister. His wife realizes that her husband regards her with indifference and is unfaithful; she is wretched, and as for himself—" Il fut grand—il fut distingué—il obtint tous les titres, tous les honneurs qu'il avoit desiré : il fut riche—il fut elevé, mais il ne fut point heureux." *Le Marquis de Cressy* was translated into English in 1763.

It should not be forgotten in regard to the Epistolary Novels of the eighteenth century, when that form, owing mainly to the influence of Richardson was so universally popular, that lengthy letters and *Conversations* comprised an integral part of the framework of the heroic romances. To go back to classical times, we have the Epistles of Philostratus, of Aristænetus (translated by Lesage), and others. One need hardly refer to the famous *Lettres portugaises* (1669), which brought forth *Réponses*, *Nouvelles lettres*, and *Réponses à ces nouvelles lettres*, together with a host of imitations such as the *Lettres Nouvelles . . . Avec Treize Lettres Amoureuses d'une Dame à un Chevalier* translated or rather paraphrased by Eliza Haywood as *Letters from a Lady of Quality to a Chevalier*, 1721. Tom Brown's *Adventures of Lindamira*, 1702, in twenty-four letters, may more certainly claim to be a consecutive narrative in epistolary form, since the Lady of Quality's epistles do not unfold any regular story merely expatiating upon the adventures of love, doubts, jealousies, disappointments, fears and joys. The Lady is married ; and in the last three letters we note that the Chevalier has left France for England.

Madame Riccoboni not unseldom placed her scenes in England, and most of her novels were very quickly translated. Thus Frances Brooke Englished the *Lettres de milady Juliette Catesby à lady Henriette Campley, son amie*, 1759, and in ten years this version reached a fifth edition. In 1759 also Madame Riccoboni published *Lettres de Mistriss Fanny Butlerd à mylord Charles Alfred, duc de Caitombridge* [26] ; and in 1764 *L'Histoire de Miss Jenny Salisbury*, another English Tale. She preferred a French setting, however, for the *Histoire d'Ernestine*; the *Histoire d'Aloise de Livarot* ; the *Lettres d'Adelaïde de Dammartin Comtesse de Sancerre à M. le Comte de Nancé*, 1766, translated 1767 ; and the *Lettres d'Elisabeth Sophie de Vallière à Louise Hortense de Canteleu*, translated 1762. Madame Riccoboni put into French *Amélie*, roman de M. Fielding, and adapted several English plays.

De Sade has derived some names from Madame Riccoboni for among his tales in *Les Crimes de l'Amour*, 2 vols., 8vo (and 4 vols., 12mo), 1800, we have *Ernestine*. *Nouvelle Suédoise* ; *La Comtesse de Sancerre, ou, la Rivale de sa Fille*, and also a *Nouvelle Anglaise, Miss Henriette Stralson, ou les Effets du Désespoir*.

It must be borne in mind that if French novels were turned into English and much admired, English novels were being translated into French with equal eagerness and equal success. Thus, to name no more, Frances Brooke's *The History of Lady Julia Mandeville*, 1763, was translated into French by Bouchaud, 1764 ; and *The History of Emily Montague*, 1769, by Robinet, 1770.

François-Thomas de Baculard D'Arnaud [27] (1716–1805) both with his romances and even more perhaps with his " drames monacales," the famous *Les Amants Malheureux, ou Comte de Comminge* (1765) and *Euphémie*, whetted his readers' sombre appetites with a veritable panorama of dungeons enlightened by expiring lamps whose last flickering flames serve but to discover terrors a profounder darkness would conceal ; awful and horror-haunted castles ; remotest abbeys peopled by swart dark-souled inquisitors grown hard and hoar with numberless persecutions ; crime-riddled vaults where are chained persons deemed to be dead years before, where the shuddering eye encounters the pale and emaciated figure of some comely youth a victim of monastic atrocity, or some hapless swooning maid who pleads in vain for pity from the stern-browed superioress.

In the *Discours préliminaires* to *Les Amants Malheureux* D'Arnaud proclaims his gospel aloud—pity, terror, love drenched in tears, in fine " cette sensibilité qui élève l'homme au-dessus des autres créatures . . . cette sensation si chère et si touchante qui nous approprie les malheurs de nos semblables."

One sudden shriek that pierces the silence, in the empty house one loud knock upon the door at midnight ; these things are well enough : but D'Arnaud will not let us off under a perfect chorus of screams, a cannonade of rapping, a veritable Donnybrook Fair of horror and noise. As Mr. Puff complained : " give these fellows a good thing, and they never know when to have done with it." D'Arnaud keeps us waiting too long for the " soft music."

Les Amants Malheureux is dramatized from a story by Madame de Tencin, *Les Mémoires du comte de Comminge*,[28] which occurs in her *Malheurs de l'amour* (1735). The locale is the Abbey of La Trappe, or rather a melodramatic caricature of La Trappe. The tyrant father of Comminge imprisons him in order to oblige him to abandon the maiden he loves. She is compelled to wed an odious fellow, who dies.

Meanwhile Comminge has immured himself in La Trappe, whither she follows him in male attire, and years pass before he recognizes in the young monk Euthime whom he loves so tenderly his lost Adelaide. In this atmosphere of graves and charnels we realize that we are not very far from Sainte-Marie-des-Bois, the Couvent de Panthemont, and the hideous cloisters of De Sade.

D'Arnaud's first novel, *L'Époux Malheureux*, 1745, is already a notable piece of work describing the ill-starred love of Agathe and the moody La Bédoyère. It should be observed how large a proportion of the stories contained in the two collections *Les Épreuves du sentiment*, 1772–80, and *Nouvelles historiques*, 1774–84, are concerned with England. *Fanny, histoire angloise*, was twice translated; in 1767 as *Fanny, or, Injur'd Innocence*, and ten years later as *Fanny; or, The Happy Repentance*. Other English stories are *Anne Bell*; *Makin, anecdote angloise*; *Clary, ou le retour à la vertu recompensé*; *Le Comte de Strafford*; *Salisbury*; *Nancy, ou les malheurs de l'imprudence et de la jalousie*; *Sidney et Volsan*, and *Adelson et Salvini*.[29]

The most famous of these is *Varbeck*, one of the *Nouvelles historiques*, which was translated into England by no less a person than Sophia Lee as *Warbeck, a pathetic tale*,[30] 1774. Here history and sentimental romance mingle to the destruction of the former, since Henry VII is Warbeck's rival in love, and it is for love's sake that Warbeck throws away a battle and wrongly confesses that he is an impostor.

Although of much later date and a far less important name, a word may perhaps not altogether unfittingly be given here to the prolific Charles Antoine Guillaume Pigault de l'Épinoy Lebrun (1753–1835),[31] some half a dozen of whose works were published in anonymous translations by the Minerva Press. *Monsieur Botte*, a prime favourite, 1802, was Englished in the following year, and Lane also furnishes *Papa Brick*, 1804; *My Uncle Thomas*, which is among Pigault Lebrun's best work; *The Barons of Felsheim*; and *The History of a Dog*. *Les Barons de Felsheim*, it may be remarked, is an extravagant book which would seem to some extent at any rate a satire on German literary taste were it not so obviously inspired by German romance. In 1797 an English version of *L'Enfant du Carnaval*, 1792, had appeared as *The Shrove-tide Child*. In 1825 Wilton and Son, 245, High Holborn, issued " The French Novelist " in weekly parts at twopence each, and here we again find *L'Enfant du Carnaval* under the more sensational title *The Amour of a Friar*; together with *L'Homme à Projets*, 1807, as *The Schemer*.

In her *Progress of Romance*, 1785, Clara Reeve wrote in reference to French novels that " the best are the most *excellent*, and the worst the most *execrable* of all others." She was speaking from a moral point of view, and it is to be feared that too often English readers craved for the worst. There was, indeed, a continual interaction, but the influence of Richardson, and a little later of Mrs. Radcliffe and Matthew Gregory Lewis in France, shows far more remarkable than anything the English novel derived from their neighbours, important names as are Marivaux, Prévost, and D'Arnaud. This, I think, hardly needs to be emphasized, and it will indeed become even more clear when we consider in detail *The Monk, The Mysteries of Udolpho,* and *The Italian.*

On September 29th, 1714, there landed at Greenwich the Elector of Hanover, to be crowned *de facto* George I of England at Westminster on the following October 31st. He was wholly German, being unable even to speak English, whence Lord Granville was the only English minister who could converse with him. With Walpole the Elector exchanged views in execrable and stuttered Latin. In fact, he did not preside at Cabinet meetings, and had no use for Great Britain save to obtain hence as much money as possible to be spent in Hanover.

It is significant that until the end of the eighteenth century the genius of Germany had no influence whatsoever upon English literature.[32] Nor is this altogether to be explained by the fact that, owing to the horrors of the Thirty Years' War and other political convulsions, German literature was somewhat imitative and inchoate rather than original and distinguished, the most notable work of fiction in the seventeenth century being *Der Abentheurliche Simplicissimus.* Anton Ulrich, Duke of Brunswick ; Bucholtz ; and Von Ziegler imitated at a distance Mlle. de Scudéry.

Robinson Crusoe, which was translated into German in 1720, inspired a host of followers, " Robinsonades," and according to Kirz [33] within the following forty years no less than sixty (and perhaps more) derivative stories appeared. Richardson was copied by Von Loen in *Mann am Hofe,* 1740, which was praised by Goethe ; whilst twenty years later Johann Karl August Musaeus ridiculed the intense admiration Germany bestowed upon *Sir Charles Grandison* in his *Grandison the Second ; or, The German Grandison,* 1760 (2nd ed., 1778), a parody which had very little real effect. J. T. Hermes, who had followed Fielding in *Miss Fanny Wilkes,* 1766, obtained considerable popularity with his *Sophia's Journey from Memel to Saxony,* 1769, which is pure Richardson throughout. The History of *Fräulein von Sternheim,* by Marie Sophie von La Roche (1731–1807), daughter of the famous physician Guterman, which appeared in 1771, is said to have been revised by Wieland, and certainly has its source in *Pamela* and *Clarissa.*

Some German novels were translated, but not immediately, into English. We may instance C. F. Gellert's [34] best known romance, *Leben der schwedischen Gräfin G.*, which in 1752 appeared, London, as *History of the Swedish Countess of Guildenstern*, and in 1776, London, 12mo, as *The Life of the Swedish Countess de G. . . .*, the original having been published in 1746. *Fraulein von Sterhneim*, again, was Englished as *The History of Lady Sophie Sternheim*, London, 8vo, 1776, only five years after the original, but then we are getting late in the century.

It is no exaggeration to say that in England before 1750 there was a complete indifference to German literature, and although by the end of the 'seventies Wieland was beginning to be read—the popular *Reason Triumphant over Fancy*, 1773, is a version of *Der Sieg der Natur über die Schäwrmerey, oder die Abentheuer des Don Sylvio von Rosalva*, and at least seven of his works appeared in translation between 1764 and 1790—whilst *Werther*,[35] at first introduced to England at second-hand from the French, proved a great success in 1779, it was mainly by means of the Scriptural poems, prose-poems, and romances that English attention was stirred and began to look with interest to German sources. The *Messias* of Klopstock, the first three cantos of which appeared in 1748, and the final portion in 1773, was translated by Joseph and Mary Collyer,[36] 1769. and imitated in English, although it did not prove so great a success as the lady's version of Gessner's *Der Tod Abels*, which was issued in 1761, *The Death of Abel*, and by 1782 had run into no less than eighteen editions. A sequel, *The Death of Cain*, by a female writer, was given to the world in 1789, and generally regarded as a most elegant composition. The more strictly orthodox, however, looked upon these works with some suspicion, and Dr. John Watkins, who was a schoolmaster in Devonshire, found it necessary in his *Scripture Biography* [37] to utter a word of warning, since " Gesner in his romance entituled ' The Death of Abel ' has made Cain a penitent, and endeavoured to excite the pity of the reader for this wretched fratricide. This is taking a very unwarrantable and dangerous liberty with the Holy Scriptures, which uniformly declare that Cain ' was of ' or belonged to ' the wicked-one.' "

At its worst in England, the imitation of Gessner may be seen in a really rather terrible production, *The Life of Joseph, Son of Israel*, in eight books, 1771, by the pastor of the Baptist meeting-house, Devonshire Square, the Rev. John MacGowan (1726–80). The style is the most abominable fustian, and the Sacred narrative is interlarded with the most bombastic impertinences. None the less *The Life of Joseph* achieved several editions, and was turned into Gaelic.

A brief mention should be made of one channel of German thought, namely, the Germans domiciled in England,[38] exiles from their own country, who were teaching their language to English (and English to Germans), compiling German Grammars for the use of English students and translating German works into English, which, as the reviewers did not fail to point out,[39] was often of a very hobbledehoy and inferior kind. Many of these writers were attached to small congregations as their ministers. Thus the Rev. Dr. G. F. Wendeborn, who published his *Elements of German Grammar* in 1774 (2nd ed. 1790 ; 3rd ed. 1797), and an *Introduction to German Grammar* in 1791, was the minister of a German church in Ludgate Hill. The Rev. Peter Will, who is the translator " From the German of Cajetan Tschink " of *The Victim of Magical Delusion*, 3 vols., 1795 ; of the famous *Horrid Mysteries*, 4 vols., 1796, " From the German of the Marquis of Grosse " ; and many more, was some time minister of the German Reformed Congregation (that is, the Lutheran Chapel) in the Savoy.

Other German propagandists were private teachers and lecturers. Dr. A. F. N. Willich, sometime physician to the Saxon Ambassador, Count Brühl, and a fervent disciple of Kant, whose lectures he had attended, was in 1792 instructor to a German class in Edinburgh. Georg Heinrich Noehden, who came to England in 1793 and died in 1826, published a *Grammar* in 1800, and in 1818 was appointed tutor to the Crown Princess of Saxe-Weimar. He is also among the translators of Schiller, who personally approved his work. In 1798 the Rev. Dr. Wilhelm Render was " Teacher of the German Language in the University of Cambridge." He published a *Grammar*, 1799 ; a *Complete Analysis of the German Language*, 1804 ; a *Complete Pocket Dictionary*, 1807 ; and translated (very badly) *Die Räuber*, 1799 ; *Der Geisterseher*, 1800 ; *Werther*, 1801 ; and several other works.

Very many more names might be recorded, but it will suffice to draw attention to a monthly paper, " The German Museum or Monthly Repository of the Literature of Germany, the North and the Continent in General. London. Printed for C. Geisweiler and the Proprietors," 3 volumes, January, 1800, to June, 1801, to which many of the German literati, and especially the prolific Rev. Peter Will, were busy contributors. *The German Museum* set out " to make the English reader more intimately acquainted with the literary labours of Germany," and, short-lived as it proved, to some extent it must have fulfilled its purpose. It is at any rate strikingly indicative of the enthusiasm and energies of the German colony in London.

A considerable impetus was given to the study of German literature by a lecture of Henry Mackenzie delivered to the Royal Society of Edinburgh on April 21st, 1788. Mackenzie (1745–1831), attorney for the Crown, comptroller of the taxes for Scotland, was widely known as the author of three novels (all published anonymously), *The Man of Feeling*, 1771 ; *The Man of the World*, 1773 ; and *Julia de Roubigné*, 1777. Mackenzie's lecture, *An Account of the German Theatre*, may be deemed superficial, since, not being acquainted with German at that time, he derived his material from the French versions of Junker and Liebault, and more particularly from the Introduction, *Histoire abrégée du Théâtre allemand*, of the *Nouveau théâtre allemand* (1782–85) of Friedel and de Bonneville. Of Lessing and Goethe he has little to say, since he sweeps on enthusiastically to a detailed account of *Die Räuber*, " *Les Voleurs*, a tragedy by Mr. Schiller," a " wonderful drama," " one of the most uncommon productions of untutored genius that modern times can boast." His periods rise to a height of burning eloquence, and Scott remarks that the paper " made much noise, and produced a powerful effect."[40]

In 1792 *Die Räuber* was translated by Alexander Fraser Tytler, whose interest in German literature did so much to attract his young friend Walter Scott to the ballads and dramas of Goethe, Schiller, Bürger, Meier and Iffland.[41] Tytler's translation which was the first— there were four versions from Schiller within ten years—reached a fourth edition in 1800. Coleridge at Cambridge in 1794 read *Die Räuber* one dark November evening at midnight, and an hour or so later threw down the book trembling like an aspen leaf and seizing a pen to pour out his heated fancies in a letter : " My God, Southey, who is this Schiller, this convulser of the heart ? . . . Upon my soul, I write to you because I am frightened. . . . Why have we ever called Milton sublime ? "[42] Peacock in his *Memoirs of Shelley* records that *Die Räuber*, Goethe's *Faust*, and four novels of Charles Brockden Brown as being " of all the works with which he was familiar, those which took the deepest root in [the poet's] mind, and had the strongest influence in the formation of his character." Byron was not carried away like the rest, but then he read *Die Räuber* late in the day : " redde the *Robbers*. Fine,—but *Fiesco* is better ; and Alfieri, and Monti's *Aristodemo best*. 20th February, 1814."[43]

Few men did more to make German literature popular in England than Matthew Gregory Lewis, who after his visit to Weimar in 1792–93, where he met Goethe, fluently acquired the language and steeped himself in ballads, folk-lore, Bürger, Kotzebue, Zschokke, and the *Schauerromane*, came back to England to win an immense vogue with *The Monk*, which was itself speedily turned into German, *The Bravo of Venice*, *Tales of Wonder*, *Tales of Terror*, *The Castle Spectre*, and melo-dramatic plays.

Weimar was also visited in November, 1801, by Henry Crabb Robinson (1775–1867), whose stay was brief indeed, only from the 17th to the 19th of that month, and yet in so short a time he contrived to meet Goethe, Schiller, Herder and Wieland. He had already become friendly with the Brentanos at Frankfurt. At Jena from 1802-05 he studied philosophy, and was able to keep up his intercourse with the great men. When he revisited Weimar in 1818 Goethe was at Carlsbad, but on the occasion of his third visit in 1829 Goethe received him most warmly and may be said to have hailed him as an apostle of German culture in England. Both during his residence abroad and after he had returned to England, Robinson published essays on German literature and translations, but it was his personal and social influence which counted more than any literary work, and there can be no doubt that his intense admiration for Goethe " the mightiest intellect that has shone on the earth for centuries " " the inimitable and incomparable poet " did much to introduce that great master to the English intellectual world.

Nor must William Taylor of Norwich be forgotten. Born in 1765, he was when aged fourteen sent by his father on a continental tour in the Netherlands, France, and Italy to study the languages of those countries. In April, 1781, immediately after his return home, he visited Germany, where he remained chiefly at Detmold, for about eighteen months, in which time by unwonted assiduity he acquired an extensive knowledge of the language which as his tutor reported, " he thoroughly understands and speaks with great fluency." [44] From 1790 onwards Taylor turned himself more and more towards literature, and owing to his extensive acquaintance with German literature he established himself as the principal English critic of German writers, contributing it has been calculated no less than 1750 articles to various Reviews between 1793 and 1824. Taylor died in 1836 leaving as his chief work the *Historic Survey of German Poetry*, 3 vols., 1828-30, but for us his translation of Bürger's *Lenore*, which was published in the *Monthly Magazine* for March, 1796, but which had been handed about in MS. for some time previously is of even greater significance. *Lenore* was first printed in 1773 in the *Göttinger Musenalmanach* for 1774, but it was not until 1794, or early in 1795, that Scott made his own excellent version of the ballad. In 1796 no less than five translations of *Lenore* separately appeared, by Taylor, Scott, J. T. Stanley, H. J. Pye, and W. R. Spencer. In *The Ghost*, an Edinburgh journal published twice weekly, which ran from April 25th, 1796, to November 16th (No. 46) of the same year under the editorship of, and indeed written by Felix Phantom, who is a Portuguese student of Edinburgh University, named

Constantia, there is an attack on *Leonore*, No. 37, September 3rd, and in No. 41, September 28th, some sharp criticism is levelled at " The rage of Bürger's productions and the swarm of translators of his witchcraft tales, sold at various prices from a guinea to one penny ! ! "[45]

It is acknowledged that Scott in the Waverley Novels has occasionally used with admirable effect a suggestion from German drama and romance. Thus the Secret Tribunal of the Vehmgericht in *Anne of Geierstein* (1829) was no doubt due in the first place to *Götz von Berlichingen* although, of course, he also knew Veit Weber's *Heilige Vehme* ; in *Old Mortality* (1816) occurs a detail from Tieck's *Phantasus* ; in *The Monastery* (1820) the White Lady of Avenel is imitated from Fouqué's *Undine* ; as Fenella in *Peveril of the Peak* (1825) is derived from Mignon. Scott himself has made a most handsome acknowledgement in the Introductions to various novels of such points as he developed from what was after all often a mere hint in a German poem or romance.

Coleridge in his *Biographia Literaria* [46] has remarked : " To understand the true character of the *Robbers*, and of the countless imitations which were its spawn, I must inform you, . . . that about that time, and for some years before it, three of the most popular books in the German language were the translations of Young's *Night Thoughts*, Hervey's *Meditations*, and Richardson's *Clarissa Harlowe*. Now we have only to combine the bloated style and peculiar rhythm of Hervey . . . with the strained thoughts, the figurative metaphysics and solemn epigrams of Young on the one hand ; and with the loaded sensibility, the minute detail, the morbid consciousness of every thought and feeling in the whole flux and reflux of the mind, in short, the self-involution and dream-like continuity of Richardson on the other hand ; and then to add the ruined castles, the dungeons, the trap-doors, the skeletons, the flesh and blood ghosts, and the perpetual moonshine of a modern author (themselves the literary brood of the Castle of Otranto . . .),— and as the compound of these ingredients duly mixed, you will recognize the so-called German Drama," for which we can equally well, nay, perhaps even more precisely, read German Romance of the *Ritter*—, *Räuber-und Schauerromane* school.

Coleridge's observations are prejudiced and exaggerated, his distaste for such masters as the sublime Young and Richardson is very clumsily and uncritically expressed, yet the passage is worth quotation as showing a good deal of truth, for the German Romance was inspired by Walpole, Richardson, Hervey and Young, and so when England translated Naubert, Wächter, Spiess, Kerndörffer, Zschokke, and the rest, we were merely taking back what we had given.

One of the earliest, if not actually the very first of the *Schauerromane* (I use rather loosely a generic term) to be translated was *Herman of Unna* : *A Series of Adventures of the Fifteenth Century, in which the Proceedings of the Secret Tribunal, under the Emperors Winceslaus and Sigismond, are Delineated,* 3 vols., 8vo, London, G. G. and J. Robinson, 1794. Although attributed to " Professor Kramer " *Herman of Unna* is the work of Naubert, and as this writer often published her romances under the name Cramer she is continually confused with Karl Gottlob Cramer, whence it may be useful here and now to distinguish these two authors.

Christiane Benedicte Eugenie Naubert, *née* Hebenstreit, the wife of an eminent physician, Johann Ernst Naubert, was born at Leipzig, September 13th, 1756. Her works, including translations from the English, exceed eighty volumes. In Meiningen she used the name Cramer ; in Leipzig, Johann Friedrich Wilhelm Müller ; at Vienna she was Professor Milbiller. She also had other aliases, assumed to veil in some sort her extraordinary prolificness. She died January 12th, 1819. Among her chief romances are : *Walther von Montbarrn,* 2 vols., 1786, English translation, *Walter de Monbary, Grand Master of the Knights Templars,* 4 vols., Minerva Press, 1803 ; *Geschichte der Gräfin Thekla von Thurn,* 2 vols., 1788 ; *Hermann von Unna,* 2 vols., 1788 ; *Konradin von Schwaben,* 1788 ; *Elisabeth, Erbin von Toggenburg,* 1789, translated by Lewis as *Feudal Tyrants,* 4 vols., J. F. Hughes, 1806 ; *Werner, Graf Bernburg,* 2 vols., 1790 ; *Konrad und Siegfried von Feuchtwanger,* 2 vols., 1792 ; *Rosalba,* 2 vols., 1817.

Karl Gottlob Cramer was born at Poedelitz, March 3rd, 1758, and died June 7th, 1817. His first novel was *Charles von Saalfeld,* 1782. *Erasmus Schleicher,* 4 vols., Leipzig, 1789, was translated into French by A. Duval as *Le Pauvre Georges,* 2 vols., Paris, 1801. *Der deutsche Alcibiades,* 3 vols., 1790 and 1814, is one of Cramer's best-known works. *Haspar a Spada, ein Sage aus den* 13 *Jahr,* 2 vols., 1792 and 1794 ; and *Leben und Abenteurer Paul Asop's eines reducirten Hofnarren,* 2 vols., 1792 and 1798, are also remembered. To say that Cramer dealt in exaggeration and violence gives only one side of the picture, he had other qualities, and a talent which was far from mediocre in its kind.

Hermann of Unna (1788) written by Naubert under the pseudonym Cramer, was very successful in the English version,[47] which ran into a second edition, 3 vols., 12mo, a few months later than the first issue, 1794, and also appeared in a Dublin edition, 2 vols., 8vo, the same year.

In the Preface we are told that " The author of the following work is known in Germany for the eminent situation he holds in one of their universities, and for his literary production, particularly his celebrated

piece of Alcibiades." Here at once we have the error of confusing the
two writers, for (as we have just noted) *Der deutsche Alcibiades* is the
work of K. G. Cramer. The translator, who prefixes an essay on the
Secret Tribunal " Extracted from the Second Volume of the Miscellaneous Works of Baron Boch " oilily congratulates himself and his readers
on being " born in an age of illumination, and at a time when the
artifices of superstition and tyranny are fated to vanish before the torch
of truth," sentiments which could certainly not be repeated with any
verisimilitude to-day.

" It was on a Monday, the Morrow of All Saints, that the emperor
Winceslaus, conducted to his palace the princess Sophia, daughter of
John Duke of Bavaria." Wenceslaus (1361–1419), German king, and
as Wenceslaus IV, King of Bohemia, married his second wife, Sophia,
daughter of John, Duke of Bavaria-Munich in 1389.

The first wife of Wenceslaus, Joanna, daughter of Albert I of
Bavaria, died December 31st, 1386. It will be remembered that
Wenceslaus, who was one of the vilest of men, " naturæ humanæ et
omnis humanitatis oblitus," says the famous Jesuit historian Aloys
Boleslas Balbinus, tortured and drowned in the Moldau, the glorious
martyr S. John Nepomucene, the confessor of the empress Joanna,
since he refused to violate the seal of confession (1393).

The first and second chapters of *Herman von Unna* describe the
nuptial festivities of Sophia and Wenceslaus, who is soon sunk in
sottish slumber owing to his potations. A number of young damsels
entertain the empress with their songs, and amongst them the bride
distinguishes by the gift of a golden chain the lovely Ida Munster, the
statuary's daughter.

Herman of Unna, a youth of eighteen of a Westphalian house, page
of honour to the emperor, falls in love with Ida. To Herman,
Wenceslaus confesses that the imperial coffers are low. Much money
has been wasted upon the vulgar and insolent Ursula von Baden, the
emperor's mistress, whose silence was only secured at a price. Munster
is wealthy, and to him Herman is dispatched to borrow money for the
emperor. The master of the house is away, but Mrs. Maria Munster
admits the young court messenger, who espies Ida at her spinning-
wheel. Munster returns and the loan is effected.

Count Victor of Milan who is at enmity with Prince Visconti
secures the friendship of Wenceslaus by the gift of a vast sum of
money, and nothing is thought of at Prague but scenes of dissipation.

Herman saves Ida from a terrible conflagration in Prague, and the
love of Herman and Ida becomes the standing jest of the palace. This
arouses the opposition of old Munster, who not unreasonably suspects

and shuns the profligacy of the court. But Wenceslaus is beginning to hate the probity of Herman, and when the latter offers to leave the imperial service no difficulty is put in his way, whilst the order of knighthood is even bestowed to speed his journey.

Herman relates his history to Munster. Of the noble house of Unna his family were so impoverished that he was obliged to make his choice between taking monastic vows in the convent of Korf or entering the service of Wenceslaus. He chose the latter, but disgusted at the foulness and brutality of his sovran's life he is now resolved to seek the protection of Sigismond, king of Hungary.

Munster approves, and the youth is permitted to take a loving farewell of Ida, " and to imprint upon her cheek his first, perhaps his last salute." Just as Herman is departing, Munster's wife whispers to him in broken accents : " Ida is not our daughter . . . I am only her nurse. Offended love, and the dread of leaving her in the hands of a wicked stepmother, induced me. . . . She is the daughter of the Count of . . ."

Maria Munster now secretly visits the court and by a lavish bribe obtains the appointment of Ida as maid of honour to the Empress. The mother of the maids, the princess of Ratisbon, is little pleased ; and Munster bitterly reproaches his wife for her folly. Deeming that Ida may be a rival to her daughter, Imago, the princess regards her with the most implacable hatred, even continuing to bring charges of witchcraft against her so that Ida receives the following summons : " Ida Munster ! sorceress ! accused of murder, of high treason ! appear ! We, the secret avengers of the Eternal, cite thee within three days before the tribunal of God ! appear ! appear ! " When she seeks comfort and counsel a priest tells her she must appear before those mysterious beings who render justice in secret, who assemble " Every where, and no where."

Munster now consoles Ida by telling her that the Secret Tribunal treats all with most impartial justice and innocent as she is her acquittal is certain. Three-quarters of an hour after midnight the party summoned must repair to a certain spot, there to be met by an unknown who leads the accused hoodwinked before the judges. On the appointed night Munster accompanies Ida to the porch of S. Bartholomew's Church, and here the masked messenger is found.

Ida is conducted alone before the tribunal, a solemn circle of several persons all in black and masked, who sit in a dim vault lit only by torches. Various charges of witchcraft, of practising against the Empress are alleged. At length the tribunal arises. Ida is allowed one and twenty days to clear herself, and meanwhile she is permitted to lodge in a convent. The following day the streets are placarded with a notice bidding any who will champion Ida Munster come forward and defend her. At the appointed time Ida is again mysteriously led before the tribunal, the proceedings of which are described in very considerable detail. Suddenly there presents himself a mask of most noble part, who announces he is the champion of Ida, and cries aloud, proclaiming her innocence, " she is not the daughter of an obscure citizen ; she is the daughter of a prince." Completely overwrought the maiden falls into a deep swoon, from which she recovers to find herself under the portico of S. Bartholomew, whilst the dawn is already chasing the last faint stars from the grey-dappled sky.

The tribunal adjudge her innocent, and she is conducted to the castle of her father, the noble Count Wirtemberg. Unhappily there is a quarrel between the houses of Wirtemberg and Unna, and the Count designs his daughter for Duke Frederick of Brunswick.

Sigismond of Hungary now falls entirely under the influence of Andrew Gara and his brother, Nicholas, who by their plots attain much the same position at Prague as the Frankish Mayors of the Palace, Erkinoald, Pepin, Otto, Grimoald and the rest held when they swayed it over the feeble Merovingian puppet-kings. In fact, the Garas imprison Sigismond at the castle of Soclos, whence owing to an intrigue with their young stepmother, Helen Gara, he is in their absence able to escape, and takes up his residence in the Castle of Cyly. The Countess Barbe Cyly, a murderous Messaline, not only enchains the King in her toils, but contrives that her husband Count Peter Cyly shall be assassinated to clear her way to sharing the throne. This abandoned woman further indulges in amorous intercourse with such knights and courtiers of Sigismond's circle who please her, and when Herman rejects her wicked love, by accusations of treason she has him thrown into a dungeon, whence he is freed by the secret offices of a maid who attends the Countess.

Through a specious combination of circumstances Herman is accused of the murder of Duke Frederick of Brunswick, who actually has been treacherously dispatched by a follower of Sigismond. Herman, owing to the exertions of Duke Albert of Austria, is acquitted by the Diet of Nobles, but his enemies are sufficiently powerful to accuse him before the Secret Tribunal, by whom he is condemned, and his adventures entail a number of hairbreadth 'scapes from the daggers of the unknown executioners, who are everywhere : " Thousands of secret executioners burn with the desire of shedding thy blood," his dear friend Ulric of Senden warns him, and it proves that the lot has fallen upon Ulric himself, who, bound by a fearful oath, stabs Herman and then turns his steel upon himself. Both eventually recover of their wounds, but it must be acknowledged that the situation is extremely poignant and developed with considerable pathos and power. It is only eventually that Herman's uncle, the Count of Unna, a secret judge of the highest rank, is able to obtain a repeal of the sentence, when the innocence of the accused has been proven beyond all question.

Meanwhile at Prague, Ida has been indiscreet enough openly to espouse the doctrines and follow the sermons of John Hus, whereupon Archbishop Zbyněk (Sbinco) " condemned her to be confined in a convent in Hungary ; a sentence which she heard with little emotion." In fact, " Ida felt no apprehension, that she was to remain eternally confined in the convent to which she was conducted."

The Convent of S. Anne in which she was immured is one of the traditional kind, and this " melancholy asylum " is described in well-worn crusted phrase. " This convent was placed in a situation to which nature had been by no means kind. The lofty mountains, covered with thick forests of gloomy pines, with which it was surrounded, could cherish no sentiments but those of grief and melancholy. The deep and narrow valley from the bottom of which rose the walls of the monastery, precluded all extent of view, and the heart seemed to shrink from the sad sterility that everywhere presented itself to the eye. Hence discontent and rancour sat brooding in every countenance ; and wearisomeness and disgust pervaded equally the parlour and the chapel, the gallery and the garden, the cell and the hall of recreation." Ida, however, " had no cause of complaint, but the tedium of her situation, a feeling which she shared in common with every nun," and which it would be unkind to suggest she contrives to convey to the pages describing her sojourn in the convent of S. Anne. For, truth to tell, the cloister episodes are not very well done, although no ingredient has been omitted, and before long when apparently bored with her first and second convents she seeks to remove to S. Emery from S. Nicholas where she is now staying, Archbishop Zbyněk, " a little red-faced old man," arrives on the scene, and proceeds to make overtures to the amazed damsel since he stands " in need of a young and obliging governante," as he is discreetly pleased to phrase it. Ida stood petrified, but " the amorous old prelate did not for this discontinue his solicitations." However, during her stay at S. Nicholas, she discovers that the wife of King Sigismond, Queen Mary, long supposed dead, is concealed here. Archbishop Zbyněk becomes pressing, and when Ida complains to the Abbess, the only reply vouchsafed is : " Abominable slanderer, thou art unworthy to live," and " Ida was conveyed to one of those subterranean dungeons vestiges of which are yet to be seen in the majority of convents." However, in a very short time, the Archbishop conveniently dies, and although " there was an intention of shutting her up in a cavern that had formerly been dug beneath the very foundations of the convent," Ida escapes " this fearful abode," and there suddenly appear on the scene her friends and relatives, who have bribed the new Archbishop to restore her to liberty. Anxious to earn his money, the good easy man actually offers to unite her to Herman upon the spot. The Abbess objects : " How horrid to think of performing such a ceremony within the sacred walls of a convent ! " she exclaims. Accordingly a little after the nuptials are celebrated with the utmost solemnity, and there is " excess of happiness ! To paint it, who will dare take the pencil ? "

I have devoted some particular attention to *Herman von Unna* because it contains so much which was afterwards developed in the Gothic romance. We have the heroine, supposed of humble (or at least not of noble) birth ; the separated lovers ; the wicked rival, a malignant and licentious woman of quality who upon being rejected by the hero involves him through her acts in trouble and captivity ; the imprisonment of the heroine in a lone convent with secret dungeons and the tenebrous *in pace* ; her persecution by the wicked monk (in this case an Archbishop) ; the tyrant abbess ; castles, adventures in forests and at midnight ; and finally the reconciliation of all parties and the nuptials of the gallant hero and the peerless heroine of the tale.

I do not say that Naubert is more talented than many other German authors of romance. *Herman von Unna* is often prolix where the action should be swift and breathless, and not infrequently it crowds into far too small a compass incidents and explanations, which are interesting in themselves, but which to be effective demand a longer description. The mystery surrounding the powerful secret society is well managed, and Naubert has certainly given us something of the atmosphere of terror and suspense, when (as indeed proves the case) the hand of the nearest and dearest may at the bidding of the masqued tribunal be directed to strike the blow. The appearance on the scene of a grave, austere, secret and silent man, who is friendly disposed and yet who is guessed to be (as ultimately proves the case) an agent of the Society, is a prominent feature in these romances.

In 1794, C. P. Kopp published at Göttingen, 8vo, *Über die Verfassung der heimlichen Gerichte in Westphalen,* a study whence Coxe drew his historical inquiry in *A Letter on the Secret Tribunal of Westphalia, addressed to Elizabeth, Countess of Pembroke,* Cadell and Davis, 8vo, 1798, 1s.

The Vehmgericht plays a great part in a romance *Die Rächenden, oder das Vehmgericht des* 18. *Jahrhunderts,* published at Leipzig in 1802. J. Powell in 1806 translated from the German of Veit Weber *Wolf, or the Tribunal of Blood,* which was reprinted as late as 1841. The historian, dramatist, and novelist Georg Philipp Ludwig Leonhard Wächter, who was born on November 25th, 1762, and died on January 8th, 1835, was wont to publish his romances under the pseudonym Veit Weber. His *Sagen der Vorzeit* extended in seven volumes from 1787 to 1798, and he further added *Romantische Sagen der Vorzeit.* Amongst his novels are : *Mannerschwur und Weibertreue* ; *Ritterwort,* 2 vols. ; *Das heilige Kleebatt* ; *Die Teufelsbeschwöring* ; and *Der Fündling von Egizheim.* In England *The Sorcerer* was very popular, and the *Monthly Mirror* for June, 1796 (Vol. II, p. 97), when reviewing *The Black Valley, A Tale from the German of Veit Weber, author of the Sorcerer,* published by Johnson, 1796, although remarking that there is more strength than elegance in the narrative, emphatically says that " Such as delight in the wilder exhibitions of romance will feel themselves deeply interested in the course of this German story."

Faust, by G. W. M. Reynolds, which concluded with Chapter XCIV its long run in *The London Journal* on July 18th, 1846, and was very shortly after published in book form, was described as " A Romance of the Secret Tribunals," but the most famous romance in which we are introduced to the Vehmgericht is, of course, Scott's *Anne of Geierstein,* 1829. Scott had previously introduced the Vehmgericht in *The House of Aspen,* probably written in 1800, and in the Catalogue of his Library appear no less than four especial studies of the Secret Tribunals.

In many of their details the German *Ritterromane* draw upon Schiller's *Der Geisterseher,* the first part of which was turned into English by D. Boileau in 1795, as *The Ghost-Seer, or Apparitionist* ; whilst the whole work appeared five years later in a translation from the pen of Dr. Render as *The Armenian, or the Ghost-seer, a History founded on Fact,* 4 vols., 1800. This novel immensely impressed English readers, and there are frequent allusions to its power. Thus Byron,[48] writing from Venice, April 2nd, 1817, to John Murray, mention " Schiller's *Armenian* a novel which took a great hold of me when a boy. It is also called the *Ghost-Seer,* and I never walked down St. Mark's by moonlight without thinking of it, and ' *at nine o'clock he died* ' ! " Rogers also in his *Italy,* " St. Mark's Place," has the following lines :

> Who answer'd me just now ? Who, when I said
> " '*Tis nine,*" turn'd round and said so solemnly,
> " *Signor, he died at nine* ' *!* '*Twas the Armenian ;*
> The mask that follows thee, go where thou wilt.

The idealization of the feudal system and the Holy Roman Empire which is so admirably imagined in the works of Tieck, Brentano, Joseph von Görres, and de la Motte Fouqué, comparable to the mediævalism and Arthurian legends of Rossetti and Morris, is very prominent but perhaps a little crudely wrought in the romances of lesser men. Their anti-clericalism, too, is all the more vulgar and grotesque when we consider that the leading romanticists, Brentano, Görres, Eichendorff, were Catholics, and that others like Friedrich Schlegel became Catholics.

In England the chivalrous element is derived from other sources—from Thomas Leland, Walpole, and Clara Reeve—but at first there was not much attention paid to feudalism in fiction, and the *Monthly Magazine*, April, 1798, in reviewing *The Knights ; or, Sketches of the Heroic Age*, remarks : " Not many romances of knighthood have as yet diversified the literature of the circulating libraries."

It were impertinent here to enter upon any discussion of the political aspects of Europe; suffice to say that the powerful Secret Societies, more or less closely knit together, with international ramifications, all clearly pointing to one great shadowed conspiracy, which play no inconspicuous part in many of these romances actually do not belong to the realm of fiction. That these societies were fantastically enough presented by the novelist is not to be denied, but one asks : Was the picture more highly coloured than the truth ? The plain statements of John Robison, Professor of Natural Philosophy at Edinburgh, in his *Proofs of a Conspiracy against all the Religions and Governments of Europe* (1797) may have been ridiculed, but they have never been rebutted, whilst Abbé Barruel has demonstrated in his *Memoires pour servir à l'histoire du Jacobinisme* (1797-98) that there was fully organized a triply co-ordinated interactive conspiracy, whose agents descended under various forms but in unbroken succession from the Manichees. One outcome of these diabolical masonries showed itself in the most hideous excesses and carnage of the French Revolution, whilst another even more terrible achievement has ravaged an Empire in our own day, and it is no exaggeration to say that the agents and grisons of the eternal movement of evil are sowing mischief and ruin in every land. Those who wish to read the tale of the foul and subversive propaganda of the societies may find it plainly set forth in Mrs. Nesta H. Webster's *World Revolution ; the Plot against Civilization*, 1922.

The most famous romance which introduces the international intrigues of these conspirators is that known in its English translation as *Horrid Mysteries*, a title entering into the Northanger canon. *Horrid*

Mysteries. "A Story. From the German of the Marquis of Grosse. *By P. Will.* In Four Volumes," was published by Lane at the Minerva Press in the autumn of 1796. A reprint, Two Volumes, with an Introduction by the present writer, appeared in 1927.

Karl Grosse, who bestowed a marquisate upon himself and who was upon occasion also wont to employ a yet more grandiloquent title, 'Marquis of Pharnusa,' published with success a good many novels between the years 1790 and 1805. He is the author of *Erzählungen und Novellen,* 1793–94; *Kleine Novellen,* 1793–95; *Spanische Novellen,* 1794–95; *Der Dolch,* 1795, translated into English as *The Dagger,* 12mo, Vernor and Hood, 1795; *Der Blumenkrantz,* 1795–96; *Chlorinde,* 1796; *Liebe und Treue,* 1796; *Versuche,* 1798; and several more. His *Der Genie, oder Memoiren des Marquis von G . . . .,* 1792–95, was twice translated into English in 1796, first as *The Genius : or the Mysterious Adventures of Don Carlos de Grandez,* by Joseph Trapp; and secondly by Peter Will, as *Horrid Mysteries.* The hero of this work, Don Carlos, is taken in the toils of the Illuminati, a secret society organized—but perhaps not founded since they were connected with the Illuminati, German Satanists of the fifteenth century—by Adam Weishaupt (Spartacus), a vile incendiary, whom Louis Blanc without exaggeration described as "the profoundest conspirator that has ever existed." The Illuminati shrouded their anarchical aims with a good deal of masquing and mummery, and there is little question that Grosse, although he may somewhat colour his episodes, is writing of actuality. When he realizes that the Illuminati are Nihilists, red-hot revolutionaries, midnight murderers, devils of the pit, hateful to God and man, Carlos seeks to escape and destroy the band, but again and again they hunt him down as he travels through first one country and now another. That *Horrid Mysteries* is fantastic exceedingly nobody would attempt to deny. The narrative is also remarkable for its sombre and fearful power, a vehemence which grips the reader and holds him fast, for even in its wildest flights he must perforce confess that the tale rings true.

A not dissimilar story is *The Victim of Magical Delusion ; or, The Mystery of the Revolution of P——l :* "A Magico-Political Tale. Founded on Historical Facts, and Translated from the German of Cajetan Tschink. By P. Will." 3 vols. 9s. Robinson, 1795. *The Monthly Review,* August, 1795, has the following critique : [49]

"This novel, like the Necromancer, is one of those numberless imitations to which the Ghost-seer of the celebrated Schiller has given rise in Germany. The author, like most copyists, seizes rather the peculiarities than the beauties of his model ; and, by overleaping too freely the fences of probability, he loses that impression of reality which is so favourable to vivid interest. Volkert and Hiermansor are feeble rivals to the incomprehensible Armenian. The translation is executed by a foreigner, and has a few peculiarities of phrase. The preface supplies some curious facts concerning the credulity of Berlin, but errs in ascribing the Ghost-seer to M. Tschink."

The Critical Review, however, for September of the same year, noticed the romance at considerable length, more than ten closely-packed pages, and was distinctly favourable and interested. In the Translator's Address, an appendix to Vol. III, it is stated that the incidents are " not the offspring of imaginary fiction, but founded on historical facts, recorded in Abbé Vertot's excellent History of the Revolution in Portugal."⁵⁰ Miguel, Duke of C——, is sent on his travels under the care of Antonio, a Portuguese count. A most extraordinary and artful impostor, The Unknown, and this tutor having deluded the youth by a series of supposed necromancies and wizard charms into a belief that the mysterious being possesses powers of the highest occult order, involve their dupe in a share of the conspiracy by which the revolution of Portugal is to be effected. All too soon Miguel finds that he is bound to the horrid authors of that desperate attempt by every tie of honour, love, pride, and gratitude. There are, it must be acknowledged, certain resemblances between The Victim of Magical Delusion and Horrid Mysteries, since in each romance the hero finds himself entangled with clandestine businesses which are murderous and bloody beneath the outworn pretext of liberty.

Sham apparitions and cozening sorceries play a great part in another book which belongs to the Northanger canon, The Necromancer : Or The Tale of the Black Forest : Founded on Facts : Translated from the German of Lawrence Flammenberg, By Peter Teuthold. 2 vols. Lane, Minerva Press. 1794.

I am glad to have the opportunity here to correct an error into which I fell twenty years since, when, in a lecture upon Ann Radcliffe delivered before the Royal Society of Literature, I threw doubt upon the German original of The Necromancer. My more recent reading in German romance of the period brought me acquaintance some ten years ago with the work whose existence I rashly questioned.⁵¹ In the first place, Lorenz Flammenberg is a pseudonym of Karl Friedrich Kahlert, who also called himself Bernhard Stein. Kahlert's romance, from which The Necromancer is translated, appeared in 1792—Der Geisterbanner, eine Wundergeschichte aus mündlichen und schriftlichen Traditionen gesammelt.

The Necromancer was reprinted as *The Necromancer ; or Wolfe the Robber,* " A Romance of the Black Forest," as No. 88, in the Fourth Volume, 1840, of *The Romancist, and Novelist's Library,* edited by William Hazlitt. There is also a recent reprint, 1927, with an Introduction by myself.

The Necromancer is a singularly disconnected narrative, and it may be presumed that various local legends of the Black Forest have been woven together without much inherent cohesion to form one tale. The incidents are often violent and even extravagant, but so wild and lawless were the times it is by no means improbable that they are founded on fact. Kahlert was no doubt describing in his pages the " Buxen," a vast secret society which from 1736 to 1779 ravaged the whole district of Limburg, parts of Lorraine and the province of Treves. These villains, whose organization was most singularly complete, not only plundered outlying manors and farms, but even invaded at midnight hamlets and the smaller villages, burning them to the ground. They were stamped out with the greatest difficulty, and in many places permanent gallows, which were never empty, were set up by the authorities. At length Leopold Leeuwerk, their chaplain as he was called, a Satanist who laid claim to occult powers, and Abraham Nathan, one of their chief leaders, an atrocious villain, were captured and put to death at Haeck, on the moor of Graed, on September 24th, 1772. When he described Volkert in his romance Kahlert clearly has Leeuwerk in view, and Nathan is drawn as Wolfe the Robber.

Wolfe's gang of fifty-three ruffians take up their headquarters in the Haunted Castle in the Black Forest, and, aided by the superstition of the credulous peasantry, soon spread the belief that this desolate fabric is the rendezvous of evil spirits. At night they sally forth disguised in the skins of goats and being taken to be demons are able to plunder the whole countryside. A great number of innkeepers and publicans are secretly leagued with this infernal sect, and thus aid their depredations, which continue year after year unchecked. Volkert acts the rôle of Necromancer, and by his subtle shifts and craft is able to deceive and delude many into the belief that he has supernatural powers, to the great advantage of his fellow freebooters.

The Necromancer is thus noticed in *The Monthly Review* [52] for April, 1795 : " The Platonic idea of influencing dæmons or disembodied spirits by human rites and adjurations, of learning secret phænomena from revelation, and of accomplishing by their intervention important purposes of this world, had scarcely been mentioned, much less credited, since the time of the old Alchemists and Rosicrucians, until

PLATE VI

[Face p. 134

THE CASTLE OF SAINT DONATS
Frontispiece, 1798

some modern novelists chose once more to familiarize the superstition.
. . . The opinion itself now seems again creeping into repute ; it is
mentioned even by philosophers without a sneer ; and it is becoming
the corner-stone of a spreading sect of visionaries, whose favoured
or impudent proselytes are said to behold by day, and in the very
streets of this metropolis, the wandering souls of holy men of other
times. It requires perhaps some leaning towards these and the
like notions, or at least a sufficient respect for them not to laugh at
but to sympathize with the curiosity and apprehensions of those
imbued with them, in order to be pleased with this novel. In Germany,
no doubt, such doctrines have made a wider impression and progress
than in our country. . . ."

It is something more than disappointing, it is bad art, to find
that in such works as *The Victim of Magical Delusion* and *The
Necromancer* all supernatural agencies, apparitions, evocations of the
dead, spectres, hauntings, phantom appearances, mysterious voices,
premonitions, warnings, are explained away by the paraphernalia
of Maskelyne and Cooke. We read in the closing chapters of trap-
doors, secret panels, stentaphrons, benumbing smoke, powder of
calophony blown by confederates through half-opened shutters,
thunder produced by large kettledrums in a cellar, burning brimstone,
a hollow pumpkin for a disfigured head, artificial lightning blazed
through chinks, *delusive miracles*, all in such abundance that the unravelment is more elaborate and more difficult to believe than ever
could be the honest supernatural.

When Cockton gives us Valentine Vox the ventriloquist or
Sylvester Sound the sonambulist we do not complain ; we are amused
and accept the various accidents of these novels with goodwill, since
the author lays his hand on the table at once. He does not build up
a structure of occultism and then betray his readers by knocking his
card castle rous to the ground.

The subject is ungrateful, but it cannot be ignored. The whole
sense of the eighteenth century was bent on " the surest means of
steering clear of the dangerous rocks and quicksands of superstition,
on which the happiness of so many mortals has been wrecked,"[53]
and hence, in spite of the authority of Shakespeare and Ossian, writers
of romance for the most part determined not to propagate a barbarous
and harmful credulity. Yet some use of supernatural agencies in their
pages seemed inevitable. A compromise then had to be effected if
phantoms and spectres were not merely to be tolerated, but to be
approved, and the only solution appeared that in the end explanations
must be proffered which, whilst not overstraining probability, accounted

for all the mysterious circumstances of the tale. In this way the complacent reader could enjoy to the uttermost the glamour and the thrill, since subconsciously he knew that his delicious tremors and comfortable apprehensions would be dissolved by a rational and enlightened *éclaircissement*.

Unfortunately, in all her works save the last, *Gaston de Blondeville*, even Mrs. Radcliffe accepted the compromise, and it is no small tribute to her genius that she is able to reconcile her readers to these anagnoristical elucidations. In his review of *The Mysteries of Udolpho* Coleridge highly commended such disingenuousness, and wrote that " The reader experiences in perfection the strange luxury of artificial terror without being obliged for a moment to hoodwink his reason, or to yield to the weakness of superstitious credulity," [54] which seems to me a most false and insipid remark. Surely Coleridge should have seen that his very phrase " artificial terror," as he intends it, cuts the ground from under his feet.

As a good example of a romance in which mysteries and hauntings are not too improbably if disappointingly explained we may take *The Horrors of Oakendale Abbey*, ' By the Author of Elizabeth,' one volume, Lane, 1797.

Laura, the adopted daughter of an eminent surgeon of Paris, Monsieur Du Frene, and his wife, was when little more than an infant captured on an English frigate by a French privateer. She is rescued from prison by Monsieur Du Frene, to whom she becomes as dear as if she were his own child. Among the pupils of Du Frene is one Eugene Rayneer, who comes from England to complete his education at Paris. Eugene and Laura soon fall in love, but he is recalled to London, and very shortly after, on August 10th, 1792, " when Paris was deluged in human gore," Du Frene, suspected of royalist tendencies, is murdered in the street. Madame Du Frene and Laura escape with difficulty to England, but are separated in the crowds of fugitives ere they land, and Laura finds herself alone at Milford Haven. Here she attracts the attention of the profligate Lord Oakendale, who, the more easily to compass his design, contrives to get her into his power and consigns her with a rustic serving-maid to his seat in remotest Cumberland, Oakendale Abbey.

The Abbey has the reputation of being fearfully haunted, and during her stay in those deserted halls Laura encounters some terrible sights. In a dark and lonely chamber she espies a huge chest, on opening which she sees a bleaching skeleton. When she enters a distant apartment " a sight more horrible than imagination can form " presented itself to her. " The dead body of a woman hung against the wall opposite to the door she had entered, with a coarse cloth pinned over all but the face; the ghastly and putrefied appearance of which bespoke her to have been some time dead. Laura gave a fearful shriek, when a tall figure, dressed only in a checked shirt, staggered towards her. The face was almost quite black; the eyes seemed starting from the head; the mouth was widely extended, and made a kind of hollow guttural sound in attempting to articulate." At length Laura is able to escape from the Abbey and is befriended and protected by a Mrs. Greville.

Lord Oakendale arrives at the Abbey to find Laura fled. A number of circumstances follow which lead to the discovery that Laura is none other than his niece, the child of his younger brother, who died at Madras. He at once instates her in position in London society.

Before her marriage to Lord Oakendale his wife had given herself to an officer named Vincent, and as the fruit of their intrigue a boy was born, who was none other than Eugene. The physician who attended her accouchement has brought up the child as his own, and he informs Lady Oakendale of his intention to discover the young man to his father, now Lord Vincent. The depraved woman, however, contrives that Eugene shall be secretly imprisoned in Oakendale Abbey, where she supposes nobody will ever come. Shortly after she expires of shame and remorse, and the unfortunate Eugene is not traced without great difficulty. Lord Vincent immediately recognizes him as his son, and owing to his influence obtains his legitimization. Even yet the path of true love is not quite smooth, but eventually Eugene wins the hand of his faithful Laura.

It is found that the supposed hauntings are due to a set of persons whose business it is to obtain dead bodies and bring them to the Abbey for dissection—resurrection men in fact. The tall figure whom Laura saw staggering through the vaults was a poor wretch hanged at Carlisle for coining, who had been cut down before life was extinct and who recovered his senses and life.

The opening scenes of *The Horrors of Oakendale Abbey*, the abrupt arrival of Laura at the deserted mansion, the chatter of the villagers Aaron Giles and old Dame Giles, the shuddering superstition, the fearful sights, are all extremely effective, and it were to be wished that the writer had boldly introduced the supernatural, for it must be confessed that towards the end of the narrative the interest begins to peter out and wear thin, whilst one feels it would not have been difficult to sustain it to the end. The commencement is plainly modelled on *The Romance of the Forest*, and the discovery by Lord Oakendale that Laura is his niece may be paralleled by the relationship of Adeline and the Marquis de Montalt. There are other details imitated from Mrs. Radcliffe, and if the author had only sustained at the same level the interest of the first fifty or sixty pages *The Horrors of Oakendale Abbey* would have been throughout an admirable romance.

In Chapter II of Mrs. Parsons' *The Mysterious Warning*, 4 vols., Lane, 1796, a book which enters into the Northanger canon, whilst Ferdinand is kneeling by the bed of his father, who has but newly expired, "a low and hollow voice pronounced the words ' *Pardon and peace !* ' " He deems that he has heard the spirit of the dead addressing him, and later the same " deep and hollow voice " warns him against his brother, Count Rhodophil, a profound dissembler, who is, in fact, the villain of the piece. The voice also upbraids Rhodophil with his crimes, and to some extent prevents worse mischief by its solemn denunciations. At length, towards the end of the tale,[55] when Rhodophil lies raving on his death-bed, his wickedness having been unmasked, the old steward Ernest confesses that it was *his voice* which the brothers heard from time to time in the old castle, and which they deemed the accents of some unearthly visitant. Concealed in a secret closet, Ernest was able to overhear interviews of the last importance, and to throw his voice in so clear yet dolorous a whisper that it was thought by all a cry coming from beyond the grave. The disclosure adds nothing to the narrative—nay, it obviously detracts—but Mrs. Parsons considered it highly fitting and proper, and her readers warmly approved what to us must seem a very weak and timid explanation of what after all proves to be a mock mystery.

There was, of course, a school of novelists who absolutely scouted these ill-judged and ineffectual attempts at compromise, who dealt boldly in the supernatural. Walpole, in the *Castle of Otranto*, had not hesitated to employ preterhuman agencies ; he rightly defended the use of the " visionary part " in fiction, and when Clara Reeve published her *Champion of Virtue*, 1777 (reissued in 1778 as *The Old English Baron ; a Gothic Story*), he damned it as a *caput mortuum*. In a letter to Mason, April 8th, 1778, he asks : " Have you seen *The Old Baron*, a Gothic story, professedly written in imitation of *Otranto*, but reduced to reason and probability ! It is so probable, that any trial for murder at the Old Bailey would make a more interesting story." [56] Later, writing to the Rev. William Cole, August 22nd, 1778, he speaks of this romance as " a professed imitation of mine only stripped of the marvellous ; and so entirely stripped, except in one awkward attempt at a ghost or two, that it is the most insipid dull nothing you ever saw." [57]

Matthew Gregory Lewis, who loved a ghost story, scorned any knock-kneed timidity, and in this he was eagerly followed by those who drew their inspiration (in part at any rate) from his work; Charlotte Dacre, William Henry Ireland, T. Bellamy, W. C. Proby, and half a hundred more. In the preface to his first novel, *Ethelwina ; or, The House of Fitz-Auburne*,[58] 3 vols., Lane, 1799, T. J. Horsley Curties made frank acknowledgement of certain articles in his literary creed : " The Author of this Work . . . in one circumstance . . . has stepped beyond the modern writers of Romance by introducing a *Real Ghost*—to many, such a circumstance will not appear unnatural or improbable ; but he neither apologizes, nor justifies on that ground —he only pleads the example of the immortal Bard of Avon, who found a spectre necessary for his purpose to heighten his story, or to ' harrow up the soul,' but never thought it necessary to account for the ' unreal mockery.' "

This stupid convention of the ' Explained Supernatural ' persisted late, and we find it even in a romance of G. P. R. James, *The Castle of Ehrenstein, Its Lord Spiritual and Temporal, its Inhabitants Earthly and Unearthly*, 3 vols., 1847, a work completely spoiled by the last chapter, since I am well assured that every reader rejects the pages where it is discovered " that the whole of this vast structure, solid as it seems, and solid as it indeed is, in reality is double," so that the phantoms were actually the Count Ferdinand and his faithful followers, who dwelt there secretly until the time was ripe for him to dispossess his usurping brother, William.

The reviewers for a considerable time highly favoured romances in which " probability " could be preserved at almost any cost, and which did not require them to hoodwink reason. By degrees, however, the bathos of the explanations forced itself upon their intelligence, and a note of dissatisfaction is heard. Thus in October, 1795, *The Monthly Review* not only grumbles (and one cannot say without reason) at the hauntings of *The Castle of Ollada*, 2 vols., Lane, 1794, which oblige Lathom " to spend a great part of the second volume in explaining mysteries, which after all are not very clearly unfolded," [59] but also proceeds to give Isabella Kelly a pretty severe jobation for the terrors in *The Abbey of Saint Asaph*, 3 vols., Lane, 1795, where " we are terrified with a fiery spectre emitting from its gaping jaws sulphurous flames, and sending forth horrid screams, and with a moving and shrieking skeleton,—only that we may afterwards have the pleasure of finding that there was no occasion to be frightened, the spectre being *only* a man, its infernal flames nothing more than a preparation of phosphorus, and the inhabitant of the skeleton not a ghost but a rat ! " [60]

Yet, curiously enough, in the very same number [61] the critic vacillates, and on reviewing *The Traditions*, A Legendary Tale, Written by a Young Lady, Lane, two vols., 1795, is huffed and says : " The principal fault of the work is that it gives too much encouragement to superstition, by connecting events with preceding predictions, and by visionary appearances, for which the reader is not enabled to account from natural causes." In his *Life of Horace Walpole*, Scott has put it excellently well. He remarks that the reader feels indignant at discovering that he has been cheated into sympathy with terrors which are finally explained as having proceeded from some very simple cause. " These substitutes for supernatural agency are frequently to the full as improbable as the machinery which they are introduced to explain away and supplant. The reader, who is required to admit the belief of supernatural interference, understands precisely what is demanded of him ; and, if he be truly a gentle reader, throws his mind into the attitude best adapted to humour the deceit which is presented for his entertainment, and grants for the time of perusal, the premises on which the fable depends."

In *The Quarterly Review*, May, 1810, there is a very admirable censure upon the " Explained Supernatural." "We disapprove of the mode introduced by Mrs. Radcliffe, and followed by Mr. Murphy [62] and her other imitators, of winding up their story with a solution by which all the incidents appearing to partake of the mystic and marvellous are resolved by very simple and natural causes. . . . We can, therefore, allow of supernatural agency to a certain extent, and for an appropriate purpose, but we never can consent that the effect of such agency shall be finally attributed to natural causes totally inadequate to its production. We can believe, for example, in Macbeth's witches, and tremble at their spells ; but had we been informed, at the conclusion of the piece that they were only three of his wife's chambermaids disguised for the purpose of imposing on the Thane's credulity, it would have added little to the credibility of the story, and entirely deprived it of the interest. In like manner we fling back upon the Radcliffe school their flat and ridiculous explanations, and plainly tell them, that they must either confine themselves to ordinary and natural events, or find adequate causes for those horrors and mysteries in which they love to involve us." [63]

It cannot, of course, be said that the Robber-Romances—die Räuber-Romane—came from Germany, as we already had very many indigenous heroes of our own, but such works as *Rinaldo Rinaldini* and *Abällino* had an immense vogue in England, and certainly set a mode for bravos and banditti.

None the less England is the home of Robin Hood, Claude Duval, Jack Sheppard, Dick Turpin, and a hundred more whose exploits form a vast library by themselves. It were superfluous to insist upon the popularity in chap-book and fiction of our native highwaymen. At their highest glory they formed, perhaps, a kind of aftermath of the Gothic Novel in the thirties and forties of the nineteenth century when Harrison Ainsworth at Rottingdean in the autumn of 1833, was writing *Rookwood*, " a story in the bygone style of Mrs. Radcliffe . . . substituting an old English squire, an old English manorial residence, and an old English highwayman for the Italian marchese, the castle, and the brigand of the great mistress of Romance." In 1839 came *Jack Sheppard* to cause a veritable furore and stir a storm of adverse criticism against the school of " criminal romance," severely but very feebly and inconsistently attacked by Thackeray and Forster. It is a sad pity that Ainsworth waited more than thirty years, until *Talbot Harland*, before he introduced Claude Duval into his novels.

Pierce Egan the younger, too, a most prolific writer, in 1838 published *Robin Hood and Little John* ; or *The Merry Men of Sherwood Forest*, which was lifted bodily into French as *Le Prince des Voleurs*, 1872, and *Robin Hood le Proscrit*, 1873, being ascribed (although incorrectly) to Alexandre Dumas.

The " criminal romance " of the nineteenth century from *Oliver Twist*, *Jack Sheppard* and *Paul Clifford* to *Charley Wag*, *Fanny White*, *Rook the Robber*, and *Blueskin*, is a long, important and most interesting study in our literature which has yet to be written, but it must not delay us here, since actually it is the German freebooter and the Italian bandit who most generally appear in the Gothic novel.

The forest scenes in Lewis' *The Monk*, when the benighted traveller, Don Alphonso d'Alvarada (who is Don Raymond de las Cisternas) encounters the Baroness Lindenberg and suite in like case at Baptiste's cottage in the wood near Strasbourg, and rescues her from the treachery of the brigands with whom their evil host is in league, may have been suggested by a German source but they have none the less, as more than one reviewer remarked, a close similarity to incidents in *Ferdinand Count Fathom*.[64]

Brigands make their appearance in many Gothic novels of the Lewis type, and within some eighteen months of its first appearance, one of the most famous German Räuber-Romane,[65] *Rinaldo Rinaldini* (1798) was translated into English by John Hinckley, *The History of Rinaldo Rinaldini, Captain of Banditti*, 3 vols., 1800, Longman and Rees, and Geisweiler. Hinckley, in his Preface, speaks of " The uncommon celebrity, on the Continent, of the work of which the following is a translation; and the numerous and ornamental editions of it, with which Germany is teeming." He adds that these chapters are not " a mere imaginary romance," but in the main an authentic record of fact.

Christian August Vulpius, the author of *Rinaldo Rinaldini*, was born on January 22nd, 1762. In 1797 he obtained a post in the Weimar Library, of which he was to become protobibliothecarius. He died at Weimar, June 25th, 1827. He was the brother-in-law of Goethe, and there is an unavouched tradition that Goethe wrote several chapters in this romance. Be that as it may, Rinaldo begat a numerous enough family, but it must suffice to give some ten titles as a specimen of the rest. In 1799, the very next year after *Rinaldo* was published, Johann Jakob Brückner issued *Dianora, Gräfin von Montagno, Rinaldo Rinaldinis Geliebte*. This lady, it may be observed, plays a very considerable part in the romance of Vulpius. Brückner also wrote *Angelika, Tochter des grossen Banditen Odoardo, Prinzen von Peschia aus den Hause Zanetti*. 1800 saw no less than three romances : a sequel, *Ferrandino, Fortsetzung der Rinaldini*, by Karl Friedrich Hensler ; and two companion-pieces, *Biandetto, der Bandit von Treviso, Seitenstück zu Rinaldo Rinaldini*, by Joseph Alois Gleich, and Theodor Jünger's *Carolo Carolini der Räuberhauptmann, Seitenstück zu Rinaldo Rinaldini*. In 1801, J. F. E. von Albrecht (1752–1816), whose earlier *Lauretta Pisana*, 1789, had dealt sensationally with Italian themes, published Rinaldo up-to-date, *Dolks der bandit, Zeitgenosse Rinaldo Rinaldinis*, whilst in the following year J. E. D. Bornschein (Christian Friedrich Möller) furnished Rinaldo with a female counterpart [66] *Das nord häusische Wundermädchen, ein weiblicher Rinaldino*, just as in England, Charley Wag, the boy thief, had his Fanny White, the young lady burglar.

There were few more prolific purveyors of romance than August Heinrich Kerndöffer (1769–1846), who in 1801–03 published *Lorenzo, der kluge Mann im Walde, oder das Banditenmädchen, ein Seitenstück zu Rinaldo Rinaldini*, and in 1804 *Karl Orsino, Räuber, ein Zeitgenosse Rinaldo Rinaldinis*. Closely imitative of Mrs. Radcliffe is his *Die Ruinen der Geisterburg, oder die warnende Stimme um Mitternacht*, 1805. In 1804 Karl August Buchholtz of Berlin made no small success with *Lutardo, oder der Banditenhauptmann*. A similar work is *Lionardo Montebello, oder der Carbonari-Bund*. Two works of Vulpius should not be omitted : *Fernando Fernandini*, 1799 ; and *Orlando Orlandini, der wunderbare Abenteurer*, 1802, in which the supernatural element looms large, Angels and devils play their part, but Cliens Mariæ nullus in æternum perit. A quarter of a century later writers such as Moritz Richter and H. Schmidt-Lisber found eager readers for their romances, *Nikanor*, *der Alte von Fronteja*; *Fortsetzung der Geschichte des Rinaldini* (1828); and *Corallo, oder die schrecklichen Geheimnisse im Moliser Thale. Ein Seitenstück zu Rinaldo Rinaldini* (1828).

Rinaldo Rinaldini is a well-told story, full of surprise and disguises, of combats with banditti, many of whom are as philosophical as any Robber in Schiller. In one sense the adventures of Rinaldo belong to the picaresque school since he travels from place to place and appears in many a masquerade. The romance opens on a tempestuous night in the Appenines, with a poetical dialogue between Rinaldo and Altaverde. We then have the encounter of Rinaldo with the friendly old anchorite, Donato ; his meeting with the gipsies from whom he purchases Rosalia for three ducats ; his timely punishment in the rôle of Count Dalbrogo of Aurelia's abominable husband, Baron Rovezzo ; his visit to Fossombrone as Marquis Soligno of Savoy ; his sojourn in Naples as Count Mandochini ; a dozen amours, and a hundred crowding incidents. Later Rinaldo takes up his quarters at Messina, and there comes upon the scene the *Old Man* of Fronteia whose " long and ample robe was like that of the Pythagoreans, of sky-blue," and who exhibits to Rinaldo " all the seven degrees of the Krata Repoa," all very much in the style of Lord Lytton, who must (I think) have known these chapters. " The Black Judges in secret " mix themselves up in the course of events, and even when Rinaldo who often has sighed for the opportunity of abandoning his bandit's career withdraws to the little island of Pantallaria to find his long desired repose, and a peaceful retreat among his worthy and honest fellow-creatures ; he is followed by the *Old Man*, who warns him that " his mortal enemy, the black man," has tracked him down, and when Rinaldo is seized by the soldiery an honourable dagger saves him from the ignominy of the scaffold.

Rinaldo Rinaldini is an intensely dramatic romance, and it was immediately seized upon by the playwrights, Karl Friedrich Hensler's *Rinaldo Rinaldini, Der Räuberhauptmann* being produced in 1799. For thirty years and more no melodramas were more popular in the German theatres than those which had Rinaldo as their hero, or which were directly derived from and imitative of his adventures.

Fra Diavolo (1760–1806), the famous bandit of the mountains of Calabria, is, of course, an historical figure, Michele Pazza, a renegade religious, whose romantic adventures were made the subject of Scribe and Auber's charming opera, *Fra Diavolo, ou l'Hôtellerie de Terracine*, produced at the Opéra Comique, Paris,[67] January 28th, 1830, with Chollet as Fra Diavolo. The original of Scribe's story is to be found in Lesueur's opera *La Caverne*, afterwards arranged as a grand spectacle and produced at Paris in 1808 by Cuvellier and Franconi, and again as a spectacular pantomime at Vienna in 1822 as *The Robber of the Abruzzi*. Owing to Auber's tuneful music, to-day Fra Diavolo is certainly the best-known of all stage brigands from Italy.

In England Rinaldo was made the hero of a ballet by John C. Cross, *Rinaldo Rinaldini ; or, The Secret Avengers*, produced at the Royal Circus, S. George's, on Monday, April 6th, 1801, the title being altered on the following Thursday to *Rinaldo Rinaldini ; or, The Black Tribunal*. The music was composed by Reeve. The songs and choruses were printed 8vo, 1801 ; in *Circusiana*,[68] 8vo, 1809 ; and in *The Dramatic Works of J. C. Cross*, 8vo, 1812.

Other plays and melodramas were founded upon the story of Vulpius, of which perhaps the most popular proved to be *Rinaldo Rinaldini ; or The Brigand and the Blacksmith*,[69] a romantic drama in two acts by T. E. Wilks,[70] produced at Sadler's Wells Theatre on January 4th, 1835, with Mrs. Wilkinson as Ermelinde, and A. L. Campbell as Rinaldo, who assumes more disguises in the course of the play than Cleanthes in *The Blind Beggar of Alexandria*, or Skink in that " pleasant Commodie " *Look About You*. It must be confessed that beyond the title, Wilks' *Rinaldo Rinaldini* has little in common with the original romance.

A serious rival to Rinaldo, and perhaps even a more popular figure, both in the pages of fiction and in the theatre, was the bravo Abellino. Zschokke's *Aballino, der grosse Bandit* (1794), when cleverly adapted by Matthew Gregory Lewis as *The Bravo of Venice* in 1804 and published the following year, achieved an immense circulation, and gave rise to a veritable Abellino saga which will be more appropriately studied in detail when dealing with the author of *The Monk*.

It is perhaps hardly necessary to mention at any length the many other German novelists who were translated and imitated in English, but two names at least cannot be suffered to pass altogether unrecorded. The actor and romanticist Christian Heinrich Speiss, who was born on April 4th, 1755, and who died August 17th, 1799, is important on account of his predilection for English sources. Thus his play, *Maria Stuart und Norfolk*, was inspired by Sophia Lee's *The Recess*, and won a considerable success. Further dramas, such as *Clara von Hoheneichen*, well received at Prague, and *Friedrich, der letze Graf von Toggenburg*, are fully in the Gothic tradition. His novels, *Der Alte überall und nirgends*, *Die zwölf schlaufenden Zungfrauen*, *Die Löwenritter*, show the influence of Schiller's *Der Geisterseher*.

In his *Morality of Fiction*,[71] 1805, Hugh Murray mentions " Schiller, Goethe, and Kotzebue " with mild approval, not distinguishing at al between the three names, but, he continues, " the best of the German novelists is La Fontaine, an interesting writer with strong pathetic power." His works " discover, in general, an amiable turn of mind, and seem to be written with very good intentions."

August Heinrich Julius Lafontaine,[72] was born at Brunswick on October 5th, 1758, and died at Halle, April 20th, 1831. Having been admitted a theological student at the University of Helmstedt on February 24th, 1777, he accompanied the Prussian General von Thadden on various campaigns from 1792 until the conclusion of the Treaty of Basel, 1795. He then obtained a Professorship in the Faculty of Philosophy at Halle, where he resided until his death, mainly occupied in the production of novels and romances, for he proved one of the most facile and most voluminous of writers, his works in all (of which a list is given in Keyser's *Index Librorum* and by more than one German bibliographer) exceeding two hundred volumes. " Tout le monde," said Madame de Staël, " a lu ses romans au moins une fois avec plaisir."

Most of his romances—in number 120—were promptly translated into French, and a very large number appeared in English versions or adaptations. It may be remarked that Lafontaine himself often drew from English and French sources, and it cannot escape notice that his favourite " Familiengeschichten " are modelled upon *The Vicar of Wakefield*.

Among the more important earlier English versions may be mentioned *Saint Julien*; or, *Memoirs of a Father*, 1 vol., Bell, 1798; *Saint Julien*, " from the German," 2 vols., Lane, 1799; *The Family of Halden*, 4 vols., 1799; *Rosaura*, 4 vols., Lane, 1800, translated into French by Madame la Comtesse De M[ontolieu] as *Rosaure, ou l'Arrêt du Destin*, 4 vols., Didot, 1818; Hemet's *Odd enough, to be sure!* 2 vols., Lane, 1802; *The Reprobate*, translated by Mary Charlton, 2 vols., Lane, 1802; *The Village Pastor and His Children*, 4 vols., 1803; *Love and Gratitude*, " prepared for the press by Mrs. Parsons," 3 vols., 1804; *Lobenstein Village*, translated by Mrs. Meeke, 4 vols., 1804, from *Der Sonderling*, 1793, which is often considered Lafontaine's best romance, and which was translated into French by Madame de Montolieu as *Le Village de Lobenstein, ou, le nouvel Enfant trouvé*, Genève et Paris, 5 vols., 1802; *Henrietta Bellmann, or, the new Family Picture*, 2 vols., 1804; *Baron De Fleming, the son*; or the *Rage of Systems*, 3 vols., 1804, being a version of *Quinctius Heymeran von Fleming*, 1795–96; *Dolgorucki and Menzikoff*, 2 vols., 1805, translated from *Fedor und Marie*, 1803; *Rodolphus of Werdenberg*, 2 vols., 1805; *Hermann and Emilia*, 4 vols., Lane, 1805, highly praised in September of that year by the *Literary*

Journal, which described Hermann as " a virtuous enthusiast, possessing all that romantic feeling and eccentricity which Fontaine delights to give to his characters " ; *Edward and Annette,* a moral tale, 1 vol., 12mo, 1807 ; *Family Quarrels,* 3 vols., Dean, 1811 ; Mrs. Green's *Raphael, or, Peaceful Life,* 2 vols., Taylor, 1812 ; and *Age and Youth ; or, The Families of Abenstedt,* 4 vols., 1813.

Yet not even Lafontaine always pleased, and the reviewers, some of whom may for a while have refrained from overtly attacking his novels, gradually but surely felt their way by their censure of feeble translations, thus in one sense bringing down two birds with one stone. So the *Monthly Review* [73] pretty sharply snibs " *Romulus, a Tale of ancient Times.* Translated from the German of August La Fontaine by the Rev. P. Will, Minister of the German Congregation in the Savoy," 2 vols., 1801, in the following terms : " Scarcely a page occurs without an instance of violated grammar, or mistaken idiom : of the substitution of one word for another, or of the introduction of words hitherto unknown in any English vocabulary."

It is worth remark that of the seven famous " horrid " Northanger Novels, two are direct translations from the German ; two are severally distinguished as " A German Story " ; one is " A German Tale " ; a sixth, by Eleanor Sleath is entitled *The Orphan of the Rhine,* and if one may venture to judge by her detail she was personally acquainted with Salzburg and the vicinity.[74]

The German vogue is alluded to by *The Critical Review,* [75] June, 1807, when noticing *Francis and Josepha, A Tale from the German of Huber by William Fardeley,* 1807. " So great is the rage for German tales, and German novels, that a cargo is no sooner imported than the booksellers' shops are filled with a multitude of translators, who seize with avidity and without discrimination, whatever they can lay their hands upon. William Fardeley, amongst other *helluones,* appears by his own confession to have possessed himself of a considerable quantity of trash of this kind, with the translation of which he intends to favour the public, should he be so fortunate as to please their palate with ' Francis and Josepha.' That the public may not be induced to squander their money upon such worthless objects, . . . we inform them that ' Francis and Josepha ' is the most uninteresting tale that ever came from Germany." This fierce attack seems effectually to have quenched Mr. Fardeley's fire, for we do not find that he again entered the field of romance.

There had, of course, already been a good deal of satire on the influence of German romances and sentiment in England, especially in the theatre, a province which we have been unable to touch upon here, but which is none the less of prime importance as exhibiting dramas of unbounded popularity, that gave the Kembles and Mrs. Siddons such vast scope for their extraordinary genius. It were almost superfluous to name Benjamin Thompson's *The Stranger* (*Menschenhass und Reue*) with Mrs. Siddons as Mrs. Haller and Sheridan's *Pizarro* with Kemble as Rolla, both from Kotzebue. There were, furthermore, the plays of poignant sentimentality, *Lovers' Vows*, adapted by Mrs. Inchbald at second hand from Kotzebue's *Das Kind der Liebe* ; as well as sensational dramas, James Boaden's *The Secret Tribunal*, which, as he acknowledges in the printed copy, 8vo, 1795, is founded upon *Herman of Unna*, and Act V of which exhibits " *a spacious Crypt, or vaulted Court of Justice, under ground, of Gothic Architecture* " with the Vehmgericht in full session, surrounded by mysterious phenomena, such as " *a luminous Cross of a deep Red*," and " *an Eye, radiated with points of Fire.*"

The Anti-Jacobin Review, or Weekly Examiner, was foremost in its indictment of those German influences it stigmatized as revolutionary and licentious, and in its pages, Nos. 30 and 31, 1798, appeared Canning's immortal burlesque, *The Rovers* ; *or, The Double Disappointment*, " A Drama, Written in imitation of the German drama."

Yet in 1811 Stephen Jones could write : " As a burlesque, *The Rovers of Weimar* was amusing : for it fastened on the most tangible absurdities of the German drama, and fastened on them laughably ; but the laugh was at a 'thing of other days' : the German drama is past and gone,—it is beyond the reach of ridicule—its absurdities cannot be revived,—and they cannot now furnish matter for even the slight ridicule of a passing burlesque." [76] Colman, too, jeered the German vogue in his mock-prologue to *The Quadrupeds of Quedlinburgh*, produced at the Haymarket, on July 26th, 1811 :

> To lull the soul by spurious strokes of art,
> To warp the genius, and mislead the heart ;
> To make mankind revere wives gone astray,—(*The Stranger*)
> Love pious sons who rob on the highway ;—(*Lovers' Vows*)
> For this the FOREIGN MUSES trod our stage,
> Commanding *German schools* to be *the rage*.

Both Jones and Colman, however, as is sometimes the wont of satirists, exaggerate, and although they might deal " soft super-Sentiment " some pretty hard knocks, German drama and romance were still influencing not a few of our great writers. Thus on November 29th, 1811, Henry Crabb Robinson was writing to Mrs. Clarkson " that Coleridge's mind is much more German than English," [77] and in 1817 Thomas Love Peacock could burlesque Shelley's Germanising tendencies as Scythrop in *Nightmare Abbey*.

In 1814 [78] Scott had written in the first chapter of *Waverley*, " had my title borne, ' Waverley, a Romance .rom the German,' what head so obtuse as not to image forth a profligate abbot, an oppressive duke, a secret and mysterious association of Rosycrucians and Illuminati, with all their properties of black cowls, caverns, daggers, electrical machines, trap-doors, and dark-lanterns ? "

It must be always borne in mind that however great a part the several influences of France and of Germany played in the development of the English novel, England in turn was all the while giving these two countries as many and as valuable treasures of romance as ever we derived and made our own. Scott, Mrs. Radcliffe, Matthew Gregory Lewis, Maturin, proved inexhaustible wells from which the novelists of France and Germany drew and drew, and came to draw yet once again, for the charities of Literature are obligatory, and certes, as the wise Sir Thomas Browne has it, " to be reserved and caitiff in this part of goodness is the sordidest piece of covetousness."

NOTES TO CHAPTER III

1. *Iconoclastes*, Prose Works, 1806, Vol. II, p. 408.
2. There is a delightful and most scholarly essay on *Pharamond* by Sir Edmund Gosse, *Gossip in a Library*, 1891, pp. 81–91.
3. I am, of course, here only able to mention the heroic romances by name. For a full treatment and consideration of their influence on English literature see *Dryden, The Dramatic Works*, edited by Montague Summers, Vol. I (1931), Introduction, pp. xl-lii, where I remark : " there are essential qualities which link the heroic tragedies with the romances of Ann Radcliffe."
4. Since *La Princesse de Clèves* appeared under the name of Segrais.
5. Mons. J. J. Jusserand, *The English Novel in the Time of Shakespeare*, English translation, 1908, p. 397, is surely mistaken when he says, " oblivion soon gathered round the ' Princess of Cleve,' and the only proof we have that it did not pass unnoticed is a clumsy play by Lee." *The Princess of Cleve* was frequently reprinted in English, was widely read and admired, and is included in several Collections of Novels. Mons. Jusserand does not notice that both *Zayde* and *La Princesse de Clève* were translated early, and the year 1688 which he quotes, is that of second editions. Moreover, Lee's play, *The Princess of Cleve*, although not printed until 1689, was actually produced in 1681.
6. For example, Bremond's *Le Pelerin*, 1670, as *The Pilgrim*, 2 vols., 12mo, 1680–81, and 8vo editions, 1684 and 1700. (For Bremond, see *Dryden, The Dramatic Works*, ed. Montague Summers, Vol. V, 1932, pp. 109–11.) Also the same author's *L'Heureux Esclave*, 1672, as *The Happy Slave*, 12mo, 1676, and several editions, as also the French, published in London ; *Le Galand Escroc*, 1672, as *The Cheating Gallant*, " a pleasant Novel," 1677. Even Bremond's satirical *roman à clef*, *Hattigè, ou Les Amours du Roy de Tamaran* (which hardly veils Charles II and the Duchess of Cleveland), Cologne, 1676, was translated into English, Amsterdam, 12mo., 1680. Mlle. de Brillac's *Agnès de Castro, nouvelle portugaise*, 1688, was adapted by Mrs. Behn as *The History of Agnes de Castro*, 1688. See *The Works of Aphra Behn*, edited by Montague Summers, 1915, Vol. V, p. 211.
7. Not acted. Printed, in *Oeuvres Meslees* De Mr. De Saint-Evremond, . . . A Londres Chez Jacob Tonson. M . DCC . IX (Second edition), 3 tomes. Tome I, pp. 251–348.

8. *Letters of Horace Walpole*, edited by Mrs. Paget Toynbee, Vol. IX (1904), p. 127.

9. There had been, of course, many accounts of English tours by French travellers; for example, le sieur Coulon's *Le fidèle Conducteur pour le Voyage d'Angleterre*, Paris, 1654; Samuel de Sorbière, *Relation d'un Voyage en Angleterre*, Paris, 1664; Balthasar de Monconys, *Journal des Voyages de M. de Monconys*, Lyons, 1665-66; Maximilian Misson's *Mémoires et Observations faites par un Voyageur en Angleterre*, La Haye, 1698; James Beeverel's *Les Délices de la Grande-Bretagne et de l'Irelande*, Leide, 1707; Béat Louis de Muralt's *Lettres sur les Anglois et les François et sur les Voiages*, 1725; and many more.

10. Mons. Henry Harrisse, *L'Abbé Prévost, Histoire de sa Vie et de ses Oeuvres*, Paris, 1896, and *La Vie Monastique de l'Abbé Prévost*, 1720-63, Paris, 1903, argues unreservedly and very cleverly in favour of Prévost's innocence, but it is difficult in the face of the evidence to accept his conclusions.

11. The terrible story that Prévost, being struck down by an apoplectic fit, was thought dead, and was really killed by a surgeon conducting the post-mortem examination, is first heard of in print, 1782, and appears to be entirely unfounded. Prévost died suddenly of the rupture of an aneurism of the aorta.

12. *Tout Pour L'Amour, ou, Le Monde Bien Perdu*; tragédie. Traduite de l'Anglois par l'Auteur des Mémoires d'un Homme de Qualité. Paris. 12mo. 1735.

13. Marivaux, *Les Fausses Confidences* (1737), I, 3.

14. *Le Genre romanesque en France*, 1922, p. 361.

15. From which, as has not previously been noticed, Colman took an important scene for *The Jealous Wife*, produced at Drury Lane, February 26th, 1761; 8vo, 1761.

16. *The Drama of Sensibility*, 1915. Mr. Bernbaum speaks (p. 218) of *The Jealous Wife* " being almost entirely free from sentimental contamination," which seems to me a curious point of view for any writer on the subject.

17. *Op. cit.*, Chapter IV.

18. The Italian translation of *Pamela* had been published by Guiseppe Bettinelli, Venice, 1744-45.

19. A. G. Spinelli, *Bibliografia goldoniana*, Milano, 1884, p. 23. *Pamela nubile* was first published in Vol. V of the *Opere*, 9 vols., Bettinelli, Venice, 1753.

20. See Giambattista Pasquali's edition of *Goldoni*, 1761-77, Vol. II, p. 10.

21. *Memorie di Carlo Goldoni*, ed. Guido Mazzoni, 2 vols., Firenze, 1907, Vol. II, p. 109. The first edition of *Pamela Maritata* is in Pasquali, Vol. I, 1761, p. 233. *La Buona Figliuola Maritata* from *Pamela Maritata*, was given at the Formigliari Theatre, Bologna, in May, 1761. Goldoni's *Pamela Nubile* was translated into English (with the Italian on facing page), London, 8vo, 1756.

22. *Marianne*, 2e partie, tome VI, p. 68 : éd. Duviquet. *Oeuvres complètes*, 1825.

23. *Marianne*, 1re partie, tome VI, p. 38.

24. The *Night Thoughts* were translated into German, Spanish, Italian, Portuguese, Swedish, Magyar, and other languages. Klopstock was enthusiastic and ranked Young as the sublimest of poets.

25. It is inevitable, but it almost seems an offence to the genius of Young to quote the delicate sarcasm of *Northanger Abbey*, Vol. I, chapter xiv : " three duodecimo volumes, two hundred and seventy-six pages in each, with a frontispiece to the first, of two tomb-stones and a lantern."

26. Compare the French efforts at English names, which were sad stumbling-blocks, such as the older travellers attempted : Ouïtal, Eyparc, Linkensin-Fils, le Strangh, Biscopgetstrut.

27. Of whom there is a separate study by D. Inklaar, 1925.

28. English translation, *Memoirs of the Count Comminge*, 1773. Cf. *Lusignan, or The Abbaye of La Trappe*, A Novel, 4 vols., Lane, 1801.

29. In *The Tears of Sensibility*, 1777, to which reference has already been made among the novels read by Miss Languish, John Murdoch translates four stories from D'Arnaud : *The Cruel Father (Anne Bell)*; *The Rival Friends (Adelson et Salvini)*; *Rosetta, or the Fair Penitent rewarded (Clary)*; and *Sidney and Salli (Sidney et Volsan)*.

30. Mrs. Shelley's *Perkin Warbeck* was published 1830.

31. Mr. George Saintsbury, *A History of the French Novel*, 1917, p. 460, has the following reference : " Indeed that *Minnigrey*, which I remember reading as a boy, and which long afterwards my friend, the late Mr. Henley, used to extol as one of the masterpieces of literature, is worth all Pigault put together and a great deal more." *Minnigrey*, an admirable romance, commenced in *The London Journal* for the week ending October 11th, 1851, and achieved an immense success. It is the work of John Frederick Smith (1804-90), who wrote a very large number of similar novels. His first novel was *The Jesuit*, 3 vols., Saunders and Otley, 1832 ; but his first elaborate serial—and his serials won him wealth and fame—was *Stanfield Hall*, an extremely long historical romance in Three Series, which commenced in *The London Journal*, of which paper he was for many years the mainstay, in the number for the week ending May 19th, 1849. *Amy Lawrence, or, The Freemason's Daughter*, a tale of contemporary life, commenced in *The London Journal* for the week ending January 25th, 1851. In October, 1852, followed *The Will and the Way*, pirated in America as *Henry Ashton ; or, The Will and the Way*. At the same time Smith supplied *The London Journal* with some highly melodramatic *Lives of the Queens of England*. *Woman and Her Master* commenced in No. 445, for the week ending September 3rd, 1853, and concluded, Chapter CLV, in No. 498, for the week ending September 9th, 1854, in which number began *Temptation*. For a time J. F. Smith joined Cassell's *Illustrated Family Paper*, but in 1865 he returned to the *London Journal*. Others of his romances are *Rochester, or, The Merry Days of Merry England*, an important fiction unknown to Herr Prinz, who in *John Wilmot, Earl of Rochester*, 1927, mentions minor work, such as Anthony Hope's *Simon Dale* (1898) and James Blyth's *The King's Guerdon* (1906). *Prince Charles, or, The Young Pretender* is another of Smith's historical romances. However we may criticize Smith's work from one point of view, he had the art of telling a good tale, and he assuredly carried his readers with him, for it is curious to reflect that in his day he could boast a far larger public than even Charles Dickens, and he was a serious rival to G. W. M. Reynolds himself.

32. One should, perhaps, in a note except the universal Faust.

33. *Bibliothek du Robinson*, Berlin, 1805-6, pt. 5.

34. C. F. Gellert, 1715-69.

35. The first version from the German text was1786 ; another translation was publishd three years later. New editions of the 1779 version were issued at intervals up to 1795. Carré lists eighteen British editions of various new translations between 1790 and 1830. See J. M. Carré, *Goethe en Angleterre*, Paris, 1920 ; also his *Bibliographie de Goethe en Angleterre*. In the " Modern Language Review," Vol. XVI, July-October, 1921, there is a *Review of Carré's Goethe en Angleterre*, by A. E. Turner, who makes some additions.

36. Mary Collyer, *née* Mitchell, died in 1763.

37. Second edition, 1809, p. 25, note.

38. See Friedrich Althaus, *Beiträge zur Geschichte der deutschen Colonie in England*. *Unsere Zeit*, N.F., 9. Jahrgang, Erste Hälfte, Leipzig, 1873. Also K. H. Schaible, *Geschichte der Deutschen in England*. Strassburg, 1885.

39. For example, *The Monthly Review*, August, 1795, Vol. XVII, pp. 462-3, in noticing *The Victim of Magical Delusion*, and again, March, 1801, Vol. XXXIV, p. 321, in noticing *Romulus* ; both translated by P. Will.

40. *Essay on Imitations of the Ancient Ballad.*

41. Although it is hardly credible that Scott " very sedulously set to work and translated right through Goethe, Schiller, Bürger, and several of the romances of Speiss." R. P. Gillies, *Recollections of Sir Walter Scott*, in *Fraser's Magazine*, September, 1835, and in book form with some alterations, 1837.

42. *Letters of S. T. Coleridge*. Ed. by E. H. Coleridge. 2 vols. London, 1895. Vol. I, pp. 96-97. Coleridge in later years, it is true, modified his impressions.

43. *Journal. Works of Byron, Letters and Journals*, ed. R. E. Prothero, 2nd impression, 1903, Vol. II, p. 388.

44. J. A. Robberds, *Memoir of the Life and Writings of the late William Taylor of Norwich*. 2 vols. London, 1843. Vol. I, p. 30.

45. It is true that J. T. Stanley's translation was issued in an *édition de luxe* at 5s., as well as the ordinary edition, 2s. 6d.

46. Two vols., London, 1817. Vol. II, p. 258.

47. *The Critical Review*, Vol. XIV, 1795, pp. 68–79, has a long review of " this singular and interesting novel."

48. *The Works of Lord Byron : Letters and Journals*, ed. by R. E. Prothero, 1904, Vol. IV, pp. 92–93.

49. Vol. XVII, pp. 462–3.

50. Réné Aubert d'Aubeuf, Sieur de Vertot, 1655–1735, a Premonstratensian. His *Histoire de la conjuration de Portugal*, first published in 1689, was afterwards expanded as *Histoire des Revolutions de Portugal*, and ran through many editions. There are several English translations, one version being published as late as 1809.

51. Herr Jakob Brauchli in his study *Der englische Schauerroman um* 1800, 1928, p. 106, whilst drawing attention to my error of twenty years ago, which he seems unaware I had since corrected, himself blunders over the names, as he consistently speaks of Peter Leuthold. He has, moreover, nothing to tell us about Kahlert. Although Herr Brauchli's book has several good points—his account of F. P. Lathy's *The Invisible Enemy, or the Mines of Wielitska* as the typical Gothic novel is quite well done—his pages are so full of mistakes and misinformation that their value must be heavily discounted. His section " Schauerroman-Autoren," three pages, is inadequate, and when he comes to deal with Ghosts and Witchcraft in the Gothic romance he proves altogether at sea. His " Lists " are not merely incomplete but muddled in their arrangement. At first they may look imposing, but there is overmuch otiose repetition of titles, and to catalogue such works as Mrs. Trollope's *Father Eustace*, 1846, or Miss Mulock's *Romantic Tales*, 1859, and a reprint of Rowe's tragedy, *The Fair Penitent*, as Gothic novels, is not a little absurd. Of such an important figure as Charlotte Dacre Herr Brauchli knows nothing, and he further ignores the recent work of scholars upon the period he essays to survey. Moreover, he is apt to cite as authorities works long since discarded and recognized as valueless, *e.g.* on p. 191, n. 3, he describes a volume which is notoriously unscholarly and eccentric as " Ein äussert vielseitiges und aufschlussreiches Buch."

52. Vol. XVI, pp. 465–6.

53. *The Victim of Magical Delusion*, Vol. III, " The Translator's Address To His Thinking Readers," Appendix, p. (i).

54. *The Monthly Review*, November, 1794.

55. Vol. IV, pp. 170–71.

56. *The Letters of Horace Walpole*, ed. by Mrs. Paget Toynbee, Oxford, 1904, Vol. X, pp. 216–17.

57. *Ibid.*, p. 302.

58. This " Romance of Former Times " was published as by T. J. Horsley.

59. *Monthly Review*, October, 1795, Vol. XVIII, pp. 223–4.

60. *Ibid*, p. 229.

61. *The Monthly Review*, Oct., 1795, Vol. XVIII, p. 229.

62. Maturin, whose pseudonym for *The Family of Montorio*, 3 vols., Longman, 1807, was Dennis Jasper Murphy.

63. Perhaps the scientific or semi-scientific explanation such as occurs in the novels of Charles Brockden Brown should be mentioned in a note. It is, of course, really the " Explained Supernatural." Thus *Wieland, or Transformation* (1798) turns on ventriloquism ; *Edgar Huntly* (1799), in the preface to which Brown speaks slightingly of " puerile superstitions and exploded manners, Gothic castles and chimeras," deals with somnambulism, which involves the sleep-walker in terrible catastrophes ; the hero of *Ormond* (1799) belongs to a secret society.

64. Chapters XX and XXI. See further the chapter upon M. G. Lewis.

65. There is a useful if rather slight monograph, *Die Ritter—und Räuberromane*, by Carl Müller-Fraureuth, Halle, 1894.

66. An Amazon, Florella, is attached to Rinaldo's band.

67. In English, adapted by Rophino Lacy at Drury Lane, London, November 3rd, 1831 ; in Italian, with some revision, by the Royal Italian Opera, at the Lyceum Theatre, London, July 9th, 1857. Sims Reeves appeared at the Haymarket in an English version, 1855. There are, further, at least four popular English burlesques.

68. *Circusiana :* A Collection of the most favourite Ballets, Spectacles, Melo-Dramas, &c., performed at the Royal Circus, St. George's Fields. 2 vols., 8vo. 1809.

69. Lacy, 1743 : Vol. 117.

70. The author of many lurid melodramas which achieved great success, such as *The Red Crow* ; *The Castle Cauldron* ; *The Raven's Nest* ; *The Demon Ship* ; *The Midnight Spell.*

71. *Morality of Fiction,* pp. 121–22.

72. See T. G. Gruber, *August Lafontaine's Leben und Werke,* Halle, 1833.

73. March, 1801, Vol. XXXIV, p. 321. Alexandre Dumas, having read a French translation of *Romulus,* wrote a comedy in one act, *Romulus,* which was produced at the Théâtre Français on January 13th, 1854.

74. Vol. XI, No. 2, p. 213.

75. As there will be occasion to note later, especially in connexion with Mrs. Radcliffe, the romantic novelists often and very adroitly made use of books of travel and local description, but—although one cannot, of course, speak with certainty—if internal evidence goes for anything, Eleanor Sleath had herself visited the districts of which she writes in *The Orphan of the Rhine.*

76. *Biographia Dramatica,* 1812, Vol. III, p. 466.

77. Henry Crabb Robinson, *Diary,* 3 vols., ed. by Thomas Sadler, 1869 (3rd ed., 2 vols., 1872), Vol. I, p. 352.

78. Scott had begun *Waverley* in 1805, and it is possible this sentence was written as early as that year.

CHAPTER IV

HISTORICAL GOTHIC

Dear, wild illusions of creative mind !
Whose varying hues arise to Fancy's art,
And by her magic force are swift combin'd
In forms that please, and scenes that touch the heart :
Oh ! whether at her voice ye soft assume
The pensive grace of Sorrow drooping low ;
Or rise sublime, on Terror's lofty plume,
And shake the soul with wildly thrilling woe ;
Or, sweetly bright, your gayer tints ye spread,
Bid scenes of pleasure steal upon my view,
Love wave his purple pinions o'er my head,
And wake the tender thought to passion true ;
O ! still—ye shadowy forms attend my lonely hours,
Still chase my real cares with your illusive powers !
ANN RADCLIFFE, *To the Visions of Fancy.*

Visions, you know, have always been my pasture ; and so far from growing old enough to quarrel with their emptiness, I almost think there is no wisdom comparable to that of exchanging what is called the realities of life for dreams. Old castles, old pictures, old histories, and the babble of old people, make one live back into centuries, that cannot disappoint one. One holds fast and surely what is past. The dead have exhausted their power of deceiving—one can trust Catherine of Medicis now.
HORACE WALPOLE to GEORGE MONTAGU (Paris, January 5th, 1766).

HOWEVER interesting, and actually indeed instructive, it were to consider the work of such writers as Mrs. Behn, Mrs. Manley, Mrs. Aubin, and Mrs. Eliza Haywood—and this latter lady, it may be remembered, published her earliest fiction, *Love in Excess*, in 1720, and her last, *The Invisible Spy*,[1] in 1755, not a decade before *Otranto*— if we are to form some idea of what we may term the mean or median novel of the first half of the eighteenth century, we shall not perhaps be ill-advised to turn to such a repertory as Samuel Croxall provided for the entertainment of his readers, and inquire what pieces we find among *A Select Collection of Novels and Histories*, issued by John Watts in six volumes, 1729. To pass in review the contents of the whole half-a-dozen were supererogatory, and we will quasi at random choose but one of these pleasant duodecimos with their attractive Van Der Gucht engravings, taking for our purpose Volume the Fourth, The Table lists : *The Happy Slave* ; *The Rival Ladies* ; *The Loves of King Henry II, and Fair* Rosamond : *The Innocent Adultery*; *The History of the Conspiracy of the* Spaniards *against the Republick of* Venice.

153

Individually, considering these five Novels and Histories, we recognize that *The Happy Slave*, " In Three Parts. Translated from the *French* Original," is a version of *L'Heureux Esclave* by Gabriel de Bremond,[2] of whom little is known save that he was living in Holland towards the end of the seventeenth century ; that his contemporaries regarded him as a " Great Wit " ; that he wrote a number of *romans à clef*, amorous and political ; and after some trouble at The Hague he obtained his liberty with the Peace of Ryswick, whereupon he travelled in the Levant, and vanishes from sight. *The Happy Slave*, Part I, first appeared in English in 1676, translated from the French, " By a Person of Quality," Magnes and Bentley, 12mo, 1*s*. The Second and Third Parts appeared in the following year. This novel proved extremely popular.

The Rival Ladies is " Translated from the *Spanish* Original of *Miguel de Cervantes Saavedra*," that is to say, from *Las Dos Doncellas*[3] in the *Novelas Ejemplares*.

The Innocent Adultery is " Translated from the *French* Original of Monsieur Scarron," that is to say, from *L'Innocent Adultère* in the *Nouvelles Tragicomiques*. These had been turned into English by John Davies of Kidwelly, *Scarron's Novels*, 8vo, 1682, in which collection *The Innocent Adultery* is duly included. It may have been (and indeed so much is hinted at) that the name proved irresistibly piquant, and certainly the tale is well told, for this novel at once became and long remained a prime favourite. When Bellmour *in Fanatick Habit* went a-wooing the frail Laetitia he carried " trusty *Scarron's* Novels " as his prayer-book, and 'twas all owing to the little volume indiscreetly opening at *The Innocent Adultery*—" the Devil's *Pater-Noster* "—that the Apocryphal Elder was discovered. Three-quarters of a century and more later, in 1775, Lydia Languish was reading the story,[4] which upon the advent of Mrs. Malaprop and Sir Anthony Absolute had to be thrust into *The Whole Duty of Man*.

There remain in the Fourth Volume of Croxall's Collection two " Histories," *The Loves of King Henry II and Fair Rosamond*, and the *History of the Conspiracy of the Spaniards against the Republick of Venice in the Year MDCXVIII*. This latter is " Translated [and abridged] from the *French* Original of the Abbot de St. Real." The Abbé César de Saint-Réal[5] published his *Conjuration des Espagnols contre la République de Venise en l'année MDCXVIII*, 12mo, 1674 (licensed December 21st, 1673). It was first translated into English, *A Conspiracie of the Spaniards against the state of Venice*, 8vo, 1675 ; and second edition, 1679. In England it was deservedly famous and popular as having been extensively used by Otway for his tragic masterpiece, *Venice Preserv'd* ; *or*,

A Plot Discover'd,[6] which, originally produced at the Duke's Theatre, Dorset Garden, on February 9th, 1682, kept the stage until 1845, and was revived[7] in 1876, 1904, and 1920.

The Loves of King Henry II and Fair Rosamond is a story which, however legendary in detail, is in feeling essentially true, and one moreover which has never lost its charm for English readers, of wit or lewd, of high or low degree. Indeed, the romance is played in a most enchanting setting, the Rose of the World blooming in the Woodstock Bower, and then (as we may well hope and believe) filling with even sweeter fragrance the holy shades of Godstow Nunnery. As a rough chap-book [8] the tale was spelled over a thousand cottage fires. As a play, *Henry the Second, King of England, With the Death of Rosamond*,[9] produced at Drury Lane in September, 1692, with Betterton as Henry II; Mrs. Barry, Queen Eleanor; and Mrs. Bracegirdle, Rosamond; " gave such universal satisfaction," to use Motteux' phrase,[10] that it was many times repeated with great applause. " It is a Tragedy, with a mixture of Comedy, and represents chiefly that part of *Henry* the Second's Life that relates to the famous *Rosamond*."

Addison's trashy opera "after the *Italian* manner," *Rosamond*, produced at Drury Lane in March, 1707, in spite of Clayton's music, met with the contempt such doggerel amply deserved.

Tennyson's fine drama *Becket*, arranged for representation, was produced at the Lyceum Theatre on February 6th, 1893, when Ellen Terry played Rosamond de Clifford; with Genevieve Ward, Queen Eleanor; William Terriss, Henry II; and Henry Irving in the title-rôle, S. Thomas.

As it appears in Croxall's Collection, *The Loves of King Henry II and Fair Rosamond* has many significant features. In the first place, we commence historically—so to speak—and rather dryly before getting to work, that is to say, before concentrating upon " the Conversation of the Ladies," so that the "Court was daily crowded with the fair Sex," all eager " to be singled out for Discourse with the King : And if the Dialogue led to Address and Assignation, there were never wanting Some, in that gay Assembly, who were willing to comply with their Prince's Inclination." " We do not hear that *Rosamond* ever made her Appearance in that wanton Circle." However, "it happen'd a rapturous Courtier struck into an *Encomium* of the Lord *Clifford's* Daughter," and albeit " this young *Inamorato's* Eloquence " fell short of the lady's beauty, 'twas enough to make the King betray " all the Symptoms of a desiring and impatient Lover." Events follow their course, related in this delightfully mannered eighteenth century prose. Henry visits my Lord Clifford's house, and becomes exceedingly amorous and fond. Alethea, an attendant "in the Nature of a

Governante " is suborned by the royal gallant, and one fine day (although Lord Clifford had packed off his daughter to a relation in Cornwall) whilst Rosamond "and her *Governante* were walking in a lonely Grove, a Chariot with a strong Retinue was seen in the neighbouring Road," and off they hie to Court. When the French Wars break out Henry takes leave of Rosamond in a scene of down-cast eyes and gushing tears which were too sentimental almost for Richardson. "There was a speaking Eloquence in the Silence of her Grief : Each Look, each Sigh, each Tear had language in Them." The Bower at Woodstock is described in a romantic, not to say Gothic, strain, and quite the most is made of the climax where Eleanor confronts the trembling fair. The death of the heroine from the poisoned cup is another great opportunity for the writer, who ends up with a little ballast from history, quoting Ranulph Higden and Holingshed, but by no means accepting the accounts which tell us that Rosamond took the veil at Godstow since these would obviously be far less to the readers' taste than the romance of her death at the hands of an injured wife.

This little novel is typical of half a hundred more. A royal intrigue ; a whiff of history ; a good deal of sentimentality, some speechifying, a tragic catastrophe. These ingredients were immensely popular, and we meet them dressed with a different sauce again and again. It were tedious to catalogue more than a few titles : *The Annals of Love ; containing twenty-one select Histories of the Amours of divers Princes' Courts*,[11] 1672 ; *The Amours of Count de Dunois*, 1676 ; *The Prince of Condé*, 1676 ; *Asteria and Tamberlain, or, The Distressed Lovers*, 1677 ; *The Novels of Queen Elizabeth, Queen of England, containing the History of Queen Ann of Bullen*, 1680 ; *The Countess of Salisbury, or The most noble Order of the Garter, An Historical Novel*, 1682 ; *The Amours of Count Teckeli and the Lady Serini*, 1686 ; Mrs. Behn's *The History of Agnes de Castro*,[12] 1688 ; *The Secret History of the Duke of Alanson and Queen Elizabeth. A true History*, 1691 ; *The Amours of Edward the IV. An Historical Novel*,[13] 1700.

Since the last of these appeared at the dawn of the eighteenth century we may give it our briefest attention. It is a duodecimo of 120 pages. The Preface points out that " *The* Theme *is the most diverting and delightful that our* English Histories *afford*," since "Edward IV. *was certainly a Prince of a most Gallant and Amorous Disposition ; and his* Court *was undoubtedly the Scene of* Love *and* Intrigue." In this little novel " *what is very uncommon in things of this Nature, you have true* History *adorn'd with the Greatest Lustre that Language and Art can add : And where* Intrigue *is introduc'd, it is with so much neatness and exactness that it neither interferes with, nor offers the least Injury to Truth.*"

The novel begins rather curiously. Queen Elizabeth, the widow of Edward IV, who is in sanctuary at Westminster, relates her Adventures—" those that are remarkable, such I reckon as have happen'd to me since the Death of my First *Lord* "—to her daughter, the Lady Elizabeth. As Lady Elizabeth Gray, the Queen was in attendance upon Queen Margaret of Anjou, who one night " treated all the Court with a Comedy, in the great Hall of *Westminster* ; after which a Ball was danced," and the Earl of Warwick makes violent love to Lady Gray. Later, however, she attracts Edward of York, and they exchange quasi-sentimental letters which lead up to a love scene. " The King's Mother, the Old Dutchess of *York*, had her Spyes in every Place," and endeavours to break the match, but when she remonstrates the King " infinitely displeas'd her, by turning the Business into Banter, which he knew how to do better than any (that pleasant sort of Wit being, more than to any, Natural to him)." Thereupon the Duchess brings forward " Lady *Lucy*, whom the King had not long before ruin'd," to swear a pre-contract, but this fails, as the lady refuses to take such an oath, her purpose being to " retire her self into a Monastry." Accordingly Elizabeth marries Edward. No sooner does Warwick, who was in France, hear of these nuptials than " He was infinitely concern'd." He " had all things ready for a Commotion before," and now openly opposes Edward, winning to his side the Duke of Clarence. Having gained the ascendancy, the ambitious Earl contrives an interview with the disconsolate Queen and long speeches are delivered in the best heroic style. Warwick, however, falls in battle, and the remaining incidents must be very quickly dispatched. The Queen praises the Earl of Richmond to the Princess, and prophesies that he will be successful in his suit, and that there will be " an everlasting Union betwixt the Two Houses " of York and Lancaster. " At these words the Lady *Elizabeth* chang'd Colours, and shiver'd like a true Lover." The final ten or twelve pages of the narrative are huddled abruptly to a conclusion, breaking off with the separation of the young Duke of York from the Queen. Not the smallest use is made of the opportunity either for pathos or drama. The Cardinal, who is come to demand the Prince's person, and the Queen exchange three or four set lifeless speeches and there the matter ends.

As we have seen, the Historical Novel—of a kind—flourished from the reign of Charles II until the beginning of the eighteenth century. Probably the best of these—certainly the best of any sustained length [14]—is *English Adventures. By a Person of Honour*, that is to say, Roger Boyle, Earl of Orrery, [15] published 8vo, 1676, and containing 129 pages. The work is in three parts. Henry VIII is supposed to be travelling *incognito* among his subjects, something very like a Western Haroun al-Raschid, with Charles Brandon, Duke of Suffolk, as his companion. Inevitably they meet with many striking experiences, which give rise to the relation of various narratives. Amongst others the Duke tells *The History of Brandon,* which falls in the First Part, and this is important as containing the incestuous motive which is the theme of Otway's *The Orphan.* Actually *English Adventures* is a romance which, interesting in itself and well written, has no relation whatsoever to history.

The first work in English which can fairly claim to be a Historical Novel is *Longsword, Earl of Salisbury,* " An Historical Romance," 2 vols., 1762, published anonymously, but written by Thomas Leland (1722–85), a Fellow of Trinity College, Dublin. Leland, inasmuch as he was both a classical scholar and an erudite historian, proved particularly well equipped to undertake such a romance, and in his work we have for the first time accuracy of detail, consistence, and a real atmosphere of chronicled antiquity, even if we allow that the archæological details are in some instances perhaps more romantic than exact. Yet in his Advertisement Leland deprecates the severity of the learned and critical, who may take umbrage at the liberties he has allowed himself, and he emphasizes that " The out-lines of the following story, and some of the incidents and more minute circumstances, are to be found in the antient English historians."

The period is of the reign of Henry III, at the time when Hubert de Burgh " had an entire ascendant over Henry, and was loaded with honours and favours beyond any other subject "—as Hume expresses it,[16] and the Novel ends with a mention of the disgrace of this Minister, which happened in 1231.

The hero, however, is William De Longespée (Lungespée), third Earl of Salisbury, the son of Henry II by an unknown mother, whom tradition, justly followed by Leland, names as Fair Rosamond. William De Longespée had joined the Dauphin Louis in 1216, but the following year he returned to the English allegiance, and until his death in 1226 he faithfully served his nephew, Henry III.

Leland has made one character of the third Earl of Salisbury and his son William De Longespée, who was born *c.* 1212 ; knighted in 1233 ; accompanied Earl Richard of Cornwall to the crusades in 1240, and Henry III to Gascony in 1242 ; who again went to the Crusades in 1247, and was killed at the battle near Mansourah in 1250.

Longsword, Earl of Salisbury, commences with some account of 'Sir Randolph, a valiant knight of Cornwall,' who, full of honour, has in his old age retired to his estate, and in the eve of his life " was engaged in the pleasing occupation of training up two youths, his sons." One genial day, whilst they are strolling by the sea, there approaches the shore a small barque whence lands a man in the garb of a humble pilgrim. This votary of religion Sir Randolph recognizes with rapturous respect as Lord William Longsword, Earl of Salisbury, thought to have been slain in the wars of Gascoigne. Longsword relates his adventures to his old friend, and tells how on the return voyage, his ship being separated from the fleet, he was driven ashore, and found himself, after much danger, fainting at the very portals of " a large and venerable pile. It's windows crowded with the foliage of their ornaments, and dimmed by the hand of the painter; it's numerous spires towering above the roof, and the Christian ensign on it's front, declared it a residence of devotion and charity." Longsword swoons, but when his languid eyes open again, " I found myself," he says, " attended by one who seemed an inhabitant ; and from him learned that I lay before the portal of an antient Abbey, where the brethren of the Cistertian order, employed their peaceful hours in orisons to heaven, and acts of humanity to their fellow creatures." The frontispiece to Volume I of the first edition, 1762, very strikingly and very Gothically depicts this episode, as I remarked in the Introduction to my reprint of *The Castle of Otranto*,[17] and this engraving I remember especially delighted Sir Edmund Gosse, when I called his attention to it. The Abbey gives Longsword most welcome hospitality, but anon he is obliged to depart owing to the malice of Count Mal-leon, who persecutes and seeks to capture him, whilst he is defended and succoured by the kind Les Roches. After many adventures, treachery, and dangers he manages to escape to England bringing under his protection Jacqueline, the daughter of Les Roches, who is reported to have been slain. Longsword and Jacqueline are disguised "as two pilgrims, engaged by solemn vows to visit the lately erected shrine of St. Thomas of Canterbury." New difficulties, however, await the Earl of Salisbury even in his native land, since he learns that " Raymond, nephew to that Hubert whose counsels govern our King now possesses his castle. There, and through all it's district, he governs with an absolute sway." Raymond even seeks the hand of the Countess Ela, now supposed a widow. " Raymond is proud and insolent ; Hubert crafty, dark, and revengeful." Again and again have the " distressed greatness, and high-born pride " of Lady Ela rejected Raymond with scorn and contumely.

Raymond now ponders evil schemes in which he is assisted by a vile confident, named Grey, who with a sullen menace plots to tear the young son of Salisbury from his mother's arms. By the good offices of loyal Oswald, warder of the castle, the child is secretly conveyed to sanctuary, and dispatches having come from Hubert de Burgh warning his nephew that the friends of Salisbury are beginning to be active, Raymond and Grey show themselves well-nigh frantic with conscious guilt and fear.

In the religious house to which Oswald has retired with the heir, there dwelt a Monk, called Reginhald, who was brother to Grey. Insolent and assuming, he holds his place owing to the favour of Lord Raymond, so that his brethren scarce dare rebuke his drunkenness, and riot, and lewdness, and other " scandalous excesses utterly subversive of holy discipline and order." They lament these enormities of their unworthy brother, but tremble lest if they punish him the vengeance of Lord Raymond fall on the house. The wicked monk, Reginhald, although rather crudely drawn is, indeed, the ancestor of a whole progeny of villainous cowlmen and friars, Schedonis, Manfronés, Conrads, Fra Udolphos, Maldichinis, Schemolis, Obandos, Malvicinos, Placido Corsos, Rovengos, Hildargos, Dorias, *cum multis aliis quos nunc perscribere longum est*.[18]   When Reginhald learns the state of affairs from his brother, he at once has Oswald and the heir closely watched, and is eager for violence. He even visits the Countess Ela and contrives to purloin an ancient and precious jewel, a ring. The lady, although admitting him when " he named the brotherhood of Sarum," viewed him with repulsion.   " His aspect, in which the sensual and malignant passions had fixed their seat, and his deportment, which was that of the rude hind or midnight brawler, not of the holy and lettered clerk, were surveyed by the Countess with sudden disgust," which is not lessened when he vehemently advocates the cause of Lord Raymond. Presently Reginhald by use of the ring induces the Abbot to entrust young William to himself and Grey, whence follows a monstrous deal of mischief. Incited by his two evil agents, Raymond proclaims his nuptials with the Lady Ela, who finds herself " the helpless and joyless prisoner of her false guest." He invades her apartments, and forcibly takes her hand, while the impious monk " suddenly began to pronounce the marriage rites," when there arrives a messenger to say that the Earl of Salisbury is hastening to the castle.

It is next contrived that the Earl shall be checked by the news his Countess has married Lord Raymond, whereupon Longsword turns from his journey to present himself before the King, at " the city of Marlborough where Henry still held his court." An overt accusation of Hubert de Burgh in the circle follows, but Henry, feeling that he too is involved by his weakness, bids fair to smooth matters over, and

PLATE VII

LONGSWORD EARL OF SALISBURY
Frontispiece, Vol. I, 1762

[*Face p.* 160

pleads for jealousies and strife to be foregone. Reginhald secretly visits Hubert de Burgh, who instructs a brave named Tyrrel to hold himself at the monk's disposal. Meanwhile he gives the monk a phial filled with a deadly poison. " Let it be thy care," said he, " to present Lord William with this fatal draught, and name the reward of so great a service." Reginhald is only too ready for the deed. He pours the venom in a bowl of wine about to be served to the Earl, and as he sees the cup raised to his victim's lips " in an extravagance of horrid and malignant joy," he fled to Lord Raymond announcing the death of Lord William.

Raymond, who now begins to feel all the horrors of remorse and who is distraught with the guilt in which he is involved, turns in anger upon his creatures, Grey and Reginhald. Some enormities of the latter, too great to be concealed or palliated, have been discovered, and the whole cloister determines to punish his accumulated baseness. Messengers from the monastery demand his instant return. Mad with rage he seeks his brother, but his partner in crime on listening to the tale, shows himself so cold and forbidding that a violent quarrel ensues, and they loudly reproach one another with their guilt. The Countess overhears their angry curses and shoutings only to learn her husband is poisoned. She is conveyed to her chamber swooning, where Raymond, full of anxiety, rushes into her presence, uttering " terrible execrations upon himself and his vile seducers." In the midst of the confusion a messenger arrives to announce that within a few hours princely Salisbury will resume his power and authority within these walls. The frontispiece to the Second Volume represents this dramatic episode.

" The soul of Raymond was harrowed with consternation." How should a dead man return ? " After a hideous pause of dismay," he calls loudly upon his servants to hasten their departure from these halls, " To horse," he loudly and frequently cried. In this state of distraction he chances to espy the monk, to whose falsehoods he ascribes his present situation. Believing that the villain has betrayed him by a false tale, he orders his followers to hang the howling wretch from the branch of an aged oak in full sight of the castle, and the sentence is forthwith performed.

It appears that just as Salisbury was about to quaff the fatal bowl the doors flew open and there entered his friend Les Roches, long since thought dead. In his glad amaze the Earl dropped the beaker, spilling the wine ere it had touched his lips.

Raymond, too great of soul to endure dishonour and shame falls upon his sword ; Grey, plotting to betray his master for all his subtle shifts and turns, is arraigned for a traitor double-dyed, " and led forth to share the fate of his wicked brother." Earl William arrives at his castle and is folded in his wife's embrace, the young heir is restored to his parents, and the memory of their past sufferings is weaned by time. Longsword " now reflected on his wrongs with less emotion. Ela, too, seemed to forget her sufferings, and each was the more endeared to the other, by the late dangers and distresses of their separation."

Longsword, Earl of Salisbury, is in many respects crude, and the conception is far better than the execution, which must be confessed often to prove a little awkward and even ill-jointed. Yet—with all faults—as the booksellers say, it is a most remarkable work, and a land-mark in English literature, since it is the first Historical Novel, of an entirely different kind from and the progenitor of quite another family than *The Castle of Otranto*. At some points, of course, the two genera meet and contact, but they are essentially separate and diverse. This must be emphasized, and needs to be urged, since certain ill-equipped and superficial sophomores [19] have devoted long otiose pages to dilating upon their preconceived fancies, and expanding notions, which are in fine the effects of too little reading and unripened judgement.

In case I am misinterpreted and misreported it may, perhaps, not altogether be impertinent to enter a caveat here and stress my keen admiration for Walpole's work [20]—as will indeed, be evident after a few pages, for *The Castle of Otranto* is of immense importance and influence, but it certainly was not the only factor in the development of the Gothic Novel, and of the Historical Novel it was not the parent and source.

Within a couple of years after publication *Longsword, Earl of Salisbury* was dramatized by Hall Hartson, a young student of Trinity College, Dublin, and a protégé of Dr. Leland. *The Countess of Salisbury*, a tragedy, produced at Crow Street, Dublin, on Friday, May 2nd, 1765, and on Friday, August 21st, 1767, at the Haymarket, London, was received with great applause, drawing crowded houses even in the hottest of dog days. It remained a stock play for some forty years.[21] At the original production Barry created Alwin (Longsword), and Mrs. Dancer (afterwards Mrs. Barry), the Countess. The author, in an ' Advertisement,' attributes his good fortune to their " animated performance." In London, at a later revival, Mrs. Siddons played the Countess to the Alwin of Smith, and Raymond of Palmer. The drama opens in "*An Avenue leading to a Gothic Castle*," and Hartson with some necessary and well-managed compression follows pretty closely the events of the novel. The diction is elegant, the numbers are smooth and easy, the scenes interesting, and if domestic yet not without some forceful strokes. The character of the wicked monk Reginhald is wisely omitted in the drama.

The Hermitage : a British Story, published in 1772, by William Hutchinson [22] (1732–1814), a solicitor practising at Barnard Castle, Durham, is as a reviewer said, "sufficiently romantic," [23] in fact, supernatural machinery, to the accompaniment of fierce lightnings and tremendous bursts of thunder is pushed to an extravagant absurdity, but the romance cannot, for all its sub-title, be esteemed historical even in the widest extent of that term, and the style is at once tumid and tame.

A distinct throw-back is Alexander Bicknell's [24] History of Lady Anne Neville, sister to the great Earl of Warwick ; in which are interspersed Memoirs of that Nobleman, and the Principal Characters of the Age in which she lived, 1776. The very title in its amplitude recalls the previous century, whilst actually it is easy to recognize that Bicknell has conveyed his material en bloc from Prévost's Histoire de Marguerite d'Anjou, reine d'Angleterre, 1740, which had actually been translated into English in 1755. Some of Bicknell's borrowings are even verbal, but he has treated episodes quite loosely as suited his aim, whilst Anne becomes the heroine in place of Margaret. The rivalry of Edward IV and Warwick, Bicknell derived from Madame D'Aulnoy's Le Comte de Warwick, translated into English in 1708, and he may have known The Amours of Edward the IV of which some account has already been given. [25]

Little attention was excited by Reginald Du Bray. An Historick Tale, " By A Late Lord, Greatly admired in the Literary World," Dublin, 1779, which acknowledges itself " the literary offspring of Longsword." The period is actually the same as that of Leland's romance, the reign of Henry III. The fair Matilda, daughter to Reginald Du Bray, a gallant knight who has served in the Crusade, is sought by Lord Ardulph. There is a feud between the houses of Du Bray and Ardulph, so the latter, never hoping to win her by honest wooing, determines to abduct the peerless heroine. Young Edmund de Clifford, who has saved the life of Reginald Du Bray in Palestine, and who is now disguised in peasant's weeds, rescues Matilda from her ravishers. Later he is captured by treachery, and borne off to durance in the castle of Lord Ardulph. Eventually the villain baron falls in a duel with Edmund, who wins the hand of the lovely Matilda Du Bray. The Critical Review [26] justly observed that this Tale " abounds with distressed damsels, disguised heroes, tilts and tournaments, and has little connection with history," save when a pseudo-mediæval colouring is essayed, and, certes, however blatantly the atmosphere may proclaim Wardour Street and the transpontine melodrama it proves in parts quite effective. The story, at any rate, is well told, and does not lack vigour and movement. It is surprising that in England it appears not to have been circulated for some seven years, and even then it passed almost unremarked.

The thought is unpleasing, and not without a saddening if salutary tinge of melancholy, when we reflect how many talented names, honoured and widely popular in their own day, are now so completely forgotten. There are few, I am told, in this third decade of the twentieth century who are familiar with *The Recess*, the chief work of Sophia Lee (1750–1824), but this romance is one of the landmarks of English literature, and it is difficult to understand how those who have not read at least *The Recess* and *The Canterbury Tales* can claim any right to be heard when they discourse upon and trace the history of English fiction.

Sophia Lee and her younger sister, Harriet (1757–1851), were two of the five daughters of John Lee, a well-known actor, who was for several years a member of Garrick's company, and in Scotland was manager at Edinburgh, 1752–56, and in the provinces at Bath, 1778–79. John Lee altered *Macbeth*,[27] his version being played at the Edinburgh theatre in 1753, and published that year, 8vo, in that city. He also grievously reduced *The Country-Wife* to a farce of two acts, produced as an after-piece at Drury Lane on Friday, April 16th, 1765, and printed 8vo (no date) the same year. He next re-fashioned *The Relapse* as *The Man of Quality*, which was given at Covent Garden on Tuesday, April 2nd, 1773, and printed 8vo, 1776. His version of *Romeo and Juliet*, produced at Covent Garden, on Monday, September 29th, 1777, was not printed. He is supposed to have maltreated several other plays, and it must be acknowledged that his adaptations are flat and insipid to the last degree. At Bath during his management he sustained many important rôles with great applause. Thus on September 29th, 1779, he played Richard III to the Anne of Mrs. Siddons ; on the following night he was Archer in *The Beaux Stratagem*. On October 30th, in Rowe's tragedy, he was Dumont to the Jane Shore of Mrs. Siddons. On November 11th, he played Jaques in *As You Like It* ; on the 13th, Benedick in *Much Ado about Nothing*. On the 18th he was Macbeth to the Lady Macbeth of Mrs. Siddons ; on the 20th Comus with Mrs. Siddons as the Lady. On December 11th, he played the Duke in *Measure for Measure*, Mrs. Siddons, Isabella ; on the 16th, Pierre in *Venice Preserv'd*, Mrs. Siddons, Belvidera ; on the 18th, Shylock, Mrs. Siddons Portia ; on the 19th, Cardinal Wolsey, with Mrs. Siddons Queen Catherine.

His last appearance was at Bristol on July 14th, 1786, as Macbeth. In the autumn, however, he was too ill to act, and he died here in the following year.

Sophia Lee lost her mother whilst she was yet very young, so that the care of the household fell upon her shoulders. Nevertheless her entrance into literature was early with *The Chapter of Accidents*, a comedy founded on Diderot's *Le Père de Famille* [28] (1760), which, being refused by Harris, was produced by Colman at the Haymarket on Saturday, August 5th, 1780, and most favourably received, as indeed so interesting and well-written a play fully deserved. *The Chapter of Accidents* ran into two editions, 8vo, 1780 ; a third edition was issued 8vo, 1781 ; a fourth, 8vo, 1782 ; a fifth, 8vo, 1792 ; and it was subsequently several times reprinted. The profits enabled her to establish a Seminary for Young Ladies at Belvidere House, Bath, where she and her sister Harriet forthwith settled their residence. Their accomplishments, elegant manners, and prudent management secured a rapid and permanent success. In fact, these two ladies took their place as most honoured and respectable members of Bath society.

In 1783, Sophia Lee published the first volume of *The Recess*, which two years later she followed with Volumes II and III. Before considering this romance in particular, it may be well rapidly to survey the work of herself and her sister. On Wednesday, April 20th, 1796, there was produced at Drury Lane a tragedy in five acts by Sophia Lee, *Almeyda ; Queen of Granada*,[29] with Kemble as Alonzo and Mrs. Siddons, to whom the printed play (8vo, 1796) is dedicated, in the title-rôle. Miss Lee in the " Advertisement " speaks of her " gratitude for the liberal acceptation it has met, and the tears with which it has been honoured." The story is fictitious, but the catastrophe is adopted from *The Cardinal*.[30] " The deep impression made on me, long since, by a similar *denouement*, in an old play of James Shirley's, determined me to apply it." The Prologue and Epilogue were written by Harriet Lee.

Sophia Lee's third and last play, *The Assignation*, a comedy in five acts, produced at Drury Lane on Wednesday, January 28th, 1807, with Elliston, Bannister, Miss Pope, and Mrs. H. Siddons in the cast, was unsuccessful and only given once, the audience taking umbrage at what they considered some very particular satire on certain public characters.

In 1786, Sophia Lee published *Warbeck, a pathetic tale*, being a translation of *Varbeck*, one of the *Nouvelles historiques* (1774–84) of Baculard d'Arnaud.

Miss Lee, having by her industry acquired a very sufficient competence, gave up her school at Bath in 1803, and after residing for some while near Tintern Abbey, Monmouthshire, she fixed her home at Clifton, Bristol.

In 1804 she published *The Life of a Lover*, an epistolary narrative in six volumes, one of her very early compositions. She died on March 13th, 1824, and is buried in the Clifton Parish Church.

Harriet Lee wrote three plays : *The New Peerage, or, Our Eyes may deceive us*, produced at Drury Lane on Saturday, November 10th, 1787, with King as Mr. Vandercrab, a merchant ; Suett, Sir John Lovelace, guardian to Lord Melville ; Bannister, Lord Melville ; Lamash, Virtu, my Lord's valet ; Miss Farren, Lady Charlotte Courtley, Sir John's niece ; Mrs. Hopkins, Miss Vandercrab, niece to Vandercrab ; and Mrs. Crouch, Miss Harley, ward to Vandercrab. This comedy proved pretty successful, being acted nine times, and running into two editions bearing the date 1787. Perhaps Genest [31] is a little severe when he says : " some parts of the dialogue are tolerably good, but on the whole this is a poor play." The scenes may be a little thin, but I imagine they would have been helped tremendously by the excellence of the performance.

The Mysterious Marriage, or, The Heirship of Rosalva, 8vo, 1798, a play in three acts, was for some reason not brought upon the stage, but is a well-written and, with its spectres and unravelling of secrets, a truly Gothic drama.

The Three Strangers, who are the Baron, Conrad, and the Hungarian, produced at Covent Garden on Saturday, December 10th, 1825, but repeated only four times, was founded by Miss Lee upon her famous story *Kruitzner*. The drama had been written (and even in the hands of the managers) before Byron's *Werner*, and hence the lady felt bound to make it public. The delay in production was due to her own desire. The piece is " far from a bad one," as Genest remarks, [32] and it is surprising that it failed to win popular favour. It was printed 8vo, 1826.

In 1786 Harriet Lee published *The Errors of Innocence* in five volumes. The theme of this novel of sensibility, which is written in letters, turns upon the dastardly scheme of an unprincipled man, who, feigning to be at the point of death, induces a lady out of pity to consent to the marriage service in order to make his last moments happy. He, of course, recovers, and since the lady has bestowed her heart upon a noble suitor, she and her lover are plunged in exquisite misery.

By far the most celebrated piece of Harriet Lee is *Canterbury Tales*, 5 vols., 8vo ; Vol. I by Harriet Lee, 1797 ; Vol. II by Sophia Lee, 1798 (2nd ed., 1799) ; Vol. III by Sophia and Harriet Lee, 1800 (two editions) ; Vol. IV, 1801, and Vol. V, 1805, both by Harriet Lee.

The plan of this work and, indeed, its accomplishment, save for two tales, must be ascribed to Harriet, who in the preface which she wrote in January, 1832, for the edition in Bentley's "Standard Novels," Vols. 12 and 13, tells us exactly under what conditions the stories were projected. The original design was that seven travellers, finding themselves snowbound in an inn at Canterbury, decided to beguile their enforced stay by relating each one " the most remarkable story he or she ever knew or heard of ! " Eventually five more stories were added over and beyond the scope of the composition as first conceived. It is interesting to note that the fourth volume (pp. 3–368) contained the German's Tale, *Kruitzner*, which so deeply impressed Lord Byron when he read it as a lad of thirteen in 1801, the date of the fourth volume of *Canterbury Tales*, that he at once set himself to dramatize the narrative as *Ulric and Ilvina*, a first attempt, which he threw into the fire. He afterwards wrote or sketched out opening scenes, but *Werner ; or The Inheritance* [33] was definitely begun at Pisa on December 18th, 1821, and finished on January 22nd, 1822.

Kruitzner is a very powerful piece of work, and it has been well said that " the *motif*—a son predestined to evil by the weakness and sensuality of his father, a father punished for his want of rectitude by the passionate criminality of his son, is the very keynote of tragedy." [34]

The *Canterbury Tales* are highly romantic rather than Gothic, although here and there we have touches of the terror-novel, but the Misses Lee were certainly not Radcliffians.

To the *Canterbury Tales* Sophia Lee contributed The Young Lady's Tale, *The Two Emilys* ; and The Clergyman's Tale, *Pembroke* ; as well as the Introduction, which serves in some sort to introduce and knit together the stories. All the rest is the work of Harriet Lee. It is perhaps worth remark that *The Two Emilys* was separately issued by Newman, 2 vols., 1827.

Miss Harriet Lee resided at Clifton, where she died at an advanced age as late as August 1st, 1851, and I have known more than one person who was acquainted with and had very distinct memories of the old lady, a brilliant conversationalist to the last, with a fund of interesting anecdotes concerning the sister whom she so greatly loved and admired. I have never heard that she spoke much of William Godwin, an ardent suitor for her hand, who in 1798 made formal and most pressing proposals of matrimony to the lady. She warmly recognized his wayward and erratic genius, but his political and religious views proved an insuperable bar to a union.

With justice and not partiality Harriet Lee observes that *The Recess* was " The first English romance that blended interesting fiction with historical events and characters, embellishing both by picturesque description. 'Cleveland,' written, as I believe, by the Abbé Prevost, had precedence of all." [35] Originally published by Cadell, *The Recess* was dedicated to Sir John Elliot, the eminent physician. Very shortly after it appeared it was turned into French by Lemare.

The title of this romance, *The Recess*, is derived from a subterranean retreat or Recess within the precincts of " the Abbey, which might rather be called a palace ; it was erected upon the ruins of a monastery, destroyed at the Reformation, and still was called by the name of St. *Vincent*. It had all the Gothic magnificence and elegance." This Recess, " once inhabited by nuns of the order of St. *Winifred*," " could not be called a cave, because it was composed of various rooms ; and the stones were obviously united by labor; yet every room was distinct, and divided from the rest by a vaulted passage with many stairs, while our light proceeded from small casements of painted glass so infinitely above our reach that we could never seek a world beyond." In these underground chambers are secretly bred up Matilda and Ellinor, the lovely twin daughters of Mary, Queen o' Scots by a private marriage with Thomas, fourth Duke of Norfolk. Both are unfortunate. Matilda loves and is passionately beloved by the Earl of Leicester, whom she clandestinely weds. They take refuge from " the savage hand of Elizabeth" at Rouen, where Lord Leicester is murdered at midnight in the very arms of his bride—a finely written scene, worthy of Ainsworth at his best. Matilda is kidnapped to the plantations of Jamaica, and here she is detained eight years, but on returning home with her little daughter Mary, wealthy and free, she discovers her sister insane.

The Life of Ellinor is written in a number of sheets addressed to Matilda. The Earl of Essex falls in love with Ellinor, who in turn delivered herself wholly up to the impulse of her ardent heart. Elizabeth " gave way to that coarse virulence which marks her manners," and unmercifully persecutes and harries the hapless heroine, who, feigning to die, in a page's habit follows Essex to Ireland, where she falls into the hands of Tiroen (Tyrone). With difficulty she evades his licentious insolence, and anon they return to England. The imprisonment and execution of Essex unsettle her reason, and there is a most effective episode when the mad Ellinor, eluding the care of her attendants, and wailing *Essex, Essex, Essex!* appears in the bedchamber of the dying Elizabeth, who groans and shudders in horrid agony, believing the sweet unfortunate to be a phantom from the tomb.

Ellinor expires, and Matilda, with her daughter Mary, live in retirement at the beautiful village of Richmond. James I is now seated upon the throne, and Richmond is a favourite resort of Henry, Prince of Wales, who meets and falls passionately in love with Mary, and is privately betrothed to her. However, the young Prince is taken ill and dies, sending with his last breath tenderest messages to Mary, who (although he knew it not) had given her heart to the handsome Somerset, and is poisoned by the jealous and vindictive Countess. The bereaved Matilda finds an asylum in France.

In the course of this long and interesting romance Sophia Lee introduces us to a very large number of historical personages in addition to those already mentioned. Thus we meet Sir Philip Sidney, Sir Francis Drake, Lord Burleigh, Lady Pembroke, Sir Francis Walsingham, Lord Brooke, Sir David Murray, and many more. We visit Kenilworth Castle, Greenwich, Windsor, Bolton Castle, Richmond Palace, and other famous places. The character of Queen Elizabeth is drawn with admirable strokes and absolutely true to fact. Indeed, it is hardly an exaggeration to say that in *The Recess* the personages for the most part act according to history, but they act from entirely different motives. *The Gentleman's Magazine* proved exceptious, and the reviewer of Sophia Lee's romance wrote that " Though Leicester, Essex, and Sidney must interest us more than those men of straw that flutter through our modern novels, we cannot entirely approve the custom of interweaving fictitious incident with historic truth." [36] This, of course, arraigns the whole claim of the historical novel and opens up immensely wide issues, questions which are still a matter for debate, since even yet there may be found precisians who suspect the propriety of the historical romance.

One thing is very clear, *The Recess* gave Sir Walter Scott some valuable suggestions for *Kenilworth*.

The Recess itself is in many important features extremely Gothic, and although strictly a historical novel, it had great influence upon the Gothic romance. Miss Lee owed much to Walpole, to Clara Reeve, and to Baculard D'Arnaud, and she gave much—more perhaps than has been acknowledged—even to her most distinguished successors.

The incidents of *The Recess* are introduced by a device which became so common and so exaggerated in the Gothic novelists as to give some inimitable strokes to the gentle satire of Jane Austen, who so used to laugh at what she loved. It will readily be remembered that in *Northanger Abbey*, when Henry is enthralling Catherine Morland with his really excellent Gothic romance—how often one has wished it might be completed—he prophesies that on the second or third night after her arrival at the Abbey she will notice in a secret chamber a large old-fashioned cabinet of ebony and gold, where an inner compartment opened by a hidden spring will discover a roll of paper : " You seize it—it contains many sheets of manuscript—you hasten with the precious treasure into your own chamber, but scarcely have you been able to decipher ' Oh ! thou—whomsoever thou mayest be, into whose hands these memoirs of the wretched Matilda may fall '—when your lamp suddenly expires in the socket, and leaves you in total darkness."[37]

In the hands of so accomplished an artist as Mrs. Radcliffe the device of the recovered manuscript, which after all is very near akin to the epistolary novel, was managed with rare skill, and is both proper and natural.   It is, however, with lesser writers a trick that can easily be overdone.   It offers some admirable facilities, but it must be employed with strict economy if it is not to seem improbable, and it may even become ludicrous.

Henry Mackenzie opens *The Man of Feeling* (1771) with an account of a chance discovery of a bundle of papers, a mutilated manuscript, which has been torn and used as wadding for a gun.   This allows him to plunge *in medias res* and to commence with Chapter XI, apologizing for what is lost.[38]   Mrs. Helme's *St. Margaret's Cave : or, The Nun's Story*, An Ancient Legend, 4 vols., Earle and Hemet, 1801, is furnished with an Introduction in which a boarder in a convent is entrusted by the Abbess with various papers and manuscripts for her perusal, and these contain the romance, which was thus noticed in *The Critical Review*[39] for February, 1802 ; " The story is artfully, and in many places very affectingly, told, and will procure Mrs. Helme considerable credit among the readers of novels."   To name only some seven or eight from scores of Gothic novels in which manuscripts are interpolated, discovered, perused, and play a prominent part, we may instance such typical works as *The Girl of the Mountains*, 1795, by Mrs. Parsons, and the same lady's *The Mysterious Warning*, 1796 ; the anonymous *Ariel, or, The Invisible Monitor*, 1801 ; *Ancient Records, or, The Abbey of Saint Oswythe*, by T. J. Horsley Curties, 1801 ; Conolly's *The Friar's Tale*, 1805 ; Sarah Wilkinson's *The Fugitive Countess, or, The Convent of St. Ursula*, 1807 ; Maturin's *Melmoth the Wanderer*, 1820. *The Convent of St. Michael*, a Tale, 2 vols., 1803, is said to be " *taken from a German MS. of the Seventeenth Century*," and thus offers a double attraction.

Perhaps the most extravagant use of the recovered manuscript is to be found in Maria Vanzee's *Fate, or Spong Castle*, 1803, where the document relating the history of a secluded prisoner in Germany is found in an iron coffer in Yorkshire.

It is, of course, possible to mention only a few of the historical novels which were inspired by and followed on *The Recess*.

In 1786 was published *St. Bernard's Priory*, An old English Tale. Being the first literary production of a Young Lady, who very obviously drew upon *The Recess* and *The Castle of Otranto*. The subterranean priory, concealed amid bramble-grown ruins, where Elgiva has dwelt for many years with her two daughters, Maud and Laura, is the Recess itself with the slightest changes. It is true that the supernatural is discreetly enough treated in comparison with Walpole's bold colouring, but there is a prominent scene where, after threading long passages, young Lord Raby enters a chamber " where, upon a high pedestal, arrayed in armour, a waving plume of feathers on his casque, and in his hand a pointed spear, stood the image of Lord Raby's father !— Riveted with astonishment, he gazed upon the lifeless statue, and, actuated by some unknown impulse, kneeled at the foot of the pedestal. . . . While in this posture a violent burst of thunder shook the place, and a terrible storm succeeded." This is the true vein of Strawberry Hill.

The same young lady two years later commended herself and *The Castle of Mowbray, An English Romance*, " to the candour of the Public." The period is the reign of Edward I, and we follow the fortunes of the amiable Elwina, who nearly falls a prey to the abandoned Edric, " when from its pedestal descended the statue of Earl Mowbray," which proves to be the Earl *in propriâ persona*, who rescues his daughter from the impetuous gallant. Eventually love and virtue triumph, and Edric's accomplice in vice and guilt, Lord Fitz Alwyn, " flung himself into a monastery, where he meant to profess the austere vows of the Benedictines."

It must be acknowledged that both *St. Bernard's Priory* and *The Castle of Mowbray* are distinctly amateurish, and although criticism is disarmed by the humility with which the Young Lady tenders her two romances, only a very partial and hoodwinked friendship could find much to praise.

William of Normandy, An Historical Novel, 2 vols., 1787, receives some very rough treatment from *The Monthly Review*, which fairly damns it as " a monstrous and misshapen birth, and such as criticism turns from in horror and disgust." Little wonder that in the same year Anne Fuller adopted a most propitiatory and apologetic tone in the Preface to her *Alan Fitz-Osborne, an Historical Tale*, 2 vols., 1787, and declared : " I mean not to offend the majesty of sacred truth by giving her but a secondary place in the following pages." The Tale is extremely Gothic and shows very clearly the influence of *Otranto*, but it is not clearly very historical, although the period is the reign of Henry III, and the hero, Alan, takes part in the Barons' Wars. Matilda, the wife of Earl Alan, is murdered by the amorous villain, her brother-in-law, Walter Fitz-Osborne, who is haunted by her pale, ghastly, and bloody apparition. The spectre stands by his bedside, and as the thunder roars and crashes without she snatches from her wounded bosom the dagger from whose points great gory gouts fall upon the sheets and coverlet.

It will be sufficient to record the names of two works belonging to this same year, 1789, *The Duke of Exeter*, An Historical Romance, in three volumes, and Anne Fuller's *The Son of Ethelwolf*, An Historical Novel, in two volumes.

Miss Rosetta Ballin's *The Statue Room* ; An Historical Tale, 2 vols., 1790, follows very closely on the lines of *The Recess*, since the heroine Adelfrida is a daughter of Henry VIII and Catherine of Aragon, born after the divorce, unacknowledged, persecuted and even poisoned by Queen Elizabeth. Adelfrida leaves a daughter, Romelia. The statue room—which is so called from being lined with statues—is of no importance in the narrative into which indeed it enters belated.

Gabrielle de Vergy, An Historical Tale, 2 vols., 1790, has the scene laid in France during the reign of Cœur de Lion. The death of the heroine was obviously suggested by Dryden's *Sigismonda and Guiscardo*, but there is little else to be deemed remarkable in the tale. *The Siege of Belgrade*, an Historical Novel, 4 vols., 1791, is offered as " Translated from a German manuscript," and we taste something of a novelty in the shape of Russian scenes, not perhaps very convincing, although the writer has been at some pains to depict various customs of the country.

In 1791, Henry, the brilliant young son of Mrs. Siddons, published *William Wallace* ; *or, The Highland Hero, A Tale, Founded on Historical Facts*, 2 volumes. The work is immature, but yet has a certain dash and vigour which more than redeem the narrative from tedium or mediocrity.

A more important romance, and one which was received with much favour, is *Monmouth*, 1790, by the prolific Mrs. Anna Maria Mackenzie of Exeter, who also wrote under the *nom de plume* Ellen of Exeter. Anna Maria Wight first married a Mr. Cox, who died very early. She then became Mrs. Johnstone, and shortly after the decease of her second husband, Mrs. Mackenzie. Her novels comprise *Burton Wood*, 1785 ; *The Gamesters*, 1786 ; *Monmouth*, 3 vols., 1790 ; *The Danish Massacre* ; *an Historical Fact*, 2 vols., 1791 ; *Mysteries Elucidated*, 3 vols., 1795 ; *The Neapolitan, or The Test of Integrity*, 3 vols., 1796 ; *Feudal Events*, 3 vols., 1797; *Dusseldorf, or the Fratricide*, 3 vols., 1798; which was translated into French as *Dusseldorf, ou le fratricide* . . . Traduit de l'anglais par L. A. Marquand, 3 tomes, 12mo, Paris, an vii [1797] ; *Martin and Mansfeldt, or, The Romance of Franconia*,[40] 3 vols., 1802 ; and *The Irish Guardian* ; *or, Errors of Eccentricity*, 3 vols., 1809.

Mysteries Elucidated is dedicated to Caroline, Princess of Wales, London, April 25th, 1795. In an address " To the Readers of Modern Romance," Anna Maria Mackenzie speaks of the success of recent historical romances :—*The Recess, Warbeck, Monmouth, The Danish Massacre, The Duke of Clarence*, all " founded on particular periods in the history of this country . . . ladies are contented to be interested and improved, without being terrified." Mrs. Mackenzie praises Mrs. Radcliffe, forcing her reader " to adopt the enthusiasm of ideas, which, like the description they are cloath'd in, are all wild, vast and terrific." She also highly commends " Burney, Bennet, Parsons." " Let every mystery thicken in the progress of the story, 'till the whole is elucidated, but let it be without the intervention of super, or preternatural appearances. Dreams and apparitions savour too much of the superstition which ought never to be encouraged. Therefore the author hopes that all ' possessing the writing influenza ' will take this to heart." Accordingly in her romance Mrs. Mackenzie very successfully combines a number of mysterious events afterwards disentangled without any loss of probability. We are in the days of Edward II. The hero of the tale is Raymond de Vallenciennes, an adopted son of De Spencer, the royal favourite. Raymond eventually is discovered to be the King's son by a clandestine marriage with Lady Lancaster. He loves Ella, daughter of Earl Fitzroy, who has been killed by Mortimer. Old Ursula, Mortimer's housekeeper, appears on the scene. Raymond is present at the deathbed of Edward II (Volume II) ; but one feels that very little is made of the capture of Mortimer in Volume III. The frontispiece of the work represents Queen Isabella, who after Mortimer has been seized and she is placed in honourable confinement, whilst walking in the gardens of Nottingham Castle threads a cypress path : " At the upper end, on a pedestal of beautiful granite, stood a bust of her late unhappy consort, Edward, which probably owed its preservation to the lonely solitude of the place." Whilst she gazes in grief and horror, her maid of honour, Lady Duval, approaches her bearing a letter from which she learns she is to be cloistered in perpetuity in a " Monastery at Warewell."

Edward de Courcy, 2 vols., Lane, 1794, is described as " an ancient figment." The period is the commencement of the Wars of the Roses, and various historical characters play a considerable part in the events.

Ann Yearsley (1756–1806), " Lactilla, the Bristol poetess-milk-woman," in 1795 published with Robinson, *The Royal Captives*,[41] *a Frag-*

ment of Secret History. Copied from an old Manuscript, 2 volumes. The story is that of the Man in the Iron Mask, his wife and son. He is supposed to be a twin-brother of Louis XIV, and one half wonders whether at some time Dumas had not glanced at Ann Yearsley's pages. Even if the incidents are improbable the book has much merit.

The Duke of Clarence by E. M. F., four volumes, 1795, with its gallant hero, Edgar, and its gentle heroine Elfrida de Clifford, has a full complement of ghosts, including the spectre of the murdered Montcalm and the phantom of Clarence in complete armour but *The Monthly Review* [42] remarks that it " has slender title to the character of an historical novel."

The anonymous *Arville Castle*, 2 vols., 1795, transports us back to the days of Boadicea, and yet even then there were ladies of exquisite sensibility and refinement, uttering the most chaste and correct sentiments. It must suffice just to record two other novels of the same year : *Montford Castle ; or The Knight of the White Rose*, " An Historical Romance of the 11th Century," 2 volumes ; and *Cicely, or The Rose of Raby*, An Historical Novel, 4 volumes, by Agnes Musgrave.

The anonymous lady who wrote *The Minstrel ; or Anecdotes of Distinguished Personages in the Fifteenth Century*, 3 volumes, 1793, has studied her authorities with perception and care, and although her archæological research does not go very deep she was evidently well upon the right track. She has gleaned romance from Shakespeare, particularly from the Historical Plays ; she has dipped into Chaucer, and she has certainly been influenced by Mrs. Radcliffe as well in the adventures of her heroine, Eleanor, who, escaping from one lover and seeking another, assumes the garb of a minstrel, a dress described in some detail with appropriate terms. A good deal is rather obvious, and as historical touches we are regaled amid anchorites, a ruined castle, and apparitions with the well-worn humour of " a travelling vendor of pardons and indulgences from the pope," " a gentil Pardoner," in fact, " That streight was comen fro the court of Rome " ; we assist at the manumission of a villein ; and visit the Duke of Suffolk's almshouses at Ewelme.

The same lady's second work, *The Cypriots ; or a Miniature of Europe in the Middle of the Fifteenth Century*, 2 volumes, 1795, follows *mutatis mutandis* precisely the same lines with its citation of authorities, and descriptions which in some sort foreshadow Scott, Ainsworth, Emma Robinson and Mrs. Bray.

The Critical Review [43] poked fun at *The Castle of Caithness : a Romance of the Thirteenth Century*, by F. H. P., 2 volumes, Lane, 1802, and observed that this romance is " the shadow of a shade—in it are contained more *ghosts* and *dreams of ghosts*, than even the Thirteenth Century could have borne."

Plantagenet, or, Secrets of the House of Anjou,[44] A Tale of the Twelfth Century, 2 volumes, 1802, by Anna Millikin, although of course pure fiction is well and interestingly told. The secret consists in the marriage of William, son of Robert, Duke of Normandy, to a daughter of the House of Anjou. In 1805 Miss Millikin published in one volume another romance, *The Rival Chiefs, or, The Battle of Mere.*

A better work is *The Witcheries of Craig Isaf*, by William Frederic Williams, 2 volumes, Lane, 1804. The period is the reign of Rufus ; the narrative is developed with some skill, especially in the management of the supernatural, for the witches keep the word of promise to the ear only. Williams wrote several other novels : *Fitzmaurice*, 2 volumes, 1800 ; *Sketches of Modern Life, Tales of an Exile*, 2 volumes, 1803 ; *The World we Live in*, 3 volumes, 1804 ; and *The Young Father*, 3 volumes, 1805.

Leslie Armstrong's *The Anglo-Saxons, or the Court of Ethelwald*, 4 volumes, published in September, 1806, by Lane, may not evince any great research or intimate knowledge of the days of Heptarchy, but it is, I think, more interestingly told than *Alvar and Seraphina* ; or *The Troubles of Mercia*, A Historical Romance, by John Canton, 2 volumes, Lane, 1804. Yet if we are content to be lenient both these " historical novels " of early English centuries are very readable. A second romance by Canton, *Don Sebastian*, is woven round the mysterious fate of that king of Portugal whom Dryden made the hero of his grand tragedy. Wisely perhaps Canton gives those characters who are attached to and affected by the destinies of Sebastian a greater prominence than the Monarch himself. The history of Don Sebastian, that digne and gallant knight of the Cross, " mystic, religious, fanatic," who disappeared, perhaps who fell on the field of Alcacerquivir, August 4th, 1578, has naturally attracted dramatists and novelists not a few.[45] Anna Maria Porter has a romance, *Don Sebastian, or, The House of Braganza*, 1809, which covers the same events, and which was by many critics regarded as the best, as it certainly proved the most popular of her works.

Francis Lathom, in the Preface to the Second Volume of *The Fatal Vow ; or, St. Michael's Monastery*, Crosby, 1807, writes : " Historical romances are the taste of the times ; and I think it a sufficient sanction for an author whose remuneration is to arise from gratifying the public taste, to apply his pen to such subjects as interest the feelings of the majority. The critics frown upon a too free use being made by novel-writers of historical facts ; but surely the most rigid cannot object to their laying claim to such events as, although mentioned in history, are doubted even by historians themselves ; of this nature will be found many of the characters and circumstances interwoven in the subsequent tale : as their ever having existed is by no means ascertained, I cannot be accused of having violated truth by having dressed them in the colours of my own fancy ; and I am equally certain that the cause of morality will not be a sufferer by the contents of my pages—the first and perhaps only important point for an author to consider, who writes only for the amusement of his readers."

The period of the narrative is very precisely fixed as in the thirty-fourth year of the reign of Henry the second of England, and the scene opens in the neighbourhood of St. Michael's Monastery, Cornwall, in which house is sojourning a gallant knight, Reginald de Brune, who falls passionately in love with the beauteous Christabelle, a maiden dwelling with her father in the utmost seclusion near the Monastery. Glencowell, her father, has shown Christabelle a miniature of her mother, but refuses to reveal his wife's rightful name or indeed to give her the slightest hint of information. After a long tangle of events, including the stay of the heroine at the Convent of St. Ursula, where she is ill treated by the traditional Abbess, it is discovered that Reginald is no other than Prince Richard the Lion-Heart, and he conveys Christabelle to court, where she is welcomed as a daughter-in-law by the Queen. Henry II is in France whither Richard, the ally of his father's enemies, resorts to take the field. Meanwhile Queen Eleanor determines to revenge herself upon Rosamond de Clifford, who has so wronged her. Accompanied by Christabelle in the disguise of a minstrel, for she has completely won all the sympathies of her future daughter-in-law, she obtains entrance into the very heart of the Bower, the Palace of Woodstock, the apartment where Rosamond receives them being described in great detail, if perhaps not strictly in the mode of the twelfth century, since it was " of the most fantastic and elegant kind ; the walls were covered with a green silk drapery ; which being drawn up at certain intervals by festoons of flowers displayed within recesses, figures of alabaster which extended from their hands, silver lamps that cast a brilliant illumination over the scene. Couches of purple velvet, adorned with silver fringe were placed around. A carpet of goat's hair, of the purest white hue, was spread upon the floor ; and on tables of rosewood, polished to the brilliancy of a mirror, were set before the guests those refreshments which had first been offered to them through the grate." Christabelle is stricken dumb to recognize in Rosamond the original of the miniature, but she is prevented from revealing herself by the Fatal Vow which her father had imposed upon her under conditions of great solemnity. At a given signal the Queen's soldiers invade the Palace, and Eleanor when Rosamond refuses to abjure Henry's love "plunged her dagger to her heart!" Since it is largely owing to Christabelle's disguise and her songs that entrance has been obtained to the Bower, Christabelle (really Matilda de Clifford) is plunged into hopeless agony. She takes shelter in the Convent of St. Ursula, whose Abbess has been replaced by one of her friends, and in spite of Richard's pleading she cannot be won to leave the cloister. She only comes forth when he is in Austrian captivity, for it is Matilda who, as the minstrel Blondel, secures his release. (For this incident Lathom seems to have drawn upon the popular play by General Burgoyne, *Richard Cœur De Lion, An Historical Romance*, produced at Drury Lane, on Tuesday, October 24th, 1786, and itself derived from Sedaine's *Richard Cœur de Lion*,[46] first given at Paris, October 21st, 1784.) Eventually when Richard is freed, Matilda, who has again sought the seclusion of St. Ursula, expires in her lover's arms.

In her *A Peep at our Ancestors*, 3 volumes, 1807, Miss Henrietta Rouvière, afterwards Mrs. Moss, "flatters herself that, aided by records and documents, she has succeeded in a correct though faint sketch of the times she treats, and in affording, if through a dim yet not distorted nor discoloured glass, A Peep at our Ancestors." I fear the lady's will was better than her achievement, and there is truth to tell little of the twelfth century in the many adventures of the peerless Adelaide and her suitor, Walter of Gloucester. Miss Rouvière also wrote *Lussington Abbey*, 2 volumes, 1804 ; and *Craig Melrose Abbey*, 4 volumes, 1818. To regard *The Catholic, or, Acts and Deeds of the Popish Church*, 3 volumes, 1807, as " A Tale of English History," which the author, William Henry Ireland, dubbed it, is more ludicrous than any of the young gentleman's Shakespearean forgeries.

In 1808 we have two historic romances by Miss C. Maxwell, *Alfred of Normandy, or, the Ruby Cross*, 2 volumes ; and *Lionel, or, the Impenetrable Command*, 2 volumes.

The events of *The Spanish Lady and the Norman Knight, A Romance of the Eleventh Century*, 2 vols., Hughes, 1810, by Kate Montalbion,[47] are laid during the pontificate of Paschal II, 1099–1118. Donna Dora Urdiales d'Ibbera is wedded to Sir Herbert de Rouen " otherwise de Beauvais " who takes the cross "under the conduct of *Peter* the *Hermit*, and *Walter* the *Pennyless*." Dora accompanies Sir Herbert, and after a battle is " carried captive to the tent of the *Soldan Soliman*, who became instantly the slave of her beauty." The young Soldan Salem proves equally amorous. Adventures abound, and we have notes historical, geographical, and ornithological to verify Miss Montalbion's allusions. Among the characters we catch glimpses of such personages as Philip I of France, Bertrade de Montfort, Godfrey of Jerusalem, and Robert of Normandy, with the romantic figures of " *Zilpala,* of the sons of *Levi* " ; Mamora, a dusky mute ; Zarood, " a *Black eunuch* . . . the terror of *Dora* " ; and Zefany, a fair minion page " with song," as the old playbills were wont to term it. William Rufus outrages " modesty and decorum " by his overtures to Dora, which seems strange in a monarch who was so well known to be entirely homosexual. Dora's reflections [48] upon her young husband's intimate charms are extremely warm, not to say grossly indecent in their suggestion.

The Spanish Lady and the Norman Knight is a curious romance, but we must needs wait until *The Talisman,* fifteen years to come, to show how the Crusades were to be handled in story.

The Loyalists ; *An Historical Novel,* published anonymously (Longmans), but by Mrs. Jane West, 3 volumes, 1812, is far more serious in its adherence to historical fact than perhaps any we have hitherto met, and the Introductory Chapter in tone becomes extremely didactic. The period is the reign of Charles I. " Public events will be stated with fidelity. Historical characters shall be but sparingly combined with feigned actions," and it must be confessed that this wise economy has greatly helped the tale, of which the interest is well sustained, many passages being admirably written. The Puritan preacher Davies, for example, is drawn with most vivid strokes, and there is not a tittle of exaggeration or caricature. In fact, *The Loyalists* is a very remarkable book, and it is strange that it should be so completely forgotten.

A popular actor of the Surrey Theatre, William Henry Hitchener, in 1813 published with a Dedication to the famous Elliston, dated August 6th, 1812, a novel of contemporary fashion *St. Leonard's Forest, or, The Child of Chance,* 2 volumes, Chapple. Inspired by the nightly melodramas in which he was much applauded, during the following year he issued with the same house a romance of earlier times, *The Towers of Ravenswold, or, the Days of Ironside,* 2 volumes ; and on July 7th of the same year was published *Waverley, or, 'Tis Sixty Years Since.*

In reviewing *Edric the Forester* ; *or The Mysteries of the Haunted Chamber. An Historical Romance,* 3 vols., Hughes, 1818, by Mrs. Anne Ker,[49] of his Grace the Duke of Roxburgh's family, *The Gentleman's Magazine,*[50] December, 1818, remarked : " Of the credulity which might prevail when ' Edric the Forester ' is represented to have run his career, in the days of William the Conqueror, we have not now to determine ; but, in the more enlightened period of the nineteenth century, the reader will require something like probability in the construction of a narrative, however ingeniously his fancy may be arrested by the imprisonment of Knights and Damsels in the turrets of a Castle, or by the effects of supernatural appearances, or a guilty conscience."

Such a romance as *Feudal Days*; or *The Freebooter's Castle*, by Mitchell Williams, 3 vols., 1826, which was "the first of an intended series illustrative of the less noticed phenomena of history.—Subject, The People, Democracy, Revival of Civilization, " shows very clearly the influence of Scott and has little of the Gothic. Unfortunately the talent of Mitchell Williams was of a very ordinary kind and his pages are jejune. It is worth noting that he expressly terms his *Legitimacy, or, The Youth of Charlemagne*, "An Heroic Romance."

Nun of St. Agatha, "An Historical Romance of the Sixteenth Century," 3 vols., Newman, 1830, is in some respects Ainsworthian, but furnishes historical "Notes and Illustrations" to certain phrases and antique words. It is a well-told interesting story of the latter years of Henry VIII and the accession of Edward VI.

It has, of course, in this quick survey of the development of the historical novel from *Longsword* to *Waverley*, a period of half a century, only been possible to call attention to the more important names and just to note an occasional milestone by the way. There are also many romances in which the historical setting is obviously so subordinate and immaterial that they must clearly be considered as the offspring of Gothic ancestry rather than in the lineage of history, however remote. Such, for example, are the works of Horsley Curties, *Ethelwina, or, The House of Fitz-Auburne*, A Romance of Former Times, the reign of Edward III, who himself appears in the story; *Ancient Records*, a tale of the reign of Henry VI, whose Queen Margaret plays an important part at the *dénouement*; and *St. Botolph's Priory, or, The Sable Mask*, where we meet Charles I, Cromwell, and are present at the death-bed of the Princess Elizabeth at Carisbrooke, although it must be confessed that in this last, history (not altogether inexact) gains a preponderance.

Yet these look back to *Otranto*, and to *Otranto* we may now well turn.

To *The Castle of Otranto* " we owe nothing less than a revolution in public taste, and its influence is strong even at the present day. It is hardly an exaggeration to say that to Walpole's romance is due the ghost story and the novel, containing so much of the supernatural and occult, than which no forms of literature are now [1923] more common and applauded. *The Castle of Otranto* is, in fine, a notable landmark in the history of English taste and English literature." [51] This is high praise, but I bate no jot of it, yet when I wrote more than a decade ago I chose my words carefully to say enough but not too much. We must not, we may not, go beyond what I have said.

As I have already shown, the tendencies of taste which culminated in the Gothic Novel had origins wider and deeper than any one book, even *The Castle of Otranto*, could develop. The dominant elements in the terror novel of the 1790's, of which the most famous exemplar is *The Monk*, came from Germany ; the historical romance, which we have just examined, accounts for much ; the French influences of Baculard d'Arnaud and his "drames monacales" are of the first importance. It is an error, and a fundamental error, to treat *The Castle of Otranto* as the one and only source of the Gothic Novel.

On June 5th, 1747, Walpole wrote to Horace Mann, I "may retire to a little new farm that I have taken just out of Twickenham," [52] which is the first mention of the famous Strawberry Hill. He first rented "this little rural *bijou*" from Mrs. Chenevix, taking over the remainder of her lease, and in 1748 he bought it by Act of Parliament, it being the property of three minors, named Mortimer. On January 10th, 1750, Walpole says to the same correspondent : "I am going to build a little Gothic castle at Strawberry Hill. If you can pick me up any fragments of old painted glass, arms, or anything, I shall be excessively obliged to you." In September, 1749, Walpole was begging the Duke of Bedford for some windows from the dilapidated Cheneys—" in half the windows are beautiful arms in painted glass. . . . They would be magnificent for Strawberry Castle." In fact his new Gothic castle gave him a new interest in life, for he had been vastly bored with most things he endured. Yet of Strawberry he never tired. In March, 1753, he proclaims that as Chiswick House "is a model of Grecian architecture, Strawberry Hill is to be so of Gothic." "My house is so monastic," he tells Mann, "that I have a little hall decked with long saints in lean arched windows and with taper columns, which we call the Paraclete, in memory of Eloise's cloister." "Under two gloomy arches, you come to the hall and staircase . . . the most particular and chief beauty of the castle. Imagine the walls covered with . . . Gothic fretwork : the lightest Gothic balustrade to the staircase, adorned with antelopes (our supporters) bearing shields ; lean windows fattened with rich saints in painted glass, and a vestibule open with three arches on the landing-place . . . the castle, when finished, will have two-and-thirty windows enriched with painted glass." The living-room had "a bow-window commanding the prospect, and gloomed with limes that shade half each window, already darkened with painted glass in chiaroscuro, set in deep blue glass." In May, 1760, Walpole had "flounced again into building—a round tower, gallery, cloister, chapel, all starting up— " and three years later, " The chapel is quite finished, except the carpet. The sable mass of the altar gives it a very sober air ; for, notwithstanding the solemnity of the painted windows, it had a gaudiness that was a little profane."

What wonder that Walpole loved to fit himself to his mock-mediæval world, that now he conceived himself as the ' sensechal ' of his castle, and now again he was a friar of orders grey or a swart-cowled monk burying manuscripts under the gnarled oak in his garden-garth or behind some secret panel in his old-new wainscot.

At first he welcomed visitors to his retreat. In May, 1755, he " gave a great breakfast to the Bedford court," the sun shone, " and Strawberry was all gold, and all green. I am not apt to think people really like it, that is understand it." Walpole hated that Strawberry Hill should be laughed at, jeered (although politely and among friends), and regarded as one of the ' lions.' In June, 1755, he writes that Princess Emily was there : " Liked it ? " " Oh no ! " but peeped and pryed into every corner, even the very offices and servants' rooms. " In short, Strawberry-Hill is the puppet-show of the times."

" The Abbot of Strawberry," as he once signed himself, withdrew more and more to Strawberry and solitude.

The fact is that Strawberry Castle—" my child Strawberry "—was infinitely precious to him, it was his own creation, the summum of his own life, the actual and external embodiment of his own dreams. Here he had built his love of Gothic, as he understood it, his romantic passion for old castles and ruined abbeys, his dreams of a mediæval world. " Tread softly," says the poet, " Tread softly because you tread upon my dreams." Strawberry, as Walpole himself wrote, " was built to please myself in my own taste, and in some degree to realize my own visions." As he wrote to Madame Du Deffand : " de tous mes ouvrages, c'est l'unique où je me sois plu ; j'ai laissé courir mon imagination ; les visions et les passions m'échauffaient." The Castle of Otranto is Strawberry in literature. As the years went by he with-drew more and more into his retreat ; the world of his dreams became more and more the real world for him, the only thing that counted. Night after night he would sit up reading into the small hours, not a little conscious of his own isolation, his mental and spiritual detach-ment, and at times not a little weary. In some such mood he began to put his dreams upon paper, his midsummer dreams. The Castle of Otranto was commenced in June, 1764, and finished on the following August 6th. It was published in an edition of five hundred copies on

Christmas Eve of the same year, the most apposite of days, and in January, 1765, sending a copy to the Earl of Hertford, he is able proudly to boast, " the enclosed novel is much in vogue."

In a letter dated March 9th, addressed to the Reverend William Cole, he gives the famous account of his original inspiration. " Your partiality to me and Strawberry have, I hope, inclined you to excuse the wildness of the story. You will ever have found some traits to put you in mind of the place. When you read of the picture quitting its panel, did you not recollect the portrait of Lord Falkland, all in white, in my gallery ? Shall I even confess to you, what was the origin of this romance ? I waked one morning, in the beginning of last June, from a dream, of which all I could recover was, that I had thought myself in an ancient castle (a very natural dream for a head like mine filled with Gothic story), and that on the uppermost banister of a great staircase I saw a gigantic hand in armour. In the evening I sat down, and began to write, without knowing in the least what I intended to say or relate. The work grew on my hands and I grew so fond of it that one evening, I wrote from the time I had drunk my tea, about six o'clock, till half an hour after one in the morning, when my hand and fingers were so weary, that I could not hold the pen to finish my sentence, but left Matilda and Isabella talking in the middle of a para-graph. In short, I was so engrossed with my Tale, which I completed in less than two months."

People, even the best people, had laughed at Strawberry Hill, and Walpole, fearing ridicule, published *The Castle of Otranto* as a " Story Translated by William Marshal, Gent. From the Original Italian of Onuphrio Muralto, Canon of the Church of St. Nicholas at Otranto." An elaborate translator's preface relates how " The following work was found in the library of an ancient Catholic family in the north of England. It was printed at Naples, in the black letter, in the year 1529 . . . the style is the purest Italian." [53]

On March 26th, 1765, Walpole, writing to the Earl of Hertford, mentions with some pride *The Castle of Otranto*, " the success of which has, at last, brought me to own it," although he was (he confesses) for a long while terribly afraid of being bantered, " but it met with too much honour, for at first it was universally believed to be Mr. Gray's."

The second edition appeared on April 11th, 1765, an issue of five hundred copies. In the Preface, Walpole entirely discards the mask ; he explains his reasons for pretending the book was a translation, and incontinently dismisses William Marshal and Canon Onuphrio Muralto. *The Monthly Review* was obviously at a loss how to treat the new romance, and whilst praising the performance as written with no common pen, allowing that the language was accurate and elegant, and proclaiming that the adventures provided considerable entertainment, the critic, forgetful of the Scriptures, objected that the moral " visiting the sins of the fathers upon the children " was useless and very insupportable.

The Critical Review was extremely unfriendly and cantankerous : " The publication of any work at this time, in England composed of such rotten materials, is a phenomenon we cannot account for," whilst the supernatural machinery is ridiculed in most clumsy fashion., None the less, the enthusiasm which greeted The Castle of Otranto permeated all ranks of society and did not wane.

In 1767 the romance was translated into French by M. E., Marc-Antoine Eidous, but the dialogue had been abbreviated, and the Amsterdam edition of 1777, Le Château d'Otrante, translated from the second English edition of 1765, is far better done and more exact. In 1791 was printed at Parma Bodoni's fine edition, whilst in 1795 Sivrac issued his well-known Italian version, Il Castello di Otranto, with seven illustrations which, beautifully coloured, were used in Jeffery's fine edition of 1796.⁵⁴

In his first Preface, 1765, the anonymous Walpole says : " The scene is undoubtedly laid in some real castle." There needs no detailed comparison between Otranto and Strawberry Hill, suffice to say that in a hundred touches the galleries, the staircases, even the very rooms, are particularized.⁵⁵ Thus in Walpole's letters there are several references to the Blue Room at Strawberry. On January 7th, 1772, he writes to the Hon. Henry Conway how an explosion injured the Castle but providentially the windows in the " gallery, and blue room, and green closet, &c.," escaped. In the romance, Chapter V, Bianca was going to the Lady Isabella's chamber—" she lies in the watchet-coloured chamber, on the right hand, one pair of stairs."

The Castle of Otranto is none other than Strawberry Hill, which, indeed, Walpole explicitly acknowledged when he said that Strawberry was " a very proper habitation of, as it was the scene that inspired, the author of the Castle of Otranto."

Yet Amédé Pichot wrote of Strawberry Hill as " ce château, modèle du gout et d'élégance, serait plutôt une miniature gothique. C'est encore plus la villa du grand seigneur homme du monde, que le manoir du baron féodal." ⁵⁶

In November, 1786, when Lady Craven sent Walpole a delightful drawing of the Castle of Otranto, made on the spot, he told her : " I did not even know that there was a castle of Otranto. When the story was finished, I looked into the map of the kingdom of Naples for a well-sounding name, and that of Otranto was very sonorous." At the same time it seems difficult to suppose that Walpole had never heard of Otranto and its castle. Perhaps during his stay in Italy he had even seen some pictures of it, and he may have retained the name and the views quite subconsciously. In his Translator's Preface to the first edition he vaguely plans the incidents as having happened "between 1095, the æra of the first crusade, and 1243, the date of the last, or not long afterwards." "Manfred, Prince of Otranto," may even have a historical counterpart in Manfred or Manfroi,[57] a natural son of the Emperor Frederick II. Manfred, who was born in 1233 and killed in battle 1266, usurped the throne of Sicily in 1258, spreading a report that Conrad II, a mere child, was dead. He also bore the title Prince of Otranto. In the romance Manfred has seized the possessions of Frederic of Vincenza, who is supposed to have perished in Palestine, but who reappears upon the scene. The historical Manfred unlawfully acquired the heritage of Frederick II, who common rumour had it did not die in 1250, as was supposed. In 1259 a certain hermit, who much resembled the late Emperor, raised a revolt against Manfred in the South of Italy, and many hostile barons espoused his cause.

It were equally easy and equally futile to suggest sources for various incidents in the story. To write that Sidney's *Arcadia* is the original of "a part of the supernatural element" is quite absurd.[58] Walpole was, moreover, very much in earnest in his narrative, and, grotesque as the vast size of the enchanted casque, of the gigantic greaved leg, and the great hand in armour may appear, it is ridiculous to suppose that Walpole had these phantoms of unwieldy horror from *Les Quatre Facardins*.[59] Actually, of course, all this is from the romances of chivalry, *Primaleon*, *Palmerin of England*, *Felixmarte of Hyrcania*, and *Tirante the White*.

To give any analysis of the plot of *The Castle of Otranto* were superfluous.

"Horace Walpole wrote a goblin tale which has thrilled through many a bosom," says Scott in the Dedicatory Epistle to *Ivanhoe*, and however awkward to modern taste may seem the handling of certain incidents, however naïve the development of the narrative in certain particulars, there can be no doubt that Walpole has achieved a great and most remarkable work. As I have said elsewhere, *The Castle of Otranto* is "a notable landmark in the history of English taste and English literature."

In his notes to Pope's *Imitations of Horace*, Warburton remarked that *The Castle of Otranto* was "a Master piece, in the Fable," at any rate. "The scene is laid in *Gothic Chivalry* where a beautiful imagination, supported by strength of judgement, has enabled the author to go beyond his subject, and to effect the full purpose of the *Ancient Tragedy*, that is, *to purge the passions by pity and terror*, in colouring as great and harmonious as in any of the best dramatic Writers." This is no light praise, at least. Scott, also, concludes his admirable Essay upon Walpole with the following : " The applause due to chastity and precision of style—to a happy combination of super-natural agency with human interest—to a tone of feudal manners and language, sustained by characters strongly drawn and well discriminated —and to unity of action, producing scenes alternately of interest and of grandeur—the applause, in fine, which cannot be denied to him who can excite the passions of fear and of pity, must be awarded to the author of *The Castle of Otranto*."

Bishop Warburton, again, in his additional notes to Pope's *Works*, pregnantly observed that " the plan of *The Castle of Otranto* was regularly a drama," and Robert Jephson, an applauded dramatist of the day, in the autumn of 1779, fitted Walpole's Romance for the stage. He duly submitted his adaptation to the author, and so far engaged Walpole's interest, and even enthusiasm, that when *The Count of Nar-bonne* went into rehearsal at Covent Garden the exquisite recluse was actually attracted from Strawberry Hill to attend and advise. Produced on Saturday, November 17th, 1781, the new tragedy proved a veritable triumph. The play kept the stage for some forty years, and it certainly is not without merit. Kemble and Mrs. Siddons were more than once seen in the principal rôles, which they acted with great power and effect.

The Castle of Otranto, " a grand romantic extravaganza " given at the Haymarket, on Monday, April 24th, 1848, by way of an Easter novelty, to us seems a vapid burletta without fun or consequence, but it was greeted with applause, which one supposes must have been due to the acting of Keeley, Priscilla Horton, and Mrs. W. Clifford. At any rate it is interesting to note that as late as the middle of the last century a burlesque founded upon *The Castle of Otranto* was received with general favour, and this goes far to show how popular the romance still remained with the larger public, for to those who were not well acquainted with Walpole's original such a travesty must have been utterly pointless and a bore.[60]

It is surprising that a decade and more passed before the influence of *The Castle of Otranto* made itself really felt in literature.[61] It is, of course, possible to trace some resemblances in *The Hermit*, by Lady Atkyns, 2 vols., 1769 ; in *The Prince of Salerno*, 1770 ; and in William Hutchinson's *The Hermitage*, 1772 ; but these are nugatory and super-ficial. The famous *Sir Bertrand*, 1773, is merely A Fragment.

In 1797, T. J. Matthias could jeer the virtuoso Walpole, who
" mus'd o'er Gothick toys through Gothick glass," and in a gloss
could declare that " his Otranto Ghosts have propagated their species
with unequalled fecundity. The spawn is in every novel shop." [62]

It was in 1777 that the eminently sedate and sensible Clara Reeve,
then nearly fifty years of age, published (Colchester) *The Champion of
Virtue*, a second edition of which appeared in the following year as
The Old English Baron; *A Gothic Story*. The work is dedicated to
Richardson's daughter, Mrs. Brigden, who had revised and corrected
these pages. In the Preface to this later issue Miss Reeve candidly
acknowledges that " This Story is the literary offspring of *The Castle of
Otranto*, written upon the same plan, . . . it is distinguished by the
appellation of a Gothic Story, being a picture of Gothic times and
manners." Notwithstanding so frank a confession of parentage, Miss
Reeve indulges in some pretty severe philippics upon Walpole's
romance when she says that " the opening excites attention very
strongly ; the conduct of the story is artful and judicious ; the characters
are admirably drawn and supported ; the diction polished and elegant ;
yet, with all these brilliant advantages, it palls upon the mind (though
it does not upon the ear) ; and the reason is obvious, the machinery is
so violent, that it destroys the effect it is intended to excite. Had the
story been kept within the utmost *verge* of probability, the effect had
been preserved, without losing the least circumstance that excites or
detains the attention.

For instance, we can conceive of a ghost, we can even dispense with
an enchanted sword and helmet, but then they must be kept within
certain limits of credibility . . ." She objects, in fine, to the vast size
of Walpole's imaginations, to the picture that walks out of its frame, a
skeleton ghost in a hermit's cowl. There is just enough of truth in
this censure to make it exceedingly unpalatable, although (as I have
said elsewhere), even if the machinery be something violent, Walpole
has managed it with such skill and invested it with such glamour of
mediæval remoteness that a little crudity may be condoned, nay, I do
not know whether it does not add to the strength and surprise of the
adventures.

Walpole himself emphatically did not approve of Clara Reeve's
way of thinking in these matters, and writing to Mason on April 8th,
1778, he asks : " Have you seen The Old Baron, a Gothic story,
professedly written in imitation of Otranto, but reduced to reason and
probability ! It is so probable, that any trial for murder at the Old
Bailey would make a more interesting story. Mrs. Barbut's Fragment
was excellent. This is a *caput mortuum*." Again, in a letter to Robert

PLATE VIII

MISS LEE.

Author of the Receſs Chapter of Accidents &c &c.

Pubᵈ for the Proprietors of the Monthly Mirror Augᵗ 1 1797 by I Bellamy King Street Covent Garden.

SOPHIA LEE
Aetat. 47

[*Face p.* 186

Jephson, the dramatist, January, 1780, he says : " I cannot compliment the author of The Old English Baron, professedly written in imitation, but as a corrective of The Castle of Otranto. It was totally void of imagination and interest ; had scarce any incidents ; and, though it condemned the marvellous, admitted a ghost. I suppose the author thought a tame ghost might come within the laws of probability." Walpole was obviously piqued, and perhaps not altogether without reason. He resented a work " a professed imitation of mine, only stripped of the marvellous, and so entirely stripped, except its one awkward attempt at a ghost or two, that it is the most insipid dull nothing you can read."

Walpole has all my sympathy, for one, but he is excessively severe, even unjust, for Miss Reeve tells a good story and makes it interesting throughout. The mystery is sustained with skill, and holds the reader. The Castle of Otranto is undeniably the finer piece of work, as it is the wilder, but he is not to be envied who cannot enjoy The Old English Baron as well. Moreover, Miss Reeve has some fine romance, for example, her description of the deserted suite of rooms is entirely in the vein of Mrs. Radcliffe, and admirably done. She has, in fact, atmosphere. I hasten to add that she can be (of set purpose, of course) quite homely and domestic.

Here we meet a knight who sups " upon new-laid eggs and rashers of bacon, with the highest relish " ; Sir Robert " complained of the toothache " ; when Edmund spends a night in the haunted apartments he determines to lie down in his clothes as " the bedding was very damp " ; and so on ; but these simple and commonplace details, introduced as they are with singular artlessness, to my mind add a touch to the narrative which is not without a very definite value, enhanced as it is by the easy and natural dialogue.

The period of The Old English Baron is the minority of Henry VI, during the protectorate of the Duke of Gloucester, and the scene is laid at Lovel Castle, the ruins of which may yet be visited at Minster Lovel, a truly romantic and most beautiful spot. The hero, Edmund Twyford, the reputed child of a cottager, is really the son of the murdered Lord Lovel, and the story tells how he is reinstated in his rank and possessions. So well was Miss Reeve's romance received that it was reprinted no less than thirteen times between 1778 and 1786. Sir Walter Scott remarks that whilst " it is no doubt true that The Old English Baron . . . is sometimes tame and tedious, not to say mean and tiresome," the romance must be allowed great merit, and even " a certain creeping and low line of narrative and sentiment," prolix, minute and unnecessary details, " do certainly add in some degree to its reality," being " precisely such as would occur in a similar story told by a grandsire or grandame to a circle assembled round a winter's fire."

In 1787 appeared a French version by de la Place, *Le Vieux Baron anglais, ou les Revenants vengés*, " histoire gothique, imitée de l'anglais de Mistress Clara Reeve," of which another edition was issued the same year as *Le Champion de la Vertu, ou le Vieux Baron anglais.* In 1800 a new translation had some success, *Édouard, ou le Spectre du Château*, Paris an VIII.

The Old English Baron was dramatized as *Edmond, Orphan of the Castle*, a tragedy, published anonymously, 8vo, 1799. This is a very poor piece, written in a kind of cripple blank verse. It was probably refused by the theatres, in any case, it was never acted.

Several chap-books prove to be alterations and abridgements of Clara Reeve's most famous romance. Of these one, at least, published in 1818, sums up the whole story on the title-page thus : " Lovel Castle, or the Rightful Heir Restored, a Gothic Tale ; Narrating how a Young Man, the Supposed Son of a Peasant, by a Train of Un-paralleled Circumstances, not only Discovers who were his Real Parents, but that they came to Untimely Deaths ; with his Adventures in the Haunted Apartment, Discovery of the Fatal Closet, and Appear-ance of the Ghost of his Murdered Father ; Relating, also, how the Murderer was Brought to Justice, with his Confession, and the Restora-tion of the Injured Orphan to his Title and Estates."

Clara Reeve can hardly be said to have repeated her success, although her novels were much admired by her contemporaries. She is perhaps too exclusively moral in her tone, too eager to impart ethical instruction, rather than to tell a story, which, notwithstanding, she could do remarkably well.

Of her five romances, *The Two Mentors*, 1783, deals with contem-porary life ; *The Exiles, or Memoirs of the Count de Crondstadt*, 1789, is founded on two stories of Baculard d'Arnaud, *L'Histoire de Comte Gleicher* and *D'Almanzi, anecdote françoise* ; *The School for Widows*, 1791, draws a paragon of wifely tact and virtue in Mrs. Strictland ; *Memoirs of Sir Roger de Clarendon*, 1793, gives us famous episodes of the reigns of Edward III and Richard II, prefaced with some pretty severe strictures on these writers who for romance sake dare to " falsify historical facts," since the consequences are mischievous and mislead young minds—the book is dull ; *Destination : or, Memoirs of a Private Family*, 1799, is a dry chip of the ultra-didactic stock.

It is a sad pity that her ghost story, *Castle Connor, an Irish story*, was lost from the London coach in May, 1787, and never recovered. It is perhaps worth noting that *Fatherless Fanny*, 1819, although often ascribed to, and even printed as by, "The Author of The Old English Baron " is not from her pen.

The Progress of Romance through Time, Countries, and Manners . . . *in a Course of evening Conversations,* 1785, is a work which suffers from self-imposed limitations. The form is a little difficult, and the extreme homiletic tone more difficult still. None the less the piece is important, and has much to say that is both interesting and valuable.[63]

Strawberry Hill was the Castle of Otranto, a most significant, indeed an essential fact, which I have repeatedly emphasized. Nor is it impertinent to note that Lovel Castle is a real building, much visited and admired by the romanticist, and this not the less because it is decayed and mouldering to ruin.

The connexion between the Gothic Romance and Gothic Architecture is, so to speak, congenital and indigenous, it goes deep down to and is vitally of the very heart of the matter.

The ruin of itself was a thing of beauty—and even more.[64] A ruin impresses the mind with tender melancholy bred from reflexion upon times long since gone ; it inspires the philosopher with meditations upon the swift passage of man, prince and peasant alike, all fallen to dust ; the ivy clambering around the broken tracery of a noble window, the grass that waves where some stately altar stood, the sky seen through the gaping rafters of some great banqueting hall, the crumbling arch of some yawning portal, the lone courtyard that so often rang with the cheery noise of horse and hound, all these bear witness to the impermanence of human things, and in their decadence are in some sense symbols of a wider liberty.

" In this turbulent life, oppressed by the urgencies of business, fettered by the cares of the world, and in the evening of my days, I wish to recall the shadows of departed joys, alas ! only the shadows of those days of my youth, in which solitude was my sole delight ; in which no retreat was more agreeable to me than the sequestered convent and the lonely cell, the lofty and awfully gloomy forests, or the ruined castles of ancient barons ; and no pleasure more lively than the converse with the *dead*." Thus wrote Johann Georg, Ritter Von Zimmermann in his celebrated *Ueber die Einsamkeit* (1755),[65] a book in England universally admired as *Zimmermann On Solitude*.

The number of romances published in the fifty years following *Otranto* which proclaimed the word *Castle* in their titles is a striking proof of the immense importance of the Castle in the Gothic Novel. When we add other such words—all connected with architecture—as *Abbey, Priory,* we may well double our list.

To catalogue these would be but to write down a hundred names, which tale might easily be increased by a hundred more, and yet a hundred again, so I will only point out that not all romances with Castle in their title are Terror Novels ; some present scenes of contemporary life as, for example, Charles Lucas' *The Castle of Saint Donats* ; or *The History of Jack Smith*, 3 vols., Minerva Press, 1798 ; and *The Castle of Tariffa*; *or, The Self-Banished Man*,[66] 4 vols., Crosby, 1812.

Sometimes Castle and Convent were combined as in *Ivey Castle*, " containing Interesting Memoirs of Two Ladies, late Nuns in a French abolished Convent," 2 vols., Owen, 1794, published at 6*s*., concerning which *The Monthly Review* [67] not untruly remarked, " When Cupid has teazed everybody all round and made them play at cross purposes he allows them to be happy."

Let us at haphazard take the date 1800 and briefly pass in review some five romances of that year whose titles are embellished by *Castle*, *Priory*, or *Abbey*.

Rimualdo, or The Castle of Badajos, 3 vols., by W. H. Ireland, is a fine type of the extremer Terror Novel, and it certainly called forth a cry from *The Monthly Review*,[68] whose critic exclaims that the oglio of the modern romance supplies : " unnatural parents,—persecuted lovers,—murders,—haunted apartments,—winding sheets, and winding staircases,—subterranean passages,—lamps that are dim and perverse, and that always go out when they should not,—monasteries,—caves,—monks, tall, thin, and withered with lank abstemious cheeks,—dreams,—groans,—and spectres." None of which things or persons are perhaps as uncommon as the critic supposed.

Humbert Castle, or, The Romance of the Rhone, 4 vols., Lane, proved deservedly popular, and won great favour in the circulating libraries. It is a well-written, cleverly-sustained romance.

Ankerwick Castle, by Mrs. Crofts, 4 vols., Lane, is an epistolary novel. The young Countess of Middleton loves the accomplished Beaumont, and after many perplexities, which lead to the discovery of malignant jealousy and enormous depravity, the hero and heroine are happily united. In the following year, 1801, Mrs. Crofts published with Lane, 2 vols., *Salvador, or Baron de Montbelliard*.

Monk Wood Priory, by Francis Tracy Thomas, a Cornet of the East and West Lothian Dragoons, published by Longman, 2 vols., is also told in a series of letters. The charms of Mrs. Sullivan are perhaps the most prominent theme, and the work is by no means unentertaining in its course.

Tales of the Abbey, founded on Historical Facts, 3 vols., 1808, Symonds, by A. Kendall,[69] whose *Derwent Priory*, 2 vols., had appeared the previous year, introduces amid Gothic surroundings and romantic scenery the widow of Sidney and the successor of Essex. The reviewer however, in *The Critical Review*,[70] remarked on the intrusion of modern manners, and added : " The sliding panel, the passing sigh, with the various paraphernalia of modern novels, have been too often repeated to interest or attract." None the less he justly allowed that the " story is not unskilfully managed," and in my opinion this romance has very considerable merit.

An Abbey in the Title continued to engage. Thus *Cordova Abbey* : *or, Lights and Shadows of the present Day*, Saunders, Otley & Co., 1860, is a clever novel dealing with the burning topics of the hour, Puseyism, ritualism and ecclesiasticism in general. The description of Lanerth Old Hall is entirely Gothic, as also is the account of the mysterious music heard in the Abbey, and the yew wreath hung by invisible hands over the rude altar tomb of the sainted Abbot Bernard : " Hic jacet Abbas Bernardus, ob. mens. Junii XXV. A.D. MDXXX."

The dark shadow of Antonio Morosini, who when supposed to be far away is seen in Rome garbed as one of the Sacconi, and who confers with Padre Azzolani, S.J., at the Gesù, and the extraordinary Padre Enrico, again, are wholly in the crusted Protestant tradition. The book which seems to be written from a rather tepid Anglican point of view, is important, and should have been included at least in the Bibliography of Joseph Ellis Barker's *The Novel and the Oxford Movement*, 1932, a somewhat superficial monograph upon an all-important subject.

In *Cordova Abbey*, Rome and Naples are written of with a sad shaking of the head, whilst the Lady Drumdo, who as a good Protestant likes things " comfortably done," a nice large pew, an arm-chair, a fireplace and a screen, is pretty sharply snibbed.

I may, perhaps not irrelevantly, be allowed to quote here a passage which I wrote more than ten years ago in reference to this very point, when I was stressing the importance of Architecture in the Gothic Novel. " In by far the greatest number of their works it would be true to say that the protagonist is not the plaintive and persecuted heroine, Elmira, Rosaline, Matilda ; nor the handsome and gallant hero, Theodore, Constantine, Rosalvo ; nor the desperate and murderous villain, Montoni, Wolfran, Gondemar ; nor even the darkly-scowling and mysterious monk, Father Heriome, Abbot Beneditto, Theodosius de Zulvin ; but rather the remote and ruined castle with its antique courts, deserted chambers, pictured windows that exclude the light, haunted galleries amid whose mouldering gloom is heard the rustle of an unseen robe, a sigh, a hurried footfall where no mortal step should tread ; the ancient manor, hidden away in the heart of a pathless forest, a home of memories of days long gone before when bright eyes glanced from casement and balcony over the rich domain, the huge-girthed oaks, the avenues and far-stretching vistas, the cool stream winding past the grassy lawns, but now tenanted only by a silver-headed retainer and his palsied dame ; the huge fortress set high upon some spar of the Apenines, dark machicolated battlements and sullen towers which frown o'er the valleys below, a lair of masterless men, through whose dim corridors prowl armed bandits, whose halls ring with hideous revelry or anon are silent as the grave ; the lone and secret convent amid the hills ruled by some proud abbess whose nod is law, a cloister of which the terraces overlook vast precipices shagged with larch and darkened by the gigantic pine, whose silences are only disturbed by the deep bell that knolls to midnight office and the ceremonies of solemn prayer."

The reviewers sometimes fretted. " In truth we are almost weary of Gothic castles, mouldering turrets and ' cloud inveloped battle-ments,' " said *The Critical Review* [71] when noticing John Palmer's *The Haunted Cavern*, 3 vols., 1795. " More abbeys with battlemented ramparts ! " peevishly cried a critic [72] when he took up T. J. Horsley Curties' *Ancient Records*.

Sir Walter Scott's delightful banter is famous : " We strolled through a variety of castles, each of which was regularly called Il Castello ; met with as many captains of condottieri, heard various ejaculations of Santa Maria and Diabolo ; read by a decaying lamp and in a tapestried chamber dozens of legends as stupid as the main history ; examined such suites of deserted apartments as might set up a reasonable barrack, and saw as many glimmering lights as would make a respectable illumination."

With very few exceptions—Mrs. Sleath and Mrs. Yorke, for example, were Catholics—the Gothic novelist beyond his vivid imaginings only knew the cloister, the Abbey, the Priory as a romantic ruin. Religious were a people unseen, unknown, of an infinite mystery. The French anti-clerical literature gave fuel for the wildest fantasies and fears. Such plays as Monvel's *Les Victimes cloîtrées, Le Couvent* of Olympe de Gouges, and *Julie ou la Religieuse de Nisme* of Pougens were all written with a purpose, definitely a bad purpose, they belong to " le Théâtre Monacal." In the same way *Les Trois Moines*, 2 vols., Paris, 1802, written by De Faverolle's sister, Madame de Guénard, baronne de Méré, which was translated by H. J. Sarratt as *The Three Monks*, 2 vols., Crosby, 1803, most bitterly and coarsely attacks the cloistered life. Indeed, the very Avant-Propos opens with a rabid truculence : " Dans les Temps ou la superstition le disputoit à l'ignorance pour ensevelir les hommes dans le dernier degré d'avilissement, l'état de moine étoit le meilleur de tous. Bonne chère, bon vin en abondance. . . ."

As we might expect, Bage in *Hermsprong*; *or, Man as he is not*, 1796, is very severe and censorious : " Up the Gron, on the right, stand the ruins of a convent, many centuries the domicile of a succession of holy drones, who buzzed about, sucked the fairest flowers of the vale, and stung where they could extract no honey."

Maturin, in *Melmoth the Wanderer*, 1820, has some extremely detailed and lurid descriptions of what he conceived monastic life in Spain might be, and in his last romance *The Albigenses*, 1824, he writes with the most deep-rooted prejudice and an entire disrespect for history. But then Maturin was of a French Protestant stock, he was curate of S. Peter's, Dublin, from which pulpit he preached Six Sermons on the Errors of the Roman Catholic Church. These were published in one volume, 8vo, Dublin, 1824, and reprinted 12mo, 1826.

Ireland, a lesser name, indulges in grossest caricature, the sort of thing which can do no kind of harm. Thus his Abbess in the romance of the same name is a lewd and practised wanton ; whilst in *Gondez the Monk*, 1805, we have the wildest and most outrageous melodrama, as, for example, in the scene when the yelling spectre of the Little Red Woman, a damned witch, appears before the full tribunal of the Holy Office to ding the villain monk to perdition.

The Holy Office often assumes terrific features in these romances. It might be supposed that *The Inquisition*, an anonymous novel, two volumes, Vernor and Hood, no date on title-page, but 1797, would prove to be at least a fertile if extravagant composition. I looked for shrouded familiars with eyes gleaming red through their black hoods, a Grand Inquisitor more imperious than Cæsar, more murderous than Tīmūr Khan. One could hear the clank of chains and hollow groans, one at least expected such tortures as the rack and cord. I regret to say that although the heroine, Ophelia, " talked much of caverns, tortures, and death," the bystanders merely think " to secure, by binding, the lovely maniac." What is more amazing is " when on a nearer examination of the countenance of the Grand Inquisitor, I found, that notwithstanding the apparent sternness of his features, yet openness and judgement were its chief characteristics." One realizes that Don Montelaski has a splendid name, but in spite of both the Inquisition and the Bastille this romance falls short. It is, in fine, a little amateurish. Perhaps *The Monthly Mirror* [73] was fairly just when the critic said that the romance was " not entirely destitute of merit," but that the " Composition is indifferent; and the fable by no means judiciously planned. . . . It may, perhaps, be permitted to pass current with the young masters and misses who subscribe for amusement to the respectable and intelligent keepers of a circulating library."

A long list of novels might be given in which the Holy Office is introduced, but it will suffice to instance the four which are the most famous. There is a powerful scene towards the conclusion of Lewis' *The Monk*, when Ambrosio and Matilda are confronted and convicted of sorcery with other horrid crimes before this tribunal. Mrs. Radcliffe uses the Inquisition with marked restraint and the greater effect in *The Italian*. Godwin's St. Leon is seized by the alguazils of the Inquisition at Madrid, and Maturin's Isidora is immured by the Spanish familiars in circumstances truly pathetic.

A very notable Gothic romance is the anonymous *Lusignan, or The Abbaye of La Trappe*,[74] four volumes, Minerva Press, 1801. The tale is exceedingly well told, and although it is true that the distresses which involve the young Marquis de Lusignan and his loved Emily are due to the malignancy and perfidy of an ecclesiastic, the villainous Abbé La Haye, the episodes—and they are many—which have their scene in cloister and in abbey are treated without offence. The author can hardly have been a Catholic. There is mention of attendance at vespers and matins, but not at mass. No difference is made between monks and friars. At the same time there are many significant details which one would hardly have expected any but a Catholic to have known and appreciated.

It is not necessary to give at length the adventures of this truly interesting work. Suffice to say that owing to the evil designs of La Haye, the Marquis de Lusignan, son of the Duke de Meronville, is betrayed and carried off upon the very eve of his marriage with Emily, daughter of the Countess de Clarival, a union to which his cruel and deceitful father had given a seeming consent. Lusignan is kept concealed in a distant dungeon, the vile plotters professing ignorance of his fate.

The Countess upon her death-bed is attended by a friar, Father du Secque, who is introduced with great reverence and respect, and through whose good offices the orphaned Emily is enabled to take refuge in the convent of St. Claire, a house very different from those usually described in Gothic romance, since the Abbess received her with the utmost courtesy, and when a nun wishes to leave the cloister she is released " by an order from the Suffragan Bishop."

In time Lusignan becomes the Duke de Meronville only to find that Emily has been wedded to the Marquis de Bentivoglio. He struggles to win her for himself, but fails, and there is some impressive writing when at last he is shown her tomb in the chapel of St. Jago. Life is utterly empty for him now and ended. He decides to become a Trappist monk, and takes his way to the Abbey of La Trappe on the confines of Perche in Normandy.

" He arrived at the outward court ; over the portal was a statue of St. Bernard." The austerities of the rule, the life of the monks, the vigils, the fasts, the prayers, are described with a correctness and, I may add, a restraint which it is truly refreshing to remark. There are, of course, some mistakes, some bad errors even, but on the whole the picture is drawn without melodrama or meretricious thrills, and gives evidence of study and research. Moreover, an unfeigned piety informs the closing pages of this striking romance. The Abbot is presented as a man of saintly character, and his fervent exhortations are expressed not only with sincerity, but even rise to a certain strain of mysticism. Among the brethren is one who although he has but newly taken the vows, is distinguished by the ardour of his devotion, Brother Ambrose. Upon the very day when he is to pronounce his solemn profession, Ambrose is found to be dying, and is carried into the chapel to be laid upon the lowly bed of ashes. As the dread moment of dissolution fast approaches, Ambrose with failing voice sighs : " Behold in me the sad victim of sensibility—behold a *woman* ! " —A general groan interrupted her.—" Yes," she continued, " a woman who has lived for man—but dies for God !—a guilty miserable woman, who calls on religion to assist her end ! "—She lifted her cowl, which had concealed her features.—" Look on me, Meronville ! listen, and recognize her who took love for her guide—her who misled you——" " Ah, heavens, my Emily ! " cried the Duke, throwing himself on the ground by her ; " here will I also die !—one tomb shall receive us ! "

The conclusion of the book as she swiftly expires is extremely poignant and pathetic, and the climax is treated with the utmost delicacy and reserve.

There are some anachronisms, it is true, but these hardly detract from the exceptional merit of this very unusual romance. For example, actually the Reform of La Trappe was not instituted until well-nigh fifty years after the period when the events of *Lusignan* are supposed to have taken place.

Although we are bound to allow that here and there a distinct " anti-Roman feeling " is to be found in the pages of certain writers, it would be foolish to insist upon any militant protestantism of the John Kensit and Chiniquy school in the Gothic novelists. These authors employed abbots and convents, friars and cloisters, " cowled monks with scapulars," " veiled nuns with rosaries," because such properties were exotic, they were mysterious, and capable of the highest romantic treatment.   There is no idea of accuracy, and shocking blunders are often made over the simplest details of ritual or attire. The ignorance of the writers is naive in the last degree, but what matter so long as the intended effect was secured !

Examples of the most incredible ineptitude might easily be cited, but I will confine myself to only a few specimens.   It is curious that these gross and laughable inaccuracies seldom, if ever, injure the romance or lessen its interest.

In Mrs. Radcliffe's *The Italian*, we meet a Dominican " monk " who appears " wrapt in the black garments of his order," and who is able to absent himself from the society for whole days together unquestioned and unchecked.   Whilst Ellena is at the convent of San Stefano, " the vesper bell, at length, summoned her to prepare for mass," which is celebrated in the evening, and the lady abbess of a Carmelite house leads a procession, " dressed in her pontifical robes, with the mitre on her head."   Ellena is a guest at " the Ursaline convent," whose abbess befriends this heroine.

In Lewis' *The Monk*, a whole community of Poor Clares leave their enclosure to go to confession in a neighbouring church, and afterwards take part in a public procession through the streets of Madrid at midnight.

In Robert Huish's *The Brothers ; or, The Castle of Niolo*, an abbot continually invokes " his holy patron, St. Benedictine " !   Ireland's Abbess rules "the convent of Santa Maria del Nova at Florence"; Theodosius de Zulvan, in *The Monk of Madrid*, belongs to the Order of St. Mark ; the monk Udolpho (of Horsley Curties) invented a new and sufficiently striking habit " of sable baize, reaching from the head and flowing round his feet, which were laced only with sandals," whilst " across his eyebrows was bound a white linen forehead cloth, upon which was displayed the ghastly grinning ensign of a Death's head."

A very singular ceremony at the burial of Eugenia is described in *The Mysteries of the Forest* : " The monks of the Order of St. Januarius, holding tapers in their hands, and chaunting a solemn requiem for the soul of the deceased, closed the procession."

In *Santa-Maria, or The Mysterious Pregnancy* by Joseph Fox of Brighton, the heroine appears to be dead but revives, when her mother informs her : " On the night, my child, of your supposed death, two Carthusian friars said mass over your sleeping body.—I occasionally mingled in their holy orisons."   There are no Carthusian *friars*.   The

sons of S. Bruno are monks, votaries of an almost perpetual silence.
Yet in *The Count di Novini, or, the Confederate Carthusians, A Neapolitan
Tale*, 3 vols., Robinson, 1800 (10s. 6d.), there are interminable dialogues,
and it is a most garrulous piece of work.

But we do not look for accuracy on these points among our writers
of the school of *Otranto*, or Lewis, or Mrs. Radcliffe. It was owing to
their melancholy and their mystery, that monasteries and cloisters had
an extraordinary fascination for the Gothic novelist. They were
remote ; they were unknown ; who in England had ever penetrated
within a convent's walls ? The very dress of their denizens, the swart
black cowl of a Benedictine, the cypress habiliments and snowy lawn
of some pallid Carmelite or Dominicaness for ever imprisoned behind
the convent grille, were in themselves romantic in the highest degree,
and allowed of the utmost exercise of perfervid imaginings. The
glamour, too, of Priory and Nunnery was not without a delicious
admixture of fear, that entrancing dread which is almost an essential
ingredient of the Gothic novel. In England, at any rate, there were
no cloisters, no convents, but there was something which was almost
better : there were the venerable ruins of the hallowed homes of days
long passed away. There were Glastonbury and Tintern, Fountains
and Whitby, Kirkstall, Jervaulx, Netley, Whalley, Welbeck, Barlings,
Beauchief, Dodford, Coverham, Tor. All of these were monuments
of most exquisite beauty ; to use a word beloved of the Gothic writer,
they were eminently "picturesque," surpassingly lovely even in their
decay where the ivy was mantling thickly over buttress and pinnacle,
the green grass growing rank in the roofless aisles, weeds and country
flowers flaunting their vivid kirtles among the broken tracery of these
empty oriels, which had once been blazoned with even fairer hues, the
crimson and gold, the topaz and the azure of richly painted glass,
dight with many a sacred picture and noble heralding. Excursions to,
and long meditations upon, scenes such these, awakened corresponding
emotions in the bosom of the Gothic enthusiast. He experienced the
most delicious sensibility, a sentiment which was amply fed by the
pages of his favourite writers. And so many readers were able, in
some slight degree, to enjoy in real life moments, at least, of that
romanticism which had become so dear to them in fiction. And this,
after all, is one of the most fundamental feelings that humanity knows.
The boy who has been reading of Robin Hood or Dick Turpin will
presently imagine the little back garden in the suburbs Sherwood
Forest or the road to York. The girl who reads of desert tents and
handsome Sheiks with flashing eyes, chieftains lithe as a leopard,
amorous as a dove, in her little back bedroom sees the ceiling vanish

away, and in its place a pavilion of dark blue sky, studded with a thousand golden stars, what time she hears the soft thud of horses' hoofs over the burning sand as her lover hastens to her side. To escape thus from humdrum reality is a primitive desire, and, in itself, it is excellent and right. The world, if we had not our dreams, would, God knows, be a very dull place. Of course, as precisians will never fail to tell you, there is danger in dreams. But, if we had not our dreams, life, I take it, would be far more dangerous ; in fact, it would not be worth while living at all. We call our dreams Romance, and it was just this that the Gothic novelists gave to their readers. This, then, is exactly the reason why I think the Gothic novelists, with all their faults and failings, have done us infinite service, and proved themselves true friends to those of us who care to withdraw, be it even for a short time, and at rare intervals, from the relentless oppression and carking cares of a bitter actuality.

NOTES TO CHAPTER IV

1. Mrs. Haywood died February 25th, 1756, and the last novel which she composed, *The History of Leonora Meadowson*, appeared posthumously, 2 vols., 1778.

2. For whom see further *Dryden The Dramatic Works*, edited by Montague Summers, Vol. V, 1932, pp. 109–11.

3. Translated by Thomas Mabbe as *The Two Damosels* in *Exemplarie Novels*, folio, 1640. Dryden's *The Rival Ladies*, acted in 1664, 4to, 1664, was to some extent suggested by this novel of Cervantes. Dryden, *The Dramatic Works*, ed. Montague Summers, Vol. I, 1931, pp. 131–32.

4. As early as 1915 I corrected in print the mistake that *The Innocent Adultery* which Lydia Languish read was Southerne's tragedy : *The Works of Aphra Behn*, ed. Montague Summers, Vol. V, 1915, p. 259. The blunder, however, has since been revived again and again, even in the Oxford University Press edition of *The Dramatic Works of Richard Brinsley Sheridan*, 1924, p. 473.
Southerne's tragedy, *The Fatal Marriage ; or, The Innocent Adultery*, is, as I was the first to discover and point out, founded upon Mrs. Behn's novel, *The History of the Nun ; or, The Fair Vow-Breaker*, 12mo, 1689, which has only once been reprinted, in my edition of Mrs. Behn, Vol. V, *ut cit. sup.* The plot of *The Fatal Marriage* is entirely different from the intrigue of Scarron's *Innocent Adultery*. In Lydia Languish's day, moreover, *The Fatal Marriage ; or, The Innocent Adultery*, with woeful alterations, had become *Isabella ; or, The Fatal Marriage.*
The Whole Duty of Man, 1658–60, by Bp. Allestree, was very frequently reprinted.

5. For a full account of the Abbé de Saint-Réal and his work see my edition of Otway, 3 vols., 1926 ; Vol. I, Introduction, pp. xl–l, lxxxvi–xcvii, and 69.

6. *Ibid.*, Vol. III, pp. 1–83, 271–87 ; and *Appendix to Venice Preserv'd*, being extracts from Saint-Réal's *Conspiracy of the Spaniards*, pp. 249–60.

7. The latest revival was by the Phoenix Society, November 28th and 30th, 1930. Jaffier, Ion Swinley ; Pierre, Baliol Holloway ; Antonio, Stanley Lathbury ; Belvidera, Cathleen Nesbitt ; and Aquilina, Edith Evans.

8. One of the most popular of these was printed about 1640 : " The Life and Death

of Fair Rosamond, King Henry the Seconds Concubine, and how she was Poysoned to death by Queen Elenor."

9. In the chapter " The Actor-Dramatists " in a forthcoming volume of my *Restoration Theatre*, I discuss the question of the authorship of this play, whether it was written by Mountford or Bancroft.

10. *The Gentleman's Journal*, October, 1692, p. 24.

11. From Part II " Constance *the fair Nun*" Dryden took a hint for the plot of his comedy, *The Assignation*, produced by Killigrew's company at Lincoln's Inn Field in 1672 ; 4to, 1673. See *Dryden, The Dramatic Works*, ed. by Montague Summers, Vol. III, 1932, pp. 271–2.

12. Reprinted in my edition of Mrs. Behn's *Works*, 1915, Vol. V, p. 209.

13. All these, with the exception of *The Amours of Edward the IV*, which is not cata-logued, appear in the Term Catalogues under " History." This novel is " By the *Author* of the *Turkish Spy*," who is spoken of as recently deceased. Dr. Robert Midgley, 1653–1723, cannot therefore be intended. Early volumes of *L'Esploratore turco* had appeared at Paris as early as 1664. There is an edition, Parigi, 1684. The first four volumes were translated into French before 1696. The author is generally supposed to have been a Genoese, Giovanni Paolo Marana. The work was translated into English by Bradshaw, and edited for the press by Midgley. Nichols in his *Literary Anecdotes* says that Dr. Manley was the original author, and that Dr. Midgley, having found the manuscript among his papers, appropriated the book, asserting he had translated it from the Italian. This does not fit the facts. The *Suite de l'Espion Turc*, which appeared in 1696, is attributed to Carlo Cotolendi. It is probable that *The Amours of Edward the IV* is to be considered the work of Manley.

14. Mrs. Behn's " sweet sentimental " *Agnes de Castro* is a novella, only occupying some 40 pages, and therefore I exclude this. *The Annals of Love* collects a number of histories.

15. For this attribution see my edition of Otway, 1926, Vol. II, pp. 313–20, where I reprint in an Appendix *The History of Brandon*. See also Vol. II, p. 157.

16. *The History of England*, A New Edition, Vol. II (1789), p. 159.

17. Constable's Edition of *The Castle of Otranto and the Mysterious Mother*, 1924, Intro-duction, p. xxiv. *Longsword* is in two volumes, and the Second Volume has a separate frontispiece.

18. K. K. Mehrotra, *Horace Walpole and the English Novel*, 1934, pp. 41–42, supposes that " the monk who was later to become so famous and so mysterious in Lewis and Mrs. Radcliffe " was derived from Father Peter in William Hutchinson's *The Hermitage*, 1772 !

19. A salient example being Mr. K. K. Mehrotra's *Horace Walpole and the English Novel*, 1934, to which reference is made in the previous note.

20. See, for example, the Introduction to my edition of *The Castle of Otranto*, to which reference has just been made, n. 17.

21. There were three editions, 8vo, 1767 ; a fourth edition, 8vo, 1769 ; and it was reprinted, 12mo, 1775 ; 8vo, 1784 ; and 12mo, 1793. It is included in John Bell's *British Theatre*, Vol. XXI, 1793 ; in Mrs. Inchbald's *British Theatre*, Vol. XX, 1808.

22. F. S. A., 1781. Of Hutchinson, who was a well-known topographer, there is some account in the *Dictionary of National Biography*.

23. *The Critical Review*, January, 1773.

24. Bicknell, a miscellaneous writer, who died in 1796, is noticed in the *Dictionary of National Biography*.

25. Bicknell's *The History of Edward, Prince of Wales, commonly termed the Black Prince*, 1776, and *The Life of Alfred the Great*, 1777, are quasi-serious biographies, a certain substratum of fact garnished with anecdote and conversations, historical hermaphrodites. This sort of narrative, or something very like it, was even to be found in professed chroniclers. With regard to *The History of Edward, Prince of Wales*, Bicknell rather naïvely remarks, p. xv, " As my chief view has been to make this work entertaining as well as instructive, I have not interrupted the narrative with references to the original authorities."

26. *The Critical Review*, 1786, Vol. LXII, p. 469.

27. Curiously enough, Professor G. C. D. Odell, in his *Shakespeare from Betterton to Irving*, 2 vols., 1921, has no mention of John Lee and his Shakespearean adaptations, which historically are important, and should not have been omitted.

28. Diderot's play was translated as *Dorval; or, The Test of Virtue*, 8vo, 1767; and gave material to General Burgoyne for his immensely popular *The Heiress*, produced at Drury Lane on Saturday, January 14th, 1786, and which ran into no less than seven editions the same year, being very frequently reprinted.

29. Produced in some haste to cover up the fiasco of Ireland's pseudo-Shakespearean *Vortigern*.

30. Licensed by Sir Henry Herbert, November 25th, 1641 ; acted at the Blackfriars ; 8vo, 1652 ; revived after the Restoration at the Theatre Royal.

31. *Some Account of the English Stage*, 10 vols., Bath, 1832 ; Vol. VI, p. 472.

32. *Ibid.*, Vol. IV, pp. 346–47.

33. Byron was emphatic that he did not intend *Werner* for the stage. It was first produced at the Park Theatre, New York, in 1826. In London, at Drury Lane, December 15th, 1830, with Macready as Werner. A special performance for the benefit of Westland Marston was given at the Lyceum on June 1st, 1887, with Henry Irving as Werner, and Ellen Terry, Josephine. *Kreutzner* was also dramatized by Georgiana, Duchess of Devonshire (1757–1806).

34. *The Works of Lord Byron*, ed. E. H. Coleridge, Vol. V (2nd ed.), 1905, p. 328.

35. *Canterbury Tales*, 1837 (Bentley's Standard Novels, No. 12), Vol. I, p. vi, note.

36. *The Gentleman's Magazine*, LVI, i, p. 327.

37. There is a much broader and rather vulgar caricature in Barrett's *The Heroine*, Colburn, 3 vols., 1813, Letter XXX, where Cherubina is entrusted with her " mother's memoirs," *Il Castello di Grimgothico*.

38. A similar device of the manuscript, with grave lacunæ, was effectively employed with some elaboration by Mgr. Robert Hugh Benson in his *Richard Raynal Solitary*, 1912. Not a few readers actually took the work to be, as the writer simulated, a transcript from ancient manuscript sources.

39. February, 1802, p. 237.

40. This romance supposed to be transcribed from an old family manuscript entrusted to Mrs. Mackenzie by a descendant of the protagonists, (Introduction, p. xxii), actually is founded on *Die Räuber*.

41. Reviewed in *The Monthly Review*, Vol. XVI, January, 1795, pp. 112–14.

42. May, 1795, Vol. XVII, p. 108.

43. December, 1802. Vol. XXXVI, Second Series, p. 478.

44. Published by Connor, price 7*s.*

45. See *Dryden The Dramatic Works*, edited by Montague Summers, Vol. VI, 1932, pp. 3–15.

46. The story is taken from the first volume of Abbé Millot's *The Literary History of the Troubadours*. Burgoyne's play was immensely popular. There are two editions, 8vo, 1786, and a fifth edition was reached in the following year. The music was by Grétry and Thomas Linley.

47. A pseudonym.

48. Vol. I, pp. 145–9.

49. Mrs. Ker also wrote : *Adeline St. Julian ; or, The Midnight Hour*, 2 vols., 1797 ; *The Heiress di Montalde ; or, The Castle of Bezanto*, 2 vols., 1799 ; *Emmeline, or, The Happy Discovery*, 2 vols., 1801 ; *The Mysterious Count ; or, Montville Castle*, 2 vols., 1803 ; and *Modern Faults, a novel, founded on facts*, 2 vols., 1814.

50. Vol. LXXXVIII, Part II, p. 617.

51. *The Castle of Otranto*, edited, with an Introduction and Notes, by Montague Summers, 1924, Introduction, p. lvii.

52. *The Letters of Horace Walpole* . . . edited . . . by Mrs. Paget Toynbee. Sixteen Volumes, Oxford, 1903–5. Vol. II, p. 278. All my references are to this edition, but I have dispensed with notes, as the passages in question can be immediately turned up from the dates and Mrs. Toynbee's indexes in Vol. XVI, whilst continual reference numbers could only serve to chafe the reader.

53. It is just possible that Walpole remembered a Croxall publication, *The Secret History of Pythagoras*, Part I. " Translated from the original copy lately found at Otranto in Italy. By J. W. M. D.," 1721. There was a reprint of this in 1751.

54. There have, of course, been a very great many reprints of *The Castle of Otranto*. " Constable's Edition of *The Castle of Otranto* and *The Mysterious Mother*," was edited by Montague Summers, 1924,

55. *A Description of the Villa of Mr. Horace Walpole*, 1784, Preface, p. iii. Walpole speaks of Miss Hickes desiring " to see The Castle of Otranto " ; in other words, visiting him at Strawberry Hill.

56. Amédé Pichot, *Voyage historique et littéraire en Angleterre et en Écosse*, Paris, 3 tomes, 1825 ; Tome I, p. 214.

57. Dante, *Purgatorio*, III, pp. 121-4.

58. Mehrotra, *Horace Walpole and the English Novel*, 1934, pp. 15-16.

59. A casual surmise of Mrs. Barbauld, 1810, echoed without acknowledgement as his own bright suggestion by Mr. Mehrotra, 1934.

60. For a fuller account of Jephson and his tragedy, and the burletta of 1848, see the Introduction to my edition of *The Castle of Otranto*.

61. In French : *Le Château d'Otrante*, trad. sur la 2e édition, by Marc-Antoine Eidous, Paris, 12mo, 1767, and 12mo, 1774 ; as *Isabelle et Théodore*, an anonymous version, Paris, 1797, 2 vols., 12mo, and 2 vols., 18mo ; *Le Château d'Otrante*, Paris, 1798.

62. *The Pursuits of Literature*, the Sixth Edition, 1798, p. 343.

63. Clara Reeve (1729-1807) also published *Original Poems*, 1769 ; *The Phoenix*, 1772, a translation of Barclay's *Argenis* ; and *Plans of Education*, 1792.

64. Ruins became an essential feature of a landscape. Thus in *The Clandestine Marriage*, produced at Drury Lane, February 20th, 1766, old Sterling the purse-proud cit, who apes the mode, carrying Lord Ogleby round his estate (Act II), cries : " I'll only show his lordship my ruins, and the cascade, and the Chinese bridge, and then we'll go in to breakfast."

" *Lord Ogleby*. Ruins, did you say, Mr. Sterling ?

" *Sterling*. Ay, ruins, my lord ! and they are reckoned very fine ones too. You would think them just ready to tumble on your head. It has just cost me a hundred and fifty pounds to put my ruins in thorough order.

65. A new edition, 4 vols., 1784-85.

66. By the Author of *The Fugitive Daughter, or, Eva of Cambria ;* and *Ora and Juliet, or Influence of First Principles.*

67. November, 1794, p. 353.

68. February, 1801, p. 203.

69. He also wrote *Tales and Poems*, which appeared in May, 1804, 12mo, price 3s. 6d.

70. March, 1801, p. 353.

71. December, 1795, Vol. XV, p. 480.

72. *Critical Review*, June, 1801 ; New Series, Vol. XXXII, p. 232.

73. July, 1797 ; Vol. IV, p. 37.

74. It is founded upon Baculard d'Arnaud's first play *Les Amans malheureux, ou le comte de Commigne* (1765), itself a dramatization of Madame de Tencin's story *Les Mémoires du comte de Commigne*, (English translation, *Memoirs of the Count Commigne*, 1773), in her *Malheurs de l'amour* (1735).

CHAPTER V

MATTHEW GREGORY LEWIS

He was a child, and a spoiled child, but a child of high imagination. . . . He had the finest ear for the rhythm of verse I ever heard—finer than Byron's. . . . He was one of the kindest and best creatures that ever lived.

Sir Walter Scott.

Lewis was a good man.
I would give many a Sugar Cane
Monk Lewis were alive again !

Byron.

"Names, madam ! names ! Whoever heard of such names as mine ?—names, madam, that have ever been my horror, my abomination . . . think ma'am, think of my two—*two* ugly names ! *Matthew* ! *Gregory* ! Heavens, madam ! not content with permitting my helpless infancy to be outraged by the name of *Matthew*, you, without a murmur, permitted the additional infliction of *Gregory* ! *Two*-fold barbarity ma'am ; I repeat, two-fold barbarity ! " Thus Lewis delighted in quizzing his mother, who used to become earnest and explanatory, " Why, really my dear, Matthew being the name of your father, and Gregory the name of——" " Barbarity, ma'am, *two*-fold barbarity ! " and so well did he use to act his imaginary grievance that Mrs. Lewis never perceived the joke, nay, more she often expressed her surprise that a sensible young man, like her son, could make so much of a trifle. All the while, perhaps his vehement expostulations had a grain of truth in their fret and fume for Lewis, indeed, felt a particular aversion to his own Christian names, and frequently avowed a decided preference for his sobriquet " Monk."

Matthew Gregory Lewis was born in London, July 9th, 1775, being the eldest son of Matthew Lewis and Frances Maria, the third daughter of Sir Thomas Sewell, K.G., Master of the Rolls, 1764–84. The Lewises, who were an ancient house, not only possessed extensive West Indian property, as did the Sewells, but also a fine estate in the immediate neighbourhood of the Sewell seat, Ottershaw Park, Surrey. Hence an acquaintance sprung up between the two families and this at length ripened into the closer relationship of marriage. At this time Matthew Lewis occupied the position of Deputy-Secretary at War, in which office he was ever held to have acquitted himself with the strictest probity and honour. Of a tall and commanding person, stately, and in his manners formal even to coldness, his was a nature more like to be respected than loved. Nor can it be denied that he was ill-matched when on February 22nd, 1773, he led Fanny Sewell to the altar. She married when very young, and her artless simplicity of character was scarcely improved by a secluded girlhood, without companionship or regular culture. Her beauty, indeed, was very remarkable, and upon her introduction to London life the lovely bride was warmly, it may even be too warmly admired by the votaries of foppery and fashion. None the less, there was also a grave and serious, even a devout side to her charcater, which further exhibited itself hereditarily in her elder son and his absorption with the supernatural. For example, one of her favourite works for more studious reading was Joseph Glanvil's *Saducismus Triumphatus*,[1] and this she happened to possess in the first complete edition, 8vo, 1681, with Faithorne's two plates, the frontispiece depicting King Saul and the Witch of Endor and the panelled illustration of several apparitions,[2] the Dæmon of Tedworth ; " *the villainous feats of that rampant hagg* Margaret Agar *of* Brewham " ; the Somersetshire witch, Julian Cox ; and other visions and sorceries. Over these engravings the young Mat used to pore with fearful interest,

> For in the wax of a soft infant's memory
> Things horrible sink deep and sternly settle.

It is significant, too, that a considerable portion of Lewis' childhood was passed at Stanstead Hall, Essex, a very ancient mansion, the family seat of a near relation on his father's side. A certain wing of the Hall had long been disused and closed, owing, it was said, to ghostly hauntings. There was, in particular, one magnificent apartment, the " Cedar Room," which the domestics expressly stipulated no one should be required to enter after dusk. The huge and strangely carved folding-doors gave on to a large landing, and in after years Lewis often recalled how when he was taken to bed at night and the moon shone palely through the painted oriel upon the sombre portals, with a quick glance of terror over his shoulder he hastened his steps, clinging closer to his companion's hand lest the leaves should fly apart and there stalk forth some grisly phantom of the dark, some bleeding apparition or carious skeleton. He added that to these dim memories he actually ascribed some of the most striking episodes in his famous play, *The Castle Spectre*.

In the *Life, Letters and Literary Remains of Edward Bulwer, Lord Lytton*,[3] by his Son, we are told that at Knebworth "two wings that contained apartments known by the name of ' The Haunted Chambers,' together with the whole character of the house, in itself a romance, powerfully and permanently influenced Lord Lytton's whole charcater. There were mysterious trap-doors and hiding-places, and in particular a kind of oubliette called ' Hell-hole.' As a child Lord Lytton was immensely impressed by the house, and himself in a letter recalled these early memories in vivid phrase : " I remember especially a long narrow gallery adjoining the great drawing-room (and hung with faded and grim portraits) which terminated in rooms that were called ' haunted.' . . . How could I help writing romances when I had walked, trembling at my own footsteps, through that long gallery, with its ghostly portraits, mused in those tapestried chambers, and peeped, with bristling hair, into the shadowy abysses of Hell-hole ? " [4]

There were four children born to Mr. and Mrs. Lewis ; Matthew ; Barrington, who having unhappily sustained an injury to the spine, lingered but died whilst a mere lad ; Maria, who married Sir Henry Lushington, Bart. ; and Sophia, the wife of Colonel John Sheddon, who survived her. Of these, Matthew was always his mother's favourite, and in return he nearly idolized her. That she petted and spoiled him was apparent to all save herself. Even as a child he was allowed to assist at the private Concerts she continually gave, collecting in her drawing-room all the virtuosi of London, for not only was she herself a skilled performer, but she " patronized musicians and composers à la folie." Often, too, Mat attended the mysteries of the toilet, and, as she recognized, so true was her little son's taste that she would at once discard a turban, wrap round her a shawl, or alter a jewel upon his suggestion.

At an early age Lewis entered as a boarder the preparatory school of an old family friend, the Rev. Dr. Fountaine, whence in due course he proceeded to Westminster, being admitted on June 19th, 1783. Here he particularly distinguished himself in the " Town Boys' Play," sustaining with great éclat Bastard Faulconbridge in *King John*, and My Lord Duke in Townley's popular farce *High Life Below Stairs*. Occasionally as a huge treat Mrs. Lewis would take him to the theatre, and she was wont to relate how on their return one evening from Covent Garden, when the lovely George Ann Bellamy had sustained the title-rôle [5] of Dodsley's *Cleone*, not only did the boy repeat with the utmost verve nearly the whole of the celebrated scene which concludes the Fourth Act, where Cleone in the wood discovers her child murdered, but he " imitated the actress's shriek with such thrilling accuracy that she could never forget her feelings at the moment." [6]

It is not at all surprising then that upon the separation of Mr. and Mrs. Lewis, at the end of his Westminster schooldays, 1790, in spite of paternal displeasure, Matthew was inclined to take his mother's part,[7]

PLATE IX

MARGIANA ; OR, WIDDRINGTON TOWER
Frontispiece, 1808

[*Face p.* 204

certainly without compromising the duty and respect he owed a father, who however reserved and undemonstrative had hitherto never shown himself ungenerous to his son, but yet with sufficient sympathy to provoke some slight degree of alienation and misunderstanding at home. Matthew, however, was eminently just, and he could not entirely approve his mother's conduct, dearly as he loved her. The temper of Mr. Lewis was not happy. He was obstinate when he prided himself upon being firm ; he was stern, and implacable in his resentments. That his wife, maybe half-unwittingly, very severely vexed him by her indiscretions and was assuredly in no small measure to blame for the jealousies and bitterness which stifled their mutual affection is quite plain from the letters that have survived, so Mr. Lewis merits a share of praise for having made her a regular and very handsome allowance, although indeed as there was no actual guilt this he was in honour bound to provide. The pecuniary embarrassments of which this lady so constantly complained, either arose then from her ill conduct of her expenses, or else were largely exaggerated and ideal. Mrs. Lewis, who at first foolishly thought of joining her son and taking up her abode at Oxford, a step which (as he was bound to point out) could only have proved needlessly disconcerting to all parties, more sensibly withdrew for a while to France upon the agreed separation, and thence she kept up a constant correspondence with her son, who systematically helped her from the annual income of £1,000 which his father had bound himself to allow him. The only time when there was an open difference between Mr. Lewis and Matthew " resulted from the discovery that Mrs. Lewis was being assisted by the regular gift of £500 a year from their son, and then with the hard remark that since he could live on the half, that moiety he should have and no more, Mr. Lewis correspondingly curtailed the promised remittances." This was cruelly unjust and unfair, but although deeply mortified, Matthew showed himself wise enough not to murmur, a spirit which so agreeably impressed the elder Lewis that the allowance was ere long restored to its former figure. Scott in speaking of Lewis mentioned that " His father and mother lived separately. Mr. Lewis allowed his son a handsome income ; but reduced it more than one half when he found that he gave his mother half of it. He restricted himself in all his expenses, and shared the diminished income with his mother as before. He did much good by stealth, and was a most generous creature." [8]

On April 16th, 1790, Matthew, aged fifteen, matriculated at Christ Church, Oxford,[9] and in the "Battels " book his name first appears on this date, although actually he did not incur any charge for food or drink before April 19th.

Mr. Lewis had now moved to No. 9, Devonshire-place, Upper Wimpole-street, a most commodious mansion, fitted up in a style of perfect elegance.   As Barrington Lewis was now evidently in a decline, he was often at Margate for the benefit of the sea air, whilst the two sisters, Marie and Sophia, spent much of their time at a country house which Mr. Lewis purchased in the neighbourhood of Barnet.

The summer vacation of 1791 Matthew Lewis spent in Paris.   He did not meet his mother as she had already returned to London, but in a letter dated September 7th, he speaks of a farce, *The Epistolary Intrigue*, which he has written, and the script of which he submits for her opinion.   He has also commenced a novel, and composed a number of verses.   This earliest essay of fiction, which was to be in the form of letters, rejoiced in the farcical mock-sentimental title *The Effusions of Sensibility* ; or, *Letters from Lady Honoria Harrowheart to Miss Sophonisba Simper*, " a Pathetic Novel in the Modern Taste, being the first literary attempt of a Young Lady of tender feelings."   The only portion which was ever printed occupies some nine and twenty pages (241–270) of the Second Volume of *The Life and Correspondence of M. G. Lewis*, 1839. It is extremely amusing and often very witty, amply sufficing to show that Lewis had a keen sense of humour.   The first letter which describes the Lady Honoria's departure for Portman Square from the antique towers and verdant bowers of Dunderhead Castle, the sensation she caused at the Duchess of Dingleton's ball, and the jealousy of Lady Mountain Mapletree, is written in a most mirthful vein and the adroit parody of such conventional openings is indeed a remarkable achievement for a boy of sixteen.   Whether the author could have completely sustained the burlesque is another matter, a question it were unjust to inquire.   Although he spoke of finishing it before his return to England, he does not appear to have carried the design beyond the second volume.

His farce, *The Epistolary Intrigue*, which he had written with the chief character Caroline intended for Mrs. Jordan, was refused by two managers, Lewis of Drury Lane, and Harris of Covent Garden, and he expresses himself in a letter to his mother as greatly mortified.   None the less, not to be lightly discouraged, he set to work upon and in the same year had ready a comedy, *The East Indian*, which, however, was not to be produced until the spring of 1799.   He also translated a play which he called *Felix*.   This was never printed and cannot certainly be identified, but it may well be *Les Deux Amis* [10] (1770) of Beaumarchais. In writing to his mother from Oxford he promises that he will bring this with him when he comes down, so that it may be sent to Lewis of the Lane, but he adds : " I have begun something which I hope, and am indeed certain, will, hereafter, produce you a little money ; though it will be some time before it is completed from the length of it, and the frequent interruption, and necessity of concealment, I am obliged to use in writing it. It is a romance, in the style of the ' Castle of Otranto.' . . . I have not yet quite finished the first volume." This romance, if completed, was never published, but Lewis subsequently founded upon these chapters the famous *Castle Spectre*.

It will not escape remark that young Lewis commenced author, translated plays, wrote a farce, composed a comedy, and employed himself upon a novel with the object of earning money for his mother. She seems at this time to have shown herself hysterical and exacting, but he never reproaches her for so frequent demands upon his purse ; [11] at the most he remarks in an Oxford letter that if he enjoyed a fixed income he would gladly act as her banker, but since he had not as yet been made any settled allowance by his father, to him he was obliged to apply to meet her requirements, and this was a humiliating and disagreeable task, since he hated encroaching on a bounty which had never failed and never shown itself less than most liberal and kind. Accordingly he could but endeavour to furnish these extra subsidies from the profits of his pen. The point is important. Not only does it show Lewis in a most amiable and unselfish light, but it also reveals the motive which made him turn so early to literature. He was no dilettante, no coxcombical undergraduate with the sophomore's eternal itch for scribbling, but a worker, a practical writer whose output meant, if not bread and butter, at any rate the complement of strawberry jam, and that not for himself but for the mother whom he loved so tenderly and so well.

Matthew Gregory was intended by his father for the diplomatic service, and since for this career a knowledge of German was not merely useful but well-nigh essential, he proceeded to Weimar in the summer of 1792 in order to acquire the language of the country. After a tedious journey, and much suffering from sea-sickness during the crossing from Harwich to Helvoet, Lewis arrived at the capital of Saxe-Weimar-Eisenach on July 27th, 1792. Here the English Ambassador, to whom he carried personal letters of introduction, was Sir Brooke Boothby, Bart., himself a poet, and well known as a friend of the Edgeworths and the Lichfield literary circle. Weimar, although a small town, was at that period, the reign of Duke Karl-August, one of the most illustrious in Europe, owing to the presence at the ducal court of Goethe,[12] who had in the previous year been appointed Director of the State Theatre ; Schiller [13] ; Johann Gottfried Herder, first preacher in the town church ; the romantic Wieland ; and many other literary and artistic figures of great fame. Indeed, within three days of his arrival Lewis writes to his mother that he has been introduced not only to the original Iphigenia, the fair court-singer, Corona Elisabeth Wihelmina Schröter, but even to " M. de Goethe, the celebrated author of Werter," adding the jest " so you must not be surprised if I should shoot myself one of these fine mornings." Of *Werther* three translations had already appeared in England [14] ; the first, a version through the medium of the French, in 1779, when it proved a huge success, new editions appearing at intervals until 1795 ; the second, this time from the author's text, in 1786 ; and the third in 1789. With one, perhaps with all of these, Lewis was familiar. He determined to read the original too. Eager and enthusiastic in his very first letter, July 30th, he says " I am now knocking my brains against German, as hard as ever I can. . . . As to my own nonsense, I write and write, and yet do not find I have got a bit further." The fact was that he could not conclude the second volume of the romance ' in the style of the *Castle of Otranto* ' which had so long occupied his thoughts. As he himself declared, " an infernal dying man " clogged his pen, and finish him off he could not. " He has talked for half a volume already," is the plaint of the poor author. This moribund but verbose gentleman was to make his appearance as the " pale and emaciated " Reginald in *The Castle Spectre*, who certainly refuses to expire and is exceedingly loquacious.

That Matthew Gregory's residence in Weimar at a most impressionable age should have had a lasting influence upon his whole life, should have moulded his taste, directed his interests, and formed his literary style is a thing neither to be wondered at nor regretted. His enthusiasm directly inspired Scott, Shelley, Byron, and Coleridge, although the latter was ungenerous enough to gird at the very poetry to which he owed not a little of his own stimulation. [15] How vitally German Romanticism energized our literature and what it lent us need not be emphasized at this point, since these correspondences are amply discussed in another chapter, but undervalued and underrated—nay, even jeered and fleered—as the work of Lewis has been, the fact remains that his mystery and terror and his German sensationalism (I do not burke the phrase) for many years permeated English romance, and they have even to-day left us a legacy in the pages of many applauded and popularly approved writers, who with all their striving and pains do not possess a spark of that genius, which dark, fantastic and wayward as it may have shown, was undoubtedly his.

During his stay at Weimar, Lewis made himself master of the German language, and his letters, in which he expresses himself as anxious about the fate of his comedy, *The East Indian*, speak of a volume of verse consisting partly of originals, partly of translations "from admired poems in Germany." "Whatever this work produces," he tells his mother, "you may reckon upon every farthing of it as your own."

Towards the end of February, 1793, Lewis returned to England, and resumed his residence at Christ Church. His keeping of terms must have been irregular, at least, on account of this absence in Germany, but none the less he proceeded B.A., 1794, and M.A., 1797. During the Easter vacation he was in Scotland, where he paid a long visit to Lord Douglas at Bothwell Castle and was also the guest of the Duke of Buccleuch. He was still occupying himself with making ballads, and was further engaged upon a translation of Schiller's *Kabale und Liebe* (1784) which, however, was not published until 1797. During the Hilary term of 1794 Lewis was at Oxford, but he did not come up for the summer since his father obtained him the position of an attaché to the British embassy at the Hague, whither Lord St. Helens [16] was returning from his ambassadorship at Madrid to succeed Lord Auckland, [17] who during the French revolution had been ambassador extraordinary to Holland.

Lewis arrived at the Hague on Thursday night, May 15th, 1794, where after a few days at an inn he removed to pleasant lodgings over a grocer's shop near the ambassador's hotel. Although eventually he got into a very agreeable Parisian coterie which used to assemble three times a week at the house of Madame de Matignon, Lewis found the Hague insupportably dull,—"I am certain that the devil *ennui* has made the Hague his favourite abode" he tells his mother—and it was only the fact that he was "horribly bit by the rage of writing," which saved him from falling into such low spirits as almost threatened to become a serious malady. His letters now are full of literary chit-chat, books he has read or is planning to write ; a refusal to allow G. G. and J. Robinson, the well-known house of Paternoster Row, to publish his poem by bits and bits in magazines ; the description of a little farce he has just penned on the subject of two twin brothers, one a rake-hell, and the other a broad-brim quaker, who are constantly mistaken for each other. The scenes were so arranged that the brothers never meet on the stage, and the dual rôle was, in fact, especially designed for a numerical actor, Jack Bannister, [18] who produced the piece, *The Twins ; or, Is it He or his Brother*, on the occasion of his benefit at Drury Lane, Monday, April 8th, 1799. "It was a whimsical and pleasant entertainment," says the *Biographia Dramatica*, but it was not adopted by the house, nor has it been printed.

At the end of April, 1794, had appeared Mrs. Radcliffe's *The Mysteries of Udolpho*, which Lewis commenced reading before he set out on his journey and finished immediately after his arrival at the Hague. It is, he cries, "in my opinion, one of the most interesting books ever published." It is significant, however, that he regarded the first nine chapters, as comparatively insipid, and yet these very passages with their exquisite descriptions of mountain scenery are among the finest of Mrs. Radcliffe's work. His imagination, however, was set afire by the lone Castle amid the far Appenines, those awful halls of dread where the dark Montoni was lord of life and death. Once more inspired to continue his own romance " in the style of *The Castle of Otranto*," he set to work to extricate the dying man from his difficulties, but finding himself unable to carry the story further, he was soon obliged yet again to lay it on one side.[19]

Not to be baffled, he wisely determined to begin altogether anew, on an entirely fresh track and this time things went smoothly, for on September 23rd. he triumphantly asks his mother : " What do you think of my having written, in the space of ten weeks, a romance of between three and four hundred pages octavo ? I have even written out half of it fair. It is called ' The Monk,' and I am myself so much pleased with it that, if the booksellers will not buy it, I shall publish it myself." Two months after, his last letter from the Hague, November 22nd, tells Mrs. Lewis that he will not send her the manuscript of *The Monk* since he prefers to hand it to her himself when they meet in London. " For my own part, I have not written a line excepting the Farce, and ' The Monk,' which is a work of some length, and will make an octavo volume of 420 pages. There is a great deal of poetry inserted," and so as a *bonne bouche* he encloses a copy of the " Inscription in an Hermitage " which occurs in Chapter II. (In the printed text of *The Monk* there are some few trifling variants.) As Lewis signed his octosyllabic Preface, Imitation of Horace,[20] Epistles, Book I, Ep. 20, " Hague, Oct. 28th, 1794," we may assume that he then completed his fair copy, and his pages were ready for the press.

Lewis' father now recalled him to England, and in December Matthew Gregory was back in London. He spent the Christmas of 1794 at Devonshire-place.

Very soon he set about finding a publisher for his romance, nor did he experience much difficulty in the quest. In March, 1796,[21] *The Monk* was first published, in three volumes, duodecimo, by John Bell, 148 Oxford Street, at nine shillings. It was re-issued in April [22] at half a guinea, whilst in October of the same year appeared a second edition, so designated on the title-page. The third, fourth, and fifth editions, all severally distinguished on their titles, followed in 1797, 1798, and 1800. In the fourth and fifth editions the title was changed to *Ambrosio, or The Monk*. Bell's advertisement, however, on the last leaf of *The Castle Spectre*, published, octavo, early in 1798, runs : *" In a few Days will be published*, By Joseph Bell, No. 148, Oxford Street, The Fourth Edition, *With considerable Additions and Alterations*, Of The Monk, A Romance, In Three Volumes. By M. G. Lewis, Esq. M.P. Author Of The Castle Spectre, Etc. *Price* 10s. 6d."

In March, 1797, Bell found it necessary to inform the public that a few copies of the Second Edition still remained. "The Book has been reported out of print, and as a Grand Ballet has been brought forward, taken from the above work, many people may wish to see the book before the performance ; and as it will be some months before a new edition can be ready to supply the demand, he has given this notice."

The Grand Ballet to which he makes reference was *Raymond and Agnes ; or, The Castle of Lindenburgh*, " a New Grand Ballet Pantomime of Action," produced at Covent Garden on Thursday, March 16th, 1797, which proved a great success and drew the whole town, so that Mathias exclaimed in horror : " And one of our publick theatres has allured the publick attention still more to this novel, by a scenick representation of an Episode in it. *O Proceres Censore opus est, an Haruspice nobis !* " [23] The Episode of the Bleeding Nun indeed immediately captured the imagination of all perfervid romantics, and as early as 1799 it was extracted and separately printed in chap-book form as *The Castle of Lindenburg; or the History of Raymond and Agnes*.[24]

The differences between the first issue of *The Monk*, March, 1796, and the second issue, April, are very evident. Several errors of the first issue will be found to be duly corrected in the second, and there are distinctive bibliographical variations into which it is hardly necessary to enter here.[25] One extremely important point remains. Volume III of the first issue concludes the text with the death of Ambrosio immediately after he is dashed upon the sharp rocks by the demon and rolls from precipice to precipice. A short horizontal line is drawn, and there follows a passage of somewhat obvious morality which begins : " Haughty Lady, why shrunk you back when yon poor frail-one drew near ? " In the second issue, after Ambrosio has fallen from a terrific height into the abyss, there follows a description of his agonies during six days, until his mangled corpse is swept away by the rising flood of waters. The paragraph of the Haughty Lady does not appear.

In the Second Edition of *The Monk* we find the shorter ending of the first issue together with the Haughty Lady paragraph. This is repeated in the third edition (1797), in the fourth edition, " with considerable additions and alterations " (1798), and in the fifth edition, " with considerable additions and alterations " (1800.)

The longer conclusion with Ambrosio's sufferings appears in the Dublin edition, 2 volumes, 1796 ; and also in the T. and H. Purkess illustrated edition of 1859.

It is difficult to surmise why Lewis should have preferred the rather abrupt ending and the little tag of trite morality to the more violent yet far more effective description. It has been suggested that possibly he thought the latter, however awesome, might be recognized as too obviously resembling the catastrophe of *Die Teufelsbeschwörung* in the *Sagen der Vorzeit* of Veit Weber (G. P. Leonhard Wächter).[26]

Mr. Louis F. Peck was, I believe, the first to point out that the well-known Waterford edition, 3 vols., 12mo, dated 1796, has 1818 watermarks, and since Lewis died in 1818 it seems tolerably certain that in consequence of his decease some enterprising printer, presaging that the obituary notices would awaken fresh interest in *The Monk*, resourcefully landed a number of " first editions " on the market.[27]

In a note, written in 1798, as an addendum to an existing note in his *Pursuits of Literature* (The Fourteenth Edition, 1808, p. 247), Matthias, quoting from *The Monk*, pp. 247–8, the passages regarded as profane, which describe how Ambrosio examines Antonia's Bible and his reflections thereon, says : " I refer to the *third* edition of *The Monk* [28] ; for it must never be forgotten, that *three* editions of this novel have been circulated through the kingdom, without *any* alteration whatsoever, which fear or, as I hope, a better principle has induced Mr. Lewis to make, since this denunciation was first published (1798)."

Ambrosio ; or the Monk, " By M. G. Lewis, Esq. M.P.   Fifth Edition, in 3 Vol.   Price 12s. in boards," is advertised by Bell in the Second Edition, 1801, of *Tales of Wonder*. Bell also advertised this Fifth Edition of *The Monk* at the end of *Adelmorn the Outlaw*, 8vo, 1801, but adds : " N.B.   The *First Edition of the above Romance* may be had at the Publisher's, price One Guinea."

To exaggerate the success and scandal of *The Monk* were impossible. Lewis at once became famous, and a celebrity he remained. " The first names in rank and talent sought his society ; he was the lion of every fashionable party." This he found extremely agreeable, for Sir Walter Scott tells us : " Lewis was fonder of great people than he ought to have been, either as a man of talent or a man of fortune. He had always dukes and duchesses in his mouth, and was particularly fond of any one who had a title. You could have sworn he had been a *parvenu* of yesterday, yet he had been all his life in good society." [29] After all, when fame comes at twenty, a little touch of snobbishness is a pardonable fault ;[30] nor was Matthew Gregory the real snob, for, even if he loved gilded salons and coronets, he did a thousand kind turns to those who were insignificant and poor ; nor did he ever treat his inferiors in purse, talent or station with the slightest discourtesy or ill-breeding. A more generous, a more civil gentleman never existed.

In these days of *Ulysses* and *Lady Chatterley's Lover*, and—for aught I know—even duller bawdry, that *The Monk* should have given offence may well seem incomprehensible. Yet such indeed proved the case. Never was such a clamour, such an outcry, heard since Troy Town fell, or the geese hissed upon the Capitol, for at the noise one might have believed that the very pillars of religion and decency were shaken to the dust and crumbled away, that the reign of Cotytto had returned, that the altars of Priapus were set up in St. Paul's. Even a hundred years after it had first appeared, at the end of the nineteenth century, I can well remember that *The Monk* was spoken of as a lewd book and still regarded with sternest disapproval. Thus in *The Imperial Dictionary of National Biography* (1890) Francis Espinasse, with a gesture of repugnance, condemned this famous fiction as "shamelessly voluptuous." *The Monk* definitely took its place with pornography, among the volumes labelled "Curious," "Facetiæ," "Erotica." It was classed with *Hic et Hæc, The Romance of Lust, Miss Coote* and *The Recollections of a Mary-Ann*. Amazing as it may appear even to-day, the crusted old tradition is sturdily maintained.[31]

There is, indeed, something a little extraordinary—one is tempted to write something morbid—in the persistence with which so uncritical and so unsound a prejudice survives ; but, instructive as the diagnosis might prove, it hardly concerns us now, for our business is with the contemporary reception of *The Monk*. The attack was not immediate, but when the storm burst it bellowed none the less tempestuous and loud. The earliest reviews were favourable. "The author of this romance has amplified the character of the Santon [32] Barsissa in the Guardian, in a most masterly and impressive manner. We really do not remember to have read a more interesting production. The stronger passions are finely delineated and exemplified in the progress of artful temptation working on self-sufficient pride, superstition, and lasciviousness. The author has availed himself of a German tradition which furnishes an episodical incident, awful, but improbable. The whole is very skilfully managed, and reflects the highest credit on the judgement and imagination of the writer. Some beautiful little ballads are interspersed, which indicate no common poetical talents." With more flippancy than politeness the *Analytical Review* [33] remarked of Matilda : " The whole temptation is so artfully contrived, that a man, it would seem, were he made as other men are, would deserve to be d——d who could resist such devilish spells, conducted with such address, and assuming such a heavenly form."

Lewis, however, was only too soon to discover how " the odious task of writing " entails upon its professors " envy, slander, and malignity," and that an author is merely " an object of newspaper animadversion and impertinence," a bitter fatality which seems as inevitable to-day as ever it was a century and a half ago. *The Critical Review* [34] suspected the writer of the new romance " of a species of brutality," whilst the abominations contained in these pages were clearly " such as no observation of character can justify, because no good man would willingly suffer them to pass, how transiently, through his own mind." It warned all fathers that *The Monk* " is a romance, which if a parent saw in the hands of a son or daughter, he might reasonably turn pale." In fine the whole work could be summed up as " a poison for youth, and a provocative for the debauchee." *The Monthly Review* [35] severely reprehended " the vein of obscenity which corrupted the entire narrative. *The Scots Magazine* [36] was indignant at the evil influence of such romances, scattered far and wide by indefatigable circulating libraries. This cant, which could be repeated to weariness, might not perhaps cause any great surprise coming from paltry reviewers, but it is painful to find that Moore affected to think *The Monk* " libidinous and impious," whilst Byron set down in his *Journal*, Monday, December 6th, 1813, such remarks as the following : " I looked yesterday at the worst parts of the *Monk*. These descriptions ought to have been written by Tiberius at Caprea—they are forced— the *philtered* ideas of a jaded voluptuary. It is to me inconceivable how they could have been composed by a man of only twenty—his age when he wrote them. They have no nature—all the sour cream of cantharides. I should have suspected Buffon of writing them on the death-bed of his detestable dotage. I had never redde this edition, and merely looked at them from curiosity and recollection of the noise they made, and the name they had left to Lewis. But they could do no harm."[37]

It is at least amusing to think of Tiberius, crowned with laurel lest the lightning should strike him, in a garden at Capri, while dwarfs and peacocks strutted round him, and the flute-player mocked the bearer of the censer, reading not the shameful books of Elephantis,[38] but writing upon his *tabulæ* with ivory style the first draft of the Gothic chapters of *The Monk*.

Keenly as Lewis felt the acrimonious and unwarranted attacks upon his romance, he was the more deeply hurt on account of the vexation thereby caused to his father, who expressed himself as in no small degree displeased and distressed. The very manly, affectionate and straightforward letter which the young author addressed to Mr. Lewis on February 23rd, 1798, has several times been printed,[39] and it must have proved more than sufficient to set his father's mind at rest. That it did so seems certain from the fact that the excellent relations existing between them were not disturbed ; and if Mr. Lewis regretted what he might consider his son's imprudence, he must at any rate have taken a just pride in his literary reputation and renown. Matthew Gregory in the course of his letter assures his father of the rectitude of his intentions ; his experience now shows him to have been in the wrong when he published the first edition of *The Monk*, but it was the lack of knowledge of a youth of twenty which gave offence ; he has made the only reparation in his power by carefully revising the work and expurging every syllable on which could be grounded the slightest construction of immorality, a charge not brought against the sentiments, characters, or general tendency of the work, but merely against some careless expressions and descriptions considered a little too warm, " a few ill-judged and unguarded passages."

The charge of irreligion was, perhaps, more serious. Yet to support this only one passage, which he is heartily sorry was ever published, had been or could be produced. In this respect he has been most unfairly treated. It is true that the expressions he used were much too strong, and he now sees that their style is irreverent. None the less the passage was only intended to convey that certain parts of the Bible should not be read before such an age as the student is capable of benefiting by its precepts and admiring its beauties. It also suggested the propriety of not putting certain passages before the eyes of very young persons. He never for a moment intended, and he believed he had sufficiently guarded against, any idea of attacking the Sacred Volume. None the less he has given offence, and he can only assure his hostile critics on this score that they have totally mistaken both himself and his principles. He is sorry for having given offence, and requests the pardon of his father for the uneasiness which this business has caused a parent whom he so regards with such true affection.

Before we examine more particularly the passage in question, which was condemned as impious and profane, it will not be impertinent to glance briefly at the censure of Lewis by Thomas James Mathias, since it was this very alleged irreverence which so grossly scandalized the satirist and stirred his hottest wrath.

Mathias, who was major-fellow of Trinity College, Cambridge, in 1776, proceeded M.A. the following year. He received the appointments of sub-treasurer and then treasurer to Queen Charlotte, the wife of George III ; was created F.S.A. and F.R.S. in 1795 ; and in 1812 became librarian of Buckingham Palace. In 1817 he visited Italy, and translated freely from the Italian into English, obtaining a wide reputation as an Italian scholar. He died in 1835.

The Pursuits of Literature, a satirical poem, was published in Four Dialogues ; the First in May, 1794 ; the Second and Third in June, 1796 ; and the Fourth in July, 1797. It was equipped with an immense lumbering apparatus of Introduction and Notes, whilst as it went on its way through sixteen editions [40] numerous alterations, corrections and additions were made, not only in the text but in the commentary. In the Fourth Dialogue, after returning to a most unreasonable and abusive onslaught on the celebrated Richard Payne Knight, and his "foul Priapus," as Mathias courteously terms this great scholar's *An Account of the Remains of the Worship of Priapus lately existing in Isernia,*[41] the poem continues :

> But though that *Garden-God* forsaken dies ;
> Another Cleland see in Lewis rise.
> Why sleep the ministers of truth and law ?
> Has the State no control, no decent awe,
> While each with each in madd'ning orgies vie,
> Panders to lust, and licens'd blasphemy ?
> Can Senates hear without a kindred rage ?
> Oh, may a Poet's light'ning blast the page,
> Nor with the bolt of Nemesis in vain
> Supply the laws, that wake not to restrain.

John Cleland, the son of Colonel Cleland, the Will Honeycomb of *The Spectator,* was born late in 1709,[42] and admitted to Westminster School in 1722. Whilst quite young he obtained the appointment of British Consul at Smyrna, and in 1736, having entered the service of the East India Company, he resided for a time at Bombay. Upon his return to London he wrote several novels and plays, the most famous of his works being that to which Mathias here refers, *Memoirs of a Woman of Pleasure.* Owing to the voluptuousness of the descriptions Cleland was called before the Privy Council and officially reprimanded, but when he pleaded his poverty, on condition that he would not write another romance of this nature he was granted an annual pension of £100. He died in Petty France, on January 23rd, 1789, aged eighty.[43]

The Memoirs of a Woman of Pleasure, which is perhaps better known under the title *Fanny Hill*, is certainly a masterpiece of English erotic literature, but to suggest that there is any comparison or point of contact between Cleland's work and *The Monk* is egregious nonsense. It would hardly be possible to name any two works of fiction which less resemble one another in every particular.

In a bombast note Mathias thus belabours *The Monk* : " The publication of this novel *by a Member of Parliament* is in itself *so serious an offence to the public* that I know not how the author can repair this breach of public decency, but by suppressing it himself : or he might omit the indecent and blasphemous passages in another edition." (This note was written in July, 1797, and in the previous year Lewis had taken his seat in Parliament for Hindon, Wilts.) " Novels of this seductive and libidinous tendency," continues Mathias, " excite disgust, fear, and horror." [44]

The Preface to this Fourth Dialogue is even more vituperative and denunciatory. " There is one publication of the time too peculiar and too important to be passed over in a general reprehension. There is nothing with which it may be compared. A legislator in our own parliament, a member of the House of Commons of Great Britain, an elected guardian and defender of the laws, the religion, and the good manners of the country, has neither scrupled nor blushed to depict, and to publish to the world, the arts of lewd and systematic seduction, and to thrust upon the nation the most open and unqualified blasphemy against the very code and volume of our religion. And all this, with his name, style, and title, prefixed to the novel or romance called ' THE MONK.' " There is appended a huffing ruffling note : " At first I thought that the name and title [M.P.] of the author were fictitious, and some of the public papers hinted it. But I have been solemnly and repeatedly assured by the Bookseller himself, that it is the writing and publication of M. LEWIS, Esq. Member of Parliament . It is sufficient for me to point out Chap. 7 of Vol. 2. As a composition, the work would have been better, if the offensive and scandalous passages had been omitted, and it is disgraced by a diablerie and nonsense fitted only to frighten children in the nursery. I believe this SEVENTH CHAPTER of Vol. 2 is indictable at Common Law." Mathias cites the prosecutions of Edmund Curll and Cleland, continuing with all the meretricious adjuvants of capitals and italics to express his horror and detestation : " To the passages of obscenity (which certainly I shall not copy in this place) Mr Lewis has added BLASPHEMY AGAINST THE SCRIPTURES." [45] He then quotes in full from *The Monk* the famous episode where Ambrosio finds Antonia reading the Bible. " ' How,' said the Prior to himself, ' Antonia reads the Bible, and is still so ignorant ? ' " The Prior discovers, however, that Antonia's mother has provided a copy of the Scriptures " copied out with her own hand," from which are omitted those passages she considered unsuitable for young persons to study.

Surely this principle, denounced by Mathias as " unqualified blasphemy," is none other than that which suggested such publications as *Line upon Line, Bible Stories for the Young*, and a hundred similar redactions. Some seven years ago, for example, the Regius Professor of Divinity in the University of Cambridge, in conjunction with two other Fellows of the University, edited not only a " Children's Bible," but even " A Little Children's Bible," both of which are most grievously mutilated, whilst the text, " That of the Authorized Version," even ventures on " occasional corrections." Moreover, the University Press did not blush to announce : " It is hoped to publish later, in the same style, a School Bible, suitable for older boys and girls. This will be, in effect, the Authorized Version with considerable omissions."

Lewis never intended anything more than this.[46] We may perhaps allow (as he himself acknowledges) that he expresses himself a little roughly and awkwardly in this passage, but that he should therefore be assailed as a blasphemer, a scoffer and unhallowed sacrilegist, threatened and coarsely denounced, can only be ascribed to an access of that fanatical exhibitionism which shatter-brained cranks so love to stimulate and indulge. This indeed is the root of the whole matter, for we can hardly read a score of lines (with their cumbrous baggage of notes) from *The Pursuits of Literature* without recognizing that we have to deal with a mind almost dangerously unbalanced. The rancour and enmity this " Satirical Poem " displays are certainly morbid, and had Max Nordau only known of these ebullitions with what glee would this *fané* journalist have instanced, in support of his pesudo-literary mock-psychiatrical theories, Thomas James Mathias as a first-class *fin-de-siècle* degenerate, with what gusto would he have dwelt upon the hysteria, the paroxysms of piety, the graphomania, ego-mania, *paraphrasia vesana*, and the whole fardel of nonsense tricks.

Lewis was very naturally chagrined at such an outrageous assault ; albeit he treated " the fury of the ' Pursuits of Literature,' &c.," with deserved contempt.

Nor did Lewis lack defenders, for in 1798 was published anony-mously " Impartial Structures on the Poem called ' The Pursuits of Literature,' and particularly a Vindication of the romance of *The*

Monk." Lewis' youngest sister, Sophia, wrote a brief defence of *The Monk*, but without her name and unacknowledged. Lewis, however, was not obliged by these champions, for, to use his own phrase, he strongly disliked " flaming eulogium," and he also entertained some degree of prejudice against female authorship.

It was acutely observed at the time that, if the composition of *The Monk* was in any way a reproach to the author, then the unbounded popularity of this romance was a far stronger reflection upon public taste.

An amusing anecdote is told : " When ' Monk ' Lewis's sensational romance was in universal request, a Mrs. Lord, who kept a circulating library in Dublin, enriched it with sufficient copies for her customers old and young. . . . A highly correct *paterfamilias* having reproved her for imperilling the morality of the metropolis by admitting such a book in her catalogue, she naively replied : ' A shocking bad book to be sure, sir ; but I have carefully looked through every copy, and *underscored* all the naughty passages, and cautioned my young ladies what they are to skip without reading it.' "

Actually about eighteen months after the appearance of *The Monk* the Attorney-General was instructed by the Society for the Suppression of Vice to move for an injunction to prevent the sale of the book. A rule *nisi* was even obtained, but it was never made absolute, and certain passages being modified, the prosecution dropped.

Famous and frequently reprinted as *The Monk* is, it may not be entirely superfluous to remind ourselves very briefly of the principal incidents in the story. Ambrosio, the Monk, is Abbot of the Capuchins at Madrid, and revered throughout the city for his sanctity. A son of mystery, his parentage is unknown, since whilst an infant he was found by the brethren laid at their abbey door, a gift, they like to think, from heaven. The youngest novice of the house, Rosario, becomes a particular favourite with the abbot, who one evening when they are together in the gardens to his horror and amaze discovers that his companion is a woman. The lady declares herself to be Matilda de Villanegas, the daughter of a noble house, passionately avowing that she has for his dear love alone penetrated the cloistral walls. As her cowl falls back he recognizes in her radiant beauty a sacred picture which some two years before had been bought by the monks, and which has been the object of his increasing adoration.[47] Matilda confesses that she thus conveyed her portrait to his notice. After a brief, but fierce struggle, the celibate yields to the overwhelming temptation and seeks satisfaction in her wanton embraces. Howbeit anon comes satiety, and then disgust. Ambrosio is requested to attend a widow, a stranger to Madrid, who is sick, Donna Elvira Dalfa. At the house of his new penitent he sees and becomes violently enamoured of her daughter, Antonia, a lovely maiden of fifteen. Matilda consents to aid his designs and help debauch the innocent object of his hot desires. In order to complete these ends she summons a fallen angel, and at midnight in the dark vaults of the monastery the monk takes part in impious rites. By means of a magic spell he gains admittance to Antonia's chamber and is about to violate her, when Elvira interrupts the ravisher. In order to escape he murders the hapless woman, and, unsuspected, regains his cloister. By Matilda's contrivance he then administers a soporific draught to the orphan Antonia, and being taken for dead she is conveyed to the vaults for sepulchre. Here Ambrosio waits her hour of wakening, and in spite of her cries effects his lustful purpose. To conceal his crime in a wild frenzy he stabs her, but the fact is almost immediately discovered. With Matilda he is thrown into the dungeons of the Inquisition, and accused of horrid crimes, murder, rape, and sorcery. Torture is applied, a full confession being extorted from the fears of his accomplice, when both are condemned to the stake. Matilda obtains freedom by devoting herself to the demon, and at the last moment Ambrosio also vows himself to the fiend on the condition of instant release. He is borne to the wilds of the Sierra Morena where the mocking spirit informs him that Elvira, whom he slew, was his mother, Antonia whom he raped and killed was his sister. The condition of release has been fulfilled, no more will be granted. The wretched monk is then hurled into the abyss.

With these main incidents is threaded the love story of Don Raymond de las Cisternas and Agnes de Medina Celi. Raymond on his travels meets Agnes in Germany at the Castle of Lindenberg, which is haunted by the Bleeding Nun. Owing to a variety of circumstances they are separated, and Agnes, at Madrid, is forced to join the sisterhood of S. Clare. Ambrosio, who discovers the secret of her love, denounces her to the domina, Mother S. Agatha, a very severe old superior, who, enraged at the scandal, gives out she is dead and condemns her to perpetual imprisonment in the vaults. A kindly nun, Mother S. Ursula, manages to convey the truth to Raymond, and Agnes is released, Ambrosio and Matilda being found in the subterranean corridors by the rescuing party.

There is one very weak point in the story which Lewis could easily have cleared up, but he apparently forgot or was not at the pains to disentangle. This results in a contradiction. Matilda is represented throughout as a woman who has fallen in love with the Monk, who has skilfully contrived that her portrait under the guise of a sacred subject shall be brought to his notice, who has recourse to magic in order to effect her ends, and who only escapes from the prisons of the Holy Office by an impious contract. At the end the fiend tells Ambrosio that his blind idolatry of the picture was made largely instrumental in his seduction and fall. " I bade a subordinate, but crafty spirit assume a similar form, and you eagerly yielded to the blandishments of Matilda." This runs counter to the whole tenour of the narrative. We cannot accept the temptress as a female Mephistopheles. If Matilda was a succubus, many of the preceding incidents are impossible and out of gear. The whole discrepancy, which is serious, could have been obviated by the omission of the one sentence quoted above, and the story would have gained. I like to think that this vaunt of the demon is a mere oversight, and, in reading, I delete it—at least mentally—from the text.[48]

There are indeed many other manifest errors. To the profound—and in the case of Lewis distorted and almost farcical—ignorance of the religious orders, of convents and the enclosed life, which marks nearly all the Gothic romances detailed attention has already been drawn, so this point need hardly be dwelt upon here. It is not impertinent perhaps to repeat that the Monk himself is not a monk, but a Franciscan friar ; and not an Abbot, but the Guardian of a Capuchin house. Incidentally the Capuchins during the course of the narrative are often described as " monks," whilst Ambrosio is called " the friar." The community of Poor Clares, than whom no nuns observe a stricter enclosure, leave their convent to visit the church, and even join in a grand procession through the midnight streets of the capital. The abbess is invariably termed the prioress, a trifling blunder in view of such grosser absurdities.

It has been shrewdly observed that in the work of Lewis " Convent life is represented from the point of view not of an ultra-Protestant but of a Voltairean freethinker," and the reviewer who announced that Matthew Gregory Lewis " is the spiritual parent of Maria Monk and all that grisly brood " was certainly very wide of the mark.

Nor is *The Monk* without some lighter strokes. Leonella is an amusing character with her exposition on the differences between the two sexes—happily interrupted by the arrival of the preacher—her amorous casting of nets for Don Christoval, the billet-doux she writes in red ink to express the blushes of her cheek, the pastoral dress she dons to receive her supposed admirer, when she is discovered simpering over the *Diana* of Jorge de Montemayor, nor is she a whit too farcical. The loquacious Jacintha is well drawn, an admirable sketch of a landlady, and indubitably from the life. There is humour too in the gossip

of the religious at the grate when Theodore sings a ballad of Denmark :
" Denmark, say you ? " mumbled an old nun.   " Are not the people
all blacks in Denmark ? "

" By no means, reverend lady ; they are of a delicate pea-green,
with flame-coloured hair and whiskers."

" Mother of God !   Pea-green ? " exclaimed sister Helena :   " Oh !
'tis impossible ! "

" Impossible," said the porteress, with a look of contempt and
exultation :   " Not at all : when I was a young woman, I remember
seeing several of them myself."

Nor does Lewis for his Spanish scene rely merely upon references
to " the Prado," Murcia, Cordova, to *Amadis de Gaul, Tirante the White,
Don Galaor*,[49] to Lope de Vega and Calderon, to pilgrimages to S.
James of Compostella, nor does he seek to obtain ' local atmosphere '
with ejaculations such as " By St. Jago ! "   His art reaches much
higher than such empty histrionics, and it has been well said : " Lewis
is content with a few dusky strokes, but they evoke the torridities of
Southern life.   Nothing could be better in this vein than the opening
of *The Monk* describing the excited crowd gathered in the Capuchin
Church at Madrid to hear the great preacher Abbot Ambrosio.   You
can almost hear the fans whir and smell the stale incense."

It is indeed a remarkable tribute to the power of *The Monk* that in
spite of all the imperfections, and indeed improprieties, in regard to the
cloister, faults and ignorances which might well have proved fatal to
the romance, the genius of Lewis shows itself so extraordinary that it
makes nothing of them, and when we are reading his pages, so great is
their fascination, the blemishes simply cease to be.   The interest of the
narrative enthralls and hurries one from incident to incident.   His
convents, his monks and nuns I regard as harmless, a mere fairyland of
melodramatic adventure, delightfully mysterious and transpontine,
having no relation at all to reality.   I will not spare to quote a severe
enough critic, although I cannot endorse his disapproval, but I echo
the final praise :   " Besides copious use of magic, incantations, and
spirits to carry on his story, and his wanton gloating over scenes of
luxury and license (hideously complicated by matricide and unconscious
incest), Lewis resorted to an even more revolting category of horrors—
loathsome images of mortal corruption and decay, the festering relics
of death and the grave.   But even when its startling defects and
blemishes are fully admitted, *The Monk* remains in every way a
marvellous production for a boy of twenty."

Mrs. Radcliffe is the romanticist of the Gothic novel ; Lewis the
realist.   His pictures of voluptuous passion are necessary to the

narrative; the violence of the orgasm but serves to balance and throw in high relief the charnel horrors. The comeliest forms of man and maid entwined in quivering embrace that Aretine might have imaged in his shameless sonnets, the long rapture of warm honeyed kisses such as Secundus sung, the full swift pulse of life, beauty, love, desire, all these are suddenly shadowed by the dark pall of mortality; those eyes that sparkled with lust's flame must fade and close in night, those hands whose touch was as a draught of heady wine must palsy, grow cold, and decay, the worm must pasture on those corrupting limbs where lovers' teeth once bit the white flesh in frenzy of sadistic appetite.

In his " Advertisement " Lewis thus acknowledges his sources : " The first idea of this Romance was suggested by the story of the *Santon Barsisa*, related in *The Guardian*. The *Bleeding Nun* is a tradition still credited in many parts of Germany ; and I have been told that the ruins of the earth of Lauenstein, which she is supposed to haunt, may yet be seen upon the borders of Thuringia. The *Water King*, from the third to the twelfth stanza, is the fragment of an original Danish ballad ; and *Belerma and Duranderte* is translated from some stanzas to be found in a collection of old Spanish poetry, which contains also the popular song of *Gayferos and Melesindra*, mentioned in *Don Quixote*. I have now made a full avowal of all the plagiarisms of which I am aware myself ; but I doubt not many more may be found of which I am at present totally unconscious."

The story of the hermit Barsisa is to be found in No. 148 of *The Guardian*, August 31st, 1713. Satan, enraged by the surpassing holiness of Barsisa, contrives that the daughter of a king shall be sent to him to heal of her sickness. The beauty of the princess tempts the santon to violate her. Afterwards, at the fiend's suggestion, he kills his victim, burying her in his grotto, where the body is found. Barsisa is seized, and upon the gallows he adores the Evil One who promises in return to save him from death, but who immediately mocks and abandons his wretched prey. " Le Santon," says the French original, " dementit en un moment une vertu de cent années."

Lewis undoubtedly found the Legend of the Bleeding Nun [50] in a tale by Johann Karl August Musaeus, [51] *Die Entführing*, published in the *Volksmärchen der Deutschen*, Gotha, 1787, Part V, pp. 247-276. Musaeus, who was a professor in the gymnasium at Weimar, was personally known to and had often discussed German literature with Lewis when " the Monk " was residing in that town. Rudolf Fürst, *Vorläufer der modernen Novelle*, Halle, 1897, pp. 88–99, draws attention to a story by Naubert in her *Die neuen Volksmärchen der Deutschen*,

1789–92, entitled *Die wiesse Frau*, which tells of Neuhaus Castle in Bohemia, haunted by the ghost of Count Rosenberg's mistress. Fürst, p. 188, also mentions a legend not unlike *The Bleeding Nun* in Gajetan Tschink's *Wundergeschichten sammt dem Schlüssel zu ihrer Erklarung*, 1792. August Sauer, the editor of Grillparzer (Vol. I, 1909) is inclined to suppose that many of these ghost stories were suggested by *Der Höllische Proteus oder tausendkünstige Versteller, vermittelst Erzahlung der vielsaltigen Bilderwechselungen erscheinender Gespenster*, of Erasmus Franciscus, first published at Nüremburg, 8vo, 1695.[52]

The Water King, the ballad sung by the disguised page, Theodore, to the nuns, is a free adaptation of *Der Wassermann* from J. T. von Herder's *Stimmen der Völker in Liedern*, for which collection it was taken from *Et Hundsede udvalde Danske viser, förögede med det andet Hundrede* of Peder Syv, Copenhagen, 1695, which derives from Andel Sörensen Vedel's 100 *udvalgte Danske viser*. It was reprinted in *Tales of Wonder*.

Belerma and Durandarte is chanted by Matilda to the convalescent Ambrosio. It will be readily remembered how Don Quixote witnesses (and interrupts) the motion of Don Gayferos and the fair Melisandra. The story, says Lockhart, is told at great length in the Spanish Cancioneros.

The Monthly Review [53] in June, 1797, angrily endeavoured to strip *The Monk* of any originality. "The form of temptation," the critic declared, " is borrowed from that of *The Devil in Love* by Cazotte ; and the catastrophe is taken from *The Sorcerer* . . . the forest scene near Strasburg brings to mind an incident in Smollett's *Ferdinand Count Fathom* . . . and the convent prison resembles the inflictions of Mrs. Radcliffe." [54]

Jacques Cazotte was born at Dijon in 1720. Most of his life was spent as a Civil Servant, and during the Reign of Terror he was arrested and executed in September, 1792. *Le Diable Amoureux*, his most famous work, appeared in 1772. An English translation was anonymously published in 1793, whilst in 1810 an inferior version, *Biondetta or the Enamoured Spirit* was " dedicated without permission to M. G. Lewis, Esq." In the ruins of Portici Don Alvaro Maravillas invokes a spirit, who appears first in the form of a camel, and then as a spaniel. The dog is changed into a page, Biondetto, who is in reality a female, that is to say a succubus, Biondetta. She exhibits the most passionate love for Alvaro, but after many adventures by a violent effort he renounces her and she vanishes as a black cloud. We learn that all that has happened was a phantasmagoria, and that the evil spirit had led Alvaro to the edge of the precipice when he was saved,

Myself I can see no sort of connexion between Cazotte's story and *The Monk*. The horrid wiles of the succubus may be read of in almost any demonologist.

The catastrophe of *The Monk* and the doom of Ambrosio (particularly, as noted before, in the amplified form) are, it is true, closely modelled upon *Der Teufelsbeschwörung*, a romance by Georg Philipp Ludgwig Leonhard Wächter,[55] who wrote under the name of Veit Weber. This work was translated into English by Robert Huish as *The Sorcerer*, " A tale from the German of Veit Weber," and published at 4s. in one volume by Johnson, 1795.

The adventures with the robbers in Baptiste's cottage may derive a hint, but nothing more than the barest hint from Chapters XX and XXI of *Ferdinand Count Fathom*,[56] when Ferdinand being " overtaken by a terrible temp st, falls upon Scylla, seeking to avoid Charybdis." The episode is conceived and related in full Gothic vein by Smollett, but Lewis not so much improves a mere outline, but gives the whole situation an entirely different and original turn. Lewis himself was copied both in fiction and upon the stage times without number.[57]

When Lewis was writing the extravagantly transpontine melodrama of his Convent scenes, he clearly had not forgotten Monvel's lurid *Les Victimes cloîtrées* and Marsollier's *Camille, ou le Souterrain*, both of which pieces he mentions in a letter to his mother [58] as having seen in Paris during his stay there in the summer of 1791, when they awakened his liveliest interest. Although he does not speak of other similar plays, it is obvious that he had also seen or read several more " anticlerical " dramas, such, for example, as Baculard d'Arnaud's *Euphémie*, the *Convent* of Olympe de Gouges, and the notorious *Julie, ou la Religieuse de Nisme* by Pougens, in which latter the description of Julie in the dungeon very nearly resembles the picture of the imprisoned Agnes in *The Monk*.

The first literary record of a doomed wanderer, the " Wandering Jew," occurs in the *Flores Historiarum* of Roger of Wendover, a monk of S. Albans, who died in 1237. Hence with some slight amplification it was incorporated in the *Historia Major* of Matthew Paris who died in 1259. The account is given on the authority of a certain Armenian Bishop who visited England in 1228 and who related how he had himself met the Wanderer. A similar version, also on the authority of the Armenian Bishop, is recorded by the Flemish chronicler, Philippe Mousket, Bishop of Tournai, about 1243.

The story was well known in Italy at the beginning of the thirteenth century, and originally came from Jerusalem, where a legend of a witness of the Crucifixion, doomed to an accursed immortality, was current in very early times. The Wanderer is given many names, and there are many variants of the tale identifying him with several characters. The popularity of the story during the last three centuries is in the first place mainly due to a German chap-book, *Kurtze Beschreibung und Erzehlung von einem Judem mit Namen Ahasverus*, 1602. The narrative is told by a Lutheran pastor, Paulus von Eitzen, who died in 1598, and who stated that at Hamburg in the year 1542 he had met the Jew Ahasuerus from whose lips he had the story. Whence or why the name Ahasuerus is not clear. In old English tradition the Wanderer is called Cartaphilus, a door-keeper of Pilate's house, who seeing the Saviour go forth carrying His Cross, struck Him crying : " Go faster, why dost Thou linger ? " Whereupon the Lord made reply : " I go indeed, but thou shalt tarry until I come again." Not a few persons have met this figure of mystery, the Wandering Jew, and have left their witness. I see no reason to doubt the facts, although naturally legend has grown up about them and literature has used them in many guises.[59]

A French version, *Histoire admirable d'un Juif Errant*, dating from the seventeenth century, adds striking particulars. The theme of the Wandering Jew attracted Goethe, and Christian Schubart's poem *Der Ewige Jude*, 1787, was read with admiration by Lewis. About 1810 it was Shelley, or Thomas Medwin, who " picked up, dirty and torn, in Lincoln's Inn Fields," a fragment of an English version of Schubart's poem in *The German Museum*, Vol. III, 1803. Shelley at once conceived and Medwin joined with him in a long metrical romance, something in the style of Scott, on the subject of the Wandering Jew. When seven or eight cantos were written, Shelley essayed various publishers, but four cantos of the poem first appeared in *The Edinburgh Literary Journal* for 1829 with Shelley's preface, dated January, 1811. The four cantos (in a different version and with the sanction of Mrs. Shelley) were also printed as " an unpublished poem " in *Fraser's Magazine* three years after they had been given in *The Edinburgh Literary Journal*. Medwin, whose account of the collaboration is unsatisfactory and inconsistent, claimed to have written almost entirely by himself the first three, if not indeed the first four, cantos, and the vision in the third canto he acknowledged was taken from *The Monk*. Shelley, we know, was a fervent admirer of *The Monk*, and many authorities believe that Shelley wrote practically the whole of this poem, *The Wandering Jew*, although as being Medwin's work it has been excluded (but improperly) from the more important editions of Shelley.

Medwin's poem, *Ahasuerus the Wanderer*, 1823, has no traces of the earlier piece.

Lewis, in addition to Schubart's poem, had read Reichardt's romance, *Der Ewige Jude*, 1785, and also Heller's *Briefe des Ewigen Juden*, two volumes, 1791. Above all, he was profoundly impressed by Schiller's *Der Geisterseher*, which was first printed in *Die Rheinische Thalia*, 1789, and which in England [60] had so powerful an influence, for as one critic asked [61] : " Who can look without awe at the inscrutable Armenian, or contemplate, unless with a heart-thrill, the terrific agony which his cunning and his science are able to evoke ? "

A well-known journalist of the day, Andrew Franklin, produced at Drury Lane on May 15th, 1797, *The Wandering Jew ; or, Love's Masquerade*. This is a mere farce, " containing much low humour, and little probability," [62] in which Atall—the name is taken from Colley Cibber's *The Double Gallant, or, The Sick Lady's Cure* [63]—disguises himself as the Wandering Jew. That this character was chosen serves to show the popularity of Lewis' work. Franklin's scenes were received with loud laughter and applause, and when printed, octavo, 1797, the little piece ran through four editions within the year.

George Daniel, the famous book collector and critic, sweepingly enough said : " The chief merit that belongs to ' The Monk ' is in bringing together an accumulation of supernatural horrors, and skilfully arranging them in an interesting tale—for it can boast of scarcely one atom of *originality*—it is *German* from beginning to end." [64]

In Ludwig Herrig's *Archiv für das Studium der Neueren Sprachen und Literaturen* (Alois Brandl und Heinrich Morf), Vol. CXI ; new Series XI ; 1903, Georg Herzfeld has an article *Die eigentliche Quelle von Lewis' ' Monk '* (pp. 316–323), in which he attempted to show that *The Monk* was for the greater part taken verbatim from an anonymous German romance *Die blutende Gestalt mit Dolch und Lampe, oder die Beschwöhrung im Schlosse Stern bei Prag*, Vienna and Prague,[65] no date. He quoted parallel passages as proving a word for word translation, and when his views were questioned by Otto Ritter [66] he did not hesitate to reassert and emphasize his supposed discovery.[67] Actually the whole question of priority is settled by an announcement of *Die blutende Gestalt* in the *Weiner Zeitung*, March 22nd, 1799, as " shortly to be published." Now Herzfeld's knowledge of *Die blutende Gestalt* was derived from an article, *Ein Schauerroman als Quelle der Ahnfrau*,[68] by L. Wyplel, who showed that Grillparzer's play *Die Ahnfrau* was taken from this source. Accordingly the editor of Grillparzer, August Sauer, compared the first German translation of *The Monk* by F. von Oertel, Leipzig, 1797–98 with the Prague romance, a collation which promptly established beyond all question that actually *Die blutende Gestalt* was derived from von Oertel's translation.[69] There are, of course, variants. Ambrosio in the German becomes a wizard astrologer; the Abbess (domina) of S. Clare is a Baroness of high lineage; the mystic myrtle is a rose-branch: names are changed; Agnes is Berta; Mother Ursula, Brigritta; and other details are altered. It is interesting to note that the anonymous author of *Die blutende Gestalt* published a sequel, no date (238 pages), *Der Geist Lurian im Silbergewand oder das Gericht über Ambrosio.*

As we have just seen, the first German translation of *The Monk* appeared in 1797–8; a second version was published at Berlin in 1799 as *Mathilde von Villanegas, oder der weibliche Faust*; a third at Magdeburg in 1806 as *Der Mönch, oder die siegende Tugend*; a fourth at Hamburg in 1810 as *Der Mönch, Eine schauerlich abentheuerliche Geschichte.* In France *Le Moine*, Paris, 4 volumes, 1797, was said to be translated from the fourth English edition by a mournival of names, Deschamps, Després, Benoît and Lamare; Paris, an VI (1797), 4 vols., *The Monk* was translated as *Le Jacobin espagnol, ou Histoire du moine Ambrosio et de la belle Antonia, sa sœur*; in 1838 was issued a new translation, *Le Moine,* said to have been made by the Abbé Morellet, who died in January, 1819; two years later *Le Moine* newly translated by Léon de Wailly from the first English edition was published by Delloye; in 1878 *The Monk* was translated as *Le Moine, ou les Nuits du Cloître*; in 1880 as *Le Moine, ou les Nuits du Couvent*; whilst in 1883 *Le Moine incestueux*, "roman imité de l'anglais," being in effect an abridgement of *The Monk* by Edouard Ploert, was published by the Libraire anticléricale. Most of these translations and adaptations ran into many editions,[70] and the popularity of *The Monk* in France is proved to have been quite extraordinary. In French literature the romance of Lewis had an immense influence.[71] In Spain a version of *The Monk*, published in 1822 as *El Fraile, o historia del padre Ambrosio y de la bella Antonia*, is taken at second-hand from *Le Jacobin espagnol. The Monk* was also translated and adapted into Italian, and also (from the French) into Swedish, and other languages.

"Raymond and Agnes; or the Castle of Lindenberg, a grand and interesting ballet, taken from the Monk, and arranged for the stage, by Mr. Farley, was performed at Covent Garden with great success on March 16th, 1797. "The music of this ballet, which was interspersed with airs and choruses" was composed by William Reeve, actor, organist, and composer.[72]

Raymond and Agnes, the Travellers benighted, or the Bleeding Nun of Lindenberg,[73] by Henry William Grosette, in two acts, was performed at the London minor theatres in 1809.[74] It is ascribed to Lewis himself, but this I think is doubtful, although in its kind it is an extremely skilful dramatization of the story. The principals in the printed cast are : Don Felix, Cooper ; Don Raymond, F. Vining ; Theodore, F. Sutton ; Conrad, Sutton ; Baptista, O. Smith ; Robert, Grimaldi ; Jaques, T. Blanchard ; Claude, Turnour ; Marco, T. Matthews ; Agnes, Miss Cawse ; Cunegonde, Mrs. Davenport ; Ursula, Miss Smith ; Marguerette, Mrs. W. Vining ; and the Bleeding Nun, Miss Nicolls. This would seem to be a Covent Garden cast of 1826.

Raymond and Agnes, a " grand romantic English Opera in three acts," the words by Edward Fitzball, and the music by E. J. Loder, was produced in Manchester, 1855, and at the S. James' Theatre, London, on June 11th, 1859.

Aurelio and Miranda, by James Boaden, " A Drama in Five Acts with Music," [75] produced at Drury Lane on Saturday, December 29th, 1798, was " *avowedly founded on the Romance of the* MONK." Boaden's attempt set out " *to dramatize the leading incidents of the Romance, without recourse to supernatural agency,*" a vital omission which has given the whole play a completely different turn from the book, and which in my opinion by depriving the incidents of their ultimate design and dominant motif, nothing less than eviscerates Lewis' chapters, leaving a very spiritless and tame performance. On the other hand, one has to recognize that this is very much in the vein of producers who prefer to eliminate the witch-scenes from *Macbeth,* and would no doubt discard the Ghost from *Hamlet.*

Aurelio and Miranda is a mixture of prose and blank verse. The licenser of plays had obliged Boaden to change the intended name of his play *Ambrosio,* thus hoping no doubt to exorcise some of the freedom of the romance. Aurelio (Ambrosio) was played by Kemble, and Miranda-Eugenio (Matilda-Rosario) by Mrs. Siddons. However, in the play Miranda is no succubus, not even a witch, but the sister of Don Christoval ; and when in the last scene Aurelio cries :

> The secret of my noble birth reveal'd, . . .
> Dispenses me from the monastic state ;

Miranda promptly rejoins :

> Away reserve, and maidenly resentment.

Wedding bells are distinctly heard, and the curtain falls upon what to me appears a very disgusting spectacle. The audience obviously shared my views for Kelly tells us : " It was no sooner found out that Miranda was a virtuous woman, instead of a demon, than many in the pit and galleries evinced dissatisfaction." [76]

The first scene is *The Cathedral Church of Madrid,* "and many thought it indecorous to represent a church on the stage," finely painted though it was by Capon. Curiously enough "the powerful objection was the unearthly appearance of Kemble as the monk." It was considered sacrilegious "for Mr. Kemble, as Aurelio, to make himself look so like a *divinity,*" to which it was wittily retorted that the play would have been all the better if Mrs. Siddons as Miranda, had only proved to be the *devil.* Boaden's drama was acted but six nights.

In France *The Monk* was frequently dramatized,[77] and the playwrights showed themselves far more mettled in their sensationalism than the English theatre. Rather than whittle away the theme like Boaden to a paltry nothing, they strove to accumulate horrors on horror's head, and they did not fall far short of their aim. In 1798, the very year that *The Monk* was translated into French, on the 7th nivoise an VI, in Christian language December 27th, 1797, at the Théâtre de l'Émulation was produced *Le Moine,* a "comédie" founded upon the romance, adapted by Cammaille Saint-Aubin, "plan et pantomime de Ribié, musique de Froment." The piece, however, proved to be too extravagant and grotesque, driving melodrama headlong into the realms of farce. Not only was a ballet interpolated in the dark monastic dungeons, but at the end Ambrosio was whirled away by a monstrous hippogriff to a Phlegthontian inferno, where fiends brandishing huge links danced the hey amid showers of golden fire.

Le Moine, for all these caperings and sulphureous effects, was poorly received, and shortly after was considerably abbreviated, but even thus failed entirely to attract.

On the 30th Thermidor, an X ; 17th August, 1802, at the opening of the Théâtre de la Gaieté under the direction of Ribié *Le Moine* was revived with alterations as a melodrama in three acts. A good deal of the ridiculous extravaganza had been wisely shorn, and, indeed, only the second act, complete in itself, of the original was presented.[78]

The fact is that *The Monk* proves so rich in incident and adventure that the practised dramatist will choose and select from Lewis' chapters, and not attempt to bring the whole story to the boards. Thus *C'est le Diable, ou la Bohemienne* by Cuvelier de Tyre produced at the Ambigu on November 18th, 1798, was very successful. A little earlier, too, *La Nonne de Lindenberg, ou, la Nuit merveilleuse,* a tragi-comedy in five acts, by Cailleran and Coupilly, given at the Théâtre des Jeunes-Artistes on June 24th, in spite of the opposition of a fierce cabal,[79] enjoyed an amazing run.[80]   From this Saint-Aubin and Ribié learned a lesson, and their next venture, an episode taken from *The Monk, Marguerite, ou, les Voleurs,* was in only one act.

Lewis' romance had naturally attracted the attention of the master melodramatist, Guilbert de Pixérécourt, who penned a *Moine, ou la victime de l'Orgueil,* which was offered to the Théâtre de la Gaieté in 1798, but not acted owing to the number of plays adapted from the English romance which were then actually running. None the less, his "drame lyrique" in two acts, *La Forêt de Sicile,* taken from *The Monk,* was produced at the Théâtre des Jeunes-Associés in the same year and achieved a veritable triumph, whilst in the following January it was transferred to the Théâtre de Montausier. The piece had caused some trouble with the authorities and was for a time prohibited, but it now appeared with various alterations and a changed catastrophe. On March 28th, 1800, *Ambrosio,* an anonymous drama in five acts, was given at the Odéon, and in the same year Prévost's *Le Jacobin espagnol* had a temporary success on the Paris stage.

As may well be believed the French theatre was sufficiently stocked from the source of *The Monk* for a good thirty years, but after the Revolution of July, 1830, *The Monk* enjoyed a veritable S. Luke's summer of popularity, for on May 28th at the Odéon, L.-M. Fontan produced *Le Moine* " drame fantastique en quatre actes et huit tableaux," a melodrama transferred on July 13th to the Porte-Saint-Martin. Frédéric Lemaître and Mlle. Juliette supported the leading characters. The catastrophe is better managed, but almost as outrageous as that of Saint-Aubin's play.

Le Dominicain, ou le Couvent de l'Annonciation, which was produced at the Ambigu-Comique on March 9th, 1832, was written by Fontan in collaboration with A. Chevalier. The principal rôle, Père Jéronimo, seems drawn from a mixture of Ambrosio and Schedoni. Jéronimo contrives to enclose in a convent a young girl whom he desires. When he attempts to rape her she poinards him, a little after to discover she has killed her own father.

La Nonne Sanglante, a drama in four acts by Anicet Bourgeois and J. Maillan, produced at the Porte-Saint-Martin, February 17th, 1835, only takes the figure of the nun from Lewis. Stella, who is believed dead, haunts Conrad her presumed assassin. This " grand et terrible mélodrame " concludes with a terrific conflagration. The spectacle had an immense success, and in May, 1864, was revived at the same theatre, achieving an equal popularity. The piece was judged very powerful and effective.

On October 18th, 1854, was produced at the Opéra, *La Nonne Sanglante,* which Gounod, who composed the music, describes in his *Mémoires d'un artiste,* Paris, 1896.

" Ma troisième tentative musicale au théâtre fut la *Nonne sanglante,* opéra en cinq actes de Scribe et Germain Delavigne . . . *La Nonne Sanglante* fut écrite en 1852–53 ; mise en répétition le 18 octobre, 1853, laissée de coté et successivement reprise à l'étude plusieurs fois, elle vit enfin la rampe le 18 octobre, 1854, un an juste après sa première répétition. Elle n'eut que onze représentations, après lesquelles Roqueplan fut remplacé à la direction de l'Opéra par M. Crosnier. Le nouveau directeur ayant déclaré qu'il ne laisserait pas jouer plus longtemps une " pareille ordure," la pièce disparut de l'affiche et n'y a plus reparu depuis. . . . Je ne sais si la *Nonne Sanglante* était susceptible d'un succès durable ; je ne le pense pas : non que ce fut une œuvre sans effet (il en avait quelques-uns de saisissants) ; mais le sujet était trop uniformément sombre ; il avait, en outre, l'inconvénient d'être plus qu'imaginaire, plus qu'invraisemblable : il était en dehors du possible, il reposait sur une situation purement fantastique, sans réalité, et par consequence sans intérêt dramatique."

The favourite *morceaux* of *La Nonne Sanglante* are the Marche Nuptiale ; " De mes Fureurs déplorable Victime " ; " Dieu nous commande l'ésperance " ; " C'est Dieu qui nous appelle " ; " Du Seigneur, pâle fiancée " ; " Un page de ma sorte " ; and " O l'erreur qui m'accable ! "

A far more famous Opera than *La Nonne Sanglante* has borrowed important matter from *The Monk*, for the libretto of Meyerbeer's *Robert le Diable*, produced at the Académie Royale, Paris,[81] on November 21st, 1831, was also written by Scribe and Delavigne. The fearfully impressive scene of the haunted convent, when, at the invocation of the demoniac Bertram, the abbess Elena and her troop of spectral nuns rise from their accursed tombs to dance in horrid revelry and tempt Robert to pluck the fateful talisman, the mystic branch of cypress from Berta's marble hand, the exultation of the fiends, the midnight horror and woe, all are from Lewis. This cypress bough which gains Robert admission to the apartment of the Princess Isabella, and enchains in slumber her attendance of knights and ladies, is, of course, the myrtle Matilda procures for Ambrosio. Unlike the monk, Robert resists his final temptation and refuses to sign the infernal scroll wherewith Bertram seeks to win him to himself.

It might seem difficult to decide whether it was Ann Radcliffe or Matthew Gregory Lewis who exerted the more powerful effect upon the temper and shaping of the Gothic Novel as it went its varied course, and since actually the influence of the former was far greater than that of the author of *The Monk*, it may appear a paradox to say that none the less it was the latter upon whom contemporary writers of fiction the more closely modelled certain prominent aspects of their work.

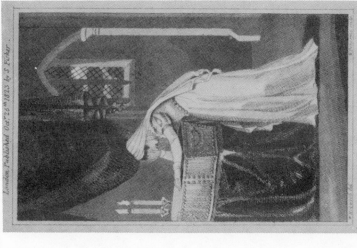

London. Published Oct.ʳ 16ᵗʰ 1823 by S Fisher.

Lady Matilda weeping over the coffin of Lord Leicester pronounced a Vow solemn and irrevocable.

THE RECESS
Edition 1824

[*Face p.* 232

THE MYSTERIOUS WARNING
Frontispiece. Edition 1824

The reason for this lies in the very practical consideration that the romances of Lewis were found to be far easier to copy, although we may add that the prentice pens showed themselves apter to reproduce and even to exaggerate his faults rather than to exhibit a tithe of his vigour and power, fastening upon his weakness and unable to reach after his strength.

The followers of both Mrs. Radcliffe and Lewis are legion, and very often the imitation is not only confined to theme, characters, incidents, all of which are repeated again and again in a hundred chapters with exemplary fidelity, but there are also very distinct verbal echoes to be heard, dialogue at second-hand which merely differs from the original by a bombast word inserted here and there, or a phrase dropped out for the worse.

In all essentials, it must be emphasized, Mrs. Radcliffe and Lewis differ very widely from one another. They have certain romantic subject-matter in common, but so entirely opposite are their several methods of approach and treatment that although casually they may appear at some points to contact this similarity is extremely superficial and proves but a deceptive glamour of resembling. Both employ picturesque properties, convents, castles, the Holy Office. Such a figure as the austere and stately Abbess of San Stephano in *The Italian*, although altogether improbable and exceptional, is barely possible ; such a figure as Lewis' domina of S. Clare, Mother St. Agatha, is altogether chimerical, fantastic, and absurd. Lewis recked nothing of Mrs. Radcliffe's suspense, her sensibility, her landscape pictures which are not the least lovely passages of her genius. Indeed, he pronounced these uncommonly dull, and fervently wished that they had been left out, and something substituted in their room.[82] Certes, *The Mysteries of Udolpho* influenced him, but not so much as he thought and liked to make himself believe. Mrs. Radcliffe shrank from the dark diablerie of Lewis ; his matricides, incests, rapes, extremely shocked her ; never did she admit his mouldering cerements and atomies ; his Paphian encounters would have cruddled her very ink. Her terrors were spiritual, and for that reason her influence has most clearly shown itself in the writings of those authors whose natural reserve and a certain delicacy of talent would not have tolerated the high colouring and eroticism of *The Monk*. By his very violence, his impassioned realism, Lewis is widely separated from Mrs. Radcliffe and her school. It is the more pity that these two great writers have been so frequently and so erroneously confounded, and their work all lumped together as if they had exhibited precisely the same characteristics, developed the same style, and elaborated the same sensationalism. It is true that in their own day many minor novelists with a curious lack of perception repeatedly endeavoured to combine *Udolpho* and *The Monk* in their pages, to make one peerless heroine of Emily and Antonia, to bring an Ambrosio Montoni upon the scene, but these attempts were foredoomed to failure ; the pieces do not fit ; there are awkward creaking joints, and untenoned mortises, discrepancy, contradictions even and incongruity both in the narrative and the springs of action.

The expert cook would have disdained to serve up so ill dressed an olio. The shrewder intelligencies were more quick to model their story either upon Mrs. Radcliffe or upon Lewis alone without commixture.

The novels which directly derive from *The Monk* are in themselves so numerous a company that rather than set down a large quota of parallel passages from a dozen writers it will be best to examine here in some detail two or three of the more important as a sample of the stuff. Other novels will be more conveniently noticed under their respective authors.

Charlotte Dacre, " better known as Rosa Matilda," was a professed disciple of *The Monk*, and her *Zofloya ; or The Moor, A Romance of the Fifteenth Century*, 3 vols., 1806,[83] shows that she had learned her lesson well.

Zofloya, the period of the tale being " about the latter end of the fifteenth century," commences upon " the birthright of the young Victoria de Loredani " when all the rank and gallantry of Venice are assembled in the " palazzo " of the Marchese de Loredani to do his daughter honour. " Beautiful and accomplished as an angel," Victoria is none the less proud and haughty, wild, ardent, implacable, revengeful and cruel. " The wildest passions predominated in her bosom ; to gratify them she possessed an unshrinking relentless soul, that would not startle at the darkest crime." She is Matilda denuded of her diabolic supernaturalism.

Upon this birthnight Count Ardolph, sceptical, cruel, dangerous, arrives as a guest at the Palazzo Loredani, and is royally welcomed, a hospitality he returns by seducing the Marchesa Laurina de Loredani, whom he persuades to an elopement, later killing her husband. The young Leonardo de Loredani in horror at his mother's shame has already fled from the paternal roof. Count Ardolph and Laurina compel Victoria to reside with them, whereupon she seeks to win the love of Count Berenza. (Her wiles to entangle him are very reminiscent of the temptation by Matilda of Ambrosio), Ardolph and Laurina now convey Victoria to the remote Il Bosco, where by a trick they leave her in charge of the austere Signora di Modena, a devotee and lynx-eyed gaoleress, closely modelled on Mother S. Agatha. Victoria, however, escapes and seeks the protection of Berenza, whom she finally entices to her arms in a scene closely reproducing the first embraces of Ambrosio and Matilda. A discarded mistress, Megalina Strozzi, nearly succeeds in procuring the assassination of Berenza, but Victoria prevents the blow, and being slightly wounded so works on her lover's feelings that he marries her. (The motive is the same as when Matilda saves Ambrosio from the fatal results of the cientipedoro's venomed sting.)

Five years pass, and in their Venetian home Berenza and Victor are visited by the young and handsome Henriquez, Berenza's brother, who is betrothed to a lovely and innocent maiden, Lilla. A guilty and devouring flame now absorbs Victoria, who determines at all costs to make Henriquez her own. In her dreams she is haunted by the figure of a noble and majestic Moor, whom she recognizes as Zofloya, the servant of Henriquez. Zofloya strangely attracts her, and after several interviews he offers to help her win Henriquez and dispose of that obstacle her husband. This is done by a slow poison administered by Victoria, and supplied by the Moor. She is struck by and frequently muses upon the mystery surrounding him, for he seems to appear suddenly even in the depths of a forest glade. Sometimes, too, his presence is heralded by sweet aerial sounds, the tremulous vibration of a double-toned flute. (Thus in *The Monk* when Matilda summons the demon in the vaults, before the spirit is seen " a full strain of melodious music sounded in the air! ") With the rage of a Brinvilliers, Victoria not only poisons Berenza, but also an aged relative of Lilla. When Henriquez rejects her with loathing she procures from Zofloya an insane drug so that in his delirium her brother-in-law will take her to his bed deeming she is Lilla, who actually is poisoned in a cave, presently to be stabbed to death by the furious Victoria. Awakening from his madness and discovering the delusion,[84] Henriquez kills himself. To escape the consequences and imminent arrest by the Inquisition Victoria, upon a promise of safety, pledges herself to Zofloya, who thereupon mysteriously conveys her to a distant ravine amid the loftiest Alps. Here they encounter a band of Condottieri or banditti with whom they companion in lawless life, and various adventures follow which conclude in the betrayal of the brigand's lair upon Mount Cenis by a traitor, Ginotti. Victoria and Zofloya are surrounded by innumerable soldiers, but upon her promise to commit herself wholly to him, Zofloya swears to protect her, and at the same moment a fearful explosion shakes the earth, the cavern crumbles, and in an instant of time she finds herself on the summit of a beetling crag, the Moor by her side. He reminds her of his past services, and demands that she shall once and for all give herself unequivocally to him. The wretched woman devotes herself to Zofloya by a fearful oath, whereupon with a loud laugh he bids her look upon him, and as she gazes in the place of the beautiful Zofloya she sees " a figure, fierce, gigantic, and hideous to behold ! ' Dost thou mark, vain fool ! ' he cried in a terrific voice, which drowned the thundering echo of the waters—' Behold me as I am !—no longer that which I appeared to be, but the sworn enemy of all created nature, by men called—SATAN ! ' " With fearful taunts " he grasped more firmly the neck of the wretched Victoria—with one push he whirled her headlong down the fearful abyss !—and as she fell his loud demoniac laugh, his yells of triumph echoed in her ears, and a mangled corse, she was received into the foaming waters below ! "

All this is exactly the catastrophe of *The Monk* when the demon hurls Ambrosio into the gulf. " Headlong fell the monk through the airy waste . . . he rolled from precipice to precipice, till, bruised and mangled he rested on the river's banks . . . the rain fell in torrents : it swelled the stream ; the waters overflowed their banks ; they reached the spot where Ambrosio lay, and, when they abated, carried with them into the river the corse of the despairing monk."

In the original issue of *The Monk*, Lewis had a final paragraph pointing a moral. Charlotte Dacre also concludes *Zofloya* with a final paragraph of moral import.

Extremely imitative of and infinitely more extravagant than *The Monk* is Edward Montague's *The Demon of Sicily*, 4 vols., Hughes, 1807. Here we have two (or it might truly be said three) separate stories, connected by the slenderest link. Thus Chapter One commences : " The clock of the monastery had told in iron notes the midnight hour," and Padre Bernardo by the glimmer of his faint lamp " fixed his large black eyes, shaded by his bushy eye-brows, on the beautiful representation " of " the Saint to whom the religious pile was dedicated, the Santa Catherina." This is closely modelled on Chapter Two of *The Monk*. Ambrosio has " eyes large, black and sparkling, and his dark brows almost joined together." He also " fixed his eyes upon a picture of the Virgin," and exclaimed : " Never was mortal formed so perfect as this picture," toying with the idea of temptation. " Sure no earthly woman can possess such charms ; if they did, passion would overcome reason, and steep in forgetfulness the cold vows of seclusion ! " cries the Padre Bernardo, and a mystic form—the demon— stands at his side. In spite of a vision of S. Catherine herself, Bernardo is led by lust and cruelty from crime to crime. He discovers that among the sisters of Santa Catherina the lovely Agatha has broken her vows. She was very beautiful—" Large expressive dark eyes, with eye-brows beautifully arched ; her cheeks the residence of the blushing rose, and her coral lips inviting the rapturous kiss." The demon had already tempted Agatha, and furnished her with a key by means of which she admits an amorous cavalier, Ferdinando de Montalino, at midnight, and allows him to possess her even in the sanctuary. " The chapel of Santa Catherina beheld the guilty pair wantoning in the fulfilment of their wishes till the grey dawn made their long untrimmed lamps almost useless."

A billet Ferdinando designs for Agatha falls into the hands of Sister Marianne, who " shrunk with horror from the view of the epistle which disclosed such a sinful distraction." To prevent discovery of her lewdness, Agatha at the instigation of the demon, poisons Marianne.

Her love for Ferdinando does not hinder Agatha giving herself to Bernardo, the cemetery of the religious being their macabre rendezvous. Here they are surprised by the sorrowing Claudine, a pious nun, who has come to weep at the grave of Marianne. " Foul votaries of vice ! " she exclaims, " I am resolved to reveal the sinful transaction which this night has discovered." The monk, however, mad with rage and fear, incontinently throttles her. (This description is plainly copied from the strangling of Elvira by Ambrosio in Antonia's chamber at night.) With the demon's aid Bernardo is enabled to convey the lovely Angelina to the dungeons of the monastery, and in these dark vaults at midnight, among circumstances of extraordinary horror, he is about to ravish her when they are surprised by the Abbot Ignazio and the community, whilst in the same hour Agatha's incontinence is discovered, just as she is about to elope with Ferdinando de Montalino, who is killed in the *mêlée*. Agatha and Bernardo are haled before the Inquisition, and there follow the most horrific scenes, which even de Sade might have envied, in the true tradition of the twopence coloured melodrame. The nun confesses all, and expires in agony, self-poisoned. Bernardo is condemned to the stake. " His body was sentenced to be consumed by flames till his soul should desert its agonized abode. The body of Agatha " now exhibiting an horrible and loathsome appearance . . . the lips black and decaying damps fast seizing on the livid corse " is cast into the same fire. The execution is described at very considerable length, and no harrowing detail, all painted in most lurid language, is spared.

On the night before the *auto-da-fé* the demon stands by the wretched monk's pallet, and cries : " That thy horrors may be complete, know that the lovely maid whom you sought in order to gratify thy abandoned desires was—thy own sister." In almost precisely the same terms did the demon proclaim to Ambrosio : " That Antonia whom you violated was your sister ! "

The description of the " festival in honor of the Santa Catherina," [85] which curiously enough took place " only twice in a century," is largely derived from the ornate description in *The Monk* of the midnight procession of nuns and friars in honour of S. Clare, in which ceremony young and lovely maidens represent S. Lucia, S. Catherine, S. Geneviève, and—comeliest of all—upon a machine fashioned like a superb throne a damsel, reclining amid silver clouds, robed as S. Clare.

The demon, again, who generally appears with dark features— dreadful was the expression of the lower part of his terrible visage, and the eyes were as glowing flame—on one occasion lays aside his terrors, and then " his form, moulded by the Divinity, was such as far excelled worldly perfection. Wings of the whiteness of the wave-washed swan shaded his lineaments . . . but his features were marked with all the raging passions . . . which bespoke him the prince of infernal horrors." [86] It is now that the monk signs a scroll with his blood. In similar fashion at Matilda's invocation, in the romance of Lewis, the demon appears as " a youth seemingly eighteen, the perfection of whose form and face was unrivalled . . . two crimson wings extended themselves on his shoulders."

The fiend carries Bernardo to the Castello, and shows him Angelina asleep.[87] Thus Matilda by means of the magic mirror reveals to Ambrosio the naked charms of Antonia, when she is about to bathe herself in the retirement of her closet.

The episodes of the wicked Marchese Roderigo de Carlentini, whose son Ricardo resides at the Castello near Pollizzi, whilst he himself riots it at Palermo with a comradeship of the sorriest rake-hells and debauches are palpably borrowed from *A Sicilian Romance*.

The Marchese aided by the confessor Father Grimaldi has many years before imprisoned his wife, Theodora, in the Southern Angle Tower, long rumoured to be haunted, in order that he may wed a wealthy heiress. Grimaldi undertakes to dispatch Theodora, and although actually she escapes the assassinate, he supposes none the less that he actually effected his horrid design. The lady is concealed in the convent of Santa Maria, but she does not long survive. Grimaldi, ere he expires, leaves a written confession of his crimes.

The boon companions of the Marchese de Carlentini are described in delicious transpontine style. Signor Roderigo de Romanzo appeared to be little better " than the captain of a banditti." His person was gigantic, " his face almost covered by a pair of enormous whiskers.

He had a long Roman nose, and black piercing eyes glared beneath his overhanging brows, while his whole countenance was shaded by a large plume of black feathers, which he wore in his military hat, and which added to the sombre appearance of his features." [88]

A hint is derived from *The Italian* for the wooing by Ricardo of the lovely Louisa de Bonini, who is abducted, but whom he rescues and eventually weds.

The domestics, old Margueretta, the voluble Annetta and her trusty swain, honest Carlo, we have oft-times met.

To the romances of Edward Montague the Gothic enthusiast will always turn secure of finding infinite entertainment, but I would hardly recommend them to any save those who can find pleasure even in the extravagances of this school.

Montague is the author of, *The Citizen*; " A Hudibrastic Poem, in Five Cantos, to which is added *Nelson's Ghost*, a Poem in two parts," Hughes, 1806; *The Castle of Berry Pomeroy*, a novel, 2 vols., Lane, 1806; *Legends of a Nunnery*, 4 vols., Hughes, 1807; *Friar Hildargo*, a romance, 4 vols., Hughes, 1807; *The Demon of Sicily*, a romance, 4 vols., Hughes, 1807; and *Modern Characters*, a novel, 3 vols., Hughes, 1807.

In her study *The Tale of Terror* [89] (1921), Chapter IV, Miss Birkhead writes : " In the second edition of *The Bravo of Venice*, a romance in four volumes by M. G. Lewis, *Legends of the Nunnery*,[90] is announced as in the press. There seems to be no record of it elsewhere." Miss Birkhead has misread the advertisement. In the Fifth Edition (1807), also, of *The Bravo of Venice*, we have the advertisement : " In the Press. Legends of a Nunnery, a Romance in Four Vols. by Mr. Montague." I corrected the error which assigns *Legends of a Nunnery* to Lewis in the Introduction [91] to my edition of *Zofloya*; or, *The Moor*, 1927. None the less it is reproduced by Herr Brauchli in the very diffuse but not very reliable bibliography appended to his *Der englische Schauerroman um* 1800, 1928. In fact, Herr Brauchli goes so far as to give Matthew Gregory Lewis, *Legends of the Nunnery*, 1805, 4 vols., Hughes, and *Legends of a Nunnery*, 1807, 4 vols., Hughes, to " E. Montagu " (pp. 208–209.)

So vast are their numbers, so rare have the romances themselves become, that a Bibliography of the Gothic Novel must be an undertaking of extraordinary difficulty and perplexity. Dilemmas and problems confront one at every step. The question continually arises whether such and such a novel is sufficiently Gothic to be included, or whether it is to be regarded as a social or a domestic novel. One is bound to be elastic in every direction. At what date may the Gothic novel be said to have begun ? At what date did the Gothic novel finally lose itself, submerged in other forms and appearing under another guise ? Such points can be argued twenty ways, and seem insoluble. Or at least they depend solely on the judgement and choice of the compiler. Yet there must be some lines of demarcation ; some rules and method must be observed ; that is to say, unless without any disposition or rationale lists are to be set down upon paper, to look after and arrange themselves as best they can. This, of course, is the line of least resistance, and the result may seem at first glance an " impressive catalogue," but actually it turns out an omnium gatherum which will almost inevitably (by the very nature of its compilation) prove not only to be gravely inaccurate but inflated to tedium with its repetitions and repeats.

In Herr Brauchli's bibliography, Schiller's *Der Geisterseher* (*The Ghost Seer*), is repeated ten times in three pages, and in all appears thirteen times ; *Rinaldo Rinaldini* is registered five times with different dates, 1798–1800 ; 1800 ; 1841 (*bis*) ; 1851 ; *Koenigsmark* is given six times ; *The Bravo of Bohemia*, thrice ; *The Horrors of Oakendale Abbey*, thrice, with an incorrect date, 1802, since this romance was published in 1797, and although Herr Brauchli lists it among " Antiklerikale Romane," it has nothing whatsoever to do with ecclesiastics of any sort or kind whatsoever, so I am afraid that " anticlerical " is a rather wild and not too happy guess. *Faust, a Romance of the Secret Tribunal* (or *Tribunals*, Herr Brauchli alternates between the singular and the plural) by " G. W. M. Reynolds " (or " G. M. W. Reynolds, Herr Brauchli again alternates) is given no less than four times under four several lists : " Mystery-Titel," " Terror-und Horror Titel," " Romance-Titel," and " Romane, deren Titel ' Germanisches ' (oder ' Slawisches ') verheissen." The date assigned is 1847.

Faust by George William MacArthur Reynolds commenced as a serial in *The London Journal* on October 4th, 1845, and concluded on July 18th, 1846. The sub-title, " A Romance of the Secret Tribunals," is a later addition. It cannot, I think, be justly argued that Reynolds' *Faust* has any place in a list of Gothic novels.

I am very certain, too, that such works as William Henry Giles Kingston's *The Circassian Chief*, and *Manco, the Peruvian Chief* ; Mrs. Trollope's *The Abbess*, and *Father Eustace* (which Herr Brauchli calls " Eustace " *tout court*) ; Samuel Warren's *Ten Thousand a Year* (que diable allait-il faire dans cette galère ?) ; Miss Hardy's ultra-protestant and very amusing *The Confessor* of 1851 ; Miss Mulock's *Romantic Tales* ; and a score beside it were tedious to particularize are absolutely inadmissible however widely the Gothic net be cast.

It might further be pointed out that neither Nathan Drake's *Literary Hours* nor Godwin's *Lives of the Necromancers* is fiction, and their presence in a bibliography of romances cannot with any reason be justified.

Such entries as "Priest, a Novel," "Robber, a Novel," seem slovenly to the last degree. I do not know whether by the latter is intended *The Robber*, A Tale, by G. P. R. James. If yes, the date assigned, 1851, is incorrect, since James' *The Robber* was published, 3 vols., 1838. The Minerva Press was not issuing romances so late as 1851, an error into which Herr Brauchli falls more than once.

It is difficult to see what purpose can be served by heaping together lists of novels under various vague and unmeaning labels, for example, "Schloss-Titel," "Turm-Titel," "Geister-Titel," "Mitternachts-Titel," "Räuber-Titel," and the like. This merely results in a number of romances which have no point of resemblance and no affinity being entered up under "Schloss-Titel" for no better reason than that the word "Castle" occurs in the title of each several romance, *The Castle of Otranto*; *Ellen, Countess of Castle Howell*; *The Castle of Tariffa*; Ainsworth's *Windsor Castle*; *Corfe Castle*; and so on *sostenuto*.

This haphazard ticketing—for haphazard the selection in greater part most unmistakably betrays itself to be—leads to some sad stumbles. Thus under "Zaubrer-und Teufels-romane" we find "1815 Marchioness, or the matured Enchantress." *The Marchioness* ! ! ! Or, "The Matured Enchantress," by Lady ——, 3 vols., Minerva Press, 1813, is a social novel depicting contemporary fashionable life, and there is not a word of magic, sorcery or necromancy in any one of the three volumes. Other instances might easily be cited.

Herr Brauchli should have been better guided in his choice of reference-books and authorities. We lose confidence when we find a particularly freakish and eccentric treatise described as "ein äussert vielseitiges und aufschlussreiches Buch."

We must therefore be pardoned if we find ourselves unable to accept Herr Brauchli's assurance that *Legends of the Nunnery*, 1805, a book whicn to the best of our knowledge nobody has ever seen, is the work of Matthew Gregory Lewis.

We believe it to be a confusion with Edward Montague's *Legends of a Nunnery*, 1807.

Montague's *The Citizen*, a burlesque poem in the metre of *Hudibras* with some variant lines, has a good deal of humour, but not enough perhaps to sustain a longer stretch. The mythological and antiquarian researches of the gentleman who dwelt in Fish-street Hill are wittily told, and the misadventures of the lady in Canto III have a distinct smack of Butler:

> The mob, who swore she was a witch,
> Wanted to throw her in the ditch,
> For if she swam, then 'twould be clear
> That they had proper cause for fear,
> But if she sank beneath the water,
> 'Twould prove they had mista'en the matter.

Nelson's Ghost is but a mediocre piece.

In Germany " the arch-priest of ultra-German romanticism," as he has been called, Ernst Theodor Wilhelm Hoffmann (1776–1822),[92] amply showed the influence of Lewis in one of his most powerfully fantastic tales, *Die Elixiere des Teufels* (1816),[93] of which an English translation appeared 2 vols., 1824, as *The Devil's Elixir*. For example, the first chapter of *The Monk* commences : " Scarcely had the abbey bell tolled for five minutes, and already was the church of the Capuchins thronged with auditors."

When a stranger makes inquiry concerning the crowds the answer is returned : " Can you possibly be ignorant that Ambrosio, Abbot of this monastery, pronounces sermon in this church every Thursday ? " In Hoffmann's novel Medardus is a Capuchin,[94] and his sermons are crowded in similar fashion, a fact which ministers inordinately to his vanity.   Thus : " An hour before the bells for assembling, the most aristocratic and cultured portion of the town's inhabitants crowded into the monastery church, no very large building, to hear the sermon of Brother Medardus." [95]   A number of other passages might be instanced especially since in *The Monk* the painting of the Madonna which Ambrosio so admired is drawn from Matilda, so in *Die Elixiere, des Teufels* Medardus hears the confession of an unknown lady who acknowledges a forbidden yearning, and suddenly cries : " Thou thyself, Medardus, art the consecrated being whom I so unspeakably love ! "   The Capuchin is racked with concupiscence.   " An impulse, till now never known, almost raged in my bosom.   A passionate desire to behold her features—to press her to my heart—to perish at once in delight and despair—wholly took possession of me ! "   In agony he flies to kneel before the altar of S. Rosalia, which is crowned by a picture of the Saint.   " In this picture which had never particularly struck me before, I now at once recognized the likeness of my beloved ! Even her dress resembled the foreign habit of the unknown ! " [96]   It may be further remarked that in *The Monk* Antonia " Knelt before a statue of St. Rosolia [*sic*] her patroness, and sang a ' Midnight Hymn.'"

The adventures of *Die Elixiere des Teufels* differ considerably, of course, from those of *The Monk* in many ways, but generally it may be remarked that Monk Medardus corresponds to Ambrosio, Euphemia to Matilda, and Aurelia to Antonia.

It has been said by J. T. Bealby that *Die Elixiere des Teufels* can " scarcely be read without shuddering," and he further describes it as a " dark maze of human emotion and human weakness—a mingling of poetry, sentimentality, rollicking humour, wild remorse, stern gloom, blind delusion, dark insanity, over all which is thrown a veil steeped in the fantastic and the horrible." [97]

At Covent Garden on April 20th, 1829, was produced *The Devil's Elixir*; *or, The Shadowless Man*, a Musical Romance in two Acts, founded upon Hoffmann's tale by Fitzball with music by G. H. Rodwell. Francesco (Medardus) was played by Warde, " a very good tragic actor in his time," [98] and Gortzburg, Demon of the Elixir, by " the terrific, terrible O. Smith, the ' creator ' of perhaps more villains and monsters than any other player to be named." [99] This drama had considerable success, and it was observed by a critic that " the *Elixir* at Covent Garden seems one of the most popular drinks of the day."

Lewis' *The Monk* very greatly influenced the prolific pen of George William MacArthur Reynolds. Father Cyprian in *The Bronze Statue or The Virgin's Kiss*, and Father Anselm in *Faust* are both reminiscent of Ambrosio, whilst the final scene of the latter romance, when the taunting demon hurls his hapless victim into the fiery bowels of Vesuvius may be nearly paralleled with the conclusion of *The Monk*. In *The Coral Island*; *or, The Hereditary Curse*, Chapter XXXII, " The Ruined Monastery." we have a legend concerning a monk of noble lineage, Lucio, who is the constant companion of a novice, Francesco. It is discovered, owing to the cries of a woman being heard during the night and the wail of a babe, that Francesco is really Francesca, who for love of Lucio has gained admittance to the house in male attire. The body of a newly buried child, strangled, is found in the garden. To avoid the doom of the guilty, Lucio and his mistress commit suicide. In *The Bronze Statue*, Chapter LXXXVI, the apparition at the bridal ceremony of a female figure in nun-like cerements seems to resemble the vision of *The Castle Spectre*, whilst the dual identity of Gloria and Satanais recalls Flodardo (Rosalvo) and Abellino, the principal figure of *The Bravo of Venice*. In *Agnes*; *or, Beauty and Pleasure*, the scene shifts from England to Naples, and here Charles de Vere, visiting a very handsome church which is described in some detail—apparently San Domenico Maggiore is intended—witnesses an extraordinary " sham-confessional " incident, when the Viscount Silvio di Camerino " hastily assuming a cowl which was hanging to a peg in the vestiary " proceeds to the box, pretending to be Father Falconara, and listens to " Ginevra's penitential outpourings." Ginevra, who is the second wife of the Count di Camerino, has borne a child to her own son-in-law. A little later by the connivance of Father Falconara, the Count himself takes the place of the priest and hears the confession of the guilty Countess. There follows swift tragedy. Although the circumstances differ, Reynolds, I think, remembered *The Monk* when he wrote these chapters.[100]

In *Wagner, The Wehr-Wolf*, the inexorable Carmelite Abbess, " noted for the austerity of her manners, the rigid discipline which she maintained in the convent," is modelled upon Mother St. Agatha, whilst the " spectre-like figures " of the recluses and the horrors of " the Chamber of Penitence," the living tomb, the destruction of the convent by fire, all very closely resemble the mysteries of St. Clare. There are Inquisition scenes, too, in *Wagner*, and detailed descriptions of the rack and other tortures. The Rosicrucian also may have been suggested by the Wandering Jew.

A " Legendary Romance," *The Black Monk ; or, The Secret of the Grey Turret*,[101] by Thomas Preskett Prest, 1844, owes much to *The Monk* as well as to Mrs. Radcliffe. Morgatani, the Black Monk, is moulded on Schedoni. " The face was that of a man who had passed the prime of life, but it would seem as if time had not succeeded in dimming the fire of his eyes, or in quenching the passions which betrayed themselves in every feature of his face. . . . Then folding his arms beneath his ample robe, he again stood fixed as a statue " (Chapter VI, p, 21). So Schedoni " remained in the same attitude fixed like a statue " (*The Italian*, 2nd ed., 1797, Chapter IX, p. 305). The aged pilgrim in *The Black Monk* was suggested by the Wandering Jew ; Agatha resembles Matilda ; the Apparition in the Southern Gallery (Chapter XXXV) is from *The Castle Spectre* ; the description of the ghastly form, half skeleton, half rotting flesh—" There were crawling things too about the body "—(Chapter XXXVII) may be paralleled in the incident of Agnes and her dead babe ; the story of the magician and Guillaume from an old romance (Chapter XLIII) is completely in the style of Lewis ; the secret passages and the vault of the dead, the Florentine convent of S. Francis, and a number of other descriptions are unmistakably elaborated from his work. In its day *The Black Monk* was immensely popular.

There are several convent scenes in the anonymous *The New Mysteries of London*,[102] where the amorous Father Anselmo may be compared with Ambrosio, and we are even regaled with a torture-room and a rack in the " convent of Saint Theresa, in —— Street " a building of the good old sort which seems to be conducted by hideous old women with long muscular arms, and which from time to time in order to give a fillip to the proceedings rings with piercing shrieks. None the less, when a novice is about to pronounce her vows, the chapel, brilliant with the golden light of myriad tall tapers, shines, whilst " a hundred voices rose and fell in measured cadence." Unfortunately a lamp bursts, scattering naptha over the decorations, and these in a moment flare in a blaze, so that the whole building is burned to the ground. " The nunnery was broken up, it is true, but only to be established in another part of London." *The Monk* is closely echoed here.

Other imitations and chapters of yet later date modelled upon *The Monk* might be described ; but enough, I think, will have been said to show how continually Lewis' romance was being drawn upon and reproduced. Even his most extravagant passages were exaggerated, his most fantastic flights outsoared. All the while, it must be remembered, the original romance was being printed again and again, although unfortunately merely in cheap and valueless editions.

It is significant, perhaps, that *The Monk* is hardly touched upon in Barrett's satirical *The Heroine* (1813),[103] but this may be accounted for by the fact that in 1798 there had appeared *The New Monk*, a Romance in three volumes, by R. S. Esq., published by Lane, which is a close parody, chapter by chapter, and almost paragraph by paragraph of Lewis' romance. Thus Ambrosio becomes Joshua Pentateuch, surnamed " the Reverend of the West End," a fanatic and hypocritical Methodist preacher. This " Boanerges of the pulpit " is attended by a young clerk with an "elegant church-drawl " in his speech, Peter, who is revealed as Betsey, the Rosario-Matilda of the original story. The crowded church of the Capuchins where Ambrosio preaches is paralleled by a Methody chapel crammed with devotees to whom Pentateuch holds forth rowzingly, roaring "like the horrors of a tempest." Antonia is Ann Maria Augusta ; and Leonella, Miss Barbara. The nunnery of S. Clare is metamorphosed to Mrs. Rod's boarding-school, and Mrs. Rod, " with four teachers at her heels," who carry off the wretched Alice Clottleberry (Agnes of *The Monk*) to the flogging apartment, bidding the porter tuck up his shirt sleeves " for he shall have a whole evening's work of it," worthily fills the rôle of the domina, Mother St. Agatha.

Willy (Theodore) sings *The Warlock Man*, *A Scotch Ballad*, to the teachers and misses in the parlour of Rod-House, the breaking-up of that seminary, " a form of great ceremony and magnificence," standing for the Festival of S. Clare. When Pentateuch pays a call upon Ann

Maria Augusta (as Ambrosio visits Antonia) he finds her reading. "The priest examined the book. . . . It was 'The Monk.' 'How!' said he to himself, 'Ann Maria Augusta reads the Monk, and yet apparently so innocent?'"[104] However Olivia (Elvira) her mother had made a fair copy of the book omitting the combustibles—for "scenes the most indecent are there worse than plainly described . . . and the ocular observations of a *brothel* could scarcely raise with more force examples of improper situations."

In due course Pentateuch finds his way to Ann Maria Augusta's bedchamber, primarily to filch some banknotes. Olivia surprises him, and he promptly godfreys her on the spot. It is in this as well as in some other incidents which too closely caricature *The Monk* our parodist fails, in that he mixes burlesque with real horrors, and the result is a little disgusting. The trial, the final scenes in Newgate, and the hanging of Pentateuch in irons on the wayside gibbet are all extremely unpleasant, the latter in particular being grimy and grue to the last degree. A lighter element should have been introduced, and some comical turn given to the affair.

The Monthly Mirror, December, 1798,[105] thus reviewed *The New Monk*, a Romance by R. S. Esq., 2 vols., Lane, 1798 : "A Parody, but not a successful one, upon Mr. Lewis's admirable romance. The writing is bad ; the humour is worse. Even on the score of *morality*, R. S. has no advantage over the *old* monk :—for his desire of burlesque has led him into indelicate descriptions of a very gross nature." With respect to religion, the exposure of the hypocrisy of a *methodist preacher* should have been treated in another vein, since without losing a whit of the serious intent and moral the effect could have been improved by a less horrid catastrophe.

In his Preface (London, May 22nd, 1798), R. S. declares "that he intends no personal attack on Mr. Lewis, but he says : "I read his 'Monk' with horror . . . I beheld obscenity decorated in all the lustre of genius, religion hooded by prejudice, and a vast phalanx of mischief levelled at the morals of mankind. . . . I have sought, by a ridicule of its worst parts, by only substituting one appetite for another, to display the grossness of the idea, and to call a blush of contrition over the cheeks of those who have dwelt with pleasure on its pages." Pentateuch is "one of those Methodists, who, possessing neither goodness nor common sense, exalting themselves as the preachers of heaven, are the will-o'-th'-wisps of society, who conduct their followers through the labyrinths of folly, to the darkest depths of fanatic terrors."[106]

In 1803 H. J. Sarratt [or Sarrat] published (Crosby) a translation of *Les Trois Moines* by Elisabeth Guénard. baronne de Méré, as *The*

Three Monks !!! *From the French.* This he dedicated, as no doubt he conceived most appropriately, to M. G. Lewis. *The Critical Review* is exceedingly severe upon the book, remarking : " It does not so properly belong to reviewers to take cognisance of this work, as it does to the Society for the suppression of vice and immorality. May we claim the indulgence of our readers, if we give one instance, from among many, of its lewdness and impiety ? Anselmo is made to lie with an artful young prostitute who lived with his friend ; and, in this double crime of treachery and whoredom he is declared to " feel that bliss which would have exalted men far above *the gods*, if the latter, through envy had not shortened its duration."[107] The *Review* sympathizes with Lewis for having his name prefixed to this " contemptible jumble of absurdity and obscenity," but at the same time declares that really he has brought this kind of attention upon himself. It also snibs Mr. Sarratt pretty sharply as a " pretended *translator.*"

Herein, however, the critic errs. *Les Trois Moines* " par l'Auteur des Forges Mystérieuses, des Capucins, et de Pauline de Ferrière " was published at Paris, " Chez Marchand, Libraire, Palais du Tribunat," two volumes, 1802.[108] This, the first edition, is embellished with a couple of engravings, each volume carrying a frontispiece. There were many subsequent editions of this popular romance which was re-issued in 1815, two volumes with coloured plates ; and again two volumes, 1821.

Les Trois Moines is one of those curious romances which cannot be truly described as " anti-clerical," but which are rather to be characterized as flippantly introducing the figures of religions and involving them in slippery and picaresque adventures to give a haut-gout to their pages. These novels are hardly to be taken seriously, although one cannot be surprised that many (and some none of the most rigorous) are extremely displeased at such liberties and indeed indecorums.

In Ferrara there dwelt three lads, boon companions, Dominico del Frazo, Silvino Fezzali (a sad scapegrace), and Anselme Georgani. " Quels étoient ses pères et mères ! en verité je n'en sais rien." Silvino is the reputed son of Petro Pezzali and his wife Clementina Ribertini. Dominico is said to be the nephew of la signora Fansonetta ; whilst Anselme was found one evening, a babe abandoned before the gates of the palace of the duc de ——, and is taken in to be brought up by the duchess who tenderly pities the poor helpless infant. As they grow up the three boys get into all kinds of mischief, Silvino being the ringleader. This young rascal even takes a mistress, Rosa, who lives with her godmother, an honest mercer's wife. Eventually Silvino becomes a Franciscan, Dominico a Cistercian, and Anselme a Benedictine monk. Silvino and Dominico are at Bologna, and here they meet after some two or three years Anselme. Rosa has established herself in the same city, and is known as a woman of pleasure. Anselme falls in love with Elise, heiress of Prince Delmonte-Tenero, and succeeds in persuading her to elope with him. It is hardly necessary, perhaps, to follow all the romantic and amorous adventures that ensue, some of which may be accounted not of the most edifying kind. Silvino dies poisoned. It is discovered that Anselme and Dominico are brothers and of high rank, wherefore the vows of the former being annulled he is able to wed Elise.

Elisabeth Guénard, who was born at Paris in 1751, and died there on February 18th, 1829, may be justly accounted one of the most prolific and amazingly versatile of all French novelists. She issued her works under various names, one of her favourite pseudonyms being M. de Faverolles. I know more than one hundred and fourteen of her works, but it must be confessed that too many of her earlier romances are not only obscene but extremely profane. Her first work, *Lise et Valcourt, ou le Bénédictin*, Paris, 2 vols., 1799, was issued as by le citoyen G—d. This was followed by some half a dozen anonymous works such, for example, as *Les Forges Mystérieuses*, " roman dans le genre de Faublas," 4 vols. ; *Les Capucins, ou le Secret du cabinet noir*, 2 vols., 1801, which ran into no less than four editions [109] ; *Pauline de Ferrière, ou Histoire de vingt jeunes filles enlevées de chez leurs parens, sous le regne de Louis XV*, 3 vols. To name a few typical examples, we also have from her pen *Mystères sur mystères, ou les onze chevaliers*, 4 vols., 1807 ; *L'Abbaye de Saint-Remy, ou la fille de l'abbesse*, 4 vols., 1807 ; *Le Château de Vauvert, ou le chariot de feu de la rue d'Enfer*, " manuscrit trouvé dans les décombres de l'ancien couvent des Chartreux," 4 vols., 1812, published under the initial B—— ; *Les Repaires du crime*, 4 vols., 1812 ; *La Duchesse de Kingston*,[110] 4 vols., 1813 ; *La Tour infernale*, 3 vols., 1819 ; *Les Souterrains de Birmingham, ou Henriette Herefort*, 4 vols., 1822 ; *Albano, ou les Horreurs de l'âbime*, 4 vols., 1824. Discarding her extravagances and improprieties, Elisabeth Guénard, baronne de Méré, also wrote a series of works such as *Saint Vincent de Paul, l'apôtre des affligées*, 4 vols., 1818, and *Contes à nos enfants*, one vol., 1824. In her later years she was known as an eminently respectable and indeed devout old lady, constant in her attendance at Mass, and she was often heard to regret the indiscretions of bygone days.

H. J. Sarratt also adapted from the German of Rudolf Erich Raspe, who puts the narrative into the mouth of Heironymus Karl Friedrich, Baron von Münchhausen, *Koenigsmark the Robber, or The Terror of Bohemia*,[111] in which is introduced " Stella, or the Maniac of the Wood, a pathetick tale," 12mo [1801].[112]   This romance, or rather this version of it, has been erroneously ascribed to Lewis himself.[113] There even exists a chap-book, *Koenigsmark the Robber*; *or, The Terror of Bohemia* : in which is included, The Affecting History of Rosenberg and Adelaide, and their Orphan Daughter.   By M. G. Lewis, Esq., M.P., 8vo, Day and Munday.   This was probably pirated about 1808.

The incidents of *Koenigsmark* are very violent, and the tale runs at a rapid pace.   Two friends Theodore and Herman resolve to avenge the fate of an Austrian officer, Adolphus Rosenberg, who was foully slain by banditti.   Rosenberg has been in the service of the famous Raimondo, Count of Montecucculi (1608–81), so, if we care, we may date the story some time about 1660 to 1675.   Now Rosenberg had married Adelaide, the daughter of old Colonel Kaempfer, and the lovely widow is the object of the mad passions of Koenigsmark, the captain of a band of fifty-four desperadoes, a circumstance not at all improbable in those days of upheaval when robber gangs roamed the country well-nigh unchecked and unresisted.   So terrible is he that rumour names Koenigsmark (and perhaps rightly) as a warlock upon whom the Prince of Darkness has bestowed a charm to render him invulnerable.   Kaempfer's manor is attacked by the banditti, and these ruffians contrive to capture Theodore and bear him off to their cave, " hung all round with black."   The shade of Rosenberg, however, who walks pretty frequently and very effectively through the piece encourages and protects Theodore.   A penitent youth, Fredrick, lieutenant of the gang, befriends Theodore, aids his escape, and materially helps in bringing the robbers to justice, himself however falling in the fray. Koenigsmark is sentenced to the question in order to compel him to reveal the whole of his horrid secrets, but as they are about to stretch him on the rack a masked Unknown sheathes a dagger in the villain's heart and instantly vanishes, thus leaving all to conclude " It was assuredly an evil spirit."

Stella, the Maniac of the Wood, is a village beauty who was betrothed to Raymond, the son of an honest carpenter, and the handsomest youth in the whole countryside.   Almost on the very eve of their nuptials it is discovered that Raymond is among the most ruthless and blood-stained of Koenigsmark's followers, and being found in the very circumstance of robbery and murder he is forthwith hanged to a branch of the nearest oak.   The hapless Stella loses her senses, and a piteous lunatic wanders through the forest glades or crouches fearfully beneath her lover's bleaching atomy, hearkening to the wail of the wind as it sighs between his bones.

Koenigsmark is full of apparitions and wizardry.   We have a werewolf, who when wounded by Count Clodimer, presently disappears amid a most noisome stench : " All that the servants remembered, who had been stunned, was that a strong sulphurous smell had suddenly issued—their sights had grown dim, and they had lost the power of perception."[114]   Romaldi encounters " a large, black horrid spider, who was slowly increasing in size and rolling two large, yellow eyes, which glared frightfully."   In this romance we further meet with a spectre who sheds three drops of boiling blood, a horrible omen.

Rudolf Erich Raspe [115] (1737–94), a scholar of some eminence, was born in Hanover, and in 1767 was appointed a Professor and Librarian at Kassel.   During the year 1775 he was travelling in Italy to buy curios for the Landgrave of Hesse, of whose collection of gems he had charge.   Raspe unhappily was tempted to sell both the antiques he had acquired and the gems to another collector.   He pocketed the proceeds and flew to England.   Here he contrived to fleece Sir John Sinclair of Ulbster of various not inconsiderable sums by pretending to find ore upon the Sinclair estates.   When the trick was discovered, Raspe evaded pursuit and escaped to Ireland.   He died at Muckross in 1794.

Hieronymus Karl Friedrich, Freiherr von Münchhausen (1720–97), of Bodenwerder in Hanover, after a long military career in which he had greatly distinguished himself by many heroic exploits, retired to his country estates where he was wont to entertain his friends with lavish hospitality.   In return they had to listen to his stories of his youth and adventures, for von Münchhausen was a famous raconteur, and justly or no he was suspected of colouring his anecdotes in very vivid hues.   Raspe had met the Baron at Göttingen, and being a wit and a good listener was often welcomed under his sociable roof.   In after years, when in England, the expatriated scholar, not desirous of drawing attention to his own whereabouts, bethought him of fathering various works on von Münchhausen.   A book of forty pages, *Baron Munchausen's Narrative of his Marvellous Travels and Campaigns in Russia* was published by Smith, London, 1785.   No copy is known, but the Second Edition, Oxford, was as far as may be judged identical.   In 1786 Kearsley of Fleet Street brought out an enlarged edition, and the *Narrative* becoming immensely popular reprint followed reprint with all sorts of additions and new adventures of the most extravagant and grotesque kind, gleaned from facetiæ, folk-lore, mock-travels and burlesques out of all quarters.   Thus was built up the book as we have it, *The Travels and Surprising Adventures of Baron Munchausen.*[116]   A free German version was made from the Fifth Edition by the poet Bürger as *Wunderbaren Reissen zu Wasse und Lande des Freyherrn von Münchhausen,*

Göttingen, 1786. The true authorship of the English *Baron Munch-hausen* was not known until the story was told in 1824 by Bürger's biographer.

There are some details concerning Sarratt in Young's *Memoirs of Mrs. Crouch.* A favourite singer at Drury Lane was Miss Dufour, whose last appearance on the stage was in the rôle of a Priestess of the Sun in Sheridan's *Pizarro*, May 24th, 1799. " She has since," the *Memoirs* tell us, " married Mr. Sarrat, a man of very great abilities ; he is known in the literary world as the author of a New Survey of London; Koningsmark the Robber, a romance, in one volume ; the Life of Buonaparte ; and he has also translated a novel from the French, called The Three Monks ! dedicated to M. G. Lewis, Esq. . . . Mrs. Sarrat has also translated a novel from the French, intitled Aurora, or the Mysterious Beauty, and written various little interesting tales for periodical publications. She engaged, some time ago, with Mr. Astley as his first singer . . . an excellent wife and mother ; it would be difficult to find a more accomplished, a more amiable, or a happier couple than Mr. and Mrs. Sarrat."[117]

In 1796 Lewis published *Village Virtues*, " A Dramatic Satire in Two Parts," large quarto, " For J. Bell." The book is uncommon, and Eino Railo, *The Haunted Castle*, rather indiscreetly observes : " At the end of the list of Lewis's works [actually it is number two, *The Monk* being first] in Mrs. Baron-Wilson's *Life*, mention is made of a work called *Village Virtues*, of which nothing is said in the text. The book is not in the British Museum Library, nor have I succeeded in tracing a copy elsewhere. Lewis never wrote such a book." Yet it does exist in private collections, and an exemplar is in the Dyce Library, Victoria and Albert Museum, South Kensington. *Village Virtues* is a satire in dialogue rather than a play. The interlocutors are : Sir David Downright ; Careful ; Farmer Sturdy ; William ; Lady Mount-Level ; Dame Sturdy ; Rose ; Phœbe. The action is supposed to pass in a Farm-house in Cornwall. Here, with Farmer Sturdy, is lodging under the name of Mrs. Harrington, Sir David's sister, Lady Mount-Level. She has informed her brother that she believes his two daughters, Julia and Louisa, whom she has barely seen, to be confirmed coquettes, whilst Lord Winworth, who is to marry one of her nieces, is an abandoned libertine. Indeed, she has left London as a vicious place, and seeks " pastoral purity." Her peace is disturbed by quarrels between Sturdy and his wife. The dame accuses her husband with Jenny Grig, the grocer's wife ; " paw-paw doings," and " The hussy should stand in a white sheet every Sunday for this year to come," she vociferates. The Farmer retaliates by jeering at her attentions to the brandy-bottle. It appears that Sturdy is the leading spirit of a Club of malcontents at the Green Dragon, and notorious for his incendiary views. Rose, Sturdy's daughter, is a fine miss, anxious to marry Tripit, gentleman to Lord Winworth's gentleman. William, a country fellow, comes a-courting Rose, but haggles coarsely about her portion. He has already entangled himself with Phœbe, a matter anent which there is a good deal of shrewish dispute. It is easy for Rose to make up her mind to jilt her swain and marry old Careful, since she consoles herself with the reflection that he "will soon go to old Nick," and then she is at liberty to make William her second spouse. A fine uproar is caused by the drunken antics of Dame Sturdy, and at length Lady Mount-Level confesses that the country is as bad as the town. Sir David then opens his sister's eyes. 'Twas all a masquerade for her benefit. Mrs. Comfit, his housekeeper, acted Mrs. Sturdy ; a friend, Mr. Wilmot, played Sturdy ; William is none other than Lord Winworth ; whilst in the brace of country wenches she may recognize her nieces twain. The conclusion which is brought about with a good deal of humour is certainly surprising and unexpected. Lady Mount-Level acknowledges the lesson : " I was wrong in confining virtue to any one rank of people."

In 1797 Lewis published 8vo, *The Minister*, an adaptation of Schiller's *Kabale und Liebe*. A second edition appeared 8vo, 1798. This " faithful and elegant translation of an excellent play," as the *Biographia Dramatica* [118] rather inaccurately describes it, since Lewis did not hesitate to alter the names of the characters, to shift the scene to Brunswick and date the period 1580, was primarily not intended for the stage.[119]

" Lewis was now mingling in the highest circles of fashion, was flatteringly noticed at court, and to add to these distinctions, almost immediately on his becoming of age, obtained a seat in Parliament." From 1796 to 1802 he represented Hindon, Wilts, succeeding William Beckford. On his introduction to the House, Charles James Fox welcomed him as a famous author, but the Senate had no charms for the young poet, and his political career proved both mute and inglorious. About this time he settled in a " cottage," " a pretty romantic retreat," which was really a charming small country house with miniature grounds, all " flowers and fragrance, books and pictures," at Barnes. He also had chambers in the Albany, and both his homes were lavishly furnished with mirrors, of which he showed himself extravagantly fond. At Barnes he often entertained persons of the highest quality, amongst others the Duchess of York, at a " Poet's fête champêtre." One of the first and firmest friends of Lewis was the

PLATE XI

"Agnès, Agnès, tu es à moi, Je suis à toi pour la vie.

Page 57

THE BLEEDING NUN

The Monk

Face p. 277

Duke of Argyle, and for several years he was wont to spend some weeks annually at Inverary Castle. It was here that rambling on a morning with Lady Charlotte Campbell,[120] the sister of his host, they met in the woods a poor maniac girl, an encounter which inspired him to write the famous ballad *Crazy Jane*.[121]

Whilst one day he was looking through the two volumes of his manuscript romance in the style of *The Castle of Otranto* with the design of completing this work for the press the idea occurred to Lewis that it might even serve better as a play, and accordingly he dramatized his chapters the result being *The Castle Spectre*, which was produced at Drury Lane on Thursday, December 14th, 1797.

The Prologue spoken by Wroughton, at once strikes the romantic note :

> Far from the haunts of men, of vice the foe,
> The moon-struck child of genius and of woe,
> Versed in each magic spell, and dear to fame,
> A fair enchantress dwells, Romance her name.
> She loathes the sun, or blazing taper's light :
> The moon-beamed landscape and tempestuous night
> Alone she loves ; and oft, with glimmering lamp,
> Near graves new-open'd, or midst dungeons damp,
> Drear forests, ruin'd aisles, and haunted towers,
> Forlorn she roves, and raves away the hours !

Michael Kelly gives the following account of this play [122] : " On December 14th, 1797, the celebrated dramatic romance, called *The Castle Spectre*, was produced at Drury Lane, written by M. G. Lewis, Esq. It had a prodigious run ; John Kemble performed in it, as did Mrs. Jordan and Mrs. Powell, who made a splendid spectre. The first night of its representation, the sinking of the Ghost in a flame of fire, and the beauty of the whole scene, had a most sublime effect. I composed the music for the piece ; but for the situation in which the Ghost first appears in the oratory to her daughter and in which the acting both of Mrs. Powell and Mrs. Jordan, without speaking, riveted the audience, I selected the chacoone of Jomelli [123] as an accompaniment to the action. . . . Mr. M. Lewis, the author of this drama, though eccentric, had a great deal of genius. I knew him well. . . . Of all dramas, *The Castle Spectre* was his favourite, perhaps from its having been the most attractive and popular." M. J. Young, in her *Memoirs of Mrs. Crouch*,[124] observes of *The Castle Spectre* : " The long run which this play had the first season, the numerous times it has been performed since, the many editions it has gone through, and the power it still retains over the feelings of the audience, prove its merit beyond any praises which have, or can be bestowed on it."

The Castle Spectre is the most famous and the most typical specimen of all Gothic melodramas. It must not indeed be judged from a purely literary point of view, for there are then very many quite palpable faults at which it is easy enough to smile with critical disdain. It has not, for example, the poetry and extraordinary power of Maturin's *Bertram*, but little imagination can be required to appreciate how upon the stage Lewis' scenes proved supremely effective. Personally, of all dramas, this " crusted grizzly skeleton melodrama " as my old friend Chance Newton who knew and loved it used to call *The Castle Spectre*, is the one I should most like to see, but unhappily the last revival in London was, more than half a century ago, at the Gaiety Theatre, for two matinée performances on May 5th and 12th, 1880, when John Hollingshead was giving " Palmy Day Neglected Dramas." [125]

The original cast was extremely fine. The principals were : Earl Osmond, Barrymore ; Earl Reginald, Wroughton ; Earl Percy, John Kemble ; Motley, young Bannister ; Hassan, Dowton ; Angela, Mrs. Jordan ; Alice, Mrs. Walcot ; and Evelina, the Spectre, Mrs. Powell.

The scene is Conway Castle, now in possession of the villainous Earl Osmond, a usurper, who has caused his brother, Earl Reginald, and his brother's wife, to be murdered some sixteen years before. Unknown to his master, however, Kenric, major-domo of the Castle and Osmond's trusted accomplice, a character curiously compounded of greed, cruelty, pity and remorse, aided Earl Reginald, whom he has immured in a dungeon of the Castle, a secret prison of which he alone has the key. The rightful heiress of Conway, a mere babe, was scarcely saved from Osmond's wrath, but at length at Kenric's prayers she was concealed in a villager's cottage, where she grew to be the lovely Angela. She was wooed, and gave her heart to the peasant Edwy, who is none other than Percy, Earl of Northumberland. Osmond, knowing this and fearing that if she were to wed so powerful a supporter his guilt would be discovered, reclaims her from her rustic guardian, and, enraptured by her charms, designs himself to marry her, giving out that she has been discovered to be the daughter of Sir Malcolm Mowbray, long since deceased. Angela rejects his suit with scorn, whilst Earl Percy who has penetrated to the Castle to bear her thence, is recognized and held in confinement by Osmond. By a stratagem he escapes, and gathers his forces. Meanwhile Osmond compels Angela to keep her chamber, the Cedar Room, until the morrow when he threatens to espouse her by force. Here Kenric visits her and tells her that Earl Reginald, her father, still lives. They are surprised by Osmond who overhears the tale. Angela, however, is encouraged by a vision of her mother. Father Philip, who is her friend, contrives her escape from the Cedar Room by a subterranean passage, which leads them out through the vaults where she meets her father. Osmond and his minions burst in upon them, but at this very moment Percy who has gained admittance with his followers drives back the assassins, and when Osmond with a frantic gesture is about to cut down Reginald, the Spectre suddenly rises between them, and as he staggers back distraught, Angela stabs him with her poniard. He is borne away about to breathe his last, soothed by the forgiveness of his long injured and suffering brother.

I am very well aware that this bald outline can only give a poor idea of the effectiveness of the play, but even in the reading it does not require much visualization to see how skilfully the incidents have been managed and how admirably adapted they are to impress an audience. I would not seem to labour this point repeatedly, but it is distressing to read such ineptitudes as " we cannot to-day esteem Lewis any other than a mediocre dramatist intent upon the cheapest of effects." [126]

In various footnotes to the printed play,[127] and in a little appendix addressed " To The Reader," Lewis quite candidly draws attention to several hints he has adopted and in some cases improved. Thus in Act II, Scene I, the animated portrait of *The Castle of Otranto* suggested a striking bit of business ; the escape of Earl Percy comes from a German play whose main incident was a similar escape of Ludwig, a Landgrave of Thuringia. When he wrote Motley's song, Lewis remembered Burgoyne's "Historical Romance" *Richard Cœur de Lion*.[128] The circumstance of Father Philip concealing himself in the bed and thus frightening Alice is from *The Mysteries of Udolpho*, where Emily and old Dorothée are alarmed when they visit at midnight the lone chamber where the Marchioness de Villeroi died.[129] In the Romance it brings forward a terrific scene. In the Play it is intended to produce an effect entirely ludicrous.[130]

Earl Reginald concealed in a secret vault may be a variation of the theme of *A Sicilian Romance*, where the Marquis of Mazzini imprisons his first wife in a subterranean abode belonging to the southern buildings of the castle of Mazzini, and gives out that she is dead. Lewis admired Marsollier's play *Camille, ou le Souterrain* [131] (1791) founded upon this very situation which is derived from the *Adèle et Theodore* (1782) of Madame de Genlis.

The Castle Spectre was most harshly criticized by those who were jealous of the young author's genius and success. Genest, who is always very severe on Lewis, is bound to allow that " Osmond, Father Philip, and Alice are very good characters—but the great run which this piece had, is a striking proof that success is a very uncertain

criterion of merit." [132]   It was said that Father Philip was copied from
Sheridan's Father Paul ; that Hassan was closely modelled on Zanga.
In fact, that Osmond should be attended by negroes was an anachronism
and yet Lewis was bold enough to protest " I by no means regret the
introduction of my *Africans*." He comically added that black servants
gave a pleasing variety to the characters, " and could I have produced
the same effect by making my heroine blue, blue I should have made
her." Against the Spectre ridiculous objections were urged. " She
ought not to appear because the belief in Ghosts no longer exists." It
was bruited abroad that if Sheridan had not advised the author to
content himself with a single Spectre, his purpose was " to have
exhibited a whole regiment of Ghosts." The managers, the actors,
the friends to whom the play was read, all begged Lewis to confine the
Ghost to the Green-room. He persisted, and " *The Spectre* was as
well treated before the curtain as she had been ill-used behind it."
The two apparition scenes were greeted with tumultuous appluase.
Lewis quite candidly and very properly adds that if he with mock-
modesty declared he thought *The Castle Spectre* very bad, what would
such an avowal be save to insult the judgement of the public " which
has given it a very favourable reception. . . . Still its success on the
stage (great enough to content even an author) does not prevent my
being very doubtful as to its reception in the closet, when divested of
its beautiful music, splendid scenery, and above all, of the acting,
excellent throughout." [133]   None the less, *The Castle Spectre* was
greeted with avidity by the reading public, and ran through no less
than seven editions in 1798, whilst an eighth edition appeared in 1799,
and a tenth edition in 1803.[134]   The prolific Miss Sarah Wilkinson
was not ill-advised when she turned the popular *The Castle Spectre* into
a prose romance (1820).

In 1799 was published *Rolla ; or The Peruvian Hero* which Lewis
translated from Kotzebue, and which ran into five editions. In 1799,
also, Lewis imitated from the thirteenth Satire of Juvenal *The Love of
Gain*, a Poem, published by Bell at 3s. 6d., some lines of which (it was
said) were from the pen of an Eton boy, a close friend of Lewis, the
Hon. George Lamb,[135] Viscount Melbourne's youngest son, whose
verse translation of Catullus won him great repute in the literary
world.

In the spring of 1798, William Erskine, who was staying in London,
met Lewis and showed him a number of ballads translated and adapted
from the German by Walter Scott. Lewis who was collecting material
for a volume of miscellaneous verse, at once proved immensely
interested and begged for further contributions. He also introduced

Scott's translation of *Gotz von Berlichingen* to his own publisher Bell, by whom it was issued in February, 1799.[136] When Lewis, who happened to be passing through Edinburgh, asked Scott (whom he had previously met at Inverary) to dine at his hotel, the invitation was accepted with pride, and years after Scott still remembered (as he told Allan Cunningham) how complimented and flattered he had been to be entertained by the author of *The Monk*. It may be remarked that Scott thought very highly of the genius of Lewis, and had a very real affection for his amiable if eccentric friend.[137]

In 1799 Lewis printed the first part of his ballad collection as *Tales of Terror* (Kelso), but actually he considered this as the second part of the *Tales of Wonder*, Bell, London, 1801, and in the second edition (same year) of the *Tales of Wonder*, Bell advertises : " Tales of Terror : with Three curious Engravings highly coloured. Price 7s. 6d. *N.B.*—This work is printed uniform with this Edition of the *Tales of Wonder*, and makes a good second volume to it." [138] The " Introductory Dialogue " to *Tales of Terror* is dated March 1st, 1801.

The *Tales of Wonder* have seventeen poems by Lewis ; five poems by Scott ; a poem apiece by H. Bunbury, J. Leyden, and (burlesque) George Colman, jun., as well as seven anonymous poems. Of the latter, one is a translation of Bürger's *Lenore* ; and another, *The Bleeding Nun*, is founded on the fourth chapter of *The Monk*.

Mingled with what is—if not fine poetry, at least exceedingly powerful and musical verse, ballads of the very first order—Lewis shows odd and even grotesque strokes of humour which can hardly fail to remind his readers of the *Ingoldsby Legends*. There is the same horror ; there are the same sudden turns of fun, almost startling in their abruptness and their incongruity. Lewis' ballads have been stupidly spoken of as " fluent doggerel," and indeed there are not many English poets among whose works passages of " fluent doggerel " might not be found. Such a banter does not harm the poet but rather makes a fool of the critic.

Some of his themes are from the old chroniclers. *The Grey Friar of Winton* is taken from a relation of William of Malmesbury ; the legend of Charles Martel is from Matthew of Westminster. Some stories have a classical origin : *The Gay Gold Ring* is the account of Philinnion and Machates as given by Phlegon of Tralles.[139] *Willy's Lady* is the Greek myth of Alcmene in labour, and how Galinthias choused the goddess Here.[140] Although described as " A Welsh Tale " and stated to be " founded on a fact, which happened at the beginning of the last century " (*circa* 1700), *The House upon the Heath* is the ghastly story of " Wild Will Darrell " of haunted Littlecote. Evil Darrell lived in the reign of Queen Elizabeth.   It is, of course, by no means impossible that similar circumstances (and the details differ) occurred in Radnorshire.[141]

On Monday, April 22nd, 1799, was produced at Drury Lane *The East Indian*, for the benefit of Mrs. Jordan, who had accepted the play, as we have noted, some half a dozen years before.   It was only performed twice that season, but being favourably received [142] it took a place in the winter repertory, although actually it never met with the enduring success so vivacious a comedy well deserved.   Lewis, with some truth, was wont to ascribe his disappointment to the inflated triumph of the famous *Pizarro*, given at Drury Lane, April 24th, 1799, and he felt the matter more keenly since Sheridan without acknowledgement appropriated a good deal of his own best material.   The title-rôle of *The East Indian*—the name is suggested by Cumberland's evergreen *The West Indian* [143]—Rivers, was created by J. P. Kemble; his daughter, Zorayda, Mrs. Jordan; Beauchamp, Charles Kemble; Lord Listless, Palmer; Modish, Barrymore; Miss Chatterall, Mrs. Pope; Lady Clara Modish, Miss Stuart; Mrs. Ormond, Mrs. Powell; Mrs. Slip-Slop, Mrs. Sparks; Lady Hubbub, Mrs. Cayler; Mrs. Blab, Miss Tidswell; and Mrs. Tiffany, Mrs. Coates.

Beauchamp has eloped from India with Zorayda, whom he is able to marry upon the death of his own wife.   There were not wanting some critics who found the moral " exceedingly questionable; in one sense indeed it may be said to be abominable." [144]   Many of the lighter scenes are extremely amusing, and there is some excellent character drawing in the fashionable scandal-mongering society, Lord Listless, Lady Clara Modish, the voluble Miss Chatterall; whilst Mrs. Slip-Slop, " a wulgarer Mrs. Malaprop," need scarcely fear comparison with " *the old weather-beaten she-dragon* " of *The Rivals* in her " nice derangement of epitaphs."   She reads a note " superdescribed, I see, to Miss Mandeville, though she knows well enough that's only a consumed name."   Miss Chatterall relates how Mrs. Punt playing at whist with Lady Cogwell, " found the ace of diamonds hid in her muff . . . so I'm going to comfort, and console, and vex and tease her and all that you know."   Certain incidents in the plot—the visits of Rivers to Modish and to Mrs. Ormond—were suggested by circumstances in Mrs. Frances Sheridan's *Memoirs of Miss Sidney Bidulph* [145] (1761), and Lewis for Lord Listless and Miss Chatterall clearly had in mind Meadows and Miss Larolles in *Cecilia* (1782).   There are also hints from Kotzebue's *Die Indianer in England* (1789).   Of *The East Indian* there are two editions, London, Bell, 1800, published at half a crown; and a Dublin edition, 12mo, the same year, as *Rivers; or, The East Indian*.

Lewis now brought out of his portfolio a drama he had written about six years before, *Adelmorn, the Outlaw*, which was produced at Drury Lane on Monday, May 4th, 1801. The Overture and Music to this ultra-romantic piece, which appropriately opens in *A Gothic Hall*, were composed by Kelly. There was an excellent cast including Powell as Sigismund ; Raymond, Ulric ; Charles Kemble, Adelmorn ; Barrymore, Father Cyprian ; Bannister, Lodowick ; Suett, Hugo ; Miss De Camp, Herman ; Mrs. Jordan, Innogen ; and Mrs. Mountain, Orrila. The scene, Saxony.

The villain, Baron Ulric, has poniarded Count Roderic of Bergen, whose nephew, Adelmorn, he contrives shall be accused of the crime. Duke Sigismund takes a solemn oath never to pardon the assassin of the Count, and Adelmorn is condemned to death. By the aid of his faithful Lodowick he escapes, whilst Ulric is acclaimed Count of Bergen. Meanwhile Adelmorn has wedded the Princess Innogen, who followed him to Britain, the Abbess of the convent where she was lodged having invented a story of her death to shield the community from the wrath of her father, Duke Sigismund. In spite of danger, Adelmorn and his bride are irresistibly impelled to return to the Castle. The outlaw is recognized and cast into a dungeon. Here he is comforted by the vision of Count Roderic, who shows him that Ulric was the murderer, and then ascends upon brilliant clouds amid the hymns of invisible spirits. Bound by his oath, Sigismund cannot pardon the supposed criminal unless indeed Ulric release him from the pledge. Almost at the moment of the execution, the Ghost of Count Roderic appears in fearful guise and compels the raving Ulric to confess his guilt.

On the first night Acts I and II were very favourably received, but the Vision [146] in Act III gave great offence. One critic even declared that " The Vision is intended to make a mockery of the Ascension, and the idea is taken from Raphael's picture of the Transfiguration." Lewis was deeply hurt, but yet another critic consoled him with the thought that " The Outlaw is written by the author of *The Monk* ; therefore it must be immoral and irreligious." ·

The third scene of Act III, which is, it must be allowed, a little difficult and liable to be misconstrued, was " hissed from the first speech to the last."

Lewis at once cut out the parts to which the audience had taken such grave exception, and further entirely altered his ghost scenes, eventually reducing the three acts to two. As might have been expected, the result was not happy, and the play was only given ten times in all during this and the following seasons, the last performance being on March 7th, 1802.[147]

As a fair specimen of the rancorous abuse which on almost every occasion Lewis had to sustain, it may be of interest to quote the notice of *Adelmorn the Outlaw* which appeared in so respectable a paper as the *European Magazine*, May 4th, 1801.

" This piece is much in the style of *The Castle Spectre* by the same Author; and ought to have been entitled ' *More Ghosts* '; for his Ghost, who in this play is a male, *appeared three times* during the performance.—Without the dialogue, which is wretched, *Adelmorn* would make a tolerable Ballet, or Pantomime; but as a Drama it is far below criticism.

" Every thing that splendid decoration and beautiful scenery could do was effected; and the music, by Kelly, was captivating in the extreme, as well in its light and airy parts, as in the choruses. Most of the songs were encored, as were also two or three glees, and a delightful duet between Mrs. Mountain and Bannister, jun. The audience, however, though they rapturously applauded the Composer and Scene Painter, hissed the dialogue almost from beginning to end; but more particularly those parts which, designed, no doubt, to be witty and humorous, were in reality absurd abortions. On being announced for repetition, much disapprobation was testified. It was, however, again performed the following evening; when, among other alterations, two appearances of the Ghost were omitted; and this *imaginary* being only appeared once (properly enough) in an *imaginary* scene representing a dream of Adelmorn's, and forming a very beautiful spectacle.

" Its extrinsic merits continued this piece on the stage, with some intermissions, till the 20th; when it was, as we presume, finally dismissed.

" When we see such a man at the head of the Concern as Mr. Sheridan, and Mr. Kemble as the Acting Manager, both highly distinguished for classical learning and correct judgement, we cannot but wonder how pieces calculated, like the above, to degrade the English stage, and vitiate the public taste, contrive to gain access."

Adelmorn the Outlaw was printed, price half-a-crown, by Bell, 8vo, 1801, and Lewis in an admirably written and dignified Preface, May 24th, 1801, defends his piece, and exposes the bitter malice and ignorance of his enemies.

In order to deprive his censurers of the plea of *involuntarily mistaking* Lewis resolved to print his next play previous to its representation, and accordingly in 1801—the Preface is dated December 12th of that year—he published 8vo, with Bell,[148] *Alfonso King of Castile*, a Tragedy in Five Acts, and in blank verse.

Although *The Castle Spectre* had replenished to overflowing the treasury of Drury Lane, Sheridan was at no pains to conceal his contempt for this play, nay, with incredible bad taste he even jeered it to the author's face, and accordingly when in addition he filched so unmercifully for *Pizarro*, it is not surprising that Lewis gave *Alfonso* to Covent Garden, where the manager, Harris, had long been soliciting him for a drama. *Alfonso*, then, was produced at this house on Friday, January 15th, 1802,[149] with Murray as Alfonso ; George Frederick Cooke, Orsino ; Henry Johnston, Cæsario ; Mrs. Litchfield, Ottilia ; and Mrs. Henry Johnston, Amelrosa. The tragedy was very well received with loud and prolonged applause,[150] and is considered by the *Biographia Dramatica*[151] the best of Lewis' plays. The scene lies in Burgos, the capital of Old Castile, and in the adjoining forest. The action is supposed to pass in the year 1345.[152] The faithful Orsino, wrongly suspected of treason, was imprisoned in the Black Tower, but the Princess Amelrosa, bribing the gaoler to give out that the captive has succumbed to his misery contrives his escape. He now drags out his days in a lone hermitage, a cave embosomed in the wildest depths of the forest. Upon his death-bed Marquis Guzman, the husband of Ottilia, confesses that he forged " those traitor-scrolls which bore Orsino's name." Amelrosa tells her father of her pious deception, and the King hastens to the lone retreat to seek Orsino's forgiveness and bid him back to honours and greatness. But the iron has entered his soul and he rejects the proffer with scorn. Amelrosa has secretly wedded Cæsario, Orsino's son, who, unknown to any, by his merit and courage has won a high place at Court. All this he has done to revenge his father, whom he seeks out, and pours forth the glad news that Alfonso is about to fall :

> Joy, joy, my father !
> My plots are ripe, the King's best troops corrupted,
> His son too through my arts declared a rebel,
> And ere two nights are past, I'll strip the tyrant
> Both of his throne and life——

In spite of all his sufferings the loyalty of Orsino revolts and he brands his son as " Villain." Furthermore, he seeks the Princess and unfolds to her the treachery of Cæsario, only to learn that the very traitor is her husband. Ottilia, who loves and has become Cæsario's mistress, discovers that he is false to her and threatens to denounce his plans, whereupon he drives a dagger to her heart. As she expires she is able to warn Amelrosa that a mine is laid in the Claudian vaults beneath the Royal Tower, which the conspirators [153] mean to spring that night.

The mine, in effect, blows up with a loud explosion,[154] but the King is saved. The magnanimous monarch assures Orsino of his son's forgiveness and that proud heart is subdued as he falls at his master's feet. The conspirators are in open revolt, and Cæsario is goaded to madness when Amelrosa who has been poisoned by the jealous Ottilia, expires in her husband's arms. In the battle which follows Cæsario has engaged the King and is about to kill him, when Orsino, himself wounded to death, to save such horrid guilt, stabs his son to the heart.

Alfonso comes very near being a great tragedy. The fidelity of Orsino and his loyalty to honour in spite of crushing wrong are very powerfully portrayed. The situations are truly poignant, and the language both poetical and dramatic. Some passages, indeed, are of striking beauty.

It is perhaps just worth remarking that in 1802 Andrew Birrell, to whom even the *Biographia Dramatica* disdains to afford more notice than the profession of contemptuous ignorance, published a tragedy, *Henry and Almeria*, the scene of which is laid in Mexico, the incidents which culminate in the heroine breaking her neck being conveyed in hobbledehoy verse. Birrell was ridiculous enough to assert that Lewis had stolen his play and brought it on to the stage !

On Tuesday, March 22nd, 1803, at Covent Garden, Mrs. Litchfield [155] recited a monodrama by Lewis entitled *The Captive*, which was printed as *The Captive* : *A Scene in a Private Mad-House*, in Lewis' *Poems*, 16mo, 1812.[156] The captive is discovered chained in a dungeon. Her reason totters on the verge of madness. " It proved too terrible for representation, and two people went into hysterics during the performance, and two more after the curtain dropped . . . as to Mrs. Litchfield, she almost fainted away." Terror threw the audience into fits, and Lewis would not allow a second performance in London, although Mrs. Litchfield recited the monodrama at Bath in May, 1810.

A not dissimilar effect in after years was created by the famous vocalist, Henry Russell (1812–1900), whose scena, *The Maniac*, almost outstripped the limits of the horrible. It was well said that Russell sang " to the mind and heart as well as to the ear of his audience."

Lewis said that *The Captive* was composed to expose the iniquity of the private madhouses, and in his recollections [157] Henry Russell tells us : "My song," *The Maniac*, " was written with the intention of exposing that great social evil—the private lunatic asylum, and, with all humility, let me say I think the song went far in achieving its object." [158] I suppose *The Maniac* is seldom if ever sung now, and perhaps scarcely remembered, but I can distinctly recall the terrific effect, after a long " misterioso " opening, of the words which begin

" Hush, 'tis the Night Watch," and the refrain that breaks in with such ghastly contrast, " I see her dancing in the hall . . . I see her dancing in the hall."

Early in the year 1802 William Lane introduced to Lewis an ardent admirer of his writings, Mrs. Isabella Kelly, herself a novelist of some repute, whose recent work, *Madeleine* ; *or, The Castle of Montgomery*, Lane, 1799, had paid the famous author the sincerest flattery by borrowing a suggestion from *The Castle Spectre*.

The name of Mrs. Kelly's father, a Captain of Marines, who for several years held an appointment at St. James, is not recorded.[159] Whilst very young, Isabella, an uncommonly beautiful girl, had met the dashing Captain Kelly, the son of General Kelly, at that time on service in India. Captain Kelly, whose father (reputed to be a very nabob) allowed him to lead a life of ease and lavish luxury, married Isabella with the fairest expectations. Unfortunately not many months later news came of the General's death, as also of the fact that with his demise most of his sources of revenue simultaneously surceased. Enough, indeed, was left to allow the young couple to continue quietly and without ostentation but Captain Kelly with a recklessness that cannot be too severely reprehended, instead of retrenching his expenses and accommodating his mode of life to his fallen fortunes, continued to pursue an idle and even dissipated course, and to mix in the highest society, leaving Mrs. Kelly to support their home and rear their two infant boys as best she might. Upon the death, at a comparatively early age of her husband, Mrs. Kelly found herself in the most straitened circumstances, and she turned to her pen for support. She had written four novels, all of which achieved some popularity, when she met Lewis. Ever generous and ready to aid, no sooner had she confided to him the pressing motives which inspired her romances and how hardly she could earn sufficient to keep a little home, than he visited her to discuss the situation. Here he met, and at once fell passionately in love with her eldest son, William, then a lad of about fourteen years old.

Lewis, who was homosexual,[160] had many affairs and intrigues, but there can be no question that William Martin Kelly was the absorbing passion of his life. This love was also his soul's tragedy, as Kelly proved to be deceitful, extravagant, ungrateful, reckless and wayward, insensible of the affection which was poured out upon him. Often a new liaison on the part of Lewis would merely be sorrow's anodyne. In the green-room his amours with many a young Antinous of the theatre were freely discussed, and gave ample point to Jane Pope's bon-mot. When *Adelmorn* was being cast at Drury Lane, and Mrs.

Jordan was named for the heroine : " Dolly Jordan, indeed ! " cried the lively Pope, " Pray who is Mr. Lewis' male love this season ? " A name was whispered with a laugh. " Take my word for it, then," quoth the lady, " The Monk will desire him, and no other to play Innogen."

Lewis was extremely fond of young Jack Dureset,[161] who came to Drury Lane, a mere boy " to learn the trade." Dureset, who was exceedingly handsome, had a very sweet voice, and in appearance resembled the boy-heroine of Restoration days, Edward Kynaston, of whom old Downes says, " it has since been Disputable among the Judicious whether any Woman that succeeded him so Sensibly touch'd the Audience as he." [162] Jack Dureset afterwards went to Covent Garden when he created Edward the page in Payne's *Charles the Second*, May 27th, 1824. In the same year he sang Figaro in Fawcett's adaptation *The Barber of Seville*.[163] In 1825 he was young Belville in *Rosina*. In 1827 he played Hippolito, the " dear pretty youth " in *The Tempest*, a rôle almost invariably acted by a woman. Thus the original Hippolito at Lincoln's Inn Fields, November 7th, 1667, was Moll Davies, and during the eighteenth century the part was sustained by actresses such as Mrs. Mountford (1714), Mrs Cibber (1729), Peg Woffington (1747), Mrs. Goodall (1787). At Covent Garden on October 31st, 1812, Mrs. Henry Johnston was the Hippolito. It will be remembered that Hippolito, the young Duke of Mantua, " one that never saw Woman," was introduced into *The Tempest* by Sir William Davenant in the Dryden-Davenant alteration of Shakespeare, and retained by Shadwell in his operatic version.[164] In 1830 at Covent Garden Dureset acted Lothair, the young peasant hero of *The Miller and his Men* with Farley, the original Grindoff. Pocock's melodrama was first produced at this house on October 21st, 1813, and was greatly liked by Lewis to whose inspiration it owed so much.

Love cannot be controlled, and Dureset who fully returned Lewis' affection, could none the less never quite take the place of William Kelly in his heart.[165]

Some very few months after they had first met, Mrs. Kelly, knowing the high position of Lewis' father in the War Office, asked the influence of her new friend to obtain for her certain arrears of half-pay due to her own dead father, monies which had accumulated and lain dormant during the time of his appointment at S. James, and which involved a considerable sum. Lewis promised to do his utmost on her behalf with regard to these claims on the Treasury, and as he informed her in a letter of August 7th 1802, he was able to set her case before the proper authorities. He even obtained an order for Mrs. Kelly to receive the money, only to learn on presenting the same that the arrears but a month before had been paid into the office for unclaimed monies and were irrecoverable. This crushing disappointment he was obliged to communicate to her; however, a very few hours afterwards on the same day, August 11th, 1802, he wrote expressing his anxiety to serve her, and offering to undertake sole charge of the education of her son William " so as to enable him to become a useful and honourable member of society," and adding " hereafter I may have interest enough to place him in the War Office." Needless to say, Mrs. Kelly accepted so generous a proposal with the utmost joy, and thenceforth Lewis continued to maintain and provide for the lad he loved.[166]

He also assisted Mrs. Kelly in her literary work. Not only did he read several of her manuscript chapters, but he gave her the entire plan of a novel, and personally introduced the lady to his own publishers, John Bell, from whose house was issued her *The Baron's Daughter, A Gothic Romance,* 4 volumes, 1802.[167]

Unhappily early in the year 1804 Lewis was much vexed by a newspaper paragraph to the effect that Mrs. Kelly was engaged upon a new romance in collaboration with the author of *The Monk.* He forthwith wrote to her saying that in order not to give the smallest foundation for such a suggestion he must in future decline even to read her manuscripts. She at once replied in great distress protesting that she had not the slightest idea how so idle gossip had found its way into print, and assuring him that she was very unhappy at having been the cause however innocent, of any annoyance to her benefactor. There the matter might have well ended, for Lewis, whilst for prudence sake adhering to his decision, exonerated her from all blame, and wholeheartedly accepted her pathetic assertion " that if she could but procure for her children the common necessaries of life by hard labour, she would prefer it to the odious task of writing, which entailed upon its professors so much envy, slander, and malignity."

It was more than unfortunate that at this very juncture his mother informed Lewis that she was herself writing a romance, which she had discussed in parties of her friends, amongst others consulting the well-known novelist, Mrs. Parsons, with whom she was on terms of intimacy. Mrs. Parsons naturally knew a great many booksellers, and Lewis shrewdly surmised that the newspaper paragraph might have taken its rise in some chance remarks. As he wrote to his mother : " Mrs. Parsons may have talked about ' a lady being employed on a novel, who could depend on having my assistance, &c. &c. ' ; and, as I recommended Mrs. Kelly to Bell, the booksellers may suppose that *she* was the lady meant." Lewis begs his mother not to publish her romance, whatever its merits. He felt that it would be everywhere advertised as by " the mother of the author of *The Monk*," and " then would follow paragraph after paragraph with all our family affairs ripped up," with every insult that scandal could suggest and malice invent. Mrs. Lewis at once relieved his anxiety by promising that her romance should never be given to the public.

About this time Mrs. Kelly married a gentleman of the name Hedgeland, and also opened a school at Chelsea. Her propsects were far more cheerful, and she further rented Cornwall Cottage, Old Brompton. It had been arranged that Mrs. Lewis should reside here with Mrs. Hedgeland, in whose society she had always shown much pleasure. Lewis was delighted with the idea, as his mother hated housekeeping, a burthen Mrs. Hedgeland was very ready to take off her shoulders. A house near the river had been offered to Mrs. Hedgeland, but this she refused, to suit the convenience of Mrs. Lewis. At the last moment, however, upon some pique, Mrs. Lewis altered her mind, relinquished the idea of being an inmate of Mrs. Hedgeland, and announced her intention of residing at Hampstead.

When William Kelly had completed his education Lewis obtained for him an excellent situation at the War Office. He was soon to be perturbed by stories that reached him of the boy's profligacy and ill-courses, gossip which he refused to believe as often as his favourite vowed the tales were false. None the less Mrs. Lewis, who took a deep interest in the lad's welfare, was unhappy owing to her knowledge of the true state of affairs, whilst Mrs. Hedgeland wept and pleaded with her wayward son in vain. In one letter Lewis assures his mother that she may tell Mrs. Hedgeland he is—if not entirely content—at least not seriously displeased with William, who has been with him at the Albany. However, young Kelly, in a moment of irritation at some deserved reprimand from his superiors for gross neglect of duty, threw up his post at the War Office, and answered the remonstrances of Lewis with open insolence.

By this act of consummate folly he at last opened his lover's eyes. There now began to pour in bills from tradesmen to whom William Kelly had described Lewis as his patron, and who had got wind of the fact that their customer was no longer in constant occupation. The next news was that he had been arrested for a debt of a considerable amount. This Lewis at once discharged. It then came out that William had drawn a draft in Lewis' name ; " a most monstrous piece of ingratitude for which I think drunkenness and debauchery no excuse," wrote the heart-broken lover. William thereupon begged to be reinstated in the War Office. " I could as soon get him into the moon ! " A little later Kelly was again in prison for debt. Lewis again extricated him, only to be whipped to fury by an insolent tradesman, Le Bas, desiring an instant settlement of Kelly's bill, since " he had only trusted him as Mr. Lewis was his friend and patron."

Crushed and suffering, Lewis wrote to William from Barnes a letter of infinite sadness and pain. " What will become of you ? Heaven only knows ! I have done all I could to serve you ; God is my witness ! I gave you a good education, I provided you not only with honest bread, but fitting for a gentleman . . . my disappointment is great and bitter . . . but you are still young enough to mend, and my nature is not implacable I shall not forget you. . . . I can say no more . . ."

To his mother Lewis in his anguish wrote of William : " In return for numerous favours heaped upon him for fourteen years, I only demanded that he should totally forget me, and never trouble me again." He strove to blot his loved face from memory, or at least only to call to mind his faults and infidelities. " He has deceived me too often and too grossly ! " At length he resolved to make William a small weekly allowance through the medium of Mrs. Lewis to whom he wrote : " Till I inquire about him *voluntarily*, I insist upon his considering me as a *total stranger*." It does not appear that Lewis ever met William again. In a codicil to his will, November 1st, 1815, he bequeathed William Martin Kelly, one hundred and four pounds yearly, that sum to be paid by weekly instalments of two pounds each, " as I have no other means of securing him from starving through his own imprudence and misconduct of every kind." A previous legacy of five shares of one hundred pounds each in Drury Lane Theatre, also £500 to be paid to him upon his twenty-first birthday, but to be invested most to his advantage, and an additional £500, was formally revoked by the later clause.

It has been necessary, but it has been painful indeed to tell the story of Lewis' love. Whatever his faults—and they were trifling— may they be forgotten and forgiven, for Matthew Gregory Lewis loved much and suffered much.

We may now retrace our steps and take up the tale of his literary achievement.

In 1804 Lewis published with J. F. Hughes of Wigmore Street what is perhaps the most popular of his lesser works, *The Bravo of Venice*, " a Romance, Translated from the German " of Zschokke's *Abællino, der grosse Bandit* (1794). The brief dedication to the Earl of Moira [168] is dated from Inverary Castle, October 27th, 1804. The fifth edition of *The Bravo of Venice* appeared in 1807. This tale is also the first number [169] of *The Romancist and Novelist's Library*, 1839, and there were constant reprints until the end of the century. In some of the later editions the form of the story is slightly altered, but although some minor details are perhaps more closely knit and the pace correspondingly quickened, the narrative can hardly be considered in every respect improved.

Lewis has pretty freely adapted from Zschokke as the fancy took him, and not without much profit to his pages. It cannot be needful to do more than remind ourselves very briefly of the theme of so famous a story. The riddling intrigue turns upon the disguise of the Neapolitan Count Rosalvo, who presents himself in Venice as Count Flodoardo, desirous of serving the Republic. He also fills the rôle of the mysterious and terrible Abellino, a monster of ugliness and ferocity, in which character he is able to penetrate the haunts of the banditti who are terrorizing Venice, and to unmask the conspirators who are plotting her downfall. As Flodoardo he wins the love of the Doge's fair niece, Rosabella of Corfu ; she clings to him even when she believes Flodoardo to be the murderous Bandit ; as Rosalvo he weds her and is acclaimed the saviour of the City.

Additions were also made by Lewis who in the Advertisement writes : " I have taken some liberties with the original—Every thing that relates to Monaldeschi (a personage who does not exist in the German romance), and the whole of the concluding chapter (with the exception of a very few sentences) have been added by myself."

The Critical Review, Series the Third, Vol. V, No. 3, July, 1805, devoted an article of several pages (pp. 252–6) to a detailed examination of *The Bravo of Venice*, although the writer confessed he was so inured as now to be able " to turn over the leaves of a Germanico-terrific Romance with an untrembling hand." He allowed that " The history of the Bravo of Venice is interesting, the language glows with animation, and the *denouement* is rapid and surprising." " Novels have commonly been divided into the pathetic, the sentimental and the humorous ; but the writers of the German school have introduced a new class, which may be called the *electric*. Every chapter contains a shock ; and the reader not only stares, but starts, at the close of every paragraph ; so that we cannot think the wit of a brother-critic far-fetched, when he compared that shelf in his library, on which the Tales of Wonder, the Venetian Bravo, and other similar productions were piled, to a galvanic battery.

Mr. Lewis possesses a fertile imagination and considerable genius : we would therefore advise him to quit the beaten track of imitation.

"'*Ohe* ! *jam satis est* !' We have had enough of ghastly visages, crawling worms, death's heads and cross-bones. When we first visited Mrs. Salmon's waxwork, Mother Shipton's sudden kick startled us, and we were terrified at the monster who darts from the corner cupboard to devour Andromeda ; but we can now visit this scene of wonders without terror or alarm, and if we affect surprise, it is merely in compliment to the woman, who exhibits them, that she may not be disappointed of her grin."

This is something more than severe, even a little ill-natured, for I do not think any reader could disentangle the thread of *The Bravo of Venice*, and he is certainly not to be envied whose interest is not held fast until the very end of this fascinating romance. Naturally when once we know the secret we peruse these chapters a second time with interest and with keenest admiration of the workmanship, but we cannot reasonably expect the same thrill.

The famous Johannes Heinrich Daniel Zschokke was born at Magdeburg, March 22nd, 1771, and died at Aarau on January 27th, 1848. He entered the University of Frankfort-on-the-Oder in 1790 as a student of theology, philosophy and jurisprudence. In 1794 he produced his celebrated romance *Abœllino, der grosse Bandit* (Frankfort and Leipzig), and the following year he dramatized it with extraordinary success, the play first being produced at Frankfort in 1795, and very soon appearing in almost every theatre of Germany.

Owing to his pronounced political opinions which were hardly acceptable to the government, Zschokke not only failed to secure a University appointment, but for some few years found it convenient to reside in France, as also at Reichnau, in Switzerland. His literary activities, however, absorbing more and more of his time, he dropped the budding statesman, and after a sojourn at the Castle of Biberstein he took up his permanent residence in Aarau, devoting himself entirely to his pen. His miscellaneous and historical works are in general more highly esteemed than his plays and romances, which none the less have very considerable merit. He was immensely prolific and even the *Sæmmtliche Schriften* published at Aarau in 1825 already ran to 40 volumes.

The name Abællino became, so to speak, generic, and in 1805–6 Zschokke published his *Giulio degli Obizzi* ; *oder, Abœllino unter den Calabrasen*. He was closely imitated in such romances as *Guido Mazzarini* ; *oder, Irlando der Verkappte*, " romantisches Gemälde," by Karl August Buckholz, and *Die Heldin der Vendée. Ein weiblicher Abœllino*. " Romantische Geschichte aus dem französischen Kriege," by H. G. Schmieder.

The play *Abællino* [170] translated into French by Lamartelière in 1799, and published Paris (1800) was promptly adapted by Guilbert de Pixérécourt, "le Shakespeare et le Corneille des boulevards," and as *L'Homme à Trois Visages, ou Le Proscrit de Venise*, produced in 1801 with overwhelming success, achieving in the course of a very few years no less than 1,022 performances. [171]   Pixérécourt has undoubtedly improved his original in several respects, not least in the detail that in his melodrama the hero has three masks or disguises, whilst Zschokke's protagonist has but two vizards.   Moreover, Pixérécourt presents his celebrated gracioso, the "comic relief," in Calgagno, "banquier juif et poltron," a rôle wherein the favourite actor Corsse achieved a triumph. [172]

The Venetian Outlaw, His Country's Friend, a drama in three acts, altered from the French (*L'Homme à Trois Visages*) by James Powell, was published, 8vo, 1805, but not given on the stage.

On April 26th, 1805, at Drury Lane, for Elliston's benefit was produced *The Venetian Outlaw*, "never acted," a version from Pixérécourt made by Elliston himself. "It was well acted, and received applause, but was not repeated many times." [173]

The Critical Review (Series the Third), Vol. V, No. 3, July, 1805, p. 332, remarks of Elliston's *Venetian Outlaw* : "We conceive that the chief ornament which Mr. Elliston has added, has been his own representation of the character of Vivaldi, and that to his merits as an actor must be attributed its success on the English stage, for with all its new decorations, the translation is a most "inveterate likeness" of the tame original. . . . The romance of Abelino, translated by Mr. Lewis, is in every person's hands, and we think that if Mr. E. had taken that work as the basis of a new drama . . . he might have produced a much more interesting and spirited performance."   This criticism is very true, but none the less such was the vogue of Abellino that even *The Venetian Outlaw* ran into three editions, being issued twice, 8vo, in 1805, and again 12mo in the following year.

The minor theatres immediately seized upon so popular a subject. It was dramatized for the Royal Circus.   On Monday, April 15th, 1805, the Coburg even preceded Elliston with a ballet, *Abelino* ; or, *The Robber's Bride*, which hugely pleased large audiences.   In later years *The Bravo and the Venetian Conspirators* [174] produced at the Royal Amphitheatre, Astley's, on Monday, November 15th, 1819, achieved a great success.   At the Surrey on Monday, July 11th, 1831, was produced an anonymous *Rugantino* ; *the Bravo of Venice*.

In New York, on February 11th, 1801, was performed *Abællino*, *The Great Bandit*, adapted from Zschokke's original romance by William Dunlap [175] with Hodgkinson in the title-rôle ; and his wife,

Rosamunda. Andrew (Jackson) Allen,[176] dubbed "the Father of the American stage," especially shone in Abællino, and often appeared in this part for his benefit. Another favourite Abællino was John R. Duff (1787–1831) the "American Elliston," who was greatly admired by the Boston public. His wife, Mary Ann Duff (1794–1857), was much applauded as Rosamunda.

Harris of Covent Garden, having read *The Bravo of Venice*, repeatedly urged Lewis himself to dramatize his work, and accordingly at this theatre on Friday, October 18th, 1805, was given *The Man of the World*, followed by *Rugantino* ; *or, The Bravo of Venice*, "a Grand Romantic Melo-Drama," "never acted," by Matthew Gregory Lewis. Henry Johnston was Rugantino; Murray the Doge; Liston, Memmo; Blanchard, Stephano ; Brunton, Contarino ; Claremont, Parozzi ; Mrs. Gibbs, Rosabella, the Doge's daughter ; and Mrs. Mattocks Camilla, a superannuated beauty. The music was by Dr. Busby [177] ; the dances arranged by Byrne ; the scenery on a scale of great beauty and magnificence was painted by Phillips and Hollogan ; the whole was under the direction of Farley. Lewis had designed Rosabella for Mrs. Henry Johnston, but owing to the illness of this lady, his close friend, another actress, Mrs. Gibbs (afterwards Mrs. Colman), "at a short notice undertook the part with much good nature, and played it with very great success." In his Advertisement to the printed edition, J. F. Hughes, 8vo, 1805,[178] Lewis says that the dialogue of the play "is taken almost *verbatim* from the Romance," and he modestly ascribes his triumph to the actors, and "to the Scenery and Decorations, than which perhaps more splendid have seldom been witnessed on an English Stage." Yet he must be given the very great credit of having done his work extremely effectively, and he certainly deserved his full measure of success, which was very gratifying, since the melodrama was acted about thirty times that season, and frequently revived, as on October 9th, 1817, at Drury Lane, after *Venice Preserv'd*, when Johnston appeared in his original rôle with Harley as Stephano; Mrs. Mardyn, Rosabella ; and Mrs. Sparks, Camilla.

With reference to *Rugantino*,[179] Eino Railo has the following extraordinary observation : "For the student of literary material a particular significance attaches to this play, owing to its inclusion of a new theme in English literature, *viz.*, the idea, in its most primitive form, of a double existence."

The disguise-play—disguises were a stock feature of Italian comedy —proved extremely popular in Elizabethan days, and has remained popular ever since. The anonymous Latin comedy, *Machiavellus*,[180] based on an Italian original, produced at S. John's College, Cambridge,

December 9th, 1597, is a play of many masquerades. In Chapman's *The Blind Beggar of Alexandria*, produced at the Rose, February 12th, 1596, are most pleasantly discoursed "his variable humours in disguised shapes," and Duke Cleanthes who does not appear *in propria persona* until towards the conclusion of the piece rings the changes upon Irus, the blind beggar ; Count Hermes ; and the usurer Leon. In the "pleasant Commodie" *Look About You*, an anonymous Admiral's Men's play, published in 1600, Skink has no less a tale than seven characters, and Gloucester five, so multiple are the changes of dress and person the intrigue requires these two individuals to support. A long catalogue of disguise plays could be readily given, but it were superfluous. As early as Chapman's *May-Day*,[181] Angelo speaks of a change of a hat or a cloak as a disguise being "the stale refuge of miserable poets" and can only approve some complete metamorphosis such as the change of Jupiter into a bull for the love of Europe.

In Mrs. Centlivre's *A Bold Stroke for a Wife*, Lincoln's Inn Fields, February 3rd, 1718, an immensely successful comedy which kept the stage until 1830 and was occasionally given even later, Colonel Fainwell adopts the dresses and characters of a Beau ; a great Traveller is "*an Egyptian Dress*" ; a Dutch Merchant ; an old Country Steward, Mr. Pillage ; and Simon Pure, the Quaker.

In the winter of 1804 there occurred an unhappy difference between Lewis and his father, which caused the former, at least, great pain and anxiety. The facts may be briefly told. The elder Mr. Lewis had commenced an acquaintance and maintained no very proper intimacy with a lady of fashion and ton, Mrs. R——, who after being a constant visitor to Devonshire Place, presently not only became an inmate of the house but was recognized as mistress of the establishment, where her son Frederick also made his home. Mr. Lewis' two daughters were now married, but Matthew could not help expressing his displeasure, not so much perhaps in words as by actions at seeing another woman installed in his mother's room. Mr. Lewis took pepper in the nose upon his son's eminently correct attitude, and with great severity informed him that he was no longer welcome under the paternal roof. It is true that Matthew occasionally visited the house, but only to be subjected to extreme mortification and open slights. At one period the father most wickedly and dishonourably curtailed his son's income by one half, contrary to his solemn promise and pledge. However the injustice, one is pleased to know, was not of long continuance, for Mr. Lewis soon came to a sense of his own gross misbehaviour in this regard, and Matthew's allowance was restored to the proper figure, as had been expressly engaged. A complete reconciliation between father and son, owing to the elder man's obstinacy and sullen brooding temper, could not be effected for some years. Matthew certainly had need of literary success to support him under these domestic trials. In 1806 he published, 8vo, a tragedy *Adelgitha*; or *The Fruits of a Single Error*, which ran into no less than three editions during the one year, and reached a fifth edition in 1817. The play, which had thus already won its way into popular favour, was not produced until Thursday, April 30th, 1807, when it was given at Drury Lane with Mrs. Powell in the title-rôle; Henry Siddons, Robert Guiscard, Prince of Apulia; Elliston, Lothair; Raymond, Michael Ducas; and Mrs. H. Siddons, Imma. The scene, Otranto. The year, 1080.

Lewis himself quite frankly acknowledged that the quasi-historical background of Guiscard and Michael of Byzantium is a flam. He had constructed his plot, sketched his characters, and then last of all fitted them into a striking framework, allowing stage pictures of " a Gothic room," " a splendidly illuminated Gothic hall," wherein an ancient minstrel strikes his harp, a grove terminated by a cloister which gives scope for that procession of nuns Lewis so loved to present.

Adelgitha, who is the wife of Guiscard, when very young had been seduced by George of Clermont, the fruit of the amour being Lothair, whom she represents to her husband as an orphan. Michael Ducas, Emperor of Byzantium, driven into exile by rebels, seeks the shelter of Guiscard's court, and here Lothair, who has risen to high honour by his valour and virtues, falls in love with the Princess Imma. Whilst Guiscard is absent waging war on behalf of Ducas, this latter attempts to win Adelgitha, and when she rejects his disloyal suit with scorn, he threatens to expose her secret which has become known to him. Immediately after Guiscard's return she resolves to acquaint him with the whole, relating her story as having happened to another. A very powerful and well-written scene follows in which Guiscard shows himself implacable and relentless in his anger against the unnamed deliquent. Adelgitha now implores Michael Ducas to return the letters which he holds and which prove her first unchastity. Mockingly he refuses, whereupon in a tumult of passion she drives a dagger to his heart. Lothair, who by the treachery of the dead emperor, is already suspect of being Adelgitha's lover, is accused of the murder, but as he is led to execution she avows the whole. After a struggle of agony her husband out of his tender love forgives, whereupon exclaiming :

> I'm happy ! Guiscard, Guiscard ! thus I thank thee
> And next *reward* thee thus !

she embraces him for the last time, and stabs herself.

Adelgitha is a very fine tragedy, and fully deserved the favour with which it was received by crowded houses. The music was composed by Michael Kelly.

There were very frequent revivals. At Covent Garden during the winter season of 1818 Miss Somerville (Mrs. Bunn) appeared as Adelgitha; " Young was not equal to himself in Guiscard, a part he did not like, and Charles Kemble made no great effort in Lothair," a rôle in which William Charles Macready had won golden opinions in the provinces, and for which he had hoped to be cast in London instead of finding himself put down to play " the old bombastic tyrant," Michael Ducas. Indeed, he protested vehemently, upon which Fawcett told him that the less he liked a part the more study it required. Macready took the hint, gave especial pains to Ducas, and was rewarded by excellent notices.[182]

At Drury Lane in 1823 Kean played Lothair; and John Cooper, Ducas. At the same theatre in April, 1828, Cooper acted Guiscard; Wallack, Ducas; and Maria Foote (afterwards Countess of Harrington), Imma.[183]

Nearly a month before the first performance of *Adelgitha* there had been produced at Drury Lane on Wednesday, April 1st, 1807, *The Wood Dæmon*; *or, The Clock has Struck*, " a Grand Romantic Melo-Drama " in two acts by Lewis, " a wonderful phantasmagoria of the supernatural, demons, witches, dragons, giants, set amid mountains and forest glooms and the great Gothic hall of a castle, illuminated by the blue lightning and heralded by the crashing thunder, with sacrifice of human victims to the Powers of Darkness—in fact, the whole armoury of legendary mystery and the Tale of Terror is here displayed with a wealth of imagination and dramatic effect that almost merit Kelly's description of ' a work of genius.' "[184] The *Biographica Dramatica* remarks that *The Wood Dæmon* " had a great run . . . the piece contained much interest of the terrific kind, arising from supernatural agency. In point of scenery, decoration, and machinery, it has hardly been surpassed." [185]

In 1808 *The Wood Dæmon* was revived for thirty performances, and in 1811 it was rewritten [186] by Lewis as *One o'Clock ! or, The Knight and the Wood Dæmon*, a " Grand Operatic Romance," " a most splendid spectacle in the performance," with music by Michael Kelly and Matthew Peter King,[187] and produced on Thursday, August 1st, of that year at the Lyceum Theatre, Strand, which from 1809 to 1812 was occupied by the Drury Lane company during the rebuilding of their own home.[188]

The Wood Dæmon has by a spell rendered Hardyknute, Count of

Holstein, invulnerable, has bestowed upon him eternal youth, and the power to fascinate all female hearts. The Count for his part is bound to offer on each seventh day of August human blood. Should the clock strike one and the sacrifice be incomplete, he is lost. As the end we are shown a Necromantic Cavern with the snake-entwined altar of darkness. Hardyknute fails to murder his victim ; " *Discordant Music —the candles on the altar light, and the snakes pour out blue flames* " ; the clock booms One ; the wood-demon suddenly appears and strikes down the magician who is carried away by four fiends and laid on the very altar. The cave vanishes, the horrors disperse, and for the conclusion is presented a Gothic hall with light and song, revelry and happiness.

"On its first appearance it had a prodigious run—scenery and decoration were lavished with magnificent profusion." In 1824 Phillips played Hardyknute ; Knight, Guelpho ; Oxberry, Willikind ; Master Doree, Leolyn ; Mrs. Mountain, Clotilda ; Miss Kelly, Una ; and Robert, Sangrida, the Wood Dæmon.

In 1833 *One o'Clock* was revived at Drury Lane. George Daniel wrote : " It is excellently acted ; the Knight of Mr. Cooper is the very mirror of Chivalry, and Una by Miss Phillips, the enchanted queen of beauty and romance. The supernatural characters were sustained and dressed with demoniacal exactness. We give our hearty commendations to Sangrida and the Giant. [Sangrida, Mr. Howell ; Giant Hacho, Mr. Hatton.] The last scene is one of the grandest and most *striking* we ever beheld on the stage. It rejoiced us to see our old friend Blanchard in the part of Guelpho. . . . Harley played Willikind with a lively humour, and was much applauded." [189]

When first published, 8vo, 1811, *One o'Clock* was dedicated to the Princess of Wales, from the Albany, August 21st, 1811.

At Birmingham and Newcastle young Macready played Hardyknute in the winter of 1811 and early in 1812 from a pirated version of the piece. He says in his *Reminiscences* [190] : " An incorrect MS. of Mr. Lewis's melodrama called ' The Wood Demon, or the Clock has Struck ' from notes taken in shorthand, I believe during its performance, was given to my father, who decided on producing it, and wished me to act Hardyknute. I re-wrote much of the character, and with the care bestowed on its rehearsals, and all the earnestness I could infuse into the performance it excited much interest, and particularly at Newcastle, proved a great attraction for many nights." [191]

The immense popularity of *The Wood Dæmon* is shown by its appearance among the Toy Theatre dramas published by M. Skelt, 11 Swan Street, Minories, London. The sheets of characters, scenes, set pieces, and tricks, are all designed with a real vigour and zesto.

A hint for *The Wood Dæmon*,[192] which in its original form was never published, is from Lewis' own ballad *The Grim White Woman* in *Tales of Wonder*.[193] Lewis in the preface to *One o'Clock*, 8vo (no date but 1811),[194] also refers to Joshua Pickersgill's romance *The Three Bothers* [195] as having afforded him a useful suggestion.

The *Three Brothers* by Joshua Pickersgill,[196] junior, was published, four volumes, 1803, by John Stockdale, Piccadilly, with appropriate verses repeated on each of the mournival of title-pages, " A Tale of Horror ! which but to hear it told . . ." This excellent and most interesting romance is especially important as having given Byron the theme of *The Deformed Transformed*,[197] which fragmentary though it remain must even so take a very high rank among that great poet's work. It will always be a matter of infinite regret that he did not finish the piece, which has a eerie and perhaps unhallowed fascination all its own. A fellow feeling certainly lent an intimate and painful vigour to Byron's drawing of the unhappy Hunchback Arnold, who sells his soul to exchange his lame cloven foot and Sublime of Humps for the beauty of " The godlike son of the sea-goddess, The unshorn boy of Peleus," the best of Greece.

In his Advertisement Byron says : " This production is founded partly on the story of a novel called ' The Three Brothers,' published many years ago, from which M. G. Lewis's ' Wood Demon ' is also taken ; and partly on the ' Faust ' of the great Goëthe."

In *The Three Brothers* [198] Arnaud, the natural son of the Marquis de Souvricour, is a child " extraordinary in Beauty and Intellect." When travelling to Languedoc, the boy, then about eight years old, is shot at by banditti, and terribly injured, so that " those perfections to which Arnaud owed his existence, ceased to adorn it." The Captain of the band nurses him, but he is now " deformed by a crooked back and an excrescent shoulder." He is found and restored to his parents, yet his life is miserable, and " The bitterest consciousness of his deformity was derived from their indelicate, though, perhaps, insensible alteration of conduct." He determines on self-destruction, his own person being an abhorrent enemy to himself, but at the last moment goes to a remote cavern and conjures up the fiend. Mysteriously he makes the evil contract, binding himself to the demon for a beautiful form. There glide past him the forms of Alexander, Alcibiades, and Hephestion : " at length appeared the supernatural effigy of a man, whose per- fections human artist never could depict or insculp—Demetrius,[199] the son of Antigonus." Arnaud finds in his hand " the resemblance of a poniard " which he is impelled to thrust through his heart. " A mere automaton in the hands of the Demon," he " underwent a painless death. During his trance, his spirit metempsychosed from the body of his detestation to that of his admiration." The hunchback Arnaud awoke a peerless Julian !

In 1806, at a date between the publication of *Adelgitha* and the production (April, 1807) of his tragedy, Lewis issued with J. F. Hughes, *Feudal Tyrants* ; *or, The Counts of Carlsheim and Sargans.* " A Romance. *Taken from the German.*²⁰⁰ In four volumes. By M. G. Lewis, Author of *The Bravo of Venice*, *Adelgitha*, *Rugantino*, &c." Upon the title-page are Gray's appropriate lines : ²⁰¹

> The portals sound, and pacing forth
> With stately steps and slow,
> High potentates, and dames of regal birth,
> And mitred fathers in long order go.

The original of *Feudal Tyrants* is Christiane Benedicte Eugenie Naubert's *Elizabeth, Erbin von Taggenburg,*²⁰² *oder Geschichte der Frauen von Sargans in der Schweiz*, published at Leipzig in 1789. This lady, the daughter of Professor Hebenstreit, was, as we have already noted, an extremely popular and prolific novelist.²⁰³

Feudal Tyrants opens with a number of letters exchanged between Conrad, Abbot of Cloister-Curwald and Elizabeth, the widowed Countess of Torrenburg. The latter, who having recently lost her husband, Count Frederick, is living in retirement at the Abbey of the Great Lady of Zurich, takes occasion to examine some old moth-eaten writings, the annals of daughters of the noble houses of Carlsheim and Sargans, whose portraits adorn the whole western side of the domina's closet. The story of Elizabeth herself is the thread upon which all these narratives depend. In the first place we have the " Memoirs of Urania Venosta " whose hand and estates are won owing to a number of ingenious devices, a prearranged rescue, a well-staged delivery from fearful danger, and the rest, by Ethelbert, Count of Carlsheim. He, however, soon shows himself in his true colours, no " angel of light " but a black and bitter tyrant. In Ravenstein Castle he keeps secretly imprisoned the Countess of Mayenfield, and here also he confines his wife, who only escapes owing to the good offices of Henric Melthal, and other patriotic Swiss. The period of this episode is presumably about the end of the thirteenth century, for the Swiss League formed by the inhabitants of the Alpine valleys enters largely into the tale, and anon we meet Hermann Gessler, the *vogt* or steward of Albert II, together with such heroes as William Tell, Walter Fürst of Uri, Arnold Melchthal of Unterwalden, and other heroes, legend and truth being skilfully blended. In Ravenstein is also prisoned Lucretia Malaspina, the first (and thus the legal) wife of Count Ethelbert. She expires in the Castle, and her son, Count Donat, arrives from Italy at the head of a large troop to avenge his mother's wrongs. Urania has been compelled by circumstances to remarry Ethelbert, who in terror at the approach of Donat, commits suicide, or at least mysteriously perishes, whilst Urania after many misfortunes and trials eventually finds peace in the Zurich Convent. We now have the " Memoirs of Adelaide of the Beacon-Tower," [204] the gentle sister of the wrathful Donat. Part the Fourth tells of Count Donat's daughters, Emmeline of Sargans and Amelberga. The former becomes a nun in the convent of S. Roswitha where she is persecuted by the wicked Abbot Luprian of Cloister-Curwald. Later Donat ravages the Convent and burns it, in punishment for which horrid crime the Bishop of Coira [205] besieges him in his castle where he comes to a fearful end. The history of " The Sisters without a Name " who are discovered to be the heiresses, Constantia and Ida, continues the tale. To these ladies Countess Elizabeth of Torrenburg resigns her estates, which she held, and what is more, she no longer opposes the union of Ida and Henry of Montfort, whom she had long loved in vain, herself taking the veil at Zurich, and being consecrated Abbess of that house, for " the Cloister is the place of enthusiasm, is the native land of visions."

Lewis has, it is true, given us in the course of this feudal romance of lawless days a quota of evil ecclesiastics, Guiderius, Luprian, and their associates, but he has more than balanced these sploaches by the presence of such holy men as the excellent Abbot of Cloister-Curwald ; the venerable Matthias ; the society of saintly hermits ; the worthy Father John ; the old Bishops of Coira, the venerable Adelfried-Herbert, the pious Thomas of Planta, and many more. It may be remarked that in the presentation of Thomas of Planta it would seem as if we have a flagrant anachronism. Thomas of Planta, Bishop of Chur, the friend of S. Carlo Borromeo, died on May 5th, 1595. He was poisoned by the fanatics, enemies to the faith.

The Critical Review, Series the Third, Vol. XI, No. 3, July, 1807, has a long article (pp. 273-7) noticing Feudal Tyrants . . . By M. G. Lewis, Author of the Bravo of Venice, Adelgitha, Rugantino, &c. " The author of the Bravo of Venice, Adelgitha, Rugantino, &c. ! It is not altogether easy to conjecture what motive should have induced Mr. Lewis to designate himself in this manner. Is he afraid to be remembered, or is he certain of not being forgotten as the parent of the lascivious Monk ? The chaster tone of his more recent compositions would induce us to prefer the former supposition were we not sure that his vanity is greatly too active a principle to suffer him to abandon his first and most popular effort. The booksellers are aware of the disadvantage of concealing the identity of the author of the Monk, and the editor of the present work, and we see advertised this fresh-wrought tissue of blood and murder as a new novel by Monk Lewis ! Mr. Lewis may just as well himself put his real designation to his name. We can venture to assure him that when the appellation of Monk Lewis is forgotten, the person to whom it belonged will not be long remembered. The Monk . . . has more merit and less morality than any of his other productions. Mr. Lewis seems to have improved himself in his knowledge of show and stage trick, but we cannot congratulate him or his admirers upon any other species of improvement. Sober reason is disgusted at the endless display of ghosts, murders, conflagrations, and crimes. . . . Of blood, vengeance, and misfortunes Mr. Lewis has indeed woven a formidable web, but not a ghost flits along the corner of a ruined hall or draws the curtain at the dead of night to delight the old or terrify the timid fair. We cannot account for this moderation : we even humbly venture to doubt of the prudence of the proceeding. To take ghosts and devils from Mr. Lewis's tales is to endanger their very existence."

When a review leads off with scomms and bitter jeers such as these, we may look for wholesale and unjust condemnations. Indeed, all German works of imagination : " ghosts, bones, chains, dungeons, castles, forests, murders, and rapine pass before us in long order, till sated with horrors and habituated to their view we regard them with as much composure as an undertaker contemplates the last melancholy rites of his mortal brethren."

" Mr. Lewis's imagination has certainly been in a languishing way when it has been unable to invent a story more interesting and terrible " than *Feudal Tyrants*. Nay, how can it be that the author ransacking the repositories of German literature can produce nothing better than this ? " It is the labour of the mountain and *Monk Lewis* has produced his mouse neither larger nor finer than has issued from the pen of many a teeming maiden in the sanctuaries of the Minerva press."

Nothwithstanding the critic finds it worth his while to give an elaborate analysis of *Feudal Tyrants*, concluding with a most unfair and (in places) violently personal attack upon Lewis, uniformly disparaging his " performances," and as a *bonne bouche* asserting that his last romance " displays a most melancholy inferiority to his former compositions."

It is very clear that the writer in the *Critical Review* would have delivered this judgement in any case. However, he convinces nobody. His bias is too bitter and too apparent in every line. *Feudal Tyrants* is an excellently told romance. The intrigues which cross one another and the weaving among the many incidents of the story of Countess

Elizabeth seem at first a little intricate, but the threads are never tangled to perplexity, and the whole is unravelled towards its regular conclusion with wonderful skill and native adroitness.

In spite of his manly and sensible attitude with regard to the reviewers, Lewis cannot but have been chagrined, not so much by the attacks upon his work as by the inveterate malice with which he was assailed as an individual. Genius and success are a double crime the reviewers cannot forgive.

In 1808—the six lines of poetical dedication inscribed to Lady Charlotte Maria Campbell are dated London, June 21st, 1808—Lewis published with Longman, Hurst, Rees and Orme of Paternoster-row *Romantic Tales* in four volumes. The first volume contains *Mistrust, or Blanche and Osbright*, a Feudal Romance, the Montague and Capulet story of Osbright of Frankheim and Blanche of Orrenberg. The opening scene, the burial at night of young Jocelyn, the swoon of Osbright, and his entertainment in the cell of old Father Peter, are particularly fine, and seem to look forward some thirty years to *Rookwood* and *Crichton*, for they are entirely in the best Ainsworthain manner. Five somewhat macabre legendary ballads complete the volume.

Volume II opens with *The Anaconda*, a horrible East-Indian tale, which Lewis tells us is " of German origin." Next is a short poem, *The Dying Bride*. In the third place we have Part I of *The Four Facardins*,[206] translated from *Les Quatre Facardins* of the famous Anthony Hamilton,[207] author of *Mémoires du Comte de Grammont*. Hamilton who left *Les Quatre Facardins* incomplete originally intended this lively extravagance as a satire upon the prevailing rage for Oriental fictions, " plus Arabes qu'en Arabie," due to Galland's *Les Mille et une Nuits*.[208]

The Second Part of *The Four Facardins*, which is quite original with Lewis, occupies the greater portion of Volume III of *Romantic Tales*. It must be acknowledged that in satire, humour, and sprightly fun this falls not a whit behind Hamilton himself, and effectually refuted those who have crassly said that the author of *The Monk* had no sense of the ludicrous. A poem of rather more than 500 lines, *Oberon's Henchman, or the Legend of the Three Sisters*," containing " The History of the Indian Boy, for whom Oberon and Titania quarrel in the ' Midsummer Night's Dream,' is not so successful, and it was indeed only written as an occasional trifle.

The Fourth Volume of *Romantic Tales* opens with *My Uncle's Garret Window*, A Pantomimic Tale, a charmingly told story, to us reminiscent of Hans Andersen. The nephew observing the opposite house from his old uncle's window is able to watch the unfolding of events in the

PLATE XII.

Voila comme je m'assure de ma proie.

Page 186

THE FATE OF AMBROSIO

The Monk

[Face p. 186

simple history of the family over the way. *Bill Jones*, "A Tale of Wonder," is a ballad founded on a " wild and singular story," says Lewis, " first related to me by my friend Mr. Walter Scott." It is extremely powerful and well written. The concluding piece, *Amorassan* ; *or, The Spirit of the Frozen Ocean*, " an Oriental romance," is freely adapted from F. M. Klinger's tale *Der Faust der Morgenländer*.

Meanwhile Lewis was working at a new tragedy. Ever since the summer of 1791 when he had seen a performance at Paris, of Monvel's *Les Victimes cloîtrées* the lurid sensationalism of this extraordinary melodrama haunted him, and he now in real earnest set about an adaptation for the English stage. On Thursday, December 1st, 1808, *Venoni* ; *or The Novice of St. Mark's*, with music by Kelly, was produced at Drury Lane.

Monvel's play shows how Madame de Saint-Alban, in order to prevent her daughter, Eugénie, from marrying the poor and honest Dorval, consigns her to a convent under the charge of the confessor Père Laurent. Eugénie is reported to be dead, whereupon Dorval enters a monastery, which, of course, adjoins the convent.

Venoni (Dorval), who is of ancient lineage and great wealth, is soon to wed Josepha (Eugénie), but her mother Hortensia, Marchioness Caprara, being a puppet in the hands of her confessor the egregious Abbot Cœlestino (Laurent) of S. Mark's, Messina, whilst on a visit to the Court of Naples, places her daughter during her absence in the Ursuline Convent at Messina. It is asserted that Josepha is dead, and Venoni promptly enters a monastery, S. Mark's, which must needs be next door to S. Ursula, and which is inevitably connected with it by a secret passage. Under the baleful influence of Abbot Cœlestino who covets Venoni's estates for the house and who also playfully intends to violate Josepha, the young novice takes the final vows. No sooner has he done so than owing to the good offices of the pious Father Michael he discovers the Abbot's intentions, with the result that when he threatens to expose the villains he is immured in a subterranean dungeon. Unknown to him, Josepha is imprisoned next door, but the two cells are divided by a thick wall. The gallant Venoni (Elliston) overhears the plaintive voice of his fair neighbour, and recognizing his Josepha commences battering the dividing wall to reach his amoret (Mrs. Harriet Siddons). As he succeeds, the Viceroy of Messina, to whom Father Michael has divulged the horrors of S. Mark's arrives upon the scene with an ample attendance of guards to the dismay of the profligate Cœlestino, who finds his power overthrown and himself devoted to immediate punishment for his black deeds, whilst Venoni and Josepha are made happy, and Father Michael loudly proclaims the concluding moral : " Be Tolerant."

The first two acts were very well received, but when in Act III the lady and her lover confined in different dungeons indulged in a sort of intermittent prose duetto, each being polite enough not seriously to interrupt the other, the audience began to giggle at the absurdity of the thing, and then not unnaturally turned from mirth to derision, and no sooner had Elliston thumped at the partition than they proceeded to give very audible and sibilant signs of displeasure.   Amid cat-calls and hisses down came the intervening wall and the drop curtain.

It says much for Lewis' pluck that he asked the manager to call a rehearsal at one o'clock the next day, and turned up with an entirely new fifth act which he had written during the night.   As the last act now stands we find in the vaults where Venoni is confined a certain friar, Lodovico, who, knowing too much of the dark secrets of the house, has been prisoned there for twenty years.   The opening has already been made, and thus when Venoni escapes he is able to gain entrance into the convent and rescue Josepha from Cœlestino and his confederates, just before the Governor of Messina and a numerous company force their way into the cloisters, and the guilty are seized, the hands of Venoni and Josepha united.

The parts were given out, good humour was restored before and behind the scenes, and the run of *Venoni* was only stopped by a catastrophe, the burning down of Drury Lane on February 24th, 1809.

In the first edition of *Venoni*, 8vo, 1809, Lewis prints both the original Third Act and the alternative.   At the production of 1809 Siddons played the Viceroy of Messina ; Powell, the Marquis Caprara ; Elliston, Venoni ; Wroughton, Cœlestino ; Jack Duruset and young Hackel, two fisher-lads ; Mrs. Powell, the Marchioness ; Harriet Siddons,[209] Josepha ; and Mrs. Mude, the Abbess Veronica.   Ten years later, in 1819, there was an important revival with Kean as Venoni ; Alexander Rae, Cœlestino ; Mrs. Glover, the Marchioness ; and Mrs. W. West from Bath, " with a fine figure, handsome face, and intelligent mind, and a voice clear and powerful," [210] Josepha.

The double scene in the original last act, formed by means of a partition passing up the centre of the stage, might have proved very effective had it been carefully managed, and it is extraordinary that so adroit and practised a dramatist as Lewis should have shown himself awkward and clumsy.   The fatal fault lay not in the new device but in the absurdity of the situation.   The trick was certainly new, for I cannot suppose that either Monvel or Lewis had any knowledge of the old *décor simultané*, the multiple scene, that curious legacy of the

Mysteries and Moralities, with its *mansions* or stationary localities simultaneously presented to the audience.[211]

George Colman in his *The Actor of All Work*; *or, First and Second Floor*, produced at the Haymarket on Wednesday, August 13th, 1817, exhibited two rooms simultaneously; whilst Edward Fitzball in his excellent melodrama *Jonathan Bradford, or, The Murder at the Roadside Inn*, Surrey Theatre, Wednesday, June 12th, 1833, presented no less than four rooms in the George at the same time, No. 1 (right) A Two Bedded Room, Dan's Room; No. 2 (left), A One Bedded Room, Mr. Hayes' Room; both above; No. 3 (right), Little Back Parlour; No. 4 (left), the Bar; both below. The action which is complicated—and violent, for Mr. Hayes is murdered in his room—is admirably managed.[212]

In *The Prisoner of Rochelle* by George Dibdin Pitt produced at the Surrey Theatre, January 23rd, 1834, Scene II shows : " *On the* L.H. *Compartment a Prison interior—Grated Window—*D[oor] *in* F[lat]—*Table, Chair, and Bed with Curtains.—*BLINVAL, *in uniform, discovered sleeping. Or the* R.H. *Compartment, a handsome Apartment, elegantly furnished—*D. *in* F.—*Table, Chairs, and Screen on.—This Compartment comprises three-fourths of the Stage, and also the Proscenium—the Partition is pannelled, and by being placed obliquely the opening is seen very distinctly on the* R.H.*"* The intrigue of the place, a brisk and amusing piece, turns on the fact that Captain Blinval, the Prisoner of Rochelle, is able to step from his prison through the secret door into the next house and hold stolen meetings with his mistress, Beatrice Belmont. He even hoodwinks General Girard, Commandant of the Prison, to whom he is introduced in the salon as another officer, and by the time the General can hurry round to the prison, he is already there having stepped through the partition. The mystification is only cleared when Blinval's pardon arrives, and he discovers the Panel door to the company.

Thomas Greenwood in his dramatization of Harrison Ainsworth's novel [213] *Jack Sheppard*; *or, The House-Breaker of the Last Century*, produced at Sadlers Wells on Monday, October 28th, 1839, as the first scene of Act IV showed : " *Newgate—*four Cells, two above and two below—grated windows in the back—a lead flat on the top—doors, leading from one cell to the other—a fire-place at the back of the condemned cell, L.—Moonlight. Jack Sheppard discovered in the condemned cell, L., heavily ironed to the floor." Hence he makes his escape, in the progress of which he " is seen traversing the different rooms."

In *Above and Below* by Edward Stirling, produced at the Lyceum Theatre, Thursday, September 16th, 1846, two floors are presented on the stage.

Of more recent years there have been quite effective sets on this principle. The most famous is the last scene, IV, 2, of Verdi's grand opera *Aida*,[214] produced in Cairo, December 24th, 1871. "Finale Ultimo : La scena è divesa in due piani. Il piano superiore rappresenta l'interno del Tempio di Vulcano, splendente d'oro e luce ; il piano inferiore, un sotterraneo." Amneris and Priestesses are in the Temple ; below in the prison vault we see Rhadames and Aida.

It was perhaps the ill success of the original third act of *Venoni*—and laughter piqued Lewis more than he cared to allow—which caused him to declare that this would probably be the last of his dramatic attempts. " The act of composing," he wrote, " has ceased to amuse me," and one can well believe what he says. He felt that he was not likely to compose any better drama than *The Castle Spectre*, and it was not worth his while " to make any further efforts at the attainment of dramatic fame." The poet and the novelist can each compose as he will to please himself ; the playwright must compose to please an audience.

Lewis was further nettled owing to the prohibition of his *Monody on the Death of Sir John Moore*,[215] which was spoken by Mrs. Powell at Drury Lane on February 16th, 1809, but upon some question being raised by a busybody, named Tierney, in the House of Commons, forbidden after the third night.

However, Lewis did not entirely keep to his resolution, and the circumstances which once again put the playwright's pen in his hand were as follows : " The Grand Dramatic Romance " of *Blue-Beard, or, Female Curiosity*! [216] the book by George Colman, and the music by Kelly, which had proved so great a success upon its first production at Drury Lane on Tuesday, January 16th, 1798, was revived at Covent Garden on February 18th, 1811, with the extra attraction of a troop of real horses.[217] "Sixteen most beautiful horses, mounted by *Spahis*, suddenly appeared before the spectators, and were received with immense applause." [218] The critics were furious and cried aloud upon the degeneracy of the times ; the house was crowded nightly.

Harris, the proprietor and manager of Covent Garden, who had always shown himself so staunch a friend, begged Lewis to write a spectacular piece, whatever it might be, in which the horses could again appear to enchant the audience. Lewis demurred, but upon the point being most earnestly pressed he felt he would be in the wrong over obstinately to refuse one to whom he was seriously obliged, and accordingly although not concealing his grave doubts as to the success a second time of the equestrian performances he composed his famous *Timour the Tartar*, arranging none the less certain scenes alternatively so that a combat on foot could be substituted for an encounter on horseback, and indeed the cavalry might even be omitted entire without injury to the play. The piece was often presented in the provinces with these alterations, and never failed to be received with considerable applause.

The account of *Timour the Tartar* given in the Appendix to the *Biographia Dramatica* [219] is extremely lively, and in particular highly praises the " white horse which carried the heroine (Mrs. H. Johnston). He played admirably. He knelt, he leaped, he tumbled, he fought, he dashed into water and up precipices, in a very superior style of acting ; and completely enraptured the audience." Nor were his fellow labourers far behind. The acting of these animals gradually softened the asperity of the critics, and " the melo-drama concluded with a general shout of approbation."

The principals were originally as follows : Timour, Khan of the Afghan Tartars, Farley ; Agib, Prince of Mingrelia, Master Chapman ; Oglon, Father of Timour, Fawceit ; Zorilda, Mrs. H. Johnston ; and Selima, Miss Bolton. At a revival, Drury Lane, May 16th, 1831, Wallack, [220] " graceful and chivalrous," was Timour, to the Zorilda of Miss Huddart.

The play was very magnificently dressed as appears by the description of the costumes in *Timour the Tartar*, Lacy's Acting Edition, Number 1182, [221] and the fascinating coloured plates to *Timour the Tartar* in Redington's Juvenile Drama. [222] Thus Timour wore : " Crimson fly, puce tunic, yellow satin shirt, red trousers, green boots, turban," all richly ornamented with addition of golden chains and beads for the neck ; Agib wore a crimson fly, white trousers, turban and slippers, all richly ornamented ; the rival chiefs Kerim and Sanballat who fight the famous duel on horseback were in burnished white chain armour and green chain armour respectively ; Selima was gorgeously attired in a pink and white satin dress with red morocco boots ; and above all the Princess Zorilda, when she first entered riding a courser richly caparisoned and attended by four African boys with huge flabella of painted feathers, was arranged as an imperial Amazon, in a white satin robe sewn with jewels, a long crimson train, yellow boots, and over all a breast-plate and helmet of gleaming gold.

The scenery was as splendid as the dresses. The mother-of-pearl chamber, and the closing scene, " The Fortress by moonlight," a fine compound of cataract and castle, were especially admired, and the Lists (Act I, Scene 3) with the decorated thrones, the gay pavilions, the Tartar tournament, was full of movement, radiant colour and life.

The action, swift and hurried, is hot with adventures and " hair-breadth 'scapes." Timour, a usurper of low origin, has murdered the Prince of Mingrelia, and keeps the heir, the boy Agib, a prisoner. Wishing to strengthen his throne by a marriage with the blood-royal of Georgia, he sends an embassy to demand the princess of that country as his bride. This gives an opportunity for Zorilda, Princess of Mingrelia, to personate the Georgian Princess in the endeavour to rescue her child. By an unlucky chance her plan is discovered, and Timour prisons her in the fortress. Her charms capture his fierce heart, and he insists that she shall wed him or see Agib slain. The boy escapes, and the Georgian warriors surround the castle. Timour appears on the battlements with Zorilda whom he threatens to poniard on the spot unless the troops retire. Springing from his grasp the Princess throws herself into the river beneath, but Agib on his trusty steed dashes into the flood and rescues her, whilst Timour, issuing from his lair, is overthrown and his soldiers routed in confusion.

Lewis tells us that he took a hint for Zorilda's disguise from a French play, *La Fausse Iseulte*.

Timour the Tartar was printed 8vo, no date, but 1811 ; and again 8vo no date, Dublin 1814.

It will not escape remark that Timour is of course none other than the fierce Mongolian Khan Timur (1336–1405), whom Marlowe introduced to the English stage as Tamburlaine the Great,[223] " a most puissant and mightye Monarque." *Tamerlane the Great*,[224] a tragedy by young Charles Saunders (1663–84) for which Dryden wrote the Epilogue, was given with success at the Theatre Royal, Bridges Street (Drury Lane), in February, 1681. Nicholas Rowe's dull *Tamerlane*,[225] with Betterton in the title-rôle, produced at Lincoln's Inn Fields in December, 1701, kept the boards on account of the political under-current, since Rowe conceived he had portrayed William of Orange in Tamerlane, and Louis XIV in Bajazet. Until well within the nineteenth century *Tamerlane* was foolishly revived once a year upon November 4th, the birthday of William. Some bright spirit even wrote a sequel or second part to Rowe's drama, and carried on the subject to the death of Bajazet, but this fortunately was neither printed nor brought upon the stage.

Timour the Tartar, as it well deserved, maintained its popularity for very many years, and in the provinces was occasionally seen until the middle of the century. At Astley's Amphitheatre, which specialized in equestrian display, a very spectacular *Timour the Tartar* exhibited on September 14th, 1829, with Military Band, Plumed Coursers, Amazons, Timour's Splendid Car drawn by Six Horses, and a Grand Tartarian

Ballet, drew the town for a whole winter especially to see the final " Castle in Flames and Overthrown of Timour." Alexander Edward Gomersal, famous as Napoleon in *The Battle of Waterloo*, was Timour ; P. King composed the music ; the Machinery was by Saul ; the dresses by Mr. Flowers and Miss Egan ; whilst a number of artists, Phillips, Pugh, Grieve, Hollogan, Hodgins, and their assistants were employed on the elaborate scenery.

Some three years earlier a spectacle *Timour Khan* ; *or, The Prince and the Mandarin* produced at the Surrey on Monday, November 27th, 1826, had been received with much favour.

It was inevitable that the Equestrian Drama [226] should be burlesqued. Not to mention such a farce as the later *Timour, Cream of all Tartars*, it will suffice to speak of a couple of contemporary parodies. On Thursday, July 18th, 1811, at the Lyceum was given *The Quadrupeds ; or, The Manager's Last Kick*, a " Heroic-Tragic-Operatic-Drama." The manager, complaining that no play will *draw* without horses, presents the mock-tragedy of *The Tailors*,[227] adapted and brought up to date, with the addition of quadrupeds, ponies, mules, asses and prancing steeds created by the property-man. George Colman's extravaganza *The Quadrupeds of Quedlinburgh ; or, The Rovers of Weimar*, a " Tragico-Comico-Anglo-Germanico-Hippo-Ono-Dramatico Romance," Haymarket, Friday, July 26th, 1811, introduced George Canning's *The Rovers* [228] and cast the net of ridicule far and wide. Lewis is especially marked down, and the conclusion a battle royal in which the last scene of *Timour the Tartar* is burlesqued, was voted amusing enough in its way. Basket [229] horses were seen on the ramparts of a castle, prancing about in all directions. The Prologue jeers at English taste, debauched by foreign quacks, but which, " Takes airings now on English horses' backs " ; and concludes :

Think that to Germans you have given no check,
Think how each actor hors'd has risk'd his neck ;
You've shown them favour—oh, then once more show it
To this night's *Anglo-German, horse-play* poet !

A dry bob which could not have been very pleasing to Lewis. *The Quadrupeds of Quedlinburgh* had a very considerable run, showing that people were prepared to fleer and laugh at what they followed and heartily enjoyed.[230]

It is much to be regretted that Lewis never printed nor brought forward his romantic drama *Zoroaster* for which Michael Kelly composed the music.[231] The " first magician " [232] and his necromancies would have afforded splendid material for Lewis' most gorgeous melodrama, and he must have shown us the evil Chaldean in a veritable blaze of supernatural phantasmagoria.[233]

One o'Clock, the alteration by Lewis of his The Wood Dæmon, given at the Lyceum in April, 1811, has already been described. At the same theatre on Wednesday, July 22nd, 1812, was produced an opera in three acts, Rich and Poor, which he adapted from The East Indian. The music by Charles Edward Horn,[234] who played Beauchamp, greatly pleased the Town, and in especial that sweetly pathetic ballad, sung by Mrs. Bland as Mrs. Secret in Act I, scene 2, " The Banks of Allan Water," [235] which so long remained popular and which even to-day is so justly and universally admired. The heroine of Rich and Poor, Zorayda, was acted by Frances Maria Kelly,[236] whose performance contributed not a little to the success of the piece. Other characters were, Listless, Oxberry ; Modish, Pyne ; Lady Clara Modish, Mrs. Orger ; Mrs. Ormond, Miss Griglietti ; and Miss Chatterall, Mrs. Harlowe. The scenery was by Morris ; the dresses by Banks and Robinson.

In 1812 Lewis published with Hatchard his Poems, 16mo, " selected from a great mass of Verses." His word of Introduction is dated— The Albany, December 9th, 1811. There are in all twenty-seven poems, occupying a slim volume of 109 pages. At the end is appended a list (not quite complete) of his works, fourteen in number. Among the poems are such pieces as Love at Sale ; Crazy Jane; Lines Written on Returning from the Funeral of the Right Hon. C. J. Fox, Friday, October 10th, 1806, addressed to Lord Holland ; The Lover's Astronomy ; The Blind Lover ; The Fate of Kings ; The Felon ; The Captive, A Scene in a Private Mad-House, the monodrama which when recited by Mrs. Litch-field was found too harrowing in the performance.

The Journal of a West-Indian Proprietor, the first edition, 1834, con-tains (pp. 261–289) The Isle of Devils, A Metrical Tale, a poem of great power and horrid fancy.[237] A number of fugitive pieces in Prose and Verse were printed for the first time in The Life and Correspondence of M. G. Lewis, Vol. II, 1839, pp. 239–355.

The Journal of a West-Indian Proprietor appeared posthumously in 1834. Coleridge is perfectly correct when he terms this book " delight-ful," for one can read and re-read it many times with unbated pleasure. The account of Lewis' two residences in Jamaica, 1815–16, and again 1817–18, although not aiming at any elegance or polished phrase, is written with a freshness and a verve that are altogether far more entertaining than the most courtly periods. His description of the Negro Play is conceived and told with rare humour. As we might have expected Lewis was particularly interested in Obeah, of which he has a good deal to say ; in Nancy stories, which contain a witch or a duppy (a Negro ghost) ; and other island superstitions. His description of the family mausoleum, " a tomb of the purest white marble, raised on a platform of ebony," and surmounted by a statue of Time, with his scythe and hour-glass, is particularly striking, and he expresses a desire that here his body might be laid.

During half a century and more, criticism of Lewis, such as it is, obvious and facile to the last degree, for the most part hardly seems to have gone beyond *The Monk*, and hence it has been necessary to consider both the romances and the ballads, and the plays at some length, since consciously or unwittingly he introduced new and essential features both by his prose works, his verse and his dramas into the Gothic novel, upon which he exercised so tremendous, one might almost say so illimitable, an influence. It is, I think, more useful for the purpose of our survey specifically to indicate (as indeed I have already done) the vast imaginative force derived from Lewis which energized and inspired numerical novels and impelled the incidence of romance in particular directions, rather than at this one point by summarizing to present what must necessarily become a vague, undefined, and in many respects incomplete and inadequate analysis of both those prominent characteristics and the many undercurrents of supernatural suggestion, which eddying fainter and fainter, it may be, through channels now brackish, now fair, until almost lost or sublimated in the chaotic spate of modern fiction, can none the less very clearly be related to and are in effect resultant from the genius, often morbid and wayward, yet ever vital and compelling, of Matthew Gregory Lewis.

It is, as I hope I have in some measure been able to indicate, far more easy to define and exactly appreciate the influence of Ann Radcliffe, which, as long-lived, no less important, and in many respects gentler, purer, and more restrained, still lends some crepuscule of colour even to the twentieth century.

It remains to acquaint ourselves with a few biographical details, of consequence and material in themselves, and also significant to us, as exhibiting the character of Lewis in a most agreeable and sympathetic light.

In November, 1811, Mr. Lewis began to show signs of weakness and before the end of the month was extremely ill. Matthew Gregory was greatly affected, and upon his son's anxiety being reported to his father, the sick man said with much emotion, " Ah ! he is a foolish boy ! " There were two physicians, Sir Walter Farquhar and Dr. Baillie in constant attendance. As it was now above nine years that

Matthew had enjoyed any filial intercourse with him, it was impossible that there should be the same grief, the same sense of imminent loss. None the less, when he was able to visit his father's bedside he broke down in tears, and it is good to know that a complete reconciliation ensued.

On May 17th, 1812, Mr. Lewis breathed his last. With the exception of a few bequests his whole estate was left to his son, who now found himself a very wealthy man. He made, as we might have judged would be the case, the best possible use of his prosperity. To his mother he allowed one thousand a year, and secured that sum to her upon his death. To his sisters and others he was equally beneficent in due to the proportion of their claims upon him, and in each case he acted not merely with ample justice but with unbounded generosity and thoughtful care.

His mother now took up her residence at " The White Cottage " near Leatherhead, Surrey. In *The Life and Correspondence of M. G. Lewis*, there is a most delightful description of this abode,[238] where she loved to entertain in a modest way but with bounteous hospitality her many friends, for she was ever peculiarly alive to the quiet joys of social life. She was often heard to regret that Mrs. Parsons, the novelist, with whom she had been very intimate, was no longer in this world to share the tranquil pleasure of this sweetest retirement.

With her music, her work-table, her garden, her dogs and cats, her books, chiefest and most prominent amongst which was ever The Bible, Mrs. Lewis passed many happy years. Much as she loved the freshness of spring mornings, the warm summer afternoons with tea upon her velvet lawn, the autumn excursions to the tinted woods, she was fain to confess that her favourite hour was that of a winter's evening, when the curtains were drawn, the fire blazed in the grate, and Cowper's " hissing urn " was set upon the table, moments to be shared by the few she esteemed more than ordinary friends.

The life of Matthew Gregory Lewis was strangely chequered. In many ways he must be accounted exceptionally fortunate. His genius was recognized young, but this circumstance only served to arouse the malevolence and undying spite of the reviewers. He was possessed of means and, in easy circumstances, able to indulge his tastes and enjoy the society which meant so much to him. Yet the separation of his father and mother, his father's cold indifference and even animosity to himself, his mother's foibles, were all a source of constant distress. He had many dear friends and comrades, but the infidelity and baseness of William Kelly came near to breaking his heart.

Although hardly accurate in some details it may not be amiss here to give the extremely interesting account of Matthew Gregory Lewis which Byron has left us, a number of remarks—not all of them over-kind—which are recorded in Thomas Medwin's *Journal of the Conversations of Lord Byron*, 2 vols., Galignani, Paris, 1824, Vol. I [239] : Talking of romances, Byron said, " ' The Monk ' is perhaps one of the best in any language, not excepting the German. It only wanted one thing, as I told Lewis, to have rendered it perfect. He should have made the demon really in love with Ambrosio : this would have given it a human interest. ' The Monk ' was written when Lewis was only twenty, and he seems to have exhausted all his genius on it. Perhaps at that age he was earnest in his belief of magic wonders. That is the secret of Walter Scott's inspiration : he retains and encourages all the superstititions of his youth. Lewis caught *his* passion for the mar-vellous, and it amounted to a mania with him in Germany ; but the groundwork of ' The Monk ' is neither original nor German : it is derived from the tale of ' Santon Barsisa.' The episode of ' The Bleeding Nun,' which was turned into a melodrama, is from the German."

There were two stories which he almost believed by telling. One happened to himself whilst he was residing at Mannheim. Every night, at the same hour, he heard or thought he heard in his room, when he was lying in bed, a crackling noise like that produced by parchment, or thick paper. The circumstance caused inquiry, when it was told him that the sounds were attributable to the following cause : The house in which he lived had belonged to a widow, who had an only son. In order to prevent his marrying a poor but amiable girl, to whom he was attached, he was sent to sea. Years passed, and the mother heard no tidings of him, nor of the ship in which he had sailed. It was supposed that the vessel had been wrecked, and that all on board had perished. The reproaches of the girl, the upbraidings of her own conscience, and the loss of her child, crazed the old lady's mind, and her only pursuit became to turn over the Gazettes for news. Hope at length left her : she did not live long—and continued her old occupation after death.

The other story that I alluded to before, was the original of his " Alonzo and Imogene," which has had such a host of imitators. Two Florentine lovers, who had been attached to each other almost from childhood, made a vow of eternal fidelity. Mina was the name of the lady—her husband's I forget, but it is not material. They parted. He had been for some time absent with his regiment, when, as his disconsolate lady was sitting alone in her chamber, she distinctly heard the well-known sound of his footsteps, and starting up beheld, not her husband, but his spectre, with a deep ghastly wound across his forehead, entering. She swooned with horror : when she recovered, the ghost told her that in future his visits should be announced by a passing-bell, and these words, distinctly whispered, ' Mina, I am here ! ' Their interviews now became more frequent, till the woman fancied herself as much in love with the ghost as she had been with the man. But it was soon to prove otherwise. One fatal night she went to a ball : what business had she there ? She danced too ; and, what was worse, her partner was a young Florentine, so much the counterpart of her lover, that she became estranged from his ghost. Whilst the young gallant conducted her in the waltz, and her ear drank in the music of his voice and words, a passing-bell tolled ! She had been accustomed to the sound till it hardly excited her attention, and now, lost in the attractions of her fascinating partner, she heard but regarded it not. A second peal !—she listened not to its warnings. A third time the bell, with its deep and iron tongue, startled the assembled company, and silenced the music ! Mina then turned her eyes from her partner, and saw reflected in the mirror, a form, a shadow, a spectre: it was her husband ! He was standing between her and the young Florentine, and whispered in a solemn and melancholy tone the accustomed accents, " Mina, I am here ! "—She instantly fell dead.

Lewis was not a very successful writer. His " Monk " was abused furiously by Mathias, in his " Pursuits of Literature," and he was forced to suppress it. " Abellino," he merely translated, " Pizarro " was a sore subject with him, and no wonder that he winced at the name. Sheridan, who was not very scrupulous about applying to himself *literary* property, at least manufactured his play without so much as an acknowledgement, pecuniary or otherwise, from Lewis's ideas. . . . He was even worse treated about "The Castle Spectre," which had also an immense run, a prodigious success. Sheridan never gave him any of its profits either.

Lewis was a pleasant companion, and would always have remained a boy in spirits and manners—(unlike me !). He was fond of the society of younger men than himself. I myself never knew a man, except Shelley, who was companionable till thirty. I remember Mrs. Pope once asking who was Lewis's male-love this season ! He possessed a very lively imagination, and a great turn for narrative, and had a world of ghost stories, which he had better have confined himself to telling. His poetry is now almost forgotten : it will be the same with that of all but two or three poets of that day."

Incidentally, it may be remarked that Byron is a little unjust to
Lewis here, many of whose ballads of the macabre order are excellent
in their kind, and were long remembered and quoted, moreover it is
scarcely correct to say that he was compelled to suppress *The Monk*,
whilst *The Bravo of Venice* is very much more than a mere translation
from Zschokke's *Abællino*.

Byron continues : " Lewis had been, or thought he had been,
unkind to a brother whom he lost young ; and when any thing disagreeable was about to happen to him, the vision of his brother
appeared : he came as a sort of monitor." In another place Byron
observed : " I am a great believer in presentiments. Socrates' demon
was no fiction. Monk Lewis had his monitor, and Napoleon many
warnings."

" Lewis was with me for a considerable period at Geneva ; and
we went to Coppet several times together : but Lewis was there
oftener than I.

Madame de Staël and he used to have violent arguments about the
Slave Trade—which he advocated strongly, for most of his property
was in negroes and plantations. Not being satisfied with three
thousand a year, he wanted to make it five ; and would go to the West
Indies ; but he died on the passage of sea-sickness, and obstinacy in
taking an emetic."

Lewis went to Jamaica as he conceived himself in duty bound
personally to see to the conditions under which his slaves worked.
He did not undertake the voyage with a view to a material increase of
income. His motives were unselfish, and is the highest degree laudable
and Christian.

On Friday, November 10th, 1815, Lewis sailed for Jamaica,
reaching the island on New Year's Day, 1816, and here he remained
for three months busily engaged in the superintendence of his estates.
It will suffice to say that he worked hard to ameliorate in every possible
way the condition of his blacks. He entirely abolished all harsh
punishments ; he increased the comforts, added to the holidays, and
mitigated the labours of all the workers on his estates. Nay, more, he
so arranged a code of penalties and misdemeanours, a time-table of
hours, a way of appeal, that even in his absence any ill-treatment of his
slaves would be impossible. The consequence was that the blacks,
not only of his own household, but well-nigh all over the island,
idolized their indulgent benefactor.

On Monday, April 1st, 1816, Lewis set sail for England, but owing
to gales and contrary winds he did not arrive home for a couple of
months, actually landing at Gravesend on Wednesday, June 5th.

A few weeks later he visited Italy, spending some time on his journey at the Villa Diodati, Geneva, in the company of Byron, Shelley, and John Polidori.

On October 1st he was at Florence, and by New Year's Day, 1817, he had reached Rome, and here he had the honour of being presented and doing homage to Pope Pius VII.

He next proceeded to Naples, "where wit walks the streets, and music fills the air," that city of exquisite loveliness and exquisite pleasure, "dear, dear Naples, beautiful Naples!" Little wonder he was so entirely charmed that he began at first to play with and then seriously to entertain the idea of permanently settling here, since, as he wrote to his mother, the delicious climate agreed so singularly well with his temper. At this time, too, his sister, Maria, Lady Lushington, was living at Naples, and he declared that she was a mortal above all to be envied. On March 13th, 1817, Lewis wrote to his mother : " I have now been here for nine weeks, and never thought it possible for me to be so much delighted with any place out of England. . . . I look upon Maria as the most fortunate person in the world, since she cannot live in England at present, that her lot is cast to live at Naples."

It was, in fact, only his sense of duty which made him return to England, for he felt that another journey to Jamaica had become imperative. He was at home in April, but not for many months, since on Wednesday, November 5th, 1817, he embarked from Gravesend for Jamaica on the same vessel and with the same captain as he had previously sailed. During his stay in England he was constantly at The White Cottage, and on Tuesday night, November 4th, he wrote to his mother an affectionate letter thanking her for the kind welcome she had always given him on his visits to her Cottage, and asking her to allow him to continue to see her in the same simple way, but begging her always to be careful to avoid all painful and agitating subjects between them either in conversation or correspondence. On this second occasion, as on the eve of his first voyage to Jamaica, he felt he could not endure the agony of a formal leave-taking.

On Saturday morning, January 24th, 1818, Lewis landed on the island, and forthwith proceeded to his estate. He was highly pleased to note that his plans had succeeded beyond even his most sanguine expectations, and he passed several months of great content among his blacks, who showed themselves loyally grateful and even enthusiastically devoted to their much-loved master.

On May 4th, 1818, he embarked on the *Sir Godfrey Webster* for his homeward voyage to England. He was attended by his Venetian valet, Baptista, or Tita, who was Byron's gondolier and also present at the poet's death. Later he was in the service of Isaac D'Israeli and chief messenger at the India Office. It was noticed that Lewis, who had previously been suffering from a slight attack of yellow fever, showed himself uneasy, restless, and extremely irritable. Nearly all the passengers were soon prostrated by sea-sickness, whilst the dreaded yellow Jack broke out among the crew. After the first few days Lewis became so ill as to be confined to his berth. Michael Kelly used to repeat a story he had heard to the effect that Lewis having solemnly promised his blacks that upon his death they should be all set free, was poisoned with some obi herb by certain of the slaves to hasten the day of their emancipation. There seems to be no foundation at all for this suggestion, which Kelly merely told as an anecdote, always being careful to add a rider that he would not vouch for the truth of the canard. Unfortunately Lewis grew worse and worse, and refusing to lie in his berth, or racked with fever, would often rush up on deck, and then totter to and fro until his strength failing, he was carried back to his bed in a state of complete collapse. His sufferings from sea-sickness were terrible. About midnight on May 10th, Lewis had the ship's steward called up and demanded a dose of James' Powders, the celebrated old nostrum of Dr. Robert James. Of this emetic he hurriedly took large quantities, and the ship's doctor, being seriously ill at the time, there was no one who could check such imprudence. At noon on May 13th, the more serious symptoms rapidly increased, and he fell into a terrible delirium. Early the next morning about four o'clock in a slumber gentle as the rest of childhood, he expired in the arms of his faithful Tita.

It was imperative that the body should be buried the same day. A slight shell of deal boards being nailed together by one of the carpenters, the corpse was laid therein, and a hammock-shroud with four eighteen-pounders enclosed wrapped all around it. At half-past eleven o'clock the body was solemnly committed to the deep with all the decencies that can be observed on such an occasion, the Burial Service as appointed in the Book of Common Prayer being read by Captain Boyes. Gently was it lowered into its ocean-tomb, only however to rise again almost immediately from the waves. The end of the hammock had become unfastened, and the weights escaped, the bellying wind, driven under the canvas acted as sail, and the body was slowly borne down the current away in the direction of Jamaica—away and away until it became a mere speck upon the ocean and vanished in the waste of many waters.

NOTES TO CHAPTER V

1. " *Saducismus Triumphatus :* Or, Full and Plain Evidence Concerning Witches And Apparitions. . . . By *Joseph Glanvil* late Chaplain in Ordinary to his Majesty, and Fellow of the Royal Society. With a Letter of Dr. *Henry More* on the same Subject." The more usual spelling (of later editions) is *Sadducismus Triumphatus.* The earliest draft, *Philosophical considerations touching Witches and Witchcraft,* was published 1666. Dr. E. A. Baker, *History of the English Novel,* Vol. V (1934), p. 208, describes *Saducismus Triumphatus* as a " chamber of horrors," which this fine work most certainly is not. Nor do I conceive that a rather flippant and wholly unapt label would have been very acceptable to the great and profoundly philosophical divine who was the author.

2. " King Saul and the Witch of Endor " was reproduced in my *History of Witchcraft and Demonology,* 1926, p. 178. The panelled illustration of several apparitions was reproduced as the frontispiece to my *Geography of Witchcraft,* 1927.

3. Two volumes, 1883. Vol. I, chapter iv, pp. 32–8.

4. Unfortunately the haunted rooms were pulled down in 1812, when, after the death of Richard Warburton Lytton, December, 1810, Mrs. Bulwer (now Bulwer-Lytton) settled at Knebworth, but resolved to demolish three sides of the great quadrangle and confine the house to the fourth side. The haunted rooms, however, are minutely described in a little story by Miss James, entitled *Jenny Spinner ; or, The Ghost of Knebworth House,* which was never published, but of which a few copies only were printed and preserved at Knebworth.

5. Which she originally created in 1758. In noticing *Cleone* the *Biographia Dramatica,* Vol. II (1812), p. 109, says : " The latter scenes, containing Cleone's madness over her murdered infant, are wrought to the highest pitch, and received every advantage they could possibly meet with from the inimitable performance of Miss Bellamy."

6. *The Life and Correspondence of M. G. Lewis,* 1839, Vol. I, pp. 41–2. This biography, which, if in many respects valuable, leaves much to be desired, is by Mrs. Baron-Wilson.

7. Yet in certain of his letters to his mother at this juncture Lewis quite frankly informs her that he cannot commend her action. He reminds her that he is unable to forget " the pain and anxiety you have occasioned to my dear, my worthy father." Her conduct at the separation he regards as " perfect frenzy." At the same time he shrinks from seeming " an umpire between my parents," and he assures her " my affection for you is as great as ever." In fact Lewis bore himself nobly in a most painful and piteous situation.

8. *The Works of Lord Byron : Letters and Journals,* ed. R. E. Prothero (Second Impression), 1903, Vol. II, p. 317, note.

9. The Dean's Admission Book, Christ Church, under Commensales, 1790, has : " 16 Apr. Matthaeus Gregory Lewis."

10. Used by the elder Colman in his *The Man of Business,* produced at Covent Garden, January 29th, 1774 ; and translated by C. H. as *The Two Friends, or, The Liverpool Merchant,* 8vo, 1800.

11. Many of Mrs. Lewis' difficulties were due to a number of persons who imposed upon her, and whose avidity she satisfied when in fact unable to supply their wants, had such even been genuine and well founded. See *The Life and Correspondence of M. G. Lewis,* 1839, Vol. I, p. 67.

12. Goethe had been invited to Weimar, where he took up his residence, November 7th, 1775, by the Duke. He died here March 22nd, 1832.

13. Actually Schiller had been appointed to a Professorship at Jena in 1789, which he resigned in 1799.

14. T. M. Carré, *Goethe en Angleterre* (1920), Chapter I ; also *Bibliographie de Goethe en Angleterre,* Chapter I. Further, see the article by A. E. Turner in the *Modern Language Review,* Vol. XVI (July–October), 1921, pp. 364–70.

15. Coleridge, *Biographia Literaria,* 2 vols., London, 1817 ; Vol. II, p. 28.

16. Alleyne Fitzherbert, Baron St. Helens (1753–1839), the famous diplomatist. He was envoy extraordinary at The Hague, 1789 ; ambassador at Madrid, 1791–94.

17. William Eden, first Baron Auckland, 1744–1814.

18. 1760–1836. He was accounted an excellent actor. Says Boaden : "I have seen no actor at all near him where he was fully himself." Oxberry considered him "the best actor on the stage." Among his many original parts were Don Ferolo Whiskerandos in *The Critic*, and Walter in *The Children in the Wood*, both of which were esteemed masterpieces.

19. In his fuliginous book with the fierce title *La Carne, La Morte e il Diavolo nella letteratura romantica !* (discreetly and appropriately translated, be it noted, into English as *The Romantic Agony*) Signor Mario Praz, amongst other errors in reference to Lewis, confuses *The Monk* with the first unfinished romance (see p. 60 of *The Romantic Agony*, English translation by Angus Davidson, 1933). I might hesitate, however, to suggest that Signor Praz is at fault, since Mr. Wyndham Lewis, in *Men Without Art*, p. 175, in reference to *The Romantic Agony*, spoke of " This gigantic pile of satanic bric-a-brac, so industriously assembled, under my directions by Professor Praz." This was repeated by Mr. Stephen Spender, *The Destructive Element*, p. 206. But Signor Praz wrote hotly to *The Times Literary Supplement*, August 8th, 1935, " to point out " that Mr. Wyndham Lewis' words were " grossly misleading." He added : " I am afraid I must disclaim the honour of being ranked as his disciple, sorry as I am to deprive him of this satisfaction." *Actum est de* Mr. Wyndham Lewis ! After all it does not in the least matter who is responsible for such disjointed gimcrack as *The Romantic Agony*.

The Sosii were celebrated booksellers in Rome. Lewis aptly has " Stockdale, Hookham, or Debrett."

21. *Monthly Magazine or British Register*, March, 1796. The List of new publications. In *The Life and Correspondence of M. G. Lewis*, 1839, Vol. I, p. 151, there is a bad blunder in regard to *The Monk* : " The first and greatest era in the literary life of Lewis was the publication of ' Ambrosio, or The Monk,' which event took place in the summer of 1795." Several writers have repeated the error that 1795 is the date of the first edition of *The Monk*. Thus Elton, *A Survey of English Literature, 1780–1830*, 1912, Vol. I, p. 215. Railo, *The Haunted Castle*, 1927, p. 89. Rudolf Schneider, *Der Mönch in der englischen Dichtung bis auf Lewis's* " *Monk*," 1795, 1927, p. 168. Herr Brauchli, *Der englische Schauerroman um* 1800, 1928, pp. 200, 235, 254. Miss J. M. S. Tompkins, *The Popular Novel in England, 1770–1800*, 1932, p. 278. E. A. Baker, *The History of the English Novel*, Vol. V (1934), p. 205. Both Baker, who is responsible for an edition of *The Monk* (1907), and Railo fall into a further mistake when they assert that the original title of Lewis' romance was *Ambrosio, or The Monk*.

22. *Monthly Magazine or British Register*, April, 1796. I have generally used the copy of *The Monk* which belonged to Francis Douce (1757–1834), and which is preserved in the Bodleian Library, Shelfmark, Douce : L. 307. This contains some interesting contemporary notes and cuttings.

23. *The Pursuits of Literature*. The Sixth Edition. 1798, pp. 196–7. The quotation is from Juvenal, Satire II, 121.

24. Printed and Sold by S. Fisher, No. 10, St. John's Lane, Clerkenwell, also Sold by T. Hurst, No. 32, Paternoster Row. The frontispiece has " London. Pub. Decr. 4th, 1799, *by S. Fisher*." 98 pages. A printer's ornament on p. 4 is the same as that upon the title-page of Will's *Horrid Mysteries*, 4 vols., Lane, 1796.

25. An interesting article upon the Bibliography of *The Monk*, by Mr. Louis F. Peck, *The Times Literary Supplement*, Thursday, March 7th, 1935, was followed by an important letter from Mr. Frederick Coykendall, who furnishes ample bibliographical details of the two issues. See also the letters in *The Times Literary Supplement*, 1935, of Mr. W. Roberts, March 14th ; and Mr. E. G. Bayford, March 28th.

26. It is not altogether easy to find a reprint of the text of the second issue of *The Monk* with the longer conclusion. Thus an " Unabridged Reprint of the First Edition," 2 vols., London, no date, but about 1890, has the shorter version and the Haughty Lady.

27. In the nineteenth century numberless reprints of *The Monk*—all cheap and some clandestine—appeared as *Rosario, or The Monk*, and *Rosario, or The Female Monk*. They were often crudely illustrated with " penny dreadful " woodcuts, and were widely read by juveniles. A copy before me, London, The Temple Company (*c.* 1899) has : *Rosario : or, The Female Monk*. A Romance. (Reprinted from the Waterford Edition.) By Monk Lewis.

28. 1797, Vol. II, pp. 247–8.

29. *Byron's Works. Letters and Journals*, ed. Rowland E. Prothero, Second Impression, 1903. Vol II, p. 317, note.

30. "His vanity is ouverte," said Byron of Lewis, "and yet not offending." *Ibid.*, pp. 356–7.

31. Miss J. M. S. Tompkins, *The Popular Novel in England, 1770–1800* (1932), p. 278, exclaims against this "scandalous book," and informs us that "the union of lasciviousness and terror . . . was first thoroughly worked by M. G. Lewis in *The Monk* (1795)." I fear that this "union" assuredly did not wait until the final decade of the eighteenth century. Miss Tompkins' distaste for Lewis' work has, unfortunately, led her into several errors. She remarks, p. 245, note 1, that "*The Monk* was begun during Lewis's stay in Germany, and finished under the influence of *The Mysteries of Udolpho*," which is not the case. She is not aware that so far from two-thirds of *The Monk* being "taken, almost word for word, from a German romance, *Die Blutende Gestalt mit Dolch und Lampe*," this very romance, published in 1799, is merely an adaptation of the German version of *The Monk*, by F. von Oertel, 1797–8. One regrets to find that, although in 1907 he furnished an Introduction to a reprint of *The Monk*, Dr. E. A. Baker with no uncertain sound lends his voice to the chorus of condemnation. Thus we are informed that Lewis "betrays the perverted lusts of a sadist." He had "not merely a voracious but a morbid appetite." The crimes of Ambrosio are described "with a gluttonous fullness." The episode of Agnes and Don Raymond "is treated with the same revolting frankness" as the main theme. And so on and so forth. *History of the English Novel*, Vol. V (1934), pp. 205–11

32. Santon, from the Spanish *santo*, a Mohammedan recluse or hermit.

33. Vol. XXIV, p. 403 ; 1796.

34. XIX, 1796, pp. 194–200.

35. February, 1799, pp. 111–15.

36. LIV, 1802, p. 548.

37. *Byron's Works, ed. cit. Letters and Journals*, Vol. II, p. 368.

38. Elephantis was a Greek poetess, quae libris suis expressit "Poikila tes Aphrodites kai akolasias schemata." See Suetonius, *Tiberius*, xliii ; Martial, XII, 43 ; Priapeia, iii.

39. *Life and Correspondence of M. G. Lewis*, Vol. I, pp. 154–8.

40. I use the Sixth Edition, 1798, and the Fourteenth Edition, 1808, as representative texts.

41. 4to, 1786, for the Dillettanti Society.

42. Nichols, *Literary Anecdotes*, Vol. II, 1812, pp. 457–8. 1707 is sometimes given as the date. See also *The New Monthly Magazine*, 1819, July 1st, p. 512. The bibliography of the *Memoirs of a Woman of Pleasure* is very obscure. The first edition, 2 vols., "for G. Fenton in the Strand," has no date, but is 1747 or 1748. The third edition is 1749. In 1750 Griffiths the bookseller (who is doubtless G. Fenton) published an expurgated edition, 12mo, as *Memoirs of Fanny Hill*. There have been numberless reprints, mostly clandestine and private. The Isidore Liseux edition was published in 1888. There are at least nine French translations, and several Italian adaptations, of which one, *La Meretrice*, Cosmopoli (Venice), about 1764, is by Count Carlo Gozzi. A German translation, *Das Frauenzimmer von Vergnugen*, is given in Volume I of *Priapische Romane*, Berlin, 1791; Leipzig, 1860 and 1872.

43. For Cleland see further *New Monthly Magazine*, July 1st, 1819, p. 512.

44. *The Pursuits of Literature*, 14th edition, 1808, p. 366. The italics are those of Mathias.

45. *Ibid.*, p. 245, and note (*b*), pp. 245–6.

46. Since I am unwilling to trench upon any theological discussion here I will merely remark in a note that I do not wish to seem to express approval of or defend the passage in *The Monk* which gave (perhaps not unjustifiably) offence on these grounds.

47. Praz, *The Romantic Agony*, English translation, 1933, pp. 180–1, suggests that this incident may have inspired a passage (omitted from the final text) in Flaubert's *La Tentation de Saint Antoine* : "Il ouvre son missel et regarde l'image de la Vierge," whereupon the devil whispers obscene thoughts in the Saint's ear.

48. Only Miss Birkhead, *The Tale of Terror*, 1921, p. 67, seems to have noticed that with regard to Matilda "Lewis changes his mind about her character during the course of the book, and fails to make her early history consistent with the ending of the story."

49. In a famous passage which gave great scandal. Rather than have allowed Antonia to read certain episodes of the Old Testament, Elvira " would have preferred putting into her daughter's hands *Amadis de Gaul*, or *The Valiant Champion, Tirante the White* ; and would sooner have authorized her studying the lewd exploits of *Don Galaor*, or the lascivious jokes of *Damsel Plazerdimivida*." Lewis had the names from Don Quixote's library, *Don Quixote*, Part I, chapters i and vi. Don Galaor is the brother of Amadis de Gaul. Plazirdemavida is a maid of honour to the Princess Carmesina in *Tirante the White*.

50. It was even suggested that he had taken the incident of the Bleeding Nun from a romance of Madame de Genlis, *Les Chevaliers du Cygne*, Hamburg, 3 vols., 1795. Two friends, Isambard and Oliver, pass the night at an inn, and the former hears gentle footsteps in his companion's room, whilst a voice murmurs : " Olivier ! C'est en vain que tu veux me fuir ; je te suivrai partout." Later attempting to catch a glimpse of this nocturnal visitant, Isambard is horrified to see a carious skeleton, all dabbled with blood, whilst tortured groans disturb the air. Tome I, ch. vi, p. 41 ; and ch. vii, pp. 60–2. Lewis however, explicitly stated that he had not read *Les Chevaliers du Cygne* until *The Monk* was printed and just about to appear, as indeed the several dates of the French and English romances amply demonstrate. Madame de Genlis was in fact drawing upon the same story by Musaeus as Lewis used.

Praz, *The Romantic Agony*, p. 209, imagines that the Bleeding Nun may have been the original of Gautier's *La Morte Amoureuse* !

51. 1735–87.

52. Also 8vo, 1708. Graesse, *Bibliotheca Magica*, Leipzig, 1843, pp. 86, 130, 134. For a reproduction of the frontispiece of this rare book see Soldan-Heppe, *Geschichte der Hexenprozesse*, München, 1912, Band II, 376.

53. Vol. XXIII, p. 451.

54. Otto Ritter, in an article " Studien zu M. G. Lewis' Roman ' Ambrosio or the Monk,' " *Archiv für das Studium der Neueren Sprachen und Literaturen*, Band CXI (New Series XI), 1903, pp. 106–21, is rather belated in drawing attention to these similarities. The influence of Bürger on Lewis' ballads the author of *The Monk* was proud openly to acknowledge. To talk of the compact with the Demon as a " Faust-theme " seems a little absurd, in view of the many historical records of such horrid bargains. See my *History of Witchcraft* and *Geography of Witchcraft, passim*.

55. Born November 25th, 1762 ; died January 8th, 1835.

56. Published in 1753.

57. Such plays as *The Woodman's Hut* and *The Miller and his Men* obviously owe their inspiration to Lewis.

58. *Life and Correspondence of M. G. Lewis*, Vol. I, pp. 60–1.

59. I have not, of course, attempted to do more than barely touch the fringe of the subject. There should further be consulted Neubaur's *Die Sage von ewigen Juden*, 2nd ed., Leipzig, 1893 ; Albert Soergel's *Ahasver-Dichtungen seit Goethe*, 1905 ; and (for literary allusions) Theodor Kapstein, *Ahasverus in der Weltpossie*, Berlin, 1906. Miss Alice M. Killen has a study *L'évolution de la légende du Juif errant* in the *Revue de littérature comparée*, January–March, 1925, pp. 5–36. Of romances upon the subject of, or which introduce the Wandering Jew, among the most famous is *Le Juif Errant* (1845), of Marie-Joseph-Eugène Sue, who read and was influenced by *The Monk*.

60. The earliest English translation was 1795, " *The Ghost-Seer, or Apparitionist*, an interesting fragment." Lewis, of course, knew the original.

61. Standard Novels, Colburn and Bentley, No. IX, 1831, *The Ghost-Seer*, Vol. I, p. 8.

62. *Biographia Dramatica*, 1812, Vol. III, p. 389 ; No. 9.

63. Produced at the Haymarket on November 1st, 1707. 4to, 1707. This comedy was a stock play throughout the eighteenth century, and was revived at the Haymarket as late as March, 1848. Although he has served the dish cleverly enough, Cibber (as his wont) offers far from original fare. Atall, the " Double Gallant," masquerades as Mr. Freeman and Colonel Standfast.

64. *Cumberland's British Theatre*, Vol. XV, 1827, *The Castle Spectre*, Remarks, p. 10. Of great significance and importance as were German influences upon the Gothic novel in general, and upon Lewis in particular, it is, of course, possible disproportionately to over-stress this point at the expense of the originality of British authors. Thus in his

The Revolutionary Ideas of the Marquis de Sade, 1934, p. 101, *Note*, Mr. Geoffrey Gorer criticizes M. Maurice Heine, who " claims priority for de Sade in the use of Gothic trappings to the adventure novel, on the historical ground of the dates of his books, compared with those of Mrs. Radcliffe and ' Monk ' Lewis." Mr. Gorer proceeds : " This seems to me difficult to justify, when the work of Clara Reeve and the wide diffusion of such German books as Boden's *Children of the Abbey* are taken into account." Clara Reeve (1729–1807) wrote : *Original Poems* (1769) ; *The Phœnix* (1772) ; *The Champion of Virtue* (1777), reprinted as *The Old English Baron* (1778) ; *The Two Mentors* (1783) ; *The Progress of Romance* (1785) ; *The Exiles* (1789) ; *The School for Widows* (1791) ; *Plans of Education* (1792) ; *Memoirs of Sir Roger de Clarendon* (1793) ; and *Destination : or Memoirs of A Private Family* (1799). *Fatherless Fanny* is not by Clara Reeve. Horace Walpole writing to the Rev. William Mason upon April 8th, 1778, jeered *The Old English Baron* as *Otranto* " reduced to reason and probability ! It is so probable, that any trial for murder at the Old Bailey would make a more interesting story." In the same letter he damns it as a " *caput mortuum*," Walpole's *Letters*, ed. Toynbee, Vol. X, Oxford, 1904, pp. 216–17. Again (*ibid.*, p. 302) Walpole speaks of *The Old English Baron* as " stripped of the marvellous " and " the most insipid dull nothing you ever saw." Miss J. M. S. Tompkins hits the mark when she emphasizes the " homely and practical streak that differentiates *The Old English Baron* from any other Gothic story whatever," *The Popular Novel in England*, 1932, p. 229. She further (p. 231) points out that Clara Reeve's *Memoirs of Sir Roger de Clarendon* " is wholly unlike the Gothic Romances in the middle of which it appeared " (1793). Professor Raleigh, in *The English Novel* (fifth edition, 1904, p. 227), justly observes that Miss Reeve deliberately diluted romance with prosiness. " In her relation to the romantic movement she thus appears as a reactionary." In fact Mr. Gorer has made such an extremely bad shot when he hazarded " the work of Clara Reeve " that one must be excused if one doubts whether he has any acquaintance at all with this lady's writing.

" Such German books as Boden's *Children of the Abbey*." This sentence I frankly do not understand. Is Boden the German author from whom a book *anglicè*, " Children of the Abbey," was translated ? Is Boden the English translator ? What is the German title of the book which he translated ? Who is this Boden ? Is he Joseph Boden, the Indian judge-advocate, who founded the Boden professorship of Sanscrit at Oxford ?

The Children of the Abbey, 4 vols., 1798, is by Mrs. Regina Maria Roche, *née* Dalton. It is certainly not a " terror " but a " sensibility " novel, and was an especial favourite, being frequently reprinted until at least the end of the nineteenth century. It is British to the core, in every page, in every turn. I have never heard of, nor can I find a German original, if that is what Mr. Gorer intends. One is entitled, I think, to express some scepticism, but should a German novel exist—whether or not by Boden—from which Mrs. Roche translated her *The Children of the Abbey*, I shall be most interested to learn all details, and I await the reading of the book with considerable curiosity.

65. Wien und Prag bey Franz Haas ; 262 pages. A copy is to be found in the Wiener Stadtbibliothek.

66. In an article, *Die angebliche Quelle von M. G. Lewis' " Monk "* ; *Archiv für das Studium*, Vol. CXIII, pp. 56–65.

67. *Noch einmal die Quelle des " Monk "* ; *Archiv*, Vol. CXV, pp. 70–3.

68. *Euphorion*, VII, p. 725.

69. Sauer, *Grillparzers Werke*, I, 1909, definitely proves that the German romance is merely an adaptation of certain chapters from *The Monk*. Rudolf Schneider, in his very superficial compilation, *Der Mönch in der englischen Dichtung bis auf Lewis's " Monk*," 1795, Leipzig, 1928 (Palaestra 155), pp. 168–75, repeats Herzfeld's errors at some length. His list of Titles influenced by *The Monk* is faulty to a degree. Evidently he had no knowledge of the books he catalogues in the most haphazard way. Misled by the word " Recluse," he regards Zara Wentworth's *The Recluse of Albyn Hall* (which he calls *Albin Hall*) as a clerical novel, and he obviously takes Mrs. Meeke's *Veiled Protectress* for a nun !

70. Alice M. Killen, *Le Roman Terrifiant*, Paris, 1923, Bibliographie, pp. 227–8.

71. Fernand Baldensperger, *Le Moine de Lewis dans la Littérature française ; Journal of Comparative Literature*, 1903.

72. M. J. Young, *Memoirs of Mrs. Crouch*, 1806, Vol. II, p. 257. S. M. Ellis, *The Life of Michael Kelly*, 1930, p. 259. note 1.

73. Cumberland's *British Theatre*, No. 38. Also Dicks' *Standard Plays*, No. 268.
74. At Norwich, November 22nd, 1809.
75. 8vo., 1798 (bis); Third Edition, 8vo, 1799. Pub. Bell.
76. S. M. Ellis, *The Life of Michael Kelly*, 1930, pp. 258–9.
77. Alexis Pitou has an interesting article, *Les Origines du mélodrame français à la fin du XVIII siècle*, in the *Revue d'Histoire littéraire de la France*, 1911.
Prosper Mérimée's *Une Femme est un Diable*, which certainly borrows the central idea from *The Monk*, was published in his *Théâtre de Clara Gazul*, 1825, and designed for the closet.
78. Alexis Pitou in the *Revue d'Histoire littéraire*, 1911, pp. 279–80.
79. *Chronique des petits théâtres de Paris*, tom. I, p. 214.
80. Ch.-M. Des Granges, *Geoffrey et la critique dramatique*, p. 402.
81. It was almost immediately given in England under various piratical forms. Edward Fitzball and J. B. Buckstone were first in the field with a Musical Drama, *Robert le Diable; or, The Devil's Son*, Adelphi Theatre, January 23rd, 1832. A few weeks later, on February 13th, Sadlers Wells followed with a burletta, *Robert le Diable; or, The Devil's Son*. On Monday, February 20th, 1832, *The Demon Duke; or, The Mystic Branch*, was produced at Drury Lane, and the following night, Tuesday, Covent Garden gave *The Fiend Father; or Robert of Normandy*. The Royal Pavilion presented a burletta, *The Demon Father; or The Devil and his Son*, on March 12th, 1832.
Robert le Diable was produced in French at Her Majesty's on June 11th, 1832; and in Italian at the same theatre on May 4th, 1847, when Jenny Lind in the rôle of Alice made her first London appearance. On March 1st, 1845, this " great Catholic work," as it has been aptly termed, arranged by Bunn, had been given at Drury Lane. The more recent English adaptation of the libretto is by John Oxenford.
Mlle. Taglioni won a supreme triumph by her mystic dance as the Abbess Elena in *Robert le Diable*.
82. Lewis in a letter from The Hague to his mother, May 18th, 1794. *Life and Correspondence of M. G. Lewis*, Vol. I, p. 123.
83. Longman, Hurst, Rees and Orme, June, 1806, 13*s*. 6*d*. There is a reprint in one volume of *Zofloya* with an Introduction by the present writer, 1927.
84. Not dissimilar is the situation in Marston's *The Wonder of Women; or, The Tragedie of Sophonisba*, 4to, 1606, where Syphax lies with the foul witch Erichto, who has by glamour assumed the shape of Sophonisba. When upon the discovery he makes at her with his sword the hell-hag vanishes. In Elkanah Settle's *The Female Prelate, Being the History of the Life and Death of Pope Joan*, 4to, 1680, Act IV, Johanna in the darkness of night enters the bed of the Duke of Saxony, who takes her to be his bride, Angeline. A fire breaks out and he discovers the horrid cheat. Johanna with difficulty escapes, as he loads her with reproaches : " Succubus ; Hag ; Horrour unspeakable ! "
85. Vol. IV, chapter 19.
86. *Ibid.*, pp. 20–5.
87. *Ibid.*, pp. 84–90.
88. Vol. I, p. 161.
89. Chapter IV, p. 71.
90. This should be *Legends of a Nunnery*. The point is trifling, but it serves to show that Herr Brauchli has taken his references secondhand from Miss Birkhead.
91. Introduction, p. xvii.
92. E. T. A. Hoffmann's *Leben und Nachlass*, " von J. G. Hitzig, herausg. von Micheline Hoffmann, geb. Rorer," 5 vols., Stuttgart, 1839. See also *Erinnerungen aus meinem Leben*, von Z. Funck [G. Kunz], Leipzig, 1836.
93. The first volume was completed in less than a month. The second volume (after a considerable interval) was finished before the end of 1815. The work is, as Hoffmann himself avowed, something disjointed.
94. It should be said that in 1812 Hoffmann paid a visit to the Kapuziner-Kloster at Bamberg, and was extremely impressed by what he saw and by the conversation of a venerable friar, Father Cyrillus. See *Erinnerungen*, p. 60, *sqq*.
95. *The Devil's Elixir*. From the German of E. T. A. Hoffmann. Blackwood and Cadell, 1824, Vol. I, p. 78.

96. *Ibid.*, pp. 87, 89. S. Rosalia "born of the royal blood of Charlemagne," is the especial patroness of Palermo. Major feast, September 4th. I suppose the name was suggested to Lewis by a certain picturesqueness and beauty. The Saint was not, however, a martyr, as Hoffmann (p. 89) represents.

97. E. T. W. Hoffmann, *Weird Tales*. A new translation by J. T. Bealby. 2 vols., Nimmo, 1885. Vol. I, Biographical Notice, p. xlviii.

98. *The Life-Work of Samuel Phelps*, by W. M. Phelps and J. Forbes-Robertson, 1886, p. 20.

99. H. Chance Newton, *Crime and the Drama*, 1927, p. 39. Richard John Smith (1786–1855) was generally known as " O. Smith " from his acting in John Fawcett's *Obi ; or Three-fingered Jack*.

100. It is remarkable that Reynolds seems to have had hardly the faintest suspicion of the appalling sacrilege involved.

101. The period is towards the end of the reign of Richard I. In Chapter XXVII Wingrove remarks : " He is,—or was a Jesuit, I have been told and they are as crafty, if not more so, than the devil himself." Agatha very properly retorts : " You speak of that you do not comprehend."

102. Illustrated by Phiz. London : E. Griffiths, 13 Catherine Street, Strand. No date, but about 1857–8.

103. The most striking parody of Lewis in *The Heroine* occurs in Letter XXX, when Cherubina learns that her mother is " confined in one of the subterranean vaults belonging to the villa." She is mysteriously conducted to a dismal cell where sits a giantess of vast bulk : " a piece of mouldy bread, a mug of water, and a manuscript, lay on the table ; some straw, strewn with dead snakes and skulls, occupied one corner, and the farther side of the cell was concealed behind a black curtain." The situation of Agnes in the subterranean dungeon is burlesqued here. The manuscript proves to be " Il Castello di Grimgothico ; or, Memoirs of Lady Hysteria Belamour."

104. *The Monk*, 3 vols., 1796, Vol. II, chapter vii, p. 247 ; Antonia has been reading. " He examined the book. . . . It was the Bible l ' How l ' said the friar to himself, ' Antonia reads the Bible, and is still so ignorant ? ' " This, it will be remembered, was one of the passages which gave greatest offence.

105. Vol. VI, p. 345.

106. R. S. has not been certainly identified, although perhaps the Brighton printer and journalist, Richard Sickelmore, may be the author of *The New Monk*.

107. Rosa " aida Anselme à saisir cet éclair de bonheur qui eût mis les hommes au-dessus des dieux, si ceux-ci, par envie, ne l'eussent rendu trop court." *Les Trois Moines*, 1802, Tome premier, p. 122.

108. Among the " Ouvrages qui se trouvent à Paris, chez le même Libraire " we find " *Crimes de l'amour*, par l'auteur *d'Aline et Valcour*, 4 vol. in 16 fig. 2 f."

109. Third edition, 2 vols., Dabot, Bordeaux and Paris, 1815 ; Fourth edition, 2 vols., Massin, 1821.

110. *Kate Chudleigh ; or, The Duchess of Kingston*, by M. J. Errym, published in fifteen numbers by John Dicks, 1864, derives little more than a suggestion from the French romance.

111. Included (not Sarratt's translation) in *Great German Short Stories*, edited by Lewis Melville and Reginald Hargreaves, 1929.

112. Miss Birkhead, *The Tale of Terror*, 1921, p. 71, incorrectly dates Sarratt's *Koenigsmark* 1818. Herr Jakob Brauchli, *Der englische Schauerroman um* 1800, p. 257, is also at fault with " 1810 ? ", since the book is mentioned in Young's *Memoirs of Mrs. Crouch*, 1806. The date is uncertain, but *circa* 1801 seems nearer the mark.

113. Miss Birkhead, *op. cit.*, p. 71 and p. 234, Index, definitely names Lewis as the adaptor or author. See also the British Museum Catalogue under " Lewis, Matthew Gregory."

114. This detail is historically and actually true. " Illos, nempe dæmones et impios, fætor turpissimus, ignis quoque suphurens amaritudinis fumosæ sine fine molestat." Anonymi Cujusdam, Tractatus III, *De Credulitate Demonibus Adhibenda*, in the collection *Malleus Maleficarum*, Lugduni, Tomus II, 1584, p. 317. See further, Montague Summers,

The History of Witchcraft, 1926, pp. 44–5 ; also Guazzo, *Compendium Maleficarum*, English translation, 1929, p. 78 ; and Remy, *Demonolatry*, Eng. tr., 1930, p. 33.

115. For Raspe see K. H. Schaible, *Geschichte der Deutschen in England*, Strassburg, 1885. Also J. L. Haney, *German Literature in England before* 1790 : Americana Germanica, Vol. IV. Raspe in 1781 translated Lessing's *Nathan der Weise*.

116. The Seventh Edition, 1793, is the text usually reprinted.

117. M. J. Young, *Memoirs of Mrs. Crouch*, 1806, Vol. II, pp. 311–12.

118. Vol. III, 1812, p. 44. *Village Virtues*, see *Monthly Review*, Nov. 1796, p. 336.

119. Adapted as *The Harper's Daughter*, it was produced at Covent Garden on May 4th, 1803, for the benefit of Henry Johnston. It was printed [Philadelphia], 12mo, 1813.

120. Mrs. Baron-Wilson in her *Life and Correspondence of M. G. Lewis* depicts Lady Charlotte as the " bright particular star " of Lewis, and invents a hopeless passion for him. There does not appear the slightest evidence that Lewis regarded the lady with any warmer feelings than friendship. In *The Haunted Castle* Railo, having delivered himself of the utterly inept remark, " In the life of every man—and especially of every poet—a woman appears," at once indulges in the most ridiculous sugary stuff about " Lady Charlotte " and Lewis.

121. Fashion even dictated a " Crazy Jane " hat. *Crazy Jane*, a " romantic play," by C. A. Somerset, produced at the Surrey Theatre, June 19th, 1827, takes only the name and a bare hint from the ballad.

122. S. M. Ellis, *The Life of Michael Kelly*, 1930, pp. 251–2.

123. Nicolo Jomelli, Neapolitan, 1714–74. He was as highly esteemed for his sacred as for his secular music. A chacoone (or a slow dance movement) was introduced into church services, and generally known as " The Sanctus of Jomelli."

124. 1806. Vol. II, pp. 282–6. There are very many anecdotes concerning *The Castle Spectre*. For some of these, and not the least amusing, see *Life and Correspondence of M. G. Lewis*, Vol. I, Chapter viii, pp. 211–16.

125. J. D. Beveridge acted Earl Osmond ; J. B. Johnstone, Earl Reginald ; Crawford, Percy ; J. L. Shine, Father Philip ; W. Elton, Motley ; T. Squire, Kenric ; Miss Louise Willes, Angela ; Mrs. Leigh, Alice ; and Miss Hobbes, the Spectre. See John Hollingshead's *Footlights*, 8vo, 1883 ; also Clement Scott and Cecil Howard, *Edward Leman Blanchard*, 2 vols., 1891 ; Vol. II, p. 501, n. 5.

126. J. R. A. Nicoll, *A History of Late Eighteenth Century Drama*, 1927, p. 100. This writer with rather heavy wit talks of the Spectre as " an exceedingly solid ghost."

127. 8vo, Printed for J. Bell, 1798 ; pp. 28, 41, 58, 69, and 100–3.

128. From the French of M. J. Sedaine. Produced at Drury Lane, October 24th, 1786. The original music by Grétry was arranged by Thomas Linley. This work proved exceedingly popular. Another adaptation from Sedaine, *Richard Cœur de Lion*, by Leonard Macnally, produced at Covent Garden, October 16th, 1786, was not so successful.

129. 1794 ; Vol. IV, chapter lv.

130. Note by Lewis. *The Castle Spectre*, 8vo, 1798, p. 58.

131. *Life and Correspondence of M. G. Lewis*, Vol. II, pp. 60–1.

132. *Some Account of the English Stage*, 1832, Vol. VII, pp. 332–3.

133. *The Castle Spectre*, 8vo, 1798, p. 103.

134. It was continually reprinted throughout the nineteenth century and appears in very many collections ; for example, Cumberland's *British Theatre*, Vol. XV, 1827, " Printed from the Acting Copy " ; Dicks Standard Plays, No. 35.

135. 1784–1834. His *Catullus* was first published 1821 : reprinted 1854.

136. Bell gave £25, and agreed upon an equal sum in the event of a second edition. Lockhart, *Memoirs* (Macmillan, 1900), Vol. I, p. 256 ; Scott, *Essay on Imitations of the Ancient Ballad*, ed. T. F. Henderson, Vol. IV, 1902, pp. 27, *sqq.*; J. A. Robberds, *Memoir . . . of . . . William Taylor of Norwich*, 2 vols., London 1843, Vol. II, pp. 353, *sqq.*

137. *Byron's Works, Letters and Journals*, Vol. II, ed. R. E. Prothero, 1903 (Second Impression), pp. 317–8, notes.

138. Early editions of both these *Tales* are uncommon. They differ very much in their contents. My copy of the Second Edition of *Tales of Wonder*, 1801, London, Bell, has 32 poems. My copy of *Tales of Wonder*, Dublin, 2 vols., 1801, has 60 poems, including *Tam*

O'Shanter; the Witches Song from Jonson's *Masque of Queens*; Parnell's *The Hermit*; Dryden's *Theodore and Honoria*; and many other additions. Henry Morley's reprint, *Tales of Terror and Wonder*, 1887, is useful. A parody is *Tales of the Devil*, 1801.

It is interesting to remember that in *Original Poetry by Victor and Cazire* (Shelley and his sister Elizabeth), published by Stockdale on September 19th, 1810, it was found that Cazire had "borrowed" in its entirety as one of her contributions to the volume "The Black Canon of Elmham; or St. Edmond's Eve," which Lewis had written as "An Old English Ballad" from *Tales of Terror*. Upon Stockdale pointing this out to Shelley, the poet, with warm resentment at the imposition, desired the destruction of all remaining copies; hence only about 110 were ever put in circulation.

139. See Montague Summers, *The Vampire in Europe*, 1929, pp. 34-8.

140. Ovid, *Metamorphoses*, IX, 306.

141. A selection from Lewis' ballads, his *Amorassan, or, The Spirit of the Frozen Ocean*, and other pieces are included in *Legends of Terror . . . In Prose and Verse*, London, 1826.

142. "The spectators found much interest, and language which spoke to the heart in this comedy." Young, *Memoirs of Mrs. Crouch*, 1806, Vol. II, p. 308.

143. Produced at Drury Lane, January 19th, 1771.

144. *Life and Correspondence of M. G. Lewis*, Vol. I, p. 219.

145. Whence also Sheridan drew for *The School for Scandal*, a comedy which has considerably influenced Lewis. None the less he treats his theme and characters with marked originality. Lewis alluded to the Novel of *Sidney Bidulph*, a reference anyone would have understood. Railo, *The Haunted Castle*, p. 105, affectedly informs us there is no "*Novel of Sidney Biddulph*, though there certainly does exist a story called *The Memoirs of Miss Sidney Biddulph*," which is inaccurate. Railo's imperfect acquaintance with English may excuse his blunders and should have spared us his cheap attempts at facetiousness. In a note on *The Cloud-King, Tales of Wonder*, p. 87, Lewis jokingly says that the moral of the ballad is to teach young ladies the value of understanding a little grammar. It will hardly be believed that Railo, *op. cit.*, p. 110, takes this quite seriously and comments on the efforts of Lewis to teach a "didactic lesson."

146. Lewis explained that this was suggested by a scene in Goethe's *Egmont*. Railo, *The Haunted Castle*, p. 111, is entirely mistaken when he says that "influences of . . . Mrs. Radcliffe's *Romance of the Forest* and *The Italian* are discernible in this play."

147. At Sadler's Wells on Tuesday, December 26th, 1843, was given *Adelmorn the Outlaw*, slightly adapted from Lewis, without acknowledgement.

148. Price 2s. 6d. Second Edition, 8vo, 1802.

149. Produced in New York, March, 1803.

150. *Richard the Third*, the next production, was even postponed, and *Alfonso* repeated. Harris was "full of civility, and compliments, and fine speeches." *Memoirs of M. G. Lewis*, Vol. I, p. 231.

151. 1812, Vol. III, p. 16.

152. Alfonso XI reigned 1310-50. The play has no historical basis.

153. "The subject of the drama is a conspiracy—and we are partial to conspiracies. They cannot but be interesting." Review of William Tennant's tragedy, *Cardinal Beaton*, 8vo, 1823 (Edinburgh), in *Blackwood's Magazine*, October, 1823; Vol. XIV, p. 422.

154 Explosions were only popular as stage effects. One of the most famous is the final blowing up of the mill that concludes *The Miller and His Men*, Covent Garden, November 21st, 1813; an explosion, blazing ruins, and a tableau are the end of Macfarren's *The Boy of Santillane*, Drury Lane, April 16th, 1827; "*the bridge blows up with a tremendous explosion . . . Picture . . . Curtain falls*" upon A. V. Campbell's *The Forest Oracle;* or *The Bridge of Tresino*, Sadler's Wells, November 9th, 1829.

155. Harriett Litchfield, *née* Hay, 1777-1854. She first appeared on the stage 1792, and retired after 1812. She was accounted one of the leading tragediennes of the day. In Belvidera, Imoinda, Zara, Roxana, Lady Randolph, Millwood, Mrs. Haller, Andromache and other heroines she was greatly applauded. She played Lady Macbeth to the Macbeth of Cooke.

156. Also again in Volume I, pp. 236-41, of *The Life and Correspondence of M. G. Lewis*, 1839. Mr. J. R. A. Nicoll, who does not know Lewis' *Poems*, erroneously supposes the reprint, 1839, to be the first edition: *Nineteenth Century Drama*, 1930, Vol. II, p. 335.

157. *Cheer ! Boys, Cheer !*, 1895, pp. 67–8 and *passim*.
158. G. W. M. Reynolds in his *Joseph Wilmot*, Charles Reade, Wilkie Collins, Sheridan Le Fanu in *The Rose and the Key* (1871), and many other novelists dealt with these abuses in private madhouses.
159. Herr Brauchli, *Der englische Schauerroman um* 1800, 1928, erroneously attributes (pp. 198 and 253) to Mrs. Kelly Sarah Lansdell's *Manfredi*, 2 vols., 1796.
160. A fact which, even were it not otherwise known, is quite apparent from his works. It has been remarked that the description of female charms in *The Monk*, however voluptuously intended, are in effect cold and merely " literary." It was in his endeavour to force the correct atmosphere that Lewis laid himself open to the accusation of lewdness when he should have been sensual and elegantly naked.
161. 1791–1842.
162. *Roscius Anglicanus*, ed. by Montague Summers, 1928, p. 19. See also *The Playhouse of Pepys*, by Montague Summers, 1935, pp. 292–7.
163. Almaviva, Jones ; Rosina, Maria Tree.
164. See *Restoration Comedies*, edited by Montague Summers, 1922, Introduction, pp. xlviii–lviii ; *The Works of Thomas Shadwell*, edited by Montague Summers, 1927, Vol. I, Introduction, pp. civ–cx, and Vol. II, pp. 187–91 ; *Dryden The Dramatic Works*, edited by Montague Summers, Vol. II, 1931, pp. 148–51.
165. Throughout the latter decades of the eighteenth century and during the Regency, as indeed for that matter in earlier and later years, homosexuality was rife in London society. Beckford, Richard Heber, Grey Bennett, Baring Wall, and other prominent persons were very notorious, as also was the Earl of Findlater and Seafield, who died about 1820, and left the whole of his estates and vast wealth to young Fischer. This legacy was disputed *ob turpem causam*, but the family eventually had to compound with Fischer for an immense sum. The " White Swan," Vere Street, was well known as a homosexual rendezvous. See *The Phœnix of Sodom, or the Vere Street Coterie*, 8vo, 1813 ; and for earlier days *Satan's Harvest Home*, 8vo, 1749. Both these are described at length by Pisanus Fraxi in his *Index Librorum Prohibitorum*, pp. 328 and 357.
166. A somewhat confused (but none the less in many respects a very valuable) account of Mrs. Kelly, referred to as Mrs. K——, and Lewis is given in the *Life and Correspondence of M. G. Lewis*, Vol. I, pp. 270–85. Several important letters are quoted. There are references to William Kelly, Vol. I, p. 361, and Vol. II, pp. 94–106, pp. 384–5, and p. 387. Unfortunately the letters are not printed entire.
167. Price 16s.
168. Francis Rawdon Hastings, first Marquis of Hastings and second Earl of Moira, 1754–1826.
169. Price 2d. J. Clements, 21 and 22 Little Pulteney Street, Regent Street.
170. *Abellino :* Schauspiel in fümf Akten, and in verse.
171. *Courier des Spectacles*, 15 Vendemiaire, an X, *i.e.*, October 6th, 1801. Pixérécourt has further introduced into his play Vivaldi and Spalatro from *The Italian*.
172. There is a Spanish translation of *L'Homme à trois Visages* as *Abelino o el Gran Bandido*, drama tragico en cinco actos, por D. T. de O., Madrid, 8vo, 1802.
173. *Biographia Dramatica*, 1812, Vol. III, pp. 376–7.
174. Given later at the same theatre as *The Conspirators ; or, The Venetian Bravo*.
175. Born, New Jersey, 1766 ; died, New York, 1839.
176. 1776–1853.
177. Thomas Busby, Mus. Doc. (Cam.) ; 1755–1838. Organist at S. Mary, Woolnoth. When *Rugantino* was given at Crow Street, Dublin, in 1814, Thomas Simpson Cooke (1782–1848) wrote new music for this production. (Cooke was musical director of Drury Lane, 1821–42.) *Rugantino* was printed, Dublin, 12mo, 1814.
178. There are many subsequent editions : Oxberry, *New English Drama*, Vol. IX, 1818 ; John Cumberland's *British Theatre*, Vol. XXXIV ; *The Acting Drama*, 1834.
179. Which Raino persists in calling a " scenic adaptation," the most awkward and uncouth of descriptions ; *The Haunted Castle*, p. 120.
180. Bodleian : Douce MSS., 234, f. 40 v.
181. 4to, 1611. Acted " probably in the spring of 1602 " : T. M. Parrott, *The Comedies of George Chapman*, 1914, p. 731.

182. Macready played Lothair at his third appearance, Theatre Royal, Birmingham, June 13th, 1810. Conway was Guiscard. *Macready's Reminiscences*, two vols., 1875, Vol. I, p. 41, and pp. 173–4.

183. At the Bowery Theatre, New York, March, 1827, Mrs. J. R. Duff acted Adelgitha. Charles Young, Guiscard ; Blake, Lothair ; G. Barrett, Ducas. *Adelgitha* was a favourite play with J. R. Duff, who had sustained Lothair, Guiscard, and Ducas.

184. S. M. Ellis, *The Life of Michael Kelly*, 1930, pp. 304–5.

185. *Biographia Dramatica*, 1812, Vol. III, p. 422.

186. "Expanded and dilated into a three act piece," *ibid.*, Vol. III, p. 463.

187. 1773–1823. A very versatile composer of and writer upon music.

188. Drury Lane was burned down on February 24th, 1809.

189. French's Acting Edition (late Lacy's), No. 1340, p. 7.

190. Edited by Sir Frederick Pollock, Bart., 1875, 2 vols., Vol. I, p. 45.

191. The Christmas pantomime, Boxing Night, 1848, at the Marylebone Theatre, Church Street, Edgware Road, was *One o'Clock ; or Harlequin Hardy Knute, the Knight and the Wooden Demon*.

192. See "First Visit to the Theatre in London," *Poems* by Hartley Coleridge, 1851, Vol. I, Appendix C, pp. cxcix–cciii.

193. Second Edition, 1801, No. XVIII, pp. 112–25.

194. Oxberry, Vol. XIX ; Cumberland, Vol. XXXII ; Lacy, Vol. XC ; Dicks, No. 128.

195. Raino, *Haunted Castle*, p. 124, mistakenly speaks of "a drama called *The Three Brothers*, by Pickersgill, produced at Drury Lane in 1807 " !

196. For references to whom see *Notes and Queries*, 1935, Vol. clxix, pp. 262, 299, 339.

197. The original MS. is dated "Pisa, 1822." Published by John Hunt, February 20th, 1824. See T. J. Wise, *A Bibliography of Byron*, London, Printed for Private Circulation Only, Vol. II, 1933, pp. 45–7, with facsimile of title-page.

198. Vol. IV, chapter xi, pp. 229–350.

199. Demetrius Poliorcetes, "the Besieger," son of Antigonus, King of Asia. He died 283 B.C. in the fifty-sixth year of his age. As a youth, his "beauty and mien were so inimitable that no statuary or painter could hit off a likeness." Plutarch's *Lives*, Langhorne's Translation, ed. 1838, p. 616. He was very licentious.

200. Raino, *Haunted Castle*, p. 122, incorrectly implies that "*Taken from the German*" was added on the title-page of the second edition. The first edition he obviously had not seen.

201. *Ode for Music*, ll. 35–8.

202. Lewis changes this to Torrenburg : "The real name is Toggenburg ; but, as this would have sounded harsh in English ears, I have taken the liberty of softening it a little." *Feudal Tyrants*, 1806, Vol. I, p. 1.

203. It may not be amiss to quote here the tribute paid to her by Wolfgang Menzel in his *German Literature*, English translation by Thomas Gordon, 1840, Vol. IV, p. 248 : "It was remarkable that a lady was the first who attempted to tell the ancient history of her country in numerous novels. This was the celebrated Christiane Benedicte Eugenie Naubert, born at Leipzig on September 13th, 1756 ; died January 12th, 1819. Her Eginhard and Emma, Conradin of Swabia, Hatto of Mainz, Elizabeth of Toggenburg, Alf von Dülnen, Konrad von Feuchtwanger, Philippine of Gueldres, Ulrich Holzer, Walther von Stadion, The League of the poor Conrad, Freidrich the Victor, &c. &c. gave to the reading public many vivid views of the past age of Germany." I have incorporated a footnote in the text. By many the most admired work of Frau Naubert was her *New Popular Tales of the Germans, Neuen Volksmärchen der Deutschen*, 1789–93.

204. Commencing Vol. II, p. 34.

205. Chur, capital of the Canton of Graubünden.

206. Facardin is the popular spelling of the Emir Fakhr-ed-Din.

207. Hamilton died at St. Germain in April, 1720, aged about 74. Lewis' translation of Part I of *Les Quatre Facardins*, together with his original Part II ; a very inferior Sequel to Part I by Mons. de Levis ; *Zénéyde* (concluded by Mons. de Levis) ; *Fleur d'Épine* ; *Le Bélier* ; and *L'Enchanteur Faustus* were published in a volume, *Fairy Tales and Romances*, written by Count Anthony Hamilton, translated from the French by M. Lewis, H. T. Ryde,

and C. Kenney, in the series " Bohn's Extra Volumes," 1849. *Le Bélier*, the first of Hamilton's *Contes*, was written about 1705 ; *Fleur d'Épine* and *Les Quatre Facardins* are to be dated 1710–15.

208. Antoine Galland, 1646–1715. The first four volumes of the *Nuits* appeared in 1704 ; vols. 5 and 6 in 1705 ; vol. 7, 1706 ; vol. 8, 1709 ; vols. 9 and 10, 1712 ; vols. 11 and 12 posthumously, 1717.

209. Who is confused by Mrs. Baron-Wilson, *Life and Correspondence of M. G. Lewis*, Vol. I, p. 57, with the great Sarah Siddons.

210. *The Biography of the British Stage*, 1824, p. 270.

211. Practically, the multiple scene is to my mind very embarrassing, as seemed the case when *Arden of Faversham* was produced by Mr. William Poel in December, 1925, and the three stationary localities simultaneously erected on the stage represented Arden's Parlour ; the High Road near Rainham Down ; and a street in London with an entrance to Franklyn's house.

212. *Jonathan Bradford*. Dicks' Standard Play. No. 370. See also Edward Fitzball, *Thirty-Five Years of a Dramatic Author's Life*, 1859, Vol. I, pp. 238–40.

213. Serial issue in *Bentley's Magazine*, 1839–40. First edition, 3 vols., 1839. See Cruikshank's illustrations, Vol. III, pp. 157 and 167. William Frederick Fenton painted the scenery for Greenwood's play, which was published by John Cumberland. R. W. Honner played Jack Sheppard, Mrs. Honner appearing as the boy Sheppard. For fuller details see S. M. Ellis, *Jack Sheppard*, 1933, pp. 101–2.

214. La Scala, Milan, February 8th, 1872 ; Théâtre Italierr, Paris, April 22nd, 1876 ; Covent Garden, London, June 22nd, 1876.

215. Mortally wounded at Corunna and buried in the citadel there, January 16th, 1809. The *Monody* is an ephemeron, and no great matter. Fifty copies only were privately printed. Reprinted, *Memoirs of M. G. Lewis*, Vol. I, pp. 378–80.

216. 8vo, 1798. For details of the original production see S. M. Ellis, *Michael Kelly*, pp. 254–8.

217. " To the King's playhouse, to see an old play of Shirley's called ' Hide Parke ' ; the first day acted ; when horses are brought upon the stage." Pepys, July 11th, 1668.

218. Boaden, *Life of J. P. Kemble*, 1825, Vol. II, p. 543. Genest, *History of the English Stage*, Vol. VIII, pp. 235–7.

219. Vol. III, 1812, pp. 469–70.

220. His first appearance with the Drury Lane company (then playing at the Lyceum) on June 22nd, 1812, was as Sangrida in *One o'clock*.

221. See also Cumberland's *British Theatre*, Vol. XXIX, No. 211.

222. Printed and published by J Redington, and then by Mr. Benjamin Pollock. *Timour the Tartar* has 8 Plates Characters, 8 Scenes, 3 Wings.

223. In a recent edition of *Tamberlain the Great*, 1930, Miss K. M. Ellis-Fermor makes no reference to *Timour the Tartar*, which certainly should have been mentioned. Miss Fermor also omits to record the early *Tamar Cam*.

224. 4to, 1681.

225. *Flying Post*, January 6th, 1702 ; *London Gazette*, January 26th, 1702.

226. *The Biographia Dramatica*, 1812, Vol. III, p. 465, remarks : " We always considered the violent opposition raised against the introduction of real horses on the stage as being, in some degree, the effect of prejudice more than of sound judgement . . . it is surely better to exhibit real horses than wooden puppets ; as living machinery is preferable to inanimate ; and fine well-trained animals to wicker-work and pasteboard."

227. First acted July 2nd, 1768, at the Haymarket. 8vo, 1778. The play was revived for Dowton's benefit at the Haymarket, August 15th, 1805, when a " Tailors' Riot " took place. Thomas Gilliland, *The Dramatic Mirror*, 1808, Vol. I, pp. 154–5, and R. B. Peake, *Memoirs of the Colman Family*, 1841, Vol. II, p. 309.

228. Originally printed in *The Anti-Jacobin : or, Weekly Examiner*, 1798. Nos. 30 and 31.

229. One is reminded of the battle in *The Rehearsal*, Act V, when " *A battel is fought between foot and great Hobby horses.*" *The Rehearsal*, ed. by Montague Summers, 1914, p. 69.

230. Byron hated horses on the stage. See *The Works of Lord Byron ; Letters and Journals*, ed. R. W. Prothero (Second Impression), 1903, Vol. II, pp. 156–8.

231. S. M. Ellis, *Michael Kelly*, p. 251, where Kelly's own statement is quoted.

232. Pliny, *Historia Naturalis*, XXX, ii, says of magic : " Sine dubio illic orta in Perside a Zoroastre, ut inter auctores convenit." See Montague Summers, *The Geography of Witchcraft*, 1927, pp. 4, 5, 35, 38.

233. There is a highly sensational *The Tragedy of Zoroastres* (unacted and unprinted), by the Earl of Orrery (1621–79), which was first noticed and described in my article, " Orrery's ' The Tragedy of Zoroastres,' " *Modern Language Review*, Vol. xii, No. 1, January, 1917, pp. 24–32. See *The Restoration Theatre* (1934), by Montague Summers, pp. 198, 250, 293. W. T. Moncrieff has a " Grand Melo-dramatic Tale of Enchantment," *Zoroaster ; or The Spirit of the Star*, produced at Drury Lane, Monday, April 19th, 1824, and printed twice, 8vo, that year.

234. 1790–1882.

235. Originally named " The Banks of Shannon Water." C. Z. Barnett has a play, *The Banks of Allan Water ; or the Death of Fair Eleanor*. Royal Pavilion, Mile End, Monday, July 25th, 1831.

236. 1786–1849.

237. In some reprints of *The Journal* this piece, *The Isle of Devils*, has unfortunately been omitted from the text. " *The Isle of Devils*, ' A Historical Tale, Founded on an Anecdote in the Annals of Portugal,' *A Faithful Reprint of the Rare Edition privately printed at Jamaica in* 1827," was issued (large and small paper) in 1912. It was stated that the poem was written by Lewis in 1817 on his last voyage to the West Indies, and that a few copies from the original manuscript were struck off at the *Advertiser* Office, Kingston, Jamaica, for certain friends in 1827. It was from one of these the 1912 reprint was done.

238. Vol. II, pp. 107–18.

239. Pp. 201–8.

CHAPTER VI

FRANCIS LATHOM ; T. J. HORSLEY CURTIES ; WILLIAM HENRY IRELAND ;
AND OTHERS

" Nothing is allowed to please generally which does not excite surprise or horror;
the simple walks of nature and probability are now despised. . . . In the relation of this
story I have endeavoured to enlist in my service those powerful assistants—novelty and
mystery."

FRANCIS LATHOM, Preface to *Mystery*, 1800.

" Trusting that of the numerous novel readers of the present day, an equal proportion
at least still retains a relish for what is natural and consistent, I feel no hesitation in quitting
the gloomy and terrific tracks of a Radcliffe for the more lively walks of a Burney or a
Robinson."

FRANCIS LATHOM, Preface to *Human Beings*, 1807.

IN many ways Francis Lathom is one of the most interesting and one
of the most typical secondary figures among the whole school of the
Gothic novelists. The illegitimate son of an English peer, he was
born at Norwich in 1777, the year of the publication of Clara Reeve's
The Champion of Virtue, and only twelve years after *The Castle of
Otranto* had first come forth in masquerade " From the Original Italian
of Onuphrio Muralto " to set the fashion in all that was eerie,
glamorous, and baroque.

In common with many other juvenals throughout the ages, young
Lathom burned with a Thespian flame, and, as is the wont in such
cases, he early penned a five-act comedy, *All in a Bustle*, which was
produced at the Norwich Theatre, 1795, and printed there, 8vo, the
same year. It even achieved the honours of a second edition, London,
1800. This light and farcical piece, which was well liked, does not,
however, seem to have ventured its fortune either at one of the London
theatres or outside the provincial circuit of the author.

All in a Bustle is a lively enough play of the school of Colman
junior, Holcroft, Mrs. Griffith, and Hannah Cowley. A hint or two
would appear to be due to *The Beaux Stratagem*, and a trifling conveyance from *The Good-Natured Man* may also be detected. The characters
of Miss Aspin, a blue-stocking Rachael Wardle, and the jack of all
trades, Smatter, are by no means badly conceived, and there is some
humour in the scene of Mrs. Palmer, a modern Mother Shipton,

and the clients she is so easily persuaded to chouse. Dame Gibbs with her colt's tooth, who was perhaps suggested by Abigail in *The Scornful Lady*, makes all too brief an appearance, for we feel that some promising material has been wasted here. The dialogue, if not brilliantly witty, is at least brisk and easy, and the action never flags. Many a worse comedy than this has been applauded in the theatre, and I have little doubt that faults which are very plain in the library would upon the stage appear but as slight blemishes and defects.

It should be remarked that even before *All in a Bustle* was given Lathom had commenced author with a romance, *The Castle of Ollada*, which was first issued, in two volumes, in 1794, and ran into a second edition, 2 vols., 12mo, London, 1799. It will be remembered that 1794 was the year of *The Mysteries of Udolpho*. Lathom was at least happy in his choice of a title for his maiden romance effort. *Castle*, as we have remarked before, was a word of power, and it was almost impossible that a romance bearing this magic name in its title should not succeed in the circulating libraries. Lathom scored heavily with his *Castle of Ollada*.

The critics even recognized merit. *The Critical Review*,[1] however, lived up to its old tradition, exclaiming : " Another haunted castle ! Surely the misses themselves must be tired of so many stories of ghosts, and murders,—though to the misses the ghosts of this novel present perhaps the most harmless part of the dramatis personæ. The heroine who could basely elope from her father's house with a young peasant whom she had only twice seen, and to whom she had scarcely ever spoken, is a personage of a far more pernicious nature. Although the heroine of a romance is always sure to know ' the true baron *upon instinct*,' young ladies cannot be recommended implicitly to follow such example."

The Monthly Review [2] October, 1795, was more genial in its appreciation. The writer remarked : " The writer appears to have a fancy plentifully stored, from former romances, with images of love and terror, and a memory not ill furnished with the terms and phrases which belong to this school of fiction. The story, which is laid in Spain, tells of a beauteous damsel, the daughter of a haughty and cruel baron, whose charms enamor Henrico, a peasant of mysterious descent. Their moonlight interviews within a friendly grove ; the hero's encounter in a well-described tournament with a wealthy duke to whom his mistress has been devoted ; with sundry miscellaneous escapes and rescues ; are in the true style of romance. Some of the inferior characters are well sketched, particularly that of the simple, credulous, prating Villetta, Matilda's waiting-woman."

In order to gratify the fashionable taste Lathom introduced a story of a castle supposed to be haunted by ghosts, but at length discovered to be inhabited by a set of coiners. " The introduction of these incidents has increased the intricacy of the general story, and has obliged the writer to spend a great part of the second volume in explaining mysteries, which after all are not very clearly unfolded, when he ought to have been interesting the feelings of his readers in the fortune of his principal characters."

His second romance has an even better title, for nobody can deny that there is something strangely fascinating about *The Midnight Bell*. It were to be wished, perhaps, that this sombre tocsin rang a little sooner than we actually hear it, but be that as it may, the book is, I think, a first-rate specimen of its kind, the " German Story," which might, or might not, have a Teutonic original. Count Cohenburg, Frederic, Anna, Baron Kardsfelt, Kroonzer, Smaldart Castle and the rest are obviously chosen because they have a German sound, but the inevitable Italian nomenclature Arieno, Bartini, Stefano, Camilla, does not, to my mind, ring quite true, and the German colour, than which nothing in its day was more relentlessly exploited and overworked, seems veriest peter and rouge. I have not been able to trace the original—if original there be—of the narrative, but this is nothing, so vast are the fields of German romance, yet I am inclined to suppose that Lathom should enjoy the full credit of the tale. The romance, " Founded on Incidents in Real Life, 3 vols., 1798, ' Printed for H. D. Symonds,' " was certainly very much to the taste of the day as a second edition was called for in 1825, and as early as 1799, the year after publication, it was translated into French and published, three volumes, 16mo, Paris. It has been said that there exists an English edition of 1800, but this I have not seen, and, although such may be the case, I am inclined to suspect an error, since the reprint of 1825, A. K. Newman and Co., Leadenhall Street, definitely bears the inscription " The Second Edition."

The Midnight Bell in itself is an important novel, and is especially famous as entering into the Northanger canon.

" Count Cohenburg was descended from one of the noblest houses in Saxony, his castle situated on a branch of the river Elbe, was one of the most magnificent in the German Empire." The Count has two sons ; Alphonsus, the elder, is twenty-six, Frederic, the younger, is nineteen. Alphonsus, who upon his father's death inherits the title and estates, marries, and his lady bears a son, named after his father. This youth, who is the hero of the tale, is remarkably handsome, and his charming person is described in some detail ; moreover, " his intellects were strong, his genius discerning, and his mind well informed." Alphonsus *père* unhappily, but quite unjustly, suspects that Frederic may love his wife, Anna, and even that this love is not unrequited. Whilst Count Alphonsus is returning home from a far journey he is assassinated, the news being brought that his body, covered with wounds, was found in the Wolf's Wood.

That night, whilst the young Count is lying awake in sorrow, his mother, in distracted guise and clasping a bloody dagger, enters his room, and bids him fly for his very life. Awed by her mysterious warning, he departs. The castle is deserted, whilst popular rumour has it that his mother has killed her son, and " directly after a ghost began to walk, and every night at twelve o'clock it tolls the great bell in the south turret, because that is the time she killed the young count."

After various adventures, Alphonsus becomes sacristan at the Convent of Saint Helena, " a large and ancient edifice ; its ivy-grown towers indicated its antiquity, and the figures carved on the walls bespoke the superstition they enclosed." Father Matthias gives Alphonsus an MS. written by a young novice, Lauretta, with whom he promptly falls in love. They are united by the obliging priest, and retire to live idyllically in a small cottage near Inspruck. Next Lauretta is abducted by two ruffians, Ralberg and the surly Kroonzer, in the pay of Theodore, the licentious nephew of Baron Smaldart. By an extraordinary event Ralberg proves to be none other than Count Byroff the father of Lauretta, so the situation is saved, and she is restored to her husband. Years before Byroff has been confined in the Bastile, through a *lettre de cachet*. Here he was tortured and condemned to death, but he contrives to escape, much after the fashion of Edmond Dantès.

Alphonsus now resolves to find out the mystery of the castle, his paternal inheritance. Eventually it is discovered that his father, Count Alphonsus had bound his brother, Frederic by a fearful oath to carry out a certain behest, and then had required him to tempt his wife, the Lady Anna by making love to her in order that he may prove her fidelity. However unwilling, Frederic, bound by his pledge, does this so effectually that the lady takes him to be a monster of profligacy and incest. The murder of the Count in the Wolf's Wood is a trick he himself devised, and returning secretly he enters his wife's bedchamber thinking that she will suppose him Frederic, whom he is persuaded she loves, and thus will infallibly betray herself. The virtuous Anna does indeed suppose that the midnight intruder is Frederic, and she drives a dagger to his heart. When she discovers that it is her husband she goes mad and rushes to her son's room with the result that on account of her horrible ravings he becomes an exile from the castle.

PLATE XIII

Il lui glissa sa Lettre dans la main,
sans avoir été apperçu.

.THE MIDNIGHT BELL
Frontispiece, Vol. I, French edition, 1799

[Face p. 312

Frederic at once retires to the monastery of Saint Paul. The mad-woman lurks all alone in the deserted castle, and as Father Nicholas explains, the Midnight Bell " was tolled by her for the double purpose of keeping idle visitants from the castle under the idea of its being haunted and to call to her two holy men of our monastery, who by turns together with myself, visited her every night to assist her prayers over the body of her husband." She now immures herself " in the convent of the Virgin Maria," whose nuns are dead to the world, so that Count Alphonsus and his Lauretta are able to establish themselves in his own fair castle of Cohenburg.

The Monthly Mirror, July, 1798 (Vol. VI, pp. 34–35), thus noticed The Midnight Bell : " To readers of a certain description this specimen of the gloomy and the horrific will be no unacceptable present," for " it is as full of mystery, suspicion, and murder, and the other alarming ingredients of modern romance, as the most ardent admirer of such compositions can wish. Yet it is a good tale, well told."

Young as he was, scarce turned twenty-one, Lathom had been for some years a most useful member of the Norwich stock company, and Norwich was still to a large extent as le sieur Chappazeau [3] had seen it in the days of Charles II, " l'une des bonnes Villes du Royaume, et le seiour de toute la Noblesse du Pays." Thus when Orlando and Seraphina ; or, The Funeral Pile (in some editions Funeral Pyre), an Heroic Drama was given at Norwich in 1799, and printed there 12mo, no date, but presumably the same year, it was received with great applause. There is also an edition, 8vo, London, 1800, which was re-issued in 1803. The story of the play is taken from Canto II of Tasso's Gerusalemme Liberata, and not only at Norwich but throughout provincial circuits generally this drama was received with considerable favour.

The Dash of the Day, a comedy in five acts, produced at Norwich on July 25th, 1800, proved very successful and ran into no less than three editions, two of which are 8vo, Norwich, that same year. The third edition, Dublin, 8vo, 1801, announces " As Perform'd with Universal Applause by His Majesty's Servants of the Theatre-Royal, Norwich." In a prefatory address Lathom thanks both the performers and the acting-manager : " And to the Public he stands indebted for the very flattering reception of a Play which was written before he had completed his eighteenth year." The scene is London, and the characters are : Sir Gabriel Hardyne (Lindoe) ; Sir Frederick Floricourt (Dwyer) ; Fretquil (Blanchard) ; Sedley (Wheatley) ; Henry Maitland (Mallinson) ; Modish (Browne) ; Simon (Mildenhall) ; Thomas (Beachem) ; Mrs. Fretquil (Mrs. Henley) ; Mrs Sedley (Mrs. Worthington) ; Harriot

(Mrs. Taylor) ; Emma (Miss Goddard) ; Mrs. Jenkins (Mrs. Powell).

Sir Frederick Floricourt, the nephew of Sir Gabriel, has dubbed himself knight, changed his name Hardyne to the fashionable Floricourt, and sets up for a man of rank and fashion. On account of her father's money-bags he is a dashing suitor to Harriot, the daughter of a broker, East of Temple Bar, one Mr. Fretquil. Her mother, a vulgar and strident worshipper of the *ton*, is all for driving on the match. Harriot, however, and Mr. Fretquil, spread the tale that her fortune is gone, whereupon Sir Frederick's ardours pretty soon cool and he offers his hand to Emma, .Fretquil's niece from the country, a completely cunning hoyden who feigns to have a plum of her own. Thus Harriot is enabled to wed her true lover Henry Maitland, who proves to be the nephew of Sir Gabriel. With these incidents are combined the sentimental but highly interesting episodes of the misfortunes of Clara Sedley, the good Sir Gabriel's niece. Mrs. Sedley has taken rooms with Mrs. Jenkins who is little other than a bawd of the Mother Needham and Mrs. Cole school. Old Fretquil privily visits her and soon attempts the most intimate familiarities, which do not go unpunished in the end. The characters of Mrs. Fretquil and Mrs. Jenkins are drawn with rich strokes of humour, and at the same time as we laugh at these pursy old women, Lathom does not allow us to forget their malice and baseness. *The Dash of the Day* is an admirable comedy with an unexceptionable moral.

Curiosity, a comedy in three acts, adapted by Lathom from the *Théâtre* of Madame de Genlis, was acted at Norwich on November 18th 1800, and printed there 8vo, 1801. (This play of Madame de Genlis was very popular, as it was translated into Italian, *La Curiosa*, by Elisabetta Caminer Turra, Tomo XVII, *Teatro moderno applaudito*, Venice 8vo, 1797.) Donna Isabella has three children, Frederick, Sophia, and Pauline. Her son has fought a duel with Antonio, the son of Don Sebastian ; both were wounded, and each believes he has killed his antagonist. Actually Frederick is concealed in his mother's castle, a secret known to the prudent Sophia and her cousin Constantia, who loves Frederick, but kept from the indiscreet Pauline. This young lady, however, who is as communicative as she is curious, is not merely all agog to unfathom the mystery, but even stoops with the aid of Rose, a servant, to open a letter addressed to Sophia. She then blabs out to Don Sebastian that there is lying perdu in the castle the Count di Parma, a name Frederick has assumed. The shrewd old fellow sends for an alquazil, and Paulina learns she has endangered her brother's life. The alquazil seizes a cloaked and muffled person, who proves to be Antonio, so that all difficulties are at an end. Frederick weds

Constantia; and Antonio Sophia. Genest [4] well remarks: "This is a good piece—considerably better than Madame Genlis—the moral is excellent—an idle curiosity is not so venial a fault as some persons imagine."

Holiday Time; or, The Schoolboy's Frolic, a farce, which was produced at Norwich, April 10th, 1801, and had been printed there, 8vo, 1800, was given at Drury Lane on October 20th, 1804, with some slight alterations and music by Reeve, as *The Dash; or, Who but He?* with the following cast: Jack Squirrel, Miss De Camp; Old Dubbs, Matthews; Morgan O'Mallawack, Johnstone; Hoddy Doddy, Collins; Miss Matilda Clementina Octavia Dubbs, sister to Dubbs, Miss Pope; and Lucy, Mrs. Mountain. Dubbs is a schoolmaster, and his daughter Lucy is in love with Jack Squirrel who is still at school. Jack Squirrel plays amusing pranks passing himself off on Dubbs first as an usher, and then as my Lady Dash. In the second act he persuades Miss Matilda Dubbs that he is an ancient critic, whereupon she reads him part of a play she has written. Jack and Lucy rehearse various scenes in the course of which with the full consent of Miss Dubbs he carries off Lucy. "This musical Farce," says Genest,[5] "was damned." It was also given during the autumn season, 1804, as *The Denouement*. Lathom, possibly, had little or nothing to do with the rehandling of the play, which may well have owed its want of success in London to the circumstance of an actress appearing in a boy's rôle. The *Biographia Dramatica* [6] sourly remarked that *The Dash; or, Who but He* is "a frivolous and uninteresting plagiarism from beginning to end," which is extremely harsh. A mere farce is not intended for the library, and on the boards with a young actor as Jack Squirrel, these scenes should surely prove not altogether unamusing.

The Wife of a Million, given at Norwich, March 3rd, 1803, was printed there 12mo the same year. It is a sprightly five-act comedy, and although Lathom may echo several other plays he certainly manages to do so in a very agreeable and amusing manner. There was a second edition of this piece 8vo, 1803. For some years it remained in the repertories of the circuit companies, and the judgement of Mr. Stephen Jones, if somewhat terse and dry, is perhaps sufficient. "The morality of this piece is unexceptionable; it affords some good situations, and contains just sentiments, generally well expressed; of novelty, however, it does not partake much; nor do we know what success it had, when acted by *His Majesty's Servants of the Theatres Royal, Norwich, Lincoln, and Canterbury*." [7]

In 1799 Lathom published *Men and Manners*, 4 volumes, 12mo, printed for J. Wright and H. D. Symonds, which attained a second edition in the following year, and proved so exceedingly popular that subsequently it ran into at least two editions more. This novel of contemporary satire is certainly a work for which scarcely any praise could be deemed excessive in its kind, and in its own day it must have proved irrestibly piquant and pointed, since even now, a century and a half after, it can be read with real interest and amusement even by those who generally are not attracted by old novels. Whether one prefers Lathom's social novels or whether one is more devoted to his Gothic romances must, of course, entirely depend upon the taste and temperament of the individual reader. At any rate, it can safely be said that he was excellent in both kinds. For all their melodrama, their artificiality, their absurdity, if you will, nay, rather on account of these very things, the Convents and Castles with their mysterious murders and subterranean secrets will always have for many an intenser fascination than the light laughter of Momus, which so thins and cracks as it grows older and older yet. Not, indeed, that this can be held to apply to *Men and Manners*, the pages of which are delightfully fresh and unfaded, and were it not for an allusion here—to the allemands, to a dash or a beau—or a scene in the theatre lobby or at a masquerade, it might well be a picture of contemporary life. The characters are the same, only the dress is changed.

Lathom's next novel had the enticing title *Mystery*, and fully lives up to its name. It was issued in two volumes, 12mo, in 1800, by H. D. Symonds at 4s., and was exceedingly well received, being shortly translated both into French and German. Lathom certainly had the art of capturing and holding his readers' attention, whether he was writing of German barons, of Italian bandits, or of contemporary English life.

It may be convenient here before completing our review of the works of this very varied and prolific author to conclude a short sketch of his life, which about the years 1802–03 divided itself, as it were, into a new part. At this time Francis Lathom, who was then only five and twenty years old, left Norwich. Details are lacking, and a good deal can only remain conjecture and surmise. The secret is that Lathom was of a homosexual temperament, and it is supposed that there had come into his life some person—in Shakespeare's phrase— " Lord of my love, to whom in vassalage " he gave " all the all of me." That his affection was reciprocated, and that he found happiness may be reasonably supposed, and it is to be believed that his friend accompanied him to his new residence.

Lathom had gained far more than the laurels of a local fame, an applause which might be suspected of partiality and interest. Not only as an actor, as a dramatist, but in the regions of romance he had won recognition, even celebrity, and it might have been supposed that this surprising person would have taken up his headquarters in London. Such was far from the case. He retired to Inveruric, where he lodged with a Scotch bailie, a municipal magistrate. Thence he removed to Bogdavic, a comfortable and commodious farm-house in Fyvie, Aberdeenshire, belonging to a shrewd Pict, one Alexander Rennie, who made it his business to study his lodger's every fad and crochet, and so became indispensible to the clever fantast. Here Lathom, who was always liberally provided with funds, developed many eccentricities. He was accustomed to dress " like a play actor," as the country folk said. It was not unnaturally a matter for surprise that in farthest Caledonia a gentleman should regularly read the London newspapers and be all agog for dramatic gossip, discussing the performances at Drury Lane or Covent Garden with rustics whose ideas of matters Thespian cannot but have been of the vaguest, and who would have shuddered at the mere thought of setting one foot within the doors of a theatre. However, so long as there was somebody to whom he could retail his quips and whimsies, Lathom seems to have been perfectly contented, and I think that in his Northern home he led a very happy life. He certainly acquired a taste for Scotch whisky, which he drank, no doubt, a little too freely and a little too often, but I suppose there was no very great harm done, and surely he was not different from any of the neighbouring cottars, or from the fine gentlemen of S. James', if it comes to that. Round the fireside he used to entertain the company with songs of his own composition, but there can be no doubt that apart from his loved comradeship his chief interests in life concentrated upon his novels. Owing to his long solitary walks he was a well-known figure throughout the whole district, where he went by the name of " Mr. Francis," or " Boggie's Lord," from the name of Rennie's farmstead. It was commonly noised that he had great wealth, and it is said that in some of his lonely excursions he ran the risk of being kidnapped to one of the manses, so anxious were they to secure such a profitable and entertaining guest. Occasionally Lathom travelled. He visited France and perhaps Italy, whilst the whole spring of 1828 he was in America, and stayed at Philadelphia. During the latter years of his life he resided with Rennie at Milnfield Farm in the parish of Monquhitter, where he died suddenly on May 19th, 1832. He was buried in Rennie's plot in the churchyard at Fyvie.

The first fiction that Lathom published after his retirement from Norwich was *Astonishment*! ! ! " a romance of a century ago," two volumes, 12mo, London, 1802. The work which followed is extremely interesting. It consists of the translation of a French narrative detailing the metamorphosis which the Tuileries underwent at the hands of the Jacobins.

The Castle of the Tuileries : " Or, A Narrative of All the Events which have taken place in the Interior of that Palace, from the Time of its Construction to the Eighteenth Brumaire of the Year VIII. Translated from the French by Francis Lathom," two volumes, London (Longman and Rees, Paternoster Row), 1803, is a spirited version of *Le Château des Tuileries, ou Récit de ce qui s'est passé dans l'interieur de ce palais depuis sa construction jusqu'au 18 brumaire*, 2 vols., 8vo, Paris, 1802, the work of Pierre-Joseph-Alexis Roussel, a fairly prolific political writer, who was born at Épinal in 1759, and died at Paris, June 10th, 1815. Lathom has done his part with elegance and vigour. He has an interesting note, Vol. I, p. 116 : " I know no English word which exactly corresponds with Roue, the nearest definition I am able to give of it is what we call a *blood*."

In 1803 we have two novels, *Very Strange but Very True*, 4 vols., 12mo, and *Ernestine*, " a tale from the French," 2 vols., 12mo. Both are good of their kind, and they serve to show Lathom's facile talent in turning almost any material to excellent account. A far better book, however, than either, is *The Impenetrable Secret, Find it Out*, 2 vols., Lane, 12mo, 1805 ; the second edition, 2 vols., 1831. To this work *The Critical Review*,[8] gives just and discriminating praise : " The story is constructed on so artful a plan, that none of the agents are left for an instant unemployed ; the events are proceeded in every quarter at once, and the interest is divided indeed, but never weakened. From the opening of the story to the discovery of the secret, our curiosity increases ; though we cannot attribute to curiosity alone a sensation which seems as closely allied to sympathy as to astonishment. The explanatory statements that follow the chief development are all satisfactory and probable." *The British Critic* of the same date, December, 1805, is equally laudatory : " We seldom remember to have met with a tale possessing so much to catch the feelings and improve the heart. The adventitious aids of declamatory dialogue and second-hand sentiments, he carefully avoids." Further, *The Monthly Mirror* adds its meed of praise : " Among the many few of our modern novels that possess anything to make amends for the labour of perusal, we are happy to class the production before us. A powerful interest is excited from the beginning. Curiosity is kept alive to the conclusion of the book. The events are romantic, but natural."

The Impenetrable Secret ; *Find It Out* ! introduces us in the first decade of the eighteenth century to the family of a Genoese merchant,

Rossano del Alvaretti ; one who places the chief value upon money and rank. His daughter Hyppolita, who is of her father's mind, he has married to a noble of the Republic, the Marchese di Bivelli. His wife, the Signora Felicia del Alvaretti, prefers the retirement of a country house, where she resides with their blind son, Felix, and Averilla, the orphan daughter of Rossano's brother Eugenio. By chance Averilla meets a young paragon, Sylvio di Rosalva, a most elegant and fascinating youth of nineteen, " in fact, Sylvio was one of those beings who are a rare instance of perfection in humanity." and Averilla is soon deeply in love with Sylvio, but Signor Rossano announces that he designs his niece for the Comte Lorenzo della Picca, a noble of immense fortune. Although Sylvio vows his passion for Averilla some mystery seems to cloud him, and he goes so far as to declare in a billet that he *never was her lover*. There can be no obstacle then to her union with Lorenzo della Picca, and indeed it is reported that Sylvio is paying his addresses to another lady, Virgilia della Bagua. The nuptials of Lorenzo and Averilla are celebrated with great splendour, and in due course they take up their residence in the Conte's palazzo at Turin.

In the passage of months Lorenzo, who is a devoted husband, confesses to his wife that he has a natural daughter, aged about eight, whose mother died at her birth. Averilla welcomes the little Flavia as an inmate of their house. The little girl, accidentally falling into the river, is rescued by Sylvio di Rosalva, who is presently proceeded against by Rodovina Martinos for reparation to be made to her daughter Vitellia, a minor, a breach of promise. In full court Sylvio relates how he has been beguiled and brought to sign the paper. Believing that he was courting the lady Lucia Eldorado, he is trapped by a courtezan, Vitellia. The case falls completely to the ground when it is found that at the time Sylvio's promise was given, Vitellia was actually wedded to an old reprobate Henrico Eldorado, a wealthy but lewd merchant, since deceased. Certain mysterious circumstances, more-over, lead to the arrest of Rodovina on a charge of poisoning her daughter's husband.

A number of intricate incidents now begin to involve the story, not the least puzzling of which appears to be that Sylvio di Rosalva is seen at numerically the same moment in two different places by separate persons. The Conte della Picca has met him driving in the suburbs, whilst the Contessa was entertaining him at dinner. Moreover, at the dinner he has seemed strange in his manner, and when the Contessa ventures to remind him of the secret he entrusted to her, namely, that he *was a woman*, Sylvio abruptly leaves her in high dudgeon. It is now clear that when Sylvio di Rosalva was supposed to be on the point of declaring his love for Averilla he in truth wished to disclose his secret to her, which he ultimately revealed under a vow of secrecy. That evening Sylvio di Rosalvo is attacked by bravoes and left wounded in the piazza whence he is carried into the palazzo. The chirurgeon Sorato discovers that Sylvio is a woman, and duly informs the Conte. The whole mystery is revealed when Sylvio di Rosalvo presents himself the next morning at the palazzo and it is revealed that actually the wo Sylvios are twins, exactly resembling one another, a boy and a girl. It is perhaps hardly necessary to detail the long and somewhat complicated history which is now unravelled, incidents wherein Rodovina Maritos has played a very considerable and very evil part. Sufficient to say that Rodovina Maritos by a cunning scheme many years before has stolen away the heir, Sylvio, whereupon the distracted Signor di Rosalva resolved to bring up his baby daughter Rosabella, as a boy, since the estate can only descend to a son.

When the wretched Rodovina Maritos is brought to trial for the murder of the merchant Eldorado, by a series of accidents, the villain Iago Zinati, who supplied her with aqua tofana, has been traced and is involved in her doom. Both perish on the scaffold. The execution is very powerfully described.

Rosabella is united to Felix del Alvaretti, whose sight is restored by a skilful operation, and Sylvio receives the hand of Virgilia della Bagua.

Personally, I find *The Mysterious Freebooter, or, The Days of Queen Bess*, which Lane issued, 4 vols., 12mo, in 1806, even more to my liking. It was well received by the critics, who often were extremely apt to sneer at and mock the obvious faults of the Gothic novelist. *The Monthly Mirror* for May, 1806, highly praises Lathom's work : " This Tale is a pleasing exception to the general opinion of critics that all novels are nonsense. If the development of interesting situations, or the inculcation of honest and honourable morality be nonsense ; if nonsense consists in the display of a lively conception, and the investigation of the human mind be nonsense ; then, indeed, the Novel before us is entitled to the name of nonsense. But if the lesson of example can instruct our understandings, or the administration of poetical justice correct our hearts, *The Mysterious Freebooter* will be read with satisfaction by a considerable portion of the public. It has already been thrown into a pantomime ballet by the proprietors of the Circus ; and we doubt not it will be as great a favourite in the closet, as it is upon the stage." Even higher praise was given by the *Annual Review* : " The author of *Men and Manners* is no inferior novelist :

nothing ought more to surprise than his unrivalled fertility : few authors have written so much who repeat themselves so little : this is the privilege of those who draw less from precedent than imagination ; who study books little and nature much. Of the plan of a romance full of incident, it would be laborious to give the story in epitome ; and would increase the reviewer's trouble only to decrease the reader's gratification. Suffice it to say, that terrorism is the predominant impression ; that this is a production of the Radcliffe school, and perhaps the best domestic imitation which has yet appeared ; and that it is full of interest, of invention, and of eloquence."

The Critical Review [9] now joins in the chorus of praise :

" Stimulated, we presume, by the applause which he obtained for his ' Impenetrable Secret,' which appeared some months ago, Mr. Lathom has speedily recovered the elasticity of his mind and returned to the charge in an ancient romance ; and a spirited charge it must be confessed to be ; for, when he fails to command our approbation, he generally seizes our attention. He has faults which we cannot but loudly condemn, yet he has merits which induce us to read. His plot is various, and not complicated ; the incidents that compose it are generally natural and simple." The reviewer regards the length of the romance as a fault, and censures some inelegancies of style. Yet he allows : " Our author has certainly the principal art of a novel writer, the knack of exciting interest " ; moreover he concludes very frankly " when we had finished the work, we forgot our displeasure at the errors of the composition, in our regret that the story was concluded."

It is curious that Lathom did not follow up The Mysterious Free-booter with a work in the same vein. His next novel, Human Beings, 3 vols., 12mo, Crosby, 1807, rather looks back to Men and Manners for its treatment and its theme. The Critical Review [10] candidly enough observed that " This novel bears very few marks of the genius which dictated Men and Manners. . . . The incident respecting the £500 note, we remember to have read in the newspapers about two years ago, which indeed seem to be the main source from whence the author has derived his whole knowledge of ' human beings.' "

In the same year, 1807, Lathom issued The Fatal Vow ; or, St. Michael's Monastery, 2 vols., Crosby, a Gothico-historical romance, which has been examined at length in a previous chapter [11] and therefore need not detain us here. There followed in 1808 The Unknown, or, The Northern Gallery, 2 vols. ; second edition, 4 vols., A. K. Newman, 1828 ; a fine romance.

1809 was a busy twelvemonth as Lathom published *London, or Truth without Treason*, 4 vols., 12mo, and *The Romance of the Hebrides, or, Wonders Never Cease*, in three volumes.

An interval of eleven years elapsed before the appearance of Lathom's next work. There was no need for him, as in the case of many other novelists, Mrs. Parsons and Mrs. Kelly, for example, " to write for bread " as Aphra Behn once phrased it, adding that such was her lot and she was " not ashamed to own it." He was in comfortable, very comfortable, circumstances. (It is believed that his father had settled a large sum upon his love-child son.) Save when he was on his travels he led a retired life in a circumscribed sphere, the petty businesses of which interested him greatly, and he had no temptation and no desire to widen or increase his ambit. He enjoyed the comradeship that meant all in all to him. His literary ambitions were amply satisfied. Time slipped by, and one day he woke up with surprise to the fact that a whole decade had flown.

Italian Mysteries, or, More Secrets than One, was published in three volumes, 12mo, 1820, A. K. Newman. The public were glad to welcome back their old favourite ; his new entrance into the literary arena was greeted with applause, and his new romance proved sufficiently popular to be translated into French by Jules Saladin, 4 vols., Paris, 1823.

In 1820 also Lathom issued *The One Pound Note and other Tales*, two volumes. The next year followed *Puzzled and Pleased, or, The Two Old Soldiers and other Tales*, three volumes.

His next piece was far more elaborate and far more carefully written. *Live and Learn ; or, The First John Brown, His Friends, Enemies, and Acquaintance in Town and Country*, a novel in four volumes, Newman, 1823, opens with the reading of the will of Mr. Oliver Clarington, Ashbank Hall, Oldham, Lincoln, recently deceased. This gentleman's sister had married a Scotch baronet, Sir Robert Brockelsbie of Dumfriesshire, but of this relation he had heard nothing for many years. Equally unknown to him is a nephew. The reading of the will is attended by Sir Malcolm Brockelsbie, the present representative of this house, and a coxcomb of the first water, who is betrayed into a fierce rage on learning he is left £500, whilst the residuary legatee, and the sole heir of all the estates, real and personal, is " the first John Brown who shall claim them." (In " A Few Words to Begin With " addressed to the " Courteous Reader," Lathom tells us that he actually knew of such an extraordinary will.) Scarcely has the lawyer read the words than a young man, of an arch and expressive countenance, forces his way through the crowd with " My name is John Brown, sir and I claim them." John Brown, then, the schoolmaster's assistant in the village, without kith or kin, is the owner of Ashbank Hall and £3,000 a year. There are conditions, however, attached. He is not to come into full possession until he is twenty-five, and if under that age he is not to marry until he reaches it. Meanwhile he is to receive £1,000 a year, and the Hall is to be his residence as he will. If before that age he contract a debt of more than £100 he forfeits all inheritance which passes to the nearest male relative of Mr. Clarington who shall appear to claim it.

Upon the Sunday morning after Mr. Clarington's funeral whilst John Brown is still at the breakfast table there visits him the mysterious " White Man," whose long hair and beard of unflecked white fall over a white habit. He has known John Brown's parents, but will enter into no particulars save warning him to be cautious in the stewardship of his unexpected wealth. A troop of strolling players, kings of shreds and patches, come to the village and give several performances. John Brown forms a close affection for Theodore Cavendish (whose name off the stage is David Ferguson). Cavendish falls ill, and upon his recovery John Brown requests him to take the place of his companion and instructor, " and from that hour commenced the date of his residence at Ashbank Hall."

The two friends visit London, and lodge at the house of Mr. Titmus, " pastry-cook and confectioner in Oxford-street, a few doors from the Regent Circus." We have exceedingly lively pictures of London life, especially masquerades, the theatres and Astleys. Here we meet Sir Frederick Lambert, a dashing dog whom Ferguson recognizes as " the polygmatic " Harry Glara, umquhile the light comedian of the Edinburgh company and a complete rogue ; the Sir Julius Maberly ; Mother Mackinflore whose bagnio is " in Liquorish court, not a hundred miles from Vere-street chapel " ; Gilbert Slapp ; Sir Malcolm Brockelsbie, and other Tom and Jerry profligates with their demireps and toys. These London adventurers set in train a very large variety of incidents which Lathom has interwoven and reticulated with no common degree of skill and interest, but which might become confusing and confused if less adroitly wrought.

By representing that he has forged a bank-bill for ten thousand pounds which when taken up must bring him to ruin and death, Sir Malcolm Brockelsbie endeavours to persuade John Brown to lend him this sum. This, however, as John Brown represents, is entirely out of his power, although he offers to interest on behalf of the criminal those whose purse and influence will effectually come between him and the law. A young man who has rendered Brown an important service appearing to be plunged on that account in the greatest distress and with his sick wife and little children in completest destitution easily obtains a promissory note from Brown of a gift of two hundred pounds. Very shortly after it comes to light that the young man, William Roberts, is an impostor instructed by Sir Malcolm when the device to obtain ten thousand pounds failed. By giving this note John Brown has broken one of the clauses of the Clarington will, and the estate therefore will go to the nearest relative who shall appear to claim it. Messrs Briefwit and Slapp of the Minories appear for Sir Malcolm Brockelsbie. The case is heard at Westminster Hall, and technically the verdict is given against John Brown. His friends are already congratulating Sir Malcolm more swollen and insolent than ever in his hour of odious triumph, when there comes forward a new figure, who declares in the face of Sir Malcolm : " By a superior right I supersede his claim : I am the son of the deceased Mr. Clarington, and consequently his nearest relation." Mr. Oliver Clarington has not only witnesses, amongst whom is Sir Julius, but also all documentary evidence to prove his claim, which the Court at once admits to the hideous discomfiture of the villainous Brockelsbie and his confederates. Oliver Clarington is none other than the mysterious " White Man," and proves to be the father of John Brown, or rather Horace Clarington, who has thus been in possession of his grandfather's estate.

To add to the downfall of Sir Malcolm, it is revealed that his birth is spurious and the true representative of the house is Sir Angus Brockelsbie, the father of David Ferguson.

Horace Clarington is united to May, the daughter of Sir Julius, whom he has long loved.

" And now, having, according to the accepted custom of fabulists, from the days of Goody Two Shoes down to the present wonderful era, distinguished by the writings of the renowned Jedediah Cleeshbotham, awarded punishment to the bad, and recompence to the meritorious, we conclude with a sincere wish, that everyone who travels through the labyrinths of the world, may arrive at the end of his journey with as perfect a prospect of happiness as John Brown and his beloved May."

In *Live and Learn*, the humours of a village—Dr. Graveton, Lawyer Slapp, Parson Clack, Mr. Dickens the anatomist, are exceedingly well drawn. The gossip of the inn is extremely realistic. Excellent strokes distinguish the characters of Molly Burkitt (Mrs. Dickens) with her cousin from Lincoln, Miss Niobe Nettle, and the fashionable Miss Jemima Clack new returned " from a Lincoln seminary of the first eminence." The supper party is of the liveliest.

It is plain that Lathom was largely drawing upon his own Norwich experience, and he obviously had a particular person in view when he depicted Theodore Cavendish (David Ferguson), the young actor who is persecuted by the hateful Mrs. Mandover. Cavendish plays Norval, and although most discreetly treated, the love between him and John Brown is clearly uranian.

An earlier and a poorer Crummles, Mr. Gag, the strolling actor, is also to the life, as is the performance of *The Poor Gentleman* and *No Song, No Supper* at the Oldham theatre, *anglice*, a barn.

Mrs. Dickens is consumedly funny when at the end of Home's tragedy she peeps behind the curtain and sees " squire Douglass that had just been stuck with a *sword*, and pretendèd to die, jump upon his feet, and run away as nimble as a rat, as much alive as I am, Oh ! I hate such *flim-flummery make-believings* ! it has taken away all my pleasure, and I really don't think I shall go *no* more."

One book appeared from Lathom's pen in 1824, *The Polish Bandit, or, Who is my Bride ? and other Tales*, 3 vols., 12mo, Newman.

In his next novel, *Young John Bull ; or, Born Abroad and Bred at Home*, 3 vols., 1828 (Newman), Lathom remarks that he is " in a very slight degree, indebted to an old French tract, ascribed to Voltaire, but never published with his works, nor, I believe, acknowledged by him."

" Oh, how true," he cries, " is the aphorism which asserts, that he who endeavours to please a multitude, invariably pleases no one ; and that he who has the resolution to please himself, has, at least, the merit of maintaining, in his own person, the good opinion of one member of society ! "

As for novels : " The soldier exclaims aloud for war—the priest demands morality—the matron desires the volumes before her to contain matter equally interesting and instructive—my lady's woman wishes them to be entertaining and fashionable—Miss, in her teens, just broken loose from a French boarding-school, hopes to meet with a great deal of love, prays that the enamoured parties may be reduced to the very brink of misery and despair, and finally, exalted to the very acme of human felicity." Every child must have its whistle, and shallow or unfriendly is he " who does not admit the difficulty to which a poor author is reduced, when called upon to produce a whistle, which shall emit a sound pleasing to everyone who blows it."

He speaks of the favour shown by the public to his work with grateful acknowledgement. The Author's Address to the Reader is signed, Philadelphia, March 1st, 1828.

Young John Bull commences with a lively discussion between Mrs. Kitty Bloom, the housekeeper at Fancy Place, a pleasant villa about three miles from Sudbury, Suffolk, and Jerry Watkins, anent the mysterious visit of a French abbé to their master, Captain Beverley. To add to their wonder, the Captain contrives that Mrs. Beverley shall go off in her carriage to pay a twenty-four hour visit to my Lady Bellington, before she knows that the abbé is in the house. Captain Beverley met in a stage-coach and was smitten by Miss Lavinia Love, the niece of Mrs. Palmerstone, a lady living in strictest retirement at York. Lavinia, as Mrs. Palmerstone informs him in telling her niece's history very briefly, is an orphan, and was born at Lisbon. The enamoured Captain proves a warm wooer, and " the happy pair were in due time to be united in that holy bond of which the end is amazement."

Shortly after the mysterious visit Captain Beverley and his lady with their near neighbour and old friend Lady Bellington, spend some weeks at Cromer, where they meet a variety of company, some of whom such as Sir Felix O'Hara, Lady Bellington's uncle ; the philosophically abstracted Sir Elliott Tankerville, and Mr. Cornelius Syndercombe are sketched with a great deal of humour.

A little later, when Captain Beverley is the guest of Sir Elliott at Richmond, he is informed by his servant, Watkins, that the abbé, who paid a visit to Fancy Place, has been inquiring for him in the vicinity, whereupon he mysteriously and immediately leaves with the hastiest farewell to his host.

Sir Felix O'Hara and his niece, Lady Bellington, who are resident in Portman Square, London, now receive a communication from a nephew of Sir Felix, John Bull; and honest Sampson Binnacle, a very stagey old tar with much nautical lingo of "shiver my timbers," "Davy Jones' locker" and "the lubber scudded out of sight," enters the story. We also meet Matty Muffin, a Cockney sailor, who exclaims, "Vell, vell," and remarks : "Ven I vas a boy, I never could abide the barking of the great hugly bull-dogs as I vent through Newport Market ; and I have many a time trembled as if I had had a hague upon me, with the fear of being run over amongst the coaches and carts, and vat not, ven I has been in a hurry to cross over from Fleet-market to Blackfriar's-bridge," and further assures the company : " I vas reckoned a wery first-rate cook . . . what a nice wenison hash I could toss up for my poor dear missus " ; and who confesses he only took to the sea because " it vas a Hirish girl as I appened of a misforturn with, and ven I told mother of it, she vould not so much as give me a single farden to help me out of my difficulty ; but said as how I and my blowing—yes, she called her that, because she said as her breath always smelt of blue ruin—might go and beg for our babby."

John Bull is the son of Captain Edward Bull, an officer in the East Indian service, and the lovely Jemima Ridgeway. The adventures of Edward and Jemima, with their voyages on the good ship *Amphitrite*, the treachery of Fanville, the second in command, who falls in love with Jemima and seeks to cuckold Edward ; the wreck ; the birth of John on the African shore, for Jemima, disguised as a midshipman, has made her way on board unknown to her husband—are all related at great length in a style not even unworthy of Marryat himself. The castaways spend fifteen years upon the African coast before an English vessel rescues them. His father and mother dying whilst he is yet a babe, John Bull is brought up by Charles Evelyn, a midshipman, and the faithful old Barnacle.

Upon regaining England, John Bull meets his two uncles, Sir Felix and Mr. Hazleton, and is assigned as his tutor and bear-leader Mr. Diogenes Index, who with his eternal lexicon and his new definitions of words is very comic and very caustic to boot.

The time now arrives when the enigma of Captain Beverley's disappearance is cleared. Whilst a young officer at Ghent, he had contracted a secret marriage with the fair Antoinette Columbine, and had fled with her to England. They are found in London by the Abbé Delaville, Antoinette's uncle, who informs Beverley that Antoinette possesses an annuity of two thousand pounds, which he will pay year by year on April 16th, appointing a rendezvous at a certain inn at Harwich. By the attendance of Beverley annually he will know his niece is alive. Unhappily Antoinette dies in childbirth, the infant being still-born. Since Beverley has to take oath to the abbé that his wife is well and upon earth, with the assistance of one Yantly, his friend, he has the corpse cunningly embalmed and placed in a coffin with a glass let in over the face. He acquires a very ancient and remote house at Castle-Acre, whither he conveys the coffin. Here an old black and his wife are stationed to guard the uninterred body of the lovely Antoinette, that Beverley may keep the letter of his oath. This house he visits annually just before his meeting with the abbé. Mrs. Beverley, learning something of the mysterious circumstances, leaps to the conclusion that her husband is a murderer, and a terrible tragedy results. Beverley, who is pursued by Sir Eugene Columbine, the brother of Antoinette, skulks in hiding for several weeks, during which time his unhappy wife, imagining he has deserted her, frivolously forms a connexion with a fop of the first water, Sir Vivian Blimp. By him she is introduced to a dissipated circle, and even gives herself to a young officer. This debauchee makes an amorous assignation at a private bordello in Leicester Square, a house of the very first quality and privacy. The lady, being first on the scene, retires to bed, and presently falls asleep waiting for her lover.

Captain Beverley, having purchased a phial of poison and distractedly seeking a night's lodging, is directed to the same house. He gives the old procuress a large vail, and she, imagining he is the expected gallant, ushers him into the chamber where Lavinia lies asleep. There is wine upon the table, and, having mixed the drug in a full glass, he drinks deeply to nerve himself to his deed. So much indeed does he quaff that he sinks in a stupor in his chair. Presently Lavinia, waking and feeling thirsty, makes her way in the firelight to the table and drinks from the full glass. Her piercing screams awake the wretched Beverley and, to his horror, he beholds his wife writhing in agony on the bed. Stunned and aghast, he " darted towards the mantel-piece—snatched one of the pistols suspended over it, and having ascertained it to be loaded, placed its muzzle to his temple, and the next moment sank a corpse to the ground." This chapter, with the scene in the midnight bagnio, the obliging matron who ushers him into the room and furnishes bottles of Madeira with many an oily smile, is very powerfully written.

The remainder of the book is concerned with the adventures of Leolin, and the *éclaircissement* concerning his sex, for Leolin proves to be a girl who has been brought up as a boy. Eventually Leolin is wedded to young John Bull. In view of what we know of Lathom, this is an interesting piece of psychology, as also is the description of Leolin O'Hara : " His form was too exquisite for his sex, his beauty too delicate for manhood ; his manners strikingly effeminate."

There are many theatrical references in *Young John Bull*, and quotations from plays.[12] One example will suffice : " They beheld in Madame Lambrette a figure which cannot be more accurately defined, than by referring the reader to the highly characteristic dress worn by the late Miss Pope, in her representation of Madame Franval in the drama of Deaf and Dumb ; and in default of their acquaintance with that most admirable piece of stage personification, in any of the old editions of Molière, they will find the prototype in the portrait of Madame Bejart, in the comedy which bears the name of its author, and is said to contain some portion of his own history." *Deaf and Dumb, or, the Orphan Protected*, was produced at Drury Lane on February 24th, 1801. It was adapted from the French *L'Abbé de l'Épée*, by

Bouilly, who himself had taken the drama from Kotzebue. " Miss Pope," says Genest, " was quite at home in Madame Franval."

In *Fashionable Mysteries ; or The Rival Duchesses (and Other Tales)*, 3 vols., 1829, 12mo, Newman, we move in the highest circles of the ton. The two peeresses are the Duchess of Zephyrlite (*née* Sophia Clarensforth) and the " darling rib of the antiquated duke of Eglantine," *née* "Lady Caroline Tamperville, a daughter of the dowager countess of Shadowley." Sophia Clarensforth and Lady Caroline were fellow-boarders at the house of Mrs. Auckland, " a seminary of a very distinguished nature, in the village of Mortlake." The romantic Horace Auckland and Sophia fall deeply in love, but the youth is scouted and pretty sharply snibbed by purse-proud Mr. Clarensforth. They elope and are married. After some months, however, her infuriated father discovers Sophia's retreat in the heart of one of the midland of the Swiss cantons, and at dead of night bears her off from her home. She is delivered of a child, but her father lodges her in a convent, having sedulously spread the rumour in London that she is visiting France to perfect herself in the French language. Here she learns that Horace has been banished to one of the Grecian islands, but that he flung himself from the boat and was drowned in the Mediterranean. As the months pass Sophia is borne down by her father's will, who tells her that her marriage—even if any such ceremony took place— was on Horace Auckland's own confession a mere mock form. Believing herself in any case a widow, she at length consents to wed the Duke of Zephyrlite.

The scenes of social rivalry between the two ladies are drawn with many witty strokes, and some smart satire that has not lost its point even to-day, but there is an undercurrent almost too grave and serious for such a tale, and the end is tragedy, for Horace Auckland returns whence he has been so long detained by the machinations of Mr. Clarensforth. He kills himself upon the sea-shore, and his unhappy Sophia, disdaining to survive, uses the same pistol to fall weltering in blood over his inanimate body.

A Month in the Highlands, which occupies Volume II and part of Volume III, is in two and twenty chapters. It is written with a very great deal of humour, and Miss Euphemia Ogilvie, of Bannockgowrie, is admirably portrayed. This lady, " a female of close and steady observation upon the actions of others," who always adhered to the broad dialect of her native country " more from a partiality to its congenial sounds, than from any difficulty which she would have experienced in exchanging her mother-tongue, for the more refined or fashionable diction of her Lowland acquaintance," is in truth a portrait not altogether unworthy of Scott himself. How shrewd is her constant reply to suitors : " That she had seen sae muckle o' the fashious lives o' married wives, that i' gude troth she considered there was indeed infinitely mair honour than pleasure i' the teetle ; . . . and syne she was determined to gang till her bed her ain gudewife, and rise out o' it agin her ain gudeman, to the end o' her days."

Poor Mary Ann, or The County Election, the remaining tale of these three volumes, is a good specimen of Lathom's keen observation and somewhat caustic humour intermingled with those episodes of pathos and tragedy he so delighted to weave. The heartless elegant seducer Sir Mirabel Maccarye is from the life, and the fact that his schemes are thwarted but little mitigates the distress and misery which proceed in the first place from his selfishness and fashionable folly.

The last of Francis Lathom's works, *Mystic Events ; or The Vision of the Tapestry,* " A Romantic Legend of the Days of Anne Boleyn," 4 vols., 1830, is a long and complicated romance. The hero, Leolin, has been brought up in remotest seclusion and secrecy by an eremite named Father Benedict, after whose death he passes, a mere lad, into the charge of a female, simply known by the name of Mabellah, whose humble dwelling is situated in the heart of a dreary forest. When he seeks to know his parentage and presses her too often and too nearly, Mabellah drives him forth, and after some wandering he passes into the service of the knight of the saffron plume, Louis of Auvignac, Count of Beaumarchais, who dwells at the Castle of the Rock in the most distant walks of Sherwood. When they lodge at the Castle of de Montford, near Peterborough, Leolin, who sleeps in a tapestried chamber, is startled by beholding, descending from the arras, the figure of a monk, who unfolds a parchment whereupon is inscribed : " The Hour of your Fate is Arrived ; Embrace it with Gratitude." Leolin, who is treated with unwonted favour by Louis of Auvignac, forms a friendship with young George Boleyn, by whom he is invited to Hever Castle, where he meets the lovely enchantress, Anne, long since adored by him from afar. A good many paragraphs are devoted to enumerating the charms and fascinations both of body and mind of the lady. Leolin's hopes are utterly crushed when the King, who has been driving on the divorce of Queen Catharine, announces his intention of wedding Anne Boleyn. Pitying his distress, with tremendous vows of secrecy, Louis of Auvignac conducts Leolin at midnight to subterranean vaults beneath the castle chapel, and introduces him into the presence of Abijah Ginnetthon, the King of the Egyptians, a master of occult science, from whom he learns : " A. B. is destined to be the wife of Sir Leolin of Auvignac." None the less

Henry VIII in jealousy sends Leolin to the Tower, whence after a brief space he is banished to France. Louis of Auvignac escorts Leolin to the château of Auvignac, and after a while sends him with George Boleyn to travel in Italy.

Eventually it falls to the lot of Sir Thomas Boleyn, the father of Anne, to reveal to Leolin the fateful secrets of his house, as told him by Louis of Auvignac. " Although my age is computed by my most intimate acquaintance to have exceeded scarcely thirty years, I have nearly attained a century ; and would to Heaven that I had never searched into those depths .of Nature, which instructed me in the baneful art of prolonging my existence ! "

When he was but two and twenty, Sir Ralph de Gastonville, as he was then called, fell violently in love with Hyppolita, the daughter of a poor Spanish musician, and upon her father's death removes her to the Castle of the Rock, intending to wed her. Hyppolita, fearing lest the union should prejudice her lover's career, prepares a fatal draught, which she swallows immediately, enclosing herself in a burial vault, deeming she will instantly expire. The poison has been changed for a harmless potion, so actually her fate is more terrible, since she breathes her last only under the devouring tortures of famine. Ralph de Gastonville plunges into profligacy, but when he realizes he has lost large sums in a debauched life, to replenish his coffers he turns to the study of alchemy and becomes at Vienna a disciple of Abijah Ginnetthon. In fine, he discovers the transmutation of metals, and the estate of Auvignac in France then falling to him, he plunges yet further into the study of occult lore and becomes the master of many curious secrets, amongst others " the art of prolonging the existence, and renovating the countenance of man." In order to suit his occasions it is given out that Sir Ralph has died at Rome, bequeathing his domains to Count Louis of Beaumarchais.

Count Louis is deep enamoured of the lovely Eloise de Foix, whose father, having no dowry for his daughter, has compelled her to take the veil. Under the name of Cecil Fairfax he contrives to win her love. She elopes from the convent, and in England they wed, where she becomes the mother of Leolin. Soon, however, Count Louis tires of his bride and feigns a hideous tale to separate from her. He relates that her father, the Count de Foix, once had a natural son, and this by-blow he has discovered himself to be. Therefore brother and sister, they are living in incest. She is soon persuaded to assume the name Mabellah and enter as a boarder a religious house near which the boy is reared by old Father Benedict, the confessor of the nuns. Count Louis carefully watches the interests of his wife and son, although the former, owing to her wrongs, is often found to be half-crazed with remorse. When the time comes he so guides and shapes events that Leolin shall encounter him and enter his service. It was Count Louis who appeared to Leolin as the monk seemingly a figure descended from the arras. So dearly has he come to love Leolin that he determines at any cost to acknowledge him before the world, and with that intent he seeks the retreat of the forsaken Eloise. As he approaches Northampton he perceives a tumultuous mob assisting at the execution of a witch. The woman is bound to a stake, heaped high with faggots, whence tongues of fire are leaping red amid clouds of dancing smoke. Oh horror! in the expiring countenance of the miserable sufferer he beholds the features of Eloise! Owing to her insanity, not without some countenance from the evil arts he himself had taught, she had been accused of and condemned for sorcery. The Count, setting his affairs in order, appointing Leolin his heir, and revealing the whole dread history to Sir Thomas Boleyn, immures himself in a monastery dedicated to S. Paul the hermit, " a community of which, although the regulations are not strictly similar to those of the penitential La Trappe, are equally severe." The reception of the new monk at midnight and his final farewell to his son are described with a good deal of emotional power. It is indeed a scene worthy of Ainsworth himself.

Leolin by a series of well-told, if somewhat surprising, events becomes the husband of Amabel, the youngest sister of Anne Boleyn. The prophecy is accordingly fulfilled.

The concluding chapters of the romance turn to a large extent upon the jealousies of Henry VIII. The final episode is the birth of Elizabeth, with some hints from Shakespeare and Fletcher. Leolin and Amabel withdraw to France and dwell on their estates at Auvignac. " Those who are acquainted with the writings of Madame Genlis, will discover in her anecdotes of the Count of St. Germain, the outline of the extraordinary life of the Count of Beaumarchais."

The description of Leolin, and his affection for the Count of Auvignac should be remarked.

Queen Catharine, Sir Thomas Wyatt, Cardinal Wolsey (who is very fully described), Thomas Crumwell, and Henry VIII cross the scene, but with the exception of the latter they have little to do with the story. Lathom apologizes for " various slight anachronisms " in his " romantic legend." It is certainly rather amazing to find a reference by George Boleyn to " our favourite poet Shakespeare," and to " a character in his excellent play of the cruel Jew of Venice."

Lighter dialogue in the romance is put in the mouths of very

Ainsworthian personages, Ovidius Longshanks, the jester at Hever; Reuben Rawbold; and Dunstan Lightbody, private fool to the noble house of Wyatt.

It is difficult to think that whilst writing his romance, *The Necromancer*, G. W. M. Reynolds had not Lathom's *Mystic Events* in view. The period of both stories is the time of Henry VIII, and they have more in common than can be ascribed to mere coincidence. Reynolds' description of the terrible Danvers, for example, may be compared with that of Louis of Auvignac in *Mystic Events*, which is as follows : " He beheld in him a man of apparently between twenty-five and thirty years of age, of a countenance so peculiarly interesting, that it riveted the eyes of the observer, and created in him an anxiety to enter into an acquaintance with the heart as well as the person of the attractive being to whom it appertained. In stature he somewhat exceeded the unusual height of man ; and in his air and deportment he appeared to blend the nerve of the warrior with the grace and dignity of the courtier. His complexion was dark ; his flowing hair of the deepest raven ; and the glow of health which tinged his cheeks added fire to the animated expression which beamed from his black and eloquent eye."

Lathom is an extremely representative figure among the novelists of the last decade of the eighteenth, and the first thirty years of the nineteenth century. At present one may look through Histories of Fiction compiled by professing scholars and find no mention of his name. This is an omission, a gross fault which should not be repeated. In his day he could appeal to all classes of readers. His social satires are light and lively ; his Gothic romances mix the ingredients of that school with a practised hand. His masterpiece is *Men and Manners*. In this book I venture to say there are characters—Jonathan Parkinson, Cranberry, Sir Gilbert Oxmondeley—which approach the shorter sketches of the young Dickens, nay, which would not be altogether out of place in the greater works themselves.

Unlike Francis Lathom, T. J. Horsley Curties never essayed a picture of contemporary life, but devoted himself entirely to the Gothic romance, and there is no author more Gothic, more romantic than he.

Of his life, practically nothing is known, beyond the facts that his first novel, *Ethelwina, or The House of Fitz-Auburne*, was published in 1799 as by T. J. Horsley, his surname, Curties, being deliberately suppressed by the novice in authorship ; and his last romance, *The Monk of Udolpho*,[13] appeared in 1807, so that eight years comprise the extent of his activities. Horsley Curties was a Londoner who mixed in literary circles. In January, 1801, he was living at No. 1 Bury Street,

Bloomsbury Square ; four years later he resided at Vale Place, Hammersmith ; in the autumn of 1806 his address was Chelsea Park, Little Chelsea. He was, as internal evidence shows, a man of some means and position.

Ethelwina, says Horsley Curties in the Preface to his second romance, was sent " into the world as an orphan, whose father feared to acknowledge it, under his *Christian* appellation of HORSLEY." The Public, however, fostered it, and accordingly in 1801 he published *Ancient Records, or, The Abbey of St. Oswythe*, in four volumes, Minerva Press. Of this work Horsley Curties tells us : " Its mysteries—its terrific illusions—its very errors must be attributed to a love of Romance, caught from an enthusiastic admiration of *Udolpho's* unrivalled Foundress.—He follows her through all the venerable gloom of horrors, not as a kindred spirit, but contented, as a shadow, in attending her footsteps."

Briefly, it may be said, that both *Ethelwina* and *Ancient Records* have a particular appeal to lovers of Gothic romance, since both are so entirely typical of their school. They are well told, full of adventure and mystery, and even if neither can claim to rise to any such heights as Mrs. Radcliffe reached, both are certainly full of interest and of that quality of " suspense " which is so essential to success in this kind.

Ancient Records was dedicated as " a mere posy of wild blossoms, gathered in the fields of fancy, and simply put together " to Mrs. Watson of Westminster. The second edition, 4 vols., A. K. Newman, 1832, omits the Dedication and Prefatory matter. The quotation from Ossian on the title-page is appropriate enough :

> A tale of the times of old——
> ——The deeds of days of other years.

It may be remarked that the opening scene, the arrival of Sir Alfred St. Oswythe and Rosaline at their ancient home amid the forest gloom, the old abbey whose spires rose " in Gothic magnificence from amidst the interior of the tallest trees " is well done. The description of the interior with its large antique rooms entered by great folding doors of church-like form would have fairly delighted Catherine Morland. Needless to say the Abbey is rumoured to be haunted o' nights, and Dame Blanche is ready enough to chatter of ghosts, and sounds, and shrieks and sights unholy.

" More abbeys, with ' battlement ramparts ' and ' heavy *Gothic* pillars of the *Saxon* order ! ' " peevishly cried a reviewer upon the appearance of T. J. Horsley Curties' *Ancient Records*.

The critic complains [14] that fifty years before a man who had a hundred miles to go conceived himself about to undertake a tiresome journey, whereas Sir Alfred St. Oswythe and his family are conveyed in a covered car through Scotland and half England in six days. With a tart scorn Mr. Curties is advised to try his hand at *A Treatise on the Mode of Posting in the Thirteenth and Fourteenth Centuries.*

In the *Ingoldsby Legends* also is a good-natured banter, where there is mention of "one of those high and pointed arches, which that eminent antiquary, Mr. Horsley Curties, has described in his ' Ancient Records ' as ' a *Gothic* window of the *Saxon* order.' " (*The Spectre of Tappington*; *The Ingoldsby Legends*, 1840, p. 19.)

The next work by Horsley Curties, *The Scottish Legend, or the Isle of St. Clothair*, A Romance, 4 vols., Lane, 1802, price 18*s*., I find entirely to my taste. Of course, there is no real knowledge of Caledonia, but the author's imagination was sufficiently vivid and picturesque. *The Critical Review* [15] observed : " We have nothing to say of this work, more than what the author has said in the title-page. *It is four volumes of* ROMANCE."

St. Botolph's Priory; *or, The Sable Mask*, An Historic Romance, five volumes, 1806, published by J. F. Hughes, was inscribed by Horsley Curties with glowing encomium to the Earl of Macclesfield, the dedication being signed from Vale Place, Hammersmith Road, October, 1805. Gothic adventure and history, some of which is correct and some not so correct, are mingled together with a vast preponderance of the former. The time is towards the end of the reign of Charles I, when the King is a prisoner. The romance commences fitly. The recluse, Odovico St. Aubespine, lives in the desert rugged walls of St. Botolph's Priory, in the Isle of Wight. His household in his retreat consists of Madame St. Aubespine ; her daughter, the beauteous Roselma ; two aged domestics, Clemence and old Pierre ; and a young girl named Cicely—eventually to be paired off with the *gracioso* Philippe, a perfect pattern of a Gothic household. The hour and weather are alike appropriate. It is night and a tempest rages ; through the " ancient Gothic casement the red and angry lightnings darted their fiery lumens," whilst Odovico St. Aubespine, recalling such another night, trembles and raves of " secrets, secrets,—damning ones." A mystery surrounds the fate of the Comte Val de Blandemonde, whom it seems that St. Aubespine has slain. Whilst the thunder crashes at its loudest and the rain pours in pitchy torrents down, there seeks shelter at St. Botolph's a stranger, sick and weary, De Rochemonde, who is in reality Adolpho Val de Blandemonde, the brother of the murdered Comte. Adolpho is a villain, a plotter deep in Cromwell's darkest scheme. Not only Cromwell and King Charles, but other historic personages have their part in the story, and the death of Princess Elizabeth at Carisbrooke is touched upon not altogether without pathos and skill. Adolpho has his feminine counterpart, a woman evil and hot for revenge. It is hardly necessary to unweave the complex incidents here, nor could the whole tale be told without diffuseness wherein the quality were lost. Suffice to say that Roselma is in danger of wedding Adolpho, who proves to be her uncle, for it is revealed that she is not the daughter of St. Aubespine. However, the incestuous match is hindered in time, and the heroine saved. For Roselma is the child of the "terrific unknown," "his visage rendered doubly ghastly by a mask bound over the upper part" who warns and wards her throughout, and proves to be Gondolpho Val de Blonde-monde, not killed, as was thought by St. Aubespine. Moreover, in right of her grandsire, she is Duchess of Rohan, and when she weds her loved Marquis of Valmont all is happiness. St. Aubespine immures himself in a monastery at Avignon.

A work of excessive rarity [16] is *The Monk of Udolpho* in four volumes by T. J. Horsley Curties, published by J. F. Hughes (Wigmore Street), 1807. The author has taken as his text

> " *Once more*
> *Let's mock the midnight bell.*"—SHAKESPEARE.[17]

In a foreword Horsley Curties commences : " The Author of these volumes, in sending before an indulgent Public, his latest literary essay under the borrowed name of ' Udolpho,' has only one plea to make against the charge of *plagiarism*, a plea which is simply the truth, and a statement of facts which will, he trusts, be credited both by the world and that Mighty Magician (Mrs. Radcliffe), as she has been aptly designated in the critique of a nervous and elegant panegyrist, to whom this apology is also justly due.

" The Publisher of these pages had long advertised a romance under the appellation of ' Monk Udolpho,' nor had its present founder the most distant idea that the fabric was to be of his rearing, till applied to, in consequence of the death of the intended composer, to retrieve him with the public, whom he must otherwise disappoint ; and not without the strongest reluctance did I assent to undertake a task so arduous, and perhaps injurious to the little fame I may have acquired by former lucubrations.

" It was my earnest wish, the Publisher should procure me a sight of the few sheets, or, more properly, the outline of the story intended to elucidate the title page ; but I was answered, that the manuscript had been lost, and that my own resources were equal to the difficulty ; that the plot and incidents must be entirely my own, but that I was at liberty to *disclaim thus publicly* any share in the title page, to which alone the promise made by the Publisher to his patrons and the world at large unavoidably compelled him to restrict me.

" Thus then, having been prevailed upon to soar once more into the regions of fancy and the dark mysteries of romance, I must continue to feel as much solicitude for the success of ' The Monk of Udolpho,' as it it had appeared under its more legitimate appellation of ' Filial Piety ' : a title which, had the nature of the above circumstances been different, I should certainly have ushered the former before its liberal and, let me hope, impartial judges." This is dated, Chelsea Park, Little Chelsea, October 20th, 1806.

The romance opens in a high flight of Gothic fancy. It is midnight when the youthful illustrious heiress of the Duchy of Placenza, the lady Hersilia, is awakened from her slumbers by the entry of her father, Duke Angelo. " The ghastly hue of death seemed impressed on the livid features of Placenza, he sank down on the couch of Hersilia, and inarticulately ejaculated, ' In the tomb my crimes will be expiated. Pronounce my pardon, oh ! most injured child.' " The unhappy Duke confesses that he has staked his birthright, his dukedom, his daughter's heritage on a gamester's throw, and all is lost. His people must soon learn to stoop under a foreign and unwelcome Lord. All that is left to Hersilia is the Castello di Alberi. The Duke then cries out : " I die, Hersilia ; the poison already chills through my blood ! " " Holy Saints ! what fiend has tempted thee, my son, to this rash act ? " pronounced in slow sepulchral tones the Father Udolpho, for the Father Confessor of the palace, privileged by his sacred office, entered the apartment.

Father Udolpho is obviously a copy of Mrs. Radcliffe's Schedoni, although Horsley Curties hardly admits the imitation.

" His dress was singular, it was of sable baize, reaching from the head and flowing round his feet, which were laced only with sandals ; his stature was tall, and even gigantic, inclined rather to the robust than meagre ! he wore a full hood, which was generally drawn over his whole face and fastened under the chin, so that the real expression of his saturnine features could never be distinguished ; across his eyebrows was bound a white linen forehead cloth, upon which was displayed in the centre the ghastly grinning ensign of a Death's head, said to be the emblem of an order of monks founded by Udolpho, and delineated in his own person with such pertinaceous exactitude as to render its first sight too horrible for a repetition."

The young Comptessa or Princess, as Hersilia is indifferently called, espies the monk " with the hood of his cowl turned aside displaying the hideous features of a demon." He stands with upraised dagger over the convulsed body of the Duke, writhing in envenomed agony, and ere Hersilia can interfere " the ferocious monk, scowling triumphantly, had plunged the poniard into the heart of her father." The Princess swoons, and lies for days ill of a frenzied fever. Meanwhile the obsequies of her father are devoutly solemnized. Shortly after " the well-known figure of a young and noble cavalier," Val Ambrosio, visits and consoles the orphan heiress. " Hersilia of Placenza and Lorenzo Val-Ambrosio of Guestella had long loved with a passion mutually pure, enthusiastic and lastingly devoted." Unhappily Hersilia learns that the Monk Udolpho and Cosmo, Duke of Parma, are her guardians, whilst the title-deeds of the principality of Placenza fell into the hands of the Unknown to whom the dead Duke lost them in play. This Unknown has given them to Cosmo. The Compte Benvoglio of Guestella, Lorenzo's father, proves Hersilia's friend, but Udolpho insists that Duke Cosmo's sanction is necessary, and almost on the very eve of the marriage informs Benvoglio that Hersilia has forfeited her rank and dower owing to her father's will, which he produces—a mysterious scroll! Compte Benvoglio now forbids the union, and the hopes of Lorenzo and Hersilia are dashed to the ground. When the youth seeks one last interview with his beloved, Udolpho would prevent it, but the impetuous amoroso seizes the monk and dashes him aside to the floor with little ceremony. " The countenance of the Confessor was now blackened with an expression of every baleful passion that could deform the human character ; it was dreadful, it was terrific, and even horrible ; as was the tremendous oath of revenge which still in his prostrate attitude issued from his gnashed teeth ! ' I will wring his heart with torments of never-ceasing anguish. . . . Audacious renegade ! in blood and ruin shalt thou rue this hour. . . . Yes ! by Heaven's host I swear to accomplish thy destruction. Escape me, if thou canst ! ' A horrible grin of demoniac exultation confirmed this impious vow."

Hersilia refuses to urge Lorenzo to disobey his father's commands, and bids him submit in everything to the parental behests. The councillors of Placenza now proceed to invest their Princess with the emblems of sovranty, disdaining to recognize Duke Angelo's will. But Parma's legions encamp beneath the walls of the palace, and Duke Cosmo claims his ward. It is useless to resist. The Duke of Parma and his followers invest Placenza, " himself and his partisans sat late carousing in the Banquet Hall, where disorder and licentious excess now reigned." Hersilia learns that she is the destined bride of Cosmo's son, Sanguedoni, who conducts his wooing in a very peremptory style.

Both Cosmo and Sanguedoni were bold and daring, treacherous and false, united in a league of iniquity, equal in atrocious guilt, as assimilated in minds. At a banquet Duke Cosmo publicly pledges the Prince and Princess of Placenza, and in private Sanguedoni proceeds to press his suit further than decency permits. Jealousy, however, now enters in the person of the Signora Hortensia delli Corsenti, a mistress of Sanguedoni, and a lady who is not easily to be discarded.

The monk Udolpho next suddenly and silently reappears in Hersilia's apartment, and urges her to accept Sanguedoni's hand. This she refuses, and at a tense moment a sepulchral hollow voice is heard : *But the grave of death cannot for ever bury in endless silence the voice which will be heard and will proclaim aloud the malefactions of the murderer Udolpho.*[18] The monk is staggered, but being a hardy villain recovers himself, and is soon followed by Duke Cosmo, who urges the ardent passion of Sanguedoni ; but soon lets her know that father and son are rivals, between whom fearful scenes of strife ensue. Sanguedoni then seeks to involve a page, Astolpho, in his schemes.

Hersilia is now persuaded by Udolpho that in order to escape a forced marriage with Duke Cosmo she must commit herself to his protection and seek safety in flight. Her guide promises to conduct her to the Castello di Alberi, which after a long and mysterious journey through the Appenines, guided by Benedotto with Astolpho in their company, they perceive. " On a lofty eminence were seen some bold gigantic towers, whose broken moss-clad battlements and walls displayed at once the ravages of time and long neglect." Beatrice, a loquacious housekeeper, admits them, talking in true Gothic style.

The journey and arrival are closely imitated from *The Mysteries of Udolpho*, and very well done at second-hand, although, of course, not in any degree comparable to the descriptions of Mrs. Radcliffe.

Beatrice shows Hersilia to a remote chamber with more than a hint it is haunted. Nor does it mend matters when with a shriek of terror at some sudden noise she cries : " The ghost ! Holy saints, it is the ghost of the murdered Eloisa ! "

In the Castle is a hall, hung with black and festooned with emblems of death, which Beatrice informs the lady is the Superior's judgement hall. The Father Udolpho, " founder of the Order of the Death's Head," has consecrated his castle to religion and holds conclave here. In the Castle Hersilia is guarded by two ruffians, Spoletto and Benedotto, and here she sees many a grim and grisly sight.

Udolpho now demands an interview with Hersilia, and bids her prepare to become Sanguedoni's bride. When she refuses with scorn, the monk throws off his black habit, " the cowl and its forehead cap, with all its horrid trappings which had so long and so well concealed his person and real countenance, disappeared, and in all his terrible attributes Sanguedoni stood revealed : bold in guilt, triumphant in the success of his dark destroying projects."

" The history of this bad man was one endless tissue of crimes and enormities, so enmeshed, that not the eye of wisdom, nor yet the keener penetration of experienced age, could develop his true character. Cruel, blood-thirsty, insidious, remorseless, and deceitful, formed to delude, and self-trained from boy to manhood in every vice, . . . hypocrisy was in him personified."

Sanguedoni di Ubaldi was the second son of the eldest sister of Duke Cosmo, and having embraced the monastic life, he proceeded to lead a double existence, as the Monk Udolpho and as Sanguedoni. In his cloud-seated fortress he had established his fearful order, supported by a band of resolutes and bravos, an order of outward sanctity and penance, but in reality of terror and rapine. Owing to various circumstances he is able to get his uncle Cosmo in his power and bend him to his whim. It is he who contrived the ruin and death of Duke Angelo of Placenza, whose will he unscrupulously forged. Hersilia learns that Cosmo has been slain, and Lorenzo di Val Ambrosio and his father the Compte are prisoners in the Castle. Here also enters the jealous and Medean Hortensia delli Corsenti.

A number of incidents follow, which are so perplexed, although clearly defined and skilfully contrived that it would require a lengthy analysis to set the adventures out in detail. It will then perhaps suffice to say that as we hasten towards the end of the tale, Sanguedoni's triumph seems complete.

Hortensia, who endeavours to poison Hersilia, is stabbed to the heart by Sanguedoni as he frustrates her vengeful malice. A meeting of the secret tribunal has been summoned, and Sanguedoni bids them bear Lorenzo to the rack, when, at a given signal, throwing aside their robes, the company are seen to be not his ruffian band but armed soldiers, headed by the Compte di Guestella, who secure and fast bind the villain. The Inquisition, having been informed of his practices, has laid a snare and trapped him in the midst of his guilt. Not least of his crimes is counted the seduction of the nun Eloisa, whom he has (as he supposes) done to death, but who now appears in the person of Astolpho. With horrid curses and the exulting laugh of a demon, Sanguedoni, having confessed his long catalogue of crime, plunges a concealed dagger into Eloisa's bosom and then stabs himself deep with the same steel. These " wonderful and awful events " are at last brought to a happy termination by the marriage of Lorenzo and Hersilia.

I have described at some length *The Monk of Udolpho*, partly because this romance is of an excessive rarity, and partly because it represents in their most flamboyant colouring all the features of the Gothic novel. They are exaggerated to a degree, and Horsley Curties would assuredly have no rival in the red of his vermilions and the yellows of his orpiments, the black of his nocturnes and shades, if it were not for William Henry Ireland, whose not unskilful pen could run to any extravagance, even to forgeries of Shakespeare.

Of William Henry Ireland, it has been remarked by a candid and none too lenient critic : " Like the man who sought to gain a name by burning the temple of Diana, he acquired renown by an act of high culpability ; but the temple he destroyed was his own fame." [19]

The son of Samuel Ireland, author, engraver, and a dealer in scarce books and prints, William Henry (of doubtful legitimacy) was born in 1777. He was partially educated in France, and articled to a conveyancer in New Inn, where he came across a number of legal Elizabethan parchments. Of a highly romantic turn and an enthusiast for the tragic style, young Ireland, who had been deeply impressed by the story of Chatterton, conceived the idea of manufacturing a number of deeds and signatures relating to Shakespeare. His father, morbidly anxious to discover some scrap of Shakespeare's writing, eagerly accepted the documents, and gradually William Henry forged a great variety of papers, including an original version of *King Lear*, some portions of *Hamlet*, and two pseudo-Shakespearean plays *Vortigern and Rowena*, and *Henry II*. All these were exhibited at the elder Ireland's house in Norfolk Street.

A fierce and tangled controversy arose as to the genuineness of the discoveries,[20] in which Malone took an energetic part in exposing the fraud. None the less, Ireland found many supporters and believers, including James Boswell, Joseph Warton, Dr. Parr, and Pye the laureate. To us it seems incredible that any should not have at once recognized the manuscripts as spurious, since the recipe for concocting original Shakespeare seems to have been the systematic and utterly erroneous doubling of final consonants, the addition of an *e* generally in an impossible termination, the substitution of *y* for *i*, a complete lack of punctuation, and the wildest vagaries with capital initial letters.

Boaden, indeed, in his letter to George Steevens, 1796, showed that the orthography was utterly unlike that of the age of Elizabeth or, in fine, of any preceding period. It is true that in a momentary enthusiasm Boaden had hoped the discoveries might prove genuine, but a deliberate consideration made him reflect with contempt upon the labours of the fabrication.

None the less, even some scholars and the cognoscenti were deceived by a smart attorney's clerk.

Vortigern, An Historical Tragedy in five acts, was published 8vo, 1799 ; and reprinted 8vo, 1832. *Henry the Second, An Historical Drama,* " Supposed to be Written by the Author of *Vortigern* " was published 8vo, 1799. Both these plays were issued in 1799 with a general title-page.[21] With regard to *Vortigern*, Genest [22] says : " No play ever came out which excited the curiosity of the public more than this, as it was pretended and by many believed, to have been written by Shakespeare." It was produced at Drury Lane, Saturday, April 2nd, 1796, with Kemble as Vortigern ; Bensley, Constantius, King of Britain ; Charles Kemble, Pascentius, son of Vortigern and Edmunda ; Benson, Hengist ; Phillimore, Horsus ; King, the Fool ; Mrs. Powell, Edmunda, wife of Vortigern (this rôle was refused by Mrs. Siddons) ; Mrs. Jordan, Flavia, daughter of Vortigern and Edmunda ; and Miss Miller, Rowena. The " Editor " of the printed play thanks Mrs. Jordan and Mrs. Powell " for their very spirited exertions and excellent acting on this occasion," and adds that could he with truth or justice make the smallest acknowledgement to Kemble and Phillimore he has little doubt that, whoever wrote the piece, it would have been well received and kept the stage. " Kemble seems to have been fully convinced that the piece was spurious," comments Genest, who further tells us that the house was crowded. " The first part of the Tragedy went off without any disapprobation, but when Kemble pronounced

——And when this solemn mockery is o'er.[23]

a most discordant howl echoed from the pit, and it was some minutes before he could again obtain a hearing—he then repeated the fatal line, which the Irelands thought was maliciously done."

The following is the passage in question. Act V, Scene 2, Vortigern's apostrophe to " sovereign death " :

> And when thou would'st be merry, thou dost chuse
> The gaudy chamber of a dying King.
> O ! then thou dost ope wide thy hideous jaws,
> And with ready laughter, and fantastic tricks,
> Thou clap'st thy rattling fingers to thy sides ;
> And when this solemn mockery is ended,
> With icy hand thou tak'st him by the feet,
> And upward go, till thou dost reach the heart,
> And wrap him in the cloak of lasting night.

It is difficult to add much to Genest's judgement of the tragedy : " Some passages in the fifth act have merit, but the play on the whole

PLATE XIV

WILLIAM HENRY IRELAND
Aetat. 25

[*Face p.* 342

is a very poor one, *Plagiarisms excepted*, there is not the least similarity between Vortigern and the genuine plays of Shakespeare." The absurdities Genest notes, such as the Fool's allusion to Bishop Bonner, Act II, Scene 4 (p. 26), were, I conceive, intentional anachronisms. As Genest further remarks, the story of Vortigern had been utilized by Middleton : " there is a considerable similarity in the incidents of the Mayor of Quinborough and Vortigern, but whether Ireland had seen Middleton's play or not, is by no means clear."

Even before the play was published, *The Monthly Mirror*,[24] August, 1797, observed : " If all other evidence were questionable the tragedy of Vortigern was decisive ; not because it was hooted from the stage, but because the very construction of the play, and the plan of the dialogue, betrayed the whole process of the writer's imitative faculty."

Whatever we may think of *Vortigern*, there can be no question that *Henry the Second*, 8vo, 1799, is a thoroughly bad piece, feeble and heavy. Here we have among the characters, Nicholas Breakespeare, and John of Salisbury, as also, of course, Queen Eleanor, Rosamond, and Nurse to Rosamond. Ireland has actually resisted the temptation of a scene between Eleanor and Rosamond in the bower, although we learn that the latter is poisoned. The caricature of S. Thomas à Becket is very gross and offensive, and the scene of the murder inexpressibly tame. Yet the " Editor " was bold enough to suggest this might be the *Henry the Second* of the Stationers' Register, September 9th, 1653 ; *Henry the first, & Hen : the* 2 , by Shakespeare and Davenport.[25]

Mutius Scævola, or the Roman Patriot, An Historical Drama, 8vo, 1801, inspired by the fact that " The historic page records the most energetic and luminous examples of public and private virtue, while it is also shadowed with the ebon tints of moral delinquency," is extremely mediocre, and neither the Roman Clelia with her heroic love for Mutius, nor the Etruscan Silvia, in love with noble Manlius and disguised as an officer, help the piece, which concludes with their " twofold nuptials." In the course of the play Manlius on the stage thrusts his hand into the glowing tripod " *looking with dauntless mien upon the astonished prince,*" Porsenna.

Upon the failure, or rather collapse of *Vortigern*, young Ireland in 1796 published an unequivocal confession of the whole affair, *An Authentic Account of the Shakespearean MSS.*, expanded in 1805 into *Confessions.* He entirely exculpates his father who, there is no question, was woefully deceived. The old man's credit none the less was badly shaken, and matters were not helped by his stoutly maintaining until his death in 1800 that he still believed the MSS. genuine, for " William Henry could not have written them." His youthful exploits at any rate show that William Henry Ireland had talents of their kind, and a most specious facility. In fact, he might have attained a very respectable place in literature, but those whom he had deceived never forgot and never forgave.

As G. P. R. James justly observes : " If Mr. W. H. Ireland committed a very great error, he suffered for it most terribly ; and, I cannot help thinking that he was pursued with an acrimony and vehemence very different from the calm assertion of truth. Petty and malevolent passions directed the scourge that chastised him ; and the object evidently was to punish and crush rather than to correct and guide." [26]

In the Preface to *The Abbess*, 4 vols., 1799, Ireland in answer to an accusation " that he had most grossly deceived the world," replies with considerable force, if not quite convincingly : "Whose fault is that ? mine, or the world's ? . . . Men of superior genius, of uncommon understanding, truly, sincerely, and firmly believed, that Shakespeare alone, and no other, wrote those papers. I knew they would believe it. . . . The number of plagiarisms from Shakespeare's plays, did not deter me—I knew this would be the last subject of investigation. I brought forth this not-undigested, not-unconnected medley—and success crowned my bold attempt. I have deceived the world you say. No : the world have deceived themselves. Whose fault is it ? I ask again : mine, or the world's ? "

Ireland's friends urged : " If you *have* been able to write, you still *are.*" A novel was suggested, and he resolved " I will try at a Novel." " My friends approved . . . I give it to the world—will the world be my friend ? "

Ireland's first romance, *The Abbess*, 4 volumes, 1799 (and Second Edition, 3 vols., A. K. Newman, 1834, price 16s. 6d.), must be distinguished from Mrs. Trollope's *The Abbess*, 3 vols., 1833. The romance was very well received,[27] and is indeed of its kind a fine piece of the more extravagant school of Lewis. There are some very detailed, very luxuriant and very incorrect descriptions of what the author imagined might be Catholic ceremonial. Hymns are chanted ; " surrounding chapels " blaze with innumerable tapers ; figures of the Saints in massive silver, globes of gold are exhibited ; a missal bound in crimson velvet is carried on a damask cushion beautifully embroidered to do honour to " the eve of the sainted day."

Much of the intrigue of *The Abbess* is, it must be confessed, exceedingly loose and voluptuous. Suffice to say that the Comte Marcello Porta falls in love with the fair Maddelena Rosa, who is a boarder in " the convent of Santa Maria del Nova at Florence," and when through the good (or bad) offices of the monk Ubaldo he obtains admittance to the cloisters at midnight and is conducted to a most elegant apartment he meets a fair nymph, whose charms are very wantonly described. Imagining her to be Maddelena Rosa, who grants him this rendezvous, he is impassioned in his embraces, only to discover that the frail who has allowed him the last favours is "the sanctified madre Vittoria Bracciano, superior of the immaculate sisterhood of Santa Maria ! " Nevertheless the lady is so beautiful that he pursues the amour.   Eventually, amid many other circumstances, the Holy Office takes cognizance of these disorders, and all concerned are promptly hailed before the Suprema, where we have some lurid scenes, and a familiar Girolamo, who proves to be a most atrocious villain.   Nor do we escape a terrific *auto-da-fé*.   There is a good deal that is repulsive in these incidents, but there is also power.

To *Rimualdo* ; *or, The Castle of Badajos*, 4 vols., Longman, 1800, *The Monthly Review*, February, 1801,[28] devotes a somewhat lengthy notice.   " We have here, in the personages of the drama, a parent and husband in the Marquis of Badajos, as wicked and as unnatural as any with whom we have before had the honour of being acquainted.—We have a son in the Condé Rimualdo, as eminent for filial piety as Æneas himself.—We have patient suffering innocence in the fair Constanza, equalling, if not transcending, any of our novel heroines.   We have *very good* haunted towers,—and a *spectre* that stands supremely eminent over the whole race of ghosts.—Hamlets and Banquos were no more than *Mawkins* in a cherry-tree, compared with that terrific vision which Rimualdo encounters on entering the old ruined chapel in the forest." What wonder, indeed, that " the brave Rimualdo, dropped down in a swoon immediately on seeing it ! "

" Murder is in this romance too much *the order of the day*.   We have murders in castles, in forests, and in cottages ; and, to borrow a word from the author, we are too frequently *enhorrored*.—*Raw head and bloody bones* is continually at our heels, so we are sincerely glad to get rid of him, and at last ' to leave our terrified fellow-travellers calmly settled in the unhaunted Castilio di Montalvan.' " Especially perhaps in this romance does Ireland's phrase tend overmuch to the picturesque, to the untramelled luxuriance, one might say, not indeed of Apuleius himself, but of the Elizabethan translator of Apuleius, stiff and quaint old William Adlington.   Morning never appears without " Aurora's tints that cover the summit of the distant mountains."   The sun never rises, but " as the imperial charioteer of day, hast'ning his car of blazing light towards green ocean's occidental flood-gate."   The moon is always full-orb'd, yet never looks *full* at us, but peeps behind fleecy clouds.   Night never forgets to assume the appropriate dignity of her sable mantle, with which (when she is not in a good humour) "she overspreads heaven's countless luminaries"; and if the hero and heroine are in a storm, God alone can help them, for then "impetuous winds blow from *every direction* (*all at once*), flakey lightning emblazons night's ebon robe, and full charged clouds *discharge* tremendous explosions."

A writer in *The Critical Review* justly observed of *Rimualdo* : "The poetry interspersed possesses a native wildness, truly interesting, and is introduced often with great effect."

Having followed up *Rimualdo* with *The Woman of Feeling*, 4 vols., 1803, a tale of sentiment, Ireland returned to the novel of terror with *Bruno, or, The Sepulchral Summons*, and a work which shall be examined in some detail, *Gondez The Monk, a Romance of the Thirteenth Century*, 4 vols., 1805. The verse Dedication (by Permission) to Lumley St. George Skeffington, Esq.,[29] of Skeffington Lodge, Leicestershire, is witty and well-turned. We may quote the following lines :

> O ! you shall hear a tale will make you start,
> For never yet had monk so black a heart.
> Never did owls and ravens scent such blood ;
> Never stood convent in so drear a wood ;
> Never was witch so foul, as you shall hear ;
> Never had damsel cause for so much fear
> As her of whom I write ;
> Never before were heroes half so fine ;
> Never did virtue half so sweetly shine ;
> Never did Cupid aim so well his dart ;
> Never did each so well enact his part ;
> Monks, heroes, witches, lovers, nobles all—
> The good, the bad, the fat, the short and tall,
> Must fill ye with delight.

Gondez the Monk commences on a high-pitched note : "Now raged on every side the direful battle's carnage : the reeking car of Mars scour'd swiftly o'er the blood-stain'd field, while on his nodding crest enthroned, sat hungry death, who seemed triumphantly to animate the furious combatants on either side."

The battle is that of Methven, near Perth, where on June 19th, 1306, Robert de Bruce VIII, King of Scotland, was defeated by the English under the Earl of Pembroke.

King Robert Bruce, Laird Douglas, and the magnanimous youth Huberto Avinzo, who had thrice rescued the king where the fray was hottest, when "the dusky veil of evening began to obscure the last bright gleam of fading day" fly the field, and after three days' wandering arrive on the shores of the Sound of Jura, whence a bark conveys them to Oronza's Isle.[30] Here they are with difficulty admitted into the mysterious monastery of Saint Columba, as truly Gothic a cloister as any built by Mrs. Radcliffe herself, and closely imitated from her pages.

Indeed, the monk who admits them has exaggerated traits of Schedoni : " His appearance was particularly meagre, and his stature far above the common level ; . . . his features, though human, had in them something so inexpressibly terrific as to appal the gaze of observation ; two eyes large and glaring, a thin aquiline nose, cheek bones remarkably high, and a mouth, whose lips through paleness seemed but a part of this petrifying countenance, the whole of which, overspread with the livid complexion of death, formed the characteristic features of this horrible figure."

His habit is as extraordinary, one might say as unique, as his person. The drapery of this father consisted of a dark brown robe, that swept along the white pavement, and hung in loose folds around his meagre limbs, while a cord slightly encircled his loins, and a broad cross of white appeared upon his breast. The religious " advanced with slow and measured step, passing and re-passing before the King and his nobles, on whom he bent his scowling eyes, as if with an intent to read the workings of their inmost souls."

This monk is named John of Dunbar, " a bosom friend " of the sanctified Gondez, the Abbot of the monastery.

The fugitives are admitted, and given food and couches of rush, although as Huberto Avinzo cries : " each object in this mansion, which should inspire my soul with thoughts of peace, is fraught with terrors that appal me," " As Avinzo spoke, the wind, as if in unison with his lugubre thoughts, moaned through the grated casement above."

The next five chapters are occupied with a retrogression. A mystery surrounds the birth of Huberto, who was brought to Scotland by a Roman, named Alzarro, At Edinburgh the stranger wins the regard of Sir Alan Macdonald, to whose care Huberto is committed when his tutor is recalled to Italy. Ere his departure Alzarro informs Sir Alan that the boy is of noble birth.

Sir Alan is slain in battle with the English, his castle razed to the ground, Huberto and Lady Macdonald sent prisoners by Edward I to London.

Lady Macdonald dies, after which Huberto contrives to escape, and painfully makes his way towards Scotland. His nights are spent under some tree or with rustics. " As the last misty hue of twilight still spreads its grey mantle over every sublunary object," Hubert's cottage hosts seek repose, " and when the shrill-gorged [31] cock first tuned his matin note he quitted his rug, and, having partook of the morning's repast, bid his kind friends farewell."

When he has made his way beyond Richmond, and is among the Yorkshire wolds, night and storm compel him to seek refuge in a ruined castle, where he witnesses the incantations and sorceries of two hags. With many obvious borrowings, sometimes almost verbal echoes, from *Macbeth*, this sabbat scene is admirably done.

" Twined within the hair of each, which was lank, coarse, and of a raven black, was the shrivelled carcase of a poisonous adder ; their visages were long, thin, loathsome and cadaverous, from each of which protruded a nose, skinny and pointed at the extremity ; their mouths from which projected sharp teeth, were hideously wide ; their lips were thin and black, while the grizzly hairs that grew around, produced the appearance of a masculine beard. Their breasts were totally bared and of a tawney hue, be'ng but a loose shrivelled covering to their projecting bones. Their arms were uncovered, and their fingers peculiarly long, each nail of which was black and pointed like an eagle's talon. Around the loins of each was a filthy jagged covering, leaving from the knees downward, quite bare : their legs were but crooked bones, thinly covered, and their feet grimed and skinny. In the hand of the one was the branch of an yew, the other grasped a deadly cypress bough ; the seat of each hag, was a mound of dead men's bones.

Between the persons of these appalling objects rose a pyramid of grinning sculls, on the summit of which was placed a brazen cauldron, from whence issued a blue lambent flame, which, casting a sickly gleam in every direction, added still more to the surrounding horrors ; while the pavement was strewed with the reeking carcasses and limbs of newly mangled reptiles, and others nailed against the walls, were in a state of putrefaction, exhaling the most nauseous stench."

The witches soon espy Huberto, " who shrunk enhorrored at their approach " and advance, hailing him as " child of mystic fate," and although he bespoke the loathsome hags : " Appalled I stand, nor know I whether to address ye as creatures of this earth, or beings of another region ; still will I dare question ye. . . . I only seek to know the mysterious fate of those who gave me being . . ." yet riddles are the reply ; he is baffled and perplexed ; whilst anon a loud yell is heard succeeded by silence and the darkness of the grave.

Huberto makes his way from the mouldering ruins, and with many a peril and scape hardly reaches the Scottish borders. His loyalty and sufferings win him the favour of King Bruce, of whose flight after the defeat at Methven he is, as we have seen, a companion.

The next morning at the monastery of Saint Columba the guests are summoned to mass, which is celebrated (as described by Ireland in fantastically picturesque detail) according to rites and with an elaborate ceremonial, wholly unknown to any liturgiologist, Western or Eastern, of any age. It were too long to quote in full, but a few of the more striking particulars may be noted. To the right of the magnificent altar " on an elevated chair, which resembled more a gaudy throne, than a monkish seat, reclined the person of the Abbot ; before whom stood two lovely boys in scarlet robes, waving to and fro large massive silver censers, that diffused the most odoriferous perfumes."

The numerous stalls were occupied by brothers of the order, each of whom " seemed to have acquired this preferment, by his long and tried adherence to the rules of the community of Saint Seoffrid [32] as the countenance of each of these fathers bore the marks of extreme age, mingled with a look of austerity and sullen reserve."

" Numerous youths arrayed in white flowing vestments, each bearing frankincense, " throng the altar steps, which must have been extremely inconvenient for the celebrant and his ministers.

" Upon the altar stood the blessed crucifix of purest virgin gold ; and on either side blazed double rows of lofty tapers cast ng a dazzling gleam upon the cushioned relicks that decorated the holy Table."

The Abbot Gondez is certainly most unfortunate in his physiognomy, since " his features were strikingly prominent and marked with every line that pourtrays internal craft, malice, cruelty and revenge . . . his nose, though short, was peculiarly acquiline, and gave to his general appearance an air of ferocity, which was in a great measure heightened by the cadaverous complexion of his countenance and the falling in of his cheeks, added to which, his mouth was hideously wide, round the falling extremities of which forever seemed to play the smile of mingled deceit and ineffable contempt." His beard was thick, short, and bushy, and Judas-coloured, as also was the corona encircling his shaven poll. " In short, every feature of the Abbot Gondez, seemed alone framed to harrow up the soul of the observer, and present to the contemplative mind some dreadful picture, replete with sin and horror."

We are hardly surprised that Robert Bruce is slow to trust this forbidding ecclesiastic whose small piercing eyes emitted " a look of malign enquiry " when he gazes on the king with the most determined effrontery.

When Huberto notices one friar at least with something of virtue in his face, and learns his name is Father Anthony, we expect to be told by the " lay friar . . . with a look of malign contempt—' And he is the outcast of the whole fraternity.' "

The monarch and his followers suspecting treachery in their interview with the Abbot, who blows hot and cold, wisely conceal their names, and resolve as soon as may be to leave the isle of Oronza.

One evening whilst in the library or scriptorium of the house, Huberto finds a manuscript : " Legend of the Little Red Woman, Written by the Monk Ingulphus at the Instigation of that Holy Father and Ghos ly Confessor Geronimo, Abbot of the Monastery of Saint Columba, in the Island of Oronza ; Wherein was displayed this Bloody Tragedy, in the Year of Grace 1152."

> The Little Old Woman was cloathed in red,
>   On a three-legged stool she sat ;
> She mutter'd, and something the old woman said ;
> She mumbled, and mumbled, and thrice shook her head,
>   And look'd on her ugly black cat.

A very good macabre ballad in the Lewis style follows. The old woman, having made a covenant with hell, essays to repent, but Satan cheats her and dings her to perdition. She has sought the Monastery of Saint Columba to win absolution from the Abbot only to find after all her endeavour the penitauncer is the fiend in the Abbot's robes, who mocks and seizes his prey. The tortured spirit of the Little Red Woman once a year at midnight flies yelling around the cloisters from the pursuing fiend. Good Christians ! pray for the soul's repose.

John of Dunbar now tempts Huberto to forsake the cause of Bruce, and is spurned by the youth with contumely.

Strange portents happen within the cloister walls. As Huberto in the midnight chapel kneels before the Crucifix, his extended right hand resting upon the entablature below, " something damp, heavy, and icy cold, dropped upon it from above." By the sickly blueish gleam of the lone lamp " the enhorror'd Avinzo was able to discern a stream of blood, that gushed from the indented wound in the side of the brass figure, of the crucified Redeemer ; three large drops of which had fallen upon and stained his hand ; the owl at that moment more dismally hooted, and the black raven rung a screeching peal that reverberated through every aile of the spacious edifice."

The youth is rapt in wonder and fear, but a few moments after, when he raises his eyes to the Cross, all appearance of the streaming blood was vanished, and, to his utter astonishment, that hand so lately tinged with blood was not quite free from stain.

Anon one of the hideous hags whom Huberto has espied at her sabbat in the mouldering tower is seen pacing the cloister and muttering words of warning and fearful mystery.

It skills not to relate at length the many other marvellous happenings in that strange monastery. Suffice to say that in the chapel Huberto meets a lovely stranger whose charms are detailed in the highest flights of Gothic imagery, a passage incidentally extremely resembling the descriptions of Clélie and Statire in the romances of Scudéry and La Calprenède.

It is pretty certain by now that the King and his friends are being speciously detained in the abbey, but the fair unknown bids Huberto " fly at midnight vespers from this haunt of terror and of blood ; and if it may be so, quit for ever, with thy brave companions, Oronza's guilty soil."

Huberto, however, shrinks from leaving the place " where he had beheld the mysterious creature who now reigned Empress of his soul." Secret means of egress from the monastery having been discovered and secured, the King with his followers by these subterranean passages eludes the troops of English Edward, who have been summoned by the treachery of Abbot Gondez to seize the person of the Scottish monarch.

A good many quasi-historical episodes follow ; Edward I dies, and is succeeded by Edward II. King Robert Bruce collects an immense army. Huberto is knighted and created Lord of the Western Isles.

Incidentally, we have a fine description of the " Proceedings at a grand festival in a convent of nuns," when the Lady Isabel, sister of the Earl of Pembroke, is to be compelled to take the vows against her will. As always in these circumstances the unwilling novice escapes. Huberto now journeys to Oronza to deliver the fair empress of his soul, and on his way beholds another sabbat with six instead of two witches. The incantations draw upon *Macbeth*, but even this second walpurgis is well done.

It appears that, after the escape of the King, Abbot Gondez has crushed his subjects with the most vindictive tyranny. Huberto obtains entrance to the monastery by a secret portal and repairs to the chapel. Here he sees " the detested form of the Abbot," whose features are " fraught with gloomy horror and malignant cruelty." The abbot, ignorant that he is being followed, by a secret stair behind the altar makes his way to the subterranean vaults, a network of gloomy and horrid chambers. In one of these Huberto finds chained to the ground " the mysterious monk John of Dunbar," whom he recognizes " notwithstanding the cadaverous and meagre hue of starvation that was imprinted on his prominent features." When released and sustained with bread and water the monk John, " while a look of fiery malignancy shot from his eyes," unfolded the tale of the enormous cruelties of the hellish Gondez.

Messengers are dispatched to King Robert Bruce requesting a number of soldiers to be sent to seize the abbot.

Meanwhile the subterranean vaults are explored to discover the lady who is confined there, and after a long and weary search through endless mazes the female stranger and another captive are found to be immured in the most secret dungeon of the abbey.

A vessel now arrives from Italy, and it is suspected that Gondez intends to convey his treasures on board and fly to a foreign shore. Howbeit, Huberty is consoled by the appearance of the spirit of Geronimo, who still prays for the tortured soul of the Little Red Woman. This spectre herself impedes Gondez, who is on the point of departure, and so alarms him that he falls in a swoon. His person is secured ; the Italian vessel is boarded by the Scottish troops ; his keys are found and the lovely captive, together with a gentle youth, her companion, are released from their durance.

In due course it appears that she is Ronilda the Fair, the daughter of Guy FitzArran, the Laird of Finalgan Castle, and that the youth is her brother, the Laird Donald FitzArran. One stormy night she was, together with Donald, through a trick captured by the detested Abbot Gondez and his crew, and borne to the vaults of Oronza, where he " revealed the extent of his abandoned desires " and informed the lady that thenceforward she was to " be the mistress of his un-bridled pleasures and abhorred licentiousness." All the liberty permitted was at night to pray in the chapel, and here she saw for the first time Huberto. With difficulty she avoided sheer rape, but, as the fair Ronilda expresses it, " still the power of innocence enshielded me with its puissant arm, and I repulsed the daring efforts of this fiend of infamy and vice."

At this point [33] " our history must needs retrograde," as Scott has it, and we are in the sumptuous palace of the family of the Marquises of Alvaroni, " within the towering walls of the noble city of Man-fredonia, in the kingdom of Naples." Here dwell the gloomy Stephano Alvaroni, a widower, with his beauteous daughter, Rosanna Valenza.

At Rome resided the detestable and depraved Cardinal Nicolo Gonzari, uncle to that noble and virtuous youth Duca Martini Gonzari, of the castle of Taranto. The Duca and his bosom friend, Count Ferdinando Ozimo, whilst visiting Rome, at an assembly of the greatest personages meet the Marquis Stephano Alvaroni.

On his journey from Rome assassins attempt the Duca's life, and his steed, taking fright, carries him to an ancient chapel. " The building was in the form of a cross, and was decorated externally and internally with the most beautiful gothic ornaments ; three lofty casements on either side, and one over the altar, at the extremity of the middle aisle, reflected around a rich and chequered light from the gaudy colours of the emblazoned and highly ornamented glass.

"In the middle of the choir stood a sculptured monument of veined marble, whereon rested the effigies of Huberto Alvaroni, the founder of that edifice. The altar was of alabaster, most curiously wrought, representing, in basso-rilievo, the beatification of the blessed Virgin Mary; and round the walls of this sacred spot were placed carved representations of the twelve Apostles."

In this sainted chapel Rosanna is offering her orisons. "The mellow radiance of the sinking sun tinged the wide expanse of the western horizon with the mingled hue of brightest gold and dye empyreal; all nature was serene, and her prolific bosom nought displayed but sweetest harmony."

At this hour the Duca enters the shrine; he sees the amiable fair; they love.

When the Duca returns to Rome suspicions awake in his heart so closely is he watched by his uncle, the Cardinal, and by a mean pander and sycophant of his uncle, Giovanni Maldachini. The noble youth, ever mindful of " the soft passion which every hour assumed a greater imperium over his soul, began to grow weary of the pretended solicitude of the Cardinal and his eleve."

The Duca now seeks the Marquis Alvaroni, who is visiting the retired Villa Serveta, and here, in the chapel where he first met Rosanna, the lovers are " united by the indissoluble bond for which they had panted with mutual ardour."

Count Ozimo is summoned to be the guest of the happy pair, but a few days after the Duca (ere his friend arrives) is called to Rome, since his uncle is dying of a dangerous fever.

On his way to the Villa Serveta, Count Ozimo rescues a lady from ruffians, but afterwards is treacherously wounded and left for dead by the ferocious employer of the murderer, a miscreant who has his countenance veiled by a black vizor.

The Count is rescued by a humble forester, who nurses him to health, and he resumes his journey to the Villa Serveta only to learn that, immediately after the Duca's departure, dispatches to hasten his journey to Rome were brought by an eleve of the Cardinal, Giovanni Maldichini. This prelate supped with the Marquis, and immediately after spurred back to Rome. That night the Marquis expired in agonies, his body assuming a livid colour, and scarcely had he breathed his last than a band of armed banditti carried off the Lady Rosanna.

The Duca himself has disappeared on his way to Rome. Ozimo suspects that the Cardinal, who has suddenly recovered, is at the bottom of these hellish practices, but he can do little against so powerful a prelate, and accordingly " he made himself master of the habilliaments of a mendicant of the Order of the Holy Cross " so that as a member of that wandering fraternity he might trace the truth.

The Abbot Gondez, under arrest, was brought before the Scottish King upon accusations of high treason. He listens to the tale of his crimes with an air of gloomy ferocity, and demands, " Are there any further charges to be adduced ? "

" The inquisition of Rome shall take cognizance of crimes as yet untold," thunders a mysterious voice when " suddenly, two male figures, enveloped in sable robes, and wearing vizors to conceal their faces, stalked forward, each presenting a folded parchment, superscribed to King Robert Bruce."

The hidden crimes are " cognizable to the fraternity of St. Dominick," and under a strong escort, commanded by Huberto Avinzo, the Abbot Gondez is conveyed to the city of Rome, " the necessary accusations having been preferred before the Abbot of the Dominican Monks of that city, who then occupied the important post of Inquisitor-General of the Italian States."

At midnight, " the Inquisitor General, and the other officers of that dreadful tribunal, being assembled, and surrounded with the usual insignias of terror," the Abbot Gondez " was brought before the tremendous table of office by two officials masked," whilst the deep and terrific voice of the Accuser-General from a secret part of the hall declared that the Abbot " was guilty of the damning crimes of Heresy, Parricide, and Murder."

When in answer to a triple exhortation Gondez maintains his innocence the most extraordinary phenomena are exhibited. " The hall resounded with a discordant yell, and the lights were suddenly extinguished ; when several officers of the inquisition rushed into the chamber, clad in sable habilliments, and wearing vizors of crimson hue, some bearing torches emitting a blood-red gleam, whilst others displayed instruments of torture, which appalled the sick'ning soul of the enhorrored delinquent."

To top these terrors, with terrific shrieks the hideous spectre of the Little Red Woman, of Oronza's monastery, rushed into the inquisitorial chamber, until the Inquisitor-General seized the crucifix and exorcised the ghastly phantom, who vanished howling, " Come, Gondez, come ! "

Guilty obduracy, seconded by shame, yet prompted the monk to deny the charges, and in consequence he is thrice racked, when finally,

the extremest torture being inflicted, Gondez makes full acknowledgement.

It now appears that Father Anthony of St. Columba's monastery
is none other than Count Ozimo, who has tracked the guilty Gondez
down the years.

One evening whilst in Rome, about eight months after the Duca
Gonzari and his bride have so mysteriously disappeared, Ozimo finds
himself in the church of the convent of the nuns of the order *Della
Pieta*. Here he is struck by a sumptuous marble monument bearing the
name CARDINAL NICOLO GONZARI. Upon the tomb reclines the full-
length marble statue of the Cardinal, and as he gazes Ozimo perceives
that the eyes of the statue are in motion and bent full upon him in
mingled anguish and horror.

" Is there not a God ? " moan the marble lips.

A little after a whisper calls him to the grate, through which a
nun thrusts a billet in his hand, begging him to attend at midnight
at the door of the cemetery of the convent. Here he is met by a nun
who, with tears and prayers, entrusts to his charge a most lovely
sleeping infant. " By the eternal ruler of Heaven, no mortal power
shall wrench from my protection this harmless babe," swears the
Count. The nun hands him a casket, which upon returning to his
room he finds to contain jewels of immense value, and a letter begging
him to deliver the child and a packet to Count Ozimo. Breaking
open the paper addressed to himself, he reads the writing of Rosanna
Valenza, and learns that the babe is the son of his friend, the Duca.

In order to escape those powerful foes who have struck the noble
house, Ozimo resolves that the child shall be nurtured in another land,
and under the feigned name Ferdinando Alzarro he sails to Scotland,
where a little later he entrusts the boy, now called Huberto Avinzo,
to Sir Allan Macdonald. Himself he returns to Italy to follow his
plans. Circumstances compelling him to quit Rome, he retires as
Father Anthony to the Monastery of Oronza.

We now read " The Substance of the several Confessions of
Giovanni Maldichini, otherwise Gondez, Abbot of the Monastery of
Saint Columba. *Taken before the Holy Dominican Fathers of the Inquisition
at Rome.*"

The Cardinal Nicolo Gonzari having formed an impious connexion
with the Madre Aluzzo, Abbess of the Convent Della Pieta, " wherein
every disgraceful scene was practiced by the vicious Cardinal," the
fruit of their amours is a male child, who early becomes habituated
to their abominable courses, and who is none other than the Cardinal's
supposed eleve, Giovanni Maldichini.

In order that the Cardinal may obtain his nephew's dukedom and domains, Maldichini attempts to assassinate the Duca in the forest, an endeavour which leads to the meeting of the latter with Rosanna.

It is Maldichini who, luring the Duca to Rome on a false report of the Cardinal's illness, waylays him and imprisons him in a dreary castle situated remote on one of the rugged mountains between Rassina and Ascoli.

It is he who poisons Marquis Alveroni, and abducts Rosanna, who actually was so nearly rescued by Count Ozimo.

In the Convent Della Pieta the Madre Aluzzo receives and jails the lovely sufferer, who is visited by the Cardinal. No sooner does he see the beauteous wife of his persecuted nephew than his guilty mind dares to entertain the most abandoned desires. Maldichini, however, burns with a similar lust for the lady, and learning from his abandoned mother the plans of the Cardinal, he will brook no rival, but, dead even to filial duty, he takes his father off by a slow poison.

He now changes his name to Gondez, and in order to further his ambitious views by assuming an air of great sanctity, and aided by the wealth of the Cardinal which has come to him, he acquires much influence.

Soon after the birth of her son, the Duchess, who has been secretly removed to the Castle which held her adored Lord, " consigned her agonized soul to the bosom of its maker."

" Fired with malignant rage, the bloody Giovanni Maldichini, anxious to terminate the existence of the amiable Duca Gonzari " as being the only person who could shake him in the possession of the Ducal estates, " determined upon giving the full rein to his vengeance, being still unsatiated with the sanguinary crimes which he had already committed." He is already nominated Abbot of Oranza, and ere he goes to take possession of his monastery he resolves to dispatch his every victim. Attended only by his vile creature Dominico, he repairs to the dismal fortress. " By day, the insidious villain would stalk with measured pace through the dreary chambers of the gothic pile, and by night, unaccustomed to enjoy the cheering balm of sweet repose, he would arise from his couch, and repairing to the battlements, pace, with folded arms, along the platform, unconscious of the tranquil hour which lulls the breast of virtue and content to balmy sleep. In vain did the orb of night throw her chaste beams upon the bosom of the procreatic earth ; in vain did the multifarious host of scintillating gems lace the dark expanse of ethereal space ; nothing could draw forth a genial thought from the sanguinary Priest, at whose heart the gnawing canker-worm of guilt unceasingly played." At length he administers to the Duca a chalice of poison, and the bodies of Gonzari and Rosanna are secretly interred in some lone and hidden spot.

It will be observed that the episode of Maldichini and Dominico, together with much of the dialogue, is closely modelled on the conduct of Schedoni and Spalatro when they debate the assassination of Ellena in *The Italian*. Gondez then betakes himself to the Monastery of Saint Columba at Oronza,where he continues his villainies, his treachery and crimes.

The awful tribunal of the Inquisition condemn the guilty Giovanni Maldichini " to be burned to.death by a slow fire," a judgement " carried into effect within the walls of the prison, in the presence only of the judges, the officials of that tribunal, and of those concerned in the prosecution.

Count Ozimo, continuing his monastic robes as Father Anthony, solemnizes the hymeneal rites of Huberto, Duca Gonzari and Marquis Alveroni, with the fair Ronilda of Finalgan, at the castle of her ancestors, the ceremony being attended by the King and the whole Court of Scotland. " The chapel was perfumed with the odour of richest incense. . . . Festoons of flowers adorned the altars, while a blaze of light issued from every chapel, proceeding from enormous waxen tapers, which were supported by candlesticks of massive silver."

At midnight, preceding the nuptials, the haggard forms of the two weird sisters suddenly draw aside the encircling drapery of the Duca's couch and prophesy good and happiness.

On the marriage day angelic forms are seen amid divine harmony, fair spirits who sanctify with their benison " the sacred bond which sealed the happiness of the Duca Huberto Avinzo Gonzari, and the lovely Ronilda, fairest of the daughters of the race of Finalgan."

Two years later, in 1807, Ireland published his next novel, *The Catholic, or Acts and Deeds of the Popish Church*, 3 volumes, which it is equally ludicrous to describe as " an historical romance " or " A Tale of English history." A second edition [34] in 1 volume, 8vo, was issued in 1826 by John Williams of 44, Paternoster Row.

In 1822 was published 8vo, *The Maid of Orleans*, Translated into English Verse by W. H. I[reland], a version of Voltaire's *La Pucelle d'Orléans*.[35]

In 1796 (Vol. II, 1797) had been printed in two volumes *La Pucelle* ; *or, The Maid of Orleans* : *A Poem in XXXI Cantos From the French of M. de Voltaire*.[36] This version is ascribed to Catherine, Countess of Charleville,[37] although it is said she indignantly denied the work was from her pen. " It was executed and printed for private circulation by her second husband, the Earl of Charleville, prior to their marriage, and was not at all in her style. She delighted in refined wit and detested coarse humour." [38] Martin, in his Catalogue of Privately Printed Books,[39] definitely says that this translation was made by Lady Charleville. Fifty copies on small and five on large paper were distributed, and the remainder were destroyed by a relation of that lady. It is believed they were burned at Lord Charleville's seat. The Rev. Henry Boyd, the translator of Dante,[40] who was domestic chaplain to the family, declared he would instantly leave the house if the thing were published.

In 1899 *La Pucelle, The Maid of Orleans* was "Printed for the Lutetian Society," [41] 2 volumes, 500 copies, "A New and Complete Translation into English Verse Revised Corrected and Augmented from the Earlier English Translation of W. H. Ireland and the One attributed to Lady Charleville . . . By Ernest Dowson."

There are famous plays on S. Joan, but quite in error Mr. John Ramsay Allardyce Nicoll in his *History of Early Nineteenth Century Drama*,[42] under the name Ireland, naïvely describes *The Maid of Orleans, or, La Pucelle of Voltaire* as a Drama !

In addition to his novels, Ireland did a vast amount of miscellaneous literary work of this kind, but the Shakespearean exploits of his youth appear (perhaps rather unfairly) to have overshadowed his career until the end, for he cannot be denied very considerable talents, and beyond his novels much of his output has decided merit. He died in 1835.

Les Brigands de l'Estramadure, ou l'Orphelin de la Forêt, 3 vols., Paris, 1823, purports to be "librement traduit de l'anglais " of William Henry Ireland, but actually it is an original work by Madame de Saint-Spérat, who wrote under the pseudonym Charles Desrosiers. In the same way a work attributed to Madame Guénard, baronne de Méré, *Les Repaires du crime, ou Histoire de brigands fameux en Espagne, en Italie, en Angleterre*, " imitation libre de l'anglais et de l'allemand," 1813 (and several times reprinted) has incorrectly been supposed to draw from Ireland's romances.

In 1849 was published in three volumes [43] (T. C. Newby) *Rizzio ; or Scenes in Europe during the Sixteenth Century*, " By the Late Mr. Ireland. Edited by G. P. R. James, Esq., Author of ' Darnley,' ' Henry Masterton,' ' Richelieu,' ' The Forgery,' &c."

In a long and interesting introduction James tells the story of Ireland's Shakespearean forgeries, and remarks of Ireland that " all the prospects of life were blighted by the errors of the boy." The present manuscript was sold by public auction to a well-known bookseller, from whom it was acquired by T. C. Newby. When James was asked to prepare it for the press, he deemed it necessary to submit the work to some pretty drastic editing. He " found the style antiquated, and the expressions often of the worst kind of the novelistic school of thirty or forty years ago," accordingly he altered the language, improved the style, omitted and amended. In fine, James turned a Gothic novel into a historical romance of his own school. " Whenever it could be done with propriety, the editor left the author's words as he found them ; but there were many passages which he felt sure the author himself would have altered had he lived to the present day." This observation is, I make no doubt, entirely true.

Rizzio is a work of very great interest. It is written in the form of an autobiography of David Rizzio, and across the crowded scene there pass such famous figures as Correggio; Pietro Aretino; Cardinal Jacopo Sadoleto ; Henry VIII of England and his jester; Cardinals Wolsey and Campeggio ; the Earl of Surrey and the fair Geraldine [44] ; Cornelius Agrippa; François I and charming Anne de Pisseleu, Duchesse d'Étampes ; Henri II and Diane de Poitiers ; Catherine de Medici ; Pier Luigi Farnese ; Queen Mary I of England and her consort ; Queen Elizabeth of England ; the Cardinal of Lorraine ; and, above all, Mary, Queen o' Scots.

Some of these portraits are sketches, some drawn full-length, but all seem admirably done, with real vigour and power. We feel that they are living folk, not mere puppets dressed in ermines, purples, and brocades, and labelled with some name.

An Ireland without talent might be a phrase fitly applied to Joseph Fox, Junior, of Brighton, who in April, 1791, dedicated his first effort, *Tancred, A Tale of Ancient Times*, Minerva Press, 2 vols., 1791, to the Duchess of Rutland. The period of this romance is discreetly indefinite. Tancred, the heir of the domain of Rochdale, is, when an infant, exposed in the forest at the command of his inhuman mother, Lady Marguerita, by her wicked squire Laurence. Lady Marguerita assassinates two husbands, the Baron of Rochdale and the Baron de Rothsay, and plans to wed a third, the Baron Murcia, who however, is enamoured of and finally espouses her daughter, the Lady Helen. Tancred, who is saved and brought up by Old Fitz-Walter, gains his castle and estate; Laurence is killed ; and the Lady Marguerita, crying out to Tancred, " Look upon me still, young hero, and looking, view thy mother and the author of thy woes ! " drives a poniard through her heart. One feels that there is plenty of the right stuff in *Tancred*, had it been skilfully wrought, for a first-rate Gothic novel, but Fox misses his opportunities at every turn and shows himself amateur and awkward.

The second work of Joseph Fox is *Santa-Maria* ; *or, The Mysterious Pregnancy*, 3 vols., G. Kearsley, 46 Fleet Street, 1797, dedicated to the Duke of Marlborough,[45] the Epistle being signed February 18th, 1797, Bright-thelmston, Sussex.

This extraordinary romance, in some ways curiously reminiscent of de Sade's *Juliette*, is composed in a spasmodic jerky style, intensely irritating to read and as if the author had written in fits and starts, but the diction well befits the incidents of the narrative.

The author is lavish of his promises : " Surmise may spread her broad expanded wings—may soar—may flutter—and then may—droop—may—aye, may, at last, fall feebly as the airblown gossamer.—Somewhat of this *hereafter*—things MAY come out, perhaps to chill—to make the sensitive soul thrill with horror—to make the very hair stand perched on its native habitual roost, where so long it had lain recumbent." [46]

We are at once whirled in a tornado of circumstance and event. John, Count Rodolph, is celebrating the nuptials of his daughter Santa-Maria with young Prince Rinaldo, but upon the wedding-morn the Lady Isabella, visiting her daughter's chamber, " discovered her offspring clasped within the icy arms of death ! ! ! "

" The usual catholic ceremonies " were performed, but Santa-Maria " with an angel's smile " recovers and " again rolled her eyes within their splendid orbs."

Lord Rinaldo " anxiously pressed a speedy consummation of their nuptials—————at the Castle ! ! ! But, how alterable are the decrees of Fate !—how strange and inconstant are the fortunes we are heirs to !—for, the next day after the arrival of the last courier, Santa-Maria was seized with the most violent agonies and continual faintings :—her body was swelled, and her beauteous countenance became again pale, languid, and sickly.—Signior Bassano being sent for he soon discovered the cause—the fatal cause, of his fair patient's malady, and, in private with Lady Isabella and her daughter, he pronounced————(with the greatest degree of concern)——THAT SANTA-MARIA—WAS PREGNANT ! ! ! "

An explanation is demanded, but Santa-Maria protests her complete innocency. The friends of Count Rodolph note " the gloomy suspence that hung upon his sable brow." Terrible scenes follow, and the good friar Matalone is summoned to examine Santa-Maria's conscience. He concludes that the lady is entirely innocent, and that the pregnancy must in effect be " some wonderful instance of supernatural agency."

In order to shield her from her father's wrath, the Countess disguises her daughter as a pilgrim, and bids her flee the house. In case of pursuit she counsels her to " take sanctuary from her father's wrath in the *Carthusian monastery* " !

Rodolph now dispatches Bernardini and Goddard to Martarono Castle, to murder Rinaldo, whom he suspects of having debauched Santa-Maria.

A good deal of intrigue and many crowding events from which " the crimson blade of dark assassination " is not absent, follow helter skelter, but it will suffice to reveal the secret of the Mysterious Pregnancy, as it is told in the written confession of Father Conrad the Carthusian, a villain in his own mind, and an outcast from mankind, who expires in a cave, once the abode of wolves, in a " recluse glen." " Secrecy, avaunt !—For lo ! methinks, I view old Time shaking his hoary head, and with his finger pointing to my pen, advance and say— *This mystery must not, shall not be buried with the dead.*"

Conrad divulges in grandiloquent periods : " Once a monk in the Carthusian monastery—Youngly initiated in the luxuries and debaucheries of that order—I dedicated my whole time and thoughts to the gratification of my lusts and passions." After various incidents of poisoning those who stood in his way, "by stratagems the most diabolical," he cried : " My blood thickens and congeals ! I shake with terror at the thought.—My flesh creeps upon my very bones as I do ruminate upon it.—But it must come forth—then forthwith let it come—deed of darkness !—hell's own direct progeny !—"

Count Philip Contarini, a villain and sworn enemy of Rodolph's house, viewed sweet Santa-Maria with a lustful eye. Conrad, during the illness of Father Matalone, a pious brother of the order and virtuous confessor of Lady Isabella, contrives to be deputed as the holy representative of the sick monk. On " the holyday of St. Januarius " he visits the palace of Rodolph, and compalining of thirst, is given some cooling beverage to drink. He invites Santa-Maria to drink also in honour of the Festa. " And alas ! you but too readily acquiesced ; for, during that short interval, I secretly contrived to mingle a strong sleeping potion, which upon its taking due effect, I too well knew would answer the seeming appearances of death—Oh ! wretched me, too well I said I knew it.—For, when (horrible remembrance) any of the virtuous females of our convent held out too rigidly against my lustful purposes, I did administer this same sleeping potion, and when dead to every sense, enjoyed my will upon them. Then satisfied and pallid, dispatch them to the silent recesses of our graves, there to awake in all the horrors of a living death. Oh ! my soul sickens at the impious recollection. . . . This same sleeping potion had all its intended effects on thee, thou loveliest sacrifice ; and as thou wert supposed to be deceased, I was dispatched for, to sing requiems over your beauteous body. In this solemn office, Count Philip attended me disguised as a brother-monk, and in the absence of thy mother, the Lady Isabella, fully and grossly satisfied his impious lusts.—Nature, however, sleeping as you were, here gave a faint struggle against—— But hold—no more—Modesty forbids me to repeat the vile abuses he made of all his opportunities, nor the horrible satisfaction he enjoyed in the idea of sending thee violated to the bed of Prince Rinaldo.—I can no more—— Stung now with remorse, guilt, fear, I fled the monastery and retired to this cave——"

Count Rodolph poniards himself; Philip, Count Contarini, suffers decapitation on the public scaffold, whilst Bernardini and Goddard, who have been his accomplices, first undergo the torture extraordinary, suffering " the most inventive torture that the rack could invent—and having expiated their heinous crimes by the most cruel death, their mangled bodies were afterwards gibbeted on the banks of the river Crati."

To conclude, " the most noble Duke Reignier gave Santa-Maria away at the sacred altar of the chapel, to Prince Rinaldo ; the suffragan of Naples officiating on this happy occasion."

It is not uninteresting to note that in Chapter IX Fox introduces a hawking scene and employs several technical terms in falconry. He sets as his motto the following lines from Spenser (*Faerie Queene*, VI, II, XXXII,) :

Nor is there hawk, which mantleth her on pearch
Whether high towring or accousting low :
But I the measure of his flight do search,
And all her prey, and all her diet know.

Reference is made to the " fleer-birds," a fleer-bird being the movable perch to which a bird is tied, and which the bird-catcher can raise by means of a long string. Valentine, a young falconer, speaks of " larks and pippets," a pipit being the particular name given by bird-catchers to a species of lark. He also cuts a " disciplinary creance," which is a long line attached to a hawk's leash in order to prevent the bird flying away whilst in training. He makes out of black cloth a rufter-hood, a form of hood used for a newly-taken hawk. " Valentine, on this, discovering the bird begin to bate, observed, ' that it might now go to jouk, for I cannot (said he) in tenderness' sake, seal the poor creature.' " *To bate* of a hawk is to flutter and beat the wings impatiently on its perch ; *to jouk* is to sleep on its perch ; seal is better written and better known in the form *seel*. Fox may perhaps have derived some of these terms from Thomas Pennant's *British Zoology*, II, 1768.

It is hardly necessary even in passing to remark upon the complete ignorance Joseph Fox, junior, shows of the Carthusian Order. The name sounded well; it was mysterious and remote, and that sufficed.

Comic relief is entrusted in *Santa-Maria* to the gracioso Drosi, who has a drunken scene, " staggering, quite overcome with the charms of favourite mistress lachryma-christi." His babble is intended by Fox to be full of wit and fun. Drosi, unable to survive the blemished honour of his master, " like a Roman lived and like a Roman died." " And now, farewell honest Drosi—thou favourite darling of my fancy ! and o'er thy grave be this thine epitaph :

> A merrier man,
> Within the limits of becoming mirth,
> I never spent an hour's talk withal.
>
> SHAKESPEARE.

It is to be feared that Joseph Fox, Junior, was utterly lacking in a sense of humour.

Another highly staccato book from the pen of another Brightonian is *Osrick ; or, Modern Horrors*, a Romance,[47] " Interspersed with a Few Anecdotes, &c. That have their Foundation in Truth, and which are occasionally pointed out to the Reader," 3 vols., Lane, 1809, by Richard Sickelmore. This novel, curiously enough, is written with headlines, not unlike an article in the cheaper modern newspapers. Thus we are confronted with *Guilt, A Spectre, A Storm, A Frightful Abyss, The Cavern, The Rescue, A Coffin, A Corpse, The Lovers, Horrors, Surprise, Agony*, and finally, *Bliss, The Conclusion*—all in boldest type arranged as captions, although the work is not even divided into chapters. Occasionally, too, conversations are given in dramatic dialogue with speech-prefixes. Lieutenant Osrick Somerton, whose home is near Brighton, during the course of his adventures visits Monte Video and Buenos Ayres, where he rescues the lovely but ill-starred Clara from the sooty bloodhounds—that is to say, the Pampas Indians with their tomahawks. Osrick weds Alethea, and Clara bestows her hand on " the honest and deserving soldier " Dreadnought.

Once we can adapt ourselves to its rather tiresome mannerisms the tale is not altogether without interest, and it is told briskly enough. Richard Sickelmore also wrote *The Dream*, a Drama, 8vo, 1797 ; *Edgar, or The Phantom of the Castle*, a novel, 2 vols., Lane, 1798 ; *Quarter Day*, an Interlude, 8vo, 1798 ; *Saltinbanco*, an Opera, 8vo, 1798 ; *The Cottage Maid*, an Opera, 1798, 8vo ; *Aboukir Bay*, a Musical Drama, 8vo, 1799 ; *Agnes and Leonora*, a Novel, 2 vols., 1799 ; *Mary Jane*, a novel, 2 vols., 1800 ; *Sketches from Life*, a Comedy, 8vo, 1802 ; *Rashleigh Abbey or the Ruin on the Rock*, a novel, 3 vols., 1805 ; *A Birth-*

day Tribute, an Interlude acted at Brighton in 1805 ; *An Epitome of Brighton, Topographical and Descriptive*, Brighton, 8vo, 1815.

The Monthly Mirror for September, 1798, warmly congratulated Sickelmore for having so successfully imitated Mrs. Radcliffe in his *Edgar, or, the Phantom of the Castle*, but the *Biographia Dramatica* [48] rather cruelly describes Sickelmore as " a person still living at Brighton, who has the merit of having raised himself from a mechanic line of life by his pen as balnean purveyor of chit-chat news for the London papers." " Apollo on Horseback," as Sickelmore was nicknamed, was none the less esteemed " a very worthy character " who " has contributed several pieces of *novel* goods to the light summer manufactory of Lane and Co."

Bath as well as Brighton gave the world a quota of writers of fiction, but although John Palmer, Jun., a typical Gothic novelist, has been described as a schoolmaster in the former town, this is an error and confuses two persons, entirely distinct and unrelated. John Palmer, the literary schoolmaster came to Bath in 1794, and in the Rate Books for the first entry for the half year ending January, 1795, Palmer's name is inserted over the name of the occupier, Mrs. Orchard, at the address Cross Bath. In the 1797 Rate Book he appears as the occupier. In the *Bath Directory* for 1800 and again for 1809 there are entries : " Palmer, John, school-master 4 Chapel-court, Cross Bath." The *Bath Chronicle* records the death of " Mrs. Palmer wife of Mr. Palmer schoolmaster in Chapel-court," on September 28th, 1809, and little more than a year after, December 13th, 1810, there appears an obituary : " In Chapel-court Mr. Palmer schoolmaster." These details concerning John Palmer, schoolmaster of Bath, were kindly given me by Mr. R. W. M. Wright, Director of the Victoria Art Gallery and Municipal Libraries, Bath.

John Palmer, Jun., the novelist, was the eldest of the eight children of the famous John Palmer, the original Joseph Surface, for whom see *The Thespian Dictionary*, 1802. John Palmer, senior, died on August 2nd, 1798, which evening he expired with awful suddenness upon the very stage during the Fourth Act of *The Stranger*. John Palmer, Jun., made his début at the Haymarket in the summer of 1791 as the Prince of Wales in *Henry IV* to his father's Falstaff. The young sprig proved himself an actor of very considerable merit, and was soon supporting characters of importance both at the Haymarket and Drury Lane. A lively account of this " chip of the old block " may be found in that extremely personal and somewhat scandalous chronicle *The Secret History of the Green Room*, 1795, Vol. II, pp. 259–61. It is true that in drawing his portrait the critic seems far more inclined to record this young Gentleman's "hereditary dissipation" and to dilate upon his amours, "already somewhat curious," than to pay a fair tribute to his remarkable histrionic talent. John Palmer, Jun., died in 1810. He wrote : *The Haunted Cavern*.[49] A Caledonian Tale. One volume, Lane, 1796. Actually this romance was issued in November, 1795. *The Mystery of the Black Tower*, 2 vols., Lane, followed in 1796. In 1800 he published a novel, *The World as It goes* ; and in 1807 *The Mystic Sepulchre* ; *or*, *Such Things have been*. A Spanish romance, 2 vols., which in 1810 was translated into French by R. J. Dardent as *Le Tombeau mystérieux* ; *ou*, *les familles de Hénarès et d'Almanza*, Paris, 2 tomes, 12 mo. A posthumous work is : *Like Master, Like Man*. A Novel. In Two Volumes. By the late John Palmer, of the Theatre Royal, in the Haymarket. Son to the deceased and celebrated John Palmer, of the Theatre Royal, Drury Lane, and of the above-mention'd Theatre. With a Preface, by George Colman, The Younger. London. Printed for the relief of the Author's Widow. 1811. 8 vo. Joseph Knight, *Dictionary of National Biography*, Vol. XLIII, (under John Palmer, the father), mistakenly attributed *Like Master, Like Man* to the famous John Palmer, senior.

The *Critical Review*, December, 1795, was unkind to *The Haunted Cavern* when it said : "The tale of shrieking spectres and bloody murder has been repeated until it palls upon the sense. It requires the genius of a Radcliffe to harrow up our souls with these visionary horrors."

The Haunted Cavern is "A Caledonian Tale," the period that of Henry VI, the scene being at once set. "In the wild and barren county of Aberdeenshire within a league of the sea-shore, and on the summit of a lofty hill, stood a gothic castle." This is occupied by the "deceitful, cruel, and designing" Sir James Wallace. Matilda, daughter of Lord Glencairn, has been compelled to become his bride. They have a child, Jane, and when Lord Archibald, the brother of Lady Wallace, mysteriously disappears, Sir James sends his trusty follower, Carrol, to bring to the castle his nephew, Eldred, now Lord of Glencairn. Eldred loves Jane, who is promised to Donald of the Isles. This fierce chief, brooking no rival, seizes Eldred and prisons him in a loathsome dungeon, "a spacious, lofty vaulted cavern." Supernatural sights are seen and strange sounds heard. The tale runs its course with some ingenuity. We have the usual skeleton, the rusty dagger and mouldering manuscript. Eventually it is discovered that Sir James Wallace has (as he believed) murdered Lord Archibald, who now casts off his pilgrim's disguise, whilst Lady Matilda, whom her husband had immured in a convent at Rouen, escaped thence to return to Scotland, and during these years has been living privily at the cottage of old Maud, hard by the castle. Most of the supposed supernatural phenomena are accounted for; Sir James expires in bitter remorse; Eldred leads the fair Jane to the altar.

The ingredients may not be new, but they are well seasoned and served, and Palmer's romance was received with great favour.

The Cavern, indeed, proved a favourite word with the Gothic novelist, and we find such titles as *The Romance of the Cavern, or, the History of Fitz-Henry and James*, by George Walker, 1792; *The Cavern of Strozzi*, 1800, one vol., Lane; *The Cavern of Horrors*, 1802; Miss E. N. Bromley's *The Cave of Cosenza*, " altered from the Italian," two vols., 1803, Robinson; Mrs. Burke's *The Secret of the Cavern*, two vols., Lane, 1805; Miss A. A. Stuart's *The Cave of Toledo*, five vols., Newman, 1812; *The Cavern of Astolpho*, an anonymous novel, 1818; Zara Wentworth's *The Hermit's Cave, or the Fugitive's Retreat*, four vols., Newman, 1821; *The Foundling of Glenthorn, or, the Smuggler's Cave*, four vols., Newman, 1829; and very many more.

Among the list of subscribers to *The Mystery of the Black Tower*, 1796, are the names of more than forty well-known actors and actresses of Drury Lane, Covent Garden, and the Haymarket, at which last house John Palmer, junior, had made his début in the summer of 1791, and was playing juveniles with such marked success. Bannister, Mrs. Bland, Mrs. Crouch, Holman, Mrs. Jordan, the two Kembles, Michael Kelly, Miss Pope, Mrs. Powell, Mrs. Siddons, Signora Storace, Suett, all bespeak the new novel, while the author's father and his uncle Robert (also of the Lane) take a couple of copies apiece.

The period of this romance is the reign of Edward III, and owing to his gallantry in the Scotch and French wars, Leonard, the rustic hero, is knighted and otherwise highly honoured by that monarch. The villain, Lord Edmund Fitzallan, employs the Black Tower, which is commonly said to be most horribly haunted, as a prison for the fair Emma whom he abducts in mysterious fashion. She is rescued, however, by Leonard who loves her, and who eventually proves to be Lord Reginald Fitzallan. His father has been murdered, his title and estates usurped by the vile Edmund, a cousin of the house. There are numberless adventures and wanderings of fullest Gothic flavour, where banditti, a lascivious lady, an aged recluse, an evil steward, a low comedy tar, play their parts briskly enough amid such sets as the Pyrenean mountains, Montmorenci Castle, the Castle of St. Julian, a gothic monastery " fallen to decay," sea voyages and storms, a lonely heath. Owen, the poltroon squire, and the talkative Alice, who whilst proclaiming her secrecy and fidelity betrays her master's plans amid her endless babble are amusing and sketched with a good deal of humour. *The Mystery of the Black Tower* is a fine title, and was echoed by G. D. Hernon in his *Louisa*; or, *The Black Tower*, 2 vols., Symonds, 1805, a romance of the very first order. Here we have Mr. Gerrard, a widower, who dwells in most solitary retirement, " in the thickest part of an extensive and gloomy forest in Lancashire." His only daughter, the lovely Louisa, was " his entire companion in this most horrible retreat," locally known as the Black Tower, and by tavern repute a ghostly spot. There are many eerie mysteries, whilst a gang of robbers under one Captain Rifle (otherwise Mr. Hodges) show themselves exceedingly active during the course of the tale. They capture Louisa, but Hodges proves generous and returns her unharmed to her father. She marries young Sir Frederick Orion, who having been attacked by the ruffians and left for dead is carried into the Tower and nursed back to health. They pass many happy years at their seat Kirkham Hall. A phantom, robed in white, which wanders in the vicinity at dark proves to be the wife of Mr. Hodges, a lady of sadistic tendencies and prone most woefully to maltreat the unfortunates who fall into her power. Mr. Gerrard daily visits a secret apartment in the Black Tower whereto none but he has access. The explanation is that when his wife died he loved her so passionately that he caused the body to be embalmed, and he spends long hours in contemplation of her incrupted charms, the world having been deceived by an empty coffin.

We also have smaller fry in whose titles " Tower " occurs. Such are *The Mystic Tower*; or, *Villainy Punished*, Kaygill, *circa* 1799; and *The Round Tower*; or a Tale of Mystery, Roe and Lemoine, 1803. In France, *Les Mystères de la Tour Saint-Jean*, 4 vols., Paris, 1818, by the Baron de La Mothe-Houdancourt (later de La Mothe-Langon) was published as a translation from Monk Lewis.

In France, also, the title *The Mystic Sepulchre* was imitated. The Baron de La Mothe-Houdancourt boldly issued his *L'Hermite de la Tombe mystérieuse, ou le Fantôme du Vieux Château*, 3 vols., Paris, 1816, as " anecdote extraite des Annales du XIIIe siècle par Mme Anne Radcliffe." Very popular was *Le Tombeau*, Paris, 1799, by Hector Chaussier and Bizet, a work they proclaimed to be " Ouvrage Posthume d'Anne Radcliffe, Auteur de L'Abbaye de Sainte-Claire, des Mystères d'Udolphe, de L'Italien, etc. *Traduit sur le Manuscrit.*" *Le Tombeau* was reprinted, 2 vols., Paris, 1835, A. Pougin, and at Avignon, 1850, Peyri, as translated from Mrs. Radcliffe by the Abbé Morellet. *Le Tombeau* even appeared in a Portuguese version, Paris, Pommeret, 1842, but the *Journal de la Librairie* in noticing the book pointed out that it was not from the pen of Mrs. Radcliffe, but almost certainly an original romance of Chaussier and Bizet.

After the publication of Mrs. Radcliffe's *The Romance of the Forest*, 1792, Forests also became greatly in vogue, and a tale dealing with a forest was sure of a warm welcome. Thus we have Miss Charlton's *Phedora, or, the Forest of Minski*, 1798 ; Mrs. Eleanor Sleath's *Who is the Murderer ? or Mysteries of the Forest*, 1802, the anonymous *The Forest of Hohenelbe*, 1803 ; Miss Hill's *The Forest of Comalva*, 1809 ; Miss Cuthbertson's *The Forest of Montalbano*, 1810 ; Miss Houghton's *Mysteries of the Forest*, 1810 ; and Miss Smith's *The Banditti of the Forest*, 1818, all of which are Gothic in the highest degree.

The Forest of Hohenelbe, three volumes, Minerva Press, 1803, is by the author of *Humbert Castle, or The Romance of the Rhone*, and *Correlia, or The Mystic Tomb*, so the writer had a pretty taste in titles and a shrewd. Castle, Tomb, and Forest are very appetizing. In *The Forest of Hohenelbe* the Baron Miltitz adopts Josephina, the daughter of Joseph Keyser, who has saved his life in battle by the sacrifice of his own. Keyser, who was a young jeweller, had eloped with and married the Lady Louisa Tremain, whose father, the proud Earl of Tremain, at once cast her off with scorn. The Baron, at first, is passionately enamoured of the fair Josephina, but he will not seek her dishonourably, and he shrinks from a mésalliance. In time, however, he comes to love her as his daughter. Josephina, whilst riding in the Forest of Hohenelbe is rescued from danger and certain death by a young stranger, Albert, around whom hangs a mystery. She gives him her heart, and when the Count Zorembeg, a man of the highest quality, is received at the Castle Miltitz as the Baron's honoured guest she is amazed to recognize in Zorembeg her Albert. Zorembeg, however, greets her as a perfect stranger. After a long chain of adventures it comes to light that Albert, who is a captain of banditti, has assumed the rôle of Zorembeg and deceived the Baron. The banditti's home is in the Forest. In the end Albert weds Josephina, but through the treachery of the Baron's umquhile steward, the villain Muller, he is betrayed to justice, put on his trial and condemned. Rather than perish on the scaffold the luckless youth pistols himself in the prison. It is found by papers he left that he is the son of Baron Miltitz, Frederick, long thought dead, but who was kidnapped by the Baron's brother and in horrid revenge brought up as a bandit among the outlaws of the Forest. The Baron and Josephina retire to Castle Miltitz, their only joy being young Frederick, whom his grandfather and mother train in every virtue.

The Castle of Hohenelbe is altogether an exceptional Gothic romance, in that we have this departure from the conventional happy ending.

It is undeniable that this comes as something of a surprise, and it is extremely well managed by the author, who indeed shows no mean talent throughout what is a striking and in many respects a very original tale.

In reading the romances of William Child Green, it is not difficult to see why he was for so long a favourite of the circulating libraries. In the first place he takes as his model some well-known author, Sir Walter Scott, Maturin, Mrs. Radcliffe, whom he follows but by no means slavishly imitates ; he always writes with ease and often with elegance ; and it is quite obvious to us how thoroughly he enjoyed relating his story, a zesto which goes far to make his readers enjoy it too. Of his life nothing is known save that he resided at Walworth, and that he mixed in both literary and social circles of no mean standing. His portrait, painted by that gifted dilettante, le Comte de Carné, has fortunately been preserved.

Green wrote *The Woodland Family* ; *or, the Sons of Error and Daughters of Simplicity*, 8vo, 1824 ; *The Fays of Loch Lomond* ; *The Sicilian Boy* ; *The Prophecy of Duncannon, or, The Dwarf and the Seer*, 1824 ; *Abbot of Montserrat, or The Pool of Blood*, 2 vols., A. K. Newman, 1826 ; and *Alibeg, the Tempter, a Tale wild and wonderful*, 4 vols., A. K. Newman, 1831.

The Prophecy of Duncannon " is intended to represent the numerous and unavoidable straits and dangers, to which irreproachable virtue, and unsullied innocence may occasionally be reduced," not only by deliberate and wicked malice, but by the force of untoward circumstances which seem to present an overwhelming mass of evidence. " The galling and oppressive grievances of the high-spirited Lorrimond, are designedly contrasted with the milder, but not less pitiable sufferings of Rosilda Dinwiddie." The narrative is very lengthy, and indeed complicated, but there are some excellent scenes. No inconsiderable part of the dialogue is in the Scotch dialect, which Green uses with force and fluency, showing evidence of a long residence in Scotland, even if he were not (as seems more likely the case) a native of that country. The influence of Sir Walter Scott is very marked in *The Prophecy of Duncannon*, but it is only fair to add that there has been no slavish and futile imitation.

Had not Green himself mentioned in his Preface to *Abbot of Montserrat* that the first idea of his tale " was suggested to me by a purely accidental perusal of Mr. Maturin's elegant and powerful work, entitled ' Melmoth the Wanderer,' wherein he so admirably depicts the immeasurable value of an immortal soul," one might have guessed that he had his inspiration from Matthew Gregory Lewis. " Unlike that able author," he continues, "I have chosen to rescue my hero from the snare of darkness."

The scowling Obando the malecontent, a "pale monk" who regarded any whom he fancied were commenting on his conduct "with an aspect of horrible malignancy," invokes Zatanai, and there are some terrific incantation episodes which are not without a certain repulsive power. By the aid of Zatanai Obando "despite the apparent abhorrence of the brotherhood," contrives to have himself created Abbot, having previously strangled the holy Abbot Ambrose whose mitre he covets, and who has discovered him in the midnight cloister holding communion with the spirit of evil. He also essays to murder his brother Roldan, the leader of a band of desperadoes who harry the neighbouring mountains. The crisis comes when the familiars of the Inquisition, before which tribunal Abbot Obando has been "accused of the practice of almost every enormous crime," descend upon the monastery. Trusting to his familiar to deliver him, Obando commits himself to Zatanai and is borne away by the exulting fiend. At the last moment, however, he repents, and Zatanai hurls him from a vast height to fall a crushed and bleeding mass upon the gory pavement of the chapel. He expires, confessing a long life of blackest iniquity, but he had renounced the cacodemon at the last, and not too late. It is obvious that this catastrophe is taken from *The Monk*.

Green is careful to inform us he has carefully read up "various works, tours, essays, etc., that have been written respecting the Monastery of Montserrat," and he places his story "In the romantic 'olden time,' when chivalry was flourishing at its height," but he has fantastic ideas of a cloistered life, in fact, he gives full rein to his imagination and a sturdy Protestantism which (quite unwittingly I am willing to believe) does not stop short of scandalous profanity.

With regard to The Pool of Blood, since he did not hesitate to introduce the supernatural, it is disappointing to find that this is a mere trick, the "sanguine-tinted pool is in reality bloodless," and instead of being the blood of the late abbot it is incarnadined by a chemical preparation, "well calculated to delude the eyes of vulgar superstition and conventual ignorance." But I regret that pool!

Alibeg, the Tempter, "A Tale Wild and Wonderful," 4 vols., A. K. Newman & Co., 1831, commences with Oriental scenes in an oasis hard by the Euphrates. "A young and graceful Arab," a "son of the desert," Almaket, is listening to the sweet melodies of his sister, the lovely Mohara. Here a mysterious visitant encounters them, Alibeg, whose exterior is most venerable with an ample beard of silvery whiteness. Alibeg, who is none other than the demon (1 Peter v, 8) "the

tempter—the devourer," entices Almaket into his thrall, and we pass
through a veritable panorama of scenes and events. We are taken to
Sicily for the " festival of saint Rosolia " ; to Moscow, to the palace of
Count Alexander Smolensko ; to St. Ives in Cornwall ; to Circassia
amid the Tartars ; and in each place Almaket meets with extraordinary
adventures which, however, always end in death and doom to those he
loves : Seraphina, Agatha Smolensk, the beauteous Ora, his blooming
Indian bride, his once-prized Amelia Tregonning, and the rest. At the
end Alibeg shows him what he has in his folly thrown away, how
impious was his presumption to interfere with his own destiny.

When the Gothic novel approaches the 'twenties and 'thirties of
the nineteenth century we find that it tends more and more to become
definitely historical, which is, of course, due to the immense influence
of Sir Walter Scott.

Thus *The Wizard Priest and the Witch* by Quintin Poynet, dedicated
to Mrs. Richardson of Evreux, Normandy, 3 vols., A. K. Newman and
Co., 1822, is a romance of the days of James I. The narrative opens
with a hunting party, which introduces us to Sir Harbottle Cutts of
Cutts Castle, comitatu Northan, Lady Margaret, his wife, their son
and heir Reginald, and in their train Alison Fawkes, a waiting-woman
upon Lady Margaret, for which position she was chosen for her
extreme beauty. The costumes of the characters as they emerge from
the woods that border Round Copse Pond are described in ample
detail, and with a profusion of technical terms extremely Ainsworthian
in manner. The falconer of Sir Harbottle is Rob Ptarmigan. Alison
and Reginald, being separated from the party, encounter a gipsy, Sibyl,
who tells the damsel's fortune in octosyllabic rhymes, recalling the
Lancashire Witches.

Chapter II is occupied with three brothers, Nicholas, Walter, and
Herbert Wharton, of Wharton House, near Thrapton. Nicholas the
eldest is a hard-hearted and ferocious profligate ; Walter, dependent
on his brother, is hypocritical and cunning. He has been steward to
the estate, but is dismissed to his bitter chagrin and the anger of his
wife Gillian. This formidable lady forces her way into the presence of
Nicholas to demand his brother's reinstatement, but is curtly dismissed
" with schreeching violence of voice—' Spider of hell, begone ! ' "

Walter Wharton has, however, furnished himself secretly with keys
that admit him to the treasure-room of Wharton House, which he
enters secretly at night, loading himself with plunder. Moreover, he
hears Nicholas plotting his assassination, and feeing Brito Spadrone
and Captain Hacco, thereto, and accordingly decamps with his wife
from the neighbourhood.

We now turn to Oxford and Herbert Wharton, who, although weakly in body, is in mind able and acute. He finds in his College Library " dangerous and forbidden volumes " " which contained, in their unhallowed pages, the learning and secrets of necromancy, conjuration, and magic." After long toil he renders himself an adept of the black art, and meanwhile, assuming a cloak of sanctity and demureness, is admitted by the Bishop as Rector of a living in his brother's gift, about a mile and a half distant from Wharton House. Here he lives in the isolated rectory, once part of an old Franciscan house. He dwells secret and alone. " There was something inconceivably horrible in the fixed gaze of his heavy and sullen eye, which, sunk deeply in his head, scowled slowly on the object to which its vision was directed." Here he is attended by Gundred Wolfe, the notorious witch of Thistledown Copse, a fearful hag, whom the villagers would have ducked and hanged.

Reginald Cutts who rides out to interview Walter Wharton on business, never returns, and since his purse, his hat, and other incriminating evidences are found in the lozel hut of certain churlish hinds, the wretched peasants are tried and hanged for the murder.

Nicholas Wharton now cunningly abducts Alison whose charms have captivated his lustful heart and bears her off to Wharton House.

He has, however, a rival in his brother Herbert, who determines to possess the maid and summons " to his aid the minions of that being, before whose tremendous iniquity and power the whole of created nature trembles and quails." On a night of woe and dread he invokes the demon Azazel who bids him seek the aid of Gundred Wolfe and her familiar Howlet. Herbert succeeds in effecting Alison's escape, but she only finds she has fallen into worser hands. Retribution is following swiftly upon the wizard's path, and suddenly he and Gundred Wolfe are arrested on charges of sorcery. " The guilty rector, however, avoided the ignominy of a public trial and execution by destroying himself in prison. . . . His guilty compeer, Gundred, was tried and cast for death, and the dreadful sentence of the law, namely, that she should be burnt at the stake, was carried into execution "—as novelists use.

Brito Spadrone has for his own purposes deceived his employer, and instead of killing Walter Wharton they capture him to hold to ransom. The robbers find that it is not Walter Wharton whom they have seized but Reginald Cutts. Reginald, until they can develop their plans, they kidnap to France in the Gosshawk, and he is imprisoned in the subterranean dungeons adjoining the venerable nunnery of Notre Dame. Here a fearful ruffian, ranger and verderer of the

PLATE XV

WILL^M CHILD GREEN, ESQ^R.

LONDON

WILLIAM CHILD GREEN

[Face p. 372

forest of Notre Dame, Monsieur Becasse, is his jailer. The wretched cell where he is confined was "contrived as a place of penitence, and for the imprisonment and punishment of those who might render themselves obnoxious to the vengeance of monastic cruelty and sacerdotal rage." This affords occasion for a good deal of ultra-romantic anti-clericalism in the style of *The Monk*, especially when Reginald, who has secreted a poniard, perseveringly works his way through the rubbled wall of his miserable den and penetrates into "a narrow apartment, in the furniture and decorations of which neither elegance nor comfort had been consulted." Here he perceives the form of a female in "the conventual garments of a nun," a victim (of course) of the Prioress of Notre Dame. This "victim of priestly malice and pride—no matter wherefore" is furnished with coarsest food by "the nun Agatha, a wicked minion of the will of the prioress." Needless to say that when Sister Agatha arrives she is all that commends itself to Protestant prejudice and ignorance. In one hand a basket containing "the stinted meal of her prisoner," in the other a flambeau whose light "gave her an appearance somewhat infernal and terrific," she enters in most melodramatic fashion. "She was a woman of tall and haggard appearance, in age, as nearly as he could judge, full fifty, but of a strong and stubborn frame, and features whose primitive ugliness defied the hand of time to add ought to their repulsiveness. Her dress, the habit of a professed sister of the rigid order of St. Benedict, was not calculated to lessen the want of natural grace, or mend and mellow the hard outline of her sharp and querulous countenance."

Suffice to say that Reginald "in spite of her resort to nails, teeth, and kicking," surprises and overpowers the nun Agatha leaving her chained where umquhile "the victim of priestly malice" was pinioned. The rescued nun—to use a phrase so dearly beloved of Protestants—and her liberator after some hairbreath scapes arrive in England. It is discovered that Agnes Montcalm, for so the vagrom lady is called, was forced to take the veil—"a ceremony, replete with senseless mummery, was performed over me," she mews in true Kensit—Horton vein—in spite of which she was married by a "Hugonot clergyman" to Nicholas Wharton, who helped her fly from the convent, and when he tired of her dispatched her back with a letter to her superiors bidding them have a better watch over their subjects. Naturally, Agnes Montcalm is vexed at such treatment, and now she proceeds to attempt her revenge in very summary fashion. Upon being confronted with her, the countenance of Nicholas Wharton "flushed as it had been an instant before with wine and passion, assumed the pallid, the cadaverous tint of the cold tenant of the grave." Nevertheless he recovers himself sufficiently to pass his toledo through her body.

Accused of murder upon murder and other heinous crimes, Nicholas Wharton refuses to surrender, and is besieged in his house. After a terrific struggle he falls and his myrmidons are cut to pieces about him.

It comes to light that Alison is none other than the daughter of Agnes Montcalm and her thrice-guilty husband. She " is recognized as heiress of the large domains of Wharton House," and in the course of a year or two she is wedded to Reginald. " A long life of peace and happiness was kept in store, by Providence," for the loving pair.

Two very typical Gothic-historical romances of the latest period are C. A. Bolen's *The Mysterious Monk ; or, The Wizard's Tower* (time of King John), 3 vols., 1826 ; and *Walter the Murderer ; or, The Mysteries of El Dorado* (Henry VII), 3 vols., 1827 ; both published by A. K. Newman.

> I love to sing of courtly dames,
> And Knights y'clad in mail ;
> And thread the mystic clue that binds
> The legendary Tale.

This is the motto inscribed on the title-pages of *The Mysterious Monk*, which commences most excellently : " The bleak November blast whistled shrill through the half-decayed turrets of the Castle Caerphilly, and the pale moon, with intermitting ray, cast its fantastic glimmering light through the stained casements of its Gothic gallery, as with light step Ella passed to the chamber of the lady Gertrude."

The lady Gertrude is dying, and by her bed kneels a strange monk to whose charge she solemnly commits Eric di Montimar, with his sister Ella, as she expires. Eric and Ella have been brought up in seclusion at Caerphilly by Lady Elinor, " princess of Bretaigne, the sister of the deceased prince Arthur," and Lady Gertrude. When the latter fell sick to death, Eric was dispatched to summon Earl Pembroke. Almost immediately after the decease of Lady Gertrude, Ella is seized by two armed men, who assert that their warrant is from the king and peremptory, and conveyed from the Castle in a close litter. She is rescued by Philip Fauconbridge, a true preux chevalier, who conducts her to his mother's castle, where she is warmly welcomed. Not the least notable feature of the noble gallery of this edifice is a full-length portrait of Richard Cœur de Lion. Philip Fauconbridge, repairing to Caerphilly, finds the place deserted, and only left in the charge of some drunken menials from whom he can glean nothing. He returns perplexed, but in time to save Ella from the amorous overtures of Sir Gervase Osterly, a visitor to Fauconbridge Castle. Upon the occasion

of young Fauconbridge being summoned to appear before the King at
Lynn, Sir Gervase becomes more pressing in his advances, and is with
difficulty foiled. Lady Fauconbridge and Ella now resolve to repair
to Lynn, sailing from Bristol port.

The vessel is attacked and Ella carried off to the fortress belonging
to the baron Osmanville, who assigns her to the Count Volquessen, a
lewd fellow, who very soon declares his intentions. During the night
Ella is mysteriously rescued by the monk Adolphe, and by means of a
secret passage conveyed to the Convent of S. Margaret. The sacred
building is shortly invested by a troop of soldiers, but among the
officers appears Philip Fauconbridge, now Richard Plantagenet, Earl
of Monmouth. Ella and the Earl exchange mutual vows, but on the
appearance of King John, the shrinking maiden recognizes the hateful
Count Volquessen in the monarch. In truth, Volquessen is one of the
Norman princes owning the sovranty of John, and Fort Osmanville
is the secret scene of his debaucheries.

Ella, in order to secure her safety, is now placed in attendance upon
the Queen Mother, Elinor of Provence, with whom she becomes a
great favourite for a while, although when the young princesses notice
her too much, the Queen Mother arranges that she shall visit Longholm
Castle as the guest of Lady Pembroke, the mother of Lady Matilda
Marsham, Ella's friend and confidante.

Longholm Castle, " a magnificent pile of Gothic architecture," is
well described. " A little to the left rose the spires of a monastery of
Benedictines, and on the right appeared among the clustering trees,
one solitary tower." This lonely tower, known as the Wizard's Tower,
had the reputation of being haunted by unquiet spirits, and at night
flames were seen to flicker, amid these dilapidated turrets.

At Longholm events begin to crowd swiftly. A billet is conveyed
to Ella from her brother Eric, whom she meets secretly. He tells her
that for many months he has been the prisoner of banditti, but finally
was released by a monk who conveyed him to the monastery near
Longholm. As they are talking two figures approach, one Lady
Pembroke, who is deep in converse with a mysterious sibyl. To Lady
Pembroke the weird woman gives a seal, bidding her show it Pembroke, and ask to whom it belonged, " and he will tell you *the murdered
Di Montimar*. Ask yet again, whose hand gave the death blow. . . .
Then say thou thus: Hipolita still lives, and vengenance sleeps
not ! "

The next day Lady Pembroke carelessly addresses her husband,
" You are a judge of antiques, my lord—what think you of this ring ? "
The earl glanced his eye on the ring, but the instant he saw it, he

exclaimed,—"Oh God! it is the Signet of the murdered Di Montimar!" and rushed out of the saloon.

Ella naturally conjectures that the extreme agitation of Pembroke points to this nobleman as the assassin of her father. That evening when Ella passes through the postern of the castle she is seized and carried off to the Wizard's Tower where she is confined in a small romantic chamber. The ruffian Giovanni, her abductor, leaves her to the company of the sybil, that eerie woman who on hearing her name leads her back by a subterranean passage and through a panel into the very picture-gallery of Longholm. "Secrecy or death," whispers the sybil, as she retires. Ella, half-swooning, now overhears a colloquy between Lady Pembroke and the monk Adolphe, in which the siren reveals that she has loved passionately, and implores the inflexible penitent "by all the guilt our headlong passions gendered" to return to her arms.

The heir of Pembroke, young Lord William Marsham, who has long been wasting away, dies not without suspicion of poison, and there is a fine midnight funeral scene, sketched briefly though it be, and not of course comparable to those magnificent chapters in *Rookwood* when Sir Piers is gathered to his fathers amid tempest and storm.

By a subtle device Lady Pembroke, persuading Ella to follow her to the vaults of the castle, immures the unsuspecting heroine in a secret dungeon.

Meanwhile Father Leopold, of the Benedictine monastery of S. Stephen, has desired Eric to accompany him to France on a mission of the first importance, and the lad has only spared a moment to trace a few lines to his sister advising her of his journey. At Dieppe Dom Leopold leaves Eric, whom he has introduced to Richard of Monmouth, under whose tutelage the gallant youth enters the service of the King.

After numerous adventures, Ella succeeds in escaping from her dungeon, and to her joy encounters the Lady Fauconbridge, or rather as she now is, the Countess of Caerphilly, Monmouth's mother. This lady has wrung the Queen's consent to the transfer of Ella from Lady Pembroke's care to her own wardship.

None the less Lady Pembroke still continues to persecute the hapless Ella, and mysteries thicken on every side. In several interfluous chapters dealing with the French campaigns and the prowess of Eric and Monmouth, with the talk of soldiers and camp-followers, the echo of Scott is very distinct.

He is also imitated in the progress of the Princess Isabella with Ella in her train to Germany. In the company is a page, Theodore, who proves to be Virginia. During an Alpine journey, Ella and

Virginia are carried off to the castle Del Raimondo a fief of the Conte Osterius, who is Sir Gervase Osterly, the uncle of Virginia. The ruffian Giovanni now appears, and is indeed a scion of the same house. There next follow a number of very complicated family histories which would require at least a genealogical table to explain in a small compass and which in their unravelment occupy many pages of the narrative. It must suffice to say very briefly that the Marchese di Montimar had two sons, Ernulpho and Albert. Ernulpho on his father's death succeeds to the estates and quality of his father, who is estranged from Albert owing to the latter having contracted a marriage with Ipollita del Castro. This lady dies giving birth to twins, Enrico and Ipollita, who are reared by their uncle, Albert expiring of sorrow a few months after his loss. Enrico at the age of eighteen is befriended by Lord Charles Marsham, ambassador of Richard Cœur de Lion, and a relation of his mother's house. Ipollita, who has taken the veil, flees her convent to join Lord Charles, whom she loves, and who is now become Earl of Pembroke. He has sworn to marry her, upon which she does not hesitate to accompany him to England, only to find that he weds the daughter of Baron Monteagle. Ipollita, who dwells in retirement, bears Pembroke a son, Giovanni di Montimar, and a daughter, Urbanina. The Countess of Pembroke accompanied by her lord's sister, Lady Gertrude Marsham and her brother Enrico, is sojourning abroad. Lord William Marsham, the heir of Pembroke, is born about this time. Meanwhile Enrico and Gertrude, deeply in love, wed clandestinely. This is discovered by Pembroke, whose treachery to Ipollita is, however, revealed when that lady, escaping from the convent where she has been confined, tells her tale to Enrico. Pembroke in an access of fury, kills Enrico, but the Countess resolves to retire to Normandy in the company of Lady Gertrude. The vessel is wrecked, and only Lady Gertrude saved. In secret, hearing her brother has murdered her husband, she withdraws to Caerphilly and dwells forgotten and unknown.

Giovanni di Montimar has been brought up in the country by a retainer, but Urbanina is under the protection of a Roman lady of high rank. Ipollita tells her two children of her wrongs and tutors them to revenge. She learns, moreover, that Pembroke has married (a second time) to the heiress of Rayo. Sir Gervase Osterly, as Conte Osterius, is now claiming the estates of the late Conte, Ipollita's uncle, and when she puts in her claim the matter is settled by his marriage to the lady, since then the property must devolve on her son and daughter.

The Countess Ipollita, in whom Ella recognizes the *sibyl of the Wizard's Tower*, is planning to marry Giovanni to Ella, and Urbanina to

Eric. The matter is complicated by the fact that Virginia is posing as Eric, and "an eclaircisement would infallibly doom her to instant destruction." Moreover Urbanina, who is enamoured of Richard of Monmouth, recognizes Virginia. There is much treachery, and the Countess Ipollita uses every tyrannous cruelty to effect her ends, whilst the licentious conte who is nightly exhilarated by copious draughts of wine, mocks at the rules of decorum in his pursuit of the heroine. She is, however, mysteriously protected by a retainer named Ulric, who after many adventures and hairbreadth scapes, proves to be none other than Enrico di Montimar, for eighteen years numbered with the dead, the father of Eric and Ella.

De Montimar assists his daughter's escape, but they are pursued by Giovanni. Some dramatic and exceedingly well-told incidents which follow culminate in the seizure of Ostorius and Giovanni by the Holy Inquisition, and shortly the scene shifts to Rome, nor are we sorry that various episodes are briefly described since Innocent III appears in terrible caricature. A further mystery is revealed when Adolphe the Monk proves that Eric and Ella are not the children of Enrico di Montimar and Lady Gertrude, but of the Earl Pembroke and his first wife the Lady Enningarde Mounteagle, who was not indeed drowned (as reported) when sailing to Normandy with Lady Gertrude, but rescued, although she expired in giving birth to the children, whom their aunt, to avenge her husband, Enrico's murder by her brother, reared in seclusion at Caerphilly. Adolphe is the brother of Lady Enningarde. The sudden death of the Earl Pembroke affords the enemies opportunity to accuse her of witchcraft, but the charges fall to the ground, and Stephen Langton, Archbishop of Canterbury, himself undertakes her defence and liberation, since it is shown that Earl Pembroke is not dead but has been drugged with a draught which brough completest insensibility, in which state he was hidden away and held captive by his own Countess. The wretched woman, frantic with her passion for Adolphe, drives a dagger to her heart.

Events rapidly clear. Ella is wedded to Richard of Monmouth ; whilst Osmanville, as well as Ipollita and Giovanni, "paid the forfeit of their crimes : all perished miserably."

The influence of Scott and Mrs. Radcliffe, are very clearly marked in this extremely typical romance. Scott is particularly discernible in the chapter which deals with the French campaigns ; whilst the adventures of Ella at Del Raimondo in many instances may be paralleled by the sojourn of Emily at Udolpho. There is some attempt at historical "atmosphere." We met with King John and Eleanor of Acquitaine, Isabella of Angoulême and her daughter, Isabella, wife of the Emperor Frederic II, Pope Innocent III and Stephen Langton. Moreover, there are some brief historical notes. Thus a scene is well described commencing : " It was Sunday, and the fête of St. Blaise ; yet the doors of the churches were closed—not a single bell was heard— a general hue of desolation seemed to cover the land. . . . The kingdom was under an interdict," and we are referred to " Berington's *Life of Henry the Second and his Sons.*" The licentiousness of King John is remarked and his seduction of a lady from her father's castle, for " King John was accused of many similar intrigues.—See Hume." When the Inquisitors seize Giovanni we are reminded in a footnote, " The Inquisition was first established at this period, by Pope Innocent the Third." Various details are given of the battle of Bouvines, July 25th, 1214, " *Vide* Anquetil's *Histoire de France.*" We must not, of course, look for any regular accuracy, that is, indeed, far enough to seek, but there are at any rate evidences that some care has been taken, some authorities have been read. The lesson of Scott could not now be entirely ignored.

The same remarks may be applied to Bolen's second novel, *Walter the Murderer ; or, The Mysteries of El Dorado*, where with appropriate, and in some cases lengthy, notes mention is made of the whirlicot, a coach or carriage, for which the author has drawn upon Stow ; the Exchange at Antwerp Gresham's model for the Royal Exchange ; Dr. Faustus and the printer Fust ; the Emperor Maximilian and his love of venery ; various details of the fall of Granada ; the duplicity of Sir Robert Clifford, who in 1494 was betraying Perkin Warbeck to Henry VII ; and several other pertinently topical allusions. The story itself which need not be examined in detail, is well and briskly told ; the narrative is interesting and not extravagant ; whilst the conversations are written with great liveliness, and as occasion serves with character and humour. As a whole this romance is an advance on *The Mysterious Monk*, and must be pronounced an exceedingly creditable performance.

In 1827 the new era had already begun. William Harrison Ainsworth had lent his help to John Partington Aston in writing *Sir John Chiverton*, published by Ebers in 1826 ; *Rookwood*, avowedly inspired by Mrs. Radcliffe, was to follow in 1834.

Devereux, Lord Lytton's first historical romance was published in 1829, and in the same year came the *Richelieu, A Tale of France*, of George Payne Rainsford James, a romance commenced in 1825, and completed owing to the encouragement of Sir Walter Scott.

Ainsworth, Lytton, and James. All three are thoroughly in the Gothic tradition ; are, in fact, Gothic novelists. All three are among the greatest romanticists of the last Golden Age of Literature, the palmier days of good Queen Victoria.

NOTES TO CHAPTER VI

1. Second Series, Vol. XIV, p. 352.
2. Vol. XVIII, pp. 223–4.
3. *L'Europe Vivante*, 1667, p. 215.
4. *Some Account of the English Stage*, Vol. V, p. 223.
5. *Ibid.*, Vol. VII, pp. 640–1.
6. Baker, Read and Jones, 3 vols., 1812, Vol. I, p. 153, No. 27.
7. *Ibid.*, Vol. III, p. 408, No. 125.
8. Series the Third, Vol. VII, No. 4, December, 1805, p. 438.
9. Series the Third, Vol. VIII, No. 3, July, 1806, p. 327.
10. Series the Third, Vol. X, No. 1, January, 1807.
11. See pp. 175–7.
12. A reference to Wycherley, Vol. II, p. 125 ; to Colman's " Dramatick Romance " *Blue-Beard*, Drury Lane, January 16th, 1798 ; to Mrs. Centlivre's *The Wonder*, *A Woman keeps a Secret*, Vol. II, p. 231. The passage quoted in the text is from Vol. I, p. 147.
13. Not *The Bloody Monk of Udolpho*, a blunder made by some few early bibliographers, and frequently repeated, as by Miss Birkhead in *The Tale of Terror*, 1921, pp. 75 and 230.
14. *The Critical Review*, June, 1801 ; New Series, Vol. XXXII, p. 232.
15. September, 1802.
16. I know of only two copies, one of which is in the Bodleian Library.
17. *Anthony and Cleopatra*, III, xiii, l. 185.
18. Vol. II, p. 191.
19. G. P. R. James, Preface to *Rizzio*, 1849, Vol. I, p. 22.
20. See *The Monthly Mirror*, January, 1796, Vol. I, pp. 169–77 ; also pp. 291–2.
21. Malone's copy in the Bodleian ; Malone, B. 320.
22. *Some Account of the English Stage*, Vol. VII, pp. 245–52. James Payn's *The Talk of the Town*, 1885, is founded on the incidents of the forgeries by Ireland, called Erin in the novel, and has a vivid description of the " first night " of *Vortigern*.
23. The 8vo reads " is ended."
24. Vol. IV, p. 99.
25. *Registers of the Stationers' Company*, Roxburghe Club, Vol. I, 1640–55, London, 1913, p. 429.
26. Preface to *Rizzio*, 1849, Vol. I, p. 25. On p. 22 James, giving an account of Ireland, says : " He afterwards wrote several novels, which, I believe, proved very successful." See also *Precious Relics or the Tragedy of Vortigern Rehearsed. A Dramatic Piece.* 8vo. 1796.
27. " Such gen'rous praise as bade my ABBESS live " ; Preface to the Reader, *Gondez the Monk*, Vol. I, p. vii. *The Abbess* was reviewed in *The Gentleman's Magazine*, July, 1799, Vol. LXIX, Part II, pp. 601–2.
28. Vol. XXXIV, pp. 203–4. *Rimualdo* is also briefly noticed in *The Critical Review*, Vol. XXXI, April, 1801, pp. 474–5. The writer judged the story " artfully complicated, but too artificially developed."
29. 1771–1850, the famous Carlton House buck and regency dramatist, whom Henry Vizetelly remembered as " an ancient fop." Horace Smith dubbed him " an admirable specimen of the florid Gothic."
30. Actually after the battle Robert de Bruce first sought safety in the mountain districts of Athole and Breadalbane, and a little later took refuge in Rathlin, an island on the Antrim coast.

31. *King Lear* IV, 6, "Shrill-gorg'd Lark."

32. Presumably, if Ireland means any Saint at all, he was thinking of S. Ceolfrid, Abbot of Jarrow and Wearmouth, *ob.* 716 ; Feast, September 25th. The Relics of S. Ceolfrid were formerly venerated at Jarrow.

33. Vol. III, chapter 9.

34. The inaccurate account of Ireland in *The Dictionary of National Biography* gives this as the first edition.

35. Begun in 1730. The first (surreptitious) edition is 12mo, Louvain, 1755. The first acknowledged edition, no place (Genève), 1762.

36. " Translated by the celebrated Lady Charleville and afterwards rigidly suppressed." MS. note in the Bodleian copy : shelfmark, Arch. Bodl. C. II, 36.

37. Charles William Bury, born June 30th, 1764, created Earl of Charleville, February 16th, 1806, married June 4th, 1798, Catherine Maria (*née* Dawson), widow of James Tisdall of Bawn, co. Louth. The Earl of Charleville died suddenly, October 31st, 1835, in his lodgings at Dover, aged 71. His widow, who had been educated in a French convent, died February 24th, 1851, in Cavendish Square, Middlesex, aged 90. She was long a leader in Dublin society.

38. *Diaries of a Lady of Quality*, 1797–1844. London, 1864. One vol., 8vo. P. 109, note, where it is incorrectly stated that Catherine was the wife of the *first* earl, and that she died in 1849.

39. Second ed., 8vo, London, 1854.

40. *The Inferno of Dante Alighieri in English*, 2 vols., 1785. Boyd, who was vicar of Rathfriland, translated the *Divina Commedia*, 3 vols., 1802. He also made other versions from the Italian, and wrote many original pieces. Watt, *Bibliotheca Britannica*, 1824, Vol. I, pp. 142*b* and *c*. *Biographical Dictionary of Living Authors*, 1816, p. 35.

41. Leonard Smithers.

42. 1930, Vol. II, p. 319.

43. Reprinted, C. H. Clarke, one vol., 12mo, 1858.

44. It is interesting to compare the scenes at Windsor and Hampton Court with similar episodes in Ainsworth's fine romance, *Windsor Castle*, 1842–43.

45. George Spencer, fourth Duke of Marlborough, 1739–1817.

46. Vol. I, chapter iii, pp. 27–8.

47. Dedicated to the Countess Craven, the lovely Louisa Brunton (1785–1860).

48. 1812 ; Vol. I, Part I, p. 669.

49. Reprinted in *The Romancist, and Novelist's Library*, ed. by William Hazlitt, Vol. IV (1840), p. 401.

SURREALISM AND THE GOTHIC NOVEL

" THE source of bad criticism, as universally of bad philosophy,"
shrewdly remarks Bishop Hurd, "is the abuse of terms." It is
necessary, then, before any serious inquiry can be usefully essayed or
profitable discussion entered upon that we should in the very first place
ascertain exactly what is implied by Surrealism, and so we begin by
asking what, briefly but adequately summed up, are the qualities and
values, the inspiration, the method and aims of this " conscious and
deliberate artistic principle." Now the answer proves not at all easy
to find, since the various definitions and even essential formulas which
Surrealist leaders, both in literature and art, freely give us are almost
invariably so conditioned and companioned by qualifying statements
and pregnant if subtly elusive suggestion that although at the outset
there seems to have been put forward a precisely clear, logical and
enlightening statement when we examine a little more carefully we find
that articles in this credo which showed hard-set, dogmatical and basic
tend in some surprising way to evaporate and evanish, whilst other
facets hitherto unsuspected thrust into sight and are vehemently
forced upon our attention.

Before we have gone very far too on our intellectual journey, it
becomes impossible to shun the conviction that there must be and
manifestly is a very vast difference between precept and practice, that
too often the Surrealist achievement does not in any way follow upon
or even remotely relate to the conception, that in not a few quite typical
instances of Surrealist prose, poetry and painting there has in effect
taken place a violent and volcanic disruption of thought and ideas,
which not infrequently drops to bathos and expresses itself by flat
contradictions, burgeoning out into even more extravagant phenomena
which are neither beautiful, wondrous, symbolical nor true.

This general statement, I am very well aware, does not of itself
hurtfully affect Surrealism, nor indeed any other movement concerning
which it might legitimately be advanced. Again and again the disciple
betrays his master. He is weak and incompetent where the master is
sure and strong. Misinterpretations, prejudice, caricature, malice
prepense beset the lot of all, whether the movement or the individual.
An insulting Sinon is always ready to throw open to the foe the gates
of every Troy.

So Mr. Herbert Read is emphatic that there is "*good Surrealism and bad Surrealism*," and he quite frankly acknowledges that "the Surrealists are . . . aware . . . of undesirable elements in our midst." He meets and argues this fact, which has been rather short-sightedly cast as a slur on the movement, with the utmost fairness and is soon able to dispose of it. None the less such a general censure as I have hinted at does carry weight if it appears that the most considerable output of any movement—Surrealism for example—which might be supposed to be the raw rhapsodies and exuberant hallucinations of some greenhorn clique or the klaxons of some loose hangers-on, a heresy in fact, is so very far from any such thing, so very far from any repudiation and disownment, that it is actually the work of the masters *en haut*, the leaders and evangelists, sponsored, approved and acclaimed by them, and enthusiastically accepted by their whole following.

Material contradictions existing synthetically within a work of art are irrational and destructive. The subject ceases to be a work of art. Mr. Herbert Read, in his *Surrealism* (1936; pp. 87–88), says that he is "often accused of contradictions " in his critical writings, and that he is "not particularly uneasy about them." (To avoid any sort of misconception, I would remark that we are not of course considering the position in which a man has revised his judgement—literary or otherwise—and holds contrary opinions to those he once maintained, it may be years before, it may be in ignorance and youth. We are treating of simultaneous contradiction.) I cannot think Mr. Read very happy in his explanation and defence. He is content to observe : " I do not choose to present a falsely regular façade. I have a strong dislike for people with symmetrical faces." There is no contradiction in irregularity. A face may be far from symmetrical without contradiction. In fact, to support his contention Mr. Read has confused his terms.

It may seem that we have wandered out of the way from our quest for the definition of Surrealism, but the path is vague and difficult, and it will be all the easier for a little preliminary clearing of the ground.

Mr. David Gascoyne commences his Introduction to *A Short Survey of Surrealism* (1935) with these words : " Confined from early childhood in a world that almost everything he ever hears or reads will tell him is the one and only *real* world and that, as almost no one, on the contrary, will point to him, is a prison, man . . . is for ever barred except in sleep " from other planes of existence. This is a most surprising assertion, and it strikes me as demonstrably false and mistaken. Even in the realms of pure imagination, the earliest stammered wisdom of the human family, folklore, fable and fairy tale all paint another world. Deep-seated conviction has its uneradicable place in man's heart, although it express itself betimes in metaphor and apologue. Personally, I should have said that almost everything man ever hears or reads will tell him that this is *not* the one and only world, it is not the real world, but only the shadowed entry to the house, our abiding home. Everything points out to him that the material is a prison. There is not a philosopher worthy of the name, not a mystic of the East or of the West, hardly a poet who does not say as much. Nature herself, as that great and holy Pope, the saintly Pio Nono so explicitly instructed us, teaches this. What of the Bible, still a best-seller ? Nay, the simplest child's Catechism sets this forth as a vital, perhaps the first truth. The world is a theatre, but as Jean Paul observes—I think in his *Hesperus, oder 45 Hundsposttage*—this is not the play, only the rehearsal.

Following on so amazing a premise Mr. Gascoyne has an eloquent plea for the recognition of the dream-world, or " oniric domain," and urges a revaluation of its importance, stressing the large part it occupies in this life where sleep demands so much of our time. " It is the avowed aim of the surrealist movement," he continues, " to dispose altogether of the flagrant contradictions that exist between dream and waking life, the ' unreal ' and the ' real ', " and thus to make the dream-world " the acknowledged common property of all." Such then is the chief objective of this " strange new ' modern ' movement."

But, we ask ourselves, what is there strange, what is there new, what is there modern in all this ? Is this " avowed aim " anything other than what romanticism has achieved throughout the ages ? Is it not what Æschylus showed upon the Greek stage when in mighty verse he unfolded " the vast, the incorporeal, the ideal " ? In his dramas mountains are made to speak ; Brute Force is a living person with bitter gibes in his mouth, possessed of a horrible vitality ; when the Titan is hung on the Scythian crags old Father Ocean, ruler of the deep, converses with him and there gather round the maiden daughters of Ocean, powers of primitive nature. As John Addington Symonds has so admirably said : " It is no episode of real or legendary history which forms the subject-matter of the play. The powers of heaven and earth are in action." Has Æschylus not given us other planes of existence ? A terrible domain, indeed, a world of elemental suffering ; the problem of conflict between a noble (if perchance a mistaken) resistance and the sovran will. All count of time is lost. The struggle is not for years, but centuries. How it was solved we can never know.

In lighter vein Aristophanes has built for us Cloudcuckootown

where King Epops rules and the Birds have their own language singing
in " native wood notes wild " that Welcome to the Nightingale which
is one of the most liquid and loveliest melodies in all lyric poetry, and
in the end Peisthetaerus is wedded to Basileia amid a riot of Hymen's
revelry. Trugaios too mounts to heaven upon a beetle, and after he
has seen the demon giant War and his foul servant Tumult braying
up the Grecian states in their infernal mortar, with his comrades
heaves the fair goddess Peace from the well into which she has been
thrown whilst the Chorus sing " Yoho ! yoho ! " as they all strain at
the cable. Dionysus visits the lower regions, and as in Charon's
barque he crosses the lake all around the Frogs are hoarsely croaking
" Brekekekex, koax, koax," and on the further shore he is met by the
rout of Eleusinian mystics chanting their ritual hymns to Iacchus,
Demeter, and Lady Persephone. Socrates invokes the Clouds,
begotten by the Sun on the myriad smiling waters of the Sea and shaped
by immeasureable Air, and they come in swift silent procession, so
lovely yet so illusive in their robes of vapour, mantled with mist.
The Greek comic poet gave us a veritable world of dreams which take
actual form and voice.

Does not Shakespeare bring us into a world where Bohemia has a
wild sea-coast, to an Illyria where dwells a noble lady whose uncle and
suitor bear good old English names and carouse in good old English
fashion ? He leads us through the glades of Arden by the murmuring
stream, where stands " a sheep-cote fenc'd about with olive trees " to
ramble with Silvius and old Corin, to meet Phebe and Audrey and Sir
Oliver Mar-text and Hymen ; or again we wander all one summer's
night in the fairy-haunted wood a mile without the town of Athens.
With him we hoist sail for that uninhabited isle, set amid what mystic
ocean ? On the battlements of Elsinore at midnight stalks "the majesty
of buried Denmark"; at the pit of Acheron Hecate and the weird
sisters deceive Macbeth with fair-seeming shows. Have we not another
world here ? A world of romance that mingles— so vivid is it—with
reality.

Beaumont and Fletcher take us to Rhodes to assist at proud Evadne's
spotted nuptials and hear sad Aspasia sing her song of the dismal yew,
or again to Sicily where love lies a-bleeding, or to Lycia to mark the
relentless working of Cupid's revenge. On the fat plains of fruitful
Thessaly we company with the holy shepherdess Clorin whom the
Satyr delights to serve, with wanton Cloe and Alexis, what time the
river god rescues wounded Amoret from his silver stream, and falls
doting on her loveliness. We lodge with Mercury's mother at the
farm and rise early of a morning to go milking with Nan and Madge,

and are pleased to watch our busy hostess setting out against company
comes the new stools

> and boughes and rushes,
> And flowers for the window, and the Turkey Carpet,
> And the great parcell salt, with the Cruets.

To the sound of trumpets and atabals Dryden shows us Granada
besieged, and the traitor Zegrys fighting with the Abencerrages in the
streets whilst Spain thunders at the gate ; or the usurping Indian
Queen distraught with passionate desire as she seeks the dismal cave
of the warlock Ismeron and calls from his sleepy mansions the dark
God of Dreams only to hear the fearful warning " Fate and Misfortune
will too quickly come " ; or again we mingle with the hot intrigues of
an Oriental harem the zenana, whilst four sons contend in pitched field
around the tottering throne of their ancient sire, and Nourmahal burns
with incestuous fire for the gallant Aureng-Zebe.   In gentler mood,
almost divine, we hear sweet S. Catharine disputing with the pagan
philosophers whose masters she puts to silence and to shame, nay
more, she wins them to the truth, dear martyred Saint whom Angels
watch and ward whilst she slumbers, whose dreams are of Paradise and
Heaven.

What new worlds does not the romantic fervour of that " Arab
soul in Spanish feathers ," Pedro Calderon de la Barca give us.   What
depths of profoundest philosophy in *La Devocion de la Cruz* !   How
sublime the mysticism of the *Autos Sacramentales* !   They draw their
inspiration from the very fount and source of all mysticism, the Corpus
Domini.   The poet shows us how the fables and imaginings of the
heathen foreshadowed the doctrines of Catholic Revelation.   In one
marvellous *auto* the new palace of the Retiro is taken as a type of the
celestial city, Jerusalem.   The noblest poetry celebrates the noblest
theme.   It has been admirably said that Calderon, " like Shakespeare

> Call'd up
> The obedient classicks from their marble seat,
> And led them thro' dim glen and sheeny glade,
> And over precipices, over seas
> Unknown to mariner, to palaces
> High-archt, to festival, to dance, to joust,
> And gave them golden spur and vizor barred,
> And steeds that Pheidias has turned pale to see."

On a far, far lower plane indeed, but not without much beauty and
much wit the Venetian Carlo Gozzi opened out a new world of fairy
fantasy.   Nor must it be forgotten that France and Germany regarded
Gozzi as a Romantic Poet of the first order.   Hoffmann was enthusiastic

in his praise, and one of Wagner's earliest operas *Die Feen* is founded on *La Donna Serpente*. In *L'Amore delle Tre Melarance* we are introduced to the court of Silvio, Re di Coppe, "Monarco d'un Regno immaginario, i di cui vestiti imitavano appunto quelli dei Re delle carte da giuoco." (Coppe, or Cups, are the card-pips equivalent to the English Diamonds, so here we have a figure wholly reminiscent of Lewis Carroll. From the Surrealist point of view, Lewis Carroll is to be ranked with Shakespeare ; Herbert Read, *Surrealism*, p. 56. Giuseppe Baretti, the famous critic, who was a prominent member of the Johnsonian Garrick circle was wont to maintain that Carlo Gozzi stood second to Shakespeare alone.) The Knave of Cups, Leandro, is Prime Minister, and in this land we meet a rope and a dog both of which talk in sonorous Martellian verse. When an orange is cut open there issues a lovely maiden in rich radiant robes, and a snow-white dove (an enchanted princess) gossips with the cook, Truffaldino, as he is busy at the spit. In *L'Augellino Belverde* we are introduced to Tartagliona, the wicked Queen of Tarocchi, and encounter a statue which walks and talks, and is indeed a petrified philosopher. The Green Bird itself can talk, and there are apples which sing and a golden water which plays and dances featly.

In Italian poetry Ariosto sings

> Le donne, i cavalier, l'arme, gli amori,
> Le cortesie, l'audaci imprese. . . .

he creates a world of romantic chivalry where we may roam. To quote John Addington Symonds : "The serious problem of his life was to construct a miracle of art, organically complete, harmonious as a whole and lovely in the slightest details." And so real was this wonder world to him, this realm of magic and marvels, of knight-errantry and adventure, of combat and love, so vivid and vital were his figures, the fair Angelica, Orlando and Rinaldo, Ruggiero and his mistress Bradamante, Cloridano and the handsome country-lad Medoro, Zerbino and the rest, that the poet's fancy was enraptured and enskied by them, and in their company he walked all the way from Carpi to Ferrara in his thin house-slippers, treading meanwhile the meads and forest glades of his own enchanted land. And so there is nothing grotesque, nothing absurd in Astolfo's journey to the moon, in the course of which the hero looks in on Prester John, and climbs the mountain of the Earthly Paradise where S. John Evangelist welcomes him and sets him down at a banquet furnished with all delicacies, and anon orders out the fiery chariot in which Elias Propheta rode, and himself escorts the Paladin to the lunar spheres. Only a genius, a supreme poetic genius to whom such fantasy had become a real adventure could conceive and write these thirty-fourth and thirty-fifth cantos and never once become ridiculous or trifling or profane.

What more famous in poetry than Armida's ensorcelled garden, and the forest which is guarded by the demons whom wizard Ismeno at " dead noon of night " summons from the deep ? Love-lorn Tasso lived in a world which proved less real but more cruel to him than he has painted in the pages of the *Gerusalemme Liberata*.

One might speak of the golden *Arcadia* Sannazzaro created which inspired the *Diana* of Montemayor, the six thousand pages of Honoré d'Urfé's *Astrée*, and (not forgetting earlier sources such as Longus) a whole pastoral realm, an imaginary lotus-land " des bergers oisifs . . . qui passent les jours et les nuits uniquement occupés à faire l'amour," as Bernardin de St. Pierre observes, but yet which was so intensely real that social stars and persons of the first quality dressed themselves in silks and satins as rustics and villagers, and wielded dainty crooks all beribanded and gilt. Thus they interpreted their dreams in actual life.

It were easy to continue the list of romantic writers, to refer to the supreme genius of Apuleius, whose every page is steeped in the supernatural, and who can combine erotic adventure of the starkest realism with vision that melts into an ecstasy of rapturous mysticism. There are the vast cycles of chivalrous romance, *Huon de Bordeaux*, *Milles et Amys*, *Ogier le Danois*, and the whole lineage of Amadis de Gaul and the " muy valeroso Cavallero " Palmerin. There are the heroic romances of Gomberville, La Calprenède, and Mlle de Scudéry. There is the great French romantic school so deeply influenced by Mrs. Radcliffe, Lewis, Maturin, Byron and Scott with the battles of *Henri III* and *Hernani*, *Antony* and *Marion Delorme* and the almost fanatical Cénacles of enthusiasts. What a roll of names has Germany alone to offer ! Zimmermann, the Schlegels, Goethe, Schiller, Tieck, Novalis, Körner, Brentano, Arnim, Görres, Chamisso, La Motte Foqué, Hoffmann, Zschokke, Cramer, Vulpius, Eugenie Naubert, Speiss, Buchholz, Kerndörffer. There are our own English novelists. There is the tradition of Ainsworth, Lytton, Le Fanu, Collins, Miss Braddon, Ouida, Amelia B. Edwards, the two Wardens, and many more. Did not Dickens in picaresque romance so vividly create his persons that after a hundred years visitors to Ipswich are shown the bedroom at the White Horse where Mr. Pickwick slept, and we lunch at the Hop Pole, Tewkesbury, and sample their madeira, because when Mr. Pickwick dined there he drank bottled ale, madeira, and port. Who shall say that the world of Dickens is unreal ? It needs not

Bleak House, Great Expectations, and *Edwin Drood* alone to claim Dickens as a great romantic writer.

Almost at haphazard I have mentioned the names of a few great romantic writers who have created a world—a dream-world, if you like, although as not in any way subscribing to the theoretics of Freud and his followers I use so coloured an expression with due caution and reserve—at any rate, the romanticists have created a world and flung it wide to be " the acknowledged common property of all " who list. What then becomes of " the avowed aim of the surrealist movement " ? In what sense is Surrealism strange or modern or new ?

The *Encyclopædia Britannica*, Fourteenth Edition, 1929, Vol. XVII, pp. 63–64, thus characterizes Surrealism : " The Surrealist doctrine, derived from Freudism, believed in the expression of thought without the control of reason and sought to paint dreams and states of mind by any means whatsoever. Its followers sought to suggest the mystery of the subconsciousness by translating ordinary objects into strange, horrible or sentimental forms."

The Shorter Oxford English Dictionary, 1936, defines Surrealism as " A form of art in which an attempt is made to represent and interpret the phenomena of dreams and similar experiences," and dates the word 1927. (Actually the word is said to have been invented in 1919, although perhaps the meaning as yet was somewhat undefined.) To interpret the phenomena of dreams, yes, but let us hope not nightmares.

I wish in sincerity and truth to approach an important artistic and literary subject seriously, without bias and without prejudice. Such specimens of Surrealist art as the pictorial work of Joan Miró—he cried " Je veux assassiner la peinture ! "—" Maternity," 1924, and " Carnival of Harlequins," 1924–25 ; Hans Arp's " Dancer," a piece of string, 1927 ; Len Lye's " Marks and Spencer in a Japanese Garden," 1930 ; Salvador Dali's illustrations, 1934, to "Les Chants de Maldoror," a prose work by Isidore Ducasse, who called himself Comte de Lautréamont ; the sculptures of Jacques Lipchitz, 1934 ; " Torso," 1934, " Concrétion humaine," 1935, " Configuration," 1936, " Mutilé et apatride," 1936, of Hans Arp ; the " Antartic Landscape " of W. Paalen, 1936 ; Georges Hugnet's " Poème-découpage," 1936 ; all these are ugly distortions, unshapely, repellent, conveying no suggestion, no idea.

In Surrealist literature such poems as Tristan Tzara's *L'Homme Approximatif* and *La Grande Complainte de mon Obscurité Trois* ; Pierre Reverdy's *Mon doigt saigne* ; Benjamin Péret's *Bâbord pour tous* and *De Derrière les Fagots* ; Réné Char's *Métaux Refroids* ; Marcel Duchamp's fragment *Teinturerie Rrose Sélavy* ; Philippe Soupault's

Dimanche ; Louis Aragon's 97–28 ; Valentine Penrose's *Mes bêtes capricieuses revenaient des champs* ; Henri Pastoureau's *Une fois mort on mettra un dirigeable sur mes yeux* ; all these I find a gross meaningless jargon, without sense, suggestion, music, symbolism or beauty.

Yet these artists and writers, Joan Miró, Salvador Dali, Hans Arp, Georges Hugnet, Tristan Tzara, and the rest are among the most prominent and the most representative figures in the Surrealist movement. I am all the less surprised then to find that Mr. Herbert Read writes : " For poets like Dryden and Pope, for painters like Michelangelo and Poussin, and for many lesser artists, we can only have an angry and in no sense patronizing pity."

Mr. Hugh Sykes Davies tells us how " At the beginning of our ' classical ' age, Dryden found himself in difficulties because he could not throw over entire the Elizabethan achievements." Nothing could be further from the truth, and in view of the facts I do not very well understand what Mr. Davies means. A little later (*Surrealism*, edited with an Introduction by Herbert Read, 1936, pp. 130–1), Mr. Davies talks of " that devastating reaction away from humanity which culminated in the eighteenth century of European culture, and which must be regarded as the last great attempt of the Catholic Church to establish universal oppression. Of this reaction ' classicism ' in literature is one aspect . . . in France under Louis XIV, and in England under the last Stuarts Poesy was literally stamped out by Church and State ! ! ! " In view of such extraordinary distortion it is really not worth while trying to understand what Mr. Davies means. Nothing could be more absurd, nothing could be more false than to regard ' classicism ' in literature as fostered and inculcated by the Catholic Church, which incidentally has never sought " to establish universal oppression." It is almost unnecessary to point out that in Catholic counties Romanticism has proved a very living inspiration. In fact, there is no true romanticism apart from Catholic influence and feeling. Dryden who was a romantic poet—not a classicist as Mr. Read and Mr. Davies suppose—was a Catholic.

Not a few critics, as I am well aware, affect to regard Dryden as a hidebound classicist, and Theodore Watts Dunton, for example, writing in *Chambers's Cyclopædia of English Literature*, 1903 (Vol. III, p. 3), speaking of " the moment when Augustanism really begins—in the latter decades of the seventeenth century " goes so far as to say " the periwig poetry of Dryden and Pope ousted all the natural singing of the true poets." This is extremely partial, so much so indeed as to be untrue. The fact is that certain of Dryden's poems, acknowledged masterpieces, have focussed the attention of reviewers and biographers who thus entirely lose sight of the fact that other of his poems are essentially romantic, not to mention his theatre of nine-and-twenty plays, of which sixteen are tragedies (or dramatic operas) and far from being hedged by any set rules, whilst of the rest such tragi-comedies as *The Rival Ladies, Secret-Love, Marriage A-la-Mode, The Assignation, The Spanish Fryar*, and *Love Triumphant*, have serious scenes of the most romantic cast. It is true that, adopting a rigidly purist outlook, Dryden in his *A Parallel betwixt Painting and Poetry* prefixed to *The Art of Painting*, 4to, 1695, a translation from Du Fresnoy, speaks of " our *English Tragi comedy* " as " wholly *Gothique* "—a significant phrase—and confesses that " Neither can I defend my *Spanish Fryar*, as fond as otherwise I am of it, from this Imputation." In his manuscript notes on his copy of Rymer's *Remarks on the Tragedies of the Last Age*, 1678, he is more free and warmly defends the English plays " which have both under-plot and a turned design," arguing that they are more pleasing than the Greek dramas, " more adorned with episodes, and larger . . . consequently more diverting."

Incidentally it may be observed—and this point carries weight—that the incest-theme which was so frequently worked in sentimental and Gothic fiction appears in no less than five of Dryden's plays, *Aureng-Zebe, Œdipus, The Spanish Fryar, Don Sebastian*, and *Love Triumphant*. To name only a few out of many novels belonging to our period of which the main plots or at any rate the climax and most strikng scenes turn upon consanguinity in some kind we have *Indiana Danby*, 1765 ; *The Adventures of a Jesuit*, 1771 ; *The History of Tom Rigby*, 1773 ; *The Man of the World*, 1773 ; *Juliet Grenville*, 1774 ; *The Modern Fine Gentleman*, 1774 ; *The Morning Ramble, or, History of Miss Evelyn*, 1775 ; *The Recess*, 1783–85 ; *The Adventures of Jonathan Corncob*, 1787 ; *Zeluco*, 1789 ; *Gabrielle de Vergy*, 1790 ; *Celestina*, 1791 ; *Vancenza*, 1792 ; *The Monk*, 1796 ; *The New Monk*, 1796 ; *The Demon of Sicily*, 1800 ; *Mystery!* 1800 ; *Ancient Records*, 1801 ; *The Libertine*, 1807 ; and a great number beside. Gradually this motif came to be treated more and more gingerly, until finally it disappeared altogether or was approached with exclamations of horror in the most powerfully lurid romances such as G. W. M. Reynolds' *Agnes, or Beauty and Pleasure*, where it is further spiced with adultery and sacrilege. Thackeray ridicules the idea of consanguinity in *Our Street*, 1848, when describing the private theatricals at Mrs. Maskelyn's, he says how at Christmas they performed " a French piece by Alexandre Dumas, I believe—" La Duchesse de Montefiasco,": of which I forget the plot, but everybody was in love with everybody else's wife, except the hero, Don Alonzo, who was ardently attached to the Duchess, who turned

out to be his grandmother. The piece was translated by Lord Fiddle-
faddle . . .

Alonzo.   You know how well he loves you, and you wonder
            To see Alonzo suffer, Cunegunda ? . . . [*He staggers from the effect of the poison.*
The Duchess. Alonzo loves—Alonzo loves ! and whom ?
            His grandmother ! Oh, hide me, gracious tomb ! [*Her Grace faints away.*"

Certainly the incest theme appeared in drama at the end of the
eighteenth century. Horace Walpole's *The Mysterious Mother*, written
in 1768, was unacted, and Hoole's *Timanthes*, 1770, is based on the
Demofoonte of Metastasio, which with music by Caldara was originally
produced at Vienna on November 4th, 1733, the name-day of the
Emperor Charles VI. Cumberland's *The Mysterious Husband*, 1783,
the Town considered almost too painful for the stage. " Don't look
at it, Charlotte, don't look at it ! " cried George III to his Queen as
they sat in the royal box. Kotzebue's *Adelaide von Wölfingen* in Benjamin Thompson's translation, 1798, was promptly pirated in America,
Smith & Stephens, New York, 1800. To make more than passing
reference to Byron, and Shelley's *The Cenci* were superfluous.

Mr. Watts Dunton holds that the poets in the latter decades of the
seventeenth century, by which he indicates the poets of the Restoration,
were afflicted with what he calls " the blight of gentility," and it was
not until the eighteenth century that writers " tried to touch that old
chord of wonder," and then " not in poetry but in prose." The
Restoration poets were in a word unromantic. What of Nathaniel
Lee, of Otway, of Southerne ? Did they not touch the chord of
wonder until the harmony thrilled again ? All their tragedies are
essentially romantic, and these are three big names. It is easy, but it is
perilous to make such sweeping generalizations. The fact is that a
few poll-parrot labels have been attached to certain periods and certain
poets, half in ignorance, half in sheer carelessness, and later reviewers
emptily echo these literary slogans until they persuade themselves and
persuade others that something is meant, and eventually there crystal-
lizes a critical dogma, which as proves the wont of critical dogmas is
unfounded and untrue. To repeat is neither to think, nor to know.
There is a very great deal more to be said for Pope himself from the
romantic point of view than is generally recognized or admitted, and I
for one am surprised that the Surrealists have not claimed *The Rape of
the Lock* as their own, " the gloomy Cave of *Spleen* " in Canto IV will
be found to offer some very extraordinary fantasies, such as Fuseli and
Beardsley loved to draw, and I suggest that a good deal might be made
of the tropes and tralations of *The Dunciad.*

Many of the deepest influences and most eminent figures in the great German romantic revival were Catholics—Friedrich von Schlegel, Zacharias Werner, Joseph von Eichendorff of Silesia, Annette Elisabeth von Droste-Hülshoff, and the Heidelberg " Jüngere Romantik," Clemens Maria Brentano and Joseph von Görres. Incidentally it may be observed that in a note on p. 37 of *Surrealism*, Mr. Herbert Read, explaining that the " only individuals who protest against injustices " are the poets and artists of each age, remarks : " It is obvious that the few revolutionary priests who may be included (St. Francis of Assisi, Sir Thomas More) were in our sense of the word no less poets than priests." Unfortunately for the point made here, neither S. Francis of Assisi nor S. Thomas More was a priest.

Mr. Read suggests that in the field of English literature four tasks await the Surrealists : (1) *A fuller acknowledgement of the supreme poetic quality of our ballads and anonymous literature.* (2) *Driving home the inescapable significance of Shakespeare.* (3) *The exact relations between metaphysics and poetry.* (4) *Lifting the moral ban.*

Of these tasks the Romanticists have already accomplished three. Even during the unenlightened and reactionary reign of Charles II, Pepys was an ardent collector and admirer of old ballads. Antiquary Selden gave no little attention to this fugitive literature. *Garlands* were constantly being printed, and *Drolleries* were immensely popular under the Restoration. Even Addison thoroughly appreciated the ballad, as witness his critique of *Chevy-Chase*, *Spectator*, Nos. 70 and 74, May 21st and 25th, 1711. Again in the *Spectator* for June 7th, 1711, No. 85, he says that the ballad of *Two Children in the Wood* gave him " most exquisite pleasure," and he notes that Lord Dorset and Dryden both had large collections of ballads which they were constantly reading, whilst to his own knowledge " several of the most refined writers of our present age " were " of the same humour." Nicholas Rowe, the poet laureate, in the Prologue to *Jane Shore, Written in Imitation of Shakespeare's Style*, 1714, speaks of the ballad as a " romantick ditty," and gives it no mean praise. It must suffice to mention only a few reprints of ballads during the eighteenth century. At Edinburgh in three volumes, 1706, 1709, 1711, respectively appeared *A Choise Collection of Comic and Serious Scots Poems, both Ancient and Modern.* In 1719 Allan Ramsay published a collection of *Scots Songs.* In 1719–20 we have Tom D'Urfey's famous *Wit and Mirth*; *or Pills to Purge Melancholy* : *Being a Collection of the Best Merry Ballads and Songs Old and New.* This is the completest issue, other editions having appeared earlier. *A Collection of Old Ballads* in three volumes was published in London, Vols. I and II, 1723, and Vol. III, 1725. The editor, who is believed to be Ambrose Philips, shows himself an enthusiast for old ballad literature. In the preface to Volume I he observes : " I may, I hope, without either vanity or offence enter upon the praises of Ballads, and shew their antiquity." He adds that even " old Homer . . . was nothing more than a blind Ballad-singer. Pindar, Anacreon, Horace, Cowley, Suckling are Ballad-makers."

In 1724 Allan Ramsay published two miscellanies, the *Tea-Table Miscellany* and the *Evergreen*. The former which with its fourth volume reached a tenth edition of the whole work in 1740 was extraordinarily popular, but the latter, which appeared in two volumes, proved less successful. These two works contain some ballads of the first importance, new and old, such as Hamilton's *Braes o' Yarrow*, Lady Wardlaw's *Hardyknute*, which deceived even Gray who vowed it was a true piece of antiquity.

Other collections, *The Hive*, 1724 ; William Thomson's *Orpheus Caledonius*, 1725 ; Wakefield's *Warbling Muses*, 1749 ; the *Prolusions*, 1760, of Capell, the Shakespearean editor, it must suffice barely to mention. In 1765, Percy published his *Reliques* in three volumes. It were superfluous to carry our survey later. The work of Ebsworth, of contemporary American scholars, is sufficiently well known. Confessedly during the eighteenth century the older ballads often suffered in the reprinting, but none the less the immense interest in ballad-literature throughout the years Mr. Read considers so sterile and barren is incontestable. The eighteenth century was enthusiastic for ballads. Unable to blink this Mr. Read endeavours to save himself by a quibble and repudiates the " ghoulish activity " of recovering and editing the material. This flatly contradicts his own postulate. How can the poetic quality of ballads be recognized and acknowledged if they remain unknown ?

One conclusion is inevitable, there is no new field for Surrealists in the domain of ballad-literature approach it as they will.

It is interesting to note that in his *Tales of Wonder*, Dublin, 1805, ballads new and old, together with *Fair Margaret and Sweet William*, *Clerk Colvin*, *Tam Lin*, Lewis prints Dryden's *Theodore and Honoria* and the passage on Dreams from *The Cock and The Fox*.

The second aim of the English Surrealists is to drive " home the inescapable significance of Shakespeare." As a preliminary it seems necessary to proclaim " the rehabilitation of Shakespeare's genius, after the class and classical denigration of the seventeenth and eighteenth centuries." If there is one weary old mistake some of us had hoped was laid to rest for ever and ever—under the waves of the Red Sea, if you will, like a wicked sprite—it is this extraordinary delusion that the genius of Shakespeare was not recognized in the seventeenth and eighteenth centuries. The error has been exploded, and in detail, again and again, until one feels there really cannot be either need or justification for traversing the old ground. Poets and critics have delighted to proclaim the universal supremacy of Shakespeare.

Hear Dryden in *Of Dramatick Poesie* : Shakespeare " was the man who of all Modern, and perhaps Ancient Poets, had the largest and most comprehensive soul." It has been well said that the Preface to *Troilus and Cressida* (1679) opens with one of Dryden's " trumpet-blasts of eulogy." " *The Poet Æschylus was held in the same veneration by the* Athenians *of after Ages as* Shakespeare *is by us* ; . . . *and our reverence or* Shakespeare [*is*] *much more just then that of the* Grecians *for Æschylus.*" Of the Deposition Scene in *Richard II* he observes : " *the painting of it is so lively, and the words so moving, that I have scarce read any thing comparable to it, in any other language.*" Again : " Shakespeare *had an Universal mind, which comprehended all Characters and Passions.*"

> *But* Shakespeare's *Magick could not copy'd be,*
> *Within that Circle none durst walk but he . . .*
> *But* Shakespeare's *Pow'r is sacred as a King's.*

These lines are from the Prologue to *The Tempest*. Can praise reach further ? And perhaps what is greatest of all when he says of Ben Jonson : " I admire him, but I love *Shakespeare.*" Dryden, be it noted, gave laws unto his day. He was the supreme critic as well as the supreme poet. Edward Phillips (1675) writes that Shakespeare attained the loftiest tragic height, whilst Nahum Tate in the Dedication to his *History of King Lear* (1681) shows himself no mean psychologist when he observes that " Lear's *real and* Edgar's *pretended madness have so much of* extravagant Nature (*I know not how else to express it*), *as cou'd never have started, but from our* Shakespear's *Creating Fancy . . . whilst we grant that none but* Shakespear *cou'd have form'd such Conceptions* ; *yet we are satisfied that they were the only Things in the World that ought to be said on these Occasions.*" It has been shrewly said of the hundred years which lie between 1600 and 1700 one of the first things to strike us is the power with which Shakespeare impressed himself on the soul of the century.

The seventeenth century saw the first critical edition of Shakespeare, 1709, by Nicholas Rowe, to whom Shakespeare was a genius of the highest quality. It were altogether too long a tale to recite the praises of successive critics, John Dennis, Gildon, Pope, Theobald who exclaims : " In how many points of Light must we be obliged to gaze at this great Poet ! In how many Branches of Excellence to consider, and admire him ! " and declares himself literally lost in wonder and pleasure " Whether we respect the Force and Greatness of his Genius, the Extent of his Knowledge and Reading, the Power and Address with which he throws out and applies either Nature, or Learning," his Diction, his Thoughts, his Images and Ideas.   Lord Kames in 1761, *Elements of Criticism*, gave it as his opinion Shakespeare was the finest dramatic genius the world has ever enjoyed.   He excels all ancients and moderns, and is as great in comedy as in tragedy.   Dr. Johnson judged Shakespeare universal ;   Edward Taylor (1774) thought that for many years past Shakespeare had been extravagantly praised but he has unrivalled strokes of nature and his diction is sublime ; Kenrick recognized him as an even greater philosopher than poet, he is, in fact, the foremost man of all this world ;   Maurice Morgann (1777) argues that Shakespeare as a dramatic artist is unapproached.   We have now come to the age of Malone and Steevens, and are soon upon the very threshold of Coleridge himself.

It has, of course, been possible to glance only quite cursorily at Shakespearean criticism in the seventeenth and eighteenth centuries, but even so, I believe enough has been indicated to show how absurdly mistaken it is to talk of the " denigration " of Shakespeare during that period, hence there is no need for any rehabilitation, and if the Surrealists busy themselves with emphasizing the genius of the great poet they are merely attempting what has been done again and again, and thus their energies in this direction will prove, if not entirely superfluous, at the most a repetition and nothing new.   Why they should " claim Shakespeare as an ally " I cannot understand, nor does it appear to me that in the dramas themselves or in the history of Shakespearean criticism there exist any grounds for such confidence and sympathy. I fail to appreciate the similarity of imagination, ideas, expression, between Shakespeare and Surrealism, as shown either in the precept or practice of the latter.

Monk Lewis, Maturin, Mrs. Radcliffe, Scott, Dickens, and Hardy, Mr. Read finds "all equally difficult to read," and not unwisely dismisses them with briefest comment.   Mr. Hugh Sykes Davies, however, has something to say about the horror novel and the " black writers," " Mother Radcliffe, ' Monk ' Lewis, and the superb Maturin," although I cannot discover that his acquaintance with this genre extends much beyond the voluble but not very reliable pages of Signor Mario Praz. Parenthetically I would like to enter a mild protest against the dubbing by Mr. Davies of Mrs. Radcliffe as Mother Radcliffe.   She was neither witch nor bawd, and the thing jars.   That the works of Mrs. Radcliffe, Lewis, and Maturin " are now unread and almost forgotten " is only true as regards the uneducated and newly cultured. All men of taste, all cognoscenti, all who can have the slightest claim to literary knowledge or are fond of books have read at least *The Mysteries of Udolpho*, *The Italian*, *The Monk*, and *Melmoth the Wanderer*. What Mr. Davies means by adding that these romances are now "suppressed by a gentleman's agreement" I cannot pretend to understand. The Gothic Novel is an aristocrat of literature.

It is (I believe) unanimously allowed by the Surrealists that Monsieur André Breton stands out as the leader of the movement. He was the author of the first *Manifesto of Surrealism*, 1924, and the *Second Manifesto of Surrealism*, 1929. Mr. Gascoyne in 1935 speaks of Mons. Breton as "one of the most significant thinkers and writers in contemporary European literature," and explicitly declares that although he may have been accused of "tyrannical authoritativeness, attempted dictatorship," even hinting that there is some modicum of truth in these charges, "except for André Breton the surrealist movement could never have existed." Later he praises Mons. Breton's "energy, enthusiasm and powers of leadership" as "of inestimable value" to the movement and all its followers, emphatically repeating that Mons. Breton "is one of the most remarkable men of his time."

Monsieur André Breton is a warm admirer and a keen collector of Gothic novels. The Fifth Number of the *Revue Minotaure*, May, 1934, opens with an article, *Promenade à travers le Roman noir*, by that very distinguished scholar and bibliophile Monsieur Maurice Heine. (Of even greater importance in connexion with the Gothic Novel is Monsieur Heine's more detailed essay, *Le Marquis de Sade et le Roman noir*, 1933.) Although brief, the survey in the *Minotaure* is of no little interest, and in his three pages the writer does not fail to make several valuable points, such, for example, as the distinctive categories into which Gothic romance may be divided : (1) *le gothique noir*, where he marshals the "mediævalists," Horace Walpole and Clara Reeve, and wherein is to be placed much of the work of later writers, Lathom, Mme de Méré, and many more ; (2) *le fantastique noir*, which will include Cantwell's translation, *Le Château d'Albert, ou le Squelette ambulant*, Cullen's *Haunted Priory*, *The Demon of Sicily*, *Gondez the Monk*, *Rimualdo* ; (3) *le réalisme noir*, the chief example being de Sade's *Justine* with *Juliette*, to which group may be assigned *The Mysterious Warning*, *The Horrors of Oakendale Abbey*, *Wieland*, Ducray-Duminil's *Cœlina, ou l'Enfant du Mystère*, *The Eve of San Pietro* ; (4) *le burlesque noir*, caricature, Bellin de La Liborlière's *La Nuit anglaise* "par le R. S. Spectro Ruini, moine italien," *St. Godwin*, Sarah Green's *Romance Readers and Romance Writers*, Barrett's *The Heroine, Love and Horror*. Inevitably in some cases the categories overlap, but the four classes are a useful generalization. Now *Promenade à travers le Roman noir* is illustrated with thirteen plates reproduced from French *romans noirs*, and of these no less than seven are from volumes belonging to the Collection André Breton.

Monsieur Breton commenting upon the popularity of the Gothic novels and their subsequent neglect argues that they are " a perfect adaptation of a certain historical situation." that they were in effect the literary result of the European " revolutionary upheaval." Readers, it is presumed, delighted in imaginary terrors whilst the horrors of the French Revolution were being enacted all about them. The ruins of which the Gothic novelist is so fond were a symbol of the collapse of the feudal system. The phantoms which appear in the pages of contemporary fiction betray a subconscious but intense fear of the revendication of reactionary powers. The subterranean passages in the castles of romance typified the struggle of the individual through darkness from the tyranny of the past to the enlightenment of the present, although one may be excused for remarking that the peace and plenty, the culture and stability of the past, seem to many of us entirely preferable to the turmoil, the quarrels, the artistic sterility and chaotic depression of the present.

Mr. Michael Sadleir in an important critical essay, *The Northanger Novels*, 1927, observes that dating " the Gothic romantic epoch from (roughly) 1775 to 1815 " the Gothic Romance was in its small way " as much an expression of a deep subversive impulse as (was) the French Revolution." This statement is no doubt true, but I would emphasize that we need to be particularly nice and guarded as to the use of our terms in this connexion. They may be woefully wrested. I distinguish therefore. A revolution in literature, a revolt against a set and sapless classicism (a movement which, it must not be forgotten, could be and was productive of much that is beautiful), is a very different thing from a social Revolution, and I am afraid that the Surrealists have confused and deliberately commingled the two. In fact, the word " Revolution," owing to its political significance, to-day even more deeply than at the end of the eighteenth century, has acquired so ugly and so murderous a meaning that in art and literature it were well to avoid it altogether, and to employ some other term—the Gothic revival is a clean, untainted and expressive phrase. Mr. Sadleir is rightly emphatic that the Gothic romance " sprang from a genuine spiritual impulse." I have chosen as the title of my book " The Gothic Quest," to signify the spiritual as well as the literary and artistic seeking for beauty, for as S. Augustine reminds us : " Quae (pulchra) tamen nulla essent, nisi essent abs Te."

Mr. Sadleir shrewdly comments that the enthusiasm of the Gothic romance began as an inspiration and ended as an opiate. " The persons who launched the new romanticism . . . prophets of iconoclasm . . . lived to see . . . their once inflammatory art become a drug for harassed minds, a refuge for imaginations in flight from menacing reality."

The great Gothic novelists abhorred and denounced political revolution. Writing in 1820, in the Preface to *Marino Faliero*, Byron says : " It is the fashion to underrate Horace Walpole ; firstly because he was a nobleman, and secondly, because he was a gentleman." With what courteous and chilling disdain, with what disgust would the Abbot of Strawberry have looked down on socialism ! There has perhaps outside the cloister never been a famous writer who lived so secluded and conventual a life as Mrs. Radcliffe. Her public for a long while actually did not know whether she was dead or alive, so that when the latter proved the case her retirement was attributed to madness, and many people confidently named Derbyshire as the place of her confinement in an asylum for the insane. Such gossip she did not even take the trouble to contradict. She steadfastly refused to mix with either literary or fashionable society. She piqued herself on being excessively genteel, was more than ordinarily shy, " a little formal, reserved in manner, and too proud to enter any circle where her full equality was not acknowledged." A writer in the *Literary Gazette*, June 3rd, 1826, says : " She was ashamed (yes, ashamed), of her own talents ; and was ready to sink in the earth at the bare suspicion of anyone taking her for an author ; her chief ambition being to be thought a lady ! " When G. F. L. Marchi, the artist who assisted Sir Joshua Reynolds, dined on August 27th, 1797, with Mr. and Mrs. Radcliffe at their residence, 7 Medina Place, St. George's Fields, he told her stories of Johnson and Goldsmith visiting Sir Joshua. " Ah, those were fine times ! " she said with a sigh. She was intensely conservative. Her husband seemed " democratically inclined," and she did not like it. We must remember that this " democratism " did not imply much one hundred and forty years ago.

Matthew Gregory Lewis loved a lord. Among his associates and intimates were the Prince of Wales (George IV) ; the Duke of Clarence (William IV) ; the two Sheridans ; Lords Holland and Byron ; Sir Morton Eden ; Lord St. Helens ; Earl Grey ; Lord Melbourne ; and very many other persons of the first quality. Even when quite a lad and visiting Weimar he writes to his mother with conscious pride : " The two duchesses are extremely affable and condescending." He adds that he is very weary, " but it is always some comfort to think I am weary with the best company." A few months later he cannot help boasting of his aristocratic acquaintance : " I was perfectly astonished at the crowds of princes and princesses, dukes and duchesses, which were poured upon me from every quarter." He delighted to stay at Inverary Castle with the Duke of Argyle, whose sister Lady Charlotte Campbell was his particular friend. Lewis is " a bit too fond of a duke," Scott said. One of the happiest days of the "Monk's" life was when he entertained in his cottage at Barnes Her Royal Highness the Duchess of York and suite to a *déjeuner à la fourchette*. He was in the seventh heaven when he could write to his mother : " On Friday, the Princess of Wales (who, *sans rime ou raison*, has not spoken to me for these five years) chose to send for me into her box at the Argyle Rooms, made me sup with her, asked me to dinner yesterday, and kept me till three o'clock in the morning, and was extremely good-humoured and attentive. To-day I dine at York House, and then sup with the Princess of Wales at the Admiralty : so that, for these two days, I shall have a dose of royalty." Or again : " The Duke of Clarence (to whom I had never been presented, nor had even dined in his company in my life) came up to me on the race-course, called me ' Lewis ' *tout court*, talked to me as familiarly as if he had known me all my life." With the Duke and Duchess of Bedford he professed himself " perfectly charmed. The duke was always a favourite of mine . . . the duchess is very pretty, lively, good-humoured, and obliging." Lewis, one of the kindest and best of men, was a capitalist. To see the conditions under which the slaves on his estates worked he undertook the voyage to the West Indies. Byron was fond of him : " Poor fellow ! he died a martyr to his new riches—of a second visit to Jamaica."

Charles Robert Maturin, the Protestant Irish clergyman, for all his eccentricities had very firm political principles. In *The Wild Irish Boy* he is unsparing in his condemnation of such " wicked writers " as Godwin and Mary Wollstonecraft. On a more serious occasion, from the pulpit, he expresses himself pretty clearly : " It is an absurd and mischievous prejudice that supposes the existence of vice confined to the higher classes of life, and virtue (as they call it) the everlasting inhabitant of a cottage—it is a prejudice originating in utter ignorance of life, cherished by the silly illusions of pastoral poetry, and inflamed by the wild and wicked ravings of political enthusiasts, without any reason in nature and in life."

It is plain that no one of the four most prominent Gothic novelists, Walpole, Mrs. Radcliffe, Lewis, and Maturin, had the slightest sympathy with socialism, rather they were most strongly opposed to such movements, and viewed with horror " the wild and wicked ravings of political enthusiasts."

Yet it cannot be denied that particularly during the last decade of the eighteenth century vicious and subversive ideology had begun to infiltrate and poison fiction. Fortunately the mischief was soon stamped out and squashed, in no small part through the admirable energies of *The Anti-Jacobin Review*. Good sound work was also done in this direction by such novelists as Isaac d'Israeli in his *Vaurien*, 1797 ; George Walker with the *Vagabond*, 1799, which incidentally throws a curious light on the machinery of the Gordon Riots ; and Charles Lucas in *The Infernal Quixote*, 1800, a very fine piece, which was translated into French, 3 volumes, as *L'Infernal Don Quichotte, Histoire à l'Ordre du Jour*, A Paris, Riche, Le Normant, and Maradan, in the following year ; nor are such satires as the fore-mentioned *St. Godwin* " by Count Reginald de St. Leon," and Mrs. Hamilton's *Memoirs of Modern Philosophers*, both published in 1800, without considerable value.

One can hardly be surprised that owing to her comments on the French situation in *Desmond* (1792) Mrs. Charlotte Smith was for a while suspect, but the political features of this novel as well as of *The Banished Man* (1794) and *The Young Philosopher* (1798), which were all termed immoral, have been unduly emphasized. Mrs. Smith was liberal in her tendencies, but no more, and any indiscretions she soon learned to modify and correct. It is no specious special pleading to argue that her case is quite exceptional, and there was reason enough for that animosity and resentment which so often finds expression in her pages. Her life was one of bitter fruitless sorrow, in fact, I know no sadder biography. The victim, the persecuted victim, of legalized fraud and chicane, robbed, harried, choused and oppressed, she must have been a mortified saint if she had not turned upon her enemies and exposed their malice, although alas ! to no effect since they were entrenched in the pitiless privileges and process of the courts. Add to that a feckless and spendthrift husband, the deaths of beloved children, a heroic struggle through long weary days of disappointment and trial. "Sorrow," says Sir Egerton Brydges, "was her constant companion ; and she sang with a thorn at her bosom."

To accuse Mrs. Inchbald, a good practising Catholic, and Mrs. Robinson of incendiarism were absurd. Yet I have met with so sweeping and so false an assertion as " all of the women novelists at the turn of the century, save Hannah More and Clara Reeve, were in sympathy with the Revolution " ! Nothing could be further from the truth.

Whatever we may think of Mary Wollstonecraft's *Vindication of the Rights of Women*, her posthumous *The Wrongs of Women*; or, *Maria, A Fragment* (1798, in the *Posthumous Works*) cannot have had any effect. Only about a third of the book was written, and it seems very crude, although not uninteresting. Her earlier work *Mary, a Fiction* (1788) is undeveloped, and truly "an artless tale." *The Memoirs of Emma Courtney* (1796), and *The Victim of Prejudice* (1799), by Mary Hays, are hysterical and exaggerated, and hence unconvincing.

Whilst I would not with Saintsbury damn Holcroft's novels too summarily as a " desert of dreary declaration and propagandist puppet-mongering," there can be no question that the man was a boutefeu, and both *Anna St. Ives*, 1792, and *Hugh Trevor*, 1794-97, are—if we took them seriously as their author meant—dangerous books, and dead. This sort of thing cannot be scotched too soon. Neither is a Gothic romance, and so they hardly concern us here. Incidentally, however, we may be allowed to remark that at the end of Hugh Trevor, the hero is furnished in pudding-time with a long-lost uncle, and inherits wealth, so he weds Olivia and settles down satisfactorily as a member of the " upper ten," a *dénouement* which goes to prove how insincere and humbugging is all this philosophical cant. Practically the same thing happens in several of the doctrinaire novels of G. W. M. Reynolds, such as *Joseph Wilmot* and *Mary Price*, in which the hero valet and heroine abigail, whose births must be " wropped in mystery," are eventually discovered to be persons of the first quality, and thus they come into magnificent fortunes and grace the most brilliant aristocratic circles in the land.

Of far greater importance and interest is William Godwin's *Things as they are*; or, *the Adventures of Caleb Williams*, 1794. The wealthy and noble-minded Ferdinando Falkland from the most altruistic principles and " out of a high point of honour," as Mr. Bayes has it, quietly dispatched a blustering boor and bully, Squire Barnabas Tyrrel, a wretch who had amply earned his fate. Caleb Williams, whom Falkland has befriended and taken into his house, yielding to the idlest itch of curiosity discovers the secret of the murder. The ingenuous youth pleads : " My offence had merely been a mistaken thirst of knowledge " ! The result is not what might have been expected. Falkland, so far from being in Williams' power, completely turns the tables, and utilizing all the advantages his social position, his wealth, his integrity, afford him punishes the unhappy Caleb by a relentless menace and pursuit. Wherever he flies, in every direction he turns, the young man is harried and hallooed. He is cast into prison on a well-contrived charge of theft; he escapes only to fall in with a gang of thieves; Mr. Spurrel, a pretended friend, basely betrays him; misfortune follows misfortune, all engineered by "the colossal intelligence of Mr. Falkland." Thus at the inn near Warwick, when the landlady's father an "extremely venerable and interesting" individual sympathizes and seems ready to assist him, upon hearing the name "Caleb Williams" the old man recoils: "He was sorry that fortune had been so unpropitious to him, as for him ever to have set eyes on me! I was a monster with whom the very earth groaned!"

It will not do. The dice are too heavily loaded. The false play is too apparent. "I saw my whole species as ready, in one mode or other, to be made the instruments of the tyrant," cries Caleb. Such exaggerations, such extravagances, are unnatural. We admit them in a romance, but do not ask us to allow that they have any relation to real life. As an exposition of philosophy, a piece of didacticism, they are just naught. The significance of the title—*Things as they are*—must not escape us. It is so palpably a misnomer that by common consent we know Godwin's romance as *Caleb Williams*. It is a powerful romance, and the adventures are well told. Mrs. Inchbald found it "sublimely horrible—captivatingly frightful."

It might be asked whether Caleb Williams did not deserve—certainly not all that, but at any rate a good part of what—he got. He was befriended, and admitted into Ferdinando Falkland's house in a confidential capacity. He turns traitor. The faith placed in him and the trust he abuses, and abuses in a particularly mean and dastardly way. A character which allowed itself to be so swayed by mere meddling inquisitiveness is far from pleasant or agreeable. In fact, we shall not be far out if we dub him a nosey young blackguard.

The fact is that the philosophical Godwin for all his genius, and in some respects his clarity of vision, was an Utopian fantast. His dreams were impossible, sometimes blasphemous, and in practice actually pernicious, although of course he could never have seen this. His life was in contradiction to his dreams.

"Religion is Politics," said Blake. Certes, and there is a Divine Revelation.

Godwin died one hundred years ago. He declared: "For myself I firmly believe that days of greater virtue and more ample justice will descend upon the earth." A splendid hope. To-day good men as they look out upon the world are asking whether Antichrist is not at the very gate?

The Romanticist is not a revolutionary ; he is rather a reactionary. He turns back towards and seeks to revive—in some measure to relive the past. As I said in my Introduction to *The Castle of Otranto*, 1924 : " The Romantic writer fell in love with the Middle Ages, the vague years of long ago, the days of chivalry and strange adventure." True, " there is in the Romantic revival a certain disquietude and a certain aspiration. It was this disquietude with earth and aspiration for Heaven which inform the greatest Romance of all, Mysticism, the Romance of the Saints."

It will be remembered that in a passage which I have already quoted, Chapter I, from *The Age*, the author of that satiric poem describes the Temple of romance to which the votaries are flocking in crowds, and

> Whilst deeper mysteries are brewing
> They see at first a gothic ruin.

The ruin played a great part in Gothic atmosphere and Gothic feeling, and it is easy to see why, the more so as we appreciate that it has a very real meaning for us even to-day. It is a symbol of great significance, and certain authors were shrewd enough to introduce it into their very titles. This point has already been made in Chapter II, but at the risk of repetition I will mention here *The Ruins of Avondale Priory*, 1796 ; *Montrose, or The Gothic Ruin*, 1799 ; *The Ruins of Rigonda*, 1808 ; *The Ruins of Tivoli*, 1810 ; *The Ruins of Selinunti*, 1813 ; *The Ruins of Ruthvale Abbey*, 1826 ; whilst in 1830 Henri Duval re-translated into French Mrs. Campbell's *The Midnight Wanderer*, 1821 (itself from Mme Brayer de Saint-Léon's *Alexina* "imité de l'anglais," 1813), as *Rose d'Altenberg, ou le Spectre dans les Ruines*, boldly attributing this romance to the late Anne Radcliffe.

The importance of the ruin, emphasized in an article " The Illustrations of the ' Gothick ' Novels " which I contributed to *The Connoisseur*, November, 1936, and from this I may venture to quote a couple of paragraphs.

In their travels through Italy and Greece, their *grands tours*, the Vergilian and Horatian dilettanti of the earlier eighteenth century had been so bit with the love of antiquity, so enraptured with the survivals of Athens and Rome, that upon their return to England they proceeded to adorn their parks and fair demesnes with reproductions of the mouldering architecture beneath whose shadow they had pondered in sweet pensive mood the glory of the past. Miniature Pantheons, copies of the columns of Paestum, models of Vesta's temple at Tivoli, sprang up on English lawns or peered amid English glades in the most ncongruous surroundings. A convention of " ruins " began to prevail.

PLATE XVI

THE GOTHIC RUIN
Frontispiece.   Manfredi, 1796

[Face p. 404

The "ruin" became the sign manual of an exquisite's taste.   Not only was it something to be vastly admired in itself, but it served another purpose.   It ministered to milord's vanity and prestige, for even more publicly than his cabinet of coins with the right "price-enhancing" verdigris, his shelves of Etruscan pottery, it proclaimed that he had visited far foreign lands, that his scholarship and judgement were first-hand accomplishments, no mere pedantry of a cabined islander.

No gardens, no ground without a ruin !   Thus the purse-proud cit, old Sterling in The, Clandestine Marriage, 1766, exhibits his ruins to Lord Ogleby with much parade.   " Ruins, Mr. Sterling ? " cries his astonished guest.   " Ay, ruins, my lord ! and they are reckoned very fine ones too.   You would think them ready to tumble on your head. It has just cost me a hundred and fifty pounds to put my ruins in thorough repair."   Places of public resort, such as Vauxhall Gardens, provided their patrons with a prospect of ruins, for here a large painting representing ruins and running water, which terminated one of the walks, was among the favourite illusions, whilst the eye was also agreeably deceived by the " simulated Ruins of Palmyra " which closed the vista at the end of the South Walk.   This ingenious canvas was either the work of Hogarth's friend, Hayman, or from the skilful brush of George Lambert, the scene-painter of Covent Garden.

When those whose leisure or whose pockets would not allow them to journey to the Continent in lieu began to " explore " (as the modish phrase went) their own country, it soon came to be realized that England also had her native ruins, and that these were often to be found amid landscapes of the most romantic loveliness.   Tintern, Llanthony, Fountains, Netley, Rievaulx, Whitby, and many another fallen fane could conjure up the past even more effectively than the Pagan antiquities of Greece or Rome.

Thus the ivied ruins of Minster Lovel Priory, which lie some three miles from Witney, gave Clara Reeve the scene for her Old English Baron (originally called The Champion of Virtue).   A ruined abbey plays a great part in The Romance of the Forest by Mrs. Radcliffe, who also in The Italian very effectively used the sombre ruins of Paluzzi.   We get a glimpse of Udolpho after a stout attack by the foe, and when Emily on her return " saw again the old walls and moon-light towers, rising over the woods : the strong rays enabled her, also, to perceive the ravages which the siege had made—with the broken walls, and shattered battlements."

Mrs. Radcliffe's last work, Gaston de Blondeville, was directly inspired by a visit to Kenilworth Castle. An earlier novel, *A Sicilian Romance*, is ushered in by a most romantic description of the " magnificent remains " of the Castle of Mazzini, whilst the tale is learned from a manuscript in the library of a neighbouring cloister.

Romantic architecture and romantic ecclesiasticism exercised a tremendous influence on the Gothic Novel.

" The ruins," says Monsieur André Breton, " appear suddenly so full of significance in that they express the collapse of the feudal period." This kind of symbolism to me appears to wander wide and is quite off the track. It is true that Mr. Michael Sadleir, in explaining why to the Gothic temperament " a ruin was in itself a thing of loveliness," suggests that it " expresses the triumph of chaos over order," and in some minds, subconsciously and in quite subsidiary fashion, I will not say that this idea may have been vaguely formed. But I cannot go so far as to see in the ruin overgrown with creepers and grasses, " a small victory for liberty, a snap of the fingers in the face of autocratic power." Still less, I repeat, can I agree that the ruin conveyed a definite historical fact, the collapse of feudalism.

The appeal of the ruin lay elsewhere, and evoked quite other emotions.

" This view of the ruin was very striking ; the three chief masses, great and solemn, without being beautiful. They spoke at once to the imagination, with the force and simplicity of truth, the nothingness and brevity of this life—' generations have beheld us and passed away, as you now behold us and shall pass away : they thought of the generations before them, as you now think of them, and as future ages shall think of you. We have witnessed this, yet we remain ; the voices that revelled beneath us are heard no more, yet the winds of Heaven still sound in our ivy.' And a still and solemn sound it was as we stood looking up at those walls." Such were the meditations of Mrs. Radcliffe in that green and open area which was once the grand court of Kenilworth Castle. No thought of " the collapse of the feudal period " here, but a far deeper, purer strain.

The ruined abbey, in particular, was dight with a certain awe and ancient reverence ; that lone and roofless sanctuary could inspire mystery and a delicious melancholy. Ingoldsby has admirably expressed this very feeling : " There is a something in the very sight of an old Abbey, as Ossian says (or MacPherson for him), ' pleasing yet mournful to the soul ' ! Nor could I ever yet gaze on the roofless walls and ivy-clad towers of one of these venerable monuments of the piety of bygone days without something very like an unbidden tear rising to dim the prospect . . ."

I saw thee, Netley, as the sun
Across the western wave
    Was sinking slow,
    And a golden glow
To thy roofless towers he gave;
    And the ivy sheen,
    With its mantle of green,
That wrapt thy walls around,
    Shone lovelily bright
    In that glorious light,
And I felt 'twas holy ground.

Then I thought of the ancient time
The days of thy Monks of old,—
When to Matin, and Vesper, and Compline chime,
    The loud Hosanna roll'd,
And, thy courts and " long-drawn aisles " among,
Swell'd the full tide of sacred song.

This is the romance of ruins. This is what the ruin conveyed to the romanticist. The ruin was not a symbol of triumph, the present conqueror of the past, as Monsieur André Breton supposes. That would have been at variance with the whole Gothic idea. The ruin was a sacred relic, a memorial, a symbol of infinite sadness, of tenderest sensibility and regret.

" How happy the man who can live philosophically in the memory of what he has once been ! " wrote Robert the painter, *Robert des Ruines* as he was called. He loved to paint ruins ; crumbling arches, columns decayed, cracked mossy fountains, vast shattered urns, falling temples, broken pyramids, great gaping walls festooned with rank luscious greenery, huge masses of scattered débris where the ivy has forced the masonry to tumble down. Diderot urged him to realize that ruins, which he painted so often and so well, had a rare sentiment and a poetry of their own. " You don't know why ruins give such pleasure. I will tell you. . . . Everything vanishes, everything perishes, everything passes away ; time goes on and on. . . . How old, how very old the world is. I walk between two eternities. . . . What is my life as compared to this crumbling stone ? " Here we have the true Gothic feeling, the quintessence of romanticism.

In his recent excellent study *Bandits in a Landscape*, " Romantic Painting from Caravaggio to Delacroix," Mr. W. Gaunt has a most thoughtful and suggestive chapter, " The Annals of Ruin," in which he analyses the source of the interest in ruins. It is in fine a psychological inquiry. He tells us of the mysterious Monsú Desiderio whose works present " the curious fecundity of ruin," and of whose Legend of S. Augustine, now in the National Gallery, London, " a wild and mad picture, ruinous in essence " he gives a most striking description.

Mr. Gaunt, who deals at length with Salvator Rosa (1615–73), Claude Lorraine (1600–82), and the fantastically imaginative Alessandro Magnasco (c. 1680–1749), says that in succession to these masters came " a line of painters whose main business is ruin," many making it " the basis of a fanciful and decorative symbolism, a few inspired to a truly imaginative art." Of this school are Salvator Rosa's pupil, Ghisolfi (1623–83) ; Ricci (1660–1734), a follower of Magnasco; Giovanni Pannini (1691–1764) ; and finally Hubert Robert (1733–1808). The favourite painters of Mrs. Radcliffe were Salvator, Claude, and Gaspar Poussin. These with " Guardi of the Haunted Lagoons " and the school of ruin painters are the artists of the Gothic romance, not Hans Arp, Miró, Ernst, Paul Klee, Man Ray, and the Surrealists.

To the symbolism which Monsieur Breton reads into the Gothic novel I cannot subscribe. In all frankness I find myself entirely at a loss to imagine in what possible way The Castle of Otranto approaches " the surrealist method and adds once more to its complete justification."

On their own showing the Surrealists are devoted to automatic writing, which is in itself a very dangerous experiment. They also lay great stress on dreams, and emphasize that messages may be received through dreams. It is devoutly to be hoped that the Surrealist visions in this kind do not resemble only too nearly those " somnia et noctium phantasmata " from which night by night at Compline we pray to be delivered and assoiled. We must be very careful even in art and literature lest—if I may venture to apply in this connexion a vital phrase of S. Augustine—" dormienti falsa visa persuadeant quod vigilanti vera non possunt."

In a letter to the Rev. William Cole, dated February 28th, 1765, Walpole, speaking of The Castle of Otranto, which had been published little less than two months before, writes : " Shall I even confess to you what was the origin of this romance ? I waked one morning, in the beginning of last June, from a dream, of which all I could recover was, that I had thought myself in an ancient castle (a very natural dream for a head like mine filled with Gothic story) and that on the uppermost banister of a great staircase I saw a gigantic hand in armour. In the evening, I sat down, and began to write . . ." The Castle of Otranto, edited by Montague Summers ; Constable, 1924, Introduction, pp. xxvi–vii. Because a vague recollection of a dream suggested the romance of Otranto to Walpole it is hardly possible and certainly not reasonable to build up from this a whole Nephelokokkugia of Freudian speculation. One might multiply examples of writers who actually received, or thought they received, some such inspiration in a dream. Pausanias tells us how Æschylus whilst yet a mere lad was set to watch the vineyards in the country. At the close of a long and weary day he fell asleep. " As he slumbered Dionysus appeared, and ordered the boy to betake himself to tragedy. In the morning he made the attempt, and succeeded very easily." The legend is poetical, a little trite, but well enough. The Venerable Bede relates how when the ceorl Cædmon who was ignorant of music and the ballad, had fallen asleep in the stables, he dreamed that there stood by him one who said : " Cædmon, sing me a song." And when he pleaded that he was witless and ignorant the reply came : " Nevertheless, thou shalt sing. Sing of the beginning of all creation." Thereupon Cædmon opened his mouth and sang sweet verses, the praise of the Creator and all His wonderful works, and when he awoke from his sleep he well remembered that song and he added unto it. One May morning on the Malvern Hills, William Langland lay him down by the side of a rippling brook that sang softly as it sped on its way,

And as I lay and lened and loked in the wateres,
I slombred in a slepyng it sweyued so merye.
Thanne gan I to meten a merveilouse sweuene . . . .

I remember how the late Dr. M. R. James told me that one of his Ghost Stories—I am not sure which, but I rather fancy it might be *The Rose Garden*—was suggested to him by his recollection of a peculiarly vivid dream. One of the ridiculous canards which used to annoy Mrs. Radcliffe so much, proclaimed how that amiable lady was accustomed to sup late on underdone pork chops in order that she might gain inspiration for her next novel of terror from the resultant nightmare !

Horace Walpole's words have already been quoted, but we may well remind ourselves how he wrote to George Montagu : " Visions, you know, have always been my pasture ; and so far from growing old enough to quarrel with their emptiness, I almost think there is no wisdom comparable to exchanging what is called the realities of life for dreams." Perhaps as time goes on we all feel that, and as we grow older we love our dreams the more, and the more actual they become to us. The realities of life belong to youth.

Earlier I said that the world, if we had not our dreams, would be a very dull place. There is danger in dreams—Homer could fable the gates of ivory and of horn—but if we had not our dreams life would not be worth living at all. But there is the bad dream, an evil dream, a diseased and delirious vision, which is a dark reality. As one values one's sanity, one's spiritual safety, of that beware !

Monsieur André Breton emphasizes that there are given places particularly suitable for the manifestation of dreams and automatic writing. Precisely, just as in olden times clients would sleep in the temple of the god to receive his supernatural message more clearly and more direct. Monsieur Breton then proceeds to develop in his argument what is called by the Surrealists the *castle problem*. He mentions that Matthew Gregory Lewis spent part of his youth in an old manor house—Stanstead Hall, Essex, as I have related in detail in Chapter V. He does not refer to the parallel case of Lord Lytton which is even more striking, but speaks of *En Rade* by J.-K. Huysmans. It does not seem that Monsieur Breton is calling our attention to anything other than that well-known psychological fact, which has been personally experienced by most of us, the influence of the atmosphere of certain places. It is always good to stress this, but it must not be offered as anything new. All artists, perhaps writers more than most, are keenly susceptible to atmosphere. There are some places which (without any apparent or assignable cause) dry up and utterly exsiccate imagination, at best, a restless and irksome, at worst a positively painful state—there are other spots which prove in themselves an impetus and the happiest inspiration. Naturally places affect various persons very dissimiliarly. Some persons are, as it were, immediately and very strongly influenced ; others are almost entirely, if indeed not altogether, insensible to such impressions. Houses have an extraordinary power in this respect, and persons who are psychically energized, or (should such be the case) unbraced, by the atmosphere of a house often find themselves sensible of this magnetism in a very positive and remarkable way. It may quite well be that in not a few instances there are contributory physical causes, health, too lax a discipline of life, indiscretions of many kinds. A vast number of houses, again, like human beings, are neutral and characterless, and neither give nor receive. The subject is exceedingly wide, and it is neither necessary nor possible to pursue it in all its bearings. The importance of the *castle problem*, to use the Surrealist name which is very aptly chosen and expressive, has been recognized for a very long while. In 1931–32 I was contributing a number of articles to *Architectural Design & Construction*, " Walpole and the Castle of Otranto," " Knebworth and the First Lord Lytton," " Le Fanu and his Houses," " Huysmans and Chartres," and others, in which series my theme throughout was the influence of buildings, particularly their houses, upon great writers. I even went so far as to say that in such romances as *The Castle of Otranto* and *The Mysteries of Udolpho* the protagonists were not Prince Manfred and Theodore, Montoni and the Chevalier Valancourt, but the Castle itself with its courts and cloisters, the watchet-coloured chamber on the right hand and the galleries, or " the gothic magnificence of Udolpho, its proud irregularity, its lofty towers and battlements, its high-arched casements, and its slender watch-tower, perched upon the corners of turrets."

If the Surrealists wish to carry the castle problem to another and a higher plane, this has been done by many a holy mystic, especially by San Juan de la Cruz and the Seraphic Mother Teresa de Jesús in her *Castillo Interior*.

The connexion which the Surrealists are anxious to trace between their own paths and principles and the ideals and inspiration of the Gothic novelists, that is to say, in fine, of romanticism, to me appears to have no existence. As I can understand them, such arguments as are adduced would seem to be based upon misapprehensions, or are so far-fetched and purely fantastical in their setting-forth that they escape into vapour and mirage.

There remains one point upon which I am reluctant to touch, but which none the less it is impossible wholly to ignore. I would not smirch Surrealism nor saddle it with the vagaries of any of its followers, yet one cannot help entertaining something much more than a suspicion that there is being fostered an intimacy—and I fear an official intimacy—between Surrealism and Communism. Impartial and most trustworthy authority has assured me that such is undoubtedly the case, that Surrealism is so closely allied with Communism as to represent in fact the " Left Wing intelligentsia "—thus the vulgar phrase goes.

The Surrealist Revolution, the first number of which was issued at the end of 1924, is very bad, and what is known as the Aragon Affair caused a resounding scandal. Monsieur Louis Aragon, not merely an important figure among the Surrealists but actually one of the founders of the movement, had published a brimstone " poem " with an ominous title, *The Red Front*. This piece proved so outrageously subversive as in January, 1932, to lay the writer open to official charges of " inciting to murder " and " provoking insubordination in the army." At once the Surrealists were ruffled and raised a shriek of protest, declaring themselves seriously discomposed to think that offence should be taken at a " poetic work " ! As was pertinently remarked at the time, they seemed to be demanding political immunity for poets, and poets alone. Poetry to-day has acquired so indefinite a meaning that at this rate any incendiary manifesto calling itself a " poem " would go scot-free and scatheless, for who dare question its claim to be lyric verse of exquisite beauty ? Monsieur Aragon, however, vehemently repudiated the Surrealists and all their works, a *volte-face* which the group met by angrily attacking their former colleague in a pasquil *Clown* ! The usual pelting of pamphlets followed.

If Surrealism is knit to Communism it can have nothing to do with the Gothic novel, nor indeed with romanticism at all. The tyranny of Communism destroys and eagerly seeks to destroy all art, all culture. We know this to have been the case in Russia. Writing to *The Daily Telegraph and Morning Post* on December 13th, 1937, Dr. T. Izod Bennett informs us how in Madrid at that date " the persecution of the literate classes continues with unbated violence."

In spite of the doctrines which the Surrealists proclaim so loudly and in so very many words, in spite of their dreams and visions, their " pure " poetry, their *collage* and *frottage*, their myths and symbols, their slogan " L'image est une création pure de l'esprit," and all the rest, the fundamental weakness, nay, the very rot which cankers the whole movement, would seem to be a crass materialism. " Supremacy of matter over thought," one of the leaders has announced to be an essential principle of their scheme. They are unmystical, unromantic. They deny the supernatural. Yet everything in the last analysis depends upon the supernatural, since as S. Augustine tells us, God is the only Reality.

GENERAL INDEX

Abællino, 270
Abællino, The Great Bandit, 270
Abællino, 270
Abbé de l'Épee, L' (*Der Taubstumme*), 328
Abbeys, popular theme in Gothic fiction, 86–7
Abelino ; o el Gran Bandido, drama tragico, 305
Abelino ; or, The Robber's Bride, 271
Abingdon, 69
Aboukir Bay, 363
Above and Below, 283
Abridgements of Gothic novels, cheap (bluebooks), 82–5
Académie Royale, 232
Account of Architects and Architecture, An (John Evelyn), 37, 58
Account of the Dramatick Poets, An, 98
Account of the German Theatre, An, 121
Acton, Eugenia de, 85, 93
Actor of All Work, The, 283
Addison, Joseph, 25, 38, 39, 44, 45, 58, 155, 393
Adelaide von Wölfingen, 392
Adelgitha, 273–4, 277, 278
Adelmorn, the Outlaw, 259, 260, 264, 304
Adelphi Theatre, 301
Adlington, William, 345
Advertiser, The (Kingston, Jamaica), 308
Ægerian grot, Pope's, 20–1
Æschylus, 384, 395, 408
Age, The, A Poem, quoted, 33–7, 404
Ahasuerus the Wanderer, 226
Ahasuerus, the Wandering Jew, 226
Ahnfrau, Die, 227
Aida, 284
Aikin, Ann Lætitia, afterwards Mrs. Barbauld, 27, 48, 49, 59, 186, 201
Aikin, Dr. John, 48, 49
Aikin, Lucy, 48
Ainsworth, William Harrison, 29, 30, 31, 80, 141, 174, 241, 379, 381, 388
Albrecht, J. F. E. von, 142
Alfieri, Vittorio, 121
Alfonso, King of Castile, 260–2, 304
All For Love ; or, The World well Lost, 110
All in a Bustle, 309
Allen, Andrew (Jackson), 271
Allen and West (publishers), 88
Almeyda, Queen of Granada, 165
Amants Malheureux, ou Comte de Comminge, Les, 116–7

Ambigu, 230
Ambigu-Comique, 231
Amore delle Tre Melarance, L', 387
Anacreon, 394
Andersen, Hans, 280
Andrews, J., 64
Angler, The, a poem by Piscator (T. P. Lathy), 91
Anglers, The, a poem by Dr. Thomas Scott, 91
Ann of Swansea, 100
Annual Review, The, 320
Anquetil, Louis Pierre,
Anthony and Cleopatra, 380
Anti-Jacobin Review, The, 147, 307, 401
Anton Ulrich, Duke of Brunswick, 118
Apuleius, 345, 388
Aragon, Louis, 390, 411
Archæology in the novel, 31
Architectural Design and Construction, 410
Architecture, Gothic, 37–9, 59
Archiv für das Studium der Neueren Sprachen, 227
Arden of Faversham, 307
Argyle, George William, sixth Duke of (1766–1839), 253, 400
Ariosto, Lodovico, 33, 41, 44, 387–8
Aristænetus, 115
Aristophanes, 384–5
Armstrong, Leslie, 30, 175
Arnim, Ludwig Achim von, 388
Arp, Hans, 389, 408
Art of Painting, The, 391
As You Like It, 164
Assignation ; or, Love in a Nunnery, The, 199, 391
Assignation, The (Sophia Lee), 165
Astley's Royal Amphitheatre, 270, 286
Aston, John Partington, 31, 379
Atkyns, Lady, 185
Aubin, Mrs. Penelope, 99, 153
Auckland, Lord, 209, 296
Augellino Belverde, L', 387
Augusta Lacrimans, 97
Augusta Triumphans, 97
Augustine of Hippo, S., 398, 408, 412
Aureng-Zebe, 391
Austen, Jane, 169
Autos Sacramentales (Calderon), 386
Authentic Account of the Shakespearean MSS., An, 343

Baculard d'Arnaud, François-Thomas de, 102, 114, 116-7, 118, 149, 165, 169, 188, 201, 225
Bage, Robert, 27, 193
Baillie, Dr., 289
Baker's Library, Brighton, 69
Balbinus, S. J., Aloys Boleslas, 125
Baldensperger, Fernand, 300
Baldwin, Robert (afterwards Baldwin, Cradock & Joy), 79-80, 90
Ballad literature, 393-4
Ballin, Rosetta, 172
Bally's Library, Bath, 62, 67
Bancroft, John, 199
Bandits in a Landscape, 407-8
Banim, John, 80
Banks (costumier), 288
Banks of Allan Water, The (play), 308
Banks of Allan Water, The (song), 288
Bannister, John, 165, 209, 254, 259, 260, 297, 366
Baptista (Tita), 294
Barber of Seville, The, 264
Barclay, John, 201
Barnett, G. Z., 308
Baron-Wilson, Mrs., 296, 303, 307
Barrett, Eaton Stannard, 245, 397
Barrett, G., 306
Barrett's Library, Bath, 67
Barruel, Abbé, 131
Barry, Ann (*née* Dancer), 162
Barry, Elizabeth, 155
Barry, Spranger, 162
Barrymore (actor), 254, 258, 259
Bath, 66-8, 262, 364
Bathoe, William, 64
Bayford, E. G., 297
Bealby, J. T., 243, 302
Beardsley, Aubrey, 392
Beaumont and Fletcher, 112, 385
Beaux Stratagem, The, 25, 164
Becket, 155
Beckford, William, 252, 305
Bede the Venerable, S., 409
Bedford, Georgiana Elizabeth, Duchess of, 400
Bedford, John, sixth Duke of, 400
Beeverel, James, 149
Behn, Aphra, 99, 112, 148, 153, 156, 198, 199, 322
Bell, John, 75-6, 99, 145, 210, 211, 256, 257, 258, 260, 265, 303
Bellamy, George Ann, 204, 296
Bellamy, T., 139
Bellin de La Liborlière, 397
Bennett, Mrs. Agnes Maria (d. 13th February, 1808), 36, 89, 173

Bennett, Grey, 305
Bennett, Dr. T. Izod, 412
Bensley, William, 342
Benson, John, 342
Benson, Mgr. Robert Hugh, 200
Bentley, Richard (publisher 17th century), 99, 104, 154
Bentley, Richard (Colburn and Bentley), 80, 81, 299
Bentley's Magazine, 307
Berington, Rev. Joseph, 379
Bertram, 254
Betterton, Thomas, 155, 286
Beveridge, J. D., 303
Bible Stories for the Young, 218
Bibliography of Byron, A, 306
Bicknell, Alexander, 163, 199
Bindings, armorial and presentation, 96-7
Biographia Dramatica, 252, 261, 262, 285, 306, 307, 315, 364
Biographia Literaria, 123
Biographical Dictionary of Living Authors, A (1816; Upcott), 104, 381
Birkhead, Miss Edith, 239, 298, 301, 302
Birrell, Andrew, 262
Birthday Tribute, A, 364
Bizet (and H. Chaussier), 367, 368
Blackwood and Cadell, 302
Blackwood's Magazine, 304
Blair, Dr. Hugh, 47
Blair, Robert, 114
Blake, William, 18, 403
Blanchard, T., 229
Blanchard, William, 271, 275
Bland, Maria Theresa, 288, 366
Blind Beggar of Alexandria, The, 144, 272
Blue-Beard, 284, 380
Bluebooks, 82-5
Blyth, James, 150
Boaden, James, 147, 229, 230, 297, 307, 341
Boileau, D., 130
Boileau Despréaux, Nicolas, 39, 44
Boissy, Louis de, 113
Bold Stroke for a Wife, A, 272
Bolen, C. A., 100, 374, 379
Bolton, Miss, 285
Bornschein, J. E. D. (i.e., C. F. Möller), 142
Boston, U.S.A., 102
Boswell, James, 341
Bouchitté, H., 18
Bouilly, Jean Nicolas, 329
Bougeant, S. J., Guillaume Hyacinthe, 57
Bourgeois, Anicet, 231
Bourget, Paul, 61
Bowery Theatre, New York, 306
Boy of Santillane, The, 304
Boyd, Rev. Henry, 358, 381
Boyes, Captain, 295

Boyesen, Professor, defines Romanticism, 23–4
Boyse, Samuel, 114
Bracegirdle, Anne, 155
Braddon, Elizabeth, 388
Brauchli, Jakob, 151, 239, 240, 241, 301, 302, 305
Bravo and the Venetian Conspirators, The, 270
Bray, Anna Eliza (née Kempe, Mrs. Stothard, then Mrs. Bray), 174
Bremond, Gabriel de, 108, 148, 154
Brentano, Clemens Maria, 122, 131, 388, 393
Breton, André, 397, 398, 406, 407, 408, 409, 410
Brewer, James N., 87
Briddon's Library, Ryde, 70
Briefe des ewigen Juden, über die merkwürdigsten Begebenheiten seiner Zeit, Utopia [Offenbach], 227
Brighton, 68–9, 359, 363, 364
Brighton, An Epitome of, 364
Brillac, Mlle. S. B. de, 108, 148
British Critic, The, 318
British Zoology, 362
Bromley, Miss E. N., 366
Brook, Frances, 116
Brown, Charles Brockden, 121, 151
Brown, Tom (of Shifnall), 99, 108, 115
Browne, Sir Thomas, 148
Browne, William, 107
Bruce of Kinross, Sir John, 53
Brückner, Johann Jakob, 142
Brunton (actor), 271
Brunton, Louisa, Countess of Craven, 381
Brydges, Sir Egerton, 401
Bucholtz, Andreas Heinrich, 118
Bucholtz, Karl August, 142, 269, 388
Buckstone, John Baldwin, 301
Bull, Lewis (of Bath), 62, 67
Bunbury, H., 257
Bunn, Alfred, 301
Bunn, Mrs. 274
Bürger, Gottfried August, 47, 121, 150, 250, 251, 257, 299
Burgoyne, Lieutenant-General John, 112, 177, 200, 255
Burke, Mrs., 85, 366
Burlesque noir, le, 397
Burnet, Bishop Gilbert, 40
Burney, Frances (Madame D'Arblay), 33, 63, 89, 173
Busby, Thomas, 271, 305
Buxen (secret society), 134
Byron, George Gordon Noel Lord, 47, 121, 130, 200, 208, 214, 276, 291, 293, 294, 298, 388, 392, 399, 400

Cadell, Thomas, 77, 86, 168
Cadell, jun., Thomas, 77, 302
Cædmon, 409
Cailleran, 230
Caldara, Antonio, 392
Calderon de la Barca, Pedro, 386
Callender's Library, Boston, U.S.A., 102
Cambridge, Richard Owen, 58
Camille, ou le Souterrain, 255
Camoëns (Camões), Luiz de, 50
Campbell, A. L., 144
Campbell, A. V., 304
Campbell, Lady Charlotte Susan Maria, daughter of John, fifth Duke of Argyle (1723–90), 253, 280, 303, 400
Campbell, Mrs. Margaret, 404
Campbell and Gainsborough's Library, Bath, 67
Canning, George, 147
Canton, John, 175
Cantwell, André Samuel Michel, 397
Capell, Edward, 394
Capon, William, 230
Captive: A Scene in a Private Mad-House, The, 262
Caravaggio (Michelangelo Mensi), 407
Cardinal, The, 165
Cardinal Beaton, 304
Carné, Comte de, 369
Carroll, Lewis (Rev. C. L. Dodgson), 387
Cartaphilus, 226
Castle Cauldron, The, 152
Castle of Otranto, The (extravaganza), 185
Castle problem, The, 410
Castle Spectre, The, 121, 206, 253–6, 260, 261, 303
Castles, popular Theme in Gothic fiction, 86–7
Catholic ceremonial, the novelist's ignorance of, 238, 349, 361–2
Caverne, La, 144
Cawse, Miss H., 229
Cawthorn and Hutt, " British Library," 64, 65, 88
Cayler, Mrs., 258
Cazotte, Jacques, 224–5
Cecil, H. M., 85
Cenci, The, 392
Centlivre, Mrs., 272, 380
Ceolfrid of Jarrow, S., 381
Certosa of Pavia, the, 38 ; founded by Gian Galeazzo Visconte, 58
Cervantes Saavedra, Miguel de, 33, 154, 198
Chamisso, Adelbert von, 388
Chapman, George, 272
Chapman, Master, 285
Chapman's Library, Newport-Pagnell, 69
Chapple (publisher), 89

Chapter of Accidents, The, 165
Characteristicks of Men, Manners, Opinions and Times, 40
Char, Réné, 389
Charles II, 108, 148, 393
Charles VI of Austria, 392
Charles the Second, 264
Charleville, Catherine Maria, Countess of, 357–8, 381
Charleville, Charles William Bury, Earl of, 357–8, 381
Charlotte Sophia of Mecklenberg-Strelitz, Queen, 97
Charlton, Mary, 145, 368
Chastenay de Lanty, Comtesse Louise Marie Victorine, 100
Chateaubriand, François-René de, 47
Chaucer, Geoffrey, 112, 174
Chaussier, Hector, 367, 368
Cheer ! Boys, Cheer !, 305
Cheltenham, 69
Chevalier, A., 231
Chevy Chase, 393
Chichester, 102
Children in the Wood, The, 297
Choise Collection of Scots Poems, A, 393
Chollet, Jean-Baptiste, 143
Cibber, Colley, 112, 227, 299
Cibber, Mrs., 264
Circulating Libraries at Abingdon, 69, 98 ; Bath, 66–8 ; Brighton, 68–9 ; Boston, U.S.A., 102 ; Cheltenham, 69 ; Chichester, 102 ; Dublin, 219 ; Edmonton, 66 ; Herne Bay, 69 ; Kew, 66 ; Margate, 70 ; Moretonhampstead, 69, 96 ; Newport-Pagnell, 69 ; Ryde, 70 ; Sedbergh, 98 ; Sherborne, 70 ; Tunbridge Wells, 69 ; Wisbeach, 70 ; cheaper and humbler, 66 ; contemporary picture of, 71 ; earliest of the, in London, 64–5 ; first recorded of the, 72 ; stocked by Lane from the Minerva Press, 70
Circusiana, 144, 152
Citizen, The (Hudibrastic poem), 239
Clandestine Marriage, The, 201, 405
Clara von Hoheneichen, 144
Claremont (actor), 271
Clark, Emily, 85
Clarke, Dr. Adam, 62
Classicism, Augustan, 19, 390
Claude Duval, 141
Claude Lorraine, 52, 408
Clayton, Thomas, 155
Cleland, John, 216, 217, 298
Cleone, 214, 296
Cleveland, Barbara Villiers, Duchess of, 148
Clifford, F., 87

Clifford, Mrs. W., 185
Clown ! 411
Coates, Mrs., 258
Coburg Theatre, 270
Cockton, Henry, 81, 135
Cogan, Henry, 107
Colburn, Henry, 78, 80–1, 299
Cole, Rev. William, 138, 182, 408
Coleridge, Samuel Taylor, 47, 121, 123, 136, 147, 150, 208, 396
Coles, John, 107
Collection of Old Ballads, A, 393–4
Collins, William, 53
Collins, William Wilkie, 81, 305, 388
Collyer, Joseph, 119
Collyer, Mary, 119, 150
Colman, jun., George, 113, 147, 257, 283, 284, 309, 365, 380
Colman, sen., George, 28, 72, 149, 165, 296
Comical Revenge ; or, Love in a Tub, The, 112
Compendium Maleficarum, 303
Comstock, Anthony, 61
Confessions of a Young Man, The (George Moore), 22, 61
Congreve, William, 99
Conolly, L. A., 86
Constable's edition of *The Castle of Otranto,* 101
Constant Couple ; or, A Trip to the Jubilee, The, 25
Convent scenes in fiction, 243–5
Conway, William Augustus, 306
Cooke, A. (London circulating library), 62
Cooke, George Frederick, 304
Cooke, Thomas Simpson, 305
Cooke, William (bookseller), 64
Cooper, Fenimore, 80
Cooper, John, 229, 274, 275
Corneille, Pierre, 39, 106, 108
Corneille, Thomas, 106, 108
Corot, Jean Baptiste Camille (1796–1875), 20
Corsse (French actor), 270
Cotolendi, Carlo, 199
Cottage Maid, The, 363
Cotterell, Sir Charles, 98, 107
Coulon, le sieur, 149
Countess of Salisbury, The, 162
Count of Narbonne, The, 185
Country-Wife, The, 164
Coupilly, 230
Couvent, Le, 192
Covent Garden, 165, 206, 261, 271, 284, 296, 301, 303, 307, 366, 405
Cowley, Abraham, 394
Cowley, Hannah, 309
Coxcomb, The, 112
Coykendall, Frederick, 297

Cradock and Joy, 80
Cramer (i.e., Benedicte Naubert), 124
Cramer, Karl Gottlob, 124, 125, 388
Crashaw, Richard, 21
Crawford, Emily, 61
Crawford, J., 303
Crazy Jane (ballad), 253
Crazy Jane (romantic play), 303
Credulitate Demonibus Adhibenda, De, 302
Credulity, Superstition, and Fanaticism (Hogarth), 56
Critic, The, 297
Critical Dissertation on the Poems of Ossian, A, 47
Critical Review, The, 89, 90, 92, 94, 104, 169, 174, 183, 191, 192, 199, 201, 214, 247, 268, 270, 278–9, 310, 218, 346, 365, 380
Crofts (Croffts), Mrs., 190
Crosby, Benjamin, 79–80, 86, 93, 96, 190, 192, 246, 321
Crosnier, Mons., 232
Cross, J. C., 144
Crouch, Anna Maria, 366
Crow Street, Dublin, 305
Crowne, John, 107
Croxall, Samuel, 58, 153, 155, 201
Cullen, Stephen, 397
Cumberland, John (British Theatre), 299, 301, 303, 305, 307
Cumberland, Richard, 112, 392
Cunningham, Allan, 257
Cupid's Revenge, 112
Curiosa, La, 314
Curiosity, 314–5
Curll, Edmund, 103
Curties, T. J. Horsley, 29, 32, 33, 48, 86, 96, 100, 139, 151, 169, 179, 192, 196, 333–41
Cuthbertson, Miss, 29, 36, 40, 368

Dacre, Charlotte (Rosa Matilda), 29, 84, 85, 139, 151, 234, 236
Daily Telegraph and Morning Post, The, 412
Dali, Salvador, 389
Dalrymple, Sir David (Lord Hailes), 53
Dance, James, 113
Dangerfield, William, 65
Daniel, George, 227, 275
Dante Alighieri, 52, 201, 358, 381
Dardent, R. J., 365
Dash of the Day, The, 313–4
D'Aulnoy, Marie Catherine de la Mothe, Comtesse, 163
Davenant, Sir William, 264
Davenport, Mrs., 229
Davies, Hugh Sykes, 390, 396, 397
Davies, John, 107, 108, 154
Davies, Moll, 264

Davies, William (Cadell and Davies), 77
Day's Library, 65
De Arte Graphica, 40, 58, 391
Death, 114
De Camp, Miss, 259, 315
Deaf and Dumb, or The Orphan Protected, 328
Décor simultané, 282–3
Deffand, Madame du, 108
Deformed Transformed, The, 276
Deity, The, 114
Dekker, Thomas, 112
Delacroix, Ferdinand Victor Eugène, 407
Delavigne, Germain, 232
Délices de la Grande-Bretagne, Les, 149
Demetrius Poliorcetes, 306
Demofoonte, 392
Demon Duke; or, The Mystic Branch, The, 301
Demon Father; or, The Devil and his Son, The, 301
Demonolatry, 303
Demon Ship, The, 152
Dennis, John, 395
Denouement, The (Holiday Time), 315
Deschamps, Emile, 228
Description of a Religious House and Condition of Life, 21
Desiderio, Monsú, 407
Des Granges, Ch.-M., 301
Desmaretz, Jean, sieur de Saint-Sorlin, 107
Desrosiers, Charles (Madame de Saint-Spérat), 358
Destouches, Philippe Hericault, 113
Devocion de la Cruz, La, 386
Dickens, Charles, 388–9, 396
Dick Turpin, 141
Dicks, John (publisher), 301, 302, 303, 307
Diderot, Denis, 111, 165, 200, 407
Dillon's Library (afterwards Mudie's), 65
Disguise-plays, 271–2
Disraeli, Benjamin, 80
D'Israeli, Isaac, 295, 401
Dobson, Austin, 23
Donna Serpente, La, 387
Don Sebastian, a popular hero of romance, 175
Don Sebastian, King of Portugal, 58, 391
Doree, Master, 275
Dorset, Charles Buckhurst, Earl of, 393
Dorval; or, The Test of Virtue, 200
Double Gallant; or, The Sick Lady's Cure, The, 227
Douce, Francis, 297
Downes, John, 264
Dowson, Ernest, 358
Dowton, William, 254
Drake, Dr. Nathan, 47, 49–55, 241
Dreams and romance, 408–9

Dream, The (a drama), 363
Droste-Hülshoff, Annette Elisabeth von, 393
Drury Lane, 253, 267, 273, 275, 282, 284, 301, 303, 304, 306, 308, 315, 328, 342, 366
Dryden, John, 39–40, 58, 110, 148, 172, 175, 198, 199, 200, 264, 386, 390–1, 393, 394, 395
Duff, John R., 271, 306
Duff, Mary Ann, 271, 306
Dumas, Alexandre (père), 141
Dunlap, William, 270
Dunlop, John, 110, 111
Du Prat, l'Abbé, 99
D'Urfé, Honoré, 107, 388
D'Urfey, Thomas, 393
Ducasse, Isidore (Comte de Lautréamont), 389
Duchamp, Marcel, 389
Ducray-Duminil, François Guillaume, 397
Dunciad, The, 392
Dunton, Theodore Watts, 390, 392
Duruset, John, 264, 282
Dutton (publisher), 90, 92
Duval, Henri, 404

Earle, William, 77, 80, 85
Earle, jun., William, 78
East Indian, The, 206, 209, 258, 288
Ebsworth, Rev. Joseph Woodfall, 394
Eden, Sir Morton, 399
Edgeworth, Mrs., 100
Edinburgh Literary Journal, The, 226
Edmond, Orphan of the Castle, 188
Edmonton, 66
Edward (a ballad), 52, 55, 59
Edward Leman Blanchard, 303
Edwards, Amelia B., 388
Egan, jun., Pierce, 141
Egan, Miss, 287
Egmont, 304
Eichendorff, Joseph Freiherr von, 131, 393
Eidous, Marc-Antoine, 183, 201
Eitzen, Paulus von, 226
Elder Brother, The, 112
Elephantis, 214, 298
Ellen of Exeter (Mrs. Anna Maria Machenzie, *née* Wight; Mrs. Cox, *en secondes noces*, Mrs. Johnson, then Mrs. Mackenzie), 89, 172–3
Ellis-Fermor, Miss K. M., 307
Ellis, Stewart Marsh, 300, 301, 303, 306, 307
Elliston, Robert William, 165, 178, 273, 281, 282
Eloisa to Abelard, 21
Elton, W., 303
Encyclopædia Britannica, 389

England, described by French travellers, 148
English Novel in the Time of Shakespeare, The, 148
Enthusiasm, the term misliked, 56
Epistolary Intrigue, The, 206, 207
Epistolary novels, 115
Equestrian drama, 284, 285, 287, 307
Ernst, Max, 408
Errym, Malcolm J., 302
Erskine, William, 256
Espinasse, Francis, 213
Esploratore Turco, L', 199
Etherege, Sir George, 112
Étienne, Servais, 111
Euphémie, 116
European Magazine, The, 260
Evans, Edith, 198
Evans's Library, Abingdon, 69
Evelyn, John, 37, 38, 43
Evergreen, The (1724–7), 53, 394
Ewige Jude, Der, 226, 227
Explained supernatural, 138–40
Eyles, Francis, 109, 110
Eyles, Sir John, 109, 110

Faery Queen, The, 43, 44, 362
Fagan, Christophe, 113
Fair Rosamond, a heroine of romance, 155–6, 176–7, 199
Faithful Shepherdess, The, 112
Falconry, technicalities of, used in novel, 362
Fancourt, Samuel, 64, 65
Fantastique noir, le, 397
Fardeley, William, 146
Farley, Charles, 229, 264, 271, 285
Farquhar, Sir Walter, 289
Fatal Marriage ; or The Innocent Adultery, The, 198
Fausse Iseulte, La, 286
Faust (Goethe), 121, 276
Fawcett, John, 264, 274, 285
Fayette, Madame de la, 108
Feen, Die, 387
Felix Phantom (Constantia), 88, 122–3
Female Prelate, The (Settle), 301
Fenton, G., 298
Fenton, William Frederick, 307
Fiction, attacked by reviewers, 88–95
Fidèle conducteur, Le (Coulon), 149
Fielding, Henry, 92, 104, 115, 118
Fiend Father, The, 301
Fiesco, 121
Fisher's editions with engravings, 81, 101
Fitzball, Edward, 229, 243, 283, 301, 307

Flammenberg, Lorenz (Karl Friedrich Kahlert), 133
Flaubert, Gustave, 298
Fletcher, John, 108, 332
Flores Historiarum, 225
Flowers, Mr., 287
Flying Post, The, 307
Fontan, Louis-Marie, 231
Foote, Maria, 276
Forest Oracle, The, 304
Fortnightly Review, The, 61
Fortnum, Mrs. 100
Fouqué, Friedrich de la Motte, 131, 388
Fox, Charles James, 252
Fox, Joseph, 196, 359, 360, 362, 363
Fra Diavolo (Auber's opera), 143
Fra Diavolo (Michele Pazza), 143
Francis of Assisi, Saint, 393
Franklin, Andrew, 227
Franklin, Benjamin (*Autobiography*), 64
Frederick's Library, William (Bath), 68
Fresnoy, Charles Alphonse du, 40, 58, 391
Friedrich, der letze Graf von Toggenburg, 144
Froment (composer), 230
Fulcher's Library, Wisbeach, 70
Fuller, Anne, 32, 171, 172
Fuller, John, 62
Furetière, Antoine, 108
Fürst, Rudolf, 223, 224
Fuseli, Henry, 392

Gabrielli (Mrs. Mary Meeke), 89, 100
Galland, Antoine, 280, 307
Garrick, David, 113, 164
Gascoyne, David, 383, 384, 397
Gaunt, W., 407-8
Gautier, Théophile, 299
Geisweiler, Constantin, 78, 120, 141
Gellert, Christian Fürchtegott, 111, 119, 150
Genest, Rev. John, 255-6, 307, 315, 329, 342, 343
Genlis, Madame de, 255, 299, 315, 332
Gentleman's Journal, The, 199
Gentleman's Magazine, The, 169, 200, 380
Geography of Witchcraft, The, 296
George IV, 399
German Museum, The, 120, 226
Gerusalemme Liberata, 313, 388
Geschichte der Hexenprozesse (Soldan-Heppe), 299
Gessner, Salomon, 119
Ghisolfi, Giovanni, 408
Ghost, The (journal), 88, 122-3
Ghost stories told by Lewis, 291-2
Gibbes, Mrs. P., 63
Gibbon, Edward, 45
Gibbs, Mrs. (*née* Palmer), 271

Gildon, Charles, 395
Gilliland, Thomas, 307
Glanvil, Joseph, 203, 296
Gleave's reprints, 100
Gleich, Joseph Alois, 142
Glover, Mrs., 282
Godwin, William, 85, 167, 194, 241, 400, 402, 403
Goethe, Johann Wolfgang, 47, 118, 121, 122, 142, 144, 150, 207, 208, 226, 276, 296, 304, 388
Goldoni, Carlo, 113
Goldsmith, Oliver, 399
Golland, Mrs. C. D. (*née* Haynes), 87, 104
Gomberville, Marin Le Roy, sieur du Parc et de, 107, 388
Gomersal, Alexander Edward, 287
Goncourt, Edmond and Jules de, 22
Goodall, Mrs., 264
Gordon Riots, 401
Gordon, Thomas, 306
Görres, Joseph von, 131, 388, 393
Gosse, C. B., Sir Edmund, 61, 148, 159
Gothic, the history and various uses of the word, 37-41
Gothique noir, le, 397
Göttinger Musenalmanach, 122
Götz von Berlichingen, 123, 257
Gouges, Olympe de, 192, 225
Gounod, Charles, 231-2
Gourmont, Rémy de, 23
Gozzi, Count Carlo, 298, 386-7
Graesse, J. G. T., 299
Graglia, G. A., 89
Grave, The, 114
Gray, Thomas, 277, 394
Green, Mrs. Sarah, 98, 146, 397
Green, William Child, 29, 48, 100, 369-71
Greenwood, Thomas, 283, 307
Gresset, Jean Baptiste Louis, 113
Grétry, André Ernest Modeste, 200, 303
Grey, Charles Grey, second Earl, 399
Grieve (artist), 287
Griffith, Elizabeth, 68, 112, 309
Griffith, Richard, 68
Griffiths, E. (publisher), 302
Griglietti, Miss, 288
Grillparzer, Franz, 224, 227, 300
Grim White Woman, The, 276
Grimaldi, Joseph S., 229
Grosette, Henry William, 228
Grosse, Karl (Marquis von Grosse), 132
Guardi, Francesco, 408
Guardian, The, 223
Guazzo, Francesco-Maria, 303
Guénard, Elisabeth, baronne de Méré, 192, 246, 248, 358

Hachel (actor), 282
Hague, Lewis at The, 209–10, 301
Hamilton, Count Anthony, 108, 280, 306–7
Hamilton, Miss, 86, 100
Hamilton, Mrs., 401
Hamilton, William, 394
Hamlet, 341
Haney, J. L., 303
Hanway, Mrs. Mary A., 87
Hardyknute (ballad), 53
Hardy, Miss, 240
Hardy, Thomas, 396
Harley, John Pritt, 271, 275
Harley, Mrs. (A Young Lady, authoress of St. Bernard's Priory), 171
Harlowe, Mrs., 288
Harper's Daughter, The, 303
Harrild, R., 83
Harris, Thomas (of Covent Garden), 165, 206, 261, 271, 284, 304
Hartson, Hall, 162
Harvey, Jane, 86
Hatchard, Messrs., 288
Hatton (actor), 275
Hawkins, Laetitia M., 86
Hayes, George, 53
Hayman, Francis, 405
Haymarket Theatre, 283, 307, 366
Hays, Mary, 402
Haywood, Mrs. Eliza, 99, 115, 153, 198
Hazard, Samuel (of Bath), 62
Hazlitt, William, 134, 381
Heal, Sir Ambrose, 62, 63
Hebenstreit, Professor, 277
Heber, Richard, 305
Hedge, Dr. F. H., defines Romanticism, 23
Heine, Mons. Maurice, 300, 397
Heiress, The, 200
Heller, Wilhelm Friedrich, 227
Helme, Mrs. Elizabeth, 30, 48, 80, 86, 101, 169
Hemet, John, 77–8, 80, 103, 145
Henry and Almeria, 262
Henry II, 341, 342, 343
Henry the Second, King of England, 155
Henry the Fourth, 365
Hensler, Karl Friedrich, 142, 143
Herbert, Sir Henry, 200
Herder, Johann Gottfried von, 47, 122, 207, 224
Hermes, Johann Timotheus, 118
Hernon, G. D., 86, 367
Hervey, James, 114, 123
Herzfeld, Georg, 227, 300
Heseltine, William, 31
Hesperus, oder 45 Hundsposttage, 384
Hewlett, Joseph Thomas James (Peter Priggins), 40

Heywood, Thomas, 112
Hinckley, John, 141
Historia Major, 225
Historia Naturalis (Pliny), 308
Historical characters in Gothic romance, 30–1
Historic Survey of German Poetry, 122
History of Edward, the Black Prince, The (Bicknell), 199
History of his Own Time, A (Bp. Burnet), 40
History of King Lear, The (Tate), 395
History of the Reign of Henry the Second (Berington), 379
History of Witchcraft and Demonology, A, 296
Hitchener, William Henry, 178
Hive, The, 394
Hobbes, Miss, 303
Hodges's Library, Sherborne, 70
Hodgins (scenic artist), 287
Hodgkinson (actor), 270
Hodgkinson, Mrs., 270–1
Hoffmann, Ernst Theodor Wilhelm, 242, 301, 302, 386, 388
Hogarth, William, 23, 56, 405
Holcroft, Thomas, 309, 402
Holiday Time, 315
Holland, Henry Richard Fox (Vassall), third Lord, 399
Hollingshead, John, 254, 303
Höllische Proteus, Der, 224
Hollogan (scene painter), 271, 287
Holloway, Baliol, 198
Holman, Joseph George, 366
Home, John, 47, 325
Homer, 42, 44, 45, 58, 393, 409
Homme à Trois Visages, L', 270
Honest Whore, The, 112
Honori Sacellum, 97
Honner, Mrs., 307
Honner, R. W., 307
Hook, Sarah Ann, 85
Hook, Theodore, 80
Hookham, Thomas Jordan, 62, 63–4, 99
Hoole, John, 391
Hope, Anthony, 150
Horace (Q. Horatius Flaccus), 39, 42, 58, 394
Horn, Charles Edward, 288
Horses on stage, 284, 285, 287, 307
Horton, Priscilla (afterwards Mrs. German Reed), 185
Houghton, Miss Mary, 368
Howard, Cecil, 303
Howell (actor), 275
Huddart, Miss, 285
Hughes, J. F., 85, 99, 124, 177, 239, 267, 271, 277, 335, 336
Hughes, John, 58
Hughes, T. & R., 83

Hugnet, Georges, 389
Hugo, Victor, 22
Huish, Robert, 100, 196, 225
Hume, David, 47, 379
Humphry's Library, Chichester, 102
Hundsede udvalde Danske viser, Et, 224
Hunt, Leigh, 48
Hurd, Richard, Bishop of Worcester, 41–5, 48, 49, 58, 382
Hutchinson, William, 163, 185, 199
Huysmans, Jorris-Karl, 19, 22, 410
Hyde Park, 307

Iffland, August Wilhelm, 121
Iliff, Edward Henry, 88
Illuminati, 132–3
Inchbald, Mrs. Elizabeth, 33, 113, 147, 401,
Index Librorum Prohibitorum, 305
Indianer in England, Die, 258
Inferno of Dante Alighieri in English, The, 381
Inge, D. D., Very Rev. William Ralph, 18
Ingoldsby Legends, The, 257, 335, 406–7
Ireland, Samuel, 341
Ireland, William Henry, 29, 80, 85, 139, 177, 190, 193, 200, 341–59
Irving, Henry, 155, 200
Isabella; or, The Fatal Marriage, 198
Isle of Devils, A Metrical Tale, The, 288, 308
Italy (Rogers), 130

Jack Sheppard, 141
Jack Sheppard (S. M. Ellis), 307
Jack Sheppard; or, The House-Breaker of the Last Century, 283
Jackson, Mr. (of Louth), 80
James, G. P. R., 80, 139, 344, 358–9, 379, 380
James, Miss, 296
James, Montague Rhodes, 409
James, Samuel, 62
Jane Shore (Rowe), 393
Jaques reprints, 100
Jephson, Robert, 48, 185, 187, 201
Jerome, S., 62
John Nepomucene, S., 125
Johnson, Dr. Samuel, 17, 32, 92, 396, 399
Johnson, Charles, 112
Johnson, T. (publisher), 130, 225
Johnston, Henry, 261, 271, 303
Johnston, Mrs. Henry, 261, 264, 271, 285
Johnston, William, 75, 103
Johnstone, J. B., 303
Jomelli, Nicolo, 253, 303
Jonathan Bradford, 283, 307
Jones, Hannah Maria, 30
Jones, Richard, 305

Jones, Stephen, 147, 315
Jonson, Ben, 108, 395
Jordan, Dorothy, 206, 253, 258, 259, 342, 366
Journal des Voyages (Monconys), 149
Journal of a West-Indian Proprietor, The, 288–9, 308
Journal of the Conversations of Lord Byron, 291
Juan de la Cruz, San, 411
Julie, ou la Religieuse de Nisme, 192
Juliette, Mlle., 231
Jünger, Theodor, 142
Jusserand, Jean Adrien Antoine Jules, 148
Juvenal, 256

Kabale und Liebe, 209, 252
Kahlert, Karl Friedrich, 133–4
Kames, Lord, 396
Kapstein, Theodor, 299
Kaygill, 367
Kean, Edmund, 274, 282
Kearsley, G., 360
Keeley, Robert, 185
Kelly, Arthur, 112
Kelly, Fanny, 275, 288
Kelly, John, 113
Kelly, Michael, 229, 253, 259, 260, 274, 281, 284, 287, 295, 366
Kelly, Mrs. Isabella (afterwards Mrs. Hedgeland), 101, 139, 263–7, 305, 322
Kelly, William Martin, 263–7, 290, 305
Kemble, Charles, 258, 274, 342, 366
Kemble, John, 103, 147, 165, 185, 229, 230, 253, 254, 258, 260, 342, 366
Kendall, A., 190
Kenilworth Castle, 406
Kenney, G., 307
Kenrick, William, 396
Ker, Anne, 93, 94, 178, 200
Ker, J., 83
Kerndörffer, August Heinrich, 123, 142–3, 388
Kew, 66
Killen, Miss Alice M., 299, 300
Kind der Liebe, Das, 147
King, Matthew Peter, 274, 287
King, Thomas, 342
King Lear, 341, 381
Kingston, William Henry Giles, 240
Klee, Paul, 408
Klinger, Friedrich Maximilian, 281
Klopstock, Friedrich Gottlieb, 111, 119
Knebworth, 203, 296
Knight, Edward, 275
Knight, Joseph, 365
Knight, Richard Payne, 216
Kopp, C. P., 129

Körner, Karl Theodor, 388
Kotzebue, August Friedrich Ferdinand von, 121, 144, 147, 256, 258, 329, 392
Kramer, Professor (Benedicte Naubert), 124
Kynaston, Edward, 264

La Calprenède, Gautier de Coste, seigneur de, 25, 26, 107, 351, 388
La Chaussée, Pierre Claude Nivelle de, 113
Lacy, Michael Rophino, 151
Lafontaine, August Heinrich Julius, 85, 99, 145–6
Lamartelière, Jean Henri Ferdinand, 270
Lamb, Hon. George, 256
Lambert, George, 405
Lancashire Witches, The, 371
Lancaster, Agnes, 29, 96
Lane, William, 70, 72–3, 78, 85, 86, 87, 89, 90, 98, 99, 100, 103, 136, 139, 145, 196, 262, 318, 320, 364, 365, 366
Langbaine, Gerard, 98
Langland, William, 409
Langley and Belch, 83
Languish, Miss Lydia (her choice of novels), 67–8, 96, 154, 198
Lansdell, Sarah, 100, 305
Lara, Catherine, 89
La Roche, Marie Sophie von, 118
La Scala, Milan, 307
Lathom, Francis, 30, 32, 86, 87, 93, 99, 100, 139, 175, 177, 309–33, 397
Lathbury, Stanley, 198
Lathy, Thomas Pike, 29, 86, 90–2, 104, 151
Lee, Harriet, 164–7
Lee, John, 164–5, 200
Lee, Nathaniel, 96–7, 104, 148, 392
Lee, Sophia, 30, 144, 164–7, 169
Leeuwerk, Leopold, 134
Le Fanu, Joseph Sheridan, 81, 305, 388
Legend of S. Augustine (Desiderio), 407
Legends of Terror (1826), 304
Leigh, Mrs., 303
Leland, D.D., Rev. Thomas, 30, 131, 158, 162, 163
Lemaître, Frédéric, 231
Lemoine, Ann, 83, 367
Lennox, Mrs. Charlotte, 26–7
Lenore, English translations of, 122
Le Normant (libraire), 401
Lessing, Gotthold Ephraim, 121
Letter on the Secret Tribunal of Westphalia, A, 129
Letters on Chivalry and Romance (Bp. Hurd), 41–6

Lewis, Barrington, 204, 206, 293
Lewis, Frances Maria, 202, 203, 204–5, 290, 294, 296
Lewis, Matthew, 202, 204–5, 215, 271, 289–90
Lewis, Matthew Gregory (1775–1818); *Adelgitha*, writes, 273 ; *Adelmorn*, writes, 258–60; Albany, his chambers in the, 252, 288 ; *Alfonso*, writes, 261–2, and Byron, 291–3 ; and Scott, 256–7 ; and Shelley, 294 ; at Naples, 294 ; at Oxford, 205, 209 ; at Paris, 206, 225 ; at Weimar, 207–8 ; attaché at The Hague, 209–10 ; attacked by Mathias, 215–18 ; Barnes, his cottage at, 252, 399 ; *Bravo of Venice*, writes, 267–9 ; *Castle Spectre*, writes, 253–6 ; death of father of, 289–90 ; dies at sea, 295 ; differences between the work of Mrs. Radcliffe and the work of, 232–4 ; early influences upon, 203–4 ; *East Indian*, writes, 258 ; enters diplomatic service, 207–8 ; first novel of, 206 ; friendship with Dureset, 264 ; friendship with William Martin Kelly, 263–7 ; *Feudal Tyrants*, writes, 276–80 ; ghost stories related by, 291–2 ; imitated by Gothic novelists, 233–9, 242–5 ; influenced by Germany, 208, 223–5 ; influences Germany and France, 227–8, 230–2 ; *Journal of a West-Indian Proprietor*, posthumously published, 288–9 ; London society, a great figure in, 212, 252–3, 399–400 ; M.P. for Hindon, 252 ; *Minister* written, 252 ; *Monk* composed at The Hague and afterwards published, London, 210 ; *Monk* causes scandal, 212–19 ; *Monk* dramatized, 229–32 ; *Monk* runs into several editions, 210–12 ; *Monk* to be prosecuted, 219 ; *Monk* translated into French, 228 ; into German, 227–8 ; *One o'Clock* (*Wood Dæmon*), 274–6 ; *Poems*, 288 ; poems, 257–8, 288 (*Banks of Allan Water*), 288 ; *Rich and Poor*, 288 ; *Romantic Tales*, 280–1 ; supernatural monitor of, 293 ; *Tales of Terror*, 257 ; *Tales of Wonder*, 257 ; theatrical bent of, 204 ; *Timour the Tartar*, 284–7 ; *Venoni*, 281–2 ; *Village Virtues*, 251 ; visits France, 206, 225 ; Geneva, 293, 294 ; Germany, 207–8, 291 ; Italy, 294 ; Jamaica, 288, 293, 294 ; Mannheim, 291 ; Naples, 294 ; Rome, 294 ; Weimar, 207–8 ; *Zoroaster*, written, but not published, 288–9.
Lewis, *Matthew Gregory, The Life and Correspondence of*, by Mrs. Baron-Wilson, 206, 288, 290, 296, 299, 301, 305, 307

Lewis, M. G., other references to, 21, 29, 46, 55, 87, 88, 91, 95, 99, 109, 118, 124, 139, 141, 144, 148, 194, 196, 197, 369, 388, 394, 396, 399, 400, 410
Levis, Mons. de, 306
Leyden, J., 257
Libraire anticléricale publish *Le Moine*, 228
Life of Alfred the Great, The, 199, 251
Life of Michael Kelly, The, 303
Lillo, George, 113
Lincoln's Inn Fields, theatre, 286
Lind, Jenny, 301
Line upon Line, 218
Linley, Thomas, 200, 303
Lipohitz, Jacques, 389
Liseux, Isidore, 298
Liston, John, 271
Litchfield, Harriett (*née* Hay), 261, 262, 288, 304
Literary Anecdotes, 298
Literary Gazette, The, 399
Literary History of the Troubadours, The, 200
Literary Hours, 49–55
Lockhart, J. G., 303
Loder, E. J., 229
London Gazette, The, 307
London Journal, The, 130, 150
London Magazine (attacks the two Nobles), 63
Longman, Thomas, 78
Longman, Thomas, 78–9
Longman, Thomas Norton, 79, 99
Longman and Rees, 141, 280, 301, 318
Longus, 388
Look About You, 144, 272
Lord, Mrs. (of Dublin), 219
Loveday, Robert, 98, 107
Love in a Wood; or, St. James Park, 112
Love of Gain, The, 256
Love Triumphant, or, Nature will Prevail, 391
Lovers' Vows, 147
Love's Last Shift, 112
Lowndes, Thomas, 62, 63
Lucas, Rev. Charles, 100, 190, 401
Luckey Chance; or, An Alderman's Bargain, The, 112
Lushington, Maria, Lady (*née* Lewis), 294
Lytton, Edward Bulwer, first Lord, 80, 203–4, 379, 388, 410
Lytton, Life and Letters of Lord, 203–4

Mabbe, Thomas, 198
Macabre in literature, the, 114
Macaulay, Thomas Babington, 45
Macbeth, 42, 59, 140, 164, 351
Macfarren, George, 304
MacGowan, Rev. John, 119

Machiavellus, 271
Mackenzie, Henry, 68, 120–21, 169
Mackenzie, Mrs. Anna Maria, 30, 100, 172–3, 200
Macnally, Leonard, 303
Macpherson, James, 47, 406
Macready, William Charles, 200, 274, 275, 306
Madhouse episodes in fiction, 81
Magnasco, Alessandro, 408
Magnes and Bentley, 154
Maid of Orleans, The (translation from Voltaire), 357–8
Maillan, J., 231
Malleus Maleficarum, 303
Malone, Edmund, 96, 104, 341, 380, 396
Man of Business, The, 296
Man of Mode, or Sr Fopling Flutter, The, 112
Man of Quality, The, 164
Man of the World, The, 271
Maniac, The, 262
Manifesto of Surrealism, 397
Manley, Mrs., 153, 199
Mann am Hofe, 118
Manuscript, recovered, a theme in Gothic fiction, 169–70
Maradan (libraire), 100, 401
Marana, Giovanni Paolo, 199
Marchi, Giuseppe Filippo Liberati, 399
Mardyn, Mrs., 271
Maria Stuart und Norfolk, 144
Marino Faliero, 399
Marishall, Jean, 97
Marivaux, Pierre Carlet de Chamblain de, 113–4, 118
Marquand, L. A., 173
Marquis de Sade et le Roman noir, Le, 397
Marriage A-la-Mode, 164
Marryat, Captain Frederick, 80
Marshall's Library, Bath, 67
Marsollier, Benoît Joseph Marsollier des Vivetières, 225, 255
Marston, John, 301
Marston, Westland, 200
Marylebone Theatre, 306
Mason, Rev. William, 186, 300
Mathias, Thomas James, 33, 186, 216, 217, 218, 292
Matthew of Westminster, 257
Matthews, Benjamin (of Bath), 62
Matthews, Charlotte, 87
Matthews, T., 229
Mattocks, Mrs., 271
Maturin, Rev. Charles Robert, 29, 87, 140, 148, 151, 169, 193, 194, 254, 369, 388, 396, 400
Maupassant, Guy de, 61
Maxwell, Miss C., 177

May-Day, 272
Measure for Measure, 164
Meditations among the Tombs, 114, 123
Medwin, Thomas, 291
Meeke, Mrs. Mary, 30, 36, 85, 89, 98, 100, 145, 300
Meier, Jakob, 121
Melbourne, William Lamb, second Viscount, 399
Melville, Theodore, 87, 92, 100, 104
Memoir of William Taylor of Norwich, 303
Memoirs of Mrs. Crouch (by Mary Julia Young), 251, 253
Memoirs of the Colman Family (Peake), 307
Memoirs of the Court of Louis XIV, 91
Mémoires pour servir à l'histoire du Jacobinisme, 131
Mémoires sur l'ancienne Chevalrie, 58
Mémoires faites par un Voyagereur, 149
Menschenhass und Reue, 147
Menzel, Wolfgang, 306
Mérimée, Prosper, 301
Méré, Mme. de. *See* Guénard, Elisabeth.
Messias, 119
Metastasio, Pietro, 392
Meyerbeer, Giacomo, 232
Meyler's Library, Bath, 67
Michelangelo, 390
Middleton, Thomas, 343
Midgley, Dr. Robert, 199
Midnight Spell, The, 152
Milbiller, Professor (i.e., Benedicte Naubert), 124
Millar, Andrew, 77
Miller and his Men, The, 299, 304
Miller, Miss, 342
Millikin, Anna, 30, 175
Millot, Abbé, 200
Milton, John, 41, 42, 107, 121
Minerva Press, 70, 72, 73, 74, 96, 100, 117, 190, 241, 359, 368
Minerva Public Library Circular, 74–5
Minister, The (*Kabale und Liebe*), 252
Minors (Mynors), Willoughby, 62
Minotaure, Revue, 397
Minster Lovel, 405
Miró, Joan, 389, 408
Miscellaneous Pieces (J. and A. L. Aikin), 48
Misson, Maximilian, 149
Modern Language Review, The, 308
Modern Standard Novels (Colburn, afterwards Bentley), 80
Moira, Francis Rawdon Hastings, Second Earl of, 267, 305
Molière, Jean-Baptiste Poquelin, 106, 108
Möller, Christian Friedrich, 142
Monasticism in the Gothic Novel, 192–97, 363

Mönch in der englischen Dichtung, Der, 300
Monconys, Balthasar de, 149
Moncrieff, W. T., 308
Monody on the Death of Sir John Moore, 284
Montagu, George, 409
Montagu, Lady Mary Wortley, 19, 57
Montague, Edward, 29, 87, 236, 239, 241
Montalbion, Kate, 177–8
Montemayor, Jorge de, 388
Monthly Magazine, The, 131, 297
Monthly Mirror, The, 88, 89, 90, 92, 93, 94, 193, 246, 313, 318, 320, 343, 364, 380
Monthly Review, The, 88, 89, 91, 93, 94, 104, 134, 139, 171, 200, 214, 224, 310
Montolieu, Mlle. de, 145
Monvel, Boutet de, 192, 225, 281, 282
Moore, Edward, 112
Moore, George (1852–1933), 20, 22, 61, 101
Moore, M.D., John, 95
Moore, Thomas, 214
Morality of Fiction (Murray), 144
More, Dr. Henry, 296
More, Hannah, 401
More, S. Thomas, 393
Morellet, Abbé André, 228, 367
Moretonhampstead, 69, 96
Morgan, Lady Sydney (*née* Owenson), 40, 80, 86, 100
Morgan's Library, Conduit Street, 80
Morgann, Maurice, 396
Morley, G. T., 29, 86, 94
Morris (scene painter), 288
Morris, William, 131
Mothe-Houdancourt (Mothe-Langon), Baron de La, 367
Motteux, Peter Anthony, 155
Mountain, Mrs., 259, 260, 275
Mountford, Susanna, 264
Mountford, William, 199
Mousket, Philippe, 225
Much Ado about Nothing, 164
Mude, Mrs., 282
Mudie, Charles Edward, 65
Mudie, Thomas, 65
Mudie's Library, 60, 61, 65
Müller, J. M., 86
Müller, Johann Friedrich Wilhelm (Benedicte Naubert), 124
Mulock, Dinah Maria (Mrs. Craik), 240
Münchhausen, Hieronymus Karl Friedrich, Freiherr von, 250–1
Muralt, Béat Louis de, 149
Murdock, John, 68, 149
Murphy, Jasper Dennis (C. R. Maturin), 140, 151
Murray, Charles, 261
Murray, Hugh, 144
Musaeus, Johann Karl August, 118, 223

Museat, Miss Eliza, 93
Musgrave, Agnes, 174
Musset, Alfred de, 111
Mutius Scævola ; or the Roman Patriot, 343
Mysterious Husband, The, 392
Mysterious Marriage ; or, The Heirship of Rosalva, The, 166
Mysterious Mother, The, 52, 53, 55, 392
Mysticism, 412 ; and Romanticism, 18 ; in literature, 23

Nanine, 113
Nathan, Abraham, 134
National Vigilance Association, prurient activities of the, 61
Naubert, Christiane Benedicte Eugenie, 123, 124, 129, 223, 277, 306, 388
Nelson's Ghost, 239
Nesbitt, Cathleen, 198
Newby, C. T., 358
Newman & Co., A. K. (Minerva Press), 87, 93, 96, 98, 311, 321, 322, 325, 329, 334, 344, 366, 369, 370, 371, 374
New Monthly Magazine, The, 298
New Peerage, The, 166
Newport-Pagnell, 69
Newton, H. Chance, 254, 302
Nichols, John, 298
Nicolls, Miss, 229
Nightmare Abbey, 147
Night Thoughts, 114, 123, 149
Night-Walker ; or, The Little Thief, The, 112
Noble, Francis and John, 62–3
Noble, Samuel, 62
Noehden, Georg Heinrich, 120
Nonne Sanglante, La, 231–2
Norbury, of Brentford, 86
Nordau, Max, 56, 218
Norris, Mr., 90
Norris, Mrs., 90, 104
Northanger Novels, The, 398
No Song, No Supper, 325
Nouveau théâtre allemand, Le, 121
Novalis (Friedrich Leopold, freiherr von Hardenberg), 388
Novel, receipt to make a Romance a, 35,
Novels, illustrated ; 'original condition' of, 95–9 ; presentation copies of, 97 prices of, 98–100
Nunn, James, 79

Obscenity, The Monk accused of, 214–15, 217, 219
Odéon, 231
Ode to Fear (Collins), 53
Ode to Superstition (Drake), 51

Œdipus, 391
Oertel, F. von, 227, 298
Of Dramatick Poesie, 395
Oldham, John, 59
One o'Clock ; or, Harlequin Hardy Knute, the Knight and the Wooden Demon, 306
One o'Clock ; or, The Knight and the Wood Dæmon, 274–5, 276, 288, 307
On Solitude, 189
On the Pleasure Derived from Objects of Terror, 48
Opie, Amelia, 85
Orger, Mrs., 288
Original Poetry by Victor and Cazire, 304
Orlando and Seraphina, 313
Orlando (pseudonym), 100
Orphan, The, 113
Orpheus Caledonius, 394
Orrery, Roger Boyle, Earl of, 107, 157, 308
Ossian, 47, 48, 51, 114, 135, 406
Otway, Thomas, 113, 154, 158, 199, 392
Ouida (Louisa de la Ramée), 388
Owenson, Sydney. See Morgan, Lady.
Oxberry, William, 275, 297
Oxenford, John, 301
Oxford, Lewis at, 209, 296

Paalen, W., 389
Palmer, John (of Bath), 364
Palmer, jun., John, 192, 258, 364–6
Palmer, sen., John (1742–1798), 162, 364, 365, 366
Palmer, Robert, 366
Pamela, 113
Paméla en France, 113
Pamela Maritata, 113, 149
Pamela Nubile, 113, 149
Pamela ; or Virtue Triumphant, 113
Pamphilus of Cæsarea, S., 62
Pannini, Giovanni, 408
Paradise Lost, 114
Parallel betwixt Painting and Poetry, A (Dryden's translation from du Fresnoy), 40, 391
Parallel of Architecture, A (De Chambray), 37
Paris, Matthew, 225
Parr, Dr. Samuel, 341
Parsons, Mrs. Eliza, 28, 29, 81, 93, 98, 100, 101, 138, 145, 169, 173, 265, 322
Pastoureau, Henri, 390
Pater, Walter, 18
Pausanias, 408
Payn, James, 380
Payne, John Howard, 264
Peacock, Lucy, 96
Peacock, Thomas Love, 14

Peake, Richard Brinsley, 307
Peck, Louis F., 212, 297
Pennant, Thomas, 362
Penrose, Valentine, 390
Pepys, Samuel, 307
Percy, Thomas, Bishop of Dromore, 46, 48, 53, 394
Péret, Benjamin, 389
Père de Famille, Le, 165
Peyri (libraire, Avignon), 367
Pharnusa, Marquis of (Karl Grosse), 132
Phelps, Samuel, 402
Philaster, 112
Phillimore (actor), 342
Phillips (actor), 275
Philips, Ambrose, 394
Phillips, Edward, 395
Phillips, John, 107
Phillips, Miss, 275
Phillips, Richard, 86
Phillips (scenic artist), 271, 287
Philosophe Marié, Le, 113
Philostratus, 115
Phiz (Hablot Knight Browne), 302
Phlegon of Tralles, 257
Phœnix of Sodom, The, 305
Pichot, Amédé, 183, 201
Pickersgill, Joshua, 276
Pigault Lebrun, Charles Antoine Guillaume Pigault de l'Épinoy Lebrun, 99, 117
Pilkington, Mrs. Mary, 87, 100
Pills to Purge Melancholy (Wit and Mirth), 393
Pindar, 394
Pinkerton, John, 53
Pisanus Fraxi (Henry Spencer Ashbee), 305
Pitavel, Gayot de, 28
Pitou, Alexis, 301
Pitt, George Dibdin, 283
Pius VII, Pope (Barnaba Luigi Chiaramonti), 294
Pius IX, Pope (Giovanni Maria Mastai-Ferretti), 384
Pixérécourt, Guilbert de, 231, 270, 305
Pizarro, 147, 251, 258, 261, 292
Plain-Dealer, The, 112
Pliny the Elder, 308
Ploert, Edouard, 228
Plomer (*Dictionary of Booksellers*), 62
Pocock, Isaac, 264
Poel, William, 307
Poems (M. G. Lewis), 262
Polidori, John, 294
Pollock, Benjamin, 307
Polly Honeycombe, 28, 72
Pommeret (libraire), 367
Poor Gentleman, The, 325
Pope, Alexander, 19-21, 25, 59, 390, 392, 395; the romantic element in, 20-1, 390, 392

Pope, Jane, 165, 258, 264, 265, 292, 315, 329, 366
Pope's grotto, 20-1
Pope's villa and garden destroyed, 57
Porte-Saint-Martin, 231
Porter, Anna Maria, 175
Porteus, Bishop Beilby, 114
Pougin, A. (libraire), 367
Pougens, 192, 225
Poussin, Gaspar, 390, 408
Powell (actor), 259, 282
Powell, J., 86
Powell, Mrs., 253, 258, 273, 282, 284, 342, 366
Poynet, Quintin, 371
Pratt, Samuel Jackson (Courtney Melmoth), 71
Precious Relics, or, the Tragedy of Vortigern Rehearsed, 380
Prest, Thomas Peskett, 244
Prévost, Augustin, 231
Prévost, Dom Antoine-François, 109-11, 114, 118, 149, 163
Prickett, Miss, 31
Prisoner of Rochelle, The, 283
Proby, W. C., 139
Profanity, *The Monk* accused of, 215, 217-8
Progress of Romance, The, 189
Prolusions ; or, select Pieces of antient Poetry, 394
Promenade à travers le Roman noir, 397, 398
Proofs of a Conspiracy (Robinson), 131
Pucelle d'Orléans, La, 357-8
Pugh (scenic artist), 287
Pursuits of Literature, The, 33, 201, 212, 216-18, 292
Pye, Henry James, 341
Pyne (actor), 288

Quadrupeds of Quedlinburgh, The, 147, 287
Quarter Day, 363
Quinault, Philippe, 106, 108

Racine, Jean, 106, 108
Radcliffe, Mary Ann, 29, 98
Radcliffe, née Ward, Ann, 21, 30, 31, 33, 47, 49, 52, 54, 55, 56, 84, 86, 87, 88, 89, 91, 95, 99, 101, 118, 133, 136, 138, 140, 141, 148, 152, 174, 187, 194, 196, 197, 199, 210, 222, 232-3, 244, 289, 334, 336, 337, 364, 365, 367, 368, 369, 378, 379, 388, 396, 399, 400, 404, 405, 406, 409
Rae, Alexander, 282
Railo, Eino, 251, 271, 303, 304
Ramsay, Allan, 53, 393, 394
Rape of the Lock, The, 392

Raspe, Rudolf Erich, 248, 250, 303
Räuber, Die, 120, 121, 123, 200
Räuber-Romane, 140–44
Ravenscroft, Edward, 53, 59
Raven's Nest, The, 152
Rawlinson, Sir Thomas (Lord Mayor of London), 97, 105
Ray, Man, 408
Raymond (Grant), 259, 273
Reade, Charles, 305
Read, Herbert, 383, 390, 394, 396
Realism, 22 ; alternates with Romanticism, 23
Réalisme noir, le, 397
Red Crow, The, 152
Red Front, The, 411
Redington's Juvenile Drama, 285, 307
Rees, Owen, 79
Reeve, Clara, 40, 102, 117, 131, 138, 169, 186–89, 201, 300, 309, 397, 401, 405
Reeve, William, 228
Reeves, Sims, 151
Registers of the Stationers' Company, The, 380
Rehearsal, The, 307
Reichardt, Johann Friedrich, 227
Relapse, or Virtue in Danger, The, 164
Rélation d'un Voyage en Angleterre, 149
Reliques of Ancient English Poetry (Percy), 46, 50, 53, 394
Remarks on Several Parts of Italy (Addison), 38
Remarks on the Tragedies of the Last Age, 391
Remy, Nicolas, 303
Render, Rev. Dr. Wilhelm, 120, 130
Reparation ; or The School for Libertines, 91
Restif de la Bretonne, 114
Reverdy, Pierre, 389
Reviewers, fiction attacked by, 88–95
Reynolds, George William McArthur, 81, 130, 150, 240, 243, 244, 302, 305, 333, 391, 402
Reynolds, Sir Joshua, 399
Rheinische Thalia, Die, 227
Ribié, Mons., 230
Ricci, Sebastiano, 408
Riccoboni, Marie Jeanne Laboras de Mezieres, Madame, 114–5
Rice, C., 62
Rice, Mrs., 86
Rich and Poor, 288
Richard, Cœur de Lion, 177
Richard, Cœur De Lion, 177, 255
Richardson, Mrs. (of Evreux), 371
Richardson, Samuel, 111, 112, 114, 118, 123
Richard the Third, 304
Riche (libraire), 401
Richter, Johann Paul Friedrich (Jean Paul), 28, 384

Richter, Moritz, 142
Ridgway (publisher), 89
Riley, George, 64
Rimelli (Monthly Mirror), 94–5
Rinaldo Rinaldini, Der Räuberhauptmann, 143
Rinaldo Rinaldini ; or, The Black Tribunal, 144
Rinaldo Rinaldini ; or, The Brigand and the Blacksmith, 144
Rinaldo Rinaldini ; or, The Secret Avengers, 144
Ritter, Otto, 227, 299
Rival Ladies, The, 391
Rivals, The, 258 (Miss Languish's novels), 67–8
Rivers ; or, The East Indian, 258
Robber of the Abruzzi, The, 144
Robber romances, 140–44
Robberds, J. A., 303
Robert (actor), 275
Robert, Hubert, 407, 408
Robert le Diable, 232, 301
Roberts, W., 297
Robin Hood, 141
Robinson (costumier), 288
Robinson, Emma, 174
Robinson, George, 77, 93, 99, 366
Robinson, Henry Crabb, 122, 147, 152
Robinson, John, 77
Robinson, Mrs. Mary " Perdita," 33, 84, 401
Robinson, sen., George (G. & J. Robinson), 76–7, 79, 86, 124, 209
Robins reprints, 100
Robison, Professor John, 131
Roche, Mrs. Regina Maria, 29, 36, 96, 100, 101, 300
Rochester, John Wilmot, Earl of, 96
Rodwell, G. H., 243
Roe, J., 83, 367
Roger of Wendover, 225
Rogers, Samuel (Table Talk quoted), 73 (Italy quoted), 130
Rolla ; or, The Peruvian Hero (Die Spanier in Peru ; oder, Rollas Tod), 256
Romance, receipt to make a Novel a, 35 ; the Temple of, poetically described, 34
Romances, Heroic, long-lived popularity of and allusions to, 25–7
Romances of Chivalry, 25
Romancist and Novelist's Library, The, 93, 268, 381
Roman noir, le, 397
Romanticism, alternates in literature with realism, 23 ; contrasted with classicism, 19 ; with realism, 22 ; definition of, 18–19 ; origin of, 23–4
Romeo and Juliet, 164

Roqueplan, M., 232
Rosalia, S., 302
Rosamond, Fair, a heroine of romance, 155–6, 176–7, 199
Rosimond, Claude La Rose de, 106
Rosina, 264
Rossetti, Dante Gaebiel, 131
Rotrou, Jean, 106, 108
Rousseau, Jean Jacques, 111
Roussel, Pierre-Joseph-Alexis, 318
Rouvière, Henrietta (Mrs. Moss), 85, 86, 104, 177
Rovers, The (Canning), 147, 287
Rowe, Nicholas, 286, 393, 395
Rowley's Circulating Library, Edmonton, 66
Royal Circus, St. George's (afterwards Surrey Theatre), 144, 270
Royal Pavilion Theatre, 301, 308
Rugantino ; or, The Bravo of Venice, 271, 278
Ruins, popular theme in Gothic novels, 87, 201, 404–7
Russell, Henry, 262
Russell's Library, Bath, 67
Ryde, 70
Ryde, H. T., 306
Rymer, Thomas, 391

Sade, Donatien-Alphonse-François, Marquis de, 116, 397
Sadleir, Michael, 95, 96, 97, 103, 398, 399, 406
Sadlers Wells, 283, 301, 304
Saducismus Triumphatus, 203, 296
Sage von ewigen Juden, Die, 299
Saint-Aubin, Cammaille, 230, 231
Saint-Evremond, Charles, Seigneur De, 108, 148
St.-Germain, Comte de (*der Wundermann*), 332
St. Helens, Lord, 209, 296, 399
Saint-Léon, Mme. Brayer de, 404
St. Pierre, Bernardin de, 388
Saint-Réal, Abbé César de, 154, 198
Saint-Spérat, Madame de, 358
St. Victor, Helen, 87
Sainte-Beuve, Charles Augustin, 47
Sainte-Palaye, Jean Baptiste De La Curne De, 58
Saintsbury, George, 401
Saladin, Jules, 322
Saltinbanco, 363
Salvator Rosa, 52, 408
Sannazzaro, Jacopo, 388
Sarratt, Mrs. (*née* Dufour), 251
Sarratt (Sarrat), H. J., 192, 246–7, 248, 251, 302

Satan's Harvest Home, 305
Sauer, August, 224, 227, 300
Saul, Mr. (theatrical machinist), 287
Saunders and Otley, 80, 150, 191
Saunders, Florence, 53
Saunder's Public Library, Cheltenham, 69
Scarron, Paul, 68, 106, 107, 108, 154
Schaible, K. H., 303
Schauerromane, 124, 130, 132, 133, 142–3
Schiller, Johann Christoph Friedrich von, 47, 121, 122, 144, 150, 207, 209, 227, 240, 252, 296, 388
Schlegel, August Wilhelm, 388
Schlegel, Friedrich, 131, 388, 393
Schmidt-Lisber, H., 142
Schmieder, H. G., 269
Schneider, Rudolf, 300
School for Scandal, The, 304
Schubart, Christian, 226, 227
Scornful Lady, The, 310
Scott, Clement, 303
Scott, Sir Walter, 31, 46, 47, 59, 121, 122, 123, 140, 148, 150, 152, 169, 174, 184, 187, 192, 208, 256, 257, 281, 291, 303, 369, 371, 378, 379, 388, 396
Scots Magazine, The, 214
Scots Songs, 393
Scribe, Auguste Eugène, 143, 232
Scudéry, Georges de, 25
Scudéry, Madeleine de, 25, 26, 27, 107, 351, 388
Second Manifesto of Surrealism, 397
Secret History of the Green Room, The, 364
Secret-Love ; or, The Maiden Queen, 391
Secret Tribunal, The, 147
Sedaine, Michel Jean, 177, 303
Sedburgh Book Club, 98
Ségrais, Jean Renaud de, 148
Selden, John, 393
Sentiment and sensibility, 111–12
Sentimentalism in English drama, 112–13
Settle, Elkanah, 97, 104, 105, 301
Sévigné, Madame de, 108
Shadwell, Charles, 112
Shadwell, Thomas, 264
Shaftesbury, Anthony Cooper, third Earl of, 40, 43
Shakespeare, William, 42, 51, 52, 53, 55, 59, 108, 135, 174, 332, 341, 343, 363, 385, 387, 393, 394, 395, 396
Shelley, Elizabeth, 304
Shelley, Mary, 149, 226
Shelley, Percy Bysshe, 121, 147, 208, 226, 294, 304, 392
Sherborne, 70
Sheridan, Frances, 258
Sheridan, Richard Brinsley, 198, 251, 258, 260, 399

Shine, J. L., 303
Shirley, James, 165, 307
Skeffington, Lumley St. George, 346
Sketches from Life (comedy), 363
Sickelmore, Richard, 29, 86, 100, 302, 363–4
Siddons, Henry, 172, 273, 282
Siddons, Mrs. Henry, 165, 273, 281, 282
Siddons, Sarah, 103, 147, 162, 164, 165, 185, 229, 230, 307, 342, 366
Sidney, Sir Philip, 184
Siena, the Duomo, 39
Simpkin and Marshall, 80
Sinclair of Ulbster, Sir John, 250
Sr Martin Mar-all; or The Feign'd Innocence, 57, 58
Sivrac's *Il Castello di Otranto*, 183
Sixpenny novels, 82–3
Skelt, Matthew, 275
Sleath, Mrs. Eleanor, 29, 146, 152, 192, 368
Smith and Stephens, New York, 392
Smith, Horace, 380
Smith, John Frederick, 150
Smith, Miss Catherine, 229, 368
Smith, Mrs. Charlotte, 28, 29, 33, 36, 47, 84, 89, 100, 101, 109, 401
Smith, Richard John (O. Smith), 229, 243, 302
Smith, Samuel, 61
Smith, William, 162
Smithers, Leonard, 381
Smollett, Tobias, 67, 225
Society for the Suppression of Vice, the, 219
Soergel, Albert, 299
Soliloquy, or Advice to an Author (Shaftesbury), 43
Somerset, C. A., 303
Somerville, Margaret Agnes (Mrs. Bunn), 274
Sorbière, Samuel de, 149
Sorel, Charles, 107
Soupault, Philippe, 389
Southerne, Thomas, 113, 198, 392
Southey, Robert, 121
Spanish Fryar, The, 58, 391
Sparks, Mrs., 258, 271
Spectator, The, 25, 216, 393
Speiss, Christian Heinrich, 123, 144, 150, 388
Spencer, George, fourth Duke of Marlborough, 360, 381
Spenser, Edmund, 41, 42, 55, 362
Spenserian revival, 58–9
Squire, T., 303
Staël, Anne Louisa, Madame de, 145, 293
Stanstead Hall, Essex, 203, 410
Steevens, George, 341, 396
Stein, Bernhard, 133
Sterne, Laurence, 67

Stewart, A. A., 87
Stimmen der Völker in Liedern, 47, 224
Stirling, Edward, 283
Stockdale, John, 276, 304
Storace, Anna Selina, 366
Stow, John, 379
Stranger, The (Menschenhass und Reue), 147
Strawberry Hill, 108, 180–2, 183, 184, 189, 201
Strickland, Agnes, 80
Stuart, Miss A. A., 258, 366
Sturm, Christoph Christian, 103
Subligny, Adrien Thomas Perdou de, 27, 98
Suckling, Sir John, 394
Sue, Marie-Joseph-Eugène, 299
Suett, Richard, 259, 366
Suite de l'Espion Turc, Le, 199
Summersett, Henry, 92, 104
Summers, Montague, 296, 303, 304, 305, 307, 398, 404, 408, 410
Surrealism, aims of, 383–4, 393; defined, 389; purports to be influenced by Gothic romance, 397, 398, 411; representative art and literature of, 389–90
Surrealism, A Short Survey of (Gascoyne), 383
Surrealism (Read), 383, 390
Surrealist Revolution, The, 411
Surrey Theatre, 270, 283, 287, 303
Sussex Weekly Advertiser, The, 103
Sutton, Mr., 229
Sutton, Mr. F., 229
Swinley, Ion, 198
Symonds, H. D., 311, 316, 367
Symonds, John Addington, 384
Symons, Arthur, 22

Taglioni, Mlle., 301
Tailors, The, 287
Tales of Terror, 121, 257, 304
Tales of the Devil, from the Original Gibberish of Professor Lumpwitz, S.U.S. and C.A.C. in the University of Snoringberg, 1801 (A parody of Lewis), 304
Tales of Wonder, 121, 257, 276, 303–4, 394
Tamar Can, 307
Tamburlaine the Great, 286
Tamerlane (Rowe), 286
Tamerlane the Great (Saunders), 286
Tasso, Torquato, 41, 42, 43, 44, 50, 313, 388
Tate, Nahum, 395
Taylor, Edward, 396
Taylor's Library, Bath, 67
Taylor, William, 122, 303
Tea-Table Miscellany, The, 394
Teatro moderno applaudito, 314
Tegg, Thomas, 82–3, 84

Tempest, The (Davenant and Dryden), 264, 395
Tencin, Claudine Alexandre Guerin, Madame de, 116, 201
Tender Husband ; or, The Accomplished Fools, The, 25
Tennant, William, 304
Tennent's Library, Bath, 67
Tennyson, Alfred, Lord, 155
Teresa de Jesús, Santa, 411
Terriss, William, 155
Terry, Ellen, 155, 200
Thackeray, William Makepeace, 391
Thalia Lacrimans, 97
Théâtre de la Gaieté, 230, 231
Théâtre de l'Emulation, 230
Théâtre de Montausier, 231
Théâtre des Jeunes-Artistes, 230
Théâtre des Jeunes-Associés, 231
Théâtre Italien, 307
Théâtre monacal (anticlérical), 192
Theatre Royal, Bridges Street, 286
Theatre Royal, Norwich, 309, 313, 314, 315
Theatrical references in novels, 325, 328
Theobald, Lewis, 395
Thespian Dictionary, The, 364
Thirty-Five Years of a Dramatic Author's Life, 307
Thomas, Francis Tracy, 190
Thomas's Library, Brighton, 69, 102
Thompson, Benjamin, 147, 392
Thompson, William, 58
Thomson, William, 394
Three Strangers, The, 166
Tidswell, Miss, 258
Tieck, Johann Ludwig, 131, 388
Tierney, M.P., Mr., 284
Timanthes, 392
Timour, Cream of Tartars, 287
Timour Khan, 287
Timour the Tartar, 285-7, 307
Tipper and Richards, 86, 94
Tita (Baptista), 294-5
Titus Andronicus, 52, 53, 55
Titus Andronicus ; or, The Rape of Lavinia, 59
Tompkins, Miss J. M. S., 298, 300
Town Fop ; or, Sir Timothy Tawdrey, The, 112
Toynbee, Mrs. Paget (Walpole's *Letters*), 200
Tragedy of Zoroastres, The (Orrery), 308
Trapp, Joseph, 133
Tree, Maria, 305
Troilus and Cressida ; or, Truth Found too Late, 395
Trollope, Frances, 240, 344
Tschink, Cajetan, 132-3, 224

Tunbridge Wells, 69
Turkish Spy, The, 199
Turnour, Mr., 229
Turra, Elisabetta Caminer, 314
Twins ; or, Is it He or his Brother ? The, 209
Two Children in the Wood, 393
Two Friends ; or, The Liverpool Merchant, The, 296
Tyre, Cuvelier de, 230
Tytler, Alexander Fraser, 121
Tzara, Tristan, 389

Uber die Verfassung der heimlichen Gerichte in Westphalen, 129
Ueber die Einsamkeit, 189
Ulric and Ilvina, 167
Upcott, William, 104, 381
Upper Ossory, the Countess of, 108

Van Der Gucht, G., 153
Vanzee, Maria, 169
Vaumorière, Pierre d'Ortigue, sieur de, 107
Vauxhall Gardens, 405
Vedel, Andel Sörensen, 224
Vehmgericht, 123, 125, 126-7, 129, 130
Venetian Outlaw, The, 270
Venice Preserv'd, 154, 164, 198
Venoni, 281-2, 283
Verdi, Giuseppe, 284
Vere, Horace, 100
Vergil (P. Vergilius Maro), 44
Vergy, Pierre Henri Treyssac de, 67, 102
Vernor and Hood (publishers), 86, 90, 132, 193
Vertot, René Aubert de Vertot d'Aubeuf, C.R.P., 133, 151
Victimes cloîtrées, Les, 192
Village Virtues, 251-2
Villedieu, Madame, 108
Vining, F., 229
Vining, Mrs. W., 229
Virtue reprints, 100
Vizetelly, Henry, 61, 380
Voltaire, Marie François Arouet de, 325, 357
Vortigern and Rowena, 341, 342-3, 380
Von Hartmann, Karl Robert Eduard, 18
Von Ziegler, Heinrich Anshelm, 118
Vulpius, Christian August, 142, 144, 388

Wächter, Georg Philipp Ludwig Leonhard (Veit Weber), 86, 123, 130, 212, 225
Wagner, Richard, 387
Wailly, Léon de, 228
Wakefield, Benjamin, 394

Walcot, Mrs., 254
Wales, Caroline Amelir Elizabeth of Brunswick-Wolfenböttel, Princess of, 400
Walker, George, 29, 81–2, 366, 401
Wallack, James, 274, 285
Wall, Baring, 305
Wall's Circulating Library (Kew), 66
Walpole, Horace, Earl of Orford, 24, 46, 48, 49, 52, 56, 59, 123, 131, 138, 169, 179–87, 200, 201, 300, 391, 397, 399, 400, 408, 409
Wandering Jew, The, 225–27
Wandering Jew, The, 226
Wandering Jew; or, Love's Masquerade, The (farce), 227
Warbling Muses, 394
Warburton, William, Bishop of Gloucester, 184–5
Ward, Catherine G., 29, 36, 100
Warde, 243
Warden, Florence, 288
Warden, Gertrude, 388
Wardlaw, Lady, 394
Warren, Samuel, 240
Warton, Joseph, 24, 41, 46, 48, 341
Warton, Thomas (senior), 46
Warton, Thomas, 41, 46, 48, 58
Waterford edition of The Monk, 212
Watkins, Dr. John, 119
Watts, Alaric, 80
Way of the World, The, 40
Webb, James, 107
Weber, Veit (Georg Philipp Ludwig Leonard Wächter), 86, 212, 225
Webster, Mrs. Nesta H., 131
Weimar, Goethe at, 296; visited by Lewis, 121, 207–9, 399; by Henry Crabb Robinson, 122, 142
Weishaupt, Adam, 132
Wendeborn, Dr. G. F., 120
Wentworth, Zara, 300, 366
Werner, 166, 200
Werner, Zacharias, 393
Wesley, John, 114
West, Gilbert, 58
West Indian, The, 258
West, Mrs. Jane, 178
West, Mrs. W., 282
Westminster Town Boys' Play, 204
White's Library, Moretonhampstead, 69, 96
Whitehead, William, 112
Wieland, Christoph Matthias, 111, 118, 119, 122, 207

Wife of a Million, The, 315
Wilkinson, Mrs., 144
Wilkinson, Sarah S., 84, 170, 256
Wilks, T. E., 144
Will, Rev. Peter, 120, 132, 146, 150
Willes, Miss Louise, 303
William IV (Duke of Clarence), 399, 400
William of Malmesbury, 258
Williams, John, 357
Williams, Mitchell, 179
Williams, William Frederic, 85, 175
Willich, Dr. A. F. N., 120
Wilton and Son, High Holborn, 117
Wisbeach, 70
Wise, Thomas James, 306
Woffington, Peg, 264
Wollstonecraft, Mary, 400, 402
Woman Kill'd with Kindness, A, 112
Wonder, A Woman keeps a Secret, The, 380
Wonder of Women; or, The Tragedie of Sophonisba, The, 301
Wood Dæmon, The, 274–5, 276
Woodfall, Sophia, 85
Woodman's Hut, The, 299
Wordsworth, William, 46
World Revolutions (Mrs. Webster), 131
Wren, Sir Christopher, 38, 39, 43
Wright, R. W. M., 364
Wroughton, Robert, 253, 254, 282
Wycherley, William, 112, 380
Wyplel, L., 227

Yearsley, Anne, 30, 173–4
Yorke, Mrs. R. P. M., 80, 85, 96, 192
York, Frederica Charlotte Ulrica Catherina, Princess Royal of Prussia, Duchess of, 252, 400
Young, Charles Mayne, 274, 306
Young, Edward, 114, 123
Young, Miss Mary Julia, 93, 251, 253, 300, 3· 2, 303, 304

Zimmermann, Johann Georg, Ritter von, 189, 388
Zola, Emile, 22–3, 61, 101
Zoroaster, first magician, 308
Zoroaster, 287
Zoroaster; or, The Spirit of the Star, 308
Zschokke, Heinrich, 121, 123, 144, 267, 269, 388

Index of Novels

Abällino, der grosse Bandit, 140, 144, 267, 269, 292, 293

Abbaye de Saint-Remy, L', 248

Abbess, The (Ireland), 344–5, 380

Abbess, The (Mrs. Trollope), 240, 344

Abbess of St. Hilda, The (bluebook), 83

Abbess of Valtiera; or, The Sorrows of a Falsehood, The, 29, 96

Abbey of Saint Asaph, The, 139

Abbey of Clunedale, The (Literary Hours), 50, 54, 55

Abbey of Weyhill, The, 85

Abbot, The, 31

Abbot of Monserrat; or, The Pool of Blood, The, 29, 369–70

Abellino, the Terrific Bravo of Venice, 66

Abentheurliche Simplicissimus, Der, 118

Adela Northington, 88

Adelaide, 100

Adeline Mowbray, 85

Adeline St. Julian; or The Midnight Hour, 94, 200

Adelson et Salvini, 117, 149

Adventures of a Jesuit, The, 391

Adventures of a Rake, The, 72

Adventures of Charles Careless, The, 103

Adventures of Jonathan Corncob, The, 391

Adventures of Lindamira, The, 99, 115

Age and Youth; or, The Families of Abenstedt, 146

Agnes and Leonora, 363

Agnes de Castro, 99, 148, 156, 199

Agnès de Castro, nouvelle portugaise, 148

Agnes; or, Beauty and Pleasure, 243, 391

Alan Fitz-Osborne, 32, 171

Albano; ou, les Horreurs de l'âbime, 248

Albigenses, The, 193

Alexina, 404

Alf von Dülmen, 306

Alfred of Normandy; or, The Ruby Cross, 177

Alibeg the Tempter, 369, 370–1

Aline et Valcour, 302

All Sorts of Lovers, 104

Almagro and Claude; or, Monastic Murder (bluebook, The Monk), 84

Almahide; or, The Captive Queen, 107

Alte überall und nirgends, Der, 144

Alvar and Seraphina; or, The Troubles of Mercia, 175

Amadis de Gaul, 222, 299

Ambition, 100

Ambrosio; or The Monk, 211; and see under The Monk.

Amelia, 72

Amorassan; or, The Spirit of the Frozen Ocean, 281, 304

Amorous Abbess; or, Love in a Nunnery, The, 99

Amorous Friars; or, the Intrigues of a Convent, The, 72

Amour of a Friar, The (L'Enfant du Carnaval), 117

Amours of Count de Dunois, The, 156

Amours of Count Teckeli, The, 156

Amours of Edward the IV, The, 156–7, 199

Amy Lawrence; or, The Freemason's Daughter, 150

Anaconda, The, 280

Ancient Records; or, The Abbey of Saint Oswythe, 32, 58, 73, 100, 170, 179, 192, 334–5, 391

Anecdotes of the Delborough Family, 73

Angelika, Tochter des grossen Banditen Odoardo, 142

Angelo, 88

Anglo-Saxons, or, the Court of Ethelwald, The, 30, 175

Ankerwick Castle, 190

Annals of Love, The, 156, 199

Anna; or, Memoirs of a Welch Heiress, 73

Anna Melvil, 73

Anna St. Ives, 402

Anne Bell, 117, 149

Anne of Geierstein, 123, 130

Anthony Varnish, 73

Arcadia (Sannazzaro), 388

Arcadia (Sidney), 184

A Rebours, 22, 57

Argenis, 201

Ariane (Ariana), 107

Ariel; or, The Invisible Monitor, 29, 170

Armenian; or, the Ghost-seer, The (Der Geisterseher), 130

Artamène; ou, le Grand Cyrus, 107

Artamenes; Or, The Grand Cyrus, 25, 26, 57, 107

Arville Castle, 174

Asteria and Tamberlain, 156

Astonishment ! ! ! 93, 317

Astrée (Astræa), 25, 107, 388

Atrocities of a Convent, The, 87

Augusta, 103
Augustus and Adelina, 104
Auristella, 99

Bandit Chief; or, Lords of Urvino, The, 28, 98
Bandit's Bride; or, the Maid of Saxony, The, 103
Banditti of the Forest, The, 368
Banished Man, The, 401
Banks of the Douro; or, the Maid of Portugal, The, 85
Baron De Fleming, the Son, 145
Baron's Daughter, The, 265
Barons de Felsheim, Les, 117
Barons of Felsheim, The, 100, 117
Bélier, Le, 306, 307
Belle au Bois Dormant, La, 49
Benevolent Monk; or, The Castle of Olalla, The, 87, 92, 104
Berger Extravagant, Le, 107
Biandetto, der Bandit von Treviso, 142
Biondetta; or, The Enamoured Spirit, 224
Black Forest; or, the Cavern of Horrors, The (bluebook), 83
Black Monk; or, The Secret of the Grey Turret, The, 244
Black Valley, The, 130
Bleak House, 389
Blueskin, 141
Blumenkrantz, Der, 132
Blutende Gestalt mit Dolch und Lampe, Die, 227-8, 298
Bravo of Bohemia, The, 98, 240
Bravo of Venice, The, 85, 121, 144, 239, 243, 267, 268, 269, 271, 278, 293
Brigands de l'Estramadure, Les, 358
Bronze Statue; or, The Virgin's Kiss, The, 243
Brothers; or, The Castle of Niolo, The, 196
Brougham Castle, 86
Bruno; or, The Sepulchral Summons, 346
Burton Wood, 172

Caleb Williams (Things as they are), 402, 403
Canterbury Tales, The (Sophia and Harriet Lee), 164, 166-7, 200
Captive of Vallance, The, 85
Capucins; ou, le Secret du cabinet noir, Les, 248
Carolo Carolini, 142
Cassandra, 25, 98, 107
Cassandre, 107
Castello di Otranto, Il, 101, 183
Castle Connor, 188
Castle of Berry Pomeroy, The, 87, 239
Castle of Caithness, The, 174

Castle of Ehrenstein, The, 139
Castle of Eridan, The, 89
Castle of Lindenburg; or The History of Raymond and Agnes, The (bluebook from *The Monk*), 84, 211
Castle of Mowbray, The, 171
Castle of Niolo; or, The Brothers, The, 100
Castle of Ollada, The, 139, 310-11
Castle of Otranto, The, 24, 48, 57, 58, 59, 101, 138, 153, 159, 162, 171, 179, 180-85, 186, 187, 197, 199, 200, 201, 208, 210, 241, 253, 255, 300, 309, 404, 408, 410
Castle of Roviègo; or, Retribution, The, 86
Castle of Saint Donats, The, 100, 190
Castle of Santa Fé, The, 100
Castle of Tariffa; or The Self-Banished Man, The, 96, 190, 241
Castle of the Apennines, The (bluebook), 83
Castle of the Tuileries, The, 318
Castle of Tynemouth, The, 86
Castle of Wolfenbach, The, 101
Castle Spectre, The (Sarah Wilkinson), 256
Castles of Athlin and Dunbayne, The, 47, 99, 101
Castles of Marsange and Nuger, The, 79
Catholic; or, Acts and Deeds of the Popish Church, The (Ireland), 177, 357
Cave of Corenza, The, 93, 366
Cave of Toledo, The, 366
Cavern of Astolpho, The, 366
Cavern of Strozzi, The, 90, 366
Cecilia, 63
Celestina, 29, 391
Chamber of Death, The, 100
Champion de la Vertu, ou le Vieux Baron anglais, Le, 188
Champion of Virtue, The (The Old English Baron), 40, 138, 186-8, 300, 309, 405
Charles von Saalfeld, 124
Charley Wag, 141
Château d'Albert; ou, le Squelette ambulant, Le, 397
Château de Vauvert, Le, 248
Château d'Otrante, Le, 183, 201
Château des Tuileries, Le, 318
Cheating Gallant, The, 148
Chevaliers du Cygne, Les, 299
Children of the Abbey, The, 29, 100, 101, 300
Chrysal; or The Adventures of a Guinea, 72
Cicely; or, The Rose of Raby, 174
Cinthelia; or, The Woman of Ten Thousand, 81
Circassian Chief, The, 240
City Romance, The (trans. from Furetière), 108
Clarissa, 111, 118, 123
Clarisse Harlowe, 111

Clary, ou le retour à la vertu recompensé, 117, 149
Clelia (Clélie), 25, 26, 107
Clélie, La fausse (Histoire comique), 27, 98
Cleopatra (Hymen's Praludia), 25, 26, 98
Cléopâtre, 98, 107
Clermont, 29, 96
Cleveland, 168
Cælina ; ou, l'Enfant du Mystère, 397
Comical Romance, The (Scarron),
Comte de Strafford, Le, 117
Comte de Warwick, Le, 163
Comtesse de Sancerre, La (Les Crimes d'Amour), 116
Confessions of the Nun of St. Omers, 85
Confessor, The, 240
Conjuration des Espagnols (Saint-Réal), 154
Conspiracie of the Spaniards, A, 154
Constance the fair Nun (The Annals of Love), 199
Contes à nos enfants, 248
Contes (Hamilton), 306-7
Contradictions ; or, Who Could Have Thought It ? 78
Convent of Notre Dame ; or, Jeanette, The, 87
Convent of St. Marc, The, 87
Convent of St. Michael, The, 170
Convent Spectre, The (bluebook), 83
Coral Island ; or, The Hereditary Curse, The, 243
Corallo, oder die schrecklichen Geheimnisse im Moliser Thale, 143
Cordova Abbey ; or, Lights and Shadows of the present Day, 191
Corfe Castle, 241
Correlia ; or, The Mystic Tomb, 368
Cottage on the Cliff, The, A Sea Side Story, 29
Count di Novini ; or, the Confederate Carthusians, The, 197
Countess of Salisbury, The, 156
Craig Melrose Abbey, 177
Crichton, 31, 280
Crimes de l'Amour, Les, 116, 302
Cruel Father, The, 149
Cypriots, The, 174

Dæmon of Venice, The (bluebook from Zofloya), 84
Dagger, The, 132
D'Almanzi, anecdote françoise, 188
Danish Massacre, The, 172, 173
Daphnis and Cloe, 72
David Simple, 72
Dean of Coleraine, The (trans. from Prévost), 110
Death of Abel, The, 119
Death of Cain, The, 119

Deeds of Darkness ; or, The Unnatural Uncle, 29, 86, 94
Deeds of the Olden Time, 100
Delicate Distress, The, 68
Dellingborough Castle ; or, The Mysterious Recluse, 86
Demon of Sicily, The, 29, 236-9, 391, 397
Derwent Priory, 190
Desmond, 401
Destination ; or, Memoirs of a Private Family, 188, 300
Deutsche Alcibiades, Der, 124, 125
Devereux, 379
Devil in Love, The, 224
Devil's Elixir, The, 241, 302
Diable Amoreux, Le, 224
Diana, 221, 388
Dianora, Gräfin von Montagno, 142
Discarded Daughter, The, 103
Discarded Son ; or, Haunt of the Banditti, The, 100
Dolch, Der, 132
Dolgorucki and Menzikoff, 85, 145
Dolks der bandit, 141
Don Galaor, 222, 299
Don Quixote, 223, 299
Don Raphael, 82
Don Sebastian (Canton), 175
Don Sebastian ; or The House of Braganza, 175
Don Sylvio von Rosalba, 119
Donalda ; or, The Witches of Glenshiel, 85, 92-3
Dos Doncellas, Las, 154
Doyen de Killérine, Le, 110, 111
Duchesse de Kingston, La, 248
Duke of Clarence, The, 30, 173, 174
Duke of Exeter, The, 172
Durston Castle ; or, the Ghost of Eleonora, 85
Dusseldorf ; or, the Fratricide, 172
Dusseldorf ; ou, le fratricide, 172

Edgar ; or, The Phantom of the Castle, 363
Edgar Huntly, 151
Edmund Ironside, 85
Édouard ; ou, le Spectre du Château, 188
Edric the Forester ; or The Mysteries of the Haunted Chamber, 93, 178
Edward and Annette, 146
Edward de Courcy, 30, 173
Effusions of Sensibility, The, 206
Eginhard and Emma, 306
Eleanor ; or, The Spectre of St. Michael's, 104
Elisabeth, Erbin von Toggenburg, 124, 277, 306
Elixiere des Teufels, Die, 242, 243
Elizabeth, 136
Ellen, Countess of Castle Howell, 241
Ellen, Heiress of the Castle, 87

Eloise de Montblanc, 29, 89
Emily Moreland ; or, The Maid of the Valley, 30
Emmeline ; or the Happy Discovery (Mrs. Ker), 94, 200
Emmeline ; or, the Orphan of the Castle (Mrs. Smith), 29, 47, 94
Enchanteur Faustus, L', 306
Enfant du Carnival, L', 117
English Adventures, 157-8
En Rade, 410
Entführing, Die, 223
Epoux Malheureux, L', 117
Épreuves du sentiment, Les, 102, 117
Erasmus Schleicher, 124
Ernestine (Les Crimes de l'Amour), 116, 31
Ernestine (trans. by Lathom), 318
Errors of Innocence, The, 166
Erzählungen und Novellen, 132
Ethelinde ; or, the Recluse of the Lake, 29, 100
Ethelwina ; or, The House of Fitz-Auburne, 32, 96, 139, 179, 333, 334
Eugene and Eugenia ; or, One Night's Horrors, 86
Euphrasia ; or, The Captive, 104
Eustace Fitz-Richard, A Tale of the Barons' Wars, 73
Eventful Marriage, The, 86
Eve of San Pietro, The, 29, 397
Eversfield Abbey, 86
Ewige Jude, Der, 227
Example ; or, the History of Lucy Cleveland, The, 40
Exemplarie Novels, 198
Exiles ; or, Memoirs of the Count de Crondstadt, The, 188, 300
Extravagant Shepherd, The, 107

Fair Adulteress, The, 72
Fair Jilt, The, 99
Fairy Tales and Romances (Anthony Hamilton), 306
Falconbridge Abbey, 87
Family of Halden, The, 145
Family of Montorio, The (The Fatal Revenge), 29, 151
Family Quarrels, 146
Family Secrets, Literary and Domestic, 59, 71
Fanny Hill, 72, 216, 217, 298
Fanny, histoire angloise, 117
Fanny ; or, Injur'd Innocence, 117
Fanny ; or, The Happy Repentance, 117
Fanny White, 141
Farmer of Inglewood Forest, The, 100, 101
Fashionable Mysteries, 329
Fatal Connection, The, 68
Fatal Follies, 96

Fatal Revenge ; or, The Family of Montorio, The, 29, 151
Fatal Vow ; or, St. Michael's Monastery, The, 87, 175-7, 321
Fate ; or Spong Castle, 170
Father Eustace, 151, 240
Father Innocent, Abbot of the Capuchins (bluebook, The Monk), 84
Fatherless Fanny, 84, 188, 300
Fatherless Fanny (bluebook), 84
Faust, A Romance of the Secret Tribunals, 130, 240
Faust der Morgenländer, Der, 281
Faute de l'Abbé Mouret, La, 22
Favourite of Nature, The, 66
Fays of Loch Lomond, The, 369
Fedor und Marie, 145
Felixmarte of Hyrcania, 184
Female Quixote ; or, the Adventures of Arabella, The, 26
Ferdinand, Count Fathom, 53, 141, 224, 225
Fernando Fernandini, 142
Ferrandino, Fortsetzung der Rinaldini, 142
Feudal Days ; or, The Freebooter's Castle, 179
Feudal Events, 172
Feudal Tyrants, 99, 124, 277-80, 306
Fisherman's Hut, The, 85
Fitzmaurice, 175
Fleetwood, 85
Fleur d'Epine, 306, 307
Forest of Comalva, The, 368
Forest of Hohenelbe, The, 368-9
Forest of Montalbano, The, 29, 368
Forest of St. Bernardo, The, 86, 100
Forges Mystérieuses, Les, 248
Fortunate Country Maid, The (Love in a Nunnery), 103
Foundling of Devonshire, The, 104
Foundling of Glenthorn, The, 366
Four Facardins, The, 280
Fraile, El (The Monk), 228
Francion, 107
Francis and Josepha, 146
Frankenstein, 94
Fräulein von Sternheim, 118
Frederic and Caroline, 70
Freidrich the Victor, 306
Friar Hildargo, 239
Friar's Tale, The, 86, 170
Fugitive Countess ; or, The Convent of St. Ursula, The, 170
Fugitive Daughter ; or, Eve of Cambria, The, 201
Fündling von Egizheim, Der, 130

Gabriel Forrester ; or the Deserted Son, 91
Gabrielle de Vergy, 177, 391

Gamesters, The, 172
Galand Escroc, Le, 148
Gallant Hermaphrodite, The, 99
Gaston de Blondeville; or, The Court of
 Henry III keeping Festival in Ardenne, 31,
 80, 136, 405
Geist Lurian im Silbergewand, Der, 228
Geisterbanner, Der, 133
Geisterseher, Der, 120, 130, 144, 227, 240
Genie; oder Memorien des Marquis von G ...,
 Der, 132
Genius: or the Mysterious Adventures of Don
 Carlos de Grandez, The, 132
Genuine Memoirs of Miss Faulkner, The, 102
Geschichte der Gräfin Thekla von Thurn, 124
Ghost-Seer, or Apparitionist, The (Der
 Geisterseher), 130, 240, 299
Gil Blas, 33
Girl of the Mountains, The, 29, 170
Giulio degli Obizzi, 269
Glenmore Abbey; or, The Lady of the Rock,
 86
Gondez the Monk, 29, 75, 80, 85, 193, 346–57,
 397
Gordian Knot, The, 68
Grandison the Second; or, The German
 Grandison, 118
Great Expectations, 389
Great German Short Stories, 302
Griffith Abbey; or, The Memoirs of Eugenia,
 87
Guido Mazzarini, 269
Guiscard, 100

Hag of the Mountains, The (bluebook), 83
Happy Slave, The, 148, 153, 154
Harriet, or the Innocent Adultress, 68
Haspar a Spada, 124
Hattigè, ou les Amours du Roy de Tamaran,
 148
Hatto of Mainz, 306
Haunted Cavern, The, 192, 365–6
Haunted Palace; or The Horrors of Ventoliene,
 The, 80, 96
Haunted Priory, The, 397
Heilige Kleebatt, Das, 130
Heilige Vehme, Der, 123
Heiress Di Montalde; or, The Castle of
 Bezanto, The, 94, 200
Heirs of Villeroy, The, 86
Heldin der Vendée, Die, 269
Henrietta Bellmann; or, the new Family
 Picture, 145
Henry Ashton, or, The Will and the Way, 150
Henry Fitzowen (Literary Hours), 50, 51–2, 55
Herman of Unna, 124–9, 147
Hermann and Emilia, 99, 145

Hermann von Unna, 124
Hermit, The, 185
Hermit's Cave; or, the Fugitive's Retreat,
 The, 366
Hermitage, The, 163, 185
Hermite de la Tombe mystérieuse; ou le
 Fantome du Vieux Château, L', 367
Hermsprong; or, Man as he is not, 27, 100,
 193
Hesperus; oder 45 Hundsposttage, 384
Heroine, The, 200, 245, 302, 397
Heureux Esclave, L', 148, 154
Hic et Haec; ou, L'Art de varier les plaisirs
 de l'amour et de la volupté, 213
Histoire d'Aloise de Livarot, 115
Histoire de Comte Gleicher, L', 188
Histoire d'Ernestine, 115
Histoire de Marguerite d'Anjou, 163
Histoire de Miss Jenny Salisbury, 115
Histoire de M. le marquis de Cressy, 115
Histories and Novels of the late Mrs. Behn,
 All the, 99
History of a Dog, The, 117
History of a Woman of Quality; or, the
 Adventures of Lady Frail, The, 72
History of Brandon, The (English Adventures),
 158
History of Lady Anne Neville, The, 163
History of Lady Sophie Sternheim, The, 119
History of Leonora Meadowson, The, 198
History of Lord Aimworth and Charles Hart-
 ford, The, 67
History of Miss Betsy Thoughtless, The, 72
History of Miss Clarinda Cathcart, The, 62, 97
History of some of the Penitents in the Magdalen-
 House, The, 72
History of the Conspiracy against Venice, The,
 153, 154
History of the Nun; or, The Fair Vow-
 Breaker, The, 198
History of the Swedish Countess of Guilden-
 stern, The, 119
History of Tom Rigby, The, 391
Homme à Projets, L', 117
Horrid Mysteries, 29, 120, 131–2, 133, 297
Horrors of Oakendale Abbey, The, 136–8, 240,
 397
House of Aspen, The, 130
House of Tynian, The, 81
Hugh Trevor, 402
Human Beings, 93, 321
Humbert Castle; or, The Romance of the
 Rhone, 190, 368
Humphry Clinker, 67
Huon de Bordeaux, 388
Hymen's Præludia (Loveday's translation of
 Cléopâtre), 98
Hyppolitus, or The Wild Boy, 86

Ibrahim, ou l'Illustre Bassa, 107
Idiot Heiress, The, 86
Impenetrable Secret, The, 86, 99, 318–9
Incognita, 99
Independence, 73
Indiana Danby, 391
Infernal Don Quichotte, L', 401
Infernal Quixote, The, 401
Innocent Adultère, L', 154
Innocent Adultery, The, 67, 153, 198
Inquisition, The, 193
Invisible Enemy; or, The Mines of Wielitska, The, 29, 90, 91, 151
Invisible Spy, The, 153
Irish Assassin, The (bluebook), 83
Irish Chieftain, and his Family, The, 92, 100, 104
Irish Guardian; or, Errors of Eccentricity, The, 173
Isabelle et Theodore (The Castle of Otranto), 201
Italian; or, The Confessional of the Black Penitents, The, 43, 52, 56, 75, 84, 118, 194, 196, 233, 239, 244, 304, 305, 397, 405
Italian Mysteries, 322
Ivanhoe, 31, 184
Ivey Castle, 190

Jack Sheppard, 141
Jacobin espagnol, Le, 228
Jaqueline of Olzeburg; or Final Retribution, 89
Jemmy and Jenny Jesammy, 72
Jenny Spinner; or, The Ghost of Knebworth House, 296
Jesuit, The (J. F. Smith), 150
Joseph Andrews, 72
Joseph Wilmot; or, The Memoirs of a Man-servant, 81, 305, 402
Juif Errant, Le, 299
Julia de Roubigné, 121
Julia of England, 104
Juliet Grenville, 391
Juliette; ou, la suite de Justine, 360, 397
Justine; ou, les Malheurs de la Vertu, 397

Kate Chudleigh; or, The Duchess of Kingston, 302
Karl Osino, Räuber, 142
Kenilworth, 31, 169
King's Guerdon, The, 150
Kleine Novellen, 132
Knight of the Rose, The, 96
Knights; or, Sketches of the Heroic Age, The, 130
Koenigsmark the Robber, 240, 248–50, 302
Koenigsmark the Robber (chap-book), 249

Konrad und Siegfried von Feuchtwanger, 124, 306
Konradin von Schwaben, 124
Kruitzner (Canterbury Tales), 166, 167, 200

Là-Bas, 22
Lady Chatterley's Lover, 213
Last Man, or Omegarus and Syderia, a Romance in Futurity, The, 90
Last of the Plantagenets, The, 31
Laughton Priory, 100
Lauretta Pisana, 142
Laurette, 73
League of the poor Conrad, The, 306
Leben der schwedischen Gräfin G., 119
Leben und Abenteurer Paul Asop's, 124
Legends of a Nunnery, The, 87, 239, 241
Legitimacy; or, The Youth of Charlemagne, 179
Letters from a Lady of Quality to a Chevalier (Mrs. Haywood), 115
Lettres d' Adelaïde de Dammartin, 115
Lettres d' Elisabeth Sophie de Vallière, 115
Lettres de milady Juliette Catesby, 115
Lettres de Mistriss Fanny Butlerd, 115
Lettres nouvelles, 115
Lettres portugaises, 115
Libertine, The, 391
Liebe und Treue, 132
Life and Death of Fair Rosamond, The, 198–9
Life of a Lover, The, 166
Life of Charlotte Dupont, The, 99
Life of Joseph, Son of Israel, The, 119
Life of the Swedish Countess de G . . . , 119
Like Master, Like Man, 365
Lionardo Montebello, oder der Carbonari-Bund, 142
Lise et Valcourt, ou le Bénédictin, 248
Live and Learn; or, The First John Brown, 322–5
Lionel; or, the Impenetrable Command, 177
Lobenstein Village, 145
London; or, Truth without Treason, 322
Longsword, Earl of Salisbury, 30, 158–62, 179
Lord Aimworth (Lord Ainsworth), 67, 102
Lorenzo, der kluge Mann im Walde, 142
Louisa; or, The Black Tower, 86, 367
Louis de Boncœur, A domestic Tale, 89
Love and Gratitude, 145
Love and Horror, 397
Love, Hatred, and Revenge, a Swiss Romance, 91
Love in a Nunnery (Amorous Abbess), 103
Love in Excess, 153
Love Victorious, 99
Lovel Castle; or, the Rightful Heir Restored (bluebook, The Old English Baron), 84

*Lovers ; or the Memoirs of Lady Mary Sc——
and the Hon. Amelia B——, The* (1772.
By de Vergy. This is Part II. Part I is
1769, and Part III was announced in
1772).

*Loves of King Henry II and Fair Rosamond,
The,* 153, 154, 155–6

Lowenritter, Die, 144

Loyalists, The, 178

Lucy, 29, 81

*Ludovico's Tale ; or The Black Banner of
Castle Douglas,* 87

Lusignan ; or The Abbaye of La Trappe, 149,
194–5

Lussington Abbey, 85, 177

Lutardo, oder der Banditenhauptmann, 142

Madame Bovary, 22

Madame Gervaisais, 22

Madeleine ; or, The Castle of Montgomery, 263

Maid of Padua ; or Past Times, 104

Makin, anecdote angloise, 117

Malheurs de l'amour, Les, 116, 201

Man as he is not, see *Hermsprong.*

Man of Feeling, The, 68, 121, 170

Man of the World, The, 121, 391

Manco, the Peruvian Chief, 240

Mandeville Castle ; or, the Two Ellinors, 87

Manfredi, 100, 305

Manfroné ; or, The One-Handed Monk, 29, 66,
73, 98

Mann am Hofe, 118

Mannerschwar und Weibertreue, 130

Manon Lescaut, 109

Manon L'Escaut ; or, the Fatal Attachment,
109

Mansion-House, The, 88

Marchioness ! ! ! The, 241

Marthe, histoire d'une fille, 56

*Martin and Mansfeldt ; or, The Romance of
Franconia,* 173

*Martyn of Fenrose ; or, The Wizard and the
Sword,* 92

Mary, a Fiction, 402

Mary Jane, 363

*Mary Price ; or, The Memoirs of a Servant-
Maid,* 402

Mathilde von Villanegas, 228

Melmoth the Wanderer, 29, 170, 193, 397

Memoires du comte de Comminge, Les, 116, 201

Memoires d'un Homme de Qualité, 109, 110

Memoirs founded on Facts, 86

Memoirs of a Coxcomb, The, 72

Memoirs of an Hermaphrodite, The, 67, 102

*Memoirs of a Lady of Quality, written by
herself, The,* 67

Memoirs of a Man of Pleasure, The, 72

*Memoirs of an Unfortunate Lady of Quality,
The,* 67

*Memoirs of a Woman of Pleasure, The (Fanny
Hill),* 72, 216, 217, 298

Memoirs of Emma Courtney, 402

Memoirs of Lady Woodford, The, 67

Memoirs of Miss Sidney Bidulph, 304

Memoirs of Modern Philosophers, 401

Memoirs of Sir Roger de Clarendon, 188, 300

Memoirs of the Count Comminge, 149, 201

Men and Manners, 93, 315–6, 320, 321, 333

*Mental Recreations, Four Danish and German
Tales,* 90

Meretrice, La (Fanny Hill), 298

Microcosm, The, 103

*Midnight Assassin ; or, Confessions of the
Monk Rinaldi, The (bluebook, The
Italian),* 84

Midnight Bell, The, 84, 100, 311–3

*Midnight Bell ; or, The Abbey of St. Francis,
The (bluebook from Lathom's romance),*
84

*Midnight Horrors ; or, The Bandit's Daughter
(bluebook),* 83

Midnight Wanderer, The, 404

Mille et une Nuits, Les (Galland), 280, 307

Milles et Amys, 388

Minerva Castle, 86

Minnigrey, 150

*Minstrel ; or, Anecdotes of Distinguished
Personages in the Fifteenth Century, The,*
174

Misled General, The, 91

*Miss Coote (Confessions of Miss Coote : The
Pearl, No. 1),* 213

Miss Fanny Wilkes, 118

*Mistakes of the Heart ; or, the Memoirs of
Lady Caroline Pelham, and Lady Victoria
Nevil, The,* 67

Mistrust, or Blanche and Osbright, 280

Mock-Clelia, The, A comical History (1678),
27, 98

Modern Characters, 239

Modern Faults, 94, 200

Modern Fine Gentleman, The, 391

*Moine, Le (trans. of The Monk by Deschamps,
etc.),* 100, 228

Moine, Le (trans. by Abbé Morellet), 228

Moine, Le (trans. by de Wailly), 228

*Moine ; ou, les Nuits du Cloître, Le (trans.,
1878),* 228

*Moine ; ou, les Nuits du Couvent, Le (trans.,
1880),* 228

Moine incestueux, Le (version by Ploert),
228

Monastery, The, 31, 123

Mönch, Der (Magdeburg), 228

Mönch, Der (Hamburg), 228

Monk, The, 75, 84, 99, 101, 118, 121, 141, 144, 180, 194, 196, 210–39, 242–6, 265, 266, 280, 289, 291, 292, 293, 297, 298, 299, 300, 305, 370, 373, 391, 397
Monk of Madrid, The, 196
Monk of Udolpho, The, 29, 100, 333, 336–41, 380
Monks and the Robbers, The, 87
Monmouth, 30, 172, 173
Monsieur Botte, 117
Monteith, 86
Montford Castle ; or, The Knight of the White Rose, 174
Month in the Highlands, A, 329–30
Montmorenci (Literary Hours), 50, 52, 53–4
Montrose ; or, The Gothic Ruin, 404
Morning Ramble ; or, History of Miss Evelyn, The, 391
Morte Amoureuse, La, 299
Moss Cliff Abbey ; or The Sepulchral Harmonist, 93
Mountbrasil Abbey ; or, Maternal Trials, 87
Mountville Castle ; or, The Village Story, 87
Munchausen's Narrative, Baron, 250, 251
Munchausen, The Travels of Baron, 250
Münchhausen, Wunderbaren Reisen des Freyherrn von, 250
My Master's Secret, 85
My Uncle Thomas, 117
My Uncle's Garret Window, 280–1
Mystères de la Tour Saint-Jean, Les, 367
Mystères d'Udolpho, Les (trans. by Victorine de Chastenay), 101
Mystères sur mystères, 248
Mysteries Elucidated, 100, 172, 173
Mysteries of the Forest, The, 196, 368
Mysteries of Udolpho, The, 43, 56, 75, 99, 101, 136, 210, 233, 234, 255, 298, 310, 334, 336, 339, 397, 410
Mysterious Count, The, 94, 200
Mysterious Father ; or, Trials of the Heart, The, 85
Mysterious Freebooter ; or, The Days of Queen Bess, 30, 32, 86, 100, 320–1
Mysterious Friendship, The, 80
Mysterious Monk ; or, The Wizard's Tower, The, 100, 374–9
Mysterious Omen ; or, Awful Retribution, The (bluebook), 83
Mysterious Protector, The, 86
Mysterious Visitor ; or, Mary the Rose of Cumberland, The, 85
Mysterious Warning, The, 100, 101, 138, 170, 397
Mysterious Sisters, The, 86
Mystery, 316, 391
Mystery of Edwin Drood, The, 389
Mystery of the Black Tower, The, 365, 366–7

Mystic Events ; or, The Vision of the Tapestry, 30, 330–3
Mystic Sepulchre ; or, Such Things have been, The, 365, 367
Mystic Tower ; or, Villainy Punished, The, 367

Nancy, ou les malheurs de l'imprudence et de la jalousie, 117
Neapolitan ; or, The Test of Integrity, The, 89, 172
Necromancer, The (Reynolds), 333
Necromancer ; or, The Tale of the Black Forest, The, 29, 133, 134–5
Necromancer ; or Wolfe the Robber, The, 134
New Monk, The, 245–6, 302, 391
New Mysteries of London, The, 244–5
Neuen Volksmärchen der Deutschen, Die, 223, 306
New Popular Tales of the Germans, 306
Niece ; or, the History of Sukey Thornby, The, 63
Nightmare Abbey, 147
Nikanor, der Alte von Fronteja, 142–3
Nine Days Wonder, The, 85
Nord häusische Wundermädchen, Das, 142
Northanger Abbey, 149, 169
Nouvelle Anglaise, Miss Henriette Stralson (Les Crimes de l'Amour), 116
Nouvelles (Scarron), 107, 154
Nouvelles historiques (D'Arnaud), 117
Novelas Ejemplares, 154
Novels of Queen Elizabeth, The, 156
Novice of Saint Dominick, The, 40, 86, 100
Nuit anglaise, La, 397
Nun and her Daughter ; or, Memoirs of the Courville Family, The, 85
Nun of St. Agatha, The, 179
Nun, or the Adventures of the Marchioness de Beauville, The, 67
Nuns of the Desert ; or, The Woodland Witches, The, 85, 93

Odd enough, to be sure ! or Emilius in the World, 78, 145
Ogier le Danois, 388
Old English Baron, The, 40, 84, 138, 186–8, 300, 405
Old Manor House, The, 84
Old Mortality, 123
Oliver Twist, 141
Olivia and Marcella, 104
One Pound Note, The, 322
Ora and Juliet, or, Influence of First Principles, 201
Orlando Orlandini, der wunderbare Abenteurer, 142

Ormond, 151
Oroonoko (Mrs. Behn), 99
Orphan of the Rhine, The, 29, 146, 152
Osmond, 66
Osrick; or, Modern Horrors, 29, 100, 363
Otho and Rutha, 48
Our Street, 391–2
Oxonian, The (Adventures of Charles Careless), 103

Palmerin of England, 184
Pamela, 111, 113, 118, 149
Paméla, 111
Pandion and Amphigenia; or, the History of the Coy Lady of Thessaly, 107
Papa Brick, 117
Paraclete, The, 86, 90
Parish Clerk, The, 40
Parthenissa, 25, 107
Paul Clifford, 141
Paul of Ségovia (Quevedo, trans. 1683), 99
Pauline de Ferrière, 248
Pauvre Georges, Le, 124
Paysan Parvenu, Le, 113
Peep at our Ancestors, A, 177
Pelerin, Le, 148
Pembroke (Canterbury Tales), 167
Peregrine Pickle, 67, 72, 102
Perkin Warbeck, 150
Peveril of the Peak, 123
Phantasus, 123
Pharamond (Faramond), 25, 107, 148
Phedora; or, The Forest of Minski, 368
Philippine of Gueldres, 306
Philosophe anglais, Le (Cléveland), 109, 110
Pilgrim, The, 148
Pilgrim of the Cross, The, 86
Pilot, The, 80
Plantagenet, or Secrets of the House of Anjou, 30, 175
Polish Bandit, The, 325
Pompey the Little; or, The Life and Adventures of a Lap-dog, 72
Poor Mary Ann, 330
Pot-Bouille, 23
Priapische Romane, 298
Primaleon, 184
Prince Charles; or, The Young Pretender, 150
Prince of Condé, The, 156
Prince of Salerno, The, 185
Prince des Voleurs, Le, 141
Princesse de Clèves, La, 108, 148
Princess of Cleve, The, 148
Priory of St. Clair, The, 84
Priory of St. Clare; or, Spectre of the Murdered Nun, The (bluebook from Sarah Wilkinson), 84

Prophecy of Duncannon; or The Dwarf and the Seer, The, 48, 100, 369
Prostitutes of Quality; or, Adultery a la Mode, 72
Puzzled and Pleased, 322

Quatre Facardins, Les, 108, 184, 280, 306, 307
Quinctius Heymeran von Fleming, 145

Rächenden; oder das Vehmgericht des 18. Jahrhunderts, Die, 130
Raphael; or, Peaceful Life, 146
Rashleigh Abbey; or, The Ruin on the Rock, 86, 363
Rayland Hall (bluebook from The Old Manor House), 84
Reason Triumphant over Fancy, 119
Recess, The, 30, 101, 144, 164, 165, 167–70, 171, 172, 173, 391
Reclaimed Prostitute, The, 103
Recollections of a Mary-Ann, The (The Sins of the Cities of the Plain), 213
Recluse of Albyn Hall, The, 300
Reginald Du Bray, 163
Repaires du Crime, Les, 248, 358
Reprobate, The, 145
Rêve, Le, 22
Reward of Constancy, The, 68
Richard Raynal, Solitary, 200
Richelieu, A Tale of France, 379
Rimualdo; or, The Castle of Badajos, 190, 345–6, 380, 397
Rinaldo Rinaldini, Captain of Banditti, The History of, 29, 66, 78, 140, 141, 142, 143–4, 240
Rising Sun, The, 104
Ritterwort, 130
Rival Chiefs; or, The Battle of Mere, The, 175
Rival Friends, The, 149
Rival Ladies, The, 153, 154
Rizzio, 358, 380
Robber, The, 241
Robin Hood and Little John (Egan the younger), 141
Robin Hood le Proscrit, 141
Robinson Crusoe, 118
Rochester; or The Merry Days of Merry England, 150
Roderick Random, 67
Rodolphus of Werdenberg, 145
Roman Bourgeois, Le, 108
Roman Comique, Le, 107
Romance of Lust; or, Early Experiences, The, 213
Romance of Real Life, The, 28

Romance of Smyrna; or The Prediction Fulfilled, The, 80
Romance of the Cavern, The, 366
Romance of the Forest, The, 43, 56, 99, 137, 304, 368, 405
Romance of the Hebrides, The, 322
Romance of the Pyrenees, 29
Romance Readers and Romance Writers. 397
Romano Castle; or, The Horrors of the Forest (bluebook), 83
Romantic Facts, 98
Romantic Tales (Lewis), 280-1
Romantic Tales (Miss Mulock), 151, 240
Rome, 22
Romulus, A Tale of Ancient Times, 146, 150, 152
Rook the Robber, 141
Rookwood, 29, 141, 280, 379
Rosa; or, The Child of the Abbey, 85
Rosabella; or, A Mother's Marriage, 40
Rosalba, 124
Rosalie; or, The Castle of Montalabretti, 29
Rosario; or, The Female Monk (The Monk), 297
Rosaura, 145
Rosaure; ou, l'Arrêt du Destin, 145
Rose and the Key, The, 81, 305
Rose d'Altenberg; ou, le Spectre dans les Ruines, 404
Rose Garden, The, 409
Rosetta; or, The Fair Penitent rewarded, 149
Round Tower; or, A Tale of Mystery, The, 367
Royal Captives, The, 30, 173
Ruinen der Geisterburg, Die, 142
Ruins of Avondale Priory, The, 101, 404
Ruins of Rigonda; or the Homicidal Father, The, 87, 404
Ruins of Ruthvale Abbey, The, 87, 404
Ruins of Selinunti; or The Val de Mazzara, The, 87, 404
Ruins of Tivoli, The, 87, 404

Sagen der Vorzeit, 211
St. Bernard's Priory (by a Young Lady, i.e., Mrs. Harley), 171
St. Botolph's Priory; or, The Sable Mask, 86, 100, 179, 335-36
St. Clair of the Isles; or, The Outlaws of Barra, 48, 101
St. Godwin, 397, 401
Saint Julien, from the German, 145
Saint Julien; or Memoirs of a Father, 145
St. Leonard's Forest; or, The Child of Chance, 178
St. Margaret's Cave; or, The Nun's Story. An Ancient Legend, 80, 170

Salammbô, 22
Salisbury, 117
Salvador; or, Baron de Montbelliard, 190
Santa-Maria; or, The Mysterious Pregnancy, 71, 196, 360-3
Santo Sebastiano; or, The Young Protector, 29
Santon Barsisa, Story of the (The Guardian), 223
Scarron's Novels, 154
Schemer, The, 117
School for Widows, The, 188, 300
Scottish Legend, or The Isle of St. Clothair, The, 48, 335
Second Love; or, The Way to be Happy, 104
Secret Histories, Novels, Love-Letters and Poems (Mrs. Haywood), 99
Secret History of Pythagoras, The, 201
Secret History of Queen Elizabeth and the E. of Essex, The, 99
Secret History of the Duke of Alanson and Queen Elizabeth, The, 156
Secret Machinations, 85
Secret Oath; or, Blood-stained Dagger, The (bluebook), 83
Secret of the Cavern, The, 85, 366
Select Collection of Novels and Histories, A, 153
Self-Deceived; or, The History of Lord Byron, The, 63
Sentimental Journey, A, 67
Series of Genuine Letters between Henry and Frances, A, 68
Setting Sun, The, 104
Shrove-tide Child, The, 117
Sicilian, The, 89
Sicilian Boy, The, 369
Sicilian Pirate, or, The Pillar of Mystery, The (bluebook), 83
Sicilian Romance, A, 56, 238, 406
Sidney and Salli, 149
Sidney et Volsan, 117, 149
Sieg der Natur über die Schäwrmercy, Der, 119
Siege of Belgrade, The, 172
Simon Dale, 150
Sinclair, 100
Sir Bertrand, 48, 59, 185
Sir Charles Grandison, 111, 118
Sir Charles Grandisson, 111
Sir Egbert (Literary Hours), 50, 54-5
Sir John Chiverton, 31, 379
Sir Ralph de Bigod, 73
Sketches of Modern Life, Tales of an Exile, 175
Sonderling, Der, 145
Son of Ethelwolf, The, 172
Sopha, The (Le Sopha, Crébillon fils), 72
Sophia's Journey from Memel to Saxony, 118
Sorcerer, The, 130, 224, 225
Souterrains de Birmingham, Les, 248

Spanische Novellen, 132
Spanish Amusements, 103
Spanish Lady and the Norman Knight, The, 177
Spectre of Tappington, The, 335
Stanfield Hall, 150
Statue Room, The, 172
Strangers, The, 90, 104
Summer at Brighton, A, 99

Talbot Harland, 141
Tale of Mystery; or, Celina, A, 87
Tale without a Title, A, 103
Tales of Fault and Feeling, 100
Tales of the Abbey, 190
Talisman, The, 178
Talk of the Town, The, 380
Tancred, A Tale of Ancient Times, 358
Tears of Sensibility, The, 68, 149
Temptation, 150
Ten Thousand a Year, 240
Tentation de Saint Antoine, La, 22, 298
Teufelsbeschwöring, Die, 130, 212, 225
Thaddeus of Warsaw, 66, 99
Theatre of Love, The, 72
Theodore Cyphon; or, The Benevolent Jew, 81
Things as they Are; or, The Adventures of Caleb Williams, 402, 403
Three Brothers, The, 276-7
Three Monks, The, 192, 246-7
Three Old Maids; or, The House of Penruddock, The, 73
Three Spaniards, The, 29, 82
Tirante the White, 184, 222, 299
Tod Abels, Der, 119
Tom Jones, 33, 40, 72
Tombeau, Le, 367
Tombeau mysterieux; ou, les familles de Hènarés et d'Almanza, Le, 365
Tour infernale, La, 248
Tower of London, The, 31
Towers of Ravenswold; or, The Days of Ironside, The, 178
Tradition of the Castle; or, Scenes in the Emerald Isle, The, 29
Traditions, The, 139
Trois Moines, Les, 192, 246-8, 302
Two Damosels, The, 198
Two Emilys, The (Canterbury Tales), 167
Two Mentors, The, 188, 300

Ulrich Holzer, 205
Ulysses, 213
Unknown; or, The Northern Gallery, The, 321
Usurpation; or, The Inflexible Uncle, 91

Vagabond, The, 81, 401
Valambrosa, or The Venetian Nun, 85
Valentine Vox, 81
Vancenza (bluebook from Mrs. Robinson's novel), 84
Vancenza; or, The Dangers of Credulity, 84, 391
Varbeck (Warbeck, D'Arnaud), 117, 165
Vaurien, 401
Veiled Protectress; or The Mysterious Mother, The, 300
Venus in the Cloyster, or, The Nun in her Smock, 99
Very Strange but Very True, 318
Vesuvia; or, Anglesea Manor, 29
Vicar of Wakefield, The, 145
Victim of Magical Delusion, The, 120, 132, 133, 135, 150, 151
Victim of Prejudice, The, 402
Victor Allen, 100
Vie de Marianne, La, 113, 114
Vieux Baron anglais; ou, les Revenants vengés, Le, 188
Village de Lobenstein, Le, 145
Village of Friedewalde, The, 86
Village Pastor and His Children, The, 145
Virtuous Orphan, or The Life of Marianne, The (trans. from Marivaux), 113
Vivonio; or, The Hour of Retribution, 86
Volksmärchen der Deutschen, 223
Voluntary Exile, The, 93, 100
Voyage merveilleux du Prince Fan-Férédin dans la Romancie, 57

Wagner, The Wehr-Wolf, 244
Wakefield Castle, 86
Walter de Monbary, Grand Master of the Knights Templars, 124
Walter the Murderer; or, The Mysteries of El Dorado, 374, 379
Walther von Montbarrn, 124
Walther von Stadion, 306
Wanderer of the Alps; or, Alphonso, The, 89
Warbeck, a pathetic Tale (D'Arnaud's Varbeck), 117, 165, 173
Warwick Castle, 31
Waverley, 148, 152, 178, 179
Way to Lose him, The, 63
Way to Please him, The, 63
Weird Tales (E. T. A. Hoffmann), 302
Werner, Graf Bernburg, 124
Werther, 118, 120, 208
What Shall Be, Shall Be, 98
Which is the Man? 100
White Knight; or, The Monastery of Marne, The, 92, 104

Who Is the Bridegroom? 73, 98
Who Is the Murderer? or, Mysteries of the Forest, 368
Whole Comical Works of Mons. Scarron, The, 108
Wieland, or Transformation, 151, 397
Wiesse Frau, Die, 224
Wild Irish Boy, The, 400
Will and the Way, The, 150
William of Normandy, 171
William Wallace, the Hero of Scotland, 66
William Wallace, the Highland Hero, 172
Windsor Castle, 31, 241, 381
Witcheries of Craig Isaf, The, 85, 175
Wizard Priest and the Witch, The, 371-4
Wolf; or, The Tribunal of Blood, 86, 130
Woman and her Master, 150
Woman in White, The, 81
Woman of Feeling, The, 346
Women as They Are, 98, 100

Woodland Family; or, The Sons of Error and Daughters of Simplicity, The, 100, 369
World as It goes, The, 365
World we Live in, The, 175
Worst of Stains, The, 104
Wrongs of Women, The, 402
Wundergeschichten sammt dem Schlüssel zu ihrer Erklärung, 224

Young Father, The, 175
Young John Bull, 325-9
Young Philosopher, The, 401

Zayde, 108, 148
Zeluco, 391
Zénéyde, 306
Zofloya; or, The Moor, 29, 84, 234-6, 239
Zwölf schlaufenden Zungfrauen, Die, 144